The Press of Alabama

A HISTORY OF THE
ALABAMA PRESS ASSOCIATION

ALABAMA PRESS ASSOCIATION
125th Anniversary
1871   1996

BY KING E. (ED) WILLIAMS, JR.
DEPARTMENT OF JOURNALISM
AUBURN UNIVERSITY

Published by the Alabama Press Association
3324 Independence Drive, Suite 200
Birmingham, Alabama 35209

ISBN 1-878561-54-5

Cover and book design by Gene Mason

Dedication

*Dedicated to the newspaper
men and women of Alabama.
To them, "getting out the paper"
is a special calling and
a labor of love.*

**"No profession in all the world's kingdom has greater
call on the spiritual life of humans than does that of the
newspaper men and women of America. In your town and
our town, the newspaper man buries more people, marries
more people, and welcomes more babies than any single
undertaker, minister or physician, respectively."**

—*Ben A. Green*
APA president, 1943-1944
The Tuscaloosa News *and* The Tallassee Tribune
(Written in the Jan. 9, 1943, issue of AlaPressa
when Green was APA president)

Contents

"We newspaper people are a close knit group. We have an organization, the Alabama Press Association, which brings us together and makes lasting friends of us all. Wherever we go in Alabama we know the local editor, and it is a comfortable feeling."

— *Karl Elebash Jr.*
Publisher, The Graphic, *Tuscaloosa*
APA president, 1970-1971
(From an editorial on April 5, 1973)

A Call to Organize the Press
1871

The Early Years: Entertainment and Excursions
1872 - 1891

The Editors Get Down to Business
1892 - 1907

Stagnation and a War
1908 - 1925

APA 125th Anniversary Committee

A revised history of the Alabama Press Association was given highest priority of the APA 125th Anniversary Committee at its organizational meeting in September 1994 to plan ways to commemorate the Press Association's upcoming 125-year history in 1996. The Anniversary Committee was appointed by 1994-1995 APA president Linda Hayes Breedlove of *The South Alabamian* in Jackson.

Other activities marking APA's 125th anniversary in 1996 included a commemorative winter convention program with display of old newspapers, luncheon and interviews with some of Alabama's senior newspaper men and women, and a history and legal program. A keepsake edition of *The Alabama Publisher* was published after the 1996 winter convention. The edition featured photographs and stories about the 125th Anniversary Convention in Montgomery, the city where APA was founded in 1872.

Members of the 125th Anniversary Committee were Ann Sutton Smith, *The Eufaula Tribune,* chairman; Ralph W. Callahan, Consolidated Publishing Co., Anniston; Nonnie Stanley Hardin, formerly of *The Greenville Advocate;* Mike Breedlove, *The South Alabamian* (Jackson); Joseph H. (Joe) Adams, *The Southern Star* (Ozark); Bertie Gammell Parish, *The Clayton Record;* Lancie M. Thomas, *The Mobile Beacon;* Jim Cox, *The Clarke County Democrat* (Grove Hill); Barrett C. Shelton Jr., *The Decatur Daily;* Luke Slaton, *The Moulton Advertiser;* Jay Thornton, retired, *The Daily Home* (Talladega); Nell Metz, widow of W. H. (Bill) Metz, the *Birmingham Post-Herald;* J. C. Henderson, retired, *The Alexander City Outlook;* James E. (Jimmy) Mills, retired, the *Birmingham Post-Herald;* Don Woodward, *The Advertiser-Gleam* (Guntersville); and Jim Oakley Jr., former publisher, *The Centreville Press.*

Bill Keller, APA executive director.

Acknowledgments

"Publishing a newspaper requires lots of hard work and many long hours. First, you must want to publish a readable paper and second you have to have lots of experience gained by working and studying under the older members of the Fourth Estate. We believe we gained this experience during more than 60 years in a newspaper office.

"Working afternoons after school, we had to stand on an Octagon soap box to reach a type case or a hand press. Our pay was one dollar and a quarter a week and we worked six days a week and late into many nights. After a couple of years we received a raise, one quarter. That was not much money but it gave us much experience and confidence."

— *Robert D. Burgess, Publisher*
The Opp News
(From an editorial on Sept. 27, 1973)

125 YEARS OF ALABAMA NEWSPAPER AND APA history.

I don't think I fully realized the size of the project I was about to undertake when I was asked two years ago to write a history of the Alabama Press Association for its 125th anniversary in 1996. I agreed to compile the revised APA history after attending an organizational meeting on Sept. 16, 1994, of the 125th Anniversary Committee at the Press Association headquarters in Birmingham.

Looking back, it's a research project I'm glad I undertook because I knew APA needed a new and revised history for its 125th anniversary, and it was something lasting that I could do for the Press Association and the newspapers of Alabama. I hope APA's history will continue to be revised at frequent intervals in the years ahead.

The work of sifting through boxes of Press Association publications, correspondence and minutes, reading bound volumes of old newspapers and microfilm, and interviewing veteran leaders in the Press Association was interesting, even exciting at times — especially when I discovered facts about the Alabama Press Association that were not in the earlier APA histories in 1951, 1959 and 1971.

I am especially grateful for the help of Alabama newspaper historian Billy Jack Jones of Auburn. A retired Linotype operator and collector of newspapers, Jones has forgotten more APA and Alabama newspaper history than the rest of us will ever know. His generous and enthusiastic help — answering questions and giving suggestions, furnishing me with newspaper clippings, books and periodicals, and reading the manuscript more than once — was invaluable.

William E. (Bill) Brooks Jr., 74, APA president in 1953-1954 when he was managing editor of *The Brewton Standard*, was a great help with his fierce editing of the manuscript and proofs. Brooks, son of 1929-1930 APA president W. Emmett Brooks, retired in 1990 as editor and publisher of *The Vincennes* (Ind.) *Sun-Commercial*.

"Reading about the people and events took me both back in time and ahead to current events," Brooks wrote me after reading the manuscript. "In many ways, I was struck by the way history repeats itself, not only in general terms but specifically in the newspaper business.

"Truth, ethics and libel track through the narrative," Brooks continued. "Education, roads and economic development are as fresh in 1996 as they were in 1886. Politics and race are as tightly tied now as they were after 'the Late Unpleasantness'. Some of my sometime friends who take pride in their intellectual attainment fret over whether those who support (Newt) Gingrich, (Fob) James or (President) Clinton are 'intelligent voters'."

I received valuable advice from other APA former presidents, 90-year-old Ralph W. Callahan of *The Anniston Star* and Consolidated Publishing Co. in Anniston; Neil O. Davis, 82, retired editor and publisher of *The Auburn Bulletin* who edited the manuscript and proofs; J.C. Henderson, 92, retired publisher of *The Alexander City Outlook;* and Jimmy Mills, 96, retired editor of the *Birmingham Post-Herald.*

I am grateful for the research by the late L.O. Brackeen of Auburn.

Brackeen, information director at Auburn University when it was called Alabama Polytechnic Institute, is author of "History of the Alabama Press Association, 1871-1951" and the revised edition in 1959. Brackeen's files, which he donated to the Archives Department at the Ralph B. Draughon Library at Auburn University, were a tremendous help to me in revising and compiling the APA history.

I appreciate the help of former APA executive director Jim Hall and his wife, Martha, of Troy, who updated the history of the Press Association for APA's centennial celebration in 1971. The Halls' updated history from 1960 to 1971 was published in the APA Rate & Data Guide 100th Anniversary Edition in 1971.

I also extend thanks to a good friend and colleague in the Auburn University Department of Journalism who has been active in APA activities for a number of years, Professor Gillis Morgan, who proofread and edited the final manuscript, and provided encouragement and advice.

Finally, I thank my family, friends, and students for their patience, interest and encourage-ment during the two years that I was writing, compiling and editing this history of the Alabama Press Association.

Conventions of the Alabama Press Association are really reunions of the newspaper families of Alabama, and it has been that way practically since APA's beginning.

The following account of the 27th annual press convention was published in *The Alexander City Outlook* following an excursion to Washington, D.C., in 1898:

"A jollier or more congenial set of people could not be gotten together than the members of the Alabama Press Association. Everyone was made to feel a kinship, and the assemblage took upon it the appearance of one great family. Consequently, he who felt lonely or out of place must lay the fault at his own door."

The Alabama Press Association is an organization designed to improve the quality of the press in Alabama and protect its interests, but researching APA's 125-year history, interviewing its veteran leaders, and reading of its activities and participants — past and present — made me fully realize that APA is much more.

The strength of the APA is its people. To them, "getting out the paper" is a calling and a labor of love. This project has given me a greater appreciation of all Alabama newspaper men and women, past and present, and what they have accomplished for their communities and the state.

The achievements of the Alabama Press Association and Alabama newspapers are tremendous. They formed an important part of the foundation on which the state was built.

From the first newspaper at Fort Stoddard in 1811, the newspaper industry has increased and prospered. Today there is a healthy population of 97 weekly and 24 daily newspapers in Alabama.

It is significant that except for some 53 years since Alabama became a state, there has been an Alabama Press Association — thought to be the oldest trade association in the state, and one of the oldest press associations in the United States.

As we fast approach the next century, what is ahead for the Alabama Press Association and Alabama newspapers is more exciting than anything that has gone before. The 21st century will see changes in production methods and distribution even more extensive than those in the 1980s and 1990s. There will be a continuous expenditure of revenues for faster and better production. Computers will play an ever-increasing role in newspapers.

Despite the changes in technology, I think one thing will never change — the printed word and its impact. Technology changes over the years, but the most important things never change. Steve Stewart, former editor and publisher of the award-winning *Monroe Journal* and an outstanding newspaper man who now works at *The Decatur Daily*, told me that the real place to start in putting out a good newspaper is with thorough and factual news coverage, strong and constructive editorials, the exchange of opinions about public issues, and a phi-

losophy that puts the interests of the public — the people who read the newspaper — ahead of all other interests. These things are important whether a newspaper is produced with manual typewriters, Linotype machines, video display terminals, or computers and transmitted on the Internet.

I am reminded of a 1954 editorial by a former APA president, the late Glenn Stanley of *The Greenville Advocate*, on the 90th anniversary of his newspaper. *The Advocate* was established in 1864 by Stanley's father, Gen. James Berney Stanley, one of the 30 founders of APA.

"The world has come a long way since this newspaper came out with its first edition, but we seriously doubt that this Number 1 of Volume 90 is an improvement over Number 1 of Volume 1," Stanley wrote. "It's the printed word that makes the difference, not how it is produced."

— Ed Williams, Associate Professor
Department of Journalism
Auburn University
December 1996

PREFACE

A Call to Organize the Press

1871

"In all its existence the Alabama Press Association has striven to promote the best interests of a common country. Political partisanship and sectional animosity have no place on its calendar. It is the unrelenting foe of all things calculated to retard the advance of the country's glory and prosperity, and its great work is being felt in every state and territory of the union. As the years come and go, the Alabama Press Association's influence and power will be felt more and more. To have been the president of such an association is an honor far greater than could be conferred by any public or private preferment."

Maj. William Wallace Screws
The Montgomery Advertiser

— *Maj. William Wallace Screws (1839-1913)*
Editor, The Montgomery Advertiser *(1865-1913)*
Founder, the Alabama Press Association
APA president, 1878-1882 (four consecutive terms)
(From a speech given at the 34th annual Alabama Press Association convention in 1905 when Screws was paid tribute for his service as president of the National Editorial Association, and for his 40th anniversary with The Montgomery Advertiser)

IF THE 125-YEAR-OLD ALABAMA PRESS Association has a founding father, it would have to be William Wallace Screws, the long-time editor of *The Montgomery Advertiser.* Screws was one of the more active and influential editors of the Reconstruction era whose efforts helped bring the newspapers of the state into closer relationship with one another.

Screws was editor of *The Montgomery Advertiser* for 48 years, from 1865 to 1913. For years he was the sole owner, editor and president of *The Montgomery Advertiser.* During his tenure at the newspaper, Screws exercised his role as industry leader and political observer with all the dignity and integrity of a sage.

Born in Jernigan in Barbour County in 1839, Screws saved enough money from three years of hard labor in a store to meet his expenses while studying law. He practiced law in Montgomery until the outbreak of the Civil War.

Screws returned to Montgomery after Civil War

Following the war, Screws returned to Montgomery and accepted a position on the editorial staff of *The Montgomery Advertiser* in 1865. He was associated with the newspaper until his death on Aug. 8, 1913. *The Montgomery Advertiser* was the most important Democratic paper in the state during the nearly 50 years that Screws was to guide and control it. Screws was a power to be reckoned with in the state.

From 1878 to 1882 Screws served as secretary of state, and he was postmaster in Montgomery from 1893 to 1897. Screws received the title of major when he was appointed to the staff of Maj. Gen. Holtzalay of the state troops. He was known affectionately as "Major Screws" for the rest of his life.

Screws set his newspaper on a course that was thought "progressive." He urged the South to take advantage of its great natural resources and to be-

come a leader in the industrial revolution. In doing so, Screws followed his own conscience and
and beliefs and often found himself defending unpopular positions. For example, in all his editorals
he fearlessly opposed all propositions to repudiate
any portion of the state debt, and he contended
that the value of the property of the people de-
pended upon the maintaince of the state's credit
and honor.

The Montgomery Advertiser boycotted by Alliance

Too, when the Farmer's Alliance first appeared
in the South, Screws gave warning through *The
Montgomery Advertiser* that it was a political machine and that it would become a third party. For
this, the newspaper was boycotted by order of Alliance officials, and merchants were warned against
giving it their patronage.

Screws' forthrightness won him the respect of
his subscribers and his fellow editors. It was natural that Screws should be the one to call the editors and publishers of the state's newspapers to
Montgomery in 1871 to organize a press association.

Editor Screws saw need to organize presss

The press was young and the state was floun-
dering in the grip of Reconstruction when Screws
saw the need to organize Alabama's fledgling newspaper community. There had been talk, among a
few editors, of organizing a state press group.
Times were hard, however, and communication
between newspaers was lacking.

Finally, on March 17, 1871, some 60 years after the first newspaper began publication in what
was to become the State of Alabama, eight far-
sighted editors and publishers met in Screws' office in Montgomery and made the first definite
plans for organizing the press of Alabama. It was
from this meeting that the Alabama Press Association was formed.

Eight editors met in Montgomery on April 9, 1871

The press meeting called by Screws was infor-
mal, and its outcome was revealed on page 1 of the
Sunday edition of *The Montgomery Advertiser* on
April 9, 1871:

"At an informal meeting held in this city, of the
17th inst. (March 17, 1871) it was agreed to call a
Convention of the members of the Press of Alabama to meet in Montgomery on Thursday, the
8th of June, (1871) for the purpose of organizing
a State Press Association. It is desireable that ev-

ery newspaper and other publishing office in the
state be represented. Signed W.W. Screws, *The
Montgomery Advertiser;* M.J. Williams & Co., *The
Montgomery Mail;* P.D. Page, *The Evergreen Ob-
server;* Sidney Herbert, *The Troy Messenger;* R.H.
Powell, *The Union Springs Times and Herald;* Wil-
liam M. Lofton, *The Montgomery State Journal;* A.
Bingham, *The Talladega Sun;* and F.B. Ticknor, *The
Opelika Locomotive.*"

It was decided that the convention would be
held in Montgomery on June 8, 1871. In addition
to releasing the story, the eight editors and publishers reportedly wrote many letters about the
upcoming convention. A full month passed with
no response to the challenge of forming a state press
group. Evidently most newspaper men in the state
were not impressed as they did not reply to either
the story or the letters. However, Screws was not a
man to accept defeat so easily. The lack of interest
led him to write the following rousing editorial,
headlined "To The Press of Alabama," in the May
16, 1871, issue of *The Montgomery Advertiser:*

"To the Press of Alabama"

"A Press Convention has been called to assemble at Montgomery on the 8th of June. It is
now the middle of May and high time that there
should be some general understanding among
members of the fraternity if the mortification of a
general disappointment would be avoided. Without desiring to be, or appear, instrusive we, therefore, most respectfully request each and every editor in the State to notify us without delay whether
we may expect his paper to be represented or not.
By this means we shall be enabled to ascertain by
the first of June what the Convention will be likely
to provide. If a success we shall that day announce
it, positively — if not, we shall so state, and thus
save the few who would otherwise come, the expense and trouble of what might, to them, be a
very inconvenient and unnecessary trip to Montgomery."

Screws continued, "Our own private judgement
is that the whole affair had better be adjourned
until next October, at which time the State Fair
and other important gatherings will render a visit
to Montgomery much more pleasant and profitable to the delegates in attendance than it can be
in the heated month of June."

Editoral brought wave of response

The editorial brought a wave of response from
across the state. Plans seemed definite for once.

Many editors and publishers wrote agreeing that it would be best to delay the meeting until October. So, on May 30, 1871, *The Montgomery Advertiser* published an editoral stating that "We, of the central portion of the State…are authorized to say that the State Press Association is postponed until someday in October, to be named hereafter.

"We have received a number of letters from gentlemen of the Press fraternity advising that the Convention, announced to take place on the 8th of June, be postponed until the commencement of the Fall season, in October next," *The Montgomery Advertiser* continued. "We, of the central portion of the State, are disposed to believe that the suggestion is a good one. There could not possibly be as good an attendance in June, as there should be and, we are, therefore authorized to say that the State Press Association is postponed until someday in October, to be named hereafter. Only two or three have so far written to us in favor of holding it in June, while a great many suggest a later date."

There is some discrepency as to whether the October 1871 meeting was ever held. There is no existing record of it. But a date was finally set for Tuesday, June 18, 1872, in the rooms of the Board of Trade in Montgomery.

Screws' call to organize the press of Alabama came just 60 years after the first newspaper, *The Mobile Centinel,* was published in 1811 in what was

to become the State of Alabama. The first effort to launch a newspaper actually occurred in 1810 while Alabama was still part of the Mississippi Territory. Harry Toulmin, federal judge of the territory, framed plans to publish a paper with the grand title *Mobile Mercury,* or *Tombigbe and Alabama Advertiser;* however, no evidence exists that his project ever became a reality, according to F. Wilbur Helmbold in his paper, "Early Alabama Newspapermen, 1810-1820."

More than 100 years passed after the establishment of the first permanent settlement in the territory that became the State of Alabama before two experienced printers, Samuel Miller from Tennessee, and John B. Hood from South Carolina, published the territory's first "journal" in 1811. The two printers had obtained a printing press and hauled it by land from Chattanooga to Mims' Ferry on the Alabama River, then by boat south to Fort Stoddard, the U.S. military and customs port near Wakefield, just above the Spanish line. The temporary military station was some 20 miles north of Mobile and on the river bank east of Mount Vernon, Mississippi Territory.

When the first newspaper was published in Alabama, just four groups of American settlements were huddled along the major rivers; the Spanish held Mobile and most Alabamians were Creeks, Cherokees and Chickasaws.

First newspaper printed on May 23, 1811

It was at Fort Stoddard in the Mississippi Territory that Miller and Hood edited and printed the

first newspaper on May 23, 1811, *The Mobile Centinel,* in what is now Alabama. The weekly newspaper consisted of four pages, each with four columns, and subscribers paid an annual subscription price of $4. The paper maintained a precarious existence from May 23,1811, to June 6,1812, and was hardly more than a patriotic gesture. Four years later John B. Hood was to appear again in connection with an Alabama newspaper, this time at Huntsville when he established *The Huntsville Gazette* during the summer of 1816.

There were a number of reasons for this tardiness in journalistic endeavor. Most of the early settlers were much too occupied with building homes, clearing fields, and preparing defenses against unfriendly Indians to read newspapers. Mobile was the only town of any consequence, and its population was made up of three language groups — Spanish, French and English. Settlers who arrived with fairly comfortable means usually confined their reading to the classics, or to journals which were sent to them from their former homes.

The Mobile Centinel was short-lived

The Mobile Centinel was short-lived, as was the second newspaper, *The Madison Gazette,* founded in Huntsville in 1812 by a printer named William W. Parham. Typical of Southern newspapers of the day, *The Madison Gazette* was a four-page paper of which two pages consisted of advertisements, notices of runaway slaves, land sales, and public meetings. The remaining two pages contained practically nothing that was current or original. Reprints of articles from leading U.S. newspapers, sometimes several weeks old, apprised Alabamians of important national and world events. In 1816 its name was changed to *The Alabama Republican,* and in 1825 it was consolidated with *The Alabamian* to become *The Southern Advocate.*

John Boardman, a Massachusetts man who allied himself with the "Aristocratic Party" of Huntsville, was editor, first of *The Alabama Republican,* and later of *The Southern Advocate.* He supported John Quincy Adams for the presidency in 1824 and, though going over to Andrew Jackson in 1828, he always opposed the state bank and its adherents. In 1823 an opposition newspaper called *The Huntsville Democrat* was founded by William B. Long of Kentucky.

The first newspaper to survive more than a few years was *The Huntsville Advocate,* established in 1815. *The Huntsville Advocate* continued for 78 years, ceasing publication in 1893.

The Halcyon established in 1815

The Halcyon was established in March 1815 at St. Stephens, the growing settlement on the Tombigbee River, by one of the most interesting of the early Alabama publishers, Thomas Eastin, who was inducted into the Alabama Newspaper Hall of Honor in 1974. While in Mt. Vernon,Tenn., Eastin noticed a damaged printing press and materials piled in the streets of the town, and he was able to purchase these goods and transport them to St. Stephens.

Thomas Eastin
The Halcyon, St. Stephens

The Mobile Gazette was founded by James Lyon in 1813, and as the present-day *Mobile Register* is the oldest existing newspaper in Alabama. In 1816 ownership of *The Mobile Gazette* passed from Lyon to George B. Cotton, who continued the paper until 1822 when it was absorbed by *The Mobile Commercial Register.* The semi-weekly *Register,* founded in 1821 by John W. Townsend and Jonathan Battelle, was primarily a paper supporting the "Aristocrats" in the political battles of the state, according to Winifred Gregory in his book, "American Newspapers, 1821-1836."

In March 1819, two men named Tucker and Turner founded *The Alabama Courier* in the Monroe County town of Claiborne. The paper lasted until March 1822. The growing town of Tuscaloosa had its first newspaper in the spring of 1819 when Thomas M. Davenport of South Carolina began *The Tuscaloosa Republican.* Although the name was changed to *The American Mirror* in 1820 and then *The Tuscaloosa Chronicle* in 1827, Davenport and his son-in-law Dugald McFarlane continued to publish the newspaper until 1829.

Cahaba obtains newspaper in 1819

Cahaba, soon to be the first state capital, obtained a newspaper in 1819 when William B. Allen of Boston printed the first issue of *The Press and Alabama Intelligencer* on June 12,1819. When Alabama gained statehood on Dec.14,1819, six weekly or semi-weekly newspapers were in existence — *The Alabama Republican* of Huntsville, *The Mobile Gazette, The* (St. Stephens) *Halcyon, The Alabama Courier* in Claiborne, *The Tuscaloosa Republican* and *The Cahaba Press.*

The first newspaper established after Alabama became a state was *The Florence Gazette,* which began publication in January 1820. The paper was published by Peter Bertrand of Richmond, Ky. from 1820 until the Civil War halted publication in 1863, but the newspaper resumed publication after the war. The first newspaper in Selma was launched in 1827 when the weekly *Alabama Courier* began publication. On Jan. 6, 1821, *The Montgomery Republican* was established by John Battelle, editor, and E.W. Thompson, printer, as the first newspaper in Montgomery. In 1825 the name was changed to *The Montgomery Journal.* In 1825 there were 16 or 17 newspapers published in the state, but the following year saw the number reduced to 10, according to Thomas Perkins Abernethy in his book, "The Formative Period in Alabama,1815-1828."

The decade of the 1830s witnessed an explosion in journalism in the state with the founding of almost 50 newspapers ranging from weeklies including *The Greene County Gazette* of Erie (1831), *The Livingston Voice* of Sumter (1837), and *The Jacksonville Republican* (1837).

More obstacles other than making profits

Editors of these frontier papers faced obstacles other than making profits. Their news items were of necessity very personal, for their sources of information were limited to the immediate vicinity. Sometimes the intimate nature of the news led to altercations with offended subscribers. Editors who wished to avoid trouble confined their writings to the arrival of river packets, the movement of cotton, escape of slaves, and the opening of new inns.

During the decade after Alabama's admission to statehood in 1819, many hopeful editors and publishers set up their small presses in the settlements. Most of the papers lived briefly, failing to secure operating expenses from either subscribers or advertisers. But some were successful. By 1850, there were 82 newspapers in Alabama, nine of which were dailies.

Most Alabama newspapers in the 1810 to 1864 era were unprofitable, and many failed. From the first days of American settlement to the outbreak of the Civil War, the history of newspapers in Alabama was marked by numerous short-term ventures and large-scale mergers as the weak newspapers were destroyed or devoured by the strong. After the Civil War and Reconstruction, it was virtually impossible for a small newspaper to support itself.

Advertiser began as *Planter's Gazette*

At Montgomery, a paper was founded on Dec. 28, 1829, that was destined to become one of the most powerful in the state. It began quietly as the weekly *Planter's Gazette.* In 1833, *The Planter's Gazette* was purchased by Hugh McGuire, formerly of *The Tuscaloosa Intelligencer,* who changed the name to *The Montgomery Advertiser.* On Feb. 1, 1836, *The Montgomery Advertiser* began semi-weekly publication; some years later it became a daily. The first issue of *The Daily Alabama Journal* was published on Jan. 11, 1847.

When the capital was moved from Tuscaloosa to Montgomery, *The Montgomery Advertiser* was placed in a dominant position. Montgomery became the political as well as the geographical center of the state, enabling the newspaper to achieve a distribution far beyond that of its rivals. While the smaller journals had to be content with rumors and reprints or neighborly gossip, *The Montgomery Advertiser* presented national news.

Reconstruction brought changes in newspaper policy

The Reconstruction period brought about definite changes in newspaper policy. Vitriolic, front page editorials disappeared abruptly from most newspapers. Editors returned to recording purely local events. According to historian Richard R. Smith, in his 1941 "Alabama: A Guide to the Deep South," nearly 50 papers failed, and only the well established journals, including *The Mobile Daily Register, The Montgomery Advertiser, The Alabama Journal, The Selma Morning Times,* and *The Huntsville Advocate,* survived. An influential weekly newspaper of the state's early period was *The Moulton Advertiser,* founded in 1828. *The Moulton Advertiser* is the oldest existing weekly newspaper in Alabama.

Every political crisis saw birth of new papers

Every political crisis saw the birth of more newspapers. Minnie Clare Boyd in her book, "Alabama in the Fifties: A Social Study," wrote that the momentous year of 1860 ushered in a regular epidemic of newspapers: *The Bellefonte Era, The Cahaba Slaveholder, The Jacksonville States Rights Democrat, The Selma Issue,* and *The Somerville Democrat.* "Most of these newspapers enjoyed but a fleeting existence, but whether they lived or died, their hue and cry, while living, was politics," Boyd wrote. "Other things concerned them for a day, but politics concerned them always."

From 1865 to 1880, few publishers dared to establish papers in Alabama. The merchants, who were ruined along with the planters and small manufacturers, greatly limited or withdrew their advertising. Circulation also fell sharply, for Alabamians looked upon a newspaper as a luxury, and few were willing to pay the meager subscription price when every penny was needed to buy food.

The Mobile Nationalist was first black newspaper

The founding of the first black newspaper in Alabama, *The Mobile Nationalist,* was on Dec. 14, 1865, and was published until October 1869. Although it was edited by two white carpetbaggers, John Silsby and Albert Griffin, the newspaper was "owned entirely by colored people and managed by a Board of Directors comprised entirely of colored men."

Throughout its existence *The Mobile Nationalist* was a devoted supporter of the Republican Party and carried articles about the party's activities, conventions, candidates, platform and elections, according to Auburn University retired history professor Dr. Allen W. Jones in the chapter he wrote for the book, "The Black Press in the South, 1865-1979," edited by Henry Lewis Suggs.

By the early 1870s, the political and educational progress of blacks in Alabama generated a need for more black newspapers.

Black newspapers appeared in Mobile, Montgomery

Black newspapers appeared in Mobile and Montgomery in 1870 and 1872, where politically ambitious blacks joined white Republicans as candidates for state and national offices.

The need for a national black press association and an increase in the number of black newspapers published in Alabama inspired black editors in the state to study the feasibility of establishing press associations on regional and state levels.

Although *The Huntsville Gazette* reported an attempt by black editors in Alabama and Mississippi to organize a press association in 1883, the first serious effort in Alabama began in 1886 when the editor of *The Gazette* suggested a meeting of black journalists in Birmingham. Editors Jesse Duke of *The Montgomery Herald* and R.C.O. Benjamin of *The Birmingham Negro American* endorsed the call for such a gathering.

Alabama Colored Press Association founded in 1887

In May 1887, editors from nine papers held a two-day convention in Selma and founded the Alabama Colored Press Association. Convention delegates adopted a constitution, elected officers, and heard the reading of several papers, including one by Jesse Duke titled "The Relation of Newspapers to Politics."

But the Alabama Colored Press Association collapsed in 1889 after editors Duke and Benjamin were run out of the state by whites who objected to their "incendiary journalism," Jones wrote.

Afro-American Press Association formed

Another press association, the Afro-American Press Association, was formed in 1894 by 16 editors. The first convention was in Birmingham on Aug. 29-31,1895.The three-day meeting included the reading of papers by prominent black editors, social activities for the editors and their families, election of officers, and the adoption of resolutions protesting Jim Crow railroad cars, the crime of lynch-law, and the government's failure to secure for all citizens...legal protection of life, liberty and the pursuit of happiness," according to Jones.

Convention delegates discussed and rejected editor A.N. Johnson's proposal to organize a state newspaper union and W.H. Mixon's resolution to advise black laborers to stay away from towns and cities. Speakers praised the educational work of the black press in the state and recognized the important work of Professor T.H. Jordan, editor of *The Birmingham Broad Axe,* who published five journals in addition to his newspaper.

Proceedings published by white press in Birmingham

The white press in Birmingham published the proceedings from the Afro-American Press Association and hailed the black newspaper editors as the new social, political and educational leaders of the race. The white editor of *The Birmingham Age-Herald* advised these new leaders to avoid "becoming the tool of designing politicians and agitators" and to "educate the Negroes to a proper appreciation of their true position and opportunities." Such "common sense and fidelity to principle," wrote the editor, would "undoubtedly be profitable (and) elevate blacks in the estimation of the white people of the state."

Journalism revived in Alabama in late 1800s

With the departure of federal officials and the return of a semblance of state government, journalism was revived in Alabama in the late 1800s. By 1890, there were 179 newspapers in Alabama, 16 of them dailies. In addition, churches and colleges were issuing 21 publications, according to Richard R. Smith in his "Alabama: A Guide to the

Deep South." The newspapers returned to the antebellum policy of presenting news in the form of editorials, and politics again became dominant. *The Montgomery Advertiser* made and unmade governors and dictated policies.

Iron and steel industries contributed an important chapter to the story of Alabama journalism. The rapid rise of Birmingham, with its booms and scarcity of newspapers, attracted publishers from all parts of the South. Some of them hurriedly set up small papers that failed for lack of capital. *The Sun* was Birmingham's first newspaper. It was originally *The Herald*, published by Henry A. Hale at Elyton, at that time the county seat of Jefferson County. The newspaper was moved to Birmingham when the town was established in 1871. Robert H. Henley, Birmingham's first mayor, was the owner. The paper became a daily in 1872, but was not long continued.

But *The Iron-Age*, established in 1874, was successful from the beginning. It became *The Age-Herald* in 1888, when its rival, *The Birmingham News*, was founded. *The News* purchased *The Age-Herald* in 1927, continuing *The Age-Herald* as the moming paper and *The News* as the evening paper (with Sunday editions combined). In 1921 the Scripps Howard chain of newspapers entered the Birmingham field by establishing *The Birmingham Post*.

The Birmingham Post and *Age-Herald* were merged into a morning newspaper on May 15, 1950, to become the *Birmingham Post-Herald*.

ADVERTISER AND STATE GAZETTE.

BRITTAN & DE WOLF.   MONTGOMERY, ALABAMA, WEDNESDAY, FEBRUARY 13, 1850.   VOLUME XVI.—NUMBER 18.

CHAPTER 1

The Early Years: Entertainment and Excursions

1872 - 1891

"Times have changed. The old Washington hand press has gone into the museum; the Country Campbell (flat-bed letter-press) is making a last stand; the old hand-compositor has joined the dodo as an extinct animal; but publishing a newspaper today involves just about the same pains and labors that it did 60 years ago.

Gen. James Berney Stanley
The Greenville Advocate

"It is not a game, not a business, it is a profession and an honorable one; and in looking over you fellows of the Alabama Press Association today, I see the same brand of brilliant men that I associated with when the association was young.

"Many of you have the same names and belong to the same families; and in years to come there will be no material change in the type of men or in the editorial policy of the papers. The changes come in the back — not in the front office.

"It is sad to think of the many missing ones, but I'm happy to be with you, and I'm lucky to be able to rub shoulders with more than one generation of Alabama editors. I thank you."

— *Gen. James Berney Stanley, 1844-1934*
Founder, The Greenville Advocate
APA president, 1882-1886 (four consecutive terms)
(From a talk, "Some Reminiscences of the
Alabama Press Association," given August 1929 at APA's first
Press Institute at Alabama Polytechnic Institute in Auburn)

THE ALABAMA PRESS ASSOCIATION, UNLIKE some other state press associations, was always more than just a publisher's organization. It was formally organized in 1872 as the Editors and Publishers Association of the State of Alabama, the name it kept until 1891 when it became the Alabama Press Association. Membership was open to individual editors and publishers of any daily, weekly or monthly in the state for $2 per person, but only one vote was allowed per newspaper.

APA has held an annual convention each year since 1872. Delegates to the press conventions adopted resolutions reflecting concern about their profession and economic development of the state. They adopted resolutions against censorship, for better education, local taxation for public education, for a paper mill in Alabama, for large resorts in the state (so they would have a place to meet), for the sale of war bonds, and for and against a variety of social, economic and cultural matters. The editors and publishers of the late 1800s probably reflected well what the state's more educated leaders were thinking.

The young Press Association's leaders also led trips all over the United States, Canada, and to the Caribbean. APA members traveled via steamer to Havana, Cuba, for several conventions. These "excursions," as they were called, seemed to be a way of broadening the view of the newspaper executives and to show the rest of the country that there were civilized people in the Reconstruction South.

Business, pleasure combined at early conventions

In the early days of the Alabama Press Association, business and pleasure were combined at the once-a-year conventions. Newspaper reports, which are almost the only surviving records of the early years of APA, usually gave more space to the excursions and entertainment provided the editors and publishers than to business meetings.

Most editors held passes on the railroads and steamship lines. Thus it was convenient for trips to be made within and outside the continental limits of the United States. The delegates would adopt resolutions expressing thanks to the railroads for favors extended to newspaper men and their families and for planning excursion trips for their pleasure.

Entertainment provided for the editors and publishers at the early conventions was lavish. This was because of the prevailing practice in that period of free railroad passes being given to newspapers, and free accommodations provided by hotels and restaurants. Those dispensing hospitality expected to be rewarded with favorable comments in the press. Towns and cities, both within and outside Alabama, vied with one another for the privilege of hosting press conventions, for they knew that they would be rewarded with favorable publicity.

Screws describes hospitality given editors

A description of the hospitality given editors at conventions was provided in 1873 by Maj. William Wallace Screws, editor of *The Montgomery Advertiser:*

"An editor was hardly allowed to pay for what he bought. One instance will serve to illustrate our meaning. Mr. Strother, who keeps the refreshment room at the depot, threw open his house to the Association and invited them to help themselves. One member, with a view to recompensing such generosity, to a degree at least, was on the point of purchasing a few articles of the Clerk or Assistant when Strother from another part of the room discovered what was going on and came running up, with both hands extended, calling out as he came 'Stop! Stop! None of that! You are our guests and welcome to anything here without money and without price.'

"This we say was the prevailing rule, and if it had any exceptions we heard nothing of them. The hotels charged nothing for board, the railroads nothing for special trains, the hacks of the city were at all times ours to command and in fact everything was free as water. Nixon of the Powell House, the Bridge Bros. of the Alamo, the proprietor of the Relay and in short proprietors of all the hotels (we cannot remember the names of all) vied with

each other and with the citizens in making the editors at home.

"A lunch consisting of roast chicken, turkey, boiled ham, breads and crackers of all sorts, pickles, etc. and flanked by demijohns of whiskey and brandy and a 10-gallon cask of scuppernong wine from the neighboring vineyard of Col. W.S. Earnest, was kept constantly standing in the office of the Elyton Land Company. To this, due reverence was paid, but to the credit of the craft be it said there was not one man among them all who overstepped the inside boundaries of sobriety."
— *The Montgomery Advertiser*
May 20, 1873
Page 3, columns 2, 3

Free transportation referred to as "deadheading"

The practice of editors exchanging free transportation and reduced rates for plugs was referred to as "deadheading." Later deadheading came into disrepute, but at the time it did not violate journalistic ethics. This practice can be defended on other grounds than the prevailing morality of the times. It would have been difficult for country editors to pay for annual outings and stays at expensive hotels.

The excursions not only encouraged editors and publishers to attend the press conventions, but also gave them a chance to broaden their outlook about their state and other states. Also, the excursions substantially aided the growth of press associations, not only in Alabama, but throughout the country.

For its first 20 years of the Alabama Press Association's existence, the annual conventions were primarily social gatherings. But it must be recognized that if the newspaper men of the state had not gotten to know each other socially there would have developed no community of interest to promote the interests of the press in the state.

Political orientation affected convention attendance

The political orientation of Alabama editors often affected attendance at Press Association conventions and their tone. The conventions were usually were held when the Democratic state convention met in Montgomery. Conventions held in Montgomery, therefore, were unusually well-attended. Those editors who were not delegates to the Democratic convention were in town to cover it.

Some Press Association meetings had to be cut short because of the political interests of the members, according to *The Montgomery Advertiser* in its May 30, 1878, issue. It is probable that as much political "horse-trading" as journalistic "shop talk" went on at the annual meetings.

Business sessions marked by flowery oratory

The business sessions of the formative period of APA were marked by flowery oratory by Press Association officers and representatives of host communities. The speeches usually extolled the virtues of Alabama, the South, and the press in Alabama. Resolutions adopted in the early years of the Press Association were as likely to deal with current political and economic issues in Alabama and the nation as with specific concerns of the press.

Alabama history and the position of newspaper editors and publishers in the 1870s explain this political orientation. The state was still under and just beginning to emerge from Reconstruction government when the Alabama Press Association was founded. Most of the newspaper men felt that Alabama's most pressing need was the replacement of the Radical (Republican) regime. They viewed it as being controlled by "blacks, carpetbaggers and scalawags." Corruption in the Radical government provided them with ammunition in their campaign for the triumph of the Democratic and Conservative Party.

The editors, however, were concerned not just with the political problems of Alabama. They were dedicated to helping the state recover from the economic and social disruptions of war. The abolition of slavery forced a new agricultural system. The single-crop, sharecropper system and farm tenancy which evolved was probably inevitable, although, both economically and socially, it was to plague the South for years to come.

Editors sought improvement of agricultural system

Many Alabama editors labored diligently for improvement of the state's agricultural system through diversification, mechanization, better transportation, and abolition of the worst abuses of the sharecrop system. Other editors adopted the philosophy of the "New South" and felt that Alabama could progress most through the development of industry.

It took capital to improve agriculture and develop industry. Because of the ravages of war, the necessary capital simply was not available within the state. It was this crying need for capital that prompted the state's newspapers to promote the virtues of the people of the state and its abundant natural resources at any opportunity.

APA founders concerned about state's image

As state leaders, the founders of the Alabama Press Association also were concerned about the state's image. The excitement aroused by the APA-sponsored visit of the New York Press Association is an example of the deep concern the newspaper men had for the welfare of Alabama. On May 19, 1874, some 63 New York editors, wives and friends arrived in Birmingham to visit the fledgling industrial town and the resort at Blount Springs, as well as Montgomery, Tuscaloosa and Selma.

Of course, the Alabama editors' motives were not selfless. They realized that the press could not be prosperous if the area was not prosperous. Later, becoming more aware that prosperity in itself did not guarantee a prosperous press, they became more concerned with specific measures to improve their newspapers and increase their revenues.

Newspapers often "militantly partisan"

"The Alabama editor in the period 1871-1891 was essentially a political animal. Alabama newspapers were often militantly partisan, in order to survive," Thomas D. Clark and Albert D. Kirwan wrote in their book, "The South Since Appomattox." Clark and Kirwan noted that "Editors, especially of the weekly papers, needed the county's printing business to succeed. Thus they became active in politics and even ran for office."

Many editors and publishers were Confederate veterans who returned from the war to find their fortunes diminished, if not wiped out. Publication of a newspaper was one business that could be started with a small amount of capital. Editing a country newspaper became a prestigious profession in the New South. Where once law, medicine, and the ministry appealed to young men, many turned instead to become newspaper editors.

Editors became active in politics

"A youth with limited education could almost begin publication of a country paper if he were able to identify one type character from another," Clark and Kirwan wrote. "He needed little capital, no typographical experience, a rundown building, and a chance at the county's printing business to succeed. Thus it was that local editors became active in politics, supported hand-picked candidates, and even ran for office themselves. Because of year-round political involvements, their papers intimately reflected grass-roots Southern politics."

Editors entered politics for other than economic reasons, too. They were community leaders who would be expected to be elected to political office. Most were dedicated to improving the state in any possible way, and political activity was an effective means for determining the state's destiny.

Editors lashed out constantly at illiteracy, and in their limited ways supported movements for public schools, better-trained teachers, and opportunities for youth. Few Southern counties could have organized public schools successfully without the leadership of country editors.

1872
Col. Seaborn Jones Saffold, *The Selma Daily Times*
1872-1873 president

First press convention, Montgomery
June 18, 1872

The first official convention of the Alabama Press Association was at the Board of Trade in Montgomery on June 18, 1872. *The Montgomery Advertiser* ran the following story on the day of the convention:

"An important meeting of the Press of Alabama was fixed for this day in this city. Many members are already in the city and we presume more will arrive on the morning trains. As there will be but one day in which to do anything it has been deemed advisable to go at once to work. The officers and members of the Board of Trade have kindly tendered the use of their Hall to the Convention, and we take the liberty of stating that the Convention will meet at 10 o'clock this morning."

S I D E L I G H T S
MARKING 125 YEARS OF HISTORY

Paper mill committee appointed in 1872

A committee of five was named at the first Press Assocation convention in Montomery in 1872 to "investigate the feasibility of establishing a paper mill at some accessable point in Alabama."

Members of the paper mill committee included Sidney Herbert, *The Troy Messenger;* J.W. Grant, *The Jacksonville Republican;* Maj. William Wallace Screws, *The Montgomery Advertiser;* H.A. Hale, *The Birmingham Herald;* and J.E. Roberts, *The Opelika Locomotive.*

Newspaper men "go at once to work"

Obviously, the newspaper men did "go at once to work." Officers were elected, a constitution was drawn up, and bylaws were adopted. Col. Seaborn Jones Saffold of *The Selma Daily Times* was named chairman, and J.M. Richards of *The LaFayette Reporter* was named secretary. Under instruction of the convention, Saffold appointed two committees — one to nominate officers to serve during the convention and the other "to report business for the consideration of the convention."

Members of the nominating committee were P.D. Page, *The Evergreen Observer;* R.H. Henley, *The Birmingham Sun;* and Malcolm Clayton Burke, *The Demopolis Bigbee News.* Serving on the business committee were J.H. Francis, *The Montgomery Advance;* William Wallace Screws, *The Montgomery Advertiser;* J.M. Macon, *The Eufaula Daily Times;* Joseph Shackleford, *The Tuscumbia North Alabamian & Times;* and Willis Brewer, *The Hayneville Examiner.*

Screws writes record of first APA convention

On the day after the convention, Screws wrote an exacting record in *The Montgomery Advertiser* of what took place:

"This convention met in the rooms of the Board of Trade, in the City of Montgomery, Tuesday, the 18th day of June, 1872. On motion of R.H. Henley, of *The Birmingham Sun,* Col. Seaborn Jones Saffold, of *The Selma Daily Times,* was called to the chair and J.M. Richards of *The LaFayette Reporter* was requested to act as Secretary. Upon motion, the representatives of the Alabama Press present were requested to come forward and enroll their names.

The following names were enrolled:

"W.W. Screws, *The Montgomery Advertiser;* R.A. Mosely Jr., *The Talladega News & Our Mountain Home;* R.H. Henley, *The Birmingham Sun;* Thomas D. Osborne, semi-weekly *Stevenson News Era;* Eppes Tucker, *The Opelika Congregational Methodist;* J.E. Roberts, *The Opelika Locomotive;* E.G. Meredith, *The Evergreen Observer;* R.A. Mosely Jr., *The Oxford Chronicle;* J.R. Thames, *The Greenville South Alabamian;* J.F. Grant, *The Jacksonville Republican;* J.M. Macon, *The Eufaula Times;* Sidney Herbert, *The Troy Messenger;* W.J. Wood, *The Lauderdale Times;* M.C. Burke, *The Demopolis Bigbee News;* J.H. Francis, *The Montgomery Advance;* L.W. Grant, *The Jacksonville Republican;* Joseph Shackleford, *The Tuscumbia North Alabamian & Times;* T.J. Cox, *The Gadsden Times;* H.A. Hale, *The Birmingham Herald;* Willis Brewer,

The Hayneville Examiner; J.M. Whitehead, *The Greenville Independent Thinker;* J.M. Withers, *The Mobile Tribune;* Robert McKee, *The Selma Argus;* L.W. Matthews, *The Elyton Jefferson Independent,* J.B. Stanley, *The Greenville Advocate;* P.D. Page, late of *The Evergreen Observer;* S.J. Saffold, *The Selma Daily Times;* R. McFarland, *The Florence Journal;* J.M. Richards, *The LaFayette Reporter;* D.C. White, *The Moulton Advertiser and Courtland News."*

These 30 newspaper men, editors and publishers from every section of the state, may be considered the founders of the 125-year-old Alabama Press Association — thought to be the oldest business and trade association in Alabama, and one of the oldest press associations in the United States.

Saffold elected first APA president

The editors and publishers came together to form a fraternity of newspaper men. They elected a slate of officers to serve during the first convention in 1872 that included Gen. Jones Mitchell Withers of *The Mobile Tribune* as president. According to Press Association minutes, however, Withers "for reasons stated, which deemed to be satisfactory by the convention" asked to be excused from serving as president and Col. Seaborn Jones Saffold of *The Selma Daily Times* was elected the first president of the Alabama Press Association.

Maj. William Wallace Screws of *The Montgomery Advertiser* was elected first vice president, and J.M. Macon of *The Eufaula Daily Times* was elected second vice president. Other officers were James Freeman Grant, *The Jacksonville Republican,* treasurer; Leonidis (Lon) W. Grant (son of James Freeman Grant), *The Jacksonville Republican,* recording secretary; and J.H. Francis, *The Montgomery Advance,* corresponding secretary.

Following the nominations and elections, convention delegates set forth the original constitution of the Editors and Publishers Association of the State of Alabama:

Constitution

Upon recommendation of the "business committee," the following constitution and bylaws were adopted:

"For purposes of mutual benefits, through annual reunions, and social and business intercourse there to be had, we do hereby associate ourselves together and do adopt as follows:

"Section 1: This association shall be known as the Editors and Publishers Association of the State of Alabama.

"Section 2: Its officers shall consist of one President, five Vice Presidents, a Recording Secretary, Corresponding Secretary and Treasurer, and an Executive Committee, who shall be elected by a majority of the members voting at each annual Convention, whose term of office shall begin at the adjournment thereof, and continue until the close of the convention next ensuing, or until their successors shall be elected, and this election shall be the last business of each Convention.*

"Section 3: It shall be the duty of the President to call the annual convention, to preside thereat, and to arrange and direct the proceedings at the same time.

"Section 4: The Executive Committee shall consist of five members, and with the President and Secretary, shall constitute an Advisory Board with power to fill all official vacancies.

"Section 5: Any editor or publisher of any daily or monthly regularly published in the State, and none other, may become a member of this Association, upon the recommendation of the Executive Committee, and on payment of the initiation fee of $2.00, and subscribing to this Constitution. Application for membership and payment of initiation fees shall be made to the Secretary and Treasurer at least 30 days previous to the holding of each annual convention.

"Section 6: Annual dues shall be paid on the first day of each annual convention.

"Section 7: This Constitution may be amended by a vote of two-thirds of the members of the Association, upon one day's notice.

"Section 8: The annual meeting of the Association shall be held at such time and place as shall be determined by a majority of the members. Such other meetings may be held as the Association may determine.

"Section 9: The number of representatives to any journal entitled to membership in the Association shall not be limited, provided each member received is actually connected with said journal in the capacity of editor or publisher, and that the annual assessments are paid by each member.

"Section 10: One vote and no more shall be allowed to each journal represented."

Bylaws

"1. The ordinary rules that govern legislative bodies shall be observed in the meeting of this Association.

"2. Whenever a division is called for, the Secretary shall call the roll of the journals represented and the vote shall be given as the roll is called.

"3. Any member of the Association who is unable to attend the annual meetings may appoint a Proxy in writing, who, on payment of the annual assessment of the member he represents, shall receive a certificate from the Secretary entitling him to all the rights and privi-

leges of membership in the Association during the meeting for which he is appointed to act as proxy.

"4. Ex-members of the press and members of the press in other states can be admitted as honorary members of this Association, but such honorary members will not be entitled to vote or speak on any question before the said Association.

"5. It shall be the duty of the Secretary to keep a roll of the members of the Association — together with the names of all persons hereafter admitted to membership, and the dates of their admission.

"6. The Secretary shall call the roll at each meeting of the Association during the Annual Session, and each member shall answer to his name, or be represented by proxy.

"7. At all meetings the Secretary shall read the journal of the last annual convention.

"8. The President shall call upon the Secretary for a report of all business transactions made during interim since the last annual meeting, and all business in course of consideration."

The secretary was instructed to have 200 copies of the constitution and bylaws and the proceedings of the meeting printed for distribution to Alabama and Southern editors.

As if this was not enough work for one day, the busy editors "burned the midnight oil," adopting resolutions that would shape the destiny of the press in Alabama. Editor Screws' extensive article in the June 19, 1872, issue of *The Montgomery Advertiser* (page 3, columns 4 and 5) goes on to enumerate each of these initial resolutions:

"Resolved, that if at any time a contract between any publisher of this Association and any advertising agent, be violated by such advertising agent, upon complaint of the publisher with whom such contract has been made, he filing complaint containing the full statement of facts with the Executive Committee, such Committee is authorized to investigate the matter and if such complaint should be found to be well-founded, said agent shall be exposed through every newspaper of the organization.

"Resolved, that the newspapers of this Association charge advertising rates henceforth for communications suggesting or recommending candidates for office, and obituaries, exceeding five lines in length.

"Resolved, that we mutually aid and assist each other in business, and lose no opportunity to throw business to any member of this Association when in our power to do so.

"Resolved, that the publisher or editor of every paper in Alabama represented in this Association, shall within 10 days after the adjournment of the same, file with the Secretary thereof, his specific rates for advertising which shall continue for the next twelve months, unless notice of change shall be filed with said Secretary at an annual meeting of this Association.

"Resolved, that each member of this Association individually pledges himself to be a faithful observer of his terms so given; and on failure thereof shall be expelled from the Association.

"Resolved, that a committee of five be appointed to investigate the feasibility of establishing a paper mill at some accessible point in Alabama and to report at the next meeting of this convention.

"Be it further resolved, that the Corresponding Secretary solicit publishers and editors within the State not members of this Association to become so at once."

Resolutions also thanked the Montgomery Board of Trade, officers of the Press Association, and others for "courtesies extended the convention."

1872-1873 Press Association officers elected

Officers elected for 1872-1873 were Col. Seaborn Jones Saffold, *The Selma Daily Times*, president; Maj. William Wallace Screws, *The Montgomery Advertiser;* J.M. Macon, *The Eufaula Daily News;* Robert McFarland, *The Florence Journal;* R.D. Osbourne, *The Stevenson New Era;* and Robert Alexander Moseley Jr., *The Talladega News* and *Our Mountain Home,* vice presidents. Treasurer was James Freeman Grant, *The Jacksonville Republican;* recording secretary was Leonidis (Lon) W. Grant, *The Jacksonville Republican;* and corresponding secretary was J.H. Francis, *The Montgomery Advance.*

The Executive Committee was comprised of Willis Brewer, *The Hayneville Examiner;* Robert Alexander Moseley Jr., *The Talladega News;* J.H. Francis, *The Montgomery Advance;* Joseph Shackleford, *The Tuscumbia North Alabamian & Times;* and R.H. Henley, *The Birmingham Sun.* The president and secretary served as ex-officio members.

Delegates to the first convention of the Editors and Publishers Association of the State of Alabama adjourned to meet in Mobile on Dec. 3, 1872. (If this meeting was ever held there is no record of it in the Mobile newspapers.)

1873
Col. Seaborn Jones Saffold, *The Selma Daily Times* 1873-1874 president

Second annual press convention, Birmingham
May 15-17, 1873

"The meeting was characterized by the utmost good feeling and harmony," *The Montgomery Ad-*

vertiser commented in its account of the second annual press convention in 1873. "The press gang seemed to be on good terms with each other and with all the rest of mankind. The generous hospitality which overflowed them from all quarters did much to increase that good feeling," *The Advertiser* reported on May 20, 1873.

Delegates to the 1873 convention in Birmingham on May 15-17 took up the question of standardization of advertising rates "in an effort to form a sort of cooperative system for the mutual protection of members against advertising agencies which beat down prices and boast of their ability to advertise in scores of Southern newspapers at prices that leave all the profits in their own pockets."

Other objectives of this measure were to stop "the unprofessional cut-throat system of underbidding among the craft" and to cut off "patent outside" advertisements.

New York editors are invited

Delegates also voted to invite New York editors to visit in May 1874 for "a grand tour of the State of Alabama." They arranged for the railroad and steamship companies to give Press Association members and wives passes and made plans for carrying the New Yorkers on a tour of the state.

"The purpose of the Alabama Press Association," Maj. William Wallace Screws wrote in *The Montgomery Advertiser,* "is to bring hither the representatives of the press from abroad; to show them something of the capacities and undeveloped wealth of our great state. We desire, for instance, to take 25 to 30 New Yorkers among the ore beds

of Red Mountain and the coal mines of the Cahaba and the Warrior. We desire to fill the Empire State with advertisements of our mineral resources, and there is no better way of doing that than the way adopted. There is a practical reconstruction in that — a reconstruction which will profit Alabama more than anything else that the State press could do on such an occasion."

1874
**Col. Seaborn Jones Saffold, *The Selma Daily Times*
1874-1875 president**

**Third annual press convention, Birmingham
May 19, 1874**

The Alabama Press Association returned to Birmingham for its third annual convention on May 19, 1874. Some 63 New York editors, wives and friends spent a week in Alabama in 1874, jam-packed with tours and hospitality. The New Yorkers were greeted in Blount Springs and Birmingham by members of the Press Association and officials of Birmingham. The New York editors spent Wednesday visiting iron works and other places of interest in and near Birmingham. They visited Tuscaloosa on Thursday, Selma on Friday, and Montgomery over the weekend.

Here is how *The Alabama Beacon* of Greensboro reported the New Yorkers' visit:

"On Tuesday afternoon some forty to fifty New York editors, composing, we suppose, a portion of the New York Press Association, accompanied by a party of ladies, arrived, receiving from the citizens of the Magic City, as also from the Alabama Press Association, a most cordial welcome. Wednesday was spent visiting Iron Works, and other objects of interest, in the vicinity of Birmingham. On Thursday they visited Tuskaloosa, Selma on Friday morning, and Montgomery on Friday evening, at both of which places they were most hospitably entertained. They left Montgomery on their return home, on Monday morning via the S&N, and Selma, Rome & Dalton Railroads, doubtless pleased with their visit to Alabama." (*The Alabama Beacon,* Greensboro, May 30, 1874 edition, page 2, column 1.)

18 Alabama editors accompanied New Yorkers on tour

Eighteen Alabama newspaper men accompanied the New York editors and publishers on the tour of Alabama and then went with the New Yorkers to Washington, D.C., for a short visit. In its May 23, 1874, edition *The Montgomery Advertiser* reported that the following Alabama newspaper men made the tour:

J.F. and L.W. Grant, *The Jacksonville Republican;* R. Randolph, *The Tuscaloosa Blade;* D.W. McIver, *The Tuskegee News;* J.H. Francis, *The Selma Times;* Jourd White, *The Moulton Advertiser;* B.O. Randall and S.R. Echols, *The Gadsden Times;* J.B. Roden and C. Roberts, *The Birmingham Age;* D.B. Haynes, *The Florence Republican;* G.M. Johnson, *The Huntsville Advocate;* T.A. McLaughlin, *The Birmingham Independent;* Gen. James Berney Stanley, *The Greenville Advocate;* J.R. Rogers, *The Union Springs Herald and Times;* A.B. Persinger, *The Jasper Mountain Eagle;* C.C. NeSmith, *The Somerville Free Press;* and H.A. Hale, *The Birmingham News.*

Alabamians hoped visit would reconcile bitter feelings

The Alabama editors and publishers hoped that the New Yorkers' visit would help reconcile bitter feelings between the North and the South as well as bring about economic advancement for the state. Both the economic and social motives of the Press Association are reflected in this May 21, 1874, editorial from *The Shelby Guide of Montevallo,* a newspaper particularly interested in the mineral development of the state:

"The members of the New York Press Association are representative men of their state. A great many of these men have since the war, considered the Southern people as rebels at heart, desiring nothing but an opportunity to overthrow 'the best government the world ever saw.' When they meet the representatives of our people in social intercourse, and enjoy the unostentatious hospitality extended to them, they will ascertain that the opinions that they have heretofore entertained of the people of the South, based upon the foul and false accusations of the carpetbaggers and scalawags, are wrong; and they will return to their homes convinced that the 'white men' of the South, desire nothing but the perpetuation of the Union upon Constitutional principles, and will in the future, instead of exhausting their talents in a war against the Southern people, unite with us in an honest endeavor to dispossess the thieves and robbers of the control of the National Government.

"Alabama's future depends upon the development of her mineral resources. The owners of the mineral lands in Alabama, appreciating this fact, have spent thousands of dollars in printer's ink, in bringing these lands to the notice of the Northern capitalist(s). The visit of the New York Press Association will do more to bring the mineral resources of Alabama into public notice than all the advertising has heretofore done."

Some attempts to prejudice New Yorkers

Apparently there were some attempts by Republican officeholders and newspapers to prejudice the New Yorkers against the Democrats of Alabama. According to *The Montgomery Advertiser* in its May 26, 1874, edition, these efforts met with little success. The editor of *Our Mountain Home* in Talladega (at that time a Republican paper) sent the New York editors marked copies of his paper "containing extracts which he thought would be likely to arouse resentment, and prevent any toning down or softening of the asperities supposed to exist in the minds of Northern Republicans toward the people of the South."

The New Yorkers showed the papers to the Alabama editors, remarking that the Talladega editor must be a "scurvy fellow who had been bought with a postmastership or some such office," *The Montgomery Advertiser* reported.

Advertiser reports on minerals in state

The Montgomery Advertiser on the day of the New Yorkers' visit (May 26, 1874) to the capital city ran a long report on the minerals of Alabama for the benefit of the New Yorkers:

"Since the New York editors have crossed our borders, they have been shown (1) the most wonderful watering place on the continent, Blount Springs, where seven different waters gush from the earth in the space of an eighth of an acre; (2) the coal fields of the Warrior, and the various mines from which the coal is being taken; (3) Red Mountain, where the iron ore, averaging 50 percent metallic iron, lies piled up in such vast masses that to scale the mountain's side is a matter of extreme difficulty and where the ore is now mined by quarried from veins thirty feet in thickness, three or four hundred feet in width and seventy miles in length from Northwest to Southwest; (4) the coal mines of the Cahaba; (5) the lime works at Calera; (6) the pine forest of Bibb and Baker (now Chilton); (7) the cotton and corn lands of Dallas, Lowndes and Montgomery; (8) the iron furnaces of the South and North, and Selma, Rome and Dalton Railroads; (9) the juxtaposition of coal, sandstone, lime and ore and indeed all things needed in the making of fine iron at small cost.

"They have seen our little Eureka furnace"

"They have seen our little Eureka furnace pouring out at one draught as much molten iron as would flow from one of double its size in Pennsylvania; they have seen specimens of ore and minerals which their limited stay in our state would not permit them to visit in the mine or quarry; they have seen tangible evidence of undeveloped wealth which it required seeing to believe; they have seen half our fields laying bare and idle because there was not enough labor here to cultivate them against the day of harvest, but above all they have seen and felt that there is no spirit of 'disloyalty' in the South against anything but wrong and oppression.

"During their stay in this city several of them were interviewed by our leading Republican officials and some doleful stories were told. The editor of the *'Mountain Home'* sent them marked copies of his paper containing extracts which he thought would be likely to arouse resentment, and prevent any toning down or softening of the asperities supposed to exist in the minds of Northern Republicans toward the people of the South. They were handed over to the Southern editors, with the remark that such efforts showed the editor to be a scurvy fellow. A prominent gentlemen of the party ventured the guess that the man who sent the paper had been bought with a postmastership or some such office. This gentlemen had never before heard of *'Our Mountain Home'* and his 'guess' was therefore, all haphazard.

"Insidious efforts made to prejudice our guests"

"Other insidious efforts were made, in secret, to prejudice our guests against us. But the men upon whom the experiment was tried were generally men who had seen something of the world and who naturally looked with suspicion and distrust upon those poor creatures whose evident purpose was to prevent, if possible, any restoration of kind feeling between the sections. In their hearts they pitied them and despised such men because they saw clearly that their complaints were meant to perpetuate unkind feeling and do harm to the Southern people.

"We believe that good will will come of this visit of the representatives of the press of the Great State of New York to our beautiful, but as yet undeveloped state."

APA apparently fair to Republican editors

Although some Alabama editors were virulent in their denunciation of Republicans, the Press Association apparently was fair to Republican editors. A letter appeared in *The Montgomery Advertiser* at the time of the 1874 press convention from G.M. Johnson, editor of *The Huntsville Advocate,* a Republican paper. He took exception to a statement in *The Alabama State Journal* (the Republican paper in Montgomery) that the Press Association was a "partisan affair."

Johnson wrote that he had been treated with "cordiality and consideration." The convention had even set aside the constitutional requirement of a 60-day notice for membership to admit him, and he had been selected a member of the Executive Committee. Johnson felt that "if all the Republican editors of Alabama were members of the association, the bitterness of the press would be greatly lessened, and that there would be but little of the fierce and disgraceful personal warfare now being carried on by opposition editors."

APA visits Bryce Hospital in 1874

At some time in 1874, members of the Press Association apparently visited Tuscaloosa and Bryce Hospital. A newspaper published in the 1870s for and by patients at what was then called the Alabama Insane Hospital was found in 1988 in the State Department of Archives and History during its efforts to find and catalog all newspaper titles in the state. The newspaper, *The Meteor,* in July 1874 noted a visit to the hospital by delegates attending a meeting of the Alabama Press Association.

According to the unnamed editor, a young man ran unannounced into the hospital superintendent's office to tell him that the Press Association delegates would soon visit the hospital. "The Doctor's first decision was to telegraph in reply that the Hospital being already nearly full, there was not room for so many, and that chronic cases could not be received."

1875
Col. Richard Holmes Powell
The Union Springs Herald and Times
1875-1876 president

Fourth annual press convention, Huntsville
May 11-13, 1875

The most important business transacted at the fourth annual press convention May 11-13, 1875, at the Opera House in Huntsville was the setting of yearly dues for members of the Press Association — $2 per year.

Following the election of Col. Richard Holmes Powell of *The Union Springs Herald and Times* as president, the editors and publishers took an excursion to Louisville, Ky., according to *The Montgomery Advertiser* in its May 15, 1875, edition, and *The Alabama Journal* in its May 14, 1875, edition.

Upon invitation of New York editors who toured Alabama in 1874, about 35 Alabama editors and publishers went to New York in June 1875. "We were met at the border and carried to every place of interest in that great state," said Gen. James Berney Stanley of *The Greenville Advocate*, who made the trip. "We made a complete tour, a banquet was served every night for two weeks. It, of course, was in the days before Volstead was born or prohibition was thought of seriously, and liquors were served at every banquet; champagne and cigars were always the last course."

1876
James Freeman Grant, *The Jacksonville Republican*
1876-1877 president

Fifth annual press convention, Montgomery
May 30-June 3, 1876

At the close of the fifth annual press convention in Montgomery on May 30-June 3, 1876, the editors and publishers went to Blount Springs for a banquet and entertainment given by a Capt. Towner, proprietor of the Jackson House.

Resolutions of tribute to Col. Seaborn Jones Saffold of *The Selma Daily Times*, the Press Association's first president who had died on June 12, 1875, were adopted. *The Montgomery Advertiser*, in its May 31, 1876, issue gave full coverage to the convention and included an invaluable list of those present:

Delegates to 1876 convention

W.A. Hundley, *The Randolph County News* at Roanoke; L.R. Davis, *The Limestone News* at Athens; William M. Meeks, *The Gadsden Times*, D.C. White, *The Moulton Advertiser;* A. Monroe, *The Evergreen Star;* W.C. Bledsoe and J.M. Richards, *The LaFayette Clipper;* S.B. Smith, *The Vernon Pioneer;* F.J. Cowart, *The Troy Messenger;* W.L. Nelson, *The Athens Post;* J.M. Macon, *The Clayton Courier;* M.A. Sheehan, *The Eufaula Times;* G.R. Cather, *The Southern Aegis;* J.B. Sanford, *The Fayette Gazette;* B.A.B. Smith, *NuJoax;* R.H. English, *The Selma Daily Times;* Frank

A. Baltzell, *The Troy Enquirer;* F.M. Grace, *The Birmingham Iron Age;* W.A. Collier, *The Clanton Courier;* James B. Stanley, *The Greenville Advocate;* D.W. McIver, *The Tuskegee News;* A.H. Britton, *The Huntsville Advocate;* J.F. and L.W. Grant, *The Jacksonville Republican;* J.R. Rogers, *The Union Springs Herald and Times;* W.A. McLaughlin, *The Birmingham Independent;* P.M. Musgrove, *The Bangor Broad-Axe;* W.F. Wilkinson, *The Shelby Guide* at Montevallo; L. Hensley Grubbs, *The Decatur News;* Willis Brewer, *The Hayneville Examiner;* W.W. Screws and B.H. Screws, *The Montgomery Advertiser;* and T.C. Bingham and J.A. Farden, *The Alabama State Journal.*

While the Press Association was meeting in Montgomery, *The Alabama State Journal* noted in disgust that Mobile had been selected as the next convention site by a margin of only three votes. *The Journal* noted, probably as a jibe against its arch-rival *The Montgomery Advertiser*, that all the Montgomery members had not attended the voting session when the 1877 convention site was approved.

1877
Willis Brewer, *The Hayneville Examiner*
1877-1878 president

Sixth annual press convention, Mobile
May 2-3, 1877

The death of Col. John Forsyth, editor of *The Mobile Register*, cast a pall over the sixth annual press convention May 2-3, 1877, in Mobile. Forsyth had practiced law and edited *The Columbus* (Ga.) *Times*. Forsyth came to Mobile in 1853 and purchased *The Mobile Register* from Thaddeus Sanford, and he served as mayor of Mobile in 1860, according to "Alabama Journalism," by Maj. William Wallace Screws of *The Montgomery Advertiser* in "Memorial Record of Alabama," Chapter 10.

Forsyth died on the opening day of the convention and APA delegates attended the funeral. "Each member felt that journalism had lost a bright and shining light," *The Montgomery Advertiser* reported in its May 6, 1877, edition. "Resolutions of respect for his memory and character were adopted by a rising vote and the Association attended his funeral in a body."

The Montgomery Advertiser reported that "During the past week the Mobile Fair, the Episcopal Diocesan Convention and the Alabama Press Association were the means of drawing to the city a large number of visitors."

It is unknown the extent of the business, if any, that was transacted at the sixth annual convention, except that George Robert Cather, editor and publisher of *The Southern-Aegis* at Ashville and APA orator, gave the association's keynote address. "The Press Association was well attended," *The Montgomery Advertiser* reported. "Hon. J.F. Grant (of *The Jacksonville Republican*), its honored president, read his annual address. It was plain, fully characteristic of the man, and was warmly applauded by the members of the Association. The general business would not be of general interest to the public and we therefore make no mention of it."

George Robert Cather
The Southern-Aegis, Ashville

1878
Maj. William Wallace Screws,
The Montgomery Advertiser
1878-1879 president

Seventh annual press convention, Montgomery
May 30, 1878

"The Press Association, which meets in Montgomery on the 30th inst., should make business, rather than pleasure, their object," *The Greensboro Watchman* commented when the APA met in the capital city for its seventh annual convention in 1878. "They should endeavor to guard the fraternity against being victimized by swindling advertisers and advertising agents," *The Watchman* continued.

Not much business was transacted at the seventh annual convention held "in the parlors of the Relay House" on May 30, 1878, because of the "absorbing interest felt in the (Democratic and Conservative Party) State Convention," *The Montgomery Advertiser* reported.

Many members of the Press Association also were members of the Democratic State Convention. It was suggested that a meeting be held in late summer in Birmingham to make up for the brief meeting in Montgomery. There is no record that another meeting took place in 1878, according to *The Montgomery Advertiser* in its May 30,

1878, edition, and *The Shelby Sentinel* in Columbiana on June 6, 1878.

1879
Maj. William Wallace Screws,
The Montgomery Advertiser
1879-1880 president

Eighth annual press convention, Gadsden
May 28-29, 1879

The eighth annual press convention was in Gadsden on May 28-29, 1879. Delegates left Gadsden on June 2 for Rome, Ga. They traveled the Coosa River on the steamer "Magnolia" and were dinner guests of the Rome Chamber of Commerce.

On their return to Gadsden the editors and publishers adopted resolutions setting forth "the great value of the Coosa River to the Commerce of the World" urging the press of Alabama "to make no delay in setting forth the necessity of its speedy opening from Greensport to Wetumpka," and calling upon senators and congressmen "to use their utmost endeavors in securing appropriations necessary for this great work."

1880
Maj. William Wallace Screws,
The Montgomery Advertiser
1880-1881 president

Ninth annual press convention, Tuscaloosa
April 23-26, 1880

Tuscaloosa, which was to become the site of the state's second paper mill, was host city of the ninth annual press convention April 23-26, 1880. Delegates discussed the problems of newsprint supply and price. A committee charged with studying the feasibility of a paper mill in Alabama recommended that a mill be erected at either Birmingham or Montgomery.

A resolution was adopted requesting senators and congressmen to exert their influence toward the repeal of "the duty now levied by laws of the United States upon type, printing paper, and the materials used in the manufacture of paper and the law extending the Voelter Wood Pulp patent." These were said to operate as a "tax upon knowledge and a grievous burden upon the publishing interests of the country," according to *The Montgomery Advertiser* in a page 1 article on April 29, 1880.

In 1844 F.G. Keller and Harry Voelter had invented in Germany a process which made ground wood pulp available for use in paper manufacture. In 1866 the first machines for grinding the wood were introduced in the United States to produce the inexpensive and highly absorbent newsprint which publishers had long wanted. The first wood pulp newsprint was used in 1868. Apparently the Southern editors hoped that the patent would be allowed to expire so that the process could be used by the paper mill which they wanted for Alabama.

The editors and publishers also adopted resolutions pledging themselves to impress upon the people of the state and its legislators "the necessity of making the needed appropriations to help the University of Alabama and the Insane Hospital in Tuscaloosa," *The Montgomery Advertiser* reported.

New advertising rate schedule adopted in 1880

A new rate schedule for advertising from outside the county in which papers were published was adopted at the Tuscaloosa convention. The rates were adopted by a large majority following a lively debate on the subject. The following were the rates adopted. They applied only to weeklies:

One column of 22 inches for one year, all space taken, $100; half column for one year, $60; one-third column for one year, $40; one-fourth column for one year, $32. One inch space for one year, $7.50; one inch space for six months, $5; one inch for three months, $3; one inch space for one month, $2.

1881
Maj. William Wallace Screws, *The Montgomery Advertiser* 1881-1882 president

10th annual press convention, Blount Springs May 17-18, 1881

A resolution was adopted at the 10th annual convention held on May 17-18, 1881, in Blount Springs that urged Alabama newspapers to publish information that would encourage "foreign immigration" into the state. By "foreign" the editors and publishers meant from other sections of the country more than from abroad.

Southern businessmen during this period hoped that immigrants would provide a labor force better than that which existed in the South, and that immigrants could be encouraged to practice diversified farming.

SIDELIGHTS
MARKING 125 YEARS OF HISTORY

"How to maintain an attractive newspaper" explained by Baldwin

W.J. (Bill) Baldwin. editor of *The Lee County Bulletin* in Auburn, gave an informal talk at the 1944 APA summer convention on the "maintenance of an attractive newspaper during war conditions," *AlaPressa* reported. "Typographically and editorially, *The Lee County Bulletin* is one of the South's outstanding weeklies and all publishers can profit by the suggestions that Bill will make."

"Of the four essentials for a good-looking newspaper – Cleanliness, the Human Element, the Tympan and Speed – Baldwin placed 'cleanliness first.' He urged the use of 'plenty of gasoline and a lot of brushes. Keep your presses clean. We do not leave ink on our rollers or in our fountains after a job is printed,' Baldwin said. 'The human element is as essential as equipment and ink. You must have a pressman who takes pride in the workmanship. The tympan on the press is a most vital factor.'

"Baldwin explained the two types of tympans, the hard and the soft, and explained that he used the hard, consisting of five sheets of newsprint and six sheets of tympan paper. One danger that he warned of was in building up the tympan too high and destroying the synchronization of the press. 'Speed is also an important element,' Baldwin said. 'Too high a press speed cuts down on the quality of the print. Good paper and good ink are also essentials. It isn't the press as much as the foreman,' Baldwin added. 'A good pressman can produce an attractive newspaper on a worn out press'."

Some of the topics to which the members of the Press Association were encouraged to devote time and space were:

Position and extent of country; when organized and present rate of taxation; general contour and proportion of timber, prairie and bottom land, with streams and bodies of water; and kinds of timber and quality of soil and minerals. "Could either of the following industries be engaged in with a fair prospect of success: silk culture, honey making, dairy farming, poultry raising, tanning, saw mills, lumbering, cotton and wood factories, shoe, harness and saddle factories," according to *The Shelby Sentinel* of Columbiana in its May 26, 1881, edition.

Following the Blount Springs convention, the newspaper men and wives went to Nashville, Tenn., where they visited the Tennessee Capitol, Mrs. James K. Polk, widow of the 11th U.S. president, the Exposition, and Vanderbilt University. They met at the Maxwell House and adopted resolutions thanking the people of Nashville for courtesies extended.

1882
**Gen. James Berney Stanley, *The Greenville Advocate*
1882-1883 president**

**11th annual press convention, Montgomery
April 20-21, 1882**

Railroad expansion in Alabama was favored by the editors and publishers in a resolution adopted at the 11th annual convention at McDonald's Opera House in Montgomery April 20-21, 1882. They sought the support of the Alabama congressional delegation for a bill allowing the St. Louis, Montgomery and Florida Railroad Company to purchase federal lands along its route.

The resolution at the 1882 convention stated, "The bill recently introduced in Congress to allow the St. Louis, Montgomery and Florida Railroad Company (or similar corporations) to purchase from the United States certain lands lying along its route in order to expedite its construction, meets with the approval of this Association; and our senators and representatives in Congress are requested to zealously endeavor to effect the passage of the above mentioned bill."

A trip on a river steamer from Montgomery to Prattville provided entertainment for the editors and their families. While traveling on the steamer, Gen. James Berney Stanley, editor and publisher of *The Greenville Advocate*, was inducted into office and began the first of four consecutive terms as president.

1883
**Gen. James Berney Stanley, *The Greenville Advocate*
1883-1884 president**

**12th annual press convention, Selma
May 22-23, 1883**

Selma was the site of the 12th annual press convention May 22-23, 1883. The editors and publishers also visited Uniontown and Demopolis. From Selma, an excursion was taken to Florida. The editors visited the Navy yard at Pensacola, rode on the St. Johns River, visited Jacksonville and St. Augustine, and then returned through Georgia by way of Brunswick, Savannah, Macon and Atlanta.

"The meeting in Selma has been an eminently pleasant and successful one," *The Montgomery Advertiser* reported in its May 24, 1883, issue. "The attendance is the largest in several years, including many ladies. After transacting business yesterday they went out on a special train into the Canebrake Country and at Uniontown and Demopolis enjoyed handsome collations spread for them by the hospitable people of those pleasant places. Last night a complimentary entertainment was given them by the Harmony Club.

"They all leave Selma this morning on a special train, and will get breakfast at the Union Depot Hotel when they depart for Pensacola, reaching there this afternoon. Tomorrow will be spent there and at the Navy yards and forts. Tomorrow night they leave for Jacksonville. The trip will include a ride on the St. Johns, visit to St. Augustine, and thence to Brunswick, Macon, Savannah, Atlanta and then home," *The Montgomery Advertiser* concluded.

1884
**Gen. James Berney Stanley, *The Greenville Advocate*
1884-1885 president**

**13th annual press convention, Eufaula
May 8-10, 1884**

Expositions in various cities had been the destinations of several of the excursions taken by the Press Association. In 1884 at the 13th annual convention in Eufaula on May 8-10, the Alabama editors and publishers endorsed the World Exposition to be held in New Orleans and felt that it was "manifestly important that the resources and industries of Alabama be properly represented" there.

Reporting on the 1884 convention, *The Eufaula*

Weekly Times and News in its May 13 issue announced that "Mrs. I.M.P. Henry has been elected an honorary member of the Press Association. She is associate editor of *The Greenville Advocate* and is a rarely gifted woman." (Ina Marie Porter Henry became editor of *The Greenville Advocate* on Aug. 1, 1883, according to Rhoda Coleman Ellison in her 1954 book, "History and Bibliography of Alabama Newspapers in the 19th Century." Mrs. Henry's stories and poems were published in "The Land We Love" and in *The Mobile Register*.)

The Eufaula newspaper continued, "After the operetta last night, which was attended by a large and delighted throng of mingled visitors and citizens, the audience repaired almost in a body to Hart's Hall, where merry music invited the dancers on the floor."

1885
Gen. James Berney Stanley, *The Greenville Advocate*
1885-1886 president

14th annual press convention, Talladega
April 7-8, 1885

Excursions to Renfro, a large lumber camp, and Anniston were made during the 14th annual press convention in Talladega, April 7-8, 1885. Delegates traveled on the Talladega and Coosa Valley Railroad. They also attended a complimentary concert at city hall in Talladega.

The editors and publishers went from the convention in Talladega to the New Orleans Exposition aboard a special train. They were given a gala reception by State Commissioner Pratt at the Alabama headquarters in the Exposition Building.

1886
William M. Meeks, *The Gadsden Times and News*
1886-1887 president

15th annual press convention, Marion
May 27-28, 1886

The 15th annual press convention was in Marion on May 27-28, 1886. *The Marion Standard* gave the following account on pages 4 and 5 of its June 2 issue:

"This has been another pleasant day with the Alabama editors visiting. The members of the Press Association visited Lincoln Institute, the State University for colored people. An hour there was

spent very pleasantly. A resolution tendering the thanks of the Association to Gen. J.B. Stanley, the retiring president, for his devoted services, was adopted. A committee was appointed to present Gen. Stanley with a suitable gift as a slight testimonial of gratitude and appreciation. J.W. Henry of *The Troy Messenger* read the annual poem. A splendid essay by Mrs. I.M.P. Henry of *The Greenville Advocate* was read."

1887
William M. Meeks, *The Gadsden Times and News*
1887-1888 president

16th annual press convention, Birmingham
May 25-26, 1887

Legal incorporation of the Press Association was accomplished in 1887 by an act of the Legislature. A committee was appointed at the 16th annual convention held May 25-26, 1887, at O'Brien's Opera House in Birmingham to prepare a constitution and bylaws to go into force along with the new charter in 1888.

"The members of the Alabama Press Association are having a royal time in Birmingham," *The Montgomery Advertiser* commented in its May 26, 1887, edition. "The morning was spent in driving about the city in carriages furnished by the citizens and viewing the many wonders of development that are to be seen on every hand."

The Advertiser reported that "J.L. Burnett delivered the annual oration, taking for his subject 'The Achievements of the Press'. It was a splendid address and was met with hearty applause."

England learned in 1887 that there was an Alabama Press Association. "A resolution was passed extending sympathy to Gladstone and Parnell in the struggle for Home Rule in Ireland. Major McFarland came all the way from Florence (to Birmingham) to introduce it. The resolution was ordered cabled to Gladstone at London," *The Montgomery Advertiser* reported in its May 27, 1887, edition.

Screws comments on developments in APA

In the May 29, 1887, issue of *The Montgomery Advertiser*, Maj. William Wallace Screws commented at some length on developments in the Press Association. It's hard to tell how much of the following was meant to be serious:

"There are some changes going on in the Alabama Press Association. Among other things, the growth of prohibition sentiment is very marked to a man who has missed two consecutive meetings. A large majority of the bona fide editors present are out and out prohibitionists."

Screws continued, "Some of those who have been attending the Association meetings for a number of years have wearied of the purely social character of these gatherings and want to do something tangible, that will show results. Major Harris, in a strong speech, proposed that a beginning be made toward raising a fund for establishing a home for broken-down editors and printers. The idea was favorably received and the movement will ripen into some fruit, let us hope at no distant day."

It seems that not everyone was sober and serious at that particular meeting, for it had been reported two days earlier that "two local newspaper men got into a scrimmage over a press badge this morning, but it amounted to nothing," *The Montgomery Advertiser* reported in its May 27, 1887, edition.

Other observations were made by Screws

Among other observations made by Screws were the following:

"Alabama has one newspaper owned and run by two young ladies, Misses Susie and Virginia Clay of *The Huntsville Democrat.* Miss Susie...is a living witness that a young lady can't be none-the-less modest and pretty because she writes editorials, solicits advertisements and sets type."

The irrepressible Screws also had some compliments for the host city of Birmingham which might have needled his fellow Montgomerians a bit:

"Above all things Birmingham is an honest town. Shortly after 5 o'clock one morning I started around the principal streets, and on the door handles of business houses on First and Second Avenues I saw copies of *The Age.* The carrier, in delivering the paper, had simply stuck it through the handle and left it there in absolute security till such times as the subscriber should come down and take it inside. Now in Montgomery, if we should deliver *The Advertiser* on the outside of Commerce Street from doors, a hundred hands would be ready to seize it before the subscriber could get out of bed. All this talk of theives (sic) being over numerous in Birmingham is stuff." (*The Montgomery Advertiser,* May 29, 1887.)

At the conclusion of 1887 convention, the editors and publishers went on an excursion to Mammoth Cave in Kentucky.

1888
Harry G. McCall, *The Shelby Sentinel*, Columbiana
1888-1889 president

17th annual press convention, Selma
April 19-21, 1888

More professionalism and less politics seemed to be a theme of the 17th annual convention held April 19-21, 1888, at Gillman's Hall in Selma. A resolution was adopted not to "recognize any resolution favoring or condemning any party, policy, platform or public official." The resolution was presented by Rufus N. Rhodes of *The Birmingham News.*

Selma Mayor Simon Mass welcomed APA delegates to his city. "It becomes my highest duty, and I know I voice the sentiment of our people when I say that you are heartily welcome, and I take occasion to tender you the freedom of our city, feeling assured such will not be abused, representing, as you do, the highest art of refinement and culture," Mayor Maas told the editors and publishers. "There is no association in existence to whom the public is as much indebted as to yours for the manifold benefits that are bestowed upon the human family, in untold measures through and by the press of the country."

Dubose's response was "eloquently made"

It was reported in APA minutes that the response on the part of the Press Association was "eloquently made by Col. J.W. Dubose of *The Gadsden Times and News,*" APA historian. "After years of weary waiting and working, we have in control of the general government at Washington a party friendly to the South, a party whose interest is inseparably associated with our growth and prosperity," Dubose said.

The Montgomery Advertiser reported that outgoing APA president William M. Meeks of *The Gadsden Times and News* was "frequently interrupted by applause" when he delivered his presidential address. "At 5 o'clock the Pettus Rifles and Selma Guards marched out of their armories to the front of the St. James Hotel amid the cheers of the ladies and gentlemen of the Press Association, both companies doing credit to themselves," *The Montgomery Advertiser* reported on April 20, 1888.

1889
Harry G. McCall, The Shelby Sentinel, Columbiana
1889-1890 president

18th annual press convention, Huntsville
June 27-29, 1889

Sixty delegates attended the 18th annual press convention at the Monte Sano Hotel in Huntsville on June 27-29, 1889. Maj. William Wallace Screws of *The Montgomery Advertiser,* Professor James Archibald Bradford Lovett of *The Teacher at Work* of Huntsville (the first educational journal established in Alabama), and Rufus Napoleon Rhodes of *The Birmingham News* were selected as delegates to the National Editorial Association convention, according to *The Birmingham News* in its July 30, 1889, edition. This was the first recorded instance of the Press Association's sponsorship of delegates to a national organization.

The National Editorial Association had been organized at the New Orleans Exposition in 1889, and it is possible that Alabama editors who visited the Exposition were involved.

The June 29, 1889, issue of *The Bessemer Weekly* mentioned the APA convention in Huntsville and reported that it "was largely attended and was a most enjoyable affair from beginning to end." The newspaper reported that "Mr. (John Withers) Clay, the veteran editor of *The* (Huntsville) *Democrat,* was received with a stirring round of applause, when he tottered into the Opera House on the arm of his daughter. He was promptly invited to the stage where he was received by President (Harry G.) McCall (of *The Shelby Sentinel* at Columbiana), who surrendered to him the chair and gavel. The old gentleman was almost overcome by the courtesies shown him."

The decade of the 1880s was an era of promotion and speculation. In 1888 there appeared an ambitious man from Iowa named Henry M. Fuller who became interested in what was known as Bolen James' cave on the east side of Pulaski Pike near what later was called the Orchard Place Club. Fuller thought the cave could be developed into a money-making attraction for sightseers and bought a quarter section of the land around the cave's opening for $5,000. With the APA holding its convention in Huntsville in 1889, Fuller saw an opportunity to receive publicity for his cave.

Convention delegates attend dinner in cave

Pat Jones, writing in *The Huntsville Times* in May 1936, reviewed some of the incidents of that novel session of the Press Association. Convention delegates were taken down the steps to cave, which had been named Shelta Cavern after Fuller's daughter, for a barbecue dinner.

"Dinner was served on specially built tables in the bowels of the earth," Jones wrote in *The Huntsville Times.* "During the meal an orchestra played from a large dance platform, sending forth music that reverberated through the damp passageways of the cave.

"Arc lights and jack-o-lanterns fought against the murky blackness, and drove away a gloom that had been there forever," *The Times* continued. "While the press members ate, they looked frequently at the dark waters of a crystal lake, above which hung a faint mist which deepened as it floated into the background."

Despite his efforts, Fuller was unable to make his cave a tourist attraction, APA historian Cash M. Stanley of *The Alabama Journal* wrote in the Jan. 1, 1953, issue of *AlaPressa*. "Following the entertainment of the editors, a good many people visited the cavern for a year or so, but the 'natural wonder' never attracted the interest and popularity hoped for it," Stanley wrote. The cave was ultimately dismantled and in 1896 was sold for taxes.

"Only tourists along Pulaski Pike who know of this cavern now occasionally turn their heads in its direction, and their view goes no farther than the wooded crown of the hill," Stanley continued. "Green flies and gnats come up from the opening concealed in one end of the crater-like depression, and the odor is not pleasant."

Following the 1889 convention, delegates took an excursion to Lookout Mountain, Tenn., and then traveled to Decatur by steamboat. Cost of the trip was $8 per person.

1890

John C. Williams, *Our Mountain Home,* Talladega
1890-1891 president

19th annual press convention, Montgomery and Troy
June 11-12, 1890

"The Alabama editors will be in Montgomery this evening," *The Montgomery Advertiser* reported on June 11, 1890, the opening day of the 19th annual press convention. "They will be accompanied by their wives and daughters and sweethearts. They will have the freedom of the city."

Dissension among delegates was reported at the 19th annual convention June 11 in Montgomery and June 12 in Troy in 1890. Outgoing president Harry G. McCall of *The Shelby Sentinel* in Columbiana in his June 11 address referred to attacks made on candidates in the last election by the press of the state.

Censorship board proposed by president McCall

McCall advocated that a censorship board consisting of one lawyer, one journalist and one other individual be appointed by the Legislature to stop such attacks. Under McCall's plan, "any offensive article in any paper" would be submitted to the censors "who would be empowered to stop further utterances of the same kind."

Maj. William Wallace Screws of *The Montgomery Advertiser,* Rufus Napoleon Rhodes of *The Birmingham News* and others "indignantly protested against the outrage committed by President McCall," *The Birmingham News* reported in its June 13, 1890, edition. Screws expressed "profound astonishment that any man in this enlightened day could entertain any such idea." Screws moved to strike out of the address before publication everything in it relating to the proposed board and the censorship idea. This provoked some discussion.

Delegates expressed disagreement with the ideas of the address, but some thought what was said should be printed with dissenting resolutions on the part of the Press Association. Screws changed his resolution so as to declare in most emphatic terms that the Press Association of Alabama did not endorse anything in the address which in any degree suggested the idea of press censorship. A vote was taken by the papers, and there were 47 yeas and 2 nays.

"Terrible rebuke" for President McCall

"It was a terrible rebuke for President McCall," *The Birmingham News* reported in its June 13, 1890, edition. The next day, however, tempers cooled and the convention delegates adopted a resolution of commendation to McCall for his dedicated service during his term of office. "After the liveliest session in history a genuine love feast came along and healed all wounds," *The Birmingham News* reported.

After visiting Troy on June 12, 1890, the editors and publishers went on an excursion to Brunswick and Savannah, Ga. They were met by the City Council, Board of Trade and Cottons Exchange officials and carried to the City Exchange, the ocean steamship wharves, and other points of interest. The conventioneers then went to Tybee and South End where they were served refreshments at the Chatham Artillery Club House. They returned to Alabama the following day.

1891

John C. Williams, *Our Mountain Home,* Talladega
1891-1892 president

20th annual press convention, Anniston
June 24-26, 1891

On June 24-26, 1891, Press Association delegates met in Anniston for the 20th annual convention and took a side trip to Gadsden. At the

1891 convention, the name of the association was changed from the Editors and Publishers Association to the Alabama Press Association.

APA had been informally called the "Press Association" for some years. Changing the name was indicative of the altered nature of the Press Association at the end of its first 20 years. APA was to become less of a convivial and only occasionally productive organization of editors and publishers, and more of an organization designed to improve the quality of the press in Alabama and protect its interests.

As *The Birmingham Age-Herald* commented in an editorial on June 24, 1891, "The editors threaten to get down to business."

CHAPTER 2

The Editors Get Down to Business

1892-1907

Hunter H. Golson
The Wetumpka Herald

"Publishing a country paper is one business a man who once gets in never gets out — he never has the money to get out. The country weekly is the last resort of freedom of the press. This is true because the editor and publisher needs little capital and little or no labor outside his own toil and that of his family. He has no 'business office' and no organization to consult in the formulation of his paper's policies; more than any other source of information, he is free to say what he pleases.

"The country editor plays down crime. Its editor probably knows 90 percent of its readers. He knows the families and their problems and if a son gets into trouble, the editor, as sorry as the parents themselves, has no desire to add to their shame and sorrow."

— Hunter H. Golson (1884-1946)
Editor and publisher, The Wetumpka Herald
APA president, 1940-1941
(From a speech given to the Exchange Club in August 1943)

THAT 1892 WAS A TURNING POINT FOR THE Alabama Press Association can be seen from the program of the 21st annual convention Oct. 20-21, 1892, in Birmingham. For the first time there were what would now be called workshop sessions on various aspects of the newspaper business.

An editorial in *The Birmingham News* on Oct. 21, 1892, summed up the new atmosphere at the 21st annual convention: "Our brothers of the quill come this time not as a guest of the city nor on pleasure bent. They pay as they go, and talk business strictly. This is well! It marks a new era in their annual gatherings. Heretofore there has been too much frolic and feast, too much junket and jest to permit much business, and the annual convocations of the cofraternity have therefore fallen somewhat into discredit."

The News concluded, "There can be much profit and usefulness derived from these annual gatherings of newspaper men, and when real benefit is derived from their commingling and communion, pleasure is sure to be an accompaniment."

The first 20 years of the Alabama Press Association, while consisting primarily of social gatherings and excursions, provided a cohesive force by which the influence of the press could be felt. And the social gatherings were the base upon which the Press Association could find the strength to shift from a social status to a business one. Once this was accomplished, APA became more easily identified with the entire newspaper population, and its voice began to be recognized and listened to.

State-Herald: "Business is the watchword"

In an Oct. 8, 1895, editorial, *The Birmingham State-Herald* reinforced the impression that the Press Association had truly entered a new era: "There was a time when the city chosen as the place for holding the annual meetings of this body of distinguished ladies and gentlemen entertained the members royally and without price, but a change came. It is the purpose of the editors of Alabama to preserve intact their Association for business and not for frolic, and to this end the long time custom of accepting free entertainment was in 1892 abandoned, and since then the Association meets, attends to business and goes on it way rejoicing. Instead of frolic and fun, business is the watchword."

APA took considerable interest in public education in the late 1800s, pushing for public school taxes to support a statewide public school system. At the 1894 annual convention, the editors and publishers resolved that the state should appropriate necessary funds to run the schools since a constitutional amendment allowing local taxation for schools had been defeated. A "Committee on Education" was appointed in 1894 to frame a bill to be presented at the next session of the Legislature for the "establishment and maintenance of a public school system" for the state.

Yerby enters "plea in behalf of our public schools"

At the 1904 annual convention, outgoing APA president William E.W. Yerby of *The Greensboro Watchman* gave a speech titled "A Plea in Behalf of Our Public Schools," according to APA minutes. "No argument is needed to sustain the position that the public schools is a necessity, and that it should be liberally supported by the citizens," Yerby told convention delegates. "The old theory that it is wrong to tax one man to educate another man's children has been exploited, and it is seldom heard in this enlightened age. It is now generally accepted as a fact that the prosperity of a nation, a state or a community is measured by its intellectual enlightenment. History teaches us that ignorance and poverty — education and wealth — go hand in hand the world over."

William E. W. Yerby
The Greensboro Watchman

Yerby calls for local taxation

Calling for local taxation for education, Yerby continued, "What the common schools in Alabama need is more money. The people of Alabama must sooner or later resort to this method of increasing the school revenue — and the sooner the better for every inhabitant of the state, for it is a conceded fact that the road to success for either the state or the individual lies through education."

Public education again was discussed at the 1905 press convention, with A.W. Holstun of *The LaFayette Sun* presenting a paper titled "The Re-lation of the Press to the Public Schools."

"In discussing the relation of the press to the public school, one proposition stands preeminent," Holstun said. "The more intelligence among the masses, the better the newspaper thrives. This proposition is clearly demonstrated in those states where the least percentage of illiteracy is found — in the Dakotas, Iowa, Oklahoma, etc. — states having the largest per capita public school funds."

Holstun continued, "Such is the happy lot of the editor where from ninety-five to ninety-nine of the people in the state can read and write. What a contrast in Alabama where half our people over 10 years of age can not read and write! Under such conditions is it any wonder that half the people do not take their local paper, that most of the business people do not advertise in it, that the paper's influence is so limited, and that editors are so 'hungry'?"

1892

John C. Williams, *Our Mountain Home,* Talladega
1892-1893 president

21st annual press convention, Birmingham
Oct. 20-21, 1892

Christopher James Hildreth of *The New Decatur Advertiser* led a discussion on makeup and press work at the 21st annual press convention Oct. 20-21, 1892, in Birmingham. L. Hensley Grubbs of *The Decatur News,* Robert M. Rawls of *The Athens Courier,* Edward Louis Collen Ward of *The Bridgeport News* and Frank P. O'Brien of *The Birmingham Age-Herald* participated in the discussion.

Other papers presented included "Rudiments of Business Management" by Edward O. Neely, *The Guntersville Democrat;* "Editorial Department," Chappell Cory, *The Selma Times;* "The Afternoon Paper," James B. Simpson, *The Montgomery Journal;* "The News Department," Franklin Potts Glass, *The Montgomery Journal;* "Increasing Circulation," Gen. James Berney Stanley, *The Greenville Advocate;* and "What is the Best Form for a Weekly Paper," William H.H. Judson, *The Bessemer Weekly.*

"Running newspaper in businesslike way"

The topic of the presidential address by John C. Williams of *Our Mountain Home* in Talladega was running a newspaper in a businesslike way. Williams felt that it was necessary to separate the business and editorial sides of a newspaper. Williams went so far as to recommend refusing advertising "placed just to help out the paper." A newspaper, according to Williams, "does not need to accept charity." An Oct. 21, 1892, editorial in *The Birmingham Age-Herald* stated that "President Williams lived up to his ideals."

1893

Edward Louis Collen Ward, *The Bridgeport News*
1893-1894 president

22nd annual press convention, Bridgeport
June 14-15, 1893

Adoption of a resolution in support of public education highlighted the 22nd annual convention in Bridgeport in Jackson County June 14-15, 1893. "We note with delight," stated the resolution, "that the citizens of the state of Alabama are now thoroughly aroused as to the importance of educating their children. Be it therefore,

---

"Resolved: That the Alabama Press Association promises its encouragement and support to this great work. That we favor local taxation and request that the Legislature of Alabama to enact a law, as provided in the Constitution, giving the voters of the different counties the right to vote on this question. That we petition our school authorities to give every encouragement and support at their command to the upbuilding and strengthening of the schools in the rural districts in the state. We favor redistricting the state into more convenient school districts."

Press Association condemns foundry trusts

Along with discussions on improving their newspapers, the editors and publishers entered the trust-busting era by adopting a resolution condemning type foundry trusts. Type foundries were engaged in the manufacturing and selling of type used in printing.

The 1893 convention again featured workshop sessions. A newspaper account of the meeting by Isidore A. Levy of *The Eutaw Mirror* at Forkland singled out a paper presented by J. Asa Rountree of *The Hartselle Enquirer* on "What Not to Publish in a Newspaper" as the best at the meeting. Levy said that Rountree was "one of the best all-around newspaper men in Alabama."

The convention was followed by a trip to Chattanooga, Tenn., by N and C train and a return trip that night down the not-yet dammed Tennessee River by steamer of the Tennessee River Transportation Co.

In its June 14, 1893, issue, *The Birmingham Age-Herald* commented that the annual press conventions were "seldom productive of any practical good to the business interests of the press," but "they are most beneficial in bringing about friendly social relations between those who conduct the newspapers, and thereby establishing a community of purpose."

Levy gives account of 1893 convention

The Eutaw Mirror's Isidore Levy wrote a detailed account of the 1893 convention at Bridgeport.

"The annual address by president John C. Williams, the oration by E.L.C. Ward of *The Bridgeport News*, the poem by I.S. Barr of *The Florence Gazette*, and a paper by Miss Louise Francis of Castroville, California, were read and were very fine.

"The headquarters of *The Eutaw Mirror* were at the Inn, a cool and comfortable hotel, with accommodating attendants and a prompt and courteous manager. After a refreshing night's rest I was ready to see the city.

Editors met by citizens in carriages

"At 8 a.m. on the 15th the editors, some sixty strong, met at the Hoffman house — here they were met by the citizens in carriages who showed them the city. By stroke of good fortune I was placed in the surrey of the genial and whole-soul gentleman, Mr. Chas. McGaughey, together with Mrs. S.N. Halsey of South Pittsburg, Tenn., and Miss Louise Francis of Castroville, Calif. Then the procession moved off with Mayor Kilpatrick in a dray drawn by four handsome bays, and filled by ten or twelve of the members of the Fourth Estate, in the lead. During this ride we saw the many advantages presented by Bridgeport, not alone natural but also artificial. Up its graded hills and around the curves that gave us a view of the muddy Tennessee River and beyond, into the state from which it derives its name, the procession wound. The point on which a heavy battery was placed during the late war and which held the key to the Sequachie Valley, is now the boundary of a handsome homestead — and the edged hill, once bristling with bayonets, is now a boulevard over which countless vehicles pass and repass each day. Stops were made at the nail, wooden box and canning factories, and to those various industries we shall devote another article.

Rountree gives article on "what not to publish"

"At 11 a.m. the association met for regular business, and Mr. J.A. Rountree of *The Hartselle Enquirer* opened with an article instructing the as-sociation 'what not to publish in a newspaper.' Now, this young man is clearly one of the best all around newspaper men in Alabama, and the ability with which he handled his subjects proves this beyond a doubt. Of all the papers presented this one was perhaps more appreciated than the rest. There were several other good papers read but none that deserve special mention.

"The association decided to attend the World's Fair in a body, to leave not later than July 24.

"Mr. J.H. Johnson of Talladega, Ala., gave the body a talk on the subject of the deaf, dumb and blind institutes of Alabama. He requested the co-operation of all the newspapers to bring this matter before the people and to inform them that by addressing him, all information in regard to tuition, etc., which we think is free, will be cheerfully furnished.

"Troy and Camden both extended cordial invitations for the next meeting. Camden, however, was selected.

"Breeze stirred" over election of officers

"When the election of officers came up there was quite a breeze stirred, and that too, over your humble servant. It seemed that Mr. W.H.H. Judson of *The Bessemer Weekly*, and Mr. W.M. Meeks of *The Gadsden Times-News* were dead against the election of a certain prominent gentleman from North Alabama as president, and as they knew that the vote of *The Mirror* would be best for that one, they raised an objection to the vote being cast. But having been duly elected a member and entitled to all the privileges they failed to carry their point, and the vote when it was counted. Your representative has no hesitancy in saying that it was the exhibition of partisanship rather than desire to benefit the association, and under no circumstances would either of the gentlemen before mentioned have raised a protest if I had assented to proposition made by one of them, 'don't vote for Grubbs'."

1894

Robert M. Rawls, *The Athens Courier*
1894-1895 president

23rd annual press convention, Montgomery
Sept. 12-13, 1894

For the second consecutive year, press convention delegates adopted a resolution in support of public education in Alabama. Formation of the APA Legislative Committee was another high point of the 23rd annual convention held Sept. 12-13, 1894, in the reading room of the Exchange Hotel in Montgomery.

The Legislative Committee was formed to promote and protect the interests of the press in Alabama by being present in Montgomery during legislative sessions when necessary, and keeping in contact with state legislators. The committee was to play an important role throughout the rest of the history of the Alabama Press Association. Members of the first Legislative Committee were John C. Williams, *Our Mountain Home,* Talladega; J. Asa Rountree, *The Hartselle Enquirer;* Franklin Potts Glass, *The Montgomery Advertiser;* John C. Lawrence, *The Marion Standard;* and Gen. James Berney Stanley, *The Greenville Advocate.*

Resolution favors development of public school system

Montgomery meetings always seemed to stimulate political interest among the members of the Press Association, and 1894 was no exception. A resolution adopted by the Press Association in 1894 favoring development of an effective system of public education in the state showed that Alabama editors were in the forefront of this important movement in the state in the late 19th and early 20th centuries.

The Alabama Press Association resolved that the state should appropriate necessary funds to run the schools since a constitutional amendment allowing local taxation for schools had been defeated. It also asked the APA president to appoint a committee to present a bill for the "establishment and maintenance of a public school system for the State of Alabama" to the next session of the Legislature.

The following resolution was adopted at the 1894 convention:

"Whereas, the educational interests of Alabama are greatly neglected, especially in the country districts,

---

S I D E L I G H T S
MARKING 125 YEARS OF HISTORY

APA favors School of Journalism
The APA Executive Committee in 1949 went on record in favor of establishment of a School of Journalism at the University of Alabama. Journalism instruction at the time was provided by the Department of Journalism in the College of Arts and Sciences.

"And whereas, the public school system itself is weak, both in construction and in support,

"Be it resolved: That we pledge ourselves anew to the creation and stimulation of a healthy educational spirit.

"Be it further resolved: That, inasmuch as the proposed school amendment looking to local taxation for school purposes was defeated at our State election, we recommend that the state appropriate all available funds, over and above the amount necessary to support the State Government, economically administered, for school purposes.

"Be it further resolved: That the Chair appoint a committee to formulate and present to the next State Legislature a bill for the establishment and maintenance of a public school system for the State of Alabama."

The following Committee on Education was appointed in 1894 and was instructed to frame a bill to be presented to the Legislature: Charles P. Lane, *The Huntsville Tribune;* J.M. Dewberry, Educational Exchange, Montgomery; and J.C. Lawrence, *The Marion Standard.*

Problem of lynching in South discussed in 1894

APA also considered the problem of lynching in the South.

It condemned the arrival in the South of a "committee of foreigners" to investigate lynching, stating that "we look upon the source from which their information has been drawn as utterly irresponsible." Yet, "if they come seeking to investigate with fairness and justice, and not with already prejudiced minds to denounce, then we bid them come and our famous hospitality will be extended to them and our aid given in their undertaking."

While condemning "foreign intervention," the Press Association made it clear that it "deplored the taking of the law in their own hands by justly incensed communities, and commended the Chief Executive of Alabama in maintaining law and order and protecting the people and property of the State from mob violence."

Resolution seeks "law abiding immigrants"

APA also felt that Alabama suffered from a lack of skilled farmers and workers in the 1890s. The representatives of the Alabama press adopted resolutions encouraging the state to seek "law abiding and useful immigrants."

Outgoing APA president Edward Louis Collen Ward of *The Bridgeport News* in his address at the 1894 convention urged that the Press Association "better guard our portals and see that we have a larger membership at business meetings or a much smaller one on excursion occasions."

APA annual dues were $2 in 1894. "No paper can exceed two representatives, each male being required to pay $2 annual dues, and members may be accompanied by not exceeding two ladies, said ladies to be the mother, wives, sisters or daughters of said representatives," stated a recommendation of the Executive Committee that was adopted by APA at its 1894 annual convention.

1895

Robert M. Rawls, *The Athens Courier*
1895-1896 president

24th annual press convention, Birmingham
Oct. 8-9, 1895

A number of important matters were considered by the Press Association at its 24th annual convention at the Florence Hotel in Birmingham, Oct. 8-9, 1895. As *The Birmingham News* in its Oct. 8, 1895, issue put it, "These annual gatherings...are no longer given to fun and frolic, but are devoted strictly to promoting the interests of the Association as a whole and of the profession generally."

The secretary of the Press Association, J. Asa Rountree of *The Hartselle Enquirer,* reported to delegates that during the past year he had kept the members informed of advertising frauds that he had exposed. Rountree suggested that APA form an advertising association to help the newspapers secure out-of-state advertising and protect them from frauds.

Rountree said that for years the situation had been discussed, but nothing had been done. At the 1895 convention a committee that was appointed to study the formation of an advertising association did not recommend its formation, but suggested that a few newspapers might want to go together and hire someone to take care of their national advertising.

It was to be several years before the weekly newspapers formed an advertising association, *The Birmingham News* reported in its Oct. 8, 1895, edition.

Maj. William Wallace Screws of *The Montgomery Advertiser,* historian of the Press Association, had prepared a 300-page history of the press in Alabama. During the convention he read some excerpts to the delegates.

Legislation to protect the press

Christopher James Hildreth of *The New Decatur Advertiser* suggested that several pieces of legislation to protect the press be introduced in the Alabama Legislature. The first would be a bill making money owed a printer for advertising a preferred lien. Also discussed was the problem of county officers starting their own newspapers to take advantage of legal advertising. Hildreth proposed a bill be passed stating that a newspaper had to have been in business for a year before it was eligible for legal advertising.

The editors and publishers also discussed possible changes in the Alabama libel law.

An interesting sidelight to the 1895 convention was the presence of F. Kolb of *The Birmingham People's Tribune,* a Populist newspaper.

"Women in Journalism" paper presented in 1895

In one of the earliest references to involvement by women in the Press Association, it was reported in the minutes that a paper was presented at the 1895 convention on "Women in Journalism" by Margaret O'Brien of *The Birmingham Age-Herald.*

Immediately following the 24th annual convention, about 150 APA members attended the Atlanta Exposition. They were present for "Alabama Day" at the Exposition.

First APA-sponsored trip to Cuba in 1895

"How the Editors Took in and Got Took in, in Havana" was the headline in a newspaper article about the first APA-sponsored trip to Cuba a short time before the Spanish-American war. It was the midwinter tour on Jan. 11, 1895, and the editors and publishers came away with an appreciation of the freedoms they enjoyed in the United States.

"The Alabama Press Association party left Cuba with higher ideas of American freedom than they ever had entertained before," *The Montgomery Advertiser* reported. "They saw many evidences of oppression that are not tolerated in America. The political conditions on the island are not at all reassuring. The people are greatly oppressed in the way of taxation and a competent leader would secure an enthusiastic following to throw off the Spanish yoke."

The Montgomery Advertiser reported that while Alabamians would be "utterly ruined" if their taxes were as much as $3 million a year, the Cubans paid the Spanish government $55 million a year. Cuba's population in 1895 was about the same as Alabama's. "It (the taxation) has to come, but where from is a mystery, when one looks at the great poverty of the great bulk of the people."

The Montgomery Journal commented:

"The student of political economy cannot, I am sure, find any better object lesson for profitable thought, than Cuba affords. The frightful gulf between the gorgeous affluence to be seen in Havana, and the pitiable squalor close at hand suggests what unjust social conditions will do. When it is considered that Spain squeezes out of this island 55 million dollars per annum, to say nothing of other galling conditions when Spain controls of the island inflict, it is not a matter of surprise that Cuba is in a state of perpetual rebellion. No patriotic man can view this condition of affairs without uttering a fervent prayer that the day may speedily come when, 'From every man, according to his ability, to every many according to his needs,' shall become a glorious realization."

1896

Moncure Woodson Camper, *The Florence Times*
1896-1897 president

25th annual press convention, Huntsville
Oct. 14, 1896

In 1896, the Alabama Press Association again supported changing of the state libel law. Delegates to the 25th annual convention "in the parlors of the Huntsville Hotel" on Oct. 14, 1896, urged the Legislature to make changes and amendments in the law which would make it more in accord with laws in other states which required some element of malice to create libel.

The Press Association wanted a newspaper to be able to make a correction and give full reparation in its columns if it had published a report without intention to injure, instead of being held responsible in damages for errors or mistakes innocently made by the newspaper, according to *The Birmingham Age-Herald* in its Oct. 15, 1896, edition.

Resolution urges exhibition to promote state's resources

Realizing, as always, that it was in the best interests of the press to promote the economic development of the state, APA recommended in a resolution that the state commissioner of agriculture use funds at his disposal to advertise and develop the resources of the state and to set up a fair or exposition to exhibit Alabama's resources, according to *The Birmingham Age-Herald* in the Oct.

15, 1896, edition. The resolution was prompted by the Tennessee Centennial Exposition which APA delegates visited following the 1897 convention.

"The meeting was short and strictly business, and much enjoyed," *The Birmingham Age-Herald* reported on Oct. 16. "The citizens of Huntsville desired the body to continue in session another day, so they could extend a number of courtesies to them, but owing to the busy season now on, the members thought best to adjourn."

Gold-silver debate was divisive in 1896

Controversy both locally and nationally centered in 1896 on silver versus gold coinage, Bruce Bemis wrote in a "100 Years Ago" column in the Sept. 2, 1996, issue of *Birmingham Business Journal.* President Grover Cleveland supported the demonetizing of silver in favor of gold, which had been accomplished in 1873 by reversal of the first-ever coinage law passed by Congress. Cleveland considered the gold standard most favorable because it created "sound money."

Challenging Cleveland was the eloquent William Jennings Bryan.

Bryan's argument, which became increasingly popular, and especially in the South, was that monometallism had resulted in the appreciation of gold and a corresponding fall in the prices of commodities. The issue resulted in perhaps history's most convoluted alignment of political factions in a presidential election, splintering both the Republican and Democratic parties.

Two Alabama editors come to blows over issue

Coinage became a wedge not only in each major party's internal relations, but also in management and labor relations. In Alabama, two daily newspaper editors even came to blows over the issue.

The Birmingham State-Herald reported that during a chance meeting in Montgomery in late August 1896, James H. Nunnelee, editor of *The Selma Times,* extended his hand to Franklin P. Glass, his counterpart at *The Montgomery Advertiser.*

Glass, miffed by word that Nunnelee had branded him a Democratic Party bolter, refused to shake hands. In fact, when Nunnelee confirmed the verbal affront, Glass "popped his fellow journalist in the snout and wrestled him to the ground. The two exchanged blows, and Glass got in a few licks with his cane before the amused bystanders intervened."

1897

Moncure Woodson Camper, The Florence Times
1897-1898 president

26th annual press convention, Florence
June 8-9, 1897

In 1897, 82 of the state's newspapers were members of the Alabama Press Association, but attendance at the 26th annual convention in Florence was "not quite so large as expected," *The Montgomery Advertiser* reported in its June 11, 1897, edition.

Included on the program were John C. Williams of *Our Mountain Home* in Talladega, who spoke on advertising; J.C. Lawrence of *The Marion Standard*, who told how the press could aid the development of the state; Percy Clark of *The Selma Telegraph*, who talked about personal journalism; and Dr. L. Hensley Grubbs who reviewed two decades of journalism in Alabama.

"After three days of convention work, the editors are in fine humor to enjoy themselves," *The Montgomery Advertiser* reported. Following the Florence convention, about 140 editors and wives went to the Exposition in Nashville. One day was known as "Alabama Press Day."

1898

Moncure Woodson Camper, The Florence Times
1898-1899 president

27th annual press convention, Tuscaloosa
May 10-13, 1898

In 1898 the Press Association added its voice to those calling for a new state constitution. The

---

S I D E L I G H T S
MARKING 125 YEARS OF HISTORY

Fire damages **Advertiser-Journal** *in 1949*

AlaPressa reported in 1949 that a fire, set off by an exploding light bulb, "put presses out of service and caused damage estimated at nearly $100,000 at *The Montgomery Advertiser* and *Alabama Journal*. Limited editions of the Montgomery dailies are being printed on the presses of *The Southern Farmer*, which can handle 16 pages."

University of Alabama campus was the site of the 27th annual convention May 10-13, 1898. Sessions were held at Clark Hall.

Interest in improving the transportation of the state was reflected in resolutions rejoicing in completion of the Mobile and Ohio railroad line to Tuscaloosa and endorsing construction of a Warrior River canal, *The Birmingham Age-Herald* reported in its May 13, 1898, edition.

Some of the addresses at the 27th annual convention included "Weak Points in Business Management," R.L. O'Neil, *The Huntsville Mercury;* "The Benefits of All Home Print," C.D. Bonney, *The Edwardsville Standard News;* "Advertising Rates," William H.H. Judson, *The Bessemer Weekly;* and "How to Make a Neat Newspaper," by Christopher James Hildreth, *The New Decatur Advertiser.*

Delegates attended a public reception given by University of Alabama president Dr. James K. Powers in the President's Mansion.

Steamer excursion on Warrior River

An excursion on the steamer "Ottawa" through locks No. 2 and 3 on the Warrior River was taken during the 1898 convention. The editors and publishers returned to Tuscaloosa over the Tuscaloosa Belt Railway by way of Riverview, Lorraine, Bryce Hospital and the University of Alabama. An account of the 1898 convention was found in a scrapbook belonging to Elizabeth Cornish George of *The Demopolis Times.* The old scrapbook had been kept by Miss Iva Welch, an active member of the APA in the 1890s.

The following account of the 1898 convention, from *The Alexander City Outlook,* is in the scrapbook held by Mrs. George: "The writer has returned from one of the pleasantest trips in his experience, which same was the jaunt of the Alabama Press, to Tuscaloosa, and from there to Washington and other points of interest. A jollier or more congenial set of people could not be gotten together than the members of the Alabama Press: every one was made to feel a kinship and the assemblage took upon it the appearance of one great family, consequently he who felt lonely or out of place must lay the fault at his own door."

On Friday following the convention, the editors and publishers left on Southern Railway for Washington, D.C., to look at the workings of national legislation and "let the powers that be, know that Alabama is still on the map." They also went to New York and to Newport News for the christening of the "Alabama."

1899

Rufus Napoleon Rhodes, *The Birmingham News*
1899-1900 president

28th annual press convention, Birmingham
June 14, 1899

By 1899 the APA Legislative Committee had apparently met with success in changing the state libel law. Although not completely satisfactory, most members of the Press Association attending the 28th annual convention at the Commercial Club in Birmingham June 14, 1899, believed it represented an improvement.

William E.W. Yerby of *The Greensboro Watchman* referred to "the new libel law as a great improvement over the old one in that a man who thinks himself libeled can recover for actual damages." On an unrelated matter, Yerby said that "a weak point in Alabama journalism is the cheap price charged for advertising." Yerby thought "a higher price could be gotten if asked for."

Clark speaks for "intelligent ballot"

Percy Clark of *The Selma Telegraph* "spoke ardently for an intelligent ballot," according to reports in *The Montgomery Advertiser,* June 15, 1899, edition, and *The Birmingham Age-Herald,* June 14, 1899, edition. "Intelligent ballot" was an euphemism for restricting Negro suffrage, particularly in the use of a literacy test.

According to *The Montgomery Advertiser,* Clark "made an earnest talk, in which he charged that the press of Alabama had not shown courage on the educational question and on an intelligent ballot. He spoke ardently on the educational question and on an intelligent ballot. He spoke ardently for an intelligent ballot, and thought the press was duty bound to advocate it."

The 28th annual convention was enlivened by a speech by Gen. James Berney Stanley of *The Greenville Advocate* titled, "What is News, How to Tell It, and What Not to Tell," and a long discussion on strong points and weak points of Alabama journalism.

"Ups and Downs of a Country Editor"

J. Earl Garrison of *The Sulligent Lightning* spoke on the "Ups and Downs of a Country Editor." APA minutes noted that "Mr. Garrison's literary additions are quaint and amusing, and his paper was entertaining in the extreme, provoking much laughter in the witty presentation of sensible thoughts."

After the one-day convention in Birmingham, about 100 newspaper men and their wives left the city at midnight, June 14, 1899, for Niagara Falls and Toronto, Canada. On their homeward trip they stopped at Lake Chautauqua and Cincinnati. The special train was furnished by the Louisville and Nashville and Erie railroads.

1900

Rufus Napoleon Rhodes, *The Birmingham News*
1900-1901 president

29th annual press convention, Birmingham
July 17-18, 1900

A well-attended 29th annual convention at the Commercial Club in Birmingham marked the turn of the century for the Alabama Press Association. About 125 attended the two-day meeting that was held June 17-18, 1900.

Generally representatives of the host city each year would welcome the conventioneers and make speeches praising their cities and the accomplishments of the state press. The 1900 speech by W.H. Kettig, president of the Birmingham Commercial Club, however, is notable in that he gave concrete reasons for Birmingham's appreciation of the press.

"Birmingham, the iron city of the South (and perhaps the world), is the greatest monument to simple advertising this country has produced," *The Birmingham Age-Herald* reported in its July 18, 1900, edition covering Kettig's speech to the APA. "No patent medicine, no produce of manufacture, no matter what it owes to advertising, nothing has been more benefited by the press than the city of Birmingham," Kettig told the APA convention delegates.

"Embarrassing situation" for secretary Rountree

Some of the editors at the 1900 convention were miffed by the failure of the State Fair Association to carry out its advertising contracts with state newspapers. This was an embarrassing situation to J. Asa Rountree, secretary of the Alabama Press Association, who also was secretary of the State Fair Association.

Apparently the situation was cleared up at the meeting as a resolution was adopted stating that Rountree had acted under the orders of the Board of Directors of the Fair Association and was not responsible for the failure to carry out contracts.

An editorial in *The Birmingham Age-Herald* praised Rountree, saying that "he has practically made himself indispensable to the Association. It could scarcely get along without Mr. Rountree."

John C. Williams of *Our Mountain Home* in Talladega presented a paper, "Are Ready Prints Injurious to Weekly Papers," in which he opposed the use of ready prints. C.H. Frye of *The Pratt City Herald* defended ready prints. Frye felt that "patent outsides gave a review of all the news of the world" and that some people "of limited means" could not afford to print all the paper themselves, *The Birmingham Age-Herald* reported on July 18, 1900.

Delegates take excursion to Colorado in 1900

An excursion to Denver, Colo., followed the 1900 convention. Many of the delegates took their children. A Denver newspaper reported that the railroad agent in charge of the train "was unaware of the large proportion of wives, sisters and children in the party, and, expecting men only filled up his commissariat accordingly with liquids. He was obliged to buy many gallons of ice cream when the joke on him was discovered."

Three Pullman sleepers were run as a special for the Alabamians leaving Birmingham on Wednesday night, July 18, 1900, for Denver. Before returning to Alabama on July 25, the party visited Silver Plume, Manitou, Colorado Springs, the summit of Pike's Peak and Cripple Creek. At Cripple Creek the editors attended a luncheon and visited the gold mines.

On the return trip, the Alabama editors and publishers received many courtesies from the citizens of St. Louis and resolved to do all in their power to contribute to the success of the World's Fair in St. Louis in 1903.

1901
William Edward Wadsworth Yerby,
The Greensboro Watchman
1901-1902 president

30th annual press convention, Montgomery
June 20-21, 1901

The convention drawing up the new Alabama state constitution was meeting in Montgomery simultaneously with the APA 30th annual convention June 20-21, 1901.

Without elaboration, outgoing APA president Rufus Napoleon Rhodes of *The Birmingham News* told delegates in his presidential address that "the

Rufus Napoleon Rhodes
The Birmingham News

constitutional convention would not now be in session in the State Capitol but for the press of Alabama," it was reported in the 1901 APA minutes.

There was, of course, much contact between the two groups. The Press Association requested that the constitutional convention "incorporate in the proposed new constitution for Alabama a clause providing that all local county laws as adopted by the Legislature, be printed in one newspaper of general circulation in each county to which said local laws apply."

"No law shall curtail liberty of press"

While APA was meeting, there was added to the proposed constitution a line stating that "No law shall ever be passed to curtail or restrain the liberty of the press," *The Birmingham Age-Herald* reported in its June 22, 1901, edition. A resolution was adopted by the APA endorsing the efforts of *The Marion Standard's* Charles Herd Greer in the constitutional convention on behalf of the press of the state.

Papers that were presented during the convention included "The Country Newspaper as a Business Venture" by William H. Cather of *The Ashville Aegis* and "My Experience in Alabama Journalism" by Isaac Grant of *The Clarke County Democrat* in Grove Hill. The religious press was represented by a paper on "The Obligations of the Press to the Furtherance of Morality" by S.P. West of *The Alabama Christian Advocate* in Birmingham.

1901 excursion to San Francisco

After adjournment of the 1901 convention, "a party of 110 ladies and gentlemen" left Montgom-

---

S I D E L I G H T S
MARKING 125 YEARS OF HISTORY

Weekly paper listed at $14,000 in 1949
AlaPressa listed the following newspaper for sale in 1949: "Alabama paper is a county seat weekly, only one in county. Grossing $15,000. Circulation little under 1,000. Can be had for about $14,000."

ery on June 21 for Birmingham where arrangements were made for APA to start on a 15-day outing to San Francisco, Calif. En route the conventioneers were entertained in Memphis during a three-hour stop. Citizens' committees met them in carriages to drive them over their cities during stops at Fresno and Stockton, Calif. In San Francisco they were entertained by a ride on the bay through the Golden Gate, with musical receptions, a trolley ride over the city, inspection of the ships in the bay, and a trip through Chinatown.

The San Francisco Call featured APA's visit in a page 1 story in the newspaper's Friday, June 28, 1901, issue that was headlined "Press Club Thronged With The Editors From The Far And Famous Sunny South." *The Call* also featured artwork and photos of the trip.

"The ladies and gentlemen of the Alabama Press Association were the guests of *The Call* yesterday on a trip around the bay on board the tug 'Defiance'," *The Call* reported in its June 29 issue. "Every minute of the time from 9:30 a.m. to 1:30 p.m. was enjoyed by the agreeable and accomplished visitors from Alabama."

1902

William Edward Wadsworth Yerby,
The Greensboro Watchman
1902-1903 president

31st annual press convention, Mobile
May 22-23, 1902

The YMCA Building in Mobile was the site of the 31st annual press convention May 22-23, 1902. Mobile went all out to welcome the representatives of the press. *The Mobile Herald* issued a special edition of the paper in honor of APA.

Conditions for the 1902 convention were less than ideal. "The air was close in the room and fans were at a premium, those who had them working vigorously all the time," *The Mobile Herald* reported. "Mopping of fevered brows was also the usual thing and melted collars were common." A thundershower provided blessed relief for the members in this pre-air conditioning era. Despite the heat, a great deal of important business was transacted. Heated discussion surrounded a proposal to limit membership to two from each newspaper.

APA secretary J. Asa Rountree of *The Dixie Home Manufacturer* in Birmingham announced that 170 members were on the rolls. Rountree reported that during the year a book of the proceedings of the last

convention had been published. It had 90 pages and included the full text of all papers given and photographs of the officers. Mrs. Rountree designed a badge for the Press Association. Pins were made for delegates who wanted them.

Five issues of *The Alabama Press Reporter* had been published during the year. It contained reports on advertisers who did not pay their bills and warnings against dead-beat advertisers. This is the first reference found to an official publication of the Alabama Press Association. (Copies of *The Alabama Press Reporter* have not been located.)

Abuses of railroad passes discussed in 1902

There was some discussion of abuses of passes given by the railroads to APA members for excursions. A resolution was adopted to expel "any newspaper man who imposed on railroads." The problem of the practice of trading railroad transportation for advertising came up. The Executive Committee was instructed to inquire into some way of paying railroads for transportation by advertising in the form of an illustrated pamphlet.

The convention delegates instructed the Legislative Committee to "try to get a law requiring all laws passed to be cast in plate form and printed in every county." The Press Association went on record asking the Legislative Committee "to prepare and present to the next Legislature a measure, and urge its passage, for the publication of laws enacted by the Legislature in the newspapers in every county."

Yerby comments on personal feuds between editors

In his presidential address, William E.W. Yerby of *The Greensboro Watchman* commented on the end of personal feuds between Alabama editors:

"The old-time method of editors indulging in bitter and vicious personal controversies, has, I am delighted to note, passed into a state of 'innocuous desuetude' in Alabama," Yerby said, "and I must give the reading public the large part of the credit for putting a stop to so objectionable a style of journalism. They grew tired of it and served notice on the publishers that they wished it to cease and it did."

Yerby also pointed out "the duty of the press to expose election frauds. The new Alabama constitution had the effect of disenfranchising blacks. One of the major reasons which had been advanced for this step was ending the corruption which had often surrounded the black vote."

Yerby continued: "For 25 years past a large portion of this state was threatened with Negro domination. The only thing that kept them out of power was the manipulation of the ballot box. It was an unpleasant duty to perform, but that strategy was regarded as a better policy than bloodshed, and those men who thus protected their homes and their firesides from the inroads of the black hordes acted the parts of patriots. Old considerations no longer exist under our new organic law, and it is the duty of every editor in Alabama to expose political corruption and trickery at the ballot box, and to create a healthy moral sentiment against such practices. Let the slogan be: The honest sentiments of the white people as expressed at the polls must and shall be heard and respected...it is our plain duty to exert our influence in this behalf, regardless of our political affiliations."

Papers presented at 1902 convention

The following papers were presented at the 1902 convention in Mobile: "Circulation Booming Experience" by Edward O. Neely, *The Guntersville Democrat;* "The Relationship of the Press to Industrial Development" by R.D. Eckberger, *The Huntsville Mercury;* "Woman as a Newspaper Man" by Julia Gillespie, *The Hanceville Hustler;* "Legal Advertising" by Christopher James Hildreth, *The New Decatur Advertiser;* "The Duty of the Press" by C.W. Hare, *The Tuskegee News;* "The Art of Interviewing" by Annie Kendrick Walker, *The Birmingham Age-Herald;* "Some Essentials to Success in Journalism" by T.C. Williams, *The Dothan Siftings;* "The Effects of Rural Free Delivery on the Country Press" by W.T. Wear, *The Opelika Daily News;* and "How to Improve and Strengthen our Association" by William H.H. Judson, *The Bessemer Weekly.*

No records have been found of the Press Association's visit to Boston, Providence and New York in July 1902.

1903
William Edward Wadsworth Yerby,
The Greensboro Watchman
1903-1904 president

32nd annual press convention, Anniston
May 21-22, 1903

At the 32nd annual press convention in Anniston May 21-22, 1903, Maj. William Wallace Screws of *The Montgomery Advertiser,* Gen. James Berney Stanley of *The Greenville Advocate,* both charter members of the Press Association, and DeWitt C. White of *The Moulton Advertiser* were named life members of APA.

H.J. Gaetner of *The Pratt City Herald* spoke on "The Newspaper as an Educational Agent," and Robert Henry (Harry) Walker Sr. of *The Athens Democrat* spoke on "How to Handle Country Correspondence."

J.E. Graves of *The Brundidge News* spoke on "The Evils that Beset Country Newspapers and How to Eradicate Them." J.C. Lawrence of *The Union Springs Herald* spoke on "The Evils that Beset Country Newspaper Men," and J.C. Norwood of *The Mountain Eagle* in Jasper spoke on "The Weekly Newspaper in the Industrial Development of our State."

Patent sheets committee formed

A committee of H.Y. Brooke of *The Luverne Journal,* Edward Louis Collen Ward of *The Bridgeport News* and Rufus Napoleon Rhodes of *The Birmingham News* was appointed to plan the printing of patent sheets for Alabama papers. Stock in the company would be bought by Alabama editors.

"Of the 175 members, 73 were present" at the 1903 convention, according to APA minutes. The minutes also reflect that "130 newspapers were represented in the total membership, 24 having been added since the last meeting." The minutes continued that "since our last annual meeting, death had taken away these members: Edward O. Neely, *The Guntersville Democrat;* Sherwood Bonner, *The Camden Progressive Era;* and H.J. Whitcomb, *The Evergreen Record.*"

APA members take excursion to Canada in 1903

On Tuesday, July 14, 1903, the Alabama press delegation left the state on a special train of four Pullman sleepers and a baggage car for a tour of Canada. "The railroads will not issue transportation but for two male and two dependent female members of his family from each paper," APA secretary J. Asa Rountree of *The Dixie Home Manufacturer* in Birmingham wrote. "The male member must be a bona fide editor, publisher, proprietor, or must be actively engaged on the staff of the paper, making in all not over four people to each paper, provided that said paper runs advertising to the amount of $48.00 for each person."

On July 16 the editors and publishers arrived in Toronto where they were entertained by the civic reception committee of the Board of Alderman, the Toronto Press Association, and by the Board of Trade. The Alabamians were given a drive over the city, a boat trip on the bay, and an elaborate lunch in the pavilion on Island Park. Friday, July 15 was spent on Muskota Lakes.

Editors board steamer "Toronto" on July 18, 1903

Saturday, July 18 was spent on board the steamer "Toronto" going up the St. Lawrence. At sundown they reached Montreal. During their stay in Montreal the editors and publishers were entertained by the Press Association of the Province of Quebec, Mayor Cochrane and the Board of Aldermen.

On July 21 they reached Quebec and were entertained for two days by the local newspaper men, the mayor and aldermen, and the Quebec Railway, Light and Power Company. They visited the shrine of Ste. Anne De. Beaupre, 20 miles from the city, and then were escorted to the Falls of Montmorency.

After two days' stay in Quebec, the Alabama delegation returned to Toronto and crossed Lake Ontario to Niagara Falls. On their return trip to Toronto, Judge S.L. Fuller, on behalf of the Alabama Press Association, presented to longtime Press Association secretary J. Asa Rountree of *The Dixie Home Manufacturer* in Birmingham a handsome watch "as a token of the affection and appre-

---

S I D E L I G H T S
MARKING 125 YEARS OF HISTORY

Birmingham Post *printed with brown ink*

The Friday, Jan. 14, 1949, issue of *The Birmingham Post* "was printed with brown ink," according to *AlaPressa*. "The issue offered no explanation, but the brown ink caused curiosity and interest among readers of *The Post.*"

---

ciation of the members of the party for his unwearying efforts for their comfort and pleasure."

July 24 and 25 were spent in Chicago being entertained by the Armour and Swift packing houses. They reached Birmingham on July 26.

1904
Charles Herd Greer, *The Marion Standard*
1904-1905 president

33rd annual press convention, Bessemer
June 29-30, 1904

Dissension rocked the Alabama Press Association in 1904 when it met in Bessemer for the 33rd annual convention June 29-30.

An Executive Committee meeting in November 1903 had charged secretary J. Asa Rountree of *The Dixie Home Manufacturer* in Birmingham with abuses of free railway passes secured for the APA on its excursion to Canada in July 1903. The committee charged that Rountree had been obtaining railway passes for individuals who were not APA members. Rountree was accused of charging a higher sum than was necessary for the excursion and pocketing commissions for securing accommodations.

Formal charges against Roundtree

The formal charges were that "For personal gain he (Rountree) had charged a higher sum against the members than was necessary for the excursion to Canada, he had received commissions for personal use in securing accommodations for the party, he had encouraged violation of the bylaws and rules of the Association in securing transportation from the railroads for persons not members of the Association."

Of the three resolutions presented regarding the charges, Rountree was condemned for "using the Alabama Press Association through the trust and confidence reposed in him as its secretary for his personal graft, and consider that his conduct in such position makes him unworthy of membership in this Association." Rountree resigned, but the incident did not end there.

Complaints about abuses of railroad passes

There had been complaints for years about abuses of railroad passes. Rountree charged some APA members, all officers or members of the Executive Committee, with selling or lending their railroad passes. Rountree asked that a committee hear his charge at the 1904 convention, but he failed to attend the committee meeting. Rountree's friends within the Press Association were hoping to clear up the whole mess by absolving either side of blame.

Rountree said he did not appear at the committee meeting because he felt that all the charges and counter-charges were in the process of being settled amicably and would probably be disposed of by the Press Association. This, however, was not the case.

Incident was heatedly debated

The incident was heatedly debated for about two hours during the convention. A resolution that was presented by a friend of Rountree recommended forgetting the entire business. Another resolution was introduced to condemn Rountree and remove him from the Press Association.

After much parliamentary wrangling, a resolution was adopted which condemned Rountree "for using the Alabama Press Association through the trust and confidence reposed in him as its secretary for his personal graft," *The Birmingham Age-Herald* reported in its June 29 and 30, 1904, issues. The resolution further stated that Rountree's conduct made him "unworthy of membership in this Association."

It appears that Rountree was not actually expelled from the APA as his name appeared on the list of members attending the conventions in later years. Following his condemnation, Rountree took the floor "and in a very sensational manner renewed the charges against a number of members of the Association," according to *The Birmingham Age-Herald*. The charges were tabled and the APA proceeded with the planned program.

H. Y. Brooks delivers "clever paper"

Along with an unscheduled command performance by H.Y. Brooks of *The Luverne Journal*, who delivered a clever paper called "The Country Editor — a Medley of Contradiction, A Being Who is Absolutely Devoid of Interest in His Own Welfare," the following papers were presented: "How Two Women Can Run a Political Country Newspaper" by Virginia C. Clay of *The Huntsville Democrat;* "The Newspaper and the Negro" by Julia H. Gillespie of *The Hanceville Hustler;* "The Money, Spirit, and Press" by Olin H. Stevenson of *The Roanoke Leader;* "The Country Weekly and Its Relation to Politics" by J.H. Meigs of *The Albertville Banner;* and "The Editor, His Duties to the Community, and His Community's Obligation to Him" by Robert E. Lee Neil of *The Selma Times.*

Editor endorses movement to change words of "Dixie"

Moncure Woodson Camper of *The Florence Times* introduced a resolution endorsing the movement to change the words of "Dixie," but the resolution was tabled. Dr. J.J. Hunter of Sylacauga commented that "if the song was good enough for our fathers, it is good enough for us."

According to minutes, "Tribute was paid to members who had passed away during the year: Isaac S. Barr, first life member of the association, connected with *The Florence Gazette* and a Confederate soldier; DeWitt C. White, life member, connected with *The Moulton Advertiser;* William J. Blan, *The Troy Messenger,* also a Confederate soldier; William Neely Dale, under his management the papers of Pickens County were consolidated."

1904 was the first year in the history of the Alabama Press Association that its business was conducted under the seal of the association.

Delegates travel to St. Louis in 1904

A special train, consisting of three Pullman sleepers "with 120 members and their ladies" left Birmingham on Friday, July 1, 1904 for St. Louis, Mo. Most of the editors remained in St. Louis for a week, during which time they visited the World's Fair and other attractions including the alluring "Pike."

Through the effort of Congressman Henry Clayton of the National Democratic Executive Committee from Alabama, APA secretary Jacob Pepperman of *The Montgomery Advertiser* secured for the Alabama editors 100 session and four season tickets of admission to the Democratic National Convention then in session in St. Louis. (Pepperman replaced long-time secretary J. Asa Rountree of *The Dixie Home Manufacturer* in Birmingham.)

1905
Robert E. Lee Neil, *The Selma Times*
1905-1906 president

34th annual press convention, Coden (Mobile County) July 20-21, 1905

A friendly spirit pervaded the 34th annual convention at the Opera House in Coden in Mobile County July 20-21, 1905. An entire afternoon session turned into a huge tribute to Maj. William Wallace Screws of *The Montgomery Advertiser.* A committee of the National Editorial Association presented Screws a silver service in recognition of his outstanding service as president of the Newspaper Editorial Association the past year.

APA delegates were unaware that Screws' retirement as NEA president coincided with his 40th anniversary of his association with *The Montgomery Advertiser*. "It is a happy thought to me that, without your knowledge of that fact, this event should occur upon the day that marks the 40th anniversary of my connection with the paper to which my life, energy and whatever ability God has given me, have been devoted," Screws said. "From the day *The Montgomery Advertiser* was resurrected from the ashes of a long and bloody war, July 20, 1865, to this hour, I have known no other field of labor than that afforded by its columns."

Advertiser staff pays tribute to W.W. Screws

The Montgomery Advertiser staff took advantage of the NEA presentation to present Screws a loving cup from the staff. Screws was overwhelmed by the double presentation, but more was to come.

Spontaneously, APA members took the floor to make speeches of tribute to this outstanding newspaper man. APA minutes reported that delegates were limited to one-minute speeches of tribute to Screws. By the time the session ended, 25 editors had made speeches of tribute, and "more would have joined in had there been time," *The Montgomery Advertiser* reported in its July 21, 1905, issue.

Delegates adopted resolutions urging stronger legal notice publication laws and stronger enforcement provisions.

The major business of the 1905 convention was making minor constitutional changes and discussing formation of an advertising agency for weeklies. The weekly editors called in Victor H. Hanson of *The Montgomery Advertiser* to help them formulate plans as he was considered "a past master of getting business and advertising rates" and "the evangelist of advertising in the South," *The Montgomery Advertiser* reported in its July 22, 1905, issue.

1906
Robert E. Lee Neil, *The Selma Times*
1906-1907 president

35th annual press convention, Gadsden
July 25-26, 1906

Formation of an advertising agency for weeklies, which had been discussed at the 1905 press convention, was launched at the 35th annual convention in Gadsden July 25-26, 1906. The convention was at the Bellevue Hotel on Lookout Mountain near Gadsden.

"Weekly newspaper men subscribed for $4,000 worth of stock...a capital of $13,000 was to be raised," it was reported in APA minutes. Gov. William Dorsey Jelks and Sen. John T. Morsen spoke at the convention. Bruce Kennedy of *The Montgomery Advertiser* spoke on "What is News and How to Get It."

Kennedy: "I yearn to be a weekly newspaper editor"

Kennedy told the 1906 convention delegates that he "yearned to be editor of a weekly newspaper. When that glad time has come, I will determine what is news to the people of my community, and I will print that news, irrespective of what individuals may tell me, regardless of what my advertising patrons may think, say or do, discriminating, mayhap, occasionally in favor of the weak, but never for the strong," Kennedy said. "I will set down my opinions freely, fully and fearlessly on my editorial page. In my news columns, I will publish facts without prejudice."

(In 1912, according to APA records, Kennedy was associated with the Montgomery Chamber of Commerce. Kennedy traveled with APA members that year to the Democratic National Convention in Baltimore to lend support to Alabama's political aspirant, Oscar W. Underwood.)

Following the convention in Gadsden, the editors and publishers went on an excursion to Montgomery, Jacksonville, Fla., and Atlantic Beach, Fla.

1907
Howard S. Doster, *The Prattville Progress*
1907-1908 president

36th annual press convention, Montgomery
July 18-19, 1907

A wild and emotion-packed press convention was held in Montgomery on July 18-19, 1907. The controversy started when outgoing APA president Robert E. Lee Neil of *The Selma Times* took some pot shots at Gov. B.B. Comer in his annual address at the 36th annual convention.

After reviewing the progress of the Press Association and the press in Alabama during his year in office, Neil commented that the progress had been made despite "an unfriendly Legislature dominated for a time by a seemingly vindictive governor, suffering from 'dementia Sylacauga' or some similar hypochondriacal complaint."

The Legislative Committee had been able to get the committee considering a railroad regulation act to insert an amendment stating that "nothing contained in the pending bill should be construed as preventing the exchange of transportation for advertising space in newspapers at the regular rates charged the general public." The governor, however, used his influence to push the bill through with an anti-pass measure. According to Neil, "the constitutional right of conducting his business as he saw fit was denied the newspaper man in Alabama."

Since the APA president had been hard on the governor, *Our* (Talladega) *Mountain Home's* John C. Williams, "as if to show that no harm was intended," moved that the governor be invited to speak to the convention delegates. Charles Herd Greer of *The Marion Standard* seconded the motion. "The resolution went through like a deer in a walk," according to APA minutes.

Charles Herd Greer
The Marion Standard

Gov. B.B. Comer addresses Press Association in 1907

The governor addressed the Press Association the next day. When Gov. Comer concluded his speech, Greer offered a set of resolutions which contained about 15 sections, thanking the governor for his address, praising some of the actions of his administration, and "then severely taking him to task for some things he had done during his administration." Greer praised the governor for his work for "education, old soldiers, equality of taxes, restriction of child labor, receding from the tax loan

feature, for resenting unjust actions for corporations, and for observing party choice in the appointment of Bankhead to the Senate."

Greer then attacked the governor for "his effort to discredit the nomination of Bankhead, hostility toward the great developers of the state, especially the great arteries of commerce, his tendency to confound the executive and legislative authority, opposition to immigration laws, failure to have an exhibit of Jamestown, and his failure to recognize the unpaid and unselfish labors of the state."

APA minutes: "Then all hell broke loose"

"Then all hell broke loose," APA minutes reported. "Some of the members felt that a few editors had 'cooked up' the idea of inviting the governor just to embarrass him." Max Hamburger of *The Mobile Daily Herald* described the resolutions as "insulting" and said that if "any man should offer such resolutions at a meeting in Mobile when the governor of the state was an invited guest, that the member would be promptly thrown from the convention hall." Hamburger stated that while he had opposed the governor politically he condemned the actions of the supporters of the resolutions.

Gov. Comer thanked Hamburger, remarking that although the Mobile editor had fought him, he had fought fairly. "With this statement the governor turned from Mr. Hamburger and walked to Mr. Greer and shook his finger in his face...saying that while he himself was a fighter he had never been known to hit below the belt," *The Mobile Daily Herald* reported.

Gov. Comer renounced the resolutions, mincing no words. "I am nearly fifty-eight years old and never before in my private or public life have I been treated with such discourtesy as shown me tonight by the Alabama Press Association. I came here as your invited guest and to say that I am astonished at your treatment is putting it mildly."

William Wallace Screws acts as peacemaker

Maj. William Wallace Screws of *The Montgomery Advertiser* acted as the peacemaker. Screws offered as a substitute for the resolutions before the convention delegates one that thanked the governor for his address, but said that everyone had the right to his own opinions. All the resolutions were expunged from the records.

The hotel lobbies buzzed that night with both friends and foes of the governor denouncing the few editors who sought to embarrass the governor.

The next day many editors called on the governor to apologize.

Gen. James Berney Stanley of *The Greenville Advocate* described the 1907 press convention in Montgomery as "one of the stormiest sessions the association ever held. That was when Hon. B.B. Comer was governor, and with many of the editors he was most unpopular, for his administration had just dealt the association a hard blow by prohibiting railroad passes," Stanley said when giving "some reminiscences" years later at the 1929 press institute at Alabama Polytechnic Institute in Auburn.

APA: Legal notices should be posted

Although the Comer incident was by far the most exciting event of the convention, some important business was transacted. A motion was passed expressing the sense of the Press Association "that all legal notices that are now required to be posted or published, be published in some county newspaper and that the legislative committee of the APA be instructed to call same to the attention of the Legislature."

Another resolution favored modification of the libel laws of the state. The resolution led to a libel retraction statute in 1907.

The press honored newspaper men who had died during the past year: William Marion Meeks, life member and editor of *The Gadsden Times and News;* Col. Jefferson M. Falkner, *The Southern Planter,* Montgomery; and John Tyler Morgan, honorary member of APA. (Morgan was a member of the 1861 secession convention, a Civil War general, and U.S. senator from 1876 until his death in 1907.)

Papers on use of railroad passes

Papers were presented that expressed opposing points of view on the use of railroad passes by newspapers. Robert Henry (Harry) Walker Sr. of *The Limestone Democrat* spoke on "The Pass, a Baleful Influence to Publisher and Editor," while W.H. Parker of *The Bessemer Rustler* discussed "The Anti-Pass Legislation an Abridgement of the Constitutional Rights of Contract." W.C. Dinwiddie of *The Baldwin Times* in Bay Minette spoke on "Advantage to Weekly Newspapers of Exchanging Advertising Space for Transportation."

Other papers presented at the 1907 convention included "Why the Alabama Press Association Should Live," by W.T. Hall of *The Dothan Eagle;* "Religious News in the Secular Press," by the Rev. Frank Willis Barnett of *The Alabama Baptist;* and "Newspapers, Past, Present and Future," by Capt.William (Will) Thomas Sheehan of *The Montgomery Advertiser.*

One-week outing held on Alabama river

Despite the controversy surrounding the 36th annual convention in 1907, delegates then left Montgomery for a week's outing on the Alabama River. APA secretary Jacob Pepperman of *The Montgomery Advertiser* described the week's events:

"On Friday night at 11 o'clock, July 19, 1907, a large number of the members of the Press Association, accompanied by ladies, left Montgomery on the steamer 'City of Mobile' for a week's outing on the Alabama River. The first stop made by the press party was Selma. Committees of Selmians met the steamboat, and members of the party were escorted to waiting automobiles.

"The visitors were shown many places of interest. At 10 o'clock the citizens of Selma received the newspaper people at the Hotel Albert, and were welcomed by Hon. Leon Clay, president of the Selma City Council. A luncheon and champagne punch were served, in which the committee was assisted by a number of attractive Selma ladies.

Vaudeville entertainment provided in saloon

"The press party left Selma about 11 o'clock Saturday morning for Mobile. The first diversion on the steamer came Saturday evening, when a splendid vaudeville entertainment was given in the main saloon of the steamer, with ex-president R.E.L. Neil of *The Selma Times* acting as master of ceremonies. Four talented young musicians of Montgomery, members of the party, added to the interest of the occasion, as indeed they added to the pleasure of the trip. They were Messrs. Fred Linder, Frank M. Spangler, George Huffman, and David W.W. Fuller. They were assisted by Misses Florie and Nellie Haden, charming and attractive girls of Montgomery, who were accomplished musicians on the piano and violin.

"Readings by Mrs. R.E.L.Neil, of Selma, and Miss Donna Hamburger, of Mobile, were greatly enjoyed, and Misses Garrett and Allen, of Montgomery, contributed piano solos. Mr. J.H. Hand concluded the program with old-time melodies.

Sunday religious service had on river steamer

"On Sunday morning a religious service was held on the steamer, the principal feature of which was singing of hymns in which the entire party participated. There was no minister in the party, so ex-president R.E.L. Neil read the Scriptures, and an eloquent invocation was offered by President Howard S. Doster (of *The Prattville Progress*). The services were concluded by a delightful sacred duet by Mrs. Bruce Kennedy, of Montgomery and J.H. Hand, of Bessemer.

"Sunday night a vote of thanks was given to Capt. T.H. Moore, General Manager of the People's line of steamers, for special rates from Montgomery to Mobile and return, and for other courtesies, and to all other officers of the steamer for courtesies and kindnesses on board their steamer.

"The boat arrived at Mobile Monday morning, July the 22nd, and after partaking breakfast, the press party left for Point Clear on the steamer 'Fairhope' arriving there at 10 o'clock. Late that afternoon the entire press party left on the steamer Fairhope for a visit to the single tax colony, 'City of Fairhope.' About 11 o'clock the editors returned to Point Clear and retired for the night.

"Tuesday noon, July 23rd, the press party went aboard the steamer 'Fairhope' for a sail across the bay of Mobile. That night, the steamer with the press party aboard left Mobile, arriving at Selma Thursday night at 11:30 p.m. July 25th.

"Delightful and inexpensive" outing for APA members

"Thus came to an end one of the most delightful and most inexpensive outings in the history of the Alabama Press Association, and one that will long be remembered by all who participated in its pleasures and enjoyments," secretary Pepperman concluded.

"Messrs. Carroll & Watson, proprietors of the Point Clear Hotel, made a special rate of $2.00 a day for the members of the Association on the American plan, with the provise that the members who contemplate stopping at that hotel must notify the Secretary of the Association of that fact,

---

not later than July 7th, because the hotel is usually crowded at this season and it is the desire of Messrs. Carroll & Watson to reserve the best rooms for the members of the Press," it was reported in APA minutes.

The year 1907 ended a 15-year period in the history of the Alabama Press Association which had been marked by a new seriousness of purpose, expanding membership and constructive actions, and marred by several violent controversies. It is doubtful if the controversies did much harm to the Press Association. A good fight can lend interest to a meeting, especially when the fight is finally resolved amicably as most of those of this period were.

It is possible, however, that the anti-(railroad) pass legislation approved during Gov. B.B. Comer's administration did affect the Alabama Press Association after 1907, for, despite public statements by APA officers to the contrary, in the next few years the pace of the Press Association slowed and membership seemed to decline.

CHAPTER 3

Stagnation and a War

1908-1925

"The most enjoyable thing about running a weekly paper, and there are many, is browsing through the exchanges on Friday and Saturday, noting the make-up, printing, and general manner of getting out the paper, and in reading the paragraphs of the different writers. There are all too many weekly editors who don't write either paragraphs or editorials, but use anything to fill up the column with. Taking a good-natured crack at some friend is lots of fun, and we don't see why more of the editors over the state don't take a hand at it."

E. Cody Hall Sr.
The Alexander City Outlook

— *E. Cody Hall Sr. (1880-1941)*
Editor and Publisher, The Alexander City Outlook
APA president, 1928-1929
(From a personal column in The Alexander City Outlook*)*

THE PERIOD FROM 1908 TO 1925 WAS ONE of ups and downs for the Alabama Press Association. Attendance at annual conventions varied widely depending upon the meeting place and business conditions. The end of trading newspaper advertising for railroad passes in 1907 made it difficult for some editors and publishers of weekly newspapers to afford attending conventions far away from their hometowns.

"It was not until the administration of the late Governor (B.B.) Comer (1907-1911) that the pen pushers stopped riding on passes, and then only when the Legislature barred them from the privilege," Gen. James Berney Stanley, editor and publisher of *The Greenville Advocate*, said in a speech titled "Some Reminiscences of the Alabama Press Association" years later at the 1929 Press Institute at Alabama Polytechnic Institute in Auburn.

Stanley, one of the 30 founders of APA at the first convention in 1872, said Gov. B.B. Comer was "most unpopular" with many Alabama editors because the governor had "dealt the association a hard blow by prohibiting railroad passes." The railway passes were widely popular with most of Alabama's newspaper men, but apparently at least one editor of the early 1900s was concerned with the ethics of newspapers accepting free passes even before the practice was outlawed. Robert H. (Harry) Walker Sr. of *The Limestone Democrat* in Athens gave a speech at the 1908 convention titled "The Pass, a Detriment to the Newspaper Publisher."

Robert H. (Harry) Walker Sr.
The Limestone Democrat

Walker: Editors should pay railroad fare in cash

"In my opinion the greatest detriment the railroad pass has been to the newspaper editor is the fact that in accepting it he laid himself liable to the charge that he was influenced in his editorial expressions by the favors thus received," Walker told 1908 convention delegates. "I must confess that it would be best for the newspaper man — and more especially the country newspaper man — to be compelled to pay his railroad fare in cash just as those in other callings are forced to do," Walker said.

One year earlier, at the 1907 press convention, Walker had presented a paper titled "The Pass, a Baleful Influence to Publisher and Editor."

(Walker had the distinction of serving as both state senator and state representative. In 1931, Sen. Walker brought the inequities of the legislative apportionment to the attention of Alabamians through his newspaper. He also entered the fight for redistricting. His modified reapportionment bill passed the Senate but failed in the House. In 1934 Walker was elected to the Alabama House of Representatives. Walker became the first newspaper man to be chosen speaker of the House. In that body, he guided into law legislation which permitted Alabama municipalities to buy electricity from the Tennessee Valley Authority. He also supported New Deal measures. He voted against the sales tax and was author of a free textbook bill for the first three grades of the public schools. All of these things he advocated in *The Limestone Democrat*.)

Doster optimistic in his address

Outgoing APA president Howard S. Doster of *The Prattville Progress* optimistically commented in his opening address at the 1908 press convention that "the anti-pass law…was at one time looked on as a serious measure to the future prosperity of the Association," but that "the life of the organization did not depend upon the ability of its members to secure transportation from the railroads."

Doster seemed to have been overly optimistic; for a few years following 1908, the APA seemed to be in a period of decline The anti-pass legislation, coupled with disruptions in economic life and especially the problems of newspapers during World War I, such as newsprint shortages, did not help the Press Association. Some progress, however, was made toward reform of Alabama's libel laws, and standardization of advertising rates for the smaller newspapers.

1908
J.C. Lawrence, *The Union Springs Breeze*
1908-1909 president

37th annual press convention, Bessemer
July 22-23, 1908

The 37th annual press convention July 22-23, 1908, at Odd Fellow's Hall in Bessemer was regarded by the members to have been "one of the most successful, from a business point of view, that had been held in years," *The Birmingham Age-Herald* reported in its July 25 issue.

Reorganization of the Press Association was the chief order of business at the 1908 convention. Past APA president Robert E. Lee Neil of *The Selma Times* delivered an address on "How Best to Promote the Interest of the Alabama Press Association," which was the basis of the reorganization.

Neil suggested that APA be divided into three groups: metropolitan dailies, city dailies and weeklies. There would be three vice presidents for APA, each to be responsible for the interests of one of the groups. Before each convention, each group was to form a committee to plan business to be discussed. The three groups were to meet together and report to the Press Association.

Reorganization discussed in 1908

The reorganization which emerged from the 1908 convention was somewhat different from Neil's plan. The state was divided into five geographical groups with a vice president for each area. The five vice presidents were to hold area meetings at least once a year. During one session of the convention the association would divide into two classes, Class A, weeklies and monthlies, and Class B, dailies, to transact business affecting the two types of newspapers.

Delegates were welcomed to the press convention in Bessemer by Mayor W.L. Rush. "More than one hundred and twenty-five editors and their lady friends were seated around the banquet table at the Grand Hotel Thursday night enjoying the bountiful repast provided for them by the good people of Bessemer," it was reported in the 1908 APA minutes.

Western Union provides free use of wires

APA had 97 members in July 1908. Before convention roll call, APA secretary Jacob Pepperman of *The Montgomery Advertiser* announced that Western Union Telegraph Co. had "extended to the members of the Association the free use of their wires at their office in Bessemer for social and personal messages, to any point in the United States. Further, that the Bell Telephone Co. had also extended the free use of their lines to any point in Alabama."

In an address to the Press Association, Professor W.C. Blessingame of Demopolis "made a plea for more publicity along the lines of school libraries in every section of the state," according to the 1908 convention minutes. William E.W. Yerby of *The*

Greensboro Watchman gave a speech titled "The Press and Railroads as Factors of Civilization."

"As usual Mr. Yerby handled the subject in a masterly manner without manuscript or notes," the minutes reflected. R.L. O'Neal of *The Huntsville Mercury* read a paper titled "The Responsibility of a Daily Paper in Moulding Current Thought." Rufus N. Rhodes of *The Birmingham News* gave a paper on "The Future of Alabama and the Part to be Played by the Press."

Excursion taken to Brunswick, Ga., in 1908

Following the Bessemer convention, the editors and publishers traveled by L&N Railroad to Brunswick, Ga., on July 24, spending part of their visit on Brunswick Island, *The Birmingham Age-Herald* reported in its July 23, 24 and 25, 1908, issues. Hotel Oglethorpe was headquarters for the association during its stay at Brunswick. "The hotel is said to be the finest of the kind in the South, the regular rates are from $4.00 to $6.00 per day however the management made a special rate of $3.00 per day for our party," it was reported in the 1908 APA convention minutes.

1909
C.G. Fennell, *The Guntersville Democrat*
1909-1910 president

38th annual press convention, Dothan
June 16-17, 1909

Press Association members "vigorously used palm leaf fans while they transacted a mass of business at the Houston County Courthouse" in 1909 at the 38th annual convention June 16-17 in Dothan. The convention was followed

---

S I D E L I G H T S
MARKING 125 YEARS OF HISTORY

Clarke Stallworth hurt in streetcar accident
AlaPressa reported in October 1950 that "Clarke Stallworth Jr., 24, former *Birmingham Post-Herald* reporter, was injured seriously last week when his auto struck a streetcar in Birmingham. He received a severe concussion, broken ribs and lacerations. Stallworth last week resigned from the *Post-Herald* staff to go on active duty as a U.S. Navy officer."

---

by an outing to Panama City and St. Andrews Bay, Fla.

In his opening address, outgoing president J.C. Lawrence of *The Union Springs Breeze* commented that it would not be possible for the weeklies in the state to settle upon good advertising rates until nearly all the newspapers in the state were members of the Press Association.

Lawrence also praised the development of schools of journalism throughout the country and said he hoped there soon would be one in Alabama. "The idea is a correct one," Lawrence said, "for if doctors, lawyers and farmers and teachers must be trained for their life work, it is apparent that the journalist needs a broader and more comprehensive training than any of these, for does not the journalist presume to criticize and even to teach the doctor, lawyer, farmer and teacher and all the rest of mankind?"

Much discussion resulted from a paper by L.S. Deal of *The Dothan Home Journal* on "The Government as a Competitor in Envelope Printing." A resolution was adopted urging Alabama senators and representatives to vote to abolish the practice of printing return addresses on envelopes.

Screws submits Alabama newspaper history

Maj. William Wallace Screws of *The Montgomery Advertiser* submitted in pamphlet form a history of Alabama newspapers on which he had been working for several years.

More than 100 delegates had been expected for the 1909 convention, but only 50 attended despite the lure of an outing to Panama City and St. Andrews Bay, according to reports in *The Birmingham Age-Herald*, June 17; *The Birmingham News*, June 16; and *The Montgomery Advertiser*, June 16, 17 and 18, 1909.

1910
McLane Tilton Jr., *The Pell City Progress*
1910-1911 president

39th annual press convention, Mobile
June 16-17, 1910

Admitted to membership at the 39th annual convention in Mobile on June 16-17, 1910, were David Holt, *The Baldwin Times,* Bay Minette; W.L. Wilkinson, *The Geneva Reaper;* George A. Carleton, *The Clarke County Democrat,* Grove Hill; and W.F. Aldrich, *The Birmingham News.*

On June 18, members of the Press Association left Mobile for Fort Morgan aboard the "Winona," revenue cutter of the Treasury Department. But after traveling about 10 miles, the party found the New York steamer "Algonquin" grounded. APA minutes reported that "the 'Winona' pulled and pulled, and the Fort Morgan boat, the 'General Holland,' pulled too, but the 'Algonquin' barely budged.

"Throughout the day efforts were made to clear the 'Algonquin,' but the party had to be returned to Mobile at 6 p.m. without having reached Fort Morgan.

"The excursion was a success in many ways, especially in the good things served," according to APA minutes. "The day was perfect in every respect and the happy party gathered under the awnings where songs and stories lent the hours wings, and even the crew of the cutter joined in and added their quota of song and dance until it was time to return to the stranded steamer."

1911
Luman Handley Nunnelee, *The Centreville Press*
1911-1912 president

40th annual press convention, Montgomery
June 11-12, 1911

The 1911 press convention apparently was never held. The 40th annual convention was scheduled June 11-12, 1911, in Montgomery and was to be followed by a tour of Tuskegee. *The Prattville Progress* reported in its June 13 edition, however, that the convention was postponed because of lack of interest by members. *The Prattville Progress* commented that the Alabama press "is not exercising a great influence in Alabama" and influence of the press "is at its lowest ebb."

If the 1911 convention was ever held, there is no report of it.

"There is a lack of interest among the editors in these meetings and the prospects were not bright for a good attendance," *The Prattville Progress* reported. "So it was deemed advisable to postpone the meeting."

The Progress further commented:

"While the attendance has been small for the past two or three years, this is the first time in the history of the Association that an annual meeting has been postponed on account of lack of interest. The secretary, Mr. Jacob Pepperman (of *The Montgomery Advertiser*), has assisted in arranging a good outing and

has sent out several circulars urging a large attendance. Several answered the circulars by urging the Association to become more practical — to discuss and deal with those subjects which would be of a more practical benefit to the newspapers.

"*The Progress* regrets that the Press of Alabama is not exercising a great influence in Alabama and it wishes to warn its members for the future," the newspaper continued. "The influence of the Press is at its lowest ebb in the State. Unless there is a more thorough co-operation of its members, future governors, legislators and advertisers will not have that respect for it they should have. We need at this time, more than ever, a cooperation and a membership who are not afraid to express themselves along the lines of right and justice.

Editors "afraid to assert their rights"

"There are today more than 200 newspaper men in Alabama. More than half of these are not in a prosperous condition. They are accepting foreign and other advertising for whatever the advertisers demand. They are afraid to charge their rates on anything for fear they will not be in line with the other newspapers in Alabama. They are afraid to assert their rights in many ways for fear that they will not have the support of their contemporaries. With these conditions the Press cannot expect to exert that influence and command that respect it should. *The Progress* repeats that if there has even been at any time in the history of the Press of Alabama when it should get together, it is now.

"*The Progress* hopes that the Secretary of the Alabama Press Association will call another meeting this year and urge every representative of the Press to attend. We should to a certain extent, reorganize and revolutionize our organization and its purposes. We should discuss subjects and act on those subjects which would be of a practical benefit to the Press. We should endeavor to have the experience of those who are actually making the newspapers of Alabama. We should not only discuss the practical things pertaining to the Press, but we should resolve to stand together against too low prices along all lines."

1912
Luman Handley Nunnelee, *The Centreville Press*
1912-1913 president

41st annual press convention, Birmingham
June 22, 1912

The concerns of Alabama newspapers in 1912 were reflected in the program topics at APA's 41st annual convention on June 22 in Birmingham. The one-day session was held in the Chamber of Commerce auditorium.

The following papers were presented at the 1912 convention:

"Should We Continue the $1 Rate for Weeklies at the Present Cost of Labor and Materials?" by A.B. Tucker, *The Thomasville Echo;* "How to Increase an Interest in Our Association" by William E.W. Yerby, *The Greensboro Watchman;* "The Religious Press" by J.B. Cumming, *The Alabama Christian Advocate;* "The Relation of the Daily to the Weekly Press" by Maj. William Wallace Screws and Franklin Potts Glass, *The Montgomery Advertiser;* "The Linotype as an Investment in a Country Weekly Office" by Hunter H. Golson, *The Wetumpka Weekly Herald* and William H. H. Judson, *The Bessemer Weekly;* "Patent Insides" by E.L.C. Ward, *The News Reporter,* Talladega; "Advertising Rates: What They Should be to Pay a Profit" by W.T. Wear, *The Opelika Daily News;* "Subscribers, How to Get Them and Collect Money" by W.L. Wilkinson, *The Geneva Reaper;* "Subscription Contest" by Charles Herd Greer, *The Marion Standard;* "Patent Medicine Advertisers" by W.T. Hall, *The Dothan Eagle;* "Cost System" by Oliver Rutherford, *The Eutaw Whig and Observer;* "The Alabama Country Weekly" by Robert Henry (Harry) Walker Sr., *The Limestone Democrat,* Athens; and "Our Editorial Columns" by S.J. Darby, *The Rockford Chronicle.*

Perfectly legal to exchange advertising space

APA vice president A.B. Tucker of *The Thomasville Echo* said he had been advised by an agent of Southern Railway and also by state officials that it was perfectly legal for newspapers to exchange advertising space for railroad transportation on a dollar-for-dollar basis.

The 75 delegates attending the 1912 convention adopted resolutions favoring control of advertising and reading matter that went into newspapers, as well as expressing the sense of the Press Association that ready-print pages containing advertising be abandoned. The editors and publishers favored abolishing the use of ready-prints containing advertising "in order that the publisher(s) might control their own advertising."

"Revival of Press Association" said complete

The Birmingham News commented that the convention showed "the revival of the Press Association" to be complete. More than one-fourth of the 200 newspapers in Alabama were represented at the 1912 convention, *The News* noted. *(The Birmingham Age-Herald,* June 22-23, 1912, and *The Birmingham News,* June 21-22, 1912.)

Following the convention, many of the editors and publishers left by special train for the Democratic National Convention in Baltimore to lend their support to Alabama's political aspirant, Oscar W. Underwood. Guests on the train included Oscar Turner, Underwood Marching Club; Lt. Gov. Walter D. Seed; Gen. W.W. Brandon, probate judge of Tuscaloosa County; Adjutant Gen. Joseph B. Scully; Lt. H.A. Goodwin; Col. Gardner Green of St. Clair County; Bruce Kennedy of the Montgomery Chamber of Commerce; Phares Coleman of Birmingham and formerly of Montgomery; Culpepper Exum, mayor of Birmingham and president of the City Commission; Birmingham Police Chief George H. Bodeker; and Joseph B. Babb, secretary of the Birmingham Chamber of Commerce.

1913
Luman Handley Nunnelee, *The Centreville Press*
1913-1914 president

42nd annual press convention, Birmingham
July 29, 1913

More independence of the press from politics and politicians, increased rates for advertising, and abolishing free advertisements were the chief topics of discussion at the 42nd annual APA convention at the Chamber of Commerce auditorium in Birmingham on July 29, 1913.

Rising rates for plate advertising was discussed. The members "expressed a determination to discourage the use of much of the free advertising matter that was sent out under the guise of pure reading matter," and stated that "prices should be put on all political advertising."

Only 25 members attended the 1913 convention. The call for the meeting had not been given far enough in advance for many members to make plans to attend. It was decided that because of the poor attendance, there should be another meeting in Birmingham at State Fair time in the fall, but no records have been found indicating that the second meeting was ever held.

1914
Christopher James Hildreth,
The New Decatur Advertiser
1914-1915 president

**43rd annual press convention, Birmingham
May 29-30, 1914**

A small turnout again was reported at the 43rd annual APA convention May 29-30, 1914, in Birmingham. The question of equal suffrage was discussed at length with Julia Gillespie, editor of *The Cullman County Democrat,* and Mrs. Lee Moody of *The Bessemer Weekly* leading the fight for women's suffrage.

Mrs. Gillespie "appealed to the press of Alabama to sweep away some of the cobwebs and prejudice against suffrage." When an equal suffrage resolution was introduced, many members out of "chivalry" would not take a stand; however 11 voted for it and eight against it.

Within nine months, Mrs. Gillespie declared, the petitions asking the submission of the question of suffrage to the voters of the state would be ready for formal presentation to the Legislature. "A real sensation was then created when she asked for a vote from the convention on the question of suffrage," *The Birmingham News* reported in its May 29, 1914, issue.

"How many of you men favor suffrage?" Mrs. Gillespie asked. Eleven editors held up their hands.

"How many are indifferent?" was her next question. One editor, from Birmingham, finally eased up his hand.

"How many of you are actually opposed to suffrage?" was the last question. Eight hands were raised.

Thirty of the editors refused to declare themselves in any way.

Delegates commend Good Roads Association

Delegates to the 1914 convention commended the work of the Alabama Good Roads Association in "educational efforts to improve the people's highway system," endorsed the Alabama Good Roads Days of Aug. 14-15, and requested "that the people in their respective counties of the state assemble on those days named to give their efforts, labor, teams and contributions to improve their roads in their respective precincts."

A resolution stated that "the good women be requested to serve meals to the men on those days, while they are arranging to take the boys and girls out of mud and put them on good roads to the churches, schools, and prosperity." The editors and publishers also urged the governor "to issue a proclamation urging the people to observe Good Roads Days."

1915
Col. Harry Mell Ayers, *The Anniston Star*
1915-1916 president

**44th annual press convention, Montgomery
July 20-21, 1915**

In 1915, the effects of the war in Europe were being felt. At the 44th annual convention in Montgomery July 20-21, APA expressed a desire for presidential action to remove the embargo on cotton.

An editorial in *The Montgomery Advertiser* called upon the press to become more strongly organized: "The hour has struck not only for the press of Alabama to be self-respecting, but for the manifestation of its influence and power in a way which will command respect from others. We might as well face an unpleasant fact, and that fact is that a great many people, some occupying positions of power, are contemptuous or rather indifferent to the influence of the Alabama press."

The Montgomery Advertiser continued, "The Press Association, when united with a singleness of purpose and that singleness of purpose the welfare of the press of Alabama, can and will count heavily in all the affairs of the state. There is another unpleasant fact, of that past, that the editors might as well face, as they prepare for the future, and that is the presence of factionalism in the past. It has been political as well as unnecessary."

1916
Col. Harry Mell Ayers, *The Anniston Star*
1916-1917 president

45th annual press convention, Birmingham
July 27-28, 1916

In his opening address of the 45th annual convention at the Tutwiler Hotel in Birmingham on July 27-28, 1916, APA president Col. Harry Mell Ayers of *The Anniston Star* addressed himself not only to the problems of newspapers, but also to the problems of the state of Alabama.

Col Harry Mell Ayers
The Anniston Star

Ayers urged the editors to "emphasize more strongly the business end of our vocation; we must realize, ourselves, and must bring those in other walks to realize that journalism is governed by the rules of income and outgo that make for the success or failure of any other business.

"We have devoted too much space to political trivialities and not enough to the fundamental questions of a bigger and better commonwealth," Ayers told the editors.

Ayers also urged compulsory school attendance laws and local taxation amendments. "I believe that the most constructive service we can render our State within the next year or two will be to lend our whole-souled support to the ratification of the legislative enactments looking to local taxation and compulsory school attendance," Ayers said.

Ayers: "Education, diversification and immigration"

"Education, diversification and immigration are, to my mind, the three big words that should constitute the burden of the editorial policy of every Alabama newspaper," Ayers told the convention delegates. "Before we can successfully practice diversified agriculture on a large scale in Alabama, we must have markets; and in order to secure markets we must lend our efforts to industrial development."

Delegates endorsed locating a Federal Farm Loan Bank in Birmingham and a nitrate plant project in Muscle Shoals. In a discussion on free publicity, it developed that a "well known liquor dealer had been distributing interesting stories of baseball players and motion picture players, signing his name to the stories," *The Birmingham News* reported in its July 27, 28 and 29, 1916, issues.

"Fairly good attendance" reported at 1916 convention

The Alabama Journal in its July 30 edition reported "a fairly good attendance, probably 24 or 25 were present," at the 1916 convention, and that "practically every section of the State was represented when the first business session was opened." *The Journal* reported that Gen. James Berney Stanley of *The Greenville Advocate* was "loud in his praise of the hospitality of Birmingham and spoke hopefully of the future outlook of the Alabama Press Association, which has not prospered in recent years." Stanley said the 1916 convention "was quite a success," and there was more real enthusiasm at the convention than any he had attended in recent years.

"Gen. Stanley attributed it to a reawakening of the members to the importance of their annual meetings, and the good that grows out of them if properly attended and with appropriate programs for the discussion of those questions of interest to the fraternity," *The Alabama Journal* concluded.

Stanley's speech popular at 1916 press convention

Stanley gave a speech titled "Reminiscences of the Alabama Press" that was popular with the delegates. "No man in the state is better qualified than General Stanley to review the work and the progress of journalism, daily and weekly, and some of his remarks were particularly interesting," *The Montgomery Advertiser* commented in its July 30, 1916, edition.

"Fifty years ago there were but fifty newspapers in the state," Stanley, a Civil War veteran, said in his address. "Numbers of counties were without a single paper, and in many cases within a radius of many miles outside of a county there would be none. Fire and other causes had eliminated many of those papers which were established and running when the war began, and the lack of means and the unsettled conditions precluded the immediate resumption of many suspended during the four years of '61-65. It was some years before a general revival of the newspapers began. A Washington hand press and a few fonts of type, hope and grit and high enterprise, formed the outfit."

Stanley: "Today is the day of the Linotype"

Stanley continued, "What a great change from then to now. That was the day of the hand compositor, of hand folding, of hand feeding, of manual labor in its primary form. Today is the day of the machine with the Linotype, the stereotype, the autopress, the perfecting press, the mailing, counting, folding and all done by machines with the human equation reduced to the part of director. Even the country weekly is rapidly helping to relegate hand composition to the limbo of forgotten things.

"Newspapers are preeminently the educators and enlighteners of the people," Stanley told the 1916 convention delegates. "What the future will bring no one can foretell. You will agree with me when I say that the present year is on the turning point that marks yet another phase of history. Even as the Civil War was the period on which hinged the turn of the South toward greater usefulness and prosperity, so this year will mark the turn of the greater South toward its fuller destiny. Needless to say that the newspapers of today, no less than their predecessors of yesterday, will do their full share and more in utilizing any and all good to the greatest advantage for all the people."

1917
Edward Doty, *The Tuscaloosa News*
1917-1918 president

46th annual press convention, Gadsden
May 17-18, 1917

Patriotism was the dominant tone of the 46th annual convention in Gadsden May 17-18, 1917. "It touched everyone to hear a big steel manufacturer like Mr. Moffat of the Gulf States (Steel Company of Gadsden) refer to the son he was sending, and yet some of us protest against giving mere money in the form of taxes," it was reported in APA convention minutes.

The press was urged to publicize the campaign to raise corn for Southern consumption to replace the wheat needed for the troops. During the convention, headlines announced the ordering of the first U.S. troops to France, the putting into effect of the conscription law by President Woodrow

Wilson, and the announcement that a military camp would be built at Anniston.

A committee was appointed to secure data on the work of newspaper men serving the War Department in the Intelligence Department, censorship, propaganda, or dispatch carrying.

Cooperative buying of newsprint discussed

A major problem during war time was the high cost of newspaper production and the high price of newsprint. Having been unsuccessful in getting a paper mill built in Alabama, convention delegates endorsed the idea of cooperatively buying newsprint. Some editors complained that they were paying as high as 8 cents per pound for paper. The following committee was appointed to perfect plans for cooperative buying of newsprint: W.T. Wear, *The Opelika Daily News,* chairman; Edward Doty, *The Tuscaloosa News;* John C. Williams, *Our Mountain Home,* Talladega; Col. Harry M. Ayers, *The Anniston Star;* and A.W. McCullock, *The Gadsden Journal.*

The Birmingham News in its May 17, 1917, edition commented editorially regarding the work of the state's newspapers:

"In waging war against the manufacturer's pools and in urging conservation of every pound of white paper, the publishers of Alabama and the United States are fighting for something infinitely more than mere selfish ends," *The Birmingham News* commented. "They are working for the free press for the propagation of light, for the education of the human race at the least possible cost. If selfish interests are not thoroughly whipped, subscriptions and advertising rates will have to be increased rapidly. The Alabama Press Association is fighting for the life of the press, but it is fighting as well for the dissemination of news at the least possible cost to people."

The Birmingham Age-Herald in its May 17, 18 and 19, 1917, editions gave accounts of some of the topics discussed during the convention: "Minimum Advertising Rates," by W.T. Wear, *The Opelika Daily News;* "Co-operation for Greater Results," by incoming APA president A.W. McCullock, *The Gadsden Journal;* and "The Daily and the Weekly."

APA delegates visit lieutenant governor's home

Following the Gadsden convention, the editors and publishers boarded an L&N train furnished through courtesy of Alabama Power Co. "Upon arriving at Anniston, the newspaper men were met by Anniston citizens in automobiles, and taken to

SIDELIGHTS

MARKING 125 YEARS OF HISTORY

APA's Jack Beisner reports on paper cleanliness in 1951, 1952

APA field manager Jack Beisner visited newspapers during a one-week excursion in 1951 and filed the following report in *AlaPressa:* "I saw some mighty fine newspaper people on that visit. Wonder of all wonders, I even saw two newspaper offices which were clean – an almost unheard of condition in this business. By clean I mean that the 'junk' was neatly arranged around the shops and the floors were swept. There's no question but that all of Alabama's newspapers are 'clean' in the other way the word could be taken."

Beisner continued his commentary in the Feb. 12, 1952, issue of *AlaPressa:*

"With a few exceptions, we found that our generalization that the average Alabama newspaper was unfit for human maneuvering as far as cleanliness was concerned was not so nearly right as we first thought," Beisner wrote.

"Henry Arnold, *The Cullman Tribune,* gives all of you something to shoot at — modern, clean rest rooms that he and his help are proud of. Those rest rooms (one for men, one for women) even sport stools with covers on them! The new *Tribune* rest rooms are freshly painted, have tile floors and tile sidewalls halfway up the walls. Good lights and running water add to their attractiveness. Even sport towels instead of newsprint. Can you match that?"

Beisner again continued his commentary in the March 14, 1952, issue of *AlaPressa:*

"A couple of weeks ago, your manager made a trip to Mobile for the purpose of making some advertising solicitation calls and to visit with some of the Alabama papers that he had not previously visited. On the trip, stops were made at Eutaw (no one in at the time of the stop), Demopolis, York (Wm. Pittman, formerly editor of *Our Southern Home,* Livingston, had taken over *The Sumter Journal* and began publishing again following the paper's recent suspension), Butler (*Choctaw Advocate*), *Thomasville Times, Clarke County Democrat* (Grove Hill), *South Alabamian* (Jackson — now in the midst of a circulation campaign), *Mobile Press Register, Chickasaw News* (sorry I couldn't visit all the papers in the Mobile area, but appointments with advertisers prevented spending as much time visiting as I had hoped for), *Fairhope Courier, Foley Onlooker & Baldwin News-Herald, Brewton Standard* (Bill Brooks was broadcasting the basketball tournament), *Evergreen Courant* (missed the Bozemans), Georgiana (*Butler County News*), *Greenville Advocate,* Fort Deposit *Lowndes Signal.* (Perry was in Montgomery, missed him, too, but talked with one of his employees.)

"One very notable thing about South Alabama newspaper plants — they're in very good shape, generally. *Thomasville Times* has a front office that will make visitors sit up and take notice — nice, clean painted walls (can't find a name for the color, but not the usual white or grey), and a back shop well arranged for efficiency. *Clarke County Democrat,* as it always is, was practically spotless even though the first run was on the press. *Choctaw Advocate* is another of those plants with a clean, orderly, efficient back shop arrangement. (We're going to try to get photos of many of these plant arrangements and use them in *The Alabama Publisher* for your checking and possibly to give you some ideas on arrangements of machinery.) *Foley Onlooker* is getting a new coat of paint inside and the Howells are re-arranging for efficiency in the front office. As usual, *The Mobile Press Register* building was a showplace and the editorial room is unbelievably neat and orderly. Greenville's backshop is in fine order and is arranged for maximum efficient utilization of its facilities. (Glenn Stanley's desk, however, looked too much like your manager's desk to merit any compliments.)

"You'll notice *The Brewton Standard's* new plant was not mentioned — Bill (Brooks) was out, but I saw the office and plant, it impressed me so that my reaction was (on calling his home to locate him), 'Where's Dr. Brooks, the noted journalist-physician of the hospital staff known as *The Brewton Standard?'* We've asked Bill for some photos, inside and out, for *The Alabama Publisher.* You won't believe it until you see it — even private offices for staffers, no less."

Journalistic history in Alabama

Journalistic history in Alabama is pictured above in a powder-flash photograph believed to have been taken in the early 1920s in the shop of *Our Southern Home* in Livingston. Seated are William Hayward Lawrence and his wife, Emily Reid Lawrence. Standing are Clarence Hunter, left, and Charles Auld. (Auld later joined *The Birmingham News*.) Mrs. Lawrence was editor of the Livingston newspaper. Her husband, who died in 1938, had retired at the time the photo was taken. Emily Reid Lawrence grew up in Montgomery where her father was editor of *The Montgomery Advertiser* during the Civil War.

Mrs. Lawrence was editor of *Our Southern Home* for 61 years. "Printer's ink was in her blood, and she married an editor, spending most of her 87 years in the newspaper business," *The Alabama Publisher* noted. For eight years before her retirement in 1945, Mrs. Lawrence and one printer published the paper. Clarence Hunter, who worked on the paper more than 20 years before joining *The Greene County Democrat* in Eutaw, helped Mrs. Lawrence set the entire paper by hand and it was printed on an old hand press.

William Hayward Lawrence received his early newspaper training on *The Tuscaloosa Blade*. Lawrence established *The Chilton View* as the first newspaper in Clanton. In 1895 he bought *The Livingston Journal*, which had been founded in 1865. The Lawrences changed the name of the newspaper to *Our Southern Home*. Mrs. Lawrence died Sept. 18, 1956, at age 87.

the magnificent home of Lieutenant Governor Thomas E. Kilby," APA minutes reflect.

"Following a reception in the home, a delicious barbecue was served on the grounds by Mr. Kilby. Soon after the arrival of the party at the Kilby home, "Extra" editions of *The Anniston Star* were placed in the hands of the visitors and of the Anniston citizens present, telling of the official announcement that Anniston has been selected as the site for a great training camp. The site, proper, embraced 16,000 acres, and it will be used by infantry, machine gun and artillery companies." It was to be known as Fort McClellan.

The "Extra" also contained news of a half million dollar contract for steel cars secured by the Kilby Car and Foundry Company. Following the barbecue, convention delegates toured Anniston Steel Co. and Anniston Ordnance Co.

1918
A.W. McCullock, *The Gadsden Journal*
1918-1919 president

47th annual press convention, Birmingham
July 18-20, 1918

War-related topics again dominated discussion at the 47th annual press convention at the Civic Association headquarters in Birmingham on July 18-20, 1918. Editors expressed concern over the severe problems that war brought to newspaper publishing. The price of newsprint had increased 100 percent in two years, and the government had ordered a 10 percent reduction in the use of white paper.

In an editorial, *The Birmingham News* commented that "the APA has war problems to face, but they should be faced with confident and enthusiastic minds." *The News* urged the editors and publishers to be more businesslike, cutting out unnecessary departments and improving the necessary ones, and "to not apologize for raising rates."

Wartime problems of press discussed

Speakers at the 1918 convention concentrated on wartime problems of the press and how the press could aid the war effort. Victor H. Hanson of *The Birmingham News* spoke on "The Newsprint Situation;" APA president A.W. McCullock of *The Gadsden Journal* talked about "Newspaper Management from the Inside" and warned against making long-time advertising contracts; John Sparrow spoke on "How Newspapers Can Help in the War Savings Stamp Campaign;" and Lloyd Hooper of Selma discussed "How Newspapers Can Help the Council of Defense."

One session of the convention was an "experience meeting" where the delegates spoke four to five minutes on everything from typesetting to the war. Bays D. Cather of *The Southern Aegis* in Ashville told how he had invested all his subscription money in war bonds.

Ben Rappaport gives patriotic talk

Ben J. Rappaport of *The Pickens County Herald* in Carrollton made an intensely patriotic talk. Rappaport, a Polish immigrant, recalled repression of news in Europe and stated that "the American government can have everything I have, and my life if necessary to win the war."

Rappaport, Col. Harry M. Ayers of *The Anniston Star* and Frank N. Julian of *The Sheffield Standard* were appointed to a Ways and Means Committee to devise plans for increasing the revenue of the APA. They came up with a dues schedule of $25 for large dailies; $15 for small dailies; and $5 for weeklies, according to reports in *The Birmingham Age-Herald,* July 17 and 19, 1918, issues, and *The Birmingham News,* July 17, 18 and 29, 1918, issues.

On Saturday following the convention, the editors and publishers went to Cordova over the Frisco and then from Cordova to Tuscaloosa down the Warrior River on the boat "Neugent."

1919
Oscar M. Dugger Sr., *The Andalusia Star*
1919-1920 president

48th annual press convention, Andalusia
June 26-27, 1919

The 48th annual press convention in Andalusia June 26-27, 1919, was made especially pleasant by

the Andalusia Chamber of Commerce which paid personal expenses of all 60 of the delegates. Oscar M. Dugger Sr. of *The Andalusia Star* was inducted president at the convention.

Oscar M. Dugger Sr.
The Andalusia Star

Journalism had to share the stage with politics at the convention. The editors and publishers refused to endorse a state income tax, but they did adopt resolutions endorsing the League of Nations, the division of unused land among returning veterans, the erection of a memorial to the Alabama soldiers killed in the war, and the good roads work of the federal government.

The banquet was dominated by a discussion of women's suffrage. Mrs. Solon Jacobs spoke on the "Susan B. Anthony Amendment." Decorations for the banquet, and even the ice cream, were in suffrage colors.

Speeches were given by Webb Stanley of *The Greenville Advocate* on "The Job Office as an Adjunct to a Weekly News;" Capt. William (Will) Thomas Sheehan, editor of *The Montgomery Advertiser,* on "The Press as an Educator;" and C.H.P. Hogan on "Advantages of a Cost System for the Job End of Newspapers."

1920
Frank N. Julian, *The Sheffield Standard*
1920-1921 president

49th annual press convention, Montgomery
May 27-28, 1920

Shortage of paper and high cost of newsprint were the subjects that received the most consideration during the 49th annual press convention at the Exchange Hotel in Montgomery May 27-28, 1920.

Welcoming addresses were given by Gov. Thomas E. Kilby and Montgomery Mayor W.A. Gunter. APA first vice president Capt. William (Will) Thomas Sheehan, editor of *The Montgomery Advertiser,* responded on behalf of the Press Association.

Ed Albright, president of the National Editorial Association, led a discussion on "Newspapers and Free Propaganda." J.C. Harrison said the government and other agencies were wasting white paper on hundreds of propaganda circulars.

1920s APA meeting
This photograph was in the office of *The Clayton Record* in Clayton in 1996. *Record* editor and publisher Bertie Gammell Parish said the photograph was made at an APA convention in Montgomery in the 1920s and that her father, the late William Lee (Bill) Gammell, is in the photograph. Alabama Press Association delegates in the photograph are unidentified. Perhaps the photograph was made at the 49th annual APA convention at the Exchange Hotel in Montgomery, May 27-28, 1920. According to APA minutes, it was at the 1920 convention that occurred what is believed to be the first recorded discussion of having a permanent manager and headquarters for the Press Association. (Photograph courtesy of Bertie Gammell Parish, *The Clayton Record*)

Editors hear discussion on newsprint problem

Frank H. Miller of Montgomery, Charles Herd Greer of *The Sylacauga News,* Victor H. Hanson of *The Birmingham News* and Mrs. J.R. Rosson of *The Cullman Democrat* led a discussion on "The Newsprint Problem and How to Solve It." Some speakers recommended reducing circulation and raising advertising rates. Also discussed was the "installation of a cost system to inform publishers whether or not a profit is being made."

Other topics that were discussed at the 1920 convention included:

"Should the Editorial Page by Abolished," by Dr. Frank Willis Barnett, *The Alabama Baptist,* Chester E. Johnson and H.S. Doster, *The Prattville Progress;* "The Influence of the Press on Our State Development," by Dr. L.C. Branscomb, L.H. Nunnelee, *The Centreville Press,* and Sam H. Oliver, *The LaFayette Sun;* "Selling Job Printing at a Profit," by J.L. Meeks, Frances Golson, *The Wetumpka Herald,* and Pierce Chilton; "The Relation of the Job Department to the Country Newspaper Office," by William H.H. Judson, W.E.W. Yerby, *The Greensboro Watchman,* and W.F. McCartney; "How to Se-

cure Foreign Advertising," by Frederick I. Thompson, W.T. Hall, *The Dothan Eagle,* and B.B. Cather; "Benefits to be Derived from the State Press Association," by John F. Simmons, president of the Georgia Press Association; "Labor Shortage in the Print Shop and How to Remedy It," by W.T. Wear, *The Opelika Daily News,* Thomas G. Wilkinson, George W. Salter and Walter G. Brown; "Creating a Sentiment for Newspaper Advertising," by Fowler Dugger, *The Andalusia Star,* C.H. Allen and C.G. Fennell, *The Guntersville Democrat;* A Metropolitan Publisher's View of the Country Newspaper," by Jason Rogers of *The New York Globe;* "The Business Management of the Weekly Newspaper," by Ben Rappaport, E.V. O'Connor and Olin H. Stevenson, *The Roanoke Leader;* and The Need of New Libel Laws in Alabama," by Edward Ware Barrett, *The Birmingham Age-Herald.*

Field manager, APA headquarters first discussed in 1920

It was during the 1920 convention that occurred what is believed to be the first recorded discussion of having a permanent manager and headquarters for the APA.

Following the convention, a trip was made to Sheffield and Muscle Shoals to see construction of the dam, according to *The Birmingham Age-Herald,* May 28 edition.

1921
William Theodore Hall, *The Dothan Eagle*
1921-1922 president

50th annual press convention, Albany and Decatur
May 5-6, 1921

Reform of the state libel laws was the chief topic of discussion at the 50th annual APA convention in Albany and Decatur (the two cities later combined to become Decatur) on May 5-6, 1921. Lt. Gov. Nathan L. Miller, speaking to the convention delegates, said that "Truth should be a bar to legal punishment. It should be a complete defense."

Under the existing libel law, a newspaper could be prosecuted in any county where it circulated. If a suit failed in one county, it could be tried in a number of counties. Truth under Alabama law was only a mitigating circumstance, not a full defense. The laws on criminal libel were declared to be so ridiculous that they had been invoked in but one single instance where conviction was had. Anything which might constitute a breach of the peace was considered libelous.

In one case, prosecution had followed publication of a grand jury report. According to *The Birmingham Age-Herald,* in its May 7 issue, and *The Birmingham News* in its May 5 issue, an APA committee was appointed to draft proposed changes in the libel laws.

While meeting in Albany and Decatur in 1921, the editors toured the country areas in Morgan and Limestone counties.

1922
Capt. William Thomas Sheehan,
The Montgomery Advertiser
1922-1923 president

51st annual press convention,
Montgomery and Auburn
May 10-11, 1922

Fewer than 50 delegates, an extremely small turnout, attended the 51st annual press convention May 10-11, 1922, in Montgomery and Auburn. This led Edward Ware Barrett of *The Birmingham Age-Herald* to call again for legislation which would again permit swapping railroad passes for advertising space in newspapers.

In a roundtable discussion of newspaper problems, the question of libel laws came up again. In one instance a man who had been shot at while operating a moonshine still had sued a newspaper because it referred to him as a "shiner." An editorial in *The Montgomery Advertiser* discussed why the Alabama libel law was so harsh.

The Advertiser also quoted an attorney who was at the 1901 constitutional convention which retained the sections of the 1875 Constitution referring to the press. The attorney said the original section had been designed "to keep down fights and bloodshed."

The convention moved from Montgomery to Alabama Polytechnic Institute at Auburn, where members attended discussions on agriculture and the press. Instead of the banquet program, a special radio program was set up for the convention delegates which featured music and speeches. After a meeting in Langdon Hall on the API campus, the editors were given a barbecue by town and college officials. They spent two hours in Tuskegee on their way back to Montgomery.

A resolution was adopted asking Alabama's senators to exert themselves to have paper pulp placed on the free list in the tariff.

1923
Forney G. Stephens, *The Southern Democrat,* Oneonta
1923-1924 president

52nd annual press convention,
Mobile and Baldwin counties
May 24-26, 1923

A joint convention with the Mississippi Press Association was held May 24-26, 1923. Some meetings of the 52nd annual convention were held

---

S I D E L I G H T S
MARKING 125 YEARS OF HISTORY

Three new papers start in 1950
The following newspapers were started in 1950: *The Winston County Times* of Haleyville, by J.W. Ayers, former publisher of *The Fayette County Times; The Chickasaw News,* L.J. Smith, editor; and *The Aliceville Informer,* I.D. Brannon, editor.

Alabama and Mississippi editors meet together
   Alabama and Mississippi editors, holding a joint convention in Mobile and Baldwin counties, gathered for this group photo on May 25, 1923. Included in the photograph are Gen. James Berney Stanley, editor and publisher of *The Greenville Advocate*, and J.C. McClendon, editor and publisher of *The Luverne Journal*. (Photo courtesy of the family of J.C. McClendon, 1996 Alabama Newspaper Hall of Honor inductee)

in Mobile while others were held in the course of extensive tours by automobile and ship in Mobile and Baldwin counties.

During the business meetings, Howard S. Doster, editor of *The Prattville Progress,* led a discussion on the successful management of circulation campaigns. The appointment of an advertising rate committee was suggested. F.W. Bolt of New Orleans spoke on early typefaces and their influence on modern types.

Victor H. Hanson, publisher of *The Birmingham News,* just back from a trip to Europe, was greeted with applause when he said that Europe was in a position to pay every cent of its $10 billion war debt.

Mississippi editors meet in separate sessions

The Mississippi editors, who met in separate business sessions, stirred up quite a furor over a letter written by Mississippi Gov. Lee Russell in which he said that not one in 10 newspapers in the state dared to tell the truth. The editors retaliated with resolutions which applied the epithets "contemptible" and "political accident" to Gov. Russell, according to *The Birmingham Age-Herald,* in its May 24, 26 and 27 issues, and *The Birmingham News* in its May 24 and 26 issues.

Frances Golson, editor of *The Wetumpka Herald,* was "appointed to write the complete account of the convention, which is to be printed in newspapers throughout the state." During the joint meeting of the Alabama and Mississippi Press Associations, the editors and publishers made two tours — one to Coden and the other through Baldwin County.

Here is how Miss Golson reported the two trips.

"Automobiles were furnished for the Coden trip by the Auto Club of Mobile and driven by their owners, including many of the leading citizens of the city. The drive over graveled roads from the Battle House to Coden Hunting and Fishing Club was made in a little more than one hour and there a fish dinner was

served, the members of the two associations being the guests once more of the Mobile Chamber of Commerce. The return trip was made by way of the great fishing and seafood canning town of Bayou la Batre and through the Satsuma orange groves which line the highways of south Mobile County.

Press convention delegates board "New Daphne"

"Early Saturday morning the press representatives of the states boarded the steamer 'New Daphne' at the municipal wharf and proceeded under the leaden skies across Mobile Bay to Daphne. A short walk brought the travelers to the Daphne State Normal School, where they were welcomed by the president, Dr. Hillary Herbert Holmes.

"The Baldwin County Kiwanis Club there became host and conveyed the visitors over the roads that were dampened by recent rains, through one of the most beautiful and interesting sections of the coast country to the farms of the Greek Colony of which Jason Malbis is the ruling spirit. From there they went to Loxley, thriving town in the truck-growing region. Stops were made at Robertsdale and Summerdale and the luncheon station was the prosperous town of Foley.

"It had been planned to take the newspaper folk to Magnolia Springs where a fish fry was prepared, but a veritable cloudburst in the morning hours made this extension of the tour practically impossible, and the return was started from Foley (named for him of 'Honey and Tar' fame) by way of the Swedish colony of Silver Hill, to Fairhope, where a truly royal welcome, supper and a spacious boat awaited the voyagers; thence to Mobile and home," Miss Golson concluded.

1924

W.R. Jordan, *The Huntsville Morning Star*
(Jordan died while in office)

James S. Benson, *The Progressive Age*, Scottsboro
(Benson, first vice president,
completed Jordan's term as president)
1924-1925 presidents

53rd annual press convention, Florence
June 13-14, 1924

The Birmingham Age-Herald hailed the opening of the 53rd annual press convention June 13-

14, 1924, in Florence with an editorial in praise of small dailies and weeklies in Alabama.

The Age-Herald commented that "the country editor is thinking more for himself than ever before. He is broadening in his motives and purposes; is drawing firmer and sounder distinctions between the real and the spurious, and is more than ever speaking in terms of principle."

APA minutes reported that "a great deal of business was transacted" at the 1924 convention, and that delegates also toured the new Wilson Dam and the nitrate plant.

The Florence Times reported in its June 13 edition that the 1924 convention was held at the Elks Club with a welcoming address by W.J. Mitchell, "who told the visitors of the accomplishments of the citizens here in their work of building a city, attributing a large part of the success to the aid of the newspaper men of the community."

Full-time APA secretary again discussed

The Advertising Rate Committee that had been appointed at the 1923 convention in Mobile was given credit for a great deal of success in standardizing rates among the smaller newspapers in the state. A decision was made to draft a code of ethics for the association.

The question of employing a full-time secretary, first discussed at the 1920 convention, again was discussed.

It was decided to hold the next convention on the Gulf Coast and a tentative decision was made to establish a summer camp at some point on the coast for a permanent meeting place.

Edward Ware Barrett of *The Birmingham Age-Herald* spoke on the "History of Newspapers," and Marcy B. Darnall of *The Florence Herald* led a discussion on "How to Get and Hold Subscriptions," according to *The Birmingham Age-Herald* in its June 13, 14 and 15 issues, and *The Birmingham News* in its June 13 and 14, 1924, issues.

Banquet held on campus of Florence Normal School

The closing event of the 1924 convention was a banquet at Alumnae Hall on the campus of Florence Normal School. "The banquet was a delightful occasion, presided over by Dr. H.J. Willingham, president of Florence Normal School, who called upon everyone present to introduce themselves, several responding with appropriate and witty speeches," *The Florence Times* reported in its June 16, 1924, edition. "The repast was sumptuous, a fine tribute to the skill of the domestic science department of the school."

After touring Florence Normal School, the press convention delegates adopted a resolution commend-

---

S I D E L I G H T S
MARKING 125 YEARS OF HISTORY

The Greenville Advocate *completes 85 years*
The Greenville Advocate noted the following in October 1950: "Last week we wound up Volume 85, so this week *The Greenville Advocate* begins Volume 86. We have completed 85 years of continuous publication of this paper, and started another year. *The Advocate* has also been operated by only two generations of the same family but without the skip from grandfather to grandson (referring to *The Clarke County Democrat* at Grove Hill, which was started in the year 1856 by Isaac Grant. Upon Grant's death, the present publisher, George A. Carleton, took over. *The Democrat* celebrated its 95th birthday this year). At one time this newspaper had a world's record — and the record still stands in retrospect. The founder, the late Gen. James B. Stanley, had a record approaching 70 years as active editor of the same newspaper."

---

ing "the wonderful work that Dr. Willingham and his able faculty are doing in the training of teachers for the public schools of Alabama. We regard this type of education among the most important our state can do, in the maintenance of a system of public schools and we urge the state to give them a better support."

APA dues in 1924 were $5 for weeklies, $10 for semi-weeklies; and $15 for dailies.

Two APA presidents served in 1924

The Alabama Press Association apparently had two presidents in 1924, it was learned in 1995 while revising the APA history for the Press Association's 125th anniversary. The 1924 APA president, W.R. Jordan, who had been editor of *The Alexander City Outlook* since 1914, became associate editor of *The Huntsville Morning Star* in February 1924, according to Alabama newspaper historian Billy Jack Jones of Auburn.

The Morning Star was a new daily edited by 1917-1918 APA president Edward Doty of *The Tuscaloosa News*. Jordan died in 1924 and was succeeded as president by first vice president James S. Benson of *The Progressive Age* in Scottsboro.

In a 1949 letter to L.O. Brackeen of Alabama Polytechnic Institute, author of the 1951 and 1959 APA histories, *Jackson County Sentinel and Progressive Age* editor and publisher Parker W. Campbell wrote that "the late James S. Benson was president for half a year (in 1924). Benson succeeded a deceased president (W.R. Jordan) and served half a year, being elevated from vice president. I was working for Mr. Benson at that time and I recall he was rather disappointed when the Association did not name him for a full presidency term to follow the short term he held. However, another man (Jonathan Cincinnatus McLendon, *The Luverne Journal)* was named (in 1924), and so far as I know Mr. Benson did not affiliate with the Association after that incident."

1925

Jonathan Cincinnatus McLendon, *The Luverne Journal*
1925-1926 president

54th annual press convention, Foley
June 18-23, 1925

"Banquets, balls, trips to the Gulf of Mexico and Mobile, fish fries, barbecues, swimming, boating and fishing all come in for a share of the time in Baldwin County," *The* (Foley) *Onlooker* noted in its account of the week's activities of the APA during its 54th annual convention in Foley June 18-23, 1925.

The Onlooker reported in its June 25 edition that "Frank Barchard of *The Onlooker* offered to give the APA a site on Perdido Bay upon which to locate a summer home. The matter of building a permanent vacation place in Baldwin County has been under consideration by the state editors for some time and it is expected that some definite step will be taken."

The delegates adopted a resolution commending Gen. James Berney Stanley of *The Greenville Advocate* "who has for 60 years acted as editor of the newspaper in Greenville, Butler County, Alabama." The resolution noted that Stanley "has long been a mentor of Alabama newspaper editors and dean of the Alabama Press Association," and further commended Stanley for "long years of service in the perpetuation of the best tradition of the Fourth Estate."

S I D E L I G H T S
MARKING 125 YEARS OF HISTORY

Frank Helderman Sr. dies in 1992

The long-time publisher of *The Gadsden Times,* Frank Helderman Sr., 80, died March 19, 1992. He was publisher of *The Times* from 1951 until 1985, when he became publisher emeritus, a title he kept until his death. Helderman was succeeded as publisher by his son, Frank Helderman Jr.

Helderman came to Gadsden from Spartanburg, S.C., where he began newspaper work as a newsboy, selling copies of *The Spartanburg Herald-Journal.* His career included jobs as a printer, advertising salesman and circulation manager of that newspaper. He was into his third term as a city commissioner in Spartanburg and working as business manager of *The Herald-Journal* when he came to Gadsden.

In 1953, he formed *The Gadsden Times* Publishing Corp., which operated newspapers in Kentucky, Tennessee and Alabama.

CHAPTER 4

APA: A Press Association of Weekly Newspapers

1926-1938

"The Star-News **may not be the greatest newspaper any-where, but for the past 24 years of operations, we have been able to voice opinions that we thought should be broadcast. We may have been wrong as many times as we were right, but we have some strong evidence...that the readers want an opinion, right or wrong."**

Ed Dannelly
The Andalusia Star-News

— *Edward A. (Ed) Dannelly Jr. (1913-1984)*
Editor, The Andalusia Star-News
APA president, 1966-1967
(From Dannelly's last editorial in
The Andalusia Star-News *on his retirement in 1972)*

T HE PERIOD FROM 1926-1938 WAS AN active time for the Alabama Press Association, particularly given the economic impact of the Great Depression. Conventions were held each year, and the editors and publishers even continued their long-time practice of taking excursions, twice to New York by ocean steamer, once to Cuba, to Canada, to Washington, D.C., and to the 1934 World's Fair in Chicago.

Starting in 1929, the APA Press Institute, a "school for publishers," was held at Alabama Polytechnic Institute in Auburn for three consecutive years, but the program failed during the early days of the Depression.

In a 1935 resolution, APA pledged its support

to a bill by Rep. W.P. Calhoun of Houston County that was pending before the Legislature. The bill "would relieve newspaper reporters and employees from the necessity of divulging the sources of information and communications given them in confidence for the purpose of publication."

APA's lobbying efforts resulted in passage of a strong shield law in 1935 that protected reporters from divulging the sources of confidential information.

In the 1930s, APA took the lead in establishing a statewide chamber of commerce, a predecessor organization to the Business Council of Alabama.

The Press Association even had a field manager for a brief time in 1934-1935 under an arrangement with the federal National Recovery Act.

APA presidents who served during the late 1920s and 1930s primarily represented the state's weekly newspapers. There was not much involvement by the dailies, but one exception was *The Birmingham News* and its publisher, Victor H. Hanson. Hanson was extremely active in the Alabama Press Association and started the practice

Victor H. Hanson
The Birmingham Mews

of awarding loving cups to the state's best weeklies that was precursor to the Better Newspaper Contest that continued in 1996.

Ala-Pressa comments on Hanson's "fine public spirit"

In 1929 *The Ala-Pressa* commented on Hanson's "fine public spirit" in awarding the loving cups and noted, "Mr. Hanson has done a splendid and notable

Fire at **The Brewton Standard** *in 1951*

Because of a recent fire at *The Brewton Standard,* editor William E. (Bill) Brooks Jr. "has kindly offered to write down a few of the things he learned from his fire for the benefit of all Alabama newspaper publishers," *AlaPressa* reported in 1951. "Bill's letter speaks for itself on the subject of fire:

"All this is based on one thing," Brooks wrote. "You get to the fire before the place is in ashes. In my case, the second floor was in flames, and the ground floor was filled with smoke and had water leaking through by the gallon. It's a hard thing at three in the morning with the full excitement of a fire around you to try to decide what to grab and what to leave.

"If you get to the fire soon enough, I would suggest grabbing the following," Brooks continued. "Subscription cards (just pick up the whole filing cabinet. ABC records. Bound copies of your paper. The money or cash register, plus your general ledger, account ledger and card account files. Invoice file (you have to pay off sometime) and advertising order and contract file. Just pick up the whole shebang and run outside with it. In a small town, somebody will guard it for you. Be sure to pull out the camera with some film. I took the two lousy pictures of the fire that we used in the issue of the same week."

ated their papers primarily as an adjunct to the job print shop," 81-year-old Neil O. Davis of Auburn said in an interview in 1995. "They made their money on job printing and gave little attention to the newspaper," Davis said.

Davis: APA a "social gathering" in early years

Davis, 1947-1948 APA president and founding editor and publisher of the award-winning *Lee County Bulletin* in Auburn, said he attended his first APA convention in 1938. "It was primarily a social gathering," Davis recalled. "There was no press association at that time deserving the name."

Davis graduated from Alabama Polytechnic Institute in 1935 and helped establish *The Lee County Bulletin* in 1937. "I was dismayed at how little attention was given by the Press Association to the thing I was most interested in — putting out a quality news product," Davis said. "Many of the weekly publishers were printers. There might have been four or five editors, not publishers, who had studied a journalism course in college."

Davis recalled little involvement in APA by the state's daily newspapers in the 1930s. "The dailies belonged to the Associated Press and went to their meetings," Davis said. "*The Birmingham News* always took an interest in the APA, and *The Anniston Star.* I don't remember any other dailies being represented at the conventions. *The Montgomery Advertiser* at that time had very little interest. Practically the whole emphasis of the Press Association in the 1930s was on weekly newspapers."

Editors attend Press Institutes at API

By the late 1930s, Alabama's weekly editors were becoming more interested in producing quality newspapers as evident by the inauguration in 1929 of the APA Press Institute, held three consecutive years from 1929 to 1931 at Alabama Polytechnic Institute, now Auburn University. The editors stayed in dormitories and dined in the campus cafeteria.

When the Victor H. Hanson loving cups were awarded for the first time in 1929 to the two best Alabama weekly newspapers, the awards committee headed by P.O. Davis, director of publicity at Alabama Polytechnic Institute, selected the winning newspapers based on such criteria as clean typography, front page content, number and importance of front page news, balance of headlines, and editorial page. "Editorial page must contain editorial matter written by the editor or any member of the staff. Bought edi-

thing and one that further endears him to every newspaper in Alabama." A resolution was adopted at the 1930 Montgomery midwinter meeting expressing appreciation to Hanson "for his constructive efforts in behalf of the Alabama publishers."

Years earlier, APA minutes reflect that the major business at the 1905 convention was a discussion on the formation of an advertising agency for weeklies. The weekly editors contacted Hanson, who at that time was associated with *The Montgomery Advertiser*, to help them formulate plans as he was considered "a past master of getting business and advertising rates" and "the evangelist of advertising in the South."

Most weekly newspaper editors, until the late 1940s and 1950s, were print-oriented who "oper-

torials are taboo," *The Ala-Pressa* explained.

20th century brought changes in editorial policy

The early years of the 20th century had brought about important changes in editorial policy and the manner of presenting news. As the national press services developed and lowered their costs, editorials disappeared from the front pages and were replaced by last-minute accounts of world events. Daily newspapers began supplanting weeklies, and many of the latter, unable to compete with their larger neighbors, ceased publication. Those that survived returned chiefly to local news. They later began purchasing fiction, comics and features from the weekly syndicates.

1926-1927 APA officers
The 1926-1927 officers of the Alabama Press Association are from left, Dixie Vail, *The South Baldwin News*, poetress; the Rev. Frank Willis Barnett, *The Alabama Baptist*, Birmingham, historian; Webb Stanley, *The Greenville Advocate*, president; J.C. McLendon, *The Luverne Journal*, vice president; and Robert B. Vail, *The Baldwin Times*, Bay Minette, secretary. This photograph was taken at Alabama Polytechnic Institute, Auburn, during the 55th annual convention June 2-4, 1926. According to APA records, a business session was held at Langdon Hall on the API campus.

The 1930s was a period of consolidation rather than expansion in the state press, with the larger papers devoting their attention to improvements in makeup and service to their advertisers and subscribers. Several Alabama newspaper men achieved distinction in various fields. Franklin Potts Glass, editor of *The Montgomery Advertiser*, was rated among the great editorial writers of his day.

Grover C. Hall awarded Pulitzer Prize in 1928

Grover C. Hall Sr.
The Montgomery Advertiser

Grover Cleveland Hall Sr., as editor of *The Montgomery Advertiser*, was recognized as one of the great editorial writers of the nation. Fluently persuasive and possessing the ardor of a crusader, Hall did not hesitate to defend an unpopular issue if he was convinced that he was right. In 1928, he was awarded the Pulitzer Prize for editorial writing in recognition of his fight against flogging, and racial and religious intolerance.

At Birmingham, Osborn Zuber of *The Birmingham News* wrote several editorials that received national attention. Zuber received honorable mention from the Pulitzer committee in 1934 for his editorial, "Why We Have Lynchings in the South." John Temple Graves II, columnist for *The Birmingham Age-Herald*, became widely known in the South for his liberal analysis of social and economic subjects.

1926

F. Webb Stanley, *The Greenville Advocate*
1926-1927 president

55th annual press convention, Auburn
June 2-4, 1926

Minutes reflect little business being transacted at the 55th annual press convention in Auburn June 2-4, 1926. Webb Stanley of *The Greenville Advocate*, a graduate of Alabama Polytechnic Institute, was inducted APA president during a business session at Langdon Hall on the Auburn campus.

The International Press Foundation was discussed, and a proposal to build a Press City in Florida to be used as a convention center and a "home for retired editors" was endorsed. Only one day of business meetings was held, although two had been scheduled. The editors and publishers toured Pepperell Mills after the convention, according to *The Birmingham News* in its

June 3 edition, and *The Montgomery Advertiser* in its June 2 edition.

New meeting schedule put into effect in 1926

A new APA meeting schedule was put into effect in 1926 that remained operational until 1933. Midwinter meetings were in January in Birmingham for members from the northern half of the state, and in Montgomery for those from the southern part of the state.

About 20 editors and publishers attended the first meeting of the southern division at Montgomery's Exchange Hotel on Jan. 16, 1926. The editors discussed improvement of education in Alabama and making the Black Belt lands more productive. A state sales tax was suggested as the best way to finance education.

A resolution was adopted condemning competition from the federal government in printing and selling envelopes. It was reported that printers were being deprived of $3.5 million annually by this government competition.

Tribute paid to *Birmingham News'* Victor H. Hanson

Tribute was paid to publisher Victor H. Hanson and *The Birmingham News* for their work in promoting education and conservation in Alabama, according to reports in the Jan. 16 editions of *The Alabama Journal* in Montgomery and *The Birmingham News.*

At the Jan. 30, 1926, meeting of the northern division at Birmingham's Hillman Hotel, Hanson suggested that publishers of weekly newspapers adopt uniform advertising and subscription rates. Hanson said the weekly newspapers were not charging any more for subscriptions than 10 years earlier, although the price of newsprint had risen about two and a half times. Hanson also suggested that higher rates be charged for national advertising.

The editors and publishers discussed and approved a Cullman County educator's proposal that the county publish a free monthly journal.

Attracting much attention in the state when the group met was a program called "Advertising Ala-

New York City in 1927
    Alabama Press Association delegates toured New York City in 1927. Total cost of the trip, including rail and ocean liner, was $25.75 per person, including meals. Delegates stayed at the Waldorf-Astoria Hotel. (Photograph from scrapbook compiled by the late Catherine Brooks, *The Brewton Standard*)

bama Abroad," the idea of which had originated with APA.

1927
Robert B. Vail, *The Baldwin Times*, Bay Minette
1927-1928 president

56th annual press convention, New York City
May 7-15, 1927

APA delegates traveled to New York City and stayed at the Waldorf-Astoria Hotel for their 56th annual press convention, May 7-15, 1927. Outgoing president Webb Stanley, business manager of *The Greenville Advocate,* and Horace Hall of *The Dothan Eagle* turned out to be financiers. They worked out plans for the editors and publishers to make a round trip to New York by railroad and ocean at a cost of $25.75 per person, including meals.

"Those two figuring geniuses of the Press Association, if given a little more time, might have worked it out to the point where each editor would be given everything free and $50 to boot," *The Birmingham News* commented in its June 2, 1927, issue.

Robert B. Vail
The Baldwin Times, Bay Minette
First president elected at sea

The annual business meeting was held at sea between Savannah, Ga., and New York, including election of officers in the music room of the steamer "City of Birmingham." On the night of May 13, 1927, Robert B. Vail of *The Baldwin Times* in Bay Minette became the first APA president to be elected at sea.

Stanley gives account of 1927 trip

Webb Stanley gave the following report of the 1927 trip to New York City in *The Ala-Pressa:*

"Some 80 odd gathered in Columbus (Georgia) that first day and took the train for Savannah, reaching there early the next morning. We were met by a bunch of hospitable folks including among their number the high officials of the Central of Georgia, of the city government of Savannah and of the Savannah newspapers. After breakfast, the party gathered at the auditorium of *The Savannah Morning News* and there were welcomed in a few speeches and then taken for a wonderful drive

about that historic city, winding up at the Shrine Country Club for a shore luncheon, and then to the 'City of Birmingham' on which we sailed at 4 p.m.

Delegates stayed at Waldorf-Astoria Hotel

"On reaching New York we went immediately to the Waldorf-Astoria Hotel where reservations had been made for our party, and then entered on a three-day round of sightseeing, enjoyment and interesting experiences. Among these were trips to the factory of the American Type Foundry at Jersey City, and the factory of the Mergenthaler Linotype Co., at Brooklyn, a visit to the Brooklyn Navy Yard, a trip by motor up Riverside Drive and down Fifth Avenue, a visit to the Stock Exchange and Greenwich Village, a banquet at the McAlphin tendered by the American Press Association and a dinner in *The New York Times* building as their guests and an inspection of that wonderful newspaper's plant.

Delegates visit New York City night club

"A visit to one of New York's night clubs and a dozen other things were participated in that are not mentioned, but suffice it to say that every hour was filled to the brim with experiences that combined to make the trip one that stood out in the lives of those who went. We returned on board the same steamer, 'The City of Birmingham,' the palatial flagship of the Ocean Steamship Company's fleet," Stanley concluded.

In its Sunday, June 2, 1927, edition, *The Birmingham News* reported on the cost of the New York excursion: "The Central of Georgia Railway will transport the editors from Columbus, Ga., to Savannah without monetary outlay — for advertising. The round-trip ticket from Savannah to New York, including meals aboard ship, is $60.75, but upon arrival in Savannah, the Ocean Steamship Company will purchase advertising contracts in the amount of $35 where only one representative of a paper is present, and $70 where there are two, issuing their checks that day, in advance payment. So, deducting $35 from the cost of the ticket, leaves the cash outlay for the trip $25.75 per person."

According to the itinerary, "staterooms on the steamship 'City of Birmingham' are of the two-berth type, each room with running water. There are certain extra large rooms with bath, for which an extra charge is made. There are ten rooms with twin beds and private bath, the charge for which is $30.00 per room, or $15 per person, each way. There are also certain rooms with two berths and a private bath, for which the extra charge is $20.00 per room, or $10.00 per person, each way."

"Seagoing edition" of *The Ala-Pressa* published in 1927

The Ala-Pressa even published a "seagoing edition" on the ship to report on the 1927 New York excursion. The May 8, 1927, issue of *The Ala-Pressa*, published on the Atlantic Ocean, was in a scrapbook compiled by the late Catherine Brooks, wife of 1929-1930 APA president W. Emmett Brooks of *The Brewton Standard*. "All agree that we are off to an excellent meeting and a delightful voyage," *The Ala-Pressa* seagoing edition reported. "It is apparent that this will be a historic meeting of the Alabama Press Association."

1927 northern midwinter meeting, Birmingham

Newspaper representatives attending the 1927 northern division midwinter meeting at the Hillman Hotel in Birmingham on Jan. 8 endorsed a Senate bill to limit the amount of government envelope and printing and wired Sen. Tom Heflin, a member of the Post Office Committee, asking if he favored the bill.

The editors and publishers also recommended that financial statements of boards of education and other officials handling public funds and grand jury results be published in the state's newspapers. A law existed requiring publication of school board financial statements, but it was widely evaded "probably because of

lack of penalties in the law," *The Ala-Pressa* reported.

Establishment of Linotype training discussed

Establishment of Linotype training at the Alabama School of Trades in Gadsden was heartily endorsed by APA delegates, who asked the Legislature to enlarge the printing department, according to *The Birmingham News* in its Jan. 8 and 9 editions.

Jonathan Cincinnatus McLendon of *The Luverne Journal*, Robert B. Vail of *The Baldwin Times* and Edward Ware Barrett of *The Birmingham Age-Herald* were authorized to tour Florida to acquaint the people of other sections with Alabama and its resources. A petition was sent to the Legislature asking it to appropriate $25,000 to advertise Alabama. The Mobile Chamber of Commerce wired the APA that it had appropriated $500 for the campaign.

1927 southern midwinter meeting, Montgomery

Fewer than 20 members attended the southern division meeting on Jan. 26, 1927, in Montgomery. The small group discussed the need for changes in laws regarding printing of legal sale notices and of libel laws.

The south Alabama editors and publishers voiced vigorous opposition to the "diversion of $125 million of the taxpayers' money" for construction of Boulder Dam which would allow enough acres

---

in the Imperial Valley of California to be irrigated to add 1 million bales to the annual output of cotton. The south Alabama editors and publishers naturally disliked any idea of competition with Alabama's cotton producers.

1928
E. Cody Hall Sr., *The Alexander City Outlook*
1928-1929 president

57th annual press convention, Havana, Cuba
April 18-26, 1928

Dothan was the point of assembly for the 57th annual press convention of the APA April 18-26, 1928. Delegates were making plans for the association's first visit to Cuba since the 24th annual convention in 1895.

After being entertained by civic clubs in the city of Dothan, 108 Alabamians boarded a special train for Tampa, Fla., arriving there the next morning. A delegation of businessmen met them there and gave them a tour of the city. Plans were to board the steamship "Cuba" at 2 p.m. Thursday for the cruise to Havana.

There were several days of sightseeing, including a tour of the opulent presidential palace. Some of the editors who looked forward to seeing a bull fight were disappointed upon learning that the sport had been discontinued in 1898 by Gen. Leonard Wood, military governor. However, Havana night clubs, a Spanish ball game, the jai-alai, and cock fighting made up for the editors' disappointment somewhat.

APA reporter describes 1928 trip to Cuba

W.A. (Bill) Young of Auburn, listed in Press Association minutes as APA reporter, described the Alabamians' trip to Cuba in the following article which appeared in *The Greenville Advocate:*

"The passengers were awakened on Friday morning by the ship's bell and told that two hours would be given for seeing the city of Key West. It was here that five members of the Havana Reporters' Association met the Alabama editors and gave them official welcome from the government of Cuba and also from the Press Association. They held a conference with President Robert B. Vail and other officers of the Alabama Press Association, outlining plans for their entertainment in Havana.

"Very few suffered from seasickness, but everyone in the party was thrilled and delighted when the Island of Cuba was sighted," Young wrote. "Cars were lined along the dock waiting to take the Alabamians to the Plaza Hotel. After registering at the hotel, which is one of the most beautiful in Havana, the editors began to stir about the city."

Saturday was spent seeing various points of interest

Saturday was spent seeing the various points of interest in and near Havana. The Maine monument, where the battleship was sunk in 1898, was particularly interesting to the editors. They also visited the "most beautiful cathedral" in Havana and "the cemetery which ranks third in the world in the cost of monuments," Young reported.

A number of the Alabamians spent Sunday touring sugar, pineapple and tobacco plantations, and the sponge and fish industries. The president of Cuba was unable to meet the editors, but his palace was open for their entertainment on Monday morning. Young reported that the editors were much impressed by the elaborate furnishings which amounted to a total cost of $4.5 million.

Marble plaque to be placed in Reporters' Building

R.P. Greer of *The Sylacauga News* and Robert B. Vail of *The Baldwin Times,* Bay Minette, were appointed to secure a marble plaque to be placed by the Alabama editors in the Reporters' Building in Havana. (Records do not reflect whether the plaque was ever secured.)

Election of officers and a business meeting were held on the ship during the return trip from Cuba. E. Cody Hall Sr. of *The Alexander City Outlook* became the second APA president to be inducted to office on the high seas.

Young wrote of the Alabamians' return: "The Alabama delegation embarked for home on Tuesday morning and after a pleasant voyage reached Tampa on the following day. A trip was made by motor boat across the bay to St. Petersburg, 12 miles distance. The Chamber of Commerce and two newspapers, *The Times* and *The Evening Independent,* gave a luncheon for the Alabamians and later took them over the city."

Thirty members attended the southern division midwinter meeting in Montgomery on Jan. 14, 1928. Once again a resolution was adopted opposing the building of Boulder Dam. Outgoing APA president Robert B. Vail of *The Baldwin Times* reported that on a visit to the area, he found the dam would not greatly increase cotton production. But Vail said he opposed the project because of "state's rights, interference with private business, and the unfair use of public funds," according to reports in the Jan. 15 issues of *The Birmingham News* and *The Montgomery Advertiser.*

Victor H. Hanson presents loving cups to APA

At the 1928 midwinter meeting in Montgomery, Victor H. Hanson, publisher of *The Birmingham News,* presented two loving cups to the APA to be awarded annually to the best weekly newspapers in Alabama. They were first awarded in 1929. Purpose of the awards was "to stimulate interest in community enterprise and service by the small town weekly." Such standards as

Ocean S. S. Co. of Savannah—"SAVANNAH LINE"—S. S. City of Birmingham

Delegates travel on "City of Birmingham"
Alabama Press Association delegates traveled on the Ocean Steamship Company's flagship, "The City of Birmingham," for the 58th annual convention in 1929. Somewhere on the high seas between Savannah and New York, W. Emmett Brooks of *The Brewton Standard* became the third APA president to be inducted while on ocean liner. (Photograph from scrapbook compiled by the late Catherine Brooks, *The Brewton Standard*)

mechanical appearance, literary excellence and forcefulness of the editorial page were to be the criteria for awarding the loving cups, *The Birmingham News* reported in its Jan. 28 issue.

Presentation of the loving cups, a precursor to APA's Better Newspaper Contest, was discontinued after 1932.

The midwinter meeting for the northern division of the state reportedly was held in Birmingham on Jan. 28, 1928, but records of that meeting have not been located.

1929
W. Emmett Brooks, *The Brewton Standard*
1929-1930 president

58th annual press convention, New York City and Montreal May 10-23, 1929

A train and steamer trip to New York from Savannah on May 10-23, 1929, was a duplication of the 1927 trip, even to traveling again on the "City of Birmingham." But the 58th annual press convention was extended to include a trip by train from New York to Montreal.

The Alabamians started at Columbus, Ga., where the party assembled on the evening of May 10, 1929, and traveled by rail over the Central of Georgia Railroad to Savannah, and from there by

water on the Ocean Steamship Company's flagship, "The City of Birmingham." Somewhere on the high seas between Savannah and New York, W. Emmett Brooks, editor and publisher of *The Brewton Standard,* became the third APA president to be inducted while on ocean liner.

Brooks later had the distinction of serving as president of the Alabama Broadcasters Association. He pioneered local radio broadcasting in 1947 over WEBJ in Brewton. Brooks was a leader in both print and electronic communications during an active career from 1920 to 1958. Brooks was a strong supporter of better news and editorial content and worked to organize the

W. Emmett Brooks
The Brewton Standard
Third APA president inducted on the high seas

first APA Press Institute, which was held during his presidency.

APA delegates travel by rail to Montreal in 1929

The group traveled by rail over the New York & New Haven and Hartford line to Montreal. The return trip was made over the same route and the trip ended at Columbus, Ga., on May 23, 1929. A party of Mississippi editors joined the Alabama editors in making the trip. After arriving in

S I D E L I G H T S
MARKING 125 YEARS OF HISTORY

Human interest in **The Greenville Advocate**

The Oct. 25, 1951, issue of *The Greenville Advocate* carried a picture of such interest and so popular with readers that its use was requested by *The Alabama Churchman,* editor Glenn Stanley reported. The photo was captioned "Family attends Sunday School for a year without missing a Sunday."

The seven members of the family also stayed for church. The cutline explained that the eighth member of the family was in the Armed Forces overseas and attended Army chapels whenever possible. Pictured with the seven members of the family were their minister and Sunday School superintendent.

Montreal "the party drank to the health of the king of England and the president of the United States."

The *Ala-Pressa* gave a detailed account of the 1929 convention:

"For two days and three nights, except for 'stunt' amusements which had been planned, the ocean voyage was uneventful and land was not sighted until Tuesday morning when the New Jersey Coast was observed and the Statue of Liberty came into sight, then New York harbor was entered and Greater New York observed. The party landed at pier 46, North River, and was escorted to the Vanderbilt Hotel under a special police escort which had been arranged by Mayor Jimmy Walker of New York.

"A dinner on Tuesday, May 14, was tendered the party by the Publishers' Autocaster Company at the Hotel (Waldorf) Astoria. On Wednesday, May 14, the party was entertained in a 'never-to-be-forgotten' way by the Intertype Corporation, which was a boat trip that circled Manhattan Island. Lunch was served while riding down the Hudson River and the aquarium at Battery Park was visited after returning from the trip. Wednesday evening a theatre party was given by W.J. Baldwin, Alabama Power Company, Birmingham, and Thursday morning the editors were the guests of the Mergenthaler Linotype Company, which carried the party to Brooklyn, where that company's plant was inspected and there a delightful luncheon was served. The Linotype Company had arranged the trip from the Vanderbilt Hotel to Brooklyn in order that the party could drive about Manhattan Island, down Riverside Drive, through Chinatown,

1929 Press Institute at Auburn

APA members met at Alabama Polytechnic Institute at Auburn for their first Press Institute in 1929. The editors and publishers stayed in dormitories and ate in the campus cafeteria. The purpose of the Press Institute was to "work, study and learn." (Photograph from scrapbook compiled by the late Catherine Brooks, *The Brewton Standard*)

down the Bowery, across Brooklyn Bridge and a visit to Coney Island.

1929 delegates leave New York for Montreal

"Thursday evening, May 16, the party left New York via the New York, New Haven and Hartford's line on the 'Montrealer' for Montreal, which point was reached Friday morning. A luncheon was given by Pro-Mayor Fagen and the City of Montreal, where the party drank to the health of the king of England and the president of the United States. At a dinner that evening, Mayor Fagen was presented a proclamation and introduction from Gov. Graves of Alabama. Sunday evening at eight o'clock, the party boarded the Canadian National Railroad for the beginning of the home trip."

First Press Institute held in Auburn in August 1929

It was not until 1929 that any attempt was made to hold a Press Institute — a "school for editors and publishers." In August of that year, after the Press Association delegates returned from their trip to New York and Montreal, the first APA Press Institute was held at Alabama Polytechnic Institute on Aug. 15-17. The program was of a practical nature and dealt with the ever-important subject, "How to increase revenues."

Webb Stanley of *The Greenville Advocate* and P.O. Davis, director of publicity at Alabama Polytechnic Institute, Auburn, were in charge of arrangements. "The whole purpose of the Press Institute is to work, study and learn," *The Ala-Pressa* reported.

Editors attending Press Institute stayed in dorms

The timing for a serious session — following a pleasure junket — could not have been better. Through the cooperation of Alabama Polytechnic Institute, arrangements were made for those attending the first Press Institute to room in dormitories. Meals were served in the university cafeteria. Auburn officials also made possible a program for the spouses. For the wives, a program of "flowers, fruits, chickens and home economics" was planned, according to "A brief history of the Alabama Press Association" published in the July-August-September 1949 issue of *AlaPressa*.

The Press Institute program was of a practical nature and dealt with how to increase revenue. Topics included "News — What to Get and How to Get It," "The Editorial Page," "Circulation," "Advertising," "Costs," "Keeping Records," and "Machinery." Olin H. Stevenson of *The Roanoke*

Leader, R.P. Greer of *The Sylacauga News,* and Mack Wyatt of *The Clanton Union Banner* led a discussion on gathering and writing news.

Editors should acquire, maintain broad viewpoint

Charles N. Feidelson, associate editor of *The Birmingham News,* stressed some of the important points editors should observe. "One was that they should acquire and maintain the broad viewpoint on all subjects they discuss, and another was that they should spare no pains to be informed," according to a newspaper account of the 1929 Press Institute. "Study is quite as important to the newspaper editor as it is to the lawyer, according to Mr. Feidelson who believes that editorials will be far more convincing if written by a man who is thoroughly informed about the subject on which he is writing."

APA president Knapp speaks at Press Institute

Speakers included Dr. J. Bradford Knapp, president of Alabama Polytechnic Institute; Hugh Doak, editor of *The Times,* Manchester, Tenn.; and W.O. Saunders, editor of *The Elizabeth City* (N.C.) *Independent.* Saunders' speech was titled "The Relation of Pajamas to the Cycle of Time." In July prior to the 1929 Press Institute, Saunders attracted widespread attention in his hometown of Elizabeth City. Clad in pajamas, his picture with this story appeared throughout the country:

"ELIZABETH CITY, N.C., JULY 16 — *"Climaxing an editorial crusade for cooler summer attire for men, W.O. Saunders, editor of* The Elizabeth City Independent, *made a Sunday afternoon promenade down the principal business street here clad only in pajamas and sandals. The incident passed without excitement or molestation by police.*

"Saunders, ever fiery editorially and in his actions, precipitated a fistic battle among the members of the North Carolina delegation to the Democratic Convention at Houston last summer by attempting to seize

the banner from an 'anti-Smith' delegate and enter the parade of states that preceded the nomination of Governor Alfred E. Smith of New York while the majority of the delegation was 'anti-Smith'."

Stanley gives "some reminiscences" in 1929

During the 1929 Press Institute, Gen. James Berney Stanley, editor and publisher of *The Greenville Advocate*, gave a speech titled "Some Reminiscences of the Alabama Press Association." Stanley, one of the 30 founders of APA in 1872 and considered the "dean" of Alabama community newspapers in the early 1900s, had given a speech at the 1916 convention titled "Reminiscences of the Alabama Press."

"Times have changed," Stanley told the editors in 1929. "The old Washington hand-press has gone into the museum; the Country Campbell (flat-bed letterpress) is making a last stand; the old hand-compositor has joined the dodo as an extinct animal; but publishing a newspaper today involves just about the same pains and labors that it did 60 years ago. It is not a game, not a business, it is a profession and an honorable one," Stanley said. "And in looking over you fellows of the Alabama Press Association today, I see the same brand of brilliant men that I associated with when the association was young."

Stanley continued, "Many of you have the same names and belong to the same families; and in years to come there will be no material change in the type of men or in the editorial policy of the papers. The changes come in the back — not in the front office. It is sad to think of the many

---

S I D E L I G H T S
MARKING 125 YEARS OF HISTORY

ANAS grows stronger through the years

APA's business affiliate, the Alabama Newspaper Advertising Service, began in 1951 with two primary goals: To help make it easy to buy advertising in newspapers and to earn income to provide more services to Alabama's newspapers.

APA is the sole stockholder of ANAS.

From the 1950s through the 1970s, ANAS earned most of its income during election years every two years. That boom-and-bust income ever two years through its one-order-one bill service made financial planning a challenge.

ANAS placed about $1 million a year through its one-order-one-bill service in the late 1970s and early 1980s. By 1996, ANAS placed advertising totaling almost $4 million.

ANAS pays newspapers the next month whether it has been paid or not. ANAS also takes no commission on ads placed at retail rates, but charges the advertiser a fee. ANAS keeps a commission on ads it places at commissionable rates.

ANAS also had a strong source of cash flow with its APA Clipping Bureau. The clipping service employed most of APA's employees from the 1950s until 1987, when ANAS sold it to Magnolia Clipping Service of Jackson, Miss.

The ANAS board decided to sell the clipping service, a relatively low-profit business, after its new statewide classified advertising service, ALA-SCAN, grew rapidly from its start in June 1985.

By the late 1980s, ALA-SCAN provided as much operating income to ANAS as the one-order-one-bill service.

With ALA-SCAN, an advertiser buys a classified word ad for a flat fee, and the ANAS staff sends a typeset sheet to all participating newspapers.

In 1993, ANAS also launched a classified display program, DIS-COVER, that began slowly and began adding noticeable new income to ANAS by 1996.

ANAS's first full-time advertising manager was Craig Woodward, who started in 1979. He was succeeded by Mike Ryland in 1984. Felicia Mason, the ad manager in 1996, started work at ANAS in 1987 as Ryland's assistant and was promoted to ad manager in 1991.

In 1995, ANAS began providing the Michael T. Ryland Internships for college students interested in advertising sales. (See related articles about Ryland.)

missing ones, but I'm happy to be with you, and I'm lucky to be able to rub shoulders with more than one generation of Alabama editors. I thank you."

Gen. Stanley awarded honorary degree

At a Friday night banquet, the editors and publishers were entertained at a banquet in honor of Gen. J. B. Stanley, who was awarded the honorary degree of "Master Journalist" in recognition of his years of service as editor and publisher of *The Greenville Advocate*. Stanley was also presented a loving cup by the Greenville Lions Club.

Held at Smith Hall on the Auburn campus, the banquet meal consisted of head of lettuce with Persian dressing, saltines, fruit cocktail, broiled chicken, June peas, asparagus, candied apples, glazed yams, pickles, Parker House rolls and tea. Dessert consisted of ice cream and cake, followed by "mints and smokes," according to the published menu that was in a scrapbook compiled by the late Catherine Brooks of Brewton. Solos were given by Caroline Samford Giles of Opelika, Anna Thomas of Montgomery and Sgt. George Moxham of Auburn, and music also was provided by the Auburn Male Quartet.

Grover Hall discusses "qualities an editor should have"

Grover C. Hall Sr., editor of *The Montgomery Advertiser*, led a discussion at the 1929 Press Institute on "what qualities the present day editor should have," one newspaper reported. "Fearlessness, conviction and an ability to express himself in a forceful and colorful manner was the consensus." Hall

> ### S I D E L I G H T S
> Marking 125 Years of History
>
> #### *Air-conditioning installed at* Herald *in 1954*
> *The Union Springs Herald* plant was modernized in 1954. The improvements included new wiring, including fluorescent lights in both the office and printing department, and installation of air-conditioning and new heating unit.
>
> William H. Garner, editor and publisher of *The Herald,* said he thought his newspaper was the only weekly in Alabama with complete air-conditioning.

led a panel discussion titled "the editorial page." Joining Hall on the panel were C.L. Feidelson of *The Birmingham News;* Julian Harris, editor of *The Columbus* (Ga.) *Enquirer-Sun;* J.P. Mitchell, editor of *Wiregrass Farmer* in Headland; Jesse B. Adams, editor of *The Southern Star* in Ozark; and W.A. Moody, editor of *The Sylacauga Advance.*

Dr. George Petrie, professor of history and dean of the graduate school at Alabama Polytechnic Institute, spoke on the "influence of the editorials of today, expressing the opinion that the editorial page is losing its influence to a large extent due to the speed at which the world moves. People read the news and pass up the editor's comments because they are in such a hurry to get on to the next interest of the day," Petrie said.

Victor H. Hanson loving cups awarded in 1929

At the southern division midwinter meeting in Montgomery on Jan. 26, 1929, the Victor H. Hanson loving cups were awarded for the first time to the two best weekly newspapers. An awards committee headed by P.O. Davis, director of publicity at Alabama Polytechnic Institute, selected the winning newspapers based on clean typography, front page content, number and importance of front page news, balance of headlines, and editorial page. "Editorial page must contain editorial matter written by the editor or any member of the staff. Bought editorials are taboo," *The Ala-Pressa* reported.

One loving cup went to *The Mountain Eagle* of Jasper as the best weekly newspaper in Alabama in 1928 and the other was awarded to *The Southern Star* in Ozark for rendering the best community service of any weekly newspaper in Alabama in 1928.

The awards committee praised *The Mountain Eagle* for its editorial page, county news coverage, typography, advertising volume, dignity and good taste, and community spirit. *The Southern Star* was cited for its service in promoting the sale of farm products, "particularly of hogs, its continued interest in the improvement of modern agricultural methods, its support of education, good roads and public health, and the excellent manner in which it did all these things," Grover C. Hall Sr., editor of *The Montgomery Advertiser*, said in making the presentation.

APA commends Hanson's "fine public spirit"

Reporting on presentations of the first two loving cups and plans to continue the awards in future years, *The Ala-Pressa* commented on Hanson's "fine public spirit" and noted, "Mr. Hanson has done a splendid and notable thing and one that further endears him to every newspaper in Alabama."

During the 1929 Press Institute APA president W. Emmett Brooks of *The Brewton Standard,* on behalf of the Press Association, presented a certificate of commendation to Marcy B. Darnall Sr. of *The Florence Herald.*

Marcy B. Darnall Sr.
The Florence Herald

The Herald, edited by Darnall, won first place in the National Editorial Association's "greatest community service contest" for 1929. "This remarkable achievement was attained by honest, intelligent and courageous effort which leads to success in journalism and renders maximum service to the community being served," the certificate stated. In 1926, 1927 and 1928, *The Florence Herald* placed second in the national contest.

1929 northern midwinter meeting, Birmingham

At the northern midwinter meeting in Birmingham on Jan. 12, 1929, competition and prices and job printing as an adjunct to the newspaper were the main topics.

"It was asserted that certain publishing houses outside Alabama were in the habit of sending expensive presents to county officials at Christmas, birthday anniversaries, and on other occasions, and that the home printer was unable to get any business from these officials," it was reported in the Jan. 12 issue of *The Birmingham News.* "It was suggested that these gifts be given the widest publicity in the counties where such conditions exist and several editors approved the suggestion," *The News* reported.

According to "History of the Alabama Press Association" compiled in 1951 and revised in 1959 by L.O. Brackeen, director of publicity at Alabama Polytechnic Institute, conventions were not held during the height of the Depression, from 1930 to 1932. However, issues of *The Ala-Pressa* on file in the archives department of Auburn University's Ralph B. Draughon Library report that press conventions were held each of those years and that officers were elected.

Chandler first publisher of *The Mobile Press*

In April 1929, local business interests combined under the leadership of T.M. Stevens to publish *The Mobile Press,* naming Ralph B. Chandler as president and publisher. Chandler, who was born in Akron, Ohio, in 1891, began his newspaper career with *The Cincinnati Post* in 1909. In 1921 he founded *The Birmingham Post* and served as its publisher until 1926. He left Alabama in 1926 to join *The Greenville* (S.C.) *Piedmont* as publisher for two years.

Ralph B. Chandler
The Mobile Press Register

In 1932, *The Mobile Press* purchased *The Mobile Register & News Item,* and Chandler became president and publisher of *The Mobile Press Register,* a post he held until his death in January 1970. He was named chairman of the board and publisher emeritus of *The Press Register* in January 1970 and served in that capacity until his death three months later.

1930

Marcy B. Darnall Sr., *The Florence Herald*
1930-1931 president

59th annual press convention, Washington, D.C.
July 14-21, 1930

APA reportedly went to Washington, D.C., for its 59th annual press convention June 14-21, 1930, but minutes of the 1930 convention are not available.

On Jan. 11, 1930, a midwinter meeting for the southern division of the state was in Montgomery, and the midwinter meeting for the northern division was in Birmingham on Jan. 25, 1930. A resolution was adopted at the Montgomery midwinter meeting expressing the thanks of the Press Association to Victor H. Hanson, publisher of *The Birmingham News* "for his constructive efforts in behalf of the Alabama publishers."

Second annual Press Institute held in 1930

The second annual APA Press Institute was at Alabama Polytechnic Institute on Aug. 14-16, 1930, with the theme of "Making a Better Newspaper." Like the first one, the 1930 institute was devoted to study and work. Alabama Polytechnic president Dr. J. Bradford Knapp welcomed the editors and publishers and expressed "confidence that there is a growing appreciation in Alabama for all things worthwhile, and especially the work of the press." Knapp welcomed members of the press as "co-workers in a common cause for united progress in Alabama."

Editors of the state were praised by Knapp, who "declared that the press as a whole is one of the greatest forces for advancement and progress along all lines."

Brooks gives tribute to Alabama Polytechnic Institute

Outgoing APA president W. Emmett Brooks of *The Brewton Standard* responded with a tribute to Alabama Polytechnic Institute. Brooks said that "Alabama newspaper people selected Auburn as the place for their annual Institute because the College here is identified with the people and business of the state in a way similar to the connections between a newspaper and its readers," according to a newspaper account of the 1930 Press Institute.

"Alabama is a State where industry, agriculture and mining are the major businesses," Brooks said. "Consequently, it is proper and desirable that editors of the state come here annually in order to stay in touch with what Auburn is doing and thereby be in a better position to serve the people of the State."

Discussions heard on local and farm news

Discussions of local and farm news were heard during the afternoon in which a dozen editors took part. The opening day of the 1930 Press Institute ended with a barbecue at the home of President and Mrs. J. Bradford Knapp.

Auburn Rotary, Kiwanis and Lions clubs were the hosts.

Several specialists were invited to participate in the 1930 Press Institute, including John E. Allen, editor of *The Linotype News* in New York; Russell Kent, a Washington correspondent and former president of the National Press Club; and professor John H. Casey, community newspaper specialist from the University of Oklahoma, who spoke on "Enterprising Newspapers and Newspaper Men of the Country Field."

Field manager for APA was discussed in 1930

Casey remained at the Press Institute until it ended. During his visit he talked with many of the editors and publishers about their problems

---

S I D E L I G H T S
MARKING 125 YEARS OF HISTORY

Printers, typesetters needed in 1952

AlaPressa reported in its March 21, 1952, issue that because of a lack of an adequate number of printers and typesetters, the Press Association was working with the State Department of Education to increase the number of graduates from the state printing schools at Dothan and Gadsden.

"There is adequate dormitory space at both schools for additional students. The cost to the students who attend these printing schools is: tuition for anyone under 21 years of age is $10 per month; tuition for anyone over 21 and not a veteran is $37 per month. One suggestion is that you help get students from your area interested in printing and get them to attend these schools. You may even be in a position to help them pay their way — for example, physicians help girls taking nurses training in the trade schools financially as much as paying their tuition and three months board in return for a promise from the girls that when they finish the course they will work (at a salary) for the physicians for a year. Some similar agreement might be worked out between you and some promising young man or woman in your area seeking a good paying job in the printing industry."

and gave them advice. After he returned to Oklahoma, Casey wrote that while at the 1930 Press Institute,"I learned that there was some sentiment for undertaking the employment of a field manager for the organization in cooperation with one of the state's educational institutions, probably Alabama Polytechnic Institute at Auburn. I also was gratified to find that President (Bradford) Knapp of Auburn was kindly disposed to the idea in general. My impression was, however, that the publishers of the state would have to initiate the movement."

APA records reflect that before the 1930 Press Institute, the hiring of a field manager and establishing permanent headquarters had been discussed at two earlier press conventions, in 1920 and 1924. However, it was not until 1934 that the dream of a field manager for the Press Association was realized, and only temporarily.

"Newspaper show" held in conjunction

A "newspaper show" was held in conjunction with the 1930 Press Institute, at which some 500 newspapers from every section of the United States were displayed for inspection by the Alabama editors. The program committee believed that this was an effective means of helping some members with their problems, *The Ala-Pressa* reported.

Outgoing APA president W. Emmett Brooks of *The Brewton Standard* and Grover C. Hall Sr. of *The Montgomery Advertiser* accompanied Howard C. Smith to the local WAPI broadcasting studio where Brooks delivered a short talk over the radio to the farmers of Alabama on the relationship of the editors to the farmers.

"All-Alabama Weekly Newspaper Eleven" inaugurated

The practice of selecting the "All-Alabama Weekly Newspaper Eleven" was inaugurated at the 1930 Press Institute, although it apparently was discontinued after 1931. Newspapers making up the team included *The Florence Herald, The Sylacauga News, The Chilton County News* in Clanton, *The Mountain Eagle* in Jasper, *The Roanoke Leader, The Southern Democrat* in Oneonta, *The Alexander City Outlook, The Brewton Standard, The Cullman Tribune, The Marion Times-Standard* and *The Southern Star* in Ozark. Gen. James Berney Stanley of *The Greenville Advocate* was named coach.

The All-Alabama Eleven were selected by the following scoreboard:

Front page	10
Editorial page	10
Local news coverage	20
General reader interest	20
Advertising typography	20
Makeup and presswork	20
	100 points

Chilton News, Florence Herald awarded cups

The Chilton County News in Clanton and *The Florence Herald* were awarded the Victor H. Hanson loving cups in 1930 as the best weekly newspapers in the state. Billy Smith, editor of *The Chilton County News,* was presented his loving cup at the south Alabama midwinter session at the Greystone Hotel in Montgomery Jan. 11, 1930.

In making the presentation, the selection committee noted that through his editorials Smith had "exploited the securing of a rural school supervisor; a county welfare worker; county agent for Chilton County; that he had sponsored and contributed materially to the success of Clanton's Community Chest drive; that through his efforts a buy-at-home campaign was put over and *The Chilton County News* had taken an active part in a Farm Bureau drive."

Marcy B. Darnall Sr., publisher of *The Florence Herald,* was presented his loving cup at the northern division midwinter meeting on Jan. 25. In making the award, the selection committee "took into consideration such factors as total news content, the excellence with which it is written, its editorial page, its advertising volume and its typographical appearance."

1931
Jack M. Pratt, *The Pickens County Herald,* Carrollton
1931-1932 president

60th annual press convention, Auburn
Aug. 13-14, 1931

The 60th annual press convention was held Aug. 13-14, 1931, on the Alabama Polytechnic Institute campus in conjunction with the third annual Press Institute. The theme of the 1931 Press Institute was the same as that of 1929 — going deeper into the matter of reducing expenses, and at the same time actually doing what the 1930 slogan suggested, "Making a Better Newspaper." New developments in printing were discussed, and editors and publishers were given advice as to the best use of machinery.

The following were announced as winners of the "All-Alabama Weekly Newspaper Eleven" in 1931:

Right End, *The Atmore Advance;* Right Guard, *The Greenville Advocate;* Right Tackle, *The Sylacauga News;* Center, *The Southern Star* in Ozark; Left Tackle, *The Alexander City Outlook;* Left Guard, *The Clanton News;* Left End, *The Brewton Standard;* Quarterback, *The Dothan Herald;* Right Halfback, *The Andalusia News;* Left Halfback, *The Florence Herald;* Fullback, *The Roanoke Leader;* and Trainer, *The Dothan Wiregrass Journal.*

The Press Institute was not held after 1931 until it was revived by APA in cooperation with the University of Alabama Department of Journalism in 1941.

The Greenville Advocate awarded Hanson loving cup

The Greenville Advocate was awarded the Victor H. Hanson loving cup in 1931 as "the best all-around weekly newspaper in Alabama." *The Advocate* was published by Gen. James Berney Stanley and his sons, Webb and Glenn. Apparently only one loving cup was awarded beginning in 1931.

The loving cup was presented at a barbecue-banquet in Auburn on Aug. 14 at the close of the 60th annual convention. Presentation of the cup was made by Howard C. Smith, chairman of the committee of judges. Gen. Stanley, who died three years later, said being chosen best weekly newspaper in Alabama was "the greatest honor *The Greenville Advocate* has ever received." Stanley paid a high tribute to his sons Glenn and Webb, declaring that they were responsible for such an honor, and he asked that Glenn Stanley come to the platform to accept the loving cup. Webb Stanley was not present at the ceremony.

Glenn Stanley immediately handed the cup back to his father saying, "I present it to the man to whom it belongs." After the statement, with its dramatic touch of genuine love of son for father, there was prolonged applause. "It was the most impressive moment in connection with the two days that Alabama editors were in Auburn," wrote P.O. Davis, director of publicity at Alabama Polytechnic Institute. "A distinguished father passing an honor to a distinguished son, and the son returning it to his father."

In 1996, the loving cup was in the possession of Gen. Stanley's granddaughter, Nonnie Stanley Hardin of Greenville, daughter of the late Glenn Stanley who died in 1967.

The midwinter meeting for the northern division of the state was in Birmingham on Jan. 10, 1931, and the midwinter meeting for the southern division was in Montgomery on Jan. 14, 1931.

1932

Forney G. Stephens, *The Southern Democrat,* Oneonta 1932-1933 president

61st annual press convention, Montgomery
July 21-22, 1932

"Back to the times which were old, and maybe good," was the theme of the 61st annual APA convention July 21-22, 1932, in Montgomery. "Your committee has selected the Jefferson Davis Hotel for headquarters," *The Ala-Pressa* reported in its July issue. "The hotel has agreed to give 'hard-time' rates and has asked the privilege of making no charge for rooms for your ladies."

Forney G. Stephens
The Southern Democrat, Oneonta

"There is really no reason why the two days and one night in Montgomery should cost over $5.00 unless you are especially prosperous and inclined to be extravagant," Chamber of Commerce secretary Jesse B. Hearin wrote in *The Ala-Pressa.*

Pratt encourages "largest attendance in history" in 1932

Outgoing APA president Jack M. Pratt of *The Pickens County Herald* in Carrollton wrote in *The Ala-Pressa* that he "would like to see the largest attendance at this meeting it its history. There is no reason why it should not be just such a meeting.

Not many of you are so busy you can't spare the time to go, and I am sure the wife or the daughter would like to take an outing with the old man of the office, and see him having a good time, renewing old acquaintances and making new ones.

"You need a few days outing, and the wife does, too," Pratt continued. "So just pack up your little bag, put the lady in your old tin lizzy, or better still, secure a trade mileage book on an advertising contract with your railroad, and meet us down in the capital city July 21st."

The Covington News awarded Hanson loving cup

The Covington News in Andalusia was awarded the Victor H. Hanson loving cup as best weekly newspaper at the 1932 convention. William Henry Jones was editor and his daughter, Eloise Jones, was society editor. Awarding of loving cups apparently was discontinued after 1932.

The midwinter meeting for the northern division was in Birmingham on Jan. 16, and the midwinter meeting for the southern division was in Montgomery on Jan. 30.

The Ala-Pressa reported that there were 21 daily newspapers in Alabama in 1932, one semi-weekly *(The Andalusia Star,* published by Oscar M. Dugger), and 133 weeklies.

1933
Jesse B. Adams, *The Southern Star,* Ozark
1933-1934 president

62nd annual press convention, Tuscaloosa
July 21-22, 1933

Not wishing to have an expensive excursion for the 62nd annual convention in 1933, APA chose to meet at the University of Alabama on July 21-22. Diversions were supplied by a tour of Gulf States Paper mill and boating on the Warrior River.

J. Fisher Rothermel of *The Birmingham News* spoke on "Teaching Journalism in Colleges," pointing out that the purpose of such courses was to train readers as well as writers. Rothermel said that students, not the newspapers, were demanding journalism courses.

A resolution was adopted pledging APA "to work with renewed zeal for the advancement of our schools and our citizens, through our newspapers, realizing that education must be sold to the public," according to articles in the July 22 and July 23 issues of *The Birmingham News.*

Business problems of newspapers growing out of the Depression were the major concern of Alabama editors and publishers at the 1933 midwinter meeting in Montgomery on Jan. 28. Only one midwinter meeting was held in this Depression year. The success of the business revival campaign promoted by APA was discussed, as well as the trade day campaigns.

1934
Jesse B. Adams, *The Southern Star,* Ozark
1934-1935 president

63rd annual press convention, Chicago World's Fair
Aug. 17-20, 1934

Following its old custom of traveling, the 63rd annual APA convention was at the Hotel Sherman in Chicago on Aug. 17-20, 1934, during the World's Fair. The party of 212 made the trip with the "Alabama Press Special" that was run from Birmingham to Chicago over the Illinois Central Railway System.

"While in Chicago, the editors visited the 1934 Century of Progress, toured the city and went on a twilight cruise up the Chicago River and attended many other outstanding events," *The Ala-Pressa* reported. APA members also participated in "Alabama Day" at the World's Fair.

First field manager hired in 1934 through NRA

APA did not have a field manager until 1934 — 62 years after its founding. The Press Association's activities for more than 60 years had been planned and carried out by elected officers, appointed committees and volunteer workers.

For some time before 1930, some members of
the Press Association had expressed a desire for
employment of a full-time field manager. But because of the limited funds on which APA had to
operate, there was little serious discussion of such
a project. Most editors realized the benefits that
would result from such an arrangement, but the
Press Association could not advocate increasing
dues to hire a manager and finance a central office.
In 1939, annual dues were $12 for both weekly and
daily newspapers.

First field manager made possible by federal govt.

In 1934 the dream of a field manager for the
Alabama Press Association was realized. It was
made possible by the federal government when the
Graphic Arts Code for Alabama was put into effect. The government, through the National Recovery Act, employed an administrator for the
Graphic Arts Code, and it was through this that
the APA was able to use the same individual as its
field manager.

The field manager was W. Roy Brown. The
office temporarily was located in Ozark, hometown
of APA president Jesse B. Adams of *The Southern*

Star, but later was moved to
Montgomery. This arrange-
ment with the NRA and the
Alabama Press Association
came to an end with the close
of the federal program in
1935, and APA again was
without a field manager.

Not much information,
except a 1949 article in *The
Alabama Publisher,* "A Brief
History of the Alabama Press
Association," exists on APA's first field manager
or his contributions to the Press Association. In
fact, the 1951 and 1959 APA histories written by
the late L.O. Brackeen of Alabama Polytechnic Institute do not mention the 1934 field manager.
Brackeen wrote that Doyle L. Buckles was the first
APA field manager.

Jesse B. Adams
The Southern Star, Ozark

Brown apparently only served in the post from
1934 to 1935. A photograph was published in the
Aug. 24, 1934, issue of *The Southern Star* in Ozark
that was captioned "Alabama Editors Hold Annual Meeting in Chicago." According to *The Southern Star,* APA president Jesse B. Adams and field
manager W. Roy Brown "led the visitors from Alabama to the World's Fair in Chicago" for the 63rd
annual convention of the APA.

Brown resigned sometime in 1935

Brown resigned apparently sometime in 1935.
It was reported in the July 1935 issue of *The Ala-
Pressa* that "Secretary Brown was so hampered that
he never had an opportunity of functioning as he
could and should, and he consented when he tendered his resignation in these capacities, not to hold
the Association liable for any past indebtedness to
himself."

The Ala-Pressa continued, "It has been the desire of many of the members of the Association for
many years to have a Field Secretary, and in Roy
Brown we would have had a valuable man had the

Official Organ of the Alabama Press Association

APA visits Chicago in 1934

Following an old custom of traveling, Alabama Press Association members traveled to Chicago for their 63rd annual convention in 1934. APA president Jesse B. Adams of *The Southern Star* in Ozark and field manager W. Roy Brown led the visitors from Alabama. The party of 212 arrived in Chicago on Illinois Central special train and visited the World's Fair. This photograph appeared in the Aug. 24, 1934, issue of *The Southern Star*. (Photograph courtesy of Joseph H. Adams, *The Southern Star*)

code authority done as they proposed so far as money to operate on was concerned. The papers naturally did not feel that it was their place to pay both dues to the code through the assessments and also to pay for the service of a secretary."

Franklin P. Glass dies in 1934

Princeton-educated Franklin Potts Glass, who served on the APA Executive Committee from 1893-1895, died in 1934. Glass, harboring ambitions toward gaining a law degree, received an injection of printer's ink as editor of *The Bibb Blade* in his hometown of Six Mile, near Centreville. From his first venture as editor of *The Bibb Blade*, he became editor and publisher of large daily newspapers in Montgomery, Birmingham and St. Louis. His editorial pages bore the stamp of his

Franklin P. Glass
The Montgomery Advertiser

personality; his courage and loyalty to his principles won him a place among the "Seven Super Pens" in America in 1913.

Glass' circle of friends at Princeton included a future president of the United States, Woodrow Wilson. The friendship with Wilson was lifelong. His interest in law declined after a year as editor of *The Bibb Blade*, and he bought *The Selma Times*. For four years he was editor of *The Selma Times* before buying an interest in *The Montgomery Advertiser*. It was while he was with *The Advertiser* that he began to gain wide fame with his frequently quoted editorials.

Glass sold his interest in *The Montgomery Advertiser* in 1915 and took charge of *The Birmingham News*, a paper in which he had been acquiring shares. In 1920, he retired for two years, but the pull of the printed page was too powerful. He moved to St. Louis as editor and half-owner of *The St. Louis Star*.

In 1928, Glass returned to Alabama where he acquired control of his old love, *The Montgomery Advertiser*. He guided it until his death in 1934.

On the death of Sen. Joseph F. Johnson in 1913, Glass was appointed by Gov. Emmett A. O'Neal to fill the unexpired term, but was denied a seat. Glass was the center of controversy because Wisconsin Sen. Robert M. LaFollete contended that Alabama had made no provision for the appointment of a senator to fill an unexpired term after the adoption of the 17th Amendment. LaFollete came from a sick bed to break a tie vote in the Senate which decided against Glass.

Glass never sought office

Although active in Democratic Party politics, Glass never sought elected office except as a delegate to national conventions. He was accredited as delegate from the Virgin Islands in 1932 and was accorded full privileges by the Alabama delegation. He successfully resisted efforts to close the delegation's caucuses to reporters. President Franklin D. Roosevelt appointed him to the Board of Federal Mediation in 1933.

As early as 1918 Glass had been president of the American Newspaper Publishers Association. He was made chairman of a group of American editors that visited Europe in the closing days of World War I.

1935
W. Bruce Shelton, *The Tuscaloosa News*
(Shelton resigned after serving
first two months of 1935 term)

F. Webb Stanley, *The Greenville Advocate*
(Stanley completed Shelton's term as president)
1935-1936 presidents

64th annual press convention, Montgomery
Jan. 25-26, 1935

Delegates to the 64th annual APA convention at the Gay-Teague Hotel in Montgomery Jan. 25-26, 1935, adopted a resolution expressing sorrow at the death of Gen. James Berney Stanley of *The Greenville Advocate,* one of the 30 founders of APA who died in 1934. Stanley founded *The Greenville Advocate* and was owner and editor of the newspaper for 70 years, an APA resolution noted.

Stanley was nationally known. In 1924, *The New York Times* designated him the "dean of American newspaper editors." After Stanley's death, his son Glenn Stanley became editor, and his son Webb Stanley was business manager. The APA resolution commended the "example of his career to the coming generation of newspaper man

for his ability to uphold the finest traditions of American journalism in that he never grew old in spirit, but maintained through the noble impulse of progress and versatility," *The Montgomery Advertiser* reported in its Jan. 27 edition.

Organization of National Recovery Act codes for Alabama dominated the 64th annual convention in Montgomery on Jan. 25-16, 1935. Much discussion was centered on the organization of an Alabama regional code authority as it would affect weekly and small newspapers. Speakers from various government agencies explained such New Deal legislation as the Farm Credit Administration and the National Recovery Act.

Field manager W. Roy Brown congratulated on work

A speaker at the convention, Clayton Rand of *The Gulfport* in Gulfport, Miss., congratulated APA field manager W. Roy Brown on his "splendid work in building the organization." Rand outlined "what might be achieved for the advancement of Alabama in an association in which weekly and daily newspapers joined forces."

Webb Stanley
The Greenville Advocate
Served two terms as APA president

Bruce Shelton of *The Tuscaloosa News* was inducted APA president at the 1935 convention, but resigned after two months and was succeeded by Webb Stanley of *The Greenville Advocate.* Stanley also had served as APA president in 1926-1927. Issues of *The Ala-Pressa* at the time do not fully explain the reason for Shelton's resignation.

Ala-Pressa doesn't explain reason for resignation

"The failure of the NRA automatically throws into the discard the code and all its authorities, and until some action is taken in this matter, naturally there can be no plan made," Webb Stanley wrote in the July 1935 issue of *The Ala-Pressa.* "Under the spur of the Blue Eagle, the Alabama Press Association had itself delegated as the code authority for Alabama, and on promises from the national code authority of financial support, employed W. Roy Brown to act in the join capacity of secretary of the code authority and field representative of the Association. The promised financial support from the national authority failed to materialize and they owe us a considerable sum which I seriously doubt will ever be paid. The funds of the Alabama Press Association were exhausted and the Association is now in debt for a sum which it is our duty to liquidate as quickly as we can and which the officers believe will be done during this year," Stanley wrote.

"The resignation of president Bruce Shelton; the failure of the program adopted at the January meeting of the Alabama Press Association; the uncertainty of the actions of the code authority governing the weekly papers; and the seemingly antagonistic attitude of the present members of the Legislature were the contributing causes of this being addressed to you by the writer," Stanley continued.

Webb Stanley asked to complete Shelton's term in 1935

"Whether because of my sins, my proximity to Montgomery and the experience I have had in the Association work, the presidency of this organization has been given to me for the remainder of the existing term," Stanley wrote in *The Ala-Pressa*. "I do not feel wise enough nor big enough to again assume this place. The honor has been mine once, and I trust that you will believe that I did not seek it a second time, for I know the responsibilities that it carries."

Stanley continued, "However, when it was urged that because of geographical location and past experience that I could serve in this very crucial time in the affairs of the members of the Association, I did not refuse to take up the burden. My hope is that I can be of service and it is only on this basis that I consented."

Stanley concluded, "This has been necessarily long, but in closing I want to make a personal appeal to every member of the Alabama Press Association. Will you not help me in doing for the Association and its members what a closely-knit body of men devoted to their profession can do? I am willing to give time and effort to the work, because I am deeply interested in the welfare of the craft as a whole and each individual member, but my efforts would be futile unless I have the enthusiastic cooperation of all the members. Please do not hesitate to call on me and every officer whenever we can serve you."

APA urges passage of shield law in 1935

Delegates to the 1935 convention in Montgomery discussed bills pending before the Alabama Legislature. At the concluding session, the APA in a resolution adopted by unanimous vote pledged its support to a bill by Rep. W.P. Calhoun of Houston County that was pending before the Legislature. The bill "would relieve newspaper reporters and employees from the necessity of divulging the sources of information and communications given them in confidence for the purpose of publication," *The Montgomery Advertiser* reported in its Jan. 27 edition.

The Legislature was urged to pass the Calhoun Bill which would prohibit courts or other investigative bodies from compelling reporters to reveal their sources of information. It led to passage of the state's respected shield law that protected reporters from divulging the sources of confidential information.

J.D. Dukes, advertising specialist from Birmingham, spoke on "Advertising Rules and Practices," according to articles in the Jan. 25-26, 1935, issues of *The Birmingham News.*

Uniform system of accounting endorsed

APA also endorsed establishment of a uniform system of accounting in all counties, but went on record as being "unalterably opposed to taking away from the county governments the right to purchase printing or any other supplies from local markets."

APA declared that "certain radio stations have inserted advertising matter and propaganda in programs designed for use in the schoolrooms of the nation and for the education of pupils in their homes after school hours."

A resolution stated, "We must depreciate the use of the radio for this unfair and un-American purpose; and insist that if educational or school-sponsored programs are broadcast, they be free from commercial advertising; and that they furthermore be kept entirely free from any sentiment not definitely and entirely connected with education as carried in the schoolroom, to the end that there may be a complete separation of education from advertising and propaganda of any kind; and that features not definitely taught in the schoolroom be excluded from this type of radio program."

An important measure for the protection of Alabama publishers was reported as follows:

"In view of the facts that promoters of write-ups, special pages and projects of a similar nature involving the use of newspaper space and the endorsement of publishers are active in Alabama; and that it is alleged that some of these promoters are irresponsible or dishonest; and newspapers are held responsible for their acts; it was decided that the Secretary of the Association prepare for issuance to bona fide promoters of this type, identification cards bearing the information that the holder has been investigated, that his record is clear and that he lives up to his promises. A fee of $10 is to be charged for each card which shall be good for a period of one year. All cards will be signed by the Secretary of the Association and countersigned by the President. Publishers and the public generally will be advised to do business only with those who have these cards."

1935 "midsummer meeting" held in Alexander City

Midwinter meetings apparently were discontinued after 1933, but APA held a "midsummer meeting" in Alexander City on July 19-21, 1935. Press members were guests of Col. Benjamin Russell, owner of Camp Dixie and president of the Alexander City Chamber of Commerce. *The Montgomery Advertiser* reported in its July 21 edition that the editors and publishers spent the weekend at Camp Dixie on Lake Martin, 15 miles from Alexander City.

APA president Webb Stanley of *The Greenville Advocate* wrote of the midsummer meeting in the July 1935 issue of *The Ala-Pressa:* "An adequate supply of gas to carry you to and from your home to Camp Dixie and a $10 bill in your pocket will enable you to attend the annual outing of the Alabama Press Association this year. You will not need new clothes because this meeting is going to be an 'Old Clothes Meeting'."

Stanley: Camp Dixie is "fisherman's paradise"

Stanley continued, "The location of the camp is the prettiest imaginable body of fresh water, with plenty of boats and guides and a fisherman's paradise. The rate for a room with meals per day is only $2.00; and for $5.00 and transportation it will be possible to spend 3 days there. The program planned is simply one of rest and relaxation. No need to bring the best clothes or stay dressed up to meet strangers, listen to speeches and addresses, for unless some member feels impelled to get a load of hot hair off his chest — and this at mealtime — there will be none of the wind-jamming we have in times past had. There will be no long, tiresome talks or Code matters to worry about.

"There will, however, be plenty of fishing, swimming, eating, sleeping, dominoes, checkers, horseshoe pitching, or what have you to entertain you, your wife and your children," Stanley continued. "Come one! Come all! Let's make this an old fashioned reunion of the Alabama Press Association. This offers the opportunity of getting to know each other better — and to many of us, the biggest joy of any Association meeting is the privilege of association with our friends, the members of the craft."

1936
Robert Gaston Bozeman Sr., *The Evergreen Courant* 1936-1937 president

65th annual convention, Havana, Cuba
June 14-22, 1936

Squalls and high seas were encountered by some 400 Alabama newspaper representatives, their families and friends as they traveled to Havana from Tampa, Fla., in the summer of 1936 for the 65th annual press convention June 14-22. It was APA's third trip to Cuba. The conventioneers traveled aboard the Peninsula and Occidental Steamship Company's liner "Florida."

Robert Gaston Boseman Sr.
The Evergreen Courant
Fourth APA president inducted
on high seas

"I perhaps enjoy the distinction of the only president of the Alabama Press Association who was elected to the office on the high seas," Robert Gaston Bozeman Sr., publisher of *The Evergreen Courant,* recalled in a 1949 letter to L.O. Brackeen of Auburn, author of the 1951 and 1959 "History of the Alabama Press Associa-

1936 marked fourth trip to Cuba

Squalls and high seas were encountered by the some 400 Alabama newspaper representatives who traveled to Cuba for the 65th annual APA convention in 1936. It marked the Alabama Press Association's third trip to Cuba. While en route, Gaston Bozeman of *The Evergreen Courant* became the fourth APA president to be inducted to the office while on the high seas. (Photograph from scrapbook compiled by the late Catherine Brooks, *The Brewton Standard*)

tion." Bozeman wrote, "I was elected in a meeting of the Association held on the boat returning us from a vacation trip to Havana, Cuba. There were more than 100 on this trip which was a most enjoyable one."

Gen. Stanley inducted on river steamer

(Actually, three earlier APA presidents, Robert B. Vail of *The Baldwin Times,* E. Cody Hall Sr. of *The Alexander City Outlook* and W. Emmett Brooks of *The Brewton Standard,* were inducted into office while on ocean liner. And years earlier, an APA president was inducted into office while traveling on a riverboat steamer. The 1898 press convention featured a trip on river steamer from Montgomery to Prattville and during the trip, Gen. James Berney Stanley, editor and publisher of *The Greenville Advocate,* was inducted president and began his first of four consecutive terms.)

Arriving at the Cuban capital on Monday, June 15, 1936, the conventioneers were given a four-day round of welcomes, dinners, dances, cocktail parties, sightseeing tours, sports events, shopping trips and receptions. "It would be a breach of etiquette for a gentleman to go to one of the receptions given us by the President, Mayor or anyone else, without his coat or to be less punctilious than his hosts," convention secretary E. Cody Hall Sr. of *The Alexander City Outlook* wrote in *The Ala-Pressa.*

Itinerary of 1936 trip to Cuba

Here is the itinerary of the 1936 convention in Cuba, according to *The Ala-Pressa:*

"Monday: Welcome at the dock by representatives of the Cuban Tourist Commission and Reporters Association of Havana; cocktail party; dinner and dance on the roof of the Hotel Plaza.

"Tuesday: Visit to Santiago de las Vegas, under auspices of Cuban Department of Agriculture; luncheon at the Hotel Plaza roof garden; visits to newspaper offices in Havana; reception by the mayor of Havana in the City Hall Palace; dinner at the Hotel Plaza roof garden; night tour, including a jai-alai game.

"Wednesday: Reception by the president of the Republic of Cuba in the Presidential Palace; luncheon at the Hotel Plaza roof garden; combined city and country tour; reception at the Reporters Association of Havana, with cocktails, music and Cuban dances; dinner on the roof of the Hotel Plaza.

"Thursday: Reception by the president of the Cuban Senate at the National Capitol; reception by the Cuban House of Representatives at the National Capitol; afternoon shopping tour; banquet by the Hotel Association of Cuba under auspices of the Cuban Tourist Commission."

APA held a winter meeting in Montgomery on Jan. 10-11, 1936. A Public Relations Committee for the Press Association was named that was to compile a weekly newsletter.

A law prohibiting city, county or state officials from letting a printing contract to an out-of-state firm was suggested, according to *The Birmingham News* in its Jan. 12 edition.

It was also at the 1936 winter meeting that APA became involved in promoting a drive to form the Alabama State Chamber of Commerce, a predecessor organization to the Business Council of Alabama.

APA promoted formation of Chamber of Commerce

"The Alabama Press Association played a very important part in the organization and early history of the Alabama State Chamber of Commerce," John Ward, executive vice president, wrote in a letter dated June 21, 1951:

"The idea of a State Chamber of Commerce and the need for such an organization had been in the minds of several of the business and industrial leaders of the state for some time, but this idea was first advanced publicly and in concrete form by the Alabama Press Association," Ward wrote. "The idea of a State Chamber of Commerce was officially presented at the 1936 meeting of the Press Association by Webb Stanley setting forth the need for such an organization, calling for action, and pledging the support of the Press Association."

APA industrial committee appointed

APA had appointed an industrial committee to promote formation of a Chamber of Commerce that was comprised of Clifford L. (Cliff) Walton,

The LaFayette Sun, chairman; E. Cody Hall Sr., *The Alexander City Outlook;* George A. Carleton, *The Clarke County Democrat,* Grove Hill; Mrs. C.W. Thomas, *The Citronelle Call;* W. Emmett Brooks, *The Brewton Standard;* Hunter H. Golson, *The Wetumpka Weekly Herald;* Forney G. Stephens, *The Southern Democrat,* Oneonta; R.C. Bryan, *The Elba Clipper;* C.G. Thomason, *The Industrial Press,* Ensley; Milton C. Giles, *The Sheffield Standard;* and Webb Stanley, *The Greenville Advocate.* The com-

APA visits Cuba in 1936
　　Alabama Press Association delegates traveled to Cuba in 1936 for their 65th annual convention. Arriving in Havana on June 15, the conventioneers were given a four-day round of welcomes, dinners, dances, cocktail parties, sightseeing tours, sports events, shopping trips and receptions. (Photograph from scrapbook compiled by the late Catherine Brooks, *The Brewton Standard)*

mittee drafted the following resolution that was adopted by the APA:

"That the Alabama Press Association, through its Industrial Committee, invites the formation of a state-wide organization embracing in character the general development of Alabama to cooperate with the editors of Alabama newspapers in their program for the development of the state through the promotion of new and protection of present industries.

"That the Press Association expresses its appreciation to present sound industries for their contributions to the progress and welfare of our people and that the Association pledges itself to the fair and impartial promotion of existing industries and the same fair treatment of those which may locate here.

"That the Alabama Press Association pledges its full cooperation with the organization or body to be formed, having for its purpose the promotion of Alabama and her interests through industry."

Resolution met with enthusiasm

Ward said the resolution "met with enthusiastic response, and the Press Association threw its full support behind the movement; and, in the months which followed, did a great deal to create public sentiment in the state in favor of such an organization."

Several months after passage of the APA resolution, a meeting of some 40 odd business and industrial leaders was called to discuss ways and means of setting up the State Chamber. Webb Stanley of *The Greenville Advocate* and Clifford L. (Cliff) Walton of *The LaFayette Sun* represented APA at the meeting.

Walton, APA president in 1938-1939, did considerable traveling over the state as a representative of the Press Association, interviewing leaders and creating interest in a state chamber. The State Chamber of Commerce was officially organized in the spring of 1937.

1937
Robert Gaston Bozeman Sr., *The Evergreen Courant* 1937-1938 president

66th annual press convention, Montgomery
Jan. 15-16, 1937

"More Industries for Alabama" was the theme of the 66th annual press convention in Montgomery on Jan. 15-16, 1937. Webb Stanley of *The Greenville Advocate*, in a speech titled "The Origin

of the Idea," pointed out that young people were leaving the state because of limited job opportunities. Stanley advocated the decentralization of labor in Alabama by establishment of small industries in agricultural areas.

Clifford L. (Cliff) Walton of *The LaFayette Sun* spoke on "Alabama's Opportunity to Secure More Industries." Grover C. Hall Sr. of *The Montgomery Advertiser* continued Walton's theme with "How Can It Be Done?" Hall advocated either revival of the State Industrial Board or a State Chamber of Commerce.

As their part in recruiting industry to Alabama, *The Ala-Pressa* reported that the editors and publishers endorsed: "(1) presentation of the resources of Alabama to the outside world; (2) encouragement of the location of new industries of all kinds; (3) adoption of legislation favorable to the location of new industries; and (4) elimination of any unfair or discriminatory taxes which might handicap Alabama in its bid for new industry."

Emmett Brooks stresses audited circulation of weeklies

"Circulation Audit for Alabama Weeklies" was the topic of a speech by W. Emmett Brooks, editor and publisher of *The Brewton Standard*. Brooks stressed that audited circulation would bring about stabilization and uniformity in advertising rates. Brooks pointed out that dailies throughout the country had audits, and that advertising agencies selected newspapers by using lists from audit agencies, according to accounts in the Jan. 16 issue of *The Birmingham News* and in the Jan. 15 and 16 issues of *The Alabama Journal* in Montgomery.

S I D E L I G H T S
MARKING 125 YEARS OF HISTORY

"First class mystery" solved in Tuscaloosa
The Alabama Publisher reported in 1954 that *Tuscaloosa News* reporter Grover Smith gave the traffic department of the city "a first-class mystery the other day by picking up by mistake the keys to the cash drawer and records of the department. Discovering the keys were missing, the department had all locks changed, then thought of Smith, who, red-faced, returned the keys he had accidentally picked up, thinking them his own."

S I D E L I G H T S
MARKING 125 YEARS OF HISTORY

The Alabama Publisher *gives the origin of "30" at end of a news article*

What is the origin of the newspaper term "30" at the end of a news article? *The Alabama Publisher* gave 10 versions from varied sources in 1958:

At one place the deadline for copy was 2:30 in the morning. Time was precious to a newspaper man and 2:30 took time to say. To shorten it by a few seconds the term "30" was used and still is.

In the days before typewriters XXX (Roman for 30) on manuscript copy indicated the end of a story.

"Thirty" was used to label the last dispatch when the Associated Press was established.

Early telegraph operators developed a code in which various numbers stood for different phrases. "Thirty" meant "end of item."

The end of the "Thirty tyrants" appointed by the Spartans at the close of the Peloponnesian War to rule Athens, finally overthrown by the Athenians, was the occasion for a general rejoicing. When copywriters finish the end of a story, they supposedly rejoice similarly.

Before newspapers had direct telegraph wires the operator would write at the bottom of the last sheet "3 o'clock," which was shortened to "3 o'c" then to "30."

"Thirty" was the number of a telegraph operator who remained at his post sending messages during a major disaster. He died at his post.

Thirty pica ems was the maximum length lines used in early typesetting machines. Thus "30" was the end of a line.

"Eighty" means farewell in Bengali. An English officer used the figures at the end of a letter to the East India Company in 1785. Adopting the figures for brevity in dealings, mistakenly made them "30."

The first message sent to the central press office during the Civil War totaled 30 words. The thirty together with the words "good night," and the signature of the sender were placed at the bottom of the sheet by the telegrapher.

Journalism students at the University of Alabama selected *The Brewton Standard* in 1937 as "having the best editorial page of the 150 weekly papers they have examined during the current semester," according to a report in the May 1937 issue of the *University of Alabama Alumni News*. The paper was edited and published by W. Emmett Brooks, a graduate of the University's class of 1917.

Journalism professor Randolph (Randy) Fort said each of the students was required to obtain and analyze six weekly papers from about 40 states as part of class work. "A committee from the class inspected all the publications received and decided that in the matter of editorials *The Standard* was superior to all the others," Fort said.

Olin H. Stevenson dies in 1937

Olin Hampton Stevenson, editor and publisher of *The Roanoke Leader,* died in 1937.

Combining determination, a college education and a year's printing experience, Stevenson bought a small newspaper outfit in 1892 and made it into *The Roanoke Leader.*

Born into the parsonage home of his parents, the Rev. and Mrs. John Baxter Stevenson, in Cherokee on Jan. 10, 1871, young Stevenson lived with his parents in places designated by pastoral appointments. In 1887 the family moved to

Olin H. Stevenson
The Randolph Leader, Roanoke

Roanoke, and it remained his family home. Graduating from the old Southern University at Greensboro in 1891, Stevenson decided upon a newspaper career early in his life. That brought about a move to LaFayette where the late S.M. Richards employed him on *The LaFayette Sun* without pay for one month. In that time, he impressed his employer to the extent that he was offered a wage of $10 a month and room and board. That arrangement continued for a year, after which his further services were sought with an increase in pay.

Stevenson sought his own shop

Independence and his own shop were more appealing to Stevenson At age 22 he bought the essential equipment and moved it to Roanoke to start *The Randolph Leader*, even though *The Roanoke Herald* was being published in Roanoke at the time. "We don't know if *The Herald* folded or was bought by *The Leader;* whatever, it didn't last long," Olin H. Stevenson's son, 81-year-old John Bluford Stevenson wrote in a 1996 letter.

For the next 45 years Olin Stevenson was editor and publisher of *The Roanoke Leader* which at first was known at *The Randolph Leader.* The paper was jointly owned for the first 25 years by Olin Stevenson and his brother Leon M. Stevenson who later entered the teaching profession. During those early years, the town was small, times were difficult, and legal advertising and county printing were unobtainable because of the political situation. Populists held the county political offices. As a consequence, official county printing jobs were awarded to a Populist newspaper in another town.

Olin Stevenson married Elsie Sharp in 1908 and two children, John Bluford Stevenson and Mary Munn Stevenson, were born to them. John Bluford Stevenson succeeded his father as editor and publisher, and in 1996 at age 81, he was chief proofreader of *The Leader.*

A prolific editorial writer, Olin Stevenson ran two editorial pages each week until the pressure of advancing years ruled otherwise. *The Montgomery Advertiser* said of his editorial prowess, "Mr. Stevenson was motivated by intense moral idealism and was consistently evangelical in his editorial writing. He was true to his principles and expounded them with a charm that appealed as much to those who disagreed with him as to his followers."

Said *The Birmingham News,* "One might find in Mr. Stevenson's life an example of the truism that he who lives consistently and sincerely will always be esteemed by his fellow men. Mr. Stevenson held pronounced views on a number of questions. Often he differed with this paper. *The News* always knew that *The Leader* was sincerely following its own light. There is no higher course."

Stevenson's grandson editor in 1996

Stevenson's grandson, John Wyatt Stevenson, was editor and publisher of *The Randolph Leader* in 1996 and first vice president of APA. John W. Stevenson said of his grandfather, "As an editor, Olin Stevenson was determined to produce numerous editorials for every issue, and much of his time went into this endeavor to fill page 2 with such material — from long editorials to squibs."

John W. Stevenson continued, "Although his brothers used tobacco, almost every issue had articles or fillers keeping readers aware of the dangers of nicotine. Alcohol and immorality were other targets. On the positive side, churches, schools and community organizations had his constant support. *The Leader's* founding editor did not hesitate to take sides in political issues and in endorsing or opposing candidates."

1938
**Clifford L. (Cliff) Walton, *The LaFayette Sun*
1938-1939 president**

67th annual press convention, Birmingham
Jan. 13-14, 1938

Establishment of a circulation audit bureau for Alabama weeklies was discussed again at the 67th annual press convention at the Tutwiler Hotel in Birmingham, Jan. 13-14, 1938.

APA members also discussed a proposal to standardize advertising rates based on circulation. A tentative agreement was reached "on efforts toward standardizing advertising rates in the state," *The Ala-Pressa* reported. A plan was adopted for a voluntary assessment of $1 per member to defray costs of administering a plan of circulation audits.

"Members of the Alabama Press Association Friday night made merry at a gridiron dinner at the Tutwiler Hotel," *The Birmingham Age-Herald* reported in its Jan. 15 edition. "Karl Landgrebe, Tennessee Coal, Iron and Railroad Company vice president, was toastmaster at the fun session."

Delegates tour Tennessee Coal

Convention delegates toured Tennessee Coal, Iron and Railroad's properties in the west Birmingham district, *The Age-Herald* reported. "The tour was made aboard a special train provided by the railroad company, which left downtown Birmingham and carried the visitors to all plants of the company in that section. The tour ended with a luncheon at the Fairfield plant."

Hiring of a full-time APA executive secretary and field manager was discussed at the 1938 convention. "The initiative for a cooperative arrangement between APA and the University of Alabama came from the Press Association," Dr. Robert Earl Tidwell, dean of the Extension Division of the University, wrote in "The Extension Division of the University of Alabama, A History," published in 1944.

API made bid to locate APA on Auburn campus in 1938

Alabama Polytechnic Institute made a bid at the 1938 winter convention to get the Press Association headquarters established at Auburn rather than Tuscaloosa. However, a majority in the Press Association voted in favor of the University of Alabama as location for the new venture, Tidwell wrote in his 1944 Extension Division history.

The preamble of the joint contract between the University of Alabama and APA outlined both the purposes of the cooperative venture and duties of the field manager as follows:

"Whereas, a fundamental responsibility of a state-supported university is to work with its citizens, either as individuals or as organized groups, in promoting the search for and wider dissemination of truth. To the end that the greatest possible good, social, economic, and otherwise, may be achieved by the people of the state, and to meet the responsibility for contributing as fully as possible to the achievement of this end,

"The University from time to time has cooperated with various groups whose general objectives fall within the area of the University's responsibility; and,

"Whereas the University has a vital interest in and responsibility for the character of the work of the press of the state and more adequate fulfillment by the press of its great service to the people; and,

"Whereas, in order to assist in meeting the needs of the press the University has for many years maintained a Department of Journalism for the better preparation of those young men and young women interested in building a life career in newspaper work; and,

"Whereas, cooperating with the Alabama Press Association offers an unusual field particularly to the Department of Journalism of the University of Alabama for the practical education of students in newspaper mechanics and management, and affords an opportunity to enlarge the field of service for the University by aiding the Alabama Press Association to obtain for itself the employment of a person who shall devote a part of his time to the service of the University and thus aid the newspapers of the state more successfully to serve in their field of endeavor, and at the same time perform regular duties at the University of Alabama as a member of the faculty of the Department of Journalism or in connection with other activities at the institution, which plan of cooperation is now being successfully maintained by several (14) larger universities and press associations in the United States."

Accomplishments such as establishment of the State Chamber of Commerce in 1937 foreshadowed the full-scale revival of the Alabama Press Association as an important force which began with the appointment of Wisconsin weekly newspaper editor Doyle L. Buckles as field manager in 1939 and the cooperative arrangement with the University of Alabama to locate APA headquarters on the University campus.

CHAPTER 5

APA Goes Full Time

1939-1950

"Now this freedom of the press about which we talk so much is no privilege conferred upon the owners and publishers of newspapers, to enable them to operate without governmental interference, while all other businesses are subjected to every form of governmental interference that any political body can devise. It is not a device to protect the profits and immunities of newspaper owners.

"It is a sacred right of the American people, and newspapers and newspaper men are simply custodians of the ark of the covenant, entrusted with the preservation of the most vital of freedoms on behalf of all the people."

James E. Chappell
The Birmingham News

— *James E. Chappell (1885-1960)*
Editor, president, general manager
The Birmingham News
(From a speech in 1939 to the Associated Industries of Alabama)

A PROPOSAL TO HIRE A FULL-TIME FIELD manager dominated the business of the 68th annual convention in Montgomery in 1939. Certainly something was needed to revitalize the Alabama Press Association.

APA had become an organization of a handful of weekly newspapers. At the time that a manager was appointed in 1939, APA had only 19 paid members — 12 newspaper members and seven associate members.

The 12 newspapers were *The Collinsville New Era, The Scottsboro Sentinel and Progressive Age; The Wetumpka Herald, The Clarke County Democrat* in Grove Hill, *The Baldwin Times* in Bay Minette, *The Clanton Union Banner, The Sheffield Standard and Tuscumbia Times, The Roanoke Leader, The Cherokee County Herald, The Southern Star* in Ozark, *The Elba Clipper* and *The Greenville Advocate.*

The seven associate members were Alabama Power Company, Alabama Polytechnic Institute at Auburn, the Birmingham Chamber of Commerce, Southern Bell Telephone Co., American Founders Sales Corp., Mergenthaler Linotype Co., and Sparrow Advertising Agency.

Contract with University enhanced APA's stature

A contract in 1939 between the Alabama Press Association and the University of Alabama enhanced the stature of the Press Association and equally benefited the state's largest educational institution. Both sought the same goals: The betterment of life for the people of the state through a search for and a dissemination of truth.

The hiring of a field manager and establishing permanent headquarters for the APA in 1939 gave the Press Association prestige and stability. The preamble of the 1939 contract between the University of Alabama and APA noted that the University had a "vital interest in and responsibility for the character of the work of the press of the state" and that joint contracts were "being successfully maintained by several (14) larger universities and press associations in the United States."

APA moved from the University campus in 1973 after some newspapers began questioning the

Press Association's ties to an arm of state government, but for years the relationship between the University and APA was a good one.

Neil Davis served on 1939 committee

"I thought it was a good idea at the time," 1947-1948 APA president Neil O. Davis, founder of *The Lee County Bulletin* in Auburn, said in a 1995 interview. Davis served on the committee in 1939 that recommended the hiring of a field manager and the contract with the University of Alabama to establish APA headquarters on the Tuscaloosa campus.

"The agreement with the University of Alabama was widely popular and generally accepted because the Press Association didn't have any money (dues for both dailies and weeklies were $12 per year), and the University was going to pick up most of the cost," Davis, 81, recalled. "I think it was very smart of the University to establish a relationship with the press of the state. I thought it was a good deal for the APA and certainly couldn't hurt the University of Alabama."

Daily newspapers return to APA in 1940s

While APA's focus remained on weekly newspapers, field manager Doyle L. Buckles, a weekly newspaper editor from Medford, Wis., was successful during the 1940s in persuading most of the state's dailies to review their memberships. Buckles came to Alabama with a community newspaper background. He was hired to help the state's weekly papers, but it was under Buckles' guidance that APA began shedding its weekly image in the late 1940s to become a press association that represented all newspapers in Alabama, from weeklies to the largest dailies.

"While I believe your work is primarily with the weekly papers of the state, I have found that your bulletins offer suggestions that can be used by dailies as well," publisher Harry M. Ayers wrote in a note attached to his $12 annual dues check in 1940 when *The Anniston Star* rejoined the APA during Buckles' first full year as field manager. "Accordingly I am enclosing a check for a year's membership in your association," Ayers wrote. "I might add that, as a past president of the Alabama Press Association, you have my heartiest congratulations on the fine work that you are doing."

Nine years later, Ayers editorialized in the Sept. 23, 1949, issue of *The Anniston Star* that APA was no longer "exclusively composed of weeklies, although the organization would be strengthened if

Field manager Doyle Buckles
     Doyle L. Buckles came to Alabama with years of experience in newspapering in his native Kansas, in Nebraska, Iowa and Wisconsin. Buckles was field manager from the time that APA headquarters were established on the University of Alabama campus in 1939 until his death on Dec. 18, 1947. Buckles was extremely popular with APA members and was credited with a revitalization of the Press Association in the 1940s. (Photo from *The Alexander City Outlook*)

more of the daily editors and publishers would participate in its deliberations." Ayers also commented in 1949 that the "most striking thing about the weekly editor of today is his comparative youthfulness and his apparent air of prosperity. Probably a majority of these young Alabama journalists are college trained, and they are applying to their papers the same enlightened business practices that characterize the better dailies."

Buckles traveled the state in 1940s

As Buckles traveled the state in the 1940s and visited the weekly editors and publishers, he shared the latest ideas that were being developed throughout the country, both in newspaper business practices and editorial presentation. The "confidential bulletins" that Buckles began mailing to member newspapers in September 1939, later titled *"Ala-Pressa,"* were short courses in community journalism.

"Doyle Buckles had the mind of a typical Midwesterner, and I wondered at first, when he got here, how he was going to get along with this bunch of native Alabama editors," Neil Davis of Auburn recalled in 1995. "But after a few weeks, actually a few months, I was convinced he was just what the doctor ordered," Davis said. "Doyle brought some fresh perspectives. He was a combination really, of a hard-headed newsman — a good one — and a good businessman."

Most publishers "wanted somebody to tell them how to make a lot of money," Davis said, "how to sell more advertising and increase circulation. Doyle Buckles did that, but he also kept trying to center the interests of the editors and publishers on a quality news product.

"Buckles brought a fresh perspective, a fresh point of view," Davis added.

1939

Milton C. Giles, *The Sheffield Standard and Times,*
The Franklin County Times, Russellville,
and *The Red Bay News*
1939-1940 president

68th annual press convention, Montgomery
Jan. 6-7, 1939

Maj. Bruce McCoy, manager of the Louisiana Press Association, spoke at the 1939 press convention Jan. 6-7 at the Whitley Hotel in Montgomery, explaining the operation of Louisiana's press association.

McCoy said that some of the advantages of hiring a full-time secretary would be the "ability to establish uniform advertising rates, increase national and state advertising, obtain prepared advertising service, improve business methods, and better APA's prestige in legislative affairs."

"The best weekly newspaper in Alabama is not going to get any volume of national advertising alone," McCoy told the 1939 convention delegates. "Unified efforts and equalized advertising rates are necessary to attract national and state advertisers."

McCoy: Weeklies render state a great service

McCoy recommended that if the Alabama publishers "perfect the full-time organization, you should seek a state appropriation toward its maintenance, basing your request for such funds on the fact that weekly newspapers render the state a great service through publicizing activities of state-supported universities and colleges, the Extension Service, the agriculture department, and similar state agencies."

"Somehow I had met Bruce McCoy, who was executive director of the Louisiana Press Association, which was at Louisiana State University," 1941-1942 APA president James H. (Jimmy) Faulkner Sr., retired publisher of *The Baldwin Times,* recalled in an interview with *Birmingham News* staff writer Bill Plott in 1990. "McCoy got the journalism department at LSU to pay his salary and the Press Association office was located there," Faulkner said.

"I went to Dr. Dick Foster, the president at the University of Alabama, and sold him on the idea of doing the same thing for the Alabama Press Association," Faulkner said. "We hired Doyle Buckles, and he really put the association on the map."

Walton recommends appointment of APA manager

Outgoing APA president Clifford L. (Cliff) Walton of *The LaFayette Sun,* who had visited newspapers throughout the state during his term urging establishment of a full-time press association, recommended appointment of a field manager and permanent headquarters, saying, "I am of the opinion that, while the APA is the best 'unorganized' organization I have ever known, there is

---

S I D E L I G H T S
MARKING 125 YEARS OF HISTORY

How to commit "business suicide"

Reduced advertising was one of the best ways to "commit business suicide," Orville W. Johler, vice president in charge of advertising for 6,000 stores in the Independent Grocers Alliance, told 1,100 representatives attending IGA's 28th international convention in 1954.

"Advertising, effective service and low prices are the lifeblood of our business," Johler said. "To reduce the efficiency of any of these main arteries is one of the best ways that I know of to commit business suicide. For years it has been the standard practice of all business, large and small, to use the economy axe on the advertising budget at the first sign of a business slump. Before this month ends, I would be willing to wager that our business will show an increase of better than 20 percent over the same period last year. Advertising has made all this possible."

much to be accomplished through a more highly perfected group."

Walton continued, "If we are to maintain and magnify our powers as an organization, we must form ourselves into an organization which commands the respect of those agencies and groups which patronize us and which expect organization and methods in keeping with present-day business methods and trends."

Walton, while urging a full-time organization, said it was "necessary to obtain all information possible before completing such an organization," *The Birmingham Age-Herald* reported in its Jan. 7, 1939, edition. "The Alabama Press Association should establish a full-time organization on a practical working basis to promote the interests of its members," Walton said. "There are some newspaper activities which are common to each of us regardless of community or section."

Committee appointed to complete tentative agreement

A committee was appointed to complete a tentative agreement for a full-time organization in a permanent headquarters. Serving on the committee were Milton C. Giles, *The Sheffield Standard and Times;* Jesse B. Adams, *The Southern Star* in Ozark; J.J. Benford, *The Albertville Herald;* Hunter H. Golson, *The Wetumpka Herald;* W. Emmett Brooks, *The Brewton Standard;* C.G. Thomason, *The Industrial Press,* Ensley; Parker W. Campbell, *The Progressive Age,* Scottsboro; James H. (Jimmy) Faulkner Sr., *The Baldwin Times,* Bay Minette; Neil O. Davis; *The Lee County Bulletin,* Auburn; Marcy B. Darnall Sr., *The Florence Herald;* and W.B. Ford, *The Northwest Alabamian,* Fayette, according to accounts in the Jan. 6 and 7 issues of *The Alabama Journal* and the Jan. 5, 6, 7 and 8 issues of *The Birmingham News.*

On Sept. 1, 1939, the Alabama Press Association and the University of Alabama entered into a cooperative program which brought into being the "field manager plan" and employed Buckles as field manager. Under the arrangement, the field manager was to devote half his time as field manager and the other half as director of the University News Bureau and teaching in the Department of Journalism at the University. The APA office was located in the Union Building.

Some APA members had reservations

Some APA members had reservations about the plan. They prepared a statement setting forth their reasons:

"We don't want to appear as picayunish, but there are some aspects of the matter that we do not like. Mr. Buckles is supposed to act as Field Manager of the Association, in which his services will be at the disposal of the weekly press of the state. His duties are said to include the sending of confidential information to the weekly editors, assisting them in improving the editorial content of the papers, and aiding them in improving revenue from advertising, circulation and job printing. All of this is proper in itself. If the University employed Mr. Buckles or if the Press Association hired him, that would be entirely all right; but in the interest of maintaining the complete and absolute freedom of the press of Alabama, we are against Mr. Buckles' dual employment."

The statement continued, "Frankly, there may be nothing at all wrong in this case. But we do not like its tone or color. There is too much possibility for political finagling. Also, there is too much possibility for good in work such as Mr. Buckles, or anyone else in a like capacity, could do for the whole situation to be placed under a cloud. In our opinion, the arrangement should be placed above reproach by Mr. Buckles being employed and paid entirely by the University or the Press Association and not by both."

O'Connell said plan endangered freedom of press

Shortly after the field manager system was launched in 1939, E.T. O'Connell, editor of *The Alabama News Digest* in Birmingham, condemned the plan as endangering the freedom of the press and lending itself to "political skullduggery."

Buckles replied to the charges with a two-page, single-spaced letter which concluded:

"I accepted this job without any strings whatsoever and my orders as Field Manager will come from the members. The dues are only $12.00 a year and we would welcome your membership. And during the year if you should discover a single thing that endangered the freedom of the press or smacked of 'political skullduggery,' I will personally refund the dues you paid. I want and need the support of every publisher in the state if I am to make this Field Manager plan a success — not only their financial support, but their active cooperation and good will."

Although APA membership increased during the latter part of 1939, all was not bright. On Nov. 20, Buckles wrote APA president Milton C. Giles of *The Sheffield Standard:* "It looks like it might be a long process to build up the proper spirit of cooperation among the publishers."

Giles: "I am greatly pleased with work you are doing"

The following day, Nov. 21, Giles wrote Buckles:

"I am greatly pleased with the work you are doing and sooner or later it must win over the weekly newspapers in Alabama. I am quite sure that the situation will work out as we contemplated, but it is going to take some time to sell the idea. Rome was not built in a day even though Nero fiddled while it burned. If we can be lucky enough to get our publishers to attend our Press Association, I feel confident your ability to sell them will do the job, and from then on it will be a new day."

Giles wrote to Dr. Robert Earl Tidwell, University of Alabama Extension Division director, on Nov. 21, saying, "I know that Mr. Buckles is a bit disappointed at not receiving a 100% response from all the publishers in the state; however, we warned him of that when he took the work, as we did you when we discussed the matter; and I am confident that no other press association in the country has a better secretary than the one you chose for our Association."

In his 1958 master's degree thesis, "History of the University of Alabama News Bureau, 1928-1956," Edward Owen (Ed) Brown II wrote, "Criticism by some editors at the outset of the cooperative venture was met in a straightforward manner by Buckles."

Milton C. Giles
The Sheffield Standard

Brown continued, "When it became evident that Buckles would not use his Association position for recruitment or propaganda purposes on behalf of the University as some feared, criticism stopped."

Buckles came to Alabama with years of experience

Buckles came to Alabama with years of experience in newspapering in his native Kansas, in Iowa, Nebraska and, before coming to Alabama, in Medford, Wis. He was fully qualified to guide the newspapers of Alabama into more profitable channels, which he did, and he revitalized the Alabama Press Association.

"I started into the newspaper business at the age of 15 — serving as a printer's devil on my hometown paper in southern Kansas," Buckles wrote in his first "confidential bulletin" to APA members on Sept. 11, 1939. "I've had my finger nails eaten off with the lye water used in those days to wash off the forms. I worked my way through the state university as a printer and makeup man on *The Daily Kansan.* I believe I can still hold my own in the back shop of any country newspaper. I've worked as owner, managing editor and ad manager on newspapers located in mining towns, old lumber towns, panic-stricken agricultural communities, drought-stricken and boll weevil-infested communities. I've worked on bankrupt papers, second papers, hand-set papers and papers that have had the finest of equipment and unlimited financial backing."

Buckles returned to Midwest following war

Buckles attended Kings College and London University during World War I. He was overseas as a member of the 139th Ambulance Company. Buckles returned to the Midwest following the war to launch a long and distinguished career as a newspaper editor and publisher. For nearly 20 years before coming to Alabama, Buckles published weekly newspapers in Kansas, Iowa and Nebraska. In 1931 he was named to Professor John H. Casey's "All-American" team of newspaper editors as its quarterback and editor-in-chief. Casey was a community newspaper specialist from the University of Oklahoma who spoke at the 1930 Press Institute at Alabama Polytechnic Institute.

Buckles inaugurated the "confidential bulletins" which in many ways were a practical short course in community journalism. The "green sheet," a confidential report of legislative activity affecting newspapers, was also initiated by Buckles and was still prepared by the APA executive director in 1996.

Bill Stewart: "Buckles made tremendous impression"

Community journalist Bill Stewart, long-time publisher of *The Monroe Journal* in Monroeville who graduated from the University of Alabama in 1941, wrote in a letter in 1989 that Buckles influenced his decision to enter the weekly newspaper field. "Doyle Buckles made a tremendous impression on me in the weekly newspaper class that he

taught at the University," Stewart wrote.

"He is probably the one man who turned dozens of University (of Alabama) journalism graduates to the weekly newspaper field because he made it sound so interesting," Stewart continued. "He persuaded us that the weekly field offered fully as many opportunities for service and livelihood as did the larger daily newspapers." Stewart, APA president in 1959-1960 and owner of several Alabama community newspapers, died in 1995.

One of the principal objectives of the field manager and the Press Association was to "Sell Alabama to Itself, And to the Rest of the World." Newspapers over the state used material from the bulletins along this line for editorial comment.

The confidential bulletins proved to be useful to the weekly newspapers, as did many other activities of the field manager. Personal and group assistance was given editors and publishers on problems ranging from mechanical to editorial, and the Press Association membership was slowly won over to see the real worth of the new field manager and to share the benefits.

Hiring of field manager discussed as early as 1920

APA minutes reflect that employment of a field manager was discussed as early as 1920, again in 1924, and in 1930 at the second annual Press Institute at Alabama Polytechnic Institute at Auburn. In fact, at the 1930 Press Institute in Auburn, placing the APA headquarters on the campus of Alabama Polytechnic Institute, now Auburn University, was considered.

Journalism professor John H. Casey, community newspaper specialist at the University of Oklahoma, spoke at the 1930 Press Institute and later wrote that "I learned that there was some sentiment for undertaking the employment of a field manager for the organization in cooperation with one of the state's educational institutions, probably Alabama Polytechnic Institute at Auburn." Alabama Polytechnic Institute also made a bid at the 1938 winter convention to get the Press Association headquarters established at Auburn rather than Tuscaloosa. However, a majority in the Press Association voted in favor of the University of Alabama as the location of the new venture.

Buckles begins "confidential bulletin" on Sept. 11, 1939

On Sept. 11, 1939, Buckles started mimeographing a "confidential bulletin" with two slogans in the nameplate: "Always for Alabama, All Ways," and "It's Our Business to Help Your Business." In

---

S I D E L I G H T S
MARKING 125 YEARS OF HISTORY

APA visits Alabama Polytechnic Institute
Neil O. Davis, publisher of *The Lee County Bulletin* in Auburn, coordinated APA's visit to Alabama Polytechnic Institute on Aug. 21, 1954.

AlaPressa urged editors to bring their fishing poles to Auburn. "APA'ers will be taken to the famous experimental fishing lakes and all will get an opportunity to enjoy this fine fishing — if you use artificial bait casting, fly or spinning outfits, bring your own. From experience we can report that you'll find fishing there like none anywhere in Alabama."

January 1940, Buckles' "confidential bulletin" became *"The Ala-Pressa"* with a subtitle of "Official House Organ of the Alabama Press Association." The subtitle was changed to "Confidential Bulletin" in March 1940, and then to *"Ala-Pressa,* Confidential Bulletin of the Alabama Press Association." Some years later, the hyphen in *"Ala-Pressa"* was dropped, and the bulletin became *"AlaPressa."*

AlaPressa continued to be published in 1996 as a monthly newsletter.

Each issue of *The Ala-Pressa* prepared by Buckles was filled with "business-building and newspaper improvement ideas collected through surveys of Alabama newspapers and outstanding publications of the nation and from all of the other press association bulletins and trade publications. Many strictly confidential items are carried with a warning to publishers of the actions of irreputable persons and organizations."

J. Russell Heitman, who succeeded Buckles as field manager in 1948, wrote in 1949 that the first official printed magazine of APA was titled *The Ala-Pressa* and was established in 1920. *The Ala-Pressa* was not being published at the time that Buckles became field manager in 1939.

The first reference to an official publication of the APA was in 1902. APA records show that five issues of a publication called *The Alabama Press Reporter* were published in 1902. The publication contained reports on advertisers who did not pay their bills and warnings against "deadbeat advertisers." (Copies of *The Alabama Press Reporter* have not been located.)

The Ala-Pressa was published from 1920 through 1937

Heitman wrote that *The Ala-Pressa* was published, intermittently at least, from 1920 through 1937. Heitman wrote that no copies of *The Ala-Pressa* were among the official records of the Press Association when he came to work on July 1, 1948. A few copies, issued during 1923, 1929, 1930, 1931, 1932, 1934, 1935, 1936 and 1937 were given to the Press Association by Neil C. Cady of Western Newspaper Union in Birmingham. These copies were placed on permanent loan in the University of Alabama library.

Among the advertisers in early issues of *The Ala-Pressa* were Western Newspaper Union, Whitaker Paper Co., Sparrow Advertising Agency, Alabama Engraving Co., American Type Founders Co., Mergenthaler Linotype Co., Dodson Printers Supply Co. of Atlanta, Hi-Speed Roller Co. of New Orleans, Alabama Power Co., Enterprise

---

S I D E L I G H T S
MARKING 125 YEARS OF HISTORY

Demopolis publishes "Times Jr." Extra

"EXTRA! EXTRA! EXTRA!" was the heading across the May 21, Volume 1, Number 1 issue of *"The Demopolis Times Jr."* published May 21, 1954. A banner headline across the front page read, "It's a Girl – Elizabeth Cornish (Beth) Griffith! Martha (George) and E.P. (Buddy) Griffith Jr., proudly announce the arrival of a daughter, whom they have named Elizabeth Cornish (Beth) Griffith. Born Friday night, May 21, 1954, at 8:25 at Bryan W. Whitfield Memorial Hospital in Demopolis, Alabama, she weighed five pounds, eight ounces."

AlaPressa reported that "the rest of the four-page announcement contained the kind of pictures all proud grandparents like to put out for their grandchildren. Congrats to Ben and Libba George — hope Ben held up under the strain all right and that his advertisers that week didn't kick too much at the nervous errors which occurred or that his favorite news sources could understand why he had the wrong people at the right places at the wrong time."

Engraving Co. of Birmingham, Dixie Type and Supply Co. of Birmingham, Service Engraving Co. of Montgomery, Bond-Sanders Paper Co. of Nashville, Intertype Corp. of Birmingham, Linotype Composing Co., S.P. Richards Paper Co., and Charles Eneu Johnson and Co.

Early issues of *The Ala-Pressa,* published in four-column format on coated book stock, were edited and published by and for members of the Press Association. Except for a short time during the NRA days, there was no full-time secretary-manager during this period. W. Roy Brown, first field manager of the Press Association, was listed as editor and business manager of *The Ala-Pressa* in 1934.

Western Newspaper Union produced The Ala-Pressa

The Ala-Pressa seems to have been produced, most of the time at least, at Western Newspaper Union's Birmingham plant. Neil C. Cady is listed as business manager of the publication in most of the issues. Webb Stanley of *The Greenville*

Advocate was editor of *The Ala-Pressa* in 1929, 1930, 1931 and 1932. He was assisted by P.O. Davis, director of publicity at Alabama Polytechnic Institute in Auburn.

E. Cody Hall Sr. of *The Alexander City Outlook* was editor of *The Ala-Pressa* in 1935 and 1936, and Cullen Morgan of *The Hale County News* at Moundville was editor in 1937. Both Hall and Morgan were assisted by Alabama Polytechnic Institute's P.O. Davis, whose service as associate editor of *The Ala-Pressa* stretched at least from 1923 to 1937, with the apparent exception of about a year during the NRA period.

District meetings held in 1939

To stimulate interest in APA activities, several district meetings were held in late 1939. District meetings were at the University of Alabama and in Sheffield, Gadsden, Alexander City, Troy, Bay Minette and Wetumpka.

Buckles wrote in December 1939 that he had set a goal of 100 paid APA members by Jan. 1, 1940. "It looks as if we are on the 50-yard line with 15 days to go," Buckles wrote in his confidential bulletin. The latest dues-paying members were Mark L. Tucker, *The Chilton County News* in Clanton; Mrs. Luther Fowler, *The Shelby County Reporter* in Columbiana; Joe Jones, *The Covington News* in Andalusia; Isabel Moses, *The Phenix-Girard Journal;* Neil C. Cady, Western Newspaper Union; F.G. Crawford, *The Fairhope Courier;* Charles G. Dobbins, *The Anniston Times;* and Harry M. Ayers, *The Anniston Star.*

1940
Hunter H. Golson, *The Wetumpka Herald*
1940-1941 president

69th annual press convention, Birmingham
Jan. 19-20, 1940
First summer convention, Gulf Shores
July 1940

Despite the worst blizzard in 20 years, 124 delegates attended the 1940 annual press convention at the Molton Hotel Jan. 19-20 in Birmingham. *AlaPressa* reported than an all-Alabama program was staged, and it was "so full of practical business-building and newspaper-improvement ideas" that the members urged that a similar program be held in Montgomery in 1941.

Convention delegates were guests at the Alabama "Big Broadcast of 1940" at the Municipal

Auditorium in Birmingham, with Gov. Frank M. Dixon presenting his state to the nation in "Alabama — A Symphony of the New South." It was a nationwide broadcast over CBS of 110 stations and 13 Alabama stations. A special section was reserved for the Alabama publishers.

During 1940 the Press Association actively cooperated with the State Chamber of Commerce in promotion of Alabama Products Week; Alabama Polytechnic Institute, Auburn, in the promotion of National Better Home Week; the Women's Field Army of the American Cancer Society in its campaign for control of cancer; the State Chamber of Commerce in its safety campaign; and the Works Progress Administration (WPA) in its statewide projects. Many letters of appreciation were received, giving credit to publishers for their cooperation.

Editors take "blitz tour" of the state

While it was impossible for all editors and publishers to make the entire trip, more than 100 made a 1,500-mile "blitz tour" of Alabama during the week of July 21, 1940, to "Sell, Alabama to Itself" and to enhance the prestige of the Alabama Press Association. George Nagle, a staff writer with *The Birmingham News*, accompanied APA members on their tour and filed this report in the July 28, 1940, issue of *The News:*

"With the Alabama Editors on Tour — From the great Tennessee Valley on the north to the beautiful gulf on the south — visiting the state's parks, expanding industry, tourist attractions and the people they write about — the editors of Alabama's weekly newspapers put a journalistic '30' on their 'blitz tour' this weekend. Today, these men and women who compose the great bulk of Alabama's '4th estate' have a new concept of the state in which they live."

Publishers of south Alabama, headed by APA president Hunter H. Golson of *The Wetumpka Herald*, met in Montgomery Monday morning and visited Tuskegee Institute at Tuskegee, Alabama Polytechnic Institute at Auburn, and Russell Mills at Alexander City before joining the north Alabama newspaper executives at Talladega.

Headed by APA field manager Doyle L. Buckles, editors and publishers from north Alabama met in Birmingham and visited Avondale Mills and Alabama Marble Quarries at Sylacauga. Civic groups of Talladega gave a barbecue for the APA members at Shocco Springs Park following a brief visit to the Alabama Institute for the Deaf and Blind.

During the tour the editors visited:

Cheaha Park, Talladega; Fort McClellan, Anniston; Alabama School of Trades, Gadsden, and Goodyear Tire and Rubber Company, Gadsden; DeSoto State Park, Fort Payne; Salt Petre and Blowing Caves, Scottsboro; Monte Sano Park and historic points of Huntsville; Athens College, Athens; Wilson Dam and Muscle Shoals at Florence; Tuscumbia and Sheffield; Alabama Stone Quarries, Rockwood; Black Warrior National Park and Bankhead Farms Alabama, Tuscaloosa; Moundville State Park and Museum, Moundville; Kraft-Phoenix Cheese Corp., Uniontown; Black Belt Substation, Marion Junction; *The Selma Times Journal* and Selma Country Club, Selma; Colonial Inn, Fairhope; and Bellingrath Gardens, Alabama State Docks and Waterman Steamship Co., Mobile.

At the completion of the 1940 tour, the State Chamber of Commerce issued a special tabloid booster edition that was carried by more than 100 Alabama newspapers.

1940: First summer APA convention

Also following the tour, the editors and publishers spent two days of rest and recreation on the "Gulf Shores of Baldwin County, boat riding and deep sea fishing" in what may be considered the first summer convention of the Alabama Press Association.

Every summer since 1940, APA has held a summer outing at some point in Alabama or in a nearby state. Summer outings of 1942, 1943 and 1944 were converted into "war conferences." They were held in Montgomery, July 24-25, 1942; Birmingham, Aug. 13-14, 1943; and Birmingham, Aug. 18-19, 1944. Because of travel restrictions, no summer outing was held in 1945.

APA membership grows in 1940

When Doyle L. Buckles became field manager in 1939, there were 12 professional members and seven associate members of the association. During his first three months on the job, membership increased to 45. At the end of 1940, the APA had a membership of more than 100 who had paid dues that year. Buckles reported in the April 1940 issue of *AlaPressa* that the daily division of APA "now includes all but six of the state's dailies." Buckles wrote that *The Birmingham News* and *Age-Herald* and *The Mobile Press* and *Mobile Register* had recently joined the association.

Buckles reported in the Dec. 16, 1940, issue of *AlaPressa* that 1940 had been a year of enlistment, with APA membership at its highest in history. "But we will not be satisfied until every paper in Alabama is on our rolls." Paid dues for 1940 totaled $934.10. Buckles submitted a financial report showing that total expense for operating the association during 1940 was $2,581.06. "Of this amount the University paid $1,575.86, and the association $1,005.20. These are cold statistics."

S I D E L I G H T S

MARKING 125 YEARS OF HISTORY

Confusion reported at **The Monroe Journal**

In 1954, *The Monroe Journal* reported "confusion in its print shop – from the public, that is," *The Alabama Publisher* reported in its November 1954 issue.

"Seems the print shop and composing room are constantly being mistaken for a repair shop for everything from shoes to radios and television sets. There was the interesting case of a middle-aged gentleman who suddenly loomed in the door of the shop one day — jerked his belt from the loops around the waist of his trousers and waved it in the face of our Linotype operator and demanded that he repair it immediately. Or the one not long ago when the lady sauntered in the office and repeatedly insisted that she be sold a can of snuff. After reassuring her several times that we did not usually keep snuff or any other such vices in stock, and that the Yellow Front Store had moved several months previous, we finally gave up and suggested that she try a little printer's ink as a substitute."

This is *The Birmingham News* in a circa 1940 photograph. (Copyright *The Birmingham News*. All rights reserved. Reprinted by permission)

Buckles was reimbursed at 5 cents per mile for travel, and he was paid a monthly salary of $112.50.

"The field manager has had 100 percent cooperation from the University," Buckles wrote. "A special office was constructed for the convenience of the field manager so that he could handle both sides

of his dual job with a minimum of effort and conflict. Under the present setup the field manager devotes half his time to his duties as field manager and the other half to serving the University as director of the News Bureau and a member of the Department of Journalism, acting as assistant professor."

UA journalism department sponsors contests

In compliance with requests of many Alabama publishers, professor Randolph (Randy) Fort, head of the Department of Journalism at the University of Alabama, announced on Nov. 11, 1940, that 13 contests for Alabama newspapers would be sponsored by the journalism department. The competition was for Best Editorial (open to both daily and weekly newspapers); Best Column; Typography and Layout; Commercial Printing; Special Editions; Best Front Page; News Writing; Women's Page; Agricultural News; Best Display Advertising; Community Service; and General Excellence.

The first winners were announced at the 70th annual convention in 1941.

S I D E L I G H T S
Marking 125 Years of History

Bottle floats 220 miles from Selma

Jack Jones, compositor at *The Selma Times-Journal,* tossed a bottle out of the rear window of the newspaper's composing room, perched high on the banks of the Alabama River, in January 1955. The Associated Press reported that the bottle, which contained Jones' name and address, had been found.

The bottle had floated 220 miles down the Alabama and Mobile rivers from Selma.

SIDELIGHTS
MARKING 125 YEARS OF HISTORY

1940 Press Convention is "full of practical ideas"
The 1940 convention program included the following:

"National Advertising," by Parker W. Campbell, *The Progressive Age,* Scottsboro; John Dukes, Sparrow Advertising Agency; and A.C. Lee,*The Monroe Journal,* Monroeville; "Photography," by Jesse B. Adams,*The Southern Star;* Ozark; Ira Armfield, *The Sylacauga News;* J. Martin Smith, Sparrow Advertising Agency; Roy Hickman, Alabama Engraving Co.; and Neil C. Cady, Western Newspaper Union, Birmingham; "Circulation," by W.M. Massey, *The Jasper Advertiser;* "Premiums" by Charles W. Smith, *The Atmore Advance;* "Value of Personals" by Mae Meyers, *The Collinsville New Era;* "Country Correspondence" by J.W. (Jim) Oakley Sr., *The Centreville Press;* "Special Columns," "Old Curiosity Shop and Rural Ramblings by Veteran" by J.A. Downer, *The DeKalb Times,* Scottsboro; "Flower Garden Column," by J.P. Mitchell, *The Wiregrass Farmer,* Headland; "Commission to Clubs," by Mrs. W.F. McCartney, *The Samson Ledger;* "Company Circulation" by Hunter H. Golson, *The Tallassee Tribune;* "Produce Swaps" by Jay Thornton, *The Haleyville Advertiser;* "Classified Advertising" by James H. (Jimmy) Faulkner Sr., *The Baldwin Times,* Bay Minette; W.W. Gunter, *The* Jasper *Mountain Eagle;* Miss Wilmot Calloway, *The Birmingham Post;* and R.E. Faherty, *The Birmingham News;* "Publishers Problems" by Cody Hall, *The Alexander City Outlook;* "Legislation" by Hunter H. Golson, *The Wetumpka Herald;* "Office Supplies" by Roger W. Pride Sr., *The Butler County News,* Georgiana; "Developing Jobwork" by Mrs. L.S Richardson; "Shopping Guides," by Ira Armfield, *The Sylacauga News;* "Building Up Job Department" by Sam B. Sloane Jr., *The Sumter County Journal,* York; "Country Printing" by R.H. Walker, *The Limestone Democrat,* Athens; "Local Advertising" by Charles G. Dobbins, *The Anniston Times;* "Building Volume" by Vernon Teel, *The Chambers County News,* Lanett; "Church Advertising" by James W. Grant, *The Columbia Record;* "Christmas Ads and Club Women" by J.J. Benford, *The Albertville Herald;*

"Treasure Hunt" by F. Webb Stanley, *The Greenville Advocate;* "Anniversary Editions" by James H. (Jimmy) Faulkner Sr., *The Baldwin Times,* Bay Minette; "Best Soliciting Methods" by Marcy B. Darnall Jr., *The Florence Herald;* "Christmas Mat Service" by T.E. Wyatt, *The Clanton Union Banner;* "Special Editions" by Henry F. Arnold, *The Cullman Tribune;* "Christmas Editions" by J.R. Rosson, *The Cullman Democrat;* "Sponsors for Ads" by John H. Acker, *The Anniston Times;* "Developing Small Accounts" by A.F. Leavitt, *The Etowah Observer,* Alabama City; "Proof that Advertising gets Results" by W.M. Wyatt, *The Montevallo Times;* "Problems of Chain Store Advertising" by J.A. Downer, *The DeKalb Times,* Scottsboro; "Keeping Department Stores from Cutting Lineage" by Mark Tucker, *The Chilton County News,* Clanton; "Are Dollar Days Still Productive?" by R. Gaston Bozeman, *The Evergreen Courant;* "Reader Relationship" by Hunter H. Golson, *The Wetumpka Herald;* "Importance of Farm Page" by P.O. Davis, Extension Service director, Alabama Polytechnic Institute, Auburn; "The Public and the Press" by Professor A.P. Beedon, University of Alabama Department of Journalism; "Community Service" by Marcy B. Darnall, *The Florence Herald;* "Editorial Problems" by Neil O. Davis, *The Lee County Bulletin,* Auburn; "Streamlining the Paper" by Bruce Shelton, *The Tuscaloosa News,* and Jesse B. Adams, *The Southern Star,* Ozark; "Tabloid Papers" by H.M. Wyatt, *The Montevallo Times;* "Departmentalizing Papers" by John B. Stevenson, *The Roanoke Leader;* "Attractive Front Pages" by Mark Tucker, *The Chilton County News,* Clanton; "Front Page Editorials" by J.W. (Jim) Oakley Sr., *The Centreville Press;* "News Among Colored Folks" by D.J. Fail, *The Tuskegee News;* "Pepping up the Paper" by Jay Thornton, *The Haleyville Advertiser;* "Giving a City Personality — the Camellia City" by F. Webb Stanley, *The Greenville Advocate;* and "This Week's Appreciation" by R.K. Coffee, *The Jacksonville News.*

1941
James H. (Jimmy) Faulkner Sr.
The Baldwin Times, Bay Minette
1941-1942 president

70th annual press convention, Montgomery
Jan. 24-25, 1941
Summer convention, Decatur and Huntsville
July 18-20, 1941

On Jan. 24-25, 1941, there was "the greatest mobilization of Alabama newspaper men in the 70 years of Association activity" at the "Training Camp for Defense and Preparedness" in Montgomery as part of the 70th annual press convention.

"The 'generals' in charge of all fronts were ably assisted by their staffs and all of the publishers in attendance played an active part" in making it one of the most practical conventions ever held," *AlaPressa* reported. "It was a program 'of, for and by' Alabama publishers."

Subjects and speakers at the 70th annual convention Jan. 24-25, 1941, in Montgomery included on the morning of the opening day:

"Modernization of Alabama Newspapers" by E. Cody Hall, *The Alexander City Outlook;* "Putting Punch into the Front Pages" by Bill Foreman, *The Baldwin Times;* "More Power on the Editorial Page" by J.A. Downer, *The DeKalb Times;* "More Reader Interest in News Columns" by J. Glenn Stanley, *The Greenville Advocate;* "Strengthening Church News Department" by Jesse B. Adams, *The*

Southern Star; Ozark, "Localizing Farm News" by George A. Carleton, *The Clarke County Democrat,* Grove Hill, and Kirtley Brown, Alabama Polytechnic Institute, Auburn; "Increasing School News Service" by W.W. Gunter, *The* (Jasper) *Mountain Eagle;* "Developing Country Correspondence" by Bonnie D. Hand, *The LaFayette Sun;* "Strengthening Courthouse News Departments" by Jack M. Pratt, *The Pickens County Herald,* Carrollton; and "Greater Use of Pictures" by Sam Sloan, *The Sumter County Journal,* York.

Joe Lovett, past president of the Kentucky Press Association, spoke at the luncheon. The afternoon program included "Building Up Circulation" by C.G. Thomason, *The Industrial Press,* Ensley; "Carrier Boy Methods" by Vernie Teel, *The Chambers County News;* "Personal Solicitation" by J.W. (Jim) Oakley Sr., *The Centreville Press;* "Premiums" by Charles W. Smith, *The Atmore Advance;* "Club Campaigns" by C.G. Thomason, *The Industrial Press,* Ensley; "Self-Conducted Campaigns" by E. Cody Hall, *The Alexander City Outlook;* "Newspaper Advertising" by Charles G. Dobbins, *The Anniston Times;* "Use of Letters" by Mrs. L.S. Richardson, *The* (Jasper) *Mountain Eagle;* and "Bargain Offers" by Brooks O'Bannon, *The Flomaton Journal.*

The next day's program included: "Drive for New and More Advertising" by O.W. Coffee, *The Chattahoochee Valley Times,* Lanett; "Better Uses for Mat Services" by Neil C. Cady, Western Newspaper Union; "Christmas Editions" by J.R. Rossum, *The Cullman Democrat,* and Mae Meyers, *The Collinsville New Era;* "Special Progress Editions" by James H. (Jimmy) Faulkner Sr., *The Baldwin Times,* Bay Minette; "Developing Small Accounts" by Frances Crawford, *The Fairhope Courier;* "Special Promotion Pages" by Milton C. Giles, *The Franklin County Times,* Russellville; "Chain Store Advertising" by Jesse B. Adams, *The Southern Star,* Ozark; "Importance of Extra or Complete Coverage" by Joe Jones, *The Covington News;* "Political and Legal Advertising" by C.A. Serferovich, *The Montgomery Advertiser;* "National Advertising — Selling Yourself and Your Services" by APA field manager Doyle Buckles; "The Future of the Press of America and Especially Alabama" by Mary H. Raiford, *The Selma Times-Journal;* "Organized or Unorganized Campaign of Critics to Discredit the Press" by Harry M. Ayers, *The Anniston Star;* "Threat of Wage-Hour Legislation or Needed Legislation in Alabama" by F. Webb Stanley, *The Greenville Advocate;* "Promotion of Job Work" by Cullen Morgan, *The Hale*

S I D E L I G H T S
MARKING 125 YEARS OF HISTORY

"We haven't stooped to yeller journalism"

"We Haven't Stooped to Yeller Journalism" was the headline in *The Haleyville Advertiser* in 1955.

"The color of this issue of *The Advertiser* has no special implication," the newspaper reported. "In no respect should it be construed as a sly reference to any person in the vicinity — or anyone who may visit here from time to time. Nor is it an indication of our stand on any particular issue. The plain, untarnished truth is that we ran slap dab out of white newsprint and had to use yellow for this one issue. We hope to be back to the regular color next week."

County News, Moundville; "Promotion of National Advertising" by John Dukes, Sparrow Advertising Agency; and "Promotion of National Appreciation Week as Observed in 1940 and Suggestions for 1941" by Milton C. Giles, *The Franklin County Times*, Russellville, and W.C. Wear, *The Opelika Daily News*.

After a tour of Maxwell Field, 150 delegates attended the annual banquet at which Gov. Frank M. Dixon gave his annual report on the progress of the state. The other guest speaker was Dr. Richard Foster, president of the University of Alabama.

"Something fine has happened" to APA

"Something fine has happened to the Alabama Press Association," *The Alabama Journal* commented in its coverage of the 1941 convention on Jan. 29. "The Montgomery convention of the organization Friday and Saturday has been not only one of the most largely attended in the whole history of the body, but the session went off with a business-like precision, and with a seriousness of purpose that would be surprising to some of the editors of older days when Press Association meetings were largely frolics and were largely dominated by people entirely outside the profession. There is an entirely new spirit among weekly newspaper men of Alabama. They are alert, eager and on tip-toes. The Alabama Press is on a new road to influence, self-respect and independence; and it is one of the most gratifying things that could happen in Alabama."

The Alabama Journal continued:

"They are getting out better papers than ever; they are writing editorials that help sway and in-

form public opinion in their communities. They are giving attention to typography, news presentation and the appearance of their papers. They are operating on a more business-like basis by demanding and getting adequate recompense for the service they render.

"No other single factor can be quite so helpful in advancing Alabama's welfare as a bunch of aggressive, independent and ambitious weekly editors. Alabama is happy to have a stream-lined one, hitting rhythmically on no less than eight cylinders."

Better Newspaper Contest begins in 1941

The University of Alabama Department of Journalism began sponsoring 13 contests for Alabama newspapers, and the first winners were announced at the 1941 convention. Known as the "Better Newspaper Contest," it was discontinued in 1947 and was not resumed until 1953. Announcement of Better Newspaper Contest recipients became a tradition at APA summer conventions that continued in 1996 as part of the Saturday night banquet.

The first Better Newspaper Contest winners were announced at the 70th annual convention in Montgomery, Jan. 24-25, 1941. *The Anniston Times* was named the best all-around weekly in Alabama. *The Lee County Bulletin* in Auburn was second, *The Baldwin Times* in Bay Minette third, *The Cullman Tribune* fourth, and *The Franklin County Times* in Russellville, was fifth. Professor Randolph (Randy) Fort of the University of Alabama presented the newspaper contest awards.

Ruling made on mailing of farm section

APA president James H. (Jimmy) Faulkner Sr. of *The Baldwin Times* announced that a new ruling had been made on the mailing of a farm section called "This Month in Rural Alabama." During the past year the Extension Service of Alabama Polytechnic Institute in Auburn had been forced to make a "token" charge to comply with postal regulations. The new ruling from Ramsay S. Black, third assistant postmaster general, recognized the educational value of the publication and absence of advertising and would permit its distribution and insertion in the papers without charge, Faulkner said.

More than 80 publishers and staff members were guests of *The Jasper Advertiser* and *The Mountain Eagle* in Jasper the last Saturday in February 1941.

Huntsville and Decatur were hosts to the summer convention July 18-20, 1941. Only one short business session was held, and the remainder of the time was devoted to "boat rides on the Tennessee River, barbecues and dancing at Monte Sano Park, fishing, golfing, loafing, meeting old friends and attending banquets," according to APA minutes.

Press Institute resumes in 1941, moves to UA

The annual APA Press Institute started at Auburn in 1929 was not held after 1931 until it was revived by APA in cooperation with the University of Alabama Department of Journalism in 1941. Press Institutes were held on the campus of Alabama Polytechnic Institute at Auburn for three years, from 1929 to 1931.

In opening the May 2-3, 1941, Press Institute chairman Col. Harry M. Ayers of *The Anniston Star* said, "The inauguration of this institute is one of the finest things that the University of Alabama and Press Association have ever done. It is a milestone in the history of journalism in the state and is the beginning of closer contact between the publishers of Alabama."

AlaPressa reported that the program was headlined by such speakers as Drew Middleton, "ace Associated Press correspondent" from London; Don R. Davis, past president of the International Association of Circulation Managers; Otis A. Brumby, vice president of the Georgia Press Association; Pat Moulton, sports editor of *The Mobile Press;* T.L. Jackson, legal adviser of *The Mobile Press Register;* Charles G. Dobbins, publisher of *The Anniston Times;* and Harry Arnold, publisher of *The Cullman Tribune.*

Panel on "As Others View the Press"

The panel, "As Others View the Press," featured five press representatives: Thomas J. Twentymen, Loveman's, Birmingham; E.L. Turner, Anniston; Mrs. H.C. Pannell, Tuscaloosa; Dr. William Graham Echols, University of Alabama; and Justice J. Edwin Livingston, state Supreme Court, Montgomery. Talks were made on "Law of Libel," "Quality Circulation," "The Sports End of a Newspaper," "and many other subjects," *AlaPressa* reported.

A scientific demonstration and show, known as "Parade of Progress," by General Motors was on display during the institute.

World War II intervened, and no Press Institutes were held between 1942 and 1947, according to APA records. Many, if not most press associations, were suspended throughout the United States during the war years. The Press Institute was not held again until 1948.

> ### S I D E L I G H T S
> #### MARKING 125 YEARS OF HISTORY
>
> *He's called "Satan" instead of "printer's devil"*
> Alexander City Outlook publisher J.C. Henderson said his veteran employee, James Thornton, had been at the paper 30 years in 1955. "He's been here 30 years and knows his way around," Henderson said. "He is called 'Satan' instead of a 'printer's devil'. It sounds nicer."

Small-town publishers "mobilized"

Small-town publishers of Alabama "mobilized" in Montgomery in late September 1941 to consider plans for an all-out "recruiting crusade" to help build the greatest Navy on earth. The meeting was called by the APA in cooperation with Southern recruiting officers and their national advertising agency, Batten, Barton, Durstine & Osborn Co. of New York.

Lee County Bulletin editor and publisher Neil O. Davis was one of 15 American newspaper men to be awarded a Nieman Foundation fellowship at Harvard University in September 1941. *AlaPressa* reported that three new staff members would be in charge of *The Bulletin* during Davis' one-year absence for the coming year.

"Eugene E. Speight, who will serve as editor-manager, comes from the noted *Cobb County Times,* Marietta, Ga., Miss Naomi Kirbo, new society editor and news editor, comes from *The Lowndes County News,* Valdosta, Ga., and W.W. Corley, formerly of *The Dothan Eagle,* will be advertising solicitor," *AlaPressa* reported.

1942
Charles G. Dobbins, *The Anniston Times*
1942-1943 president

71st annual press convention, Birmingham
Jan. 16-17, 1942
Summer "war conference," Montgomery
July 24-25, 1942

To provide the editors and publishers with an opportunity to strengthen their own morale and secure new and practical ideas on meeting problems that were developing because of unusual war conditions, two well-attended conventions were held in 1942. Both conventions were devoted to business and problems of wartime newspaper production.

The 71st annual press convention was at the Redmont Hotel in Birmingham on Jan. 16-17, 1942. Among the guest speakers were Maj. Bruce McCoy, field manager of the Louisiana Press Association; Professor C.R. Smith, editor of *Folks Magazine* and a member of the Louisiana State University faculty; and Jim Seymour, manager of the Georgia Press Association.

McCoy advised publishers against having a subscription rate lower than $2 a year, or less than $2.50 for subscribers living outside the newspaper's "trade basin," *The Birmingham Age-Herald* reported in its Jan. 17, 1942, edition.

Publishers conduct panels on circulation, job printing

Alabama publishers and editors conducted panels on circulation, job printing, advertising, and modernizing news and editorial departments.

Cullen Morgan of *The Hale County News* in Moundville was panel leader of a program on job printing. Participating on the panel were Sam Slone of *The Sumter County Journal* in York and E.H. (Ed) Pierce of *The Jasper Advertiser.* Jay Thornton of *The Haleyville Advertiser* led a program on circulation and was joined by J.W. (Jim) Oakley Sr. of *The Centreville Press* and George A. Carleton of *The Clarke County Democrat* in Grove Hill. APA president Charles G. Dobbins of *The Anniston Times* led a panel discussion on modernizing news departments.

Zipp Newman, sports editor of *The Birmingham News*, "urged retention of sports during wartime, asserting they afforded a safety valve and recreation," *The Birmingham Age-Herald* reported in its Jan. 17 edition. "They (sports) are important because a keen mind goes with a healthy body," Newman said. Bill Foreman of *The Atmore Advance* discussed feature stories. Foreman said few weekly newspaper used enough local features, adding that "the publishers should encourage their correspondents to watch for unusual news."

L.O. Brackeen discusses farm news

L.O. Brackeen, director of publicity at Alabama Polytechnic Institute, Auburn, discussed farm news. Brackeen spoke on ways that weekly newspaper publishers and county farm agents might work together for the benefit of the press. Brackeen said releases from Auburn "are being kept as short as possible and confined to releases of real interest to farmers."

Other panel participants included Dan Davis, *The Birmingham News;* Florence Fisher, *The Tuskegee News;* Eugene Speight, *The Lee County Bulletin,* Auburn; J.K. Hilton, *The Haleyville Advertiser;* Bonnie D. Hand, *The LaFayette Sun;* Harry Hall, *The Dothan Eagle;* John B. Stevenson, *The Roanoke Leader;* W.C. Wear, *The Opelika Daily News;* Milton C. Giles, *The Franklin County Times,* Russellville; Vernie Teel, *The Chambers County News;* W.J. (Bill) Hearin Jr., *The Mobile Press Register;* Jack Langhorne, *The Huntsville Times;* Ben Green, *The Tuscaloosa News;* Hamner Cobbs, *The Greensboro Watchman;* McClellan Van der Veer, *The Birmingham News;* John H. Singleton, *The Enterprise Ledger;* Floyd Tillery, *The Chattahoochee Valley Times,* Lanett; Harry M. Ayers, *The Anniston Star;* Gould Beech, *The Southern Farmer,* Montgomery; W. Emmett Brooks, *The Brewton Standard;* Parker W. Campbell, *The Progressive Age,* Scottsboro; Hunter H. Golson, *The Wetumpka Herald;* and Howard Barney, *The Mobile Press.*

Faulkner presides at panel

A preview of what was ahead for Alabama was presented by a panel of state leaders. The panel, presided over by past APA president James H. (Jimmy) Faulkner Sr. of *The Baldwin Times*, included: Industries, Frank P. Samford, president, Alabama Industries; State Development, W.A. Steadham, president, Alabama State Chamber of Commerce; Labor, William Mitch, president, Alabama State Industrial Union Council; Conservation, Brooks Toler, State Forester; Agriculture, P.O. Davis, Extension director, Alabama Polytechnic Institute, Auburn; Education, Dr. A.H. Collins, state superintendent of education; New industries, Randolph Norton, president, Bradford-Norton Company;

S I D E L I G H T S
MARKING 125 YEARS OF HISTORY

Blessing only good for 35 miles per hour
From J.C. Henderson's column in *The Alexander City Outlook* in 1955: "A Catholic lad bought himself a St. Christopher medal, which is supposed to keep the owner safe from accidents. After making the purchase the boy took the medal to Father O'Malley to be blessed. The good Father took the medal, blessed it and said, 'This blessing is only good up to 35 miles per hour'."

Ozark's Vivian Adams honored by Pilot Club

More than 250 persons gathered in the Ozark Community House in 1955 to watch Vivian Brantly Adams receive honorary membership in the Pilot Club. "Miss Vivian," as she was affectionately known, was selected for the honor in recognition of more than half a century of "mothering" the county's only newspaper, the weekly *The Southern Star* in Ozark. Guest speaker Geoffrey Birt of *The Montgomery Examiner* paid tribute to Mrs. Adams:

"A hundred years from now, other newspaper reporters and history students will be scanning the 1955 pages of *The Southern Star* to learn what life and times of the mid-20th century were really like for both ordinary and famous citizens," Birt said. "In this respect, Miss Vivian will be called blessed. Year by year she has faithfully presented the news of her region for the neighbors, for the sons, for the daughters of Dale County living far, far away and for future generations."

Mrs. Adams was the wife of one Southern Star editor and the mother of two others. A Georgia native, she married the young editor, John Quincy Adams, in 1900, reared three sons, and played an active role in the newspaper. At the time of John Quincy Adams' death in 1925, she became right-hand man to her eldest son, Jesse Adams, who succeeded his father as editor and served until his death in 1952. The youngest son, John Quincy Adams Jr., was editor in 1955, and Mrs. Adams was assisting him.

Legislative outlook, Hunter H. Golson, member of the House of Representatives and editor of *The Wetumpka Herald*.

Houston Cole, executive director of the Alabama State Defense Council, was guest speaker at the banquet at the Tutwiler Hotel.

In March 1942, the Executive Committee endorsed the idea of government agencies using paid advertising and wrote Alabama senators and congressmen urging enactment of legislation giving agencies this authority.

Better Newspaper Contest winners announced

The 1941 Better Newspaper Contest winners were announced at the 1942 convention. Professor Phil Beedon, head of the University of Alabama Department of Journalism, presented the awards. *The Lee County Bulletin* in Auburn was named outstanding weekly. Other winners were *The Baldwin Times* in Bay Minette, second place; *The Cullman Tribune,* third; *The Haleyville Advertiser-Journal,* fourth; and *The Atmore Advance* and *The Franklin County Times,* Russellville, tied for fifth.

In addition to winning first place in the best all-around division, *The Lee County Bulletin* took seven first-place awards, two seconds and three honorable mentions in the 12 contests it entered.

Other first-place winners included: Best Editorial, *The Anniston Times;* Best Editorial Page, The *Lee County Bulletin;* Best Column, *The Lee County Bulletin* for Gould Beech's "Of Cabbages and Kings;" Best Front Page, *The Lee County Bulletin;* Best Typography and Layout, *The Baldwin Times;* Commercial Printing, *The Lee County Bulletin;* Special Editions, *The Alexander City Outlook;* News Writing, *The Lee County Bulletin;* Best Women's Page, *The Lee County Bulletin;* Best Agricultural News, *The Baldwin Times;* Best Display Advertising, *The Lee County Bulletin;* Best Use of Local Pictures, *The Haleyville Advertiser-Journal;* Community Service, *The Franklin County Times,* Russellville.

APA presents plaque to Doyle L. Buckles in 1942

At the banquet on Jan. 16, 1942, APA presented a plaque to field manager Doyle L. Buckles. In presenting the plaque, Milton C. Giles, APA past president and publisher of *The Franklin County Times,* said:

"Doyle, on behalf of the members of the Alabama Press Association and of the department of journalism at the University of Alabama, for what you are, for your ability and loyalty to the cause and progress of the Fourth Estate in Alabama, for molding the Alabama Press Association into one among America's best and most effective press associations and for rendering the greatest amount of professional service for dollar expended, it is my pleasure as the President of the Alabama Press Association, that brought you to Alabama with the cooperation of the University of Alabama, that I am privileged to award this plaque to you in token of the love and deep appreciation of the donors, each and every member of the Alabama Press Association; and may the years that come, bring what they may, still find the tie that binds us even more pleasant than now and the friendship sweeter and the contacts between you, our leader, and the members of the Fourth Estate be as roses cast along your pathway of life in our midst."

Giles continued, "And finally when the great scorer writes '30' over your name, may there be inscribed on the stone that marks your resting place these words: 'Doyle Buckles, God's Gift to Alabama Newspapers and the State Itself'."

Buckles given $157 on 46th birthday

Exactly one month after the winter convention presentation, on Feb. 16, 1942, association members further honored Buckles with a gift check for $157. The occasion was Buckles' 46th birthday. APA president Charles G. Dobbins of *The Anniston Times* wrote, "This letter is accompanied by a gift of money for you from your friends of the Alabama Press Association on the occasion of your birthday, February 16. We wish for you many returns of this day — and all of them as the strong right arm of the Alabama Press Association! The money is yours to do as you please with, though we have hoped that it might serve in helping provide you with a car better suited for your rambles over the state. Or would you be willing to part with that 'dream bus' of yours?"

William E. (Bill) Brooks Jr., 1953-1954 APA president, explained the reference to "dream bus" in a 1995 interview: "Doyle Buckles drove his own automobile, which was a disreputable pile of junk waiting to fall down and die on the side of the road," Brooks, 73, said. "That was why Milton Giles called

it a 'dream bus'. Also, you need to remember that the late, unlamented Depression was far from over during Buckles' time with APA. The mentality that went with that era prevailed well after World War II, as seen by the APA dues structure, convention costs, and meal charges," Brooks said.

During 1942, Buckles appeared on the programs of the Louisiana Press Association in New Orleans, the Arkansas Press Association at Hot Springs and the Mississippi Press Association at Biloxi. He also attended the annual convention of the Newspaper Association Managers in Chicago.

APA cooperates in scrap metal drive

APA cooperated in the newspaper scrap metal drive in Alabama. "It was one of the finest examples of democracy in action I have ever seen," said Col. Harry M. Ayers, publisher of *The Anniston Star,* who headed the campaign in the collection of more than 130 million pounds. In expressing appreciation of the newspapers' efforts, the executive director for the drive in Alabama said, "In addition to the gathering of considerable material valuable to the war effort, the drive was a great morale builder and its benefits will continue to be felt for a long time."

The following telegram was received from Donald M. Nelson, chairman of the War Production Board: "In meeting today with the Newspaper Scrap Metal Drive Committee, I expressed our thanks for the unprecedented results obtained in their salvage efforts. I wish now to extend our gratitude through you and to all newspapers taking part in this magnificent drive which brought in salvage far beyond our fondest expectations and urge your continuing support."

Dobbins elected 1942 president

The following officers were elected for 1942-1943 at the 71st annual convention in Birmingham Jan. 16-17, 1942: Charles G. Dobbins, editor and publisher of *The Anniston Times,* president; Marcy B. Darnall Jr., *The Florence Herald,* vice president; Neil O. Davis, *The Lee County Bulletin* in Auburn, second vice president.

Executive Committee members included Webb Stanley, *The Greenville Advocate;* Parker W. Campbell, *The Progressive Age,* Scottsboro; Ben A. Green, *The Tuscaloosa News;* Hunter H. Golson, *The Wetumpka Herald;* Henry Arnold, *The Cullman Tribune;* J. Fisher Rothermel, *The Birmingham News;* Milton C. Giles, *The Franklin Times,* Russellville; Cullen Morgan, *The*

S I D E L I G H T S
MARKING 125 YEARS OF HISTORY

Rice Howard parts with "old friend"

Rice Howard, publisher of *The Southern Democrat* in Oneonta, parted with an old friend and helper in 1955. "It was in the form of a deformed toe, broken in early childhood," Howard wrote in a column. "After 56 years of faithful service it had to be amputated. We never went broke in a marble game because of this digit; we could walk across a ring and pick up a marble, an aggie or glassie and never be detected. It could be that sins of this kleptomaniac caused its downfall."

Moundville News; Ed Pierce, *The Mountain Eagle,* Jasper; Bonnie D. Hand, *The LaFayette Sun;* Harry Hall, *The Dothan Eagle;* R.C. Bryan, *The Elba Clipper;* George M. Cox, *The Mobile Press Register;* and George A. Carleton, *The Clarke County Democrat,* Grove Hill.

Top APA officers enter Armed Forces

The three top officers of the APA resigned in 1942 to enter the Armed Forces. President Charles G. Dobbins, *The Anniston Times,* was a lieutenant in the Navy; first vice president Marcy B. Darnall Jr., *The Florence Herald,* was a lieutenant and naval aviator; and second vice president Neil O. Davis, *The Lee County Bulletin,* was a lieutenant in the Army. Ben A. Green of *The Tuscaloosa News* served as acting president from the time of Dobbins' resignation in November 1942 until the annual convention in 1943.

In 1950 for *The Alabama Publisher,* Green recalled how he had been "drafted" as acting president: "As I recall it, things first took shape at a barbecue held in Montgomery during July, 1942, at the closing session of a summer meeting of the Association. James H. Faulkner...was president. A war was going on and Jimmy (Faulkner), father of two children and mayor of Bay Minette, was on the verge of enlisting in the U.S. Air Corps.

"Charles Dobbins, then publisher of *The Anniston Star* (sic) *Times,* a weekly, was Association vice president. He was on the verge of going into the U.S. Navy. Somebody, probably the irrepressible Hunter Golson of Wetumpka (God bless his memory), suggested that a second vice president would be needed to take over if the other two officers left for military service. It seems that at the barbecue I was elected second vice president."

Summer conventions of 1942, 1943 and 1944 were called "war conferences." The 1942 summer war conference was in Montgomery on July 24-25.

Mark L. Tucker dies in 1942

Alabama newspaper man Mark L. Tucker died in 1942. Tucker began his career as a 10-year-old office boy with *The Selma Times-Mail* in 1881 and later moved to other newspapers, becoming in turn compositor, foreman and editor.

Following his departure from *The Selma Times-Mail,* Tucker was associated in one capacity or another with *The Selma Telegram, The Selma Evening Journal, The Birmingham Age-Herald, The Tusca-loosa Evening Times, The Tuscaloosa Sunday Sun, The Montgomery Evening Journal, The Tarrant City Her-*ald, *The Ashville Southern Aegis, The Union Springs Herald, The Bullock County Breeze, The Scottsboro Progressive Age, The Stevenson Chronicle, The Scottsboro Citizen, The Alabama Reporter* of Talladega, *The Hayneville Examiner, The Montgomery Plain Dealer,* and *The Little Rock* (Ark.) *Gazette.*

Mark L. Tucker
The Chilton County News

In 1938, Tucker began publishing *The Chilton County News* with his son, Marion Tucker. Tucker initiated publication of several of the newspapers listed above; others he bought while they were in poor condition. He exulted in rebuilding them, becoming a great rehabilitator along the way.

At one time Tucker represented the Western Newspaper Union.

A native of Bibb County, Tucker was married to the former Mary Julia Booth. The union produced 10 children. All five of the sons and several of his grandsons followed him into the newspaper or commercial printing fields. Two of his grandsons, Bob Tucker of *The Chilton County News* in Clanton and Vernon Payne of *The Baldwin Times* in Bay Minette, were publishers in Alabama at the time of his induction to the Newspaper Hall of Honor in 1976, while another was composing room foreman with an Alabama metropolitan daily newspaper.

1943

**Ben A. Green, *The Tuscaloosa News*
and *The Tallassee Tribune*
(Green purchased *The Tallassee Tribune*
in March 1943)
1943-1944 president**

**72nd annual press convention, Montgomery
Jan. 29-30, 1943
Summer war conference, Birmingham
Aug. 13-14, 1943**

"Let us pray!" Those three words opened the 72nd annual convention of the APA at the Whitley Hotel in Montgomery on Jan. 29, 1943. The annual convention, known as the "Third War Conference," started at 1 p.m.

"You are respectfully urged to be on hand and join in the praying, and also in the other events which will occupy the 24-hour session," APA president Ben A. Green, managing editor of *The Tuscaloosa News*, wrote in a letter published in the Jan. 9, 1943, issue of *AlaPressa*. "No profession in all the world's kingdom has greater call on the spiritual life of humans than does that of the newspaper men and women of America," Green wrote. "In your town and our town, the newspaper man buries more people, marries more people and welcomes more babies than any single undertaker, minister or physician, respectively. We come in daily contact with people who are under stress of great emotion. We must fortify our own spirits to meet these tests."

One of the highlights of the convention was the annual banquet at which more than 100 delegates listened to Gov. Chauncey Sparks pledge his sincere cooperation with the press in solving war problems and building up the state.

The Birmingham Age-Herald reported in its Jan. 30 edition that Sparks told APA members

SIDELIGHTS
MARKING 125 YEARS OF HISTORY

Mergenthaler promotes Linotype Comet
The March 1956 issue of *The Alabama Publisher* contained an advertisement by Mergenthaler Linotype Co. promoting the Linotype Comet. "In 18,000 hours the Comet never lost an hour," said L.R. McCoy, mechanical superintendent of Southern Newspapers Inc., in Hot Springs, Ark. "It produced nearly 11,000,000 slugs, and matrix costs are less than one-half cent per operating hour."

"Our nine Comets enabled a reduction in typesetting machines from 28 to 25," said L.H. Hendricks, composing room superintendent of The Union-Tribune Publishing Co., in San Diego, Calif.

that whatever he advocated would be "within the structure of the Democratic Party. I am a Democrat," Sparks declared. "I may not always agree with the party, but I will not carry my disagreements outside the party."

Gov. Sparks praises Alabama press
Sparks praised the Alabama press, saying he had "never met a finer group" and asked editors to criticize his administration frankly so that he could have "added counsel." *The Birmingham Age-Herald* reported that Sparks was chosen by APA as its "first honorary non-paying member" of the Press Association and was "presented a make-up rule to carry in his pocket and signify membership."

The 1943 convention was a 24-hour roundtable session "for, of, and by the publishers," according to *AlaPressa*. "It was enlarged by the 'hotel-lobby' discussions that are usually the most fruitful phase of a convention." APA president Ben A. Green appointed 16 "thinking committees" for 1943. "Spend 50 minutes in just thinking, and then devote the last 10 minutes of the hour to writing a letter to your committee chairman expressing your ideas," Green advised.

"I have made some changes in the committee set-up," Green said. "Past presidents, all of whom we love and appreciate, have been 'booted off' the Executive Committee to make room for other

Evergreen publisher's son leaves for college
Publisher R. Gaston Bozeman Sr., publisher of *The Evergreen Courant,* wrote in his column in 1955, "My youngest son Pace left Monday morning to return to his college work at the University (of Alabama). He and Dickey have been taking turns at working and going to college since Bob *(The Dadeville Record)* left last year. It is going to be pretty rough on me to have to do without them all the same time, but my son-in-law, Marshall Brittain, has become pretty well oriented in newspaper work by now and with the help of Bufred Johnson, Joe Hyde, W.H. Howell, Herbert Harpe and Clarence Smith we hope to be able to get *The Courant* out each week."

highly deserving members. However, I am reluctant to part with their executive services; therefore, a new past-presidents' advisory committee is being created, all members being ex-officio members of the Executive Committee."

APA unanimously adopted a resolution endorsing the Bankhead-Cannon government advertising bills and urged members to contact their congressmen during the recess to secure their active support.

Green, Buckles attend Senate hearings in Washington

Early in 1943 the Press Association was successful in getting Sen. John M. Bankhead to introduce a bill in the U.S. Senate authorizing the Treasury secretary to utilize $25 million to $30 million each year for government purchasing of advertising space to promote the sale of war bonds and other essential war programs. APA president Ben A. Green and field manager Doyle L. Buckles represented the Press Association at Senate hearings in Washington before the Banking and Currency Committee on the newspaper advertising bill.

Better Newspaper Contest winners were announced at the 1943 winter convention. *The Lee County Bulletin* in Auburn received the first place award for General Excellence for the second consecutive year. Other first-place recipients included *The Greenville Advocate,* Special Editions; *The Lee County Bulletin,* Best Editorial Page; *The Industrial*

Press, Ensley, Best Editorial; *The Northwest Alabamian* of Fayette and *Advertiser-Journal* of Haleyville, Best Editorial Column, "The Jay Walker," by Jay Thornton; *The Cullman Tribune,* Best Display Advertising; *The Alexander City Outlook,* Best Front Page; *The Lee County Bulletin,* Best Typography and Makeup; *The Haleyville Advertiser-Journal,* Best Commercial Printing; *The Franklin County Times,* Community Service; *The Lee County Bulletin,* Best Women's Page; and *The Mountain Eagle,* Jasper, Best Agricultural News.

Membership dues were $12 in 1943

APA annual membership dues in 1943 remained at $12 for both dailies and weeklies. "It's no gamble when you invest $12 a year in a membership in the Alabama Press Association, especially during these war days when there are so many changes in living and doing business," *AlaPressa* reported. "Your association, as a 'clearing house' of ideas, keeps you informed as to what others are doing to keep the presses rolling."

APA president Ben A. Green assumed new duties in March 1943 as publisher of *The Tallassee Tribune,* which he purchased from Hunter H. Golson. "Ben is most enthusiastic over the possibilities of his newspaper and community and is making plans for a special edition on April 1st to feature the Army-Navy 'E' award to the Tallassee Mills and 4,500 employees," *AlaPressa* reported.

Mergenthaler, APA hold Linotype clinics

Two mechanical clinics in Montgomery and Birmingham on March 27 and 28, sponsored by APA in cooperation with Mergenthaler Linotype Corp., were attended by more than 175 publishers, printers, and Linotype operators. Registration cards showed that 80 newspaper plants and 20 job printing plants were represented. John L. Davis, manager of the Southern Branch of Mergenthaler, explained why such clinics were being held. "The war program," he said, "forces a great retrenchment in available equipment and repairs and we must take greater care of our machines while the factories are working 24 hours a day on war supplies." Davis stressed the following three major factors in care of the Linotype: (1) Cleanliness; (2) Proper lubrication; (3) Locate your trouble then make adjustments.

"If you want to continue in the publishing business don't take any chances on losing your

Linotype operator," *AlaPressa* warned in its April 9, 1943, edition. "Only the publishers who have tried to locate operators can appreciate the seriousness of this manpower shortage. When authorities like John L. Davis, who knows every operator and shop in the South, tells you that he doesn't know of a single unemployed operator — it is time to check up on the draft status of your employees. The shortage has reached the point where the loss of a Linotype operator may mean the suspension of your publication or that of your neighbor if you lure his operator away. This is not an empty 'Wolf, Wolf' warning."

1943 summer "warvention," Birmingham

Roundtable discussions of timely war problems dominated the summer APA convention called a "warvention," at the Redmont Hotel in Birmingham on Aug. 13-14, 1943. Four outstanding headliners addressed the Alabama publishers during the business sessions and banquets.

Sen. John M. Bankhead, Alabama's senior senator and author of the widely discussed $30 million government advertising bill, was guest at the banquet staged Friday night at the Tutwiler Hotel. Bankhead's speech was printed in a four-page leaflet titled, "The Bankhead-Cannon Government Advertising Bill."

Out-of-state guest speakers included Albert Hardy, president of the National Editorial Association and publisher of *The Gainesville* (Ga.) *News,* and Matt P. Vernon, editor of *The Columbian* (Miss.) *Progress,* one of the outstanding weekly newspapers in the South and nation, APA minutes reported. John Temple Graves III, noted columnist of *The Birmingham Age-Herald* and widely known as an author and lecturer, gave an inspirational talk Saturday morning on the "Possibilities and Future of the South."

Roundtable business session held

While APA president Ben A. Green was in charge of all sessions, vice presidents Parker W. Campbell, *The Progressive Age,* Scottsboro, and *Jackson Sentinel,* and George A. Carleton, *The Clarke County Democrat,* Grove Hill, were in charge of the roundtable business session Friday afternoon and Saturday morning.

The manpower problem, which had seriously hit all newspapers, was the topic for the roundtable. Increased costs of newsprint and overhead focused attention on the importance of increasing circulation and advertising rates so very essential to the survival of newspapers during the war crisis.

SIDELIGHTS
MARKING 125 YEARS OF HISTORY

"A Smith named Joel edits lively paper"

A Smith Named Joel Edits Lively Geneva County Paper was the headline. "He'll tell you, 'I'm just a guy named Smith.' But to hundreds of people he is the Wiregrass' youngest newspaper editor," *The Alabama Publisher* reported in its April 1955 issue featuring Joel Smith. "At 26, Joel P. Smith is the guiding light behind *The Geneva County Reaper,* a 56-year-old newspaper that is going into more and more Geneva County homes each week, thanks to his efforts.

"In a way, Smith's story is that of the hometown boy who made good. He was born in Samson, only 20-plus miles away. He went to school in Samson for his early education, but jumped the Florida state lines for a background that made him into a newspaper man. Smith graduated in 1952 from Florida State University. Later in 1952, the blond-haired youngster went to Panama City where he held down two jobs — one as a teacher and promotion spark plug in the state school system, and the other as a writer for *The Panama City News-Herald.*

"In 1953, Smith recrossed the state line and came to a stop in Birmingham where he worked on *The Birmingham News* until fall 1954 when he became general manager of *The Reaper.*

"They had to go get Smith. He was happily ensconced on *The News* when *The Reaper* lost Orsen B. (Red) Spivey, who was general manager. The paper is owned by four brothers named Scott, with most of the decisions left up to Howard Scott, an attorney who lives in Chatom, near Mobile. Scott wanted someone who had a smattering of newspaper and radio background, since the brothers had high hopes for WGEA, their Geneva radio station. Someone whispered Smith, and within a few days Joel found himself back home."

Attention was also devoted to the problem of how to meet the increasing demands for wartime news and services on the home front.

How to prevent "newspaper casualties" was the major objective of the annual "warvention," the fourth war council of the APA in two years. Because of help shortages, limited hotel accommodations and transportation difficulties, the problem was condensed to a streamlined 24-hour session.

APA, University of Alabama renew contract

During the 1943-1944 academic year, APA and the University of Alabama completed the five-year contract to pay half the field manager's salary and provide office space on campus. The contract was renewed, it being the judgment of the Extension Division dean as stated in his annual report to the president that "the joint service...has afforded the University an opportunity to cooperate in one of the finest products of adult education; that is in working with the Alabama Press in improving and expanding the services to the people."

Extension Dean R.E. Tidwell reported that the standards of news service at the University had been "substantially raised" during the period in which "sufficient time has been given by a trained newspaper man to conduct the News Bureau."

1944
Parker W. Campbell,
The Progressive Age, **Scottsboro**
1944-1945 president

73rd annual press convention, Birmingham
Jan. 28-29, 1944
Summer war conference, Birmingham
Aug. 18-19, 1944

"The Alabama Press Association takes great pride in the splendid records made by its members during another long war year, filled with increasing handicaps due to manpower and newsprint shortages and other abnormal conditions over which they had no control," field manager Doyle L. Buckles wrote in his 1944 annual report.

"Despite long, weary hours and confusing rules and regulations, Alabama publishers stuck to their posts and continued to keep their presses rolling," Buckles continued. "We know of no other state in the Union that had fewer 'newspaper casualties' in 1944. And we know of no other business or professional group that gave more of their time and services to the various war programs on the home

---

> ### S I D E L I G H T S
> #### MARKING 125 YEARS OF HISTORY
>
> #### *APA begins "homemakers page" in 1956*
> APA president Ben George of *The Demopolis Times* announced in 1956 the start of a new service for APA members — a homemakers page. Noting that there had been a need for many years for a good homemakers page in Alabama newspapers designed primarily for Alabama women, George explained that APA was sponsoring a test series of five such pages for use in Alabama newspapers.
>
> The five homemaker publications were sent to APA members in copy form. "They may use the copy as the basis of good homemaker pages, either building a complete page with this copy and appropriate advertising, or spreading it over a couple of pages, with more appropriate advertising filling its pages," George said.

front. That this service, 'far beyond the call of duty,' was appreciated was indicated by the scores of letters and citations at the annual summer convention banquet from the war leaders of this state."

Green comments on fate of APA during WWII

Ben A. Green of *The Tuscaloosa News* and later *The Tallassee Tribune* commented several years later on the fate of the APA during wartime stress: "Weeklies did a fair job securing promotional wartime advertising, but they could not tap the big field that used the dailies so extensively. (Field manager Doyle) Buckles and his bulletins provided a great source of help to the weekly publishers who were faced with personnel shortages in addition to tussles for newsprint, ink, and everything else. APA members showed a wonderful willingness to help each other out in various emergencies which came along. Our membership was maintained at a remarkably high level, although many of our strongest young stalwarts were in the military services."

The 73rd annual convention at the Redmont Hotel in Birmingham on Jan. 28-29, 1944, was highlighted by inspirational and helpful addresses and roundtable discussions. Among the speakers were Matt Vernon of Mississippi, Walter Randolph, Bruce Shelton, Leon Gilbert, John Gilbert, John L. Davis, Carl B. Fritsche, Hunter H. Golson and E.H. (Ed) Pierce. An endowment fund of more than $1,400 was raised for newspaper improvement programs.

Carleton presides at reader interest roundtable

APA vice president George A. Carleton of *The Clarke County Democrat* presided over a Saturday morning roundtable on increasing reader interest and newspaper improvements. Libba Cornish George of *The Demopolis Times* stressed the great popularity of soldier news columns and "the little personal items about town people and farmers. Make your paper more local," she advised. Webb Stanley of *The Greenville Advocate* said that "the things people are most interested in are the things they know most about." He cited the popularity of one of his features, "The Farmer of the Week."

"People love it," Stanley said. "You can lead your people most easily by the indirect method." Stanley predicted that Alabama was on the verge of the greatest development era of any state and explained the great possibilities of the sweet potato industry.

Tribute paid to William Allen White of Kansas

J. Fisher Rothermel, who served on the editorial staff of *The Birmingham News,* paid tribute to William Allen White, editor of *The Emporia Gazette* in Kansas, whose death had just been announced. Rothermel stressed the importance of a local philosophy, citing the success of White and outstanding Alabama editors, whose influence was felt not only locally, but in Montgomery and Washington. Rothermel expressed the hope that there would be more editorial comment on the life of the community.

J.A. Downer of *The DeKalb Times* in Fort Payne,

in discussing his popular "Speaking at Random" column, warned of the danger of "preaching too much." Downer said he had found that soldier columns were most interesting.

"If you want people to be interested in what you say, be interested in people," advised Clark Hodgins of *The Moulton Advertiser,* in discussing the secrets of his widely quoted "Scattered Remarks." Hodgins said he had found that people were interested in almost everything, "but there is a danger of becoming too orthodox."

Rice Howard of *The Southern Democrat* in Oneonta remarked that "if you leave your readers alone, they will get out a good paper for you."

Hand: "Reader interest centers around people"

"Reader interest centers around people," said Bonnie D. Hand of *The LaFayette Sun.* "You've got it in soldier's news — they read every word of it, and it encourages you to feel that your newspaper is of real service during this war." Hand also urged giving more attention to country correspondence.

Charles Scarritt, journalism instructor at Alabama Polytechnic Institute, pointed out that the basis of the success of William Allen White of Kansas was in keeping his newspaper a local newspaper. "He loved his community and every person in his community, knew them personally; he never lost the common touch," Scarritt said. (Scarritt later joined the Department of Journalism at the University of Alabama.)

1944 summer war conference, Birmingham

The summer war conference at the Thomas Jefferson Hotel in Birmingham Aug. 18-19, 1944, featured a "citation banquet" at which tributes and citations were extended to the Alabama publishers by state and federal war leaders.

Among the citations were those from Gov. Chauncey Sparks; Haygood Patterson, Alabama Defense Council; Andrew W. Smith, Office of Price Administration; Col. J.T. Johnson, Selective Service System; James P. Barnes, War Production Board; Ben C. Morgan, State Department of Conservation; Rear Adm. A.C. Bennett, USN, Eighth Naval District; W.O. Dobbins, State of Alabama Planning Board; Ed Leigh McMillan of Brewton, War Finance Committee; Nat C. Wilson, American Red Cross; Maj. Gen. F.E. Uhl, USA, Fourth Service Command; Frank L. Grove, Alabama Education Association; Sen. Lister Hill; State Legion Commander C.C. Horton; Dr. B.F. Austin, State Health Officer; Joe N. Poole, State Department of

Agriculture and Industries; and John M. Ward, State Chamber of Commerce.

Copies of the citations were sent to all city and county officials and were made available to all publishers for use in promotional ads or for use with Selective Service and Rationing Boards.

The convention program was headlined by Ed M. Anderson, publisher of five North Carolina newspapers and chairman of the National Editorial Association's Legislative Committee, who spoke on "Opportunities of the Weekly Press." Other speakers included O. William Spoor of the Birmingham Advertising Club on war activities advertising of the Birmingham Advertising Club; possibilities of forest advertising by state and federal authorities; and Neil C. Cady of Western Newspaper Union in Birmingham on major advertising prospects ahead.

S I D E L I G H T S
MARKING 125 YEARS OF HISTORY

Publishers clash in marble tournament

It was knuckles down and circle off when two prominent newspaper men clashed on the field of marble honor on March 21, 1957, in Talladega.

Tom Abernethy, vice president of Talladega Publishing Co., publisher of *The Talladega Daily Home* and *The Talladega Daily News*, challenged Cecil Hornady, editor and publisher of the publishing company, to play a public match of marbles to determine "The middle-aged champion of Talladega — and maybe the world." Frank Wagner, Talladega recreation director, known as the "Old Agate Buster," was referee.

Jep Greer of *The Sylacauga News* wrote in his "Casual Comments" column that Abernethy and Hornady had challenged him to take on the winner of the marble match. "Of all the effrontery!" Greer wrote. "Of all the conceit! Me, who graduated at M.M.I. (Marion Marble Institute) with marble cum laud. Why, I could take on both of them and never get my knees dirty. Just let me know the date and I'll have my knickers pressed and my bobby socks laundered, but I'll have to advise you, Tom and Cecil, I play for keeps, so don't use your good marbles if they're keepsakers."

The mechanical and revenue producing round tables "brought out many good ideas from Alabama publishers," *AlaPressa* reported.

Golson presented "Lister Hill" hat

Past president Milton C. Giles of *The Franklin County Times* in Russellville presented past president Hunter H. Golson of *The Wetumpka Herald* a "Lister Hill" hat, and past president Ben A. Green of *The Tuscaloosa News* and *The Tallassee Tribune* was presented a fountain pen set and silver inlaid gavel.

The Press Association voted to continue affiliation with the National Editorial Association.

Luskin announces newspaper contest winners

Professor John Luskin, acting head of the University of Alabama Department of Journalism, announced winners of the annual state newspaper contests sponsored by the University. "It is with gratitude and confidence that we unanimously ratify a contract, proposed by our Board of Directors, calling for continuance of this cooperative arrangement for an indefinite period of time in the future," said a resolution.

The Cullman Tribune was selected as Outstanding Weekly in the 1944 contest. Other papers winning first-place awards were *The Alexander City Outlook*, Best Typography and Makeup; *The Lee County Bulletin* in Auburn, Best Front Page; *The Lee County Bulletin*, Best Editorial Page; *The Mountain Eagle* in Jasper, Best Editorial; *The Cullman Tribune*, Best Column; *The Cullman Tribune*, Best use of Local Pictures; *The Tallassee Tribune*, Special Edition; *The Cullman Tribune*, Best Women's Page; *The Atmore Advance*, Best Agricultural News; *The Franklin County Times* in Russellville, Best Service to the Community; *The Atmore Advance*, Best Display Advertising; and *The Mountain Eagle* in Jasper, Best Commercial Printing.

Buckles represents APA at two New York meetings

As president of Newspaper Association Managers Inc. in 1944, field manager Doyle L. Buckles was able to keep in close contact with all state, regional and national press association executives and their activities. Buckles represented APA at two meetings in New York "to help in the formation of the National Committee on Weekly Newspapers by the Association of Advertising Agencies — the first recognition of its kind to be given the weekly newspapers in the 1940s."

In connection with the waste paper drive in 1944, Bruce Shelton, publisher of *The Tuscaloosa News* and

APA past president, added a contribution that won heartiest applause at the annual convention. He suggested that the government be supplied with rubber stamps to be used on envelopes of the so-called news releases, reading "Please forward to the Mobile Paper Mill."

Singleton sells *The Enterprise Ledger* to Carnegie Thomas

John Henry Singleton, one of the most widely quoted editors in the state, sold *The Enterprise Ledger* to Carnegie Thomas, production superintendent of *The Miami Daily News*, in 1944.

John Henry Singleton
The Enterprise Ledger

Thomas assumed ownership on July 1.

Despite the warnings of friends that he had "too much ink under his fingernails to quit the printing business," Singleton said, "I have some hobbies that will keep me right busy, what time I'm not resting and fishing. And I'm going to get better acquainted with my children, go places and do things with my wife, and see my friends both in and out of the printing business oftener than has been the case heretofore."

1945

**George A. Carleton, *The Clarke County Democrat*
1945-1946 president**

74th annual press convention, Montgomery
May 11, 1945
(Summer convention not held in
1945 because of travel restrictions)

Because of Office of Defense Transportation restrictions, a formal convention was not held in 1945, but instead, a meeting of the Executive Committee served as the annual convention. In January 1945, the officers and directors voted 9-6 not to hold the annual convention that had been scheduled for Feb. 9-10 in Montgomery in response to an appeal by James F. Byrnes, War Mobilization director, that all organizations cancel all conventions after Feb. 1 which would attract more than 50 persons.

While the directors voted in favor of complying with Byrnes' request, they expressed the belief that no other organization had greater justification for holding a convention than did the Alabama Press Association.

One APA director commented, "If James F. Byrnes has any conception of what the press is doing in the war effort, he would recommend that the convention of the Alabama Press Association be held. If a newspaper is doing its duty, it is contributing more to the home front, and at the same time is the greatest builder of morale in the Armed Forces. There was never a time when an APA meeting was more needed, in our opinion."

Meeting held in lieu of 1945 annual convention

At the May 11, 1945, meeting at the Whitley Hotel in Montgomery, which served in lieu of the

---

S I D E L I G H T S
MARKING 125 YEARS OF HISTORY

Russellville editor and publisher only 15

The Russellville Daily Reminder, the town's only daily newspaper, was being edited and published in 1955 by Jack Morris. "Jack is 15," *The Alabama Publisher* reported in its July 1955 issue. "A junior in the Russellville High School, a town in north Alabama of about 6,000 population, Jack became interested in the newspaper field while working in a local print shop and delivering papers on a long country route. Armed with an idea, ambition and initiative, Jack polled the merchants of his town on the idea of a daily advertising sheet and found them receptive."

According to *The Alabama Publisher,* Jack used money he had saved, plus a $200 loan from the bank "and the installment plan" to purchase a large typewriter, motorized mimeograph machine, newsprint and a table. *The Russellville Daily Reminder* hit the streets for the first time on May 2, 1955, "and has been published six days a week since," *The Publisher* reported in its July 1955 edition. "Young Jack has made his paper pay off on the financial side also. Job mimeographing, circulars and advertising brought in a total of $1,116.45 for a seven-week period. After payrolls and expenses, a profit of $502 was realized. Interest in the paper remains high, people stop editor Jack on the street to congratulate him and the delivery boys are often given gifts, 'because we like that lil' ol' paper'."

74th annual convention, a Committee on Research and Promotion was authorized.

Incoming APA president George A. Carleton of *The Clarke County Democrat* in Grove Hill announced the committee's membership as Milton C. Giles, *The Franklin County Times,* Russellville, chairman; Hunter H. Golson, *The Wetumpka Herald;* Webb Stanley, *The Greenville Advocate;* W. Emmett Brooks, *The Brewton Standard;* Jack M. Pratt, *The Pickens County Herald,* Carrollton; vice president Bonnie D. Hand, *The LaFayette Sun;* and vice president E.H. (Ed) Pierce, *The Mountain Eagle* in Jasper.

Topics discussed at the meeting included the Audit Bureau of Circulation program and Victory Day Editions. Resolutions were adopted making the meeting serve as the annual convention, expressing appreciation for the cooperation of the University of Alabama, naming a State Apprenticeship Committee, appointing a committee to study circulation statements, and naming a research and promotion committee

Members of the committee to study circulation statements were Jack M. Pratt, *The Pickens County Herald,* Carrollton, chairman; J.W. (Jim) Oakley Sr., *The Centreville Press;* Vernie Teel, *The Chambers County News,* Lanett; and Ed Salter, *The Monroe Journal,* Monroeville.

Alabama papers rejoice at Japan's surrender

The surrender of Japan was received with great rejoicing by Alabama newspaper publishers. Many of the state's newspapers featured the historic event with screaming headlines, but a record was established by *The Talladega News* which issued three "Extras."

The largest weekly edition featuring the end of the war was published by Jay Thornton of *The Haleyville Advertiser-Journal,* which came out a day early with 28 packed pages "in order to speed to subscribers details of Japan's surrender." In a page-1 box, Thornton explained that "this issue represents the biggest rush job *The Advertiser-Journal* has ever tackled. All 28 pages were prepared, the advertising sold, and the papers printed since last Friday, when it became apparent the war would end within a few days."

Thornton gives employees a Friday holiday

Thornton said *The Haleyville Advertiser-Journal's* press, which printed only four pages at a time, "has been running almost continuously since Saturday. A total of approximately 25,000 sheets had to be fed into the press and folded to print the

edition." After the remarkable showing of energy and cooperation among the staff, Thornton gave them a Friday holiday.

Edmund R. (Ed) Blair of *The Pell City News* issued a "Souvenir Victory Edition" containing photos of a record number of local veterans. *The News* also celebrated the Japanese surrender with a 20-page edition.

During 1945 the "Official Apprenticeship Standard for the Printing Trade" was developed jointly by APA and the International Typographical Union in cooperation with the Apprentice Training Service in Birmingham. It was printed Sept. 8, 1945.

APA holds nine district meetings in 1945

A series of nine district meetings were held to start the apprentice training program for the printing trade. They were attended by district committeemen representing the newspapers, the unions, coordinators of schools, and representatives of the U.S. Employment Service.

APA representatives on the Apprentices Training Committee for the printing trade were Hunter H. Golson, *The Wetumpka Herald,* chairman; Rice Howard, *The Southern Democrat,* Oneonta; and Henry Arnold, *The Cullman Tribune.*

Short talks were made by visiting guests, including Ed LeMay and Maj. Steve McGinnis, T.C.I. public relations department; Fred Thornton, director, State News Bureau; and George W. Lanier, president, State Junior Chamber of Commerce.

Outgoing APA president Parker W. Campbell of *The Progressive Age* in Scottsboro nominated Annie Laurie Carleton as "Miss Alabama Press

Association for 1945," and the honor was "unanimously conferred upon the charming young daughter of Mr. and Mrs. George Carleton." Campbell expressed his appreciation of the honor of serving as APA president and turned the gavel over to the new president, George A. Carleton of *The Clarke County Democrat* in Grove Hill.

No headline speaker at 1945 banquet

According to APA minutes, "an informal banquet was held Friday evening. President Carleton presided over a most unique program that included no headline speaker, but there was plenty of speaking as each member was called upon to make a few remarks."

Members, dates and schedules of the nine district committee meetings for the apprenticeship training program in the state in 1945 and 1946 were:

Mobile-Jan. 22, Joe Jones, *The Covington News;* James H. (Jimmy) Faulkner Sr., *The Baldwin Times;* and Ralph.B. Chandler, *The Mobile Press Register.*

Montgomery-Jan. 6, Cash M. Stanley, *The Montgomery Advertiser* and *Alabama Journal;* Neil O. Davis, *The Lee County Bulletin;* and Webb Stanley, *The Greenville Advocate.*

Birmingham-Dec.18, Neil C. Cady, Western Newspaper Union; Tom Abernathy, *The Daily Home,* Talladega; and Ed Blair, *The Pell City News.*

Alexander City-Jan. 7, Ralph W. Callahan, *The Anniston Star;* J.C. Henderson, *The Alexander City Outlook;* and John B. Stevenson, *The Roanoke Leader.*

Tuscaloosa - Dec. 17, W.W. Baker, Wetherford Printing Co.; Jack Pratt, *The Pickens County Herald,* Carrollton; and J.W. (Jim) Oakley Sr., *The Centreville Press.*

Jasper - Dec. 27, Ed Pierce, *The* (Jasper) *Mountain Eagle;* Jay Thornton, *The Haleyville Advertiser;* and Bernard Guthrie, *The Jasper Union News.*

Florence - Dec. 28, Milton C. Giles, *The Franklin County Times,* Russellville; Clark Hodgins, *The Moulton Advertiser;* and Louis A. Eckl, *The Florence Times.*

Huntsville - Dec. 31, Barrett C. Shelton, *The Decatur Daily;* Jack Langhorne, *The Huntsville Times;* and Parker W. Campbell, *The Progressive Age,* Scottsboro.

Gadsden - Jan. 4, Walling Keith, *The Gadsden Times;* Arthur Downer, *The Fort Payne Times;* and Porter Harvey, *The Advertiser-Gleam,* Guntersville.

A summer convention was not held in 1945 because of travel restrictions.

S I D E L I G H T S
MARKING 125 YEARS OF HISTORY

"Where humor is divine" was the headline
"Where humor is divine" was the headline in a 1957 issue of *The Sylacauga News* in reporting a mistake in the paper.

"It is hard to tell where to find the most humor in weekly newspapers — whether in the typographical errors that crop up in the most undesirable spots, or in the unedited last minute news items that contribute to the dilemma of press-time," *The Sylacauga News* reported. "A typical such of the latter is the story of a farmer going rabbit hunting. The gun was discharged accidentally and the hunter was killed. 'He was survived,' reports the story, 'by his wife, two sons and a rabbit'."

1946
Bonnie D. Hand, *The LaFayette Sun*
1946-1947 president

75th annual press convention, Birmingham
Jan. 18-19, 1946
Summer convention, Panama City, Fla.
July 18-20, 1946

Nationally known newspaper men were the principal speakers at the 75th annual (victory) convention Jan. 18-19, 1946, at the Thomas Jefferson Hotel in Birmingham. Speakers gave suggestions for greater community service, tips on improved business methods, suggestions for enhancing typographical appearance of newspapers, and discussed the need for greater leadership and unit.

The four headline speakers were Fred W. Hill, publisher of *The Hamburg* (Iowa) *Reporter* and vice president of the National Editorial Association; Vernon T. Sanford, manager of the Oklahoma Press Association and past president of Newspaper Association Managers; John Temple Graves, author, lecturer and columnist for *The Birmingham Age-Herald;* and John E. Allen, editor of *The Linotype News* in Brooklyn, N.Y.

Allen urged the editors to use "conversational headlines." He said simplified makeup is taking hold in more and more papers and that the trend is toward headlines that will be "easy for the copy desk to write, easy for the printer to set up, and easy for the reader to read," *The Birmingham News* reported in its Jan. 20 edition.

Tribute paid to Marcy B. Darnall Jr.

The 1946 convention was opened by outgoing APA president George A. Carleton of *The Clarke County Democrat* with a prayer and silent standing tribute to publishers who had made the "supreme sacrifice" on the battle and home fronts. Tribute was paid to the memory of the late Lt. Marcy B. Darnall Jr. of *The Florence Herald* who entered service in the U.S. Navy while serving as vice president of the APA. Darnall was reported missing in action.

Delegates also adopted a resolution of condolences to the family of Horace Wilkinson, editor of *The Geneva Reaper*, who "died recently while putting out his newspaper, a weekly," *The Birmingham News* reported in its Jan. 20 edition.

Roundtable sessions were conducted by vice presidents Bonnie D. Hand of *The LaFayette Sun* and E.H. (Ed) Pierce of *The Mountain Eagle* in Jasper. Minutes reflect that "vice president Hand yielded part of his time to an explanation of the apprenticeship training program by L.O. Petree, state director. Maj. Charles R. Phillips, representing the Army Recruiting Service in Alabama, spoke briefly, expressing appreciation to the publishers for their help in meeting all quotas."

Bonnie D. Hand
The LaFayette Sun

According to minutes, "Past president Hunter H. Golson of *The Wetumpka Herald*, chairman of the Executive Committee, presented a five-year plan which had been suggested by Gould Beech, editor of *The Southern Farmer* in Montgomery that each member could afford to contribute, or invest, a certain number of inches of space for use and sale by the association. A motion, made by Chairman Golson and seconded by J.A. Downer, *The Fort Payne Times*, that the Committee on Research and Promotion was unanimously authorized to establish a reasonable goal, ascertain the amount of space to be needed, as to se-

E. H. (Ed) Pierce
The Mountain Eagle, Jasper

cure the required pledges from members was passed unanimously."

The secretary recording the minutes also reported that "the Birmingham entertainment committee, headed by editor C.J. Thomason of the Associated Suburban Press, arranged a banquet program featuring 10 attractive and talented artists in a floor show and John Temple Graves as guest speaker."

Lee County Bulletin best weekly newspaper

The Lee County Bulletin in Auburn was named Best Weekly Newspaper at the 1946 winter convention. *The Cullman Tribune* was chosen for second place in the Better Newspaper Contest competition. Third place went to *The Advertiser-Journal*, Haleyville, and fourth place to *The Shades Valley Sun*.

The Shades Valley Press, *The Ensley Industrial Press* and *The Franklin County Times* in Russellville won honorable mention awards.

Jay Thornton of *The Haleyville Advertiser* won first place for Best Local Column for "The Jay Walker." Other winners in the Best Local Column category were Nancy Dickson of *The Lee County Bulletin*, second place, for "Talk of the Times; Fred Turbyville of *The Lee County Bulletin*, third place, for "Columns," and Martha Shillite of *The Shades Valley Sun*, Homewood, fourth place, for "Sunstrokes."

In late 1946 the APA cooperated with the American Legion in sponsoring the state oratorical contest.

1946 summer convention, Panama City

An "informal three-day summer recreational convention" was attended by 100 members and guests in Panama City, Fla., on July 18-20, 1946. The members were housed in three leading hotels and resorts. The one and only informal business session was opened Friday morning in the Dixie Sherman roof garden by APA president Bonnie D. Hand of *The LaFayette Sun*.

Vice presidents Neil O. Davis, *The Lee County Bulletin* in Auburn, and E.H. (Ed) Pierce, *The Mountain Eagle* in Jasper, led a session which dealt primarily with better local news coverage. A basic problem for the press, pointed out Maj. Bruce McCoy, manager of the Louisiana Press Association, was better news coverage of the communities' forms of government.

McClellan Van der Veer, chief editorial writer for *The Birmingham News,* gave a report on a survey he had been making on the state senatorial race. "The most remarkable thing in connection with this campaign is the lack of interest being shown by the voters," Van der Veer said.

Field manager Doyle L. Buckles briefly explained the state publicity campaign, adopted by the APA directors. Buckles said that John Ward, executive vice president of the Alabama State Chamber of Commerce, "has pledged the wholehearted cooperation of that organization which will help provide pictures, materials and help underwrite the cost of putting them in plate form."

1947
Neil O. Davis, *The Lee County Bulletin,* Auburn
1947-1948 president

76th annual press convention, Montgomery
Feb. 14-15, 1947
Summer convention, Biloxi, Miss.
July 18-20, 1947
  Problems of newspaper production and advertising dominated the 76th annual press con-

vention, held Feb. 14-15, 1947, at the Whitley Hotel in Montgomery.

A panel on press photography was conducted by John Faber, art director of the photography department of *The Birmingham News* and *Age-Herald,* and Bob Faerber of Alabama Engraving Co. Kenneth Burchard, manager of American Type Founders Corporation's offset department, spoke on offset printing. Burchard urged weekly publishers to "study the possibilities of offset printing, both for their newspapers and for job printing."

Incoming APA president Neil O. Davis of *The Lee County Bulletin* led a roundtable session on newspaper improvements, and professor C.E. (Ed) Bounds of the University of Alabama Department of Journalism gave a brief review of the newspaper industry during the previous year and possibilities for the future.

Roundtable held on revenue-producing ideas
  APA vice president E.H. (Ed) Pierce of *The Mountain Eagle* in Jasper was in charge of a roundtable discussion on revenue-producing ideas.

A panel on the possibilities of the statewide publicity campaign, "Alabama, Unlimited," was held with the cooperation of the State Chamber of Commerce. Appearing on the panel were John M. Ward, State Chamber of Commerce; Haygood Paterson, commissioner of Agriculture and Industries; R.R. Wade, State Department of Labor; Dr. D.J. Gill, state health officer; and Dr. Austin Meadows, state superintendent of education.

Need of free and uncontrolled press
  Outgoing president Bonnie D. Hand of *The LaFayette Sun* presided over the annual banquet at which Congressman Albert Rains was principal speaker. Rains asserted that there was a need for a "worldwide free and uncontrolled press. Here in America, a free press stands more strongly entrenched by general acceptance, by statutory law, and by judicial decision, than ever before," Rains told the Press Association, according to a Feb. 15, 1947, article in *The Birmingham Age-Herald.*

Professor C.E. (Ed) Bounds of the University of Alabama announced winners in the state newspaper contests. *The Lee County Bulletin* in Auburn again won first place for General Excellence among Alabama weekly newspapers in the Better Newspaper Contest. Second place went to *The Shades Valley Sun* of Homewood, and third place was awarded to *The Baldwin County Times* in Bay Minette. Honorable mention went to *The Cullman*

Thomasville's Earl Tucker becomes author

Humorist Earl L. Tucker, editor of *The Thomasville Times,* became an author in 1958 when Strode Publishers of Huntsville purchased reprint rights to Tucker's humorous newspaper and magazine columns. The selections were published in book form under the column's title, "Rambling Roses and Flying Bricks."

The Alabama Publisher reported in 1958 that Tucker had given more than 500 speeches since 1953. "His lectures," according to *The Publisher,* "fall roughly in four categories. One lecture is for conventions; another is for Methodist Clubs, Ladies Missionary Societies and Boy Scouts; a third is for V.F.W. and American Legion groups; and a fourth is for miscellaneous people such as bankers and small loan associations and treasurers and others."

In addition to his writing and speaking, Tucker was a "sometime teacher of journalism." In such classes, Tucker said his major contribution was to "emphasize double spacing." Excerpts from "Rambling Roses and Flying Bricks" were used in at least one journalism textbook.

Tribune, *The Industrial Press* of Ensley, *The Talladega News* and *The Franklin County Times* of Russellville. Jay Thornton of *The Haleyville Advertiser-Journal* again won first place for his column, "The Jay Walker."

(The Better Newspaper Contest was discontinued after 1947 and was not resumed until 1953.)

At a special meeting in Birmingham April 13, 1947, the Executive Committee recommended that the Legislature provide an adequate budget for the State Division of Records and Reports in Montgomery. The afternoon program ended with a "get acquainted" party sponsored by "Birmingham friends of the APA" under chairmanship of Roy Hickman of Alabama Engraving Co.

Field manager Doyle L. Buckles dies Dec. 18, 1947

APA field manager Doyle L. Buckles died Dec. 18, 1947, in a Birmingham hospital. In August 1947, illness had caused a siege of hospitalization. Buckles finally underwent surgery and then apparently was recovering when he was suddenly and fatally stricken. Death came in the morning hours of Dec. 18.

"The newspaper profession in Alabama lost a fine scholar and wise counselor," *The Anniston Star* editorialized. "A tireless worker, he gave freely of his time and talent toward the upbuilding of the press in this state, using his wisdom to an advantage in helping to improve the style and general content of the Alabama press."

Word of Buckles' death caused "sudden sadness" in the offices of newspapers in Alabama," *The Birmingham News* commented. "A good friend, a cheerful fellow worker, has gone. His life had been filled with activity; he lived and breathed newspapers — and had since graduation from college."

The Birmingham Post wrote, "Doyle Buckles built up the Alabama Press Association from a small membership to a thriving organization. He helped to feed life-giving advertising to the smaller papers. In his pleasant way he did much to help the press of Alabama improve its product and its standing."

Comments were equally as eloquent in the weekly newspapers.

Lee County Bulletin: " 'Buck' of the Press Passes"

" 'Buck' of the Press Passes" was the headline of an editorial in *The Lee County Bulletin,* which reviewed Buckles' work since coming to Alabama in 1939. "From the Tennessee line to the Gulf, people in the front shops and the back shops learned of Buckles' death with great shock," *The Bulletin* commented. "The improved position of Alabama's weekly press stands as testimony to the work Buck did in Alabama."

"Newspaper men throughout Alabama lost their dearest friend and helpmate" when Buckles died, *LaFayette Sun* publisher Bonnie D. Hand, immediate past president of APA, wrote. " '30' in the newspaper language means the end, and so it is '30' for Doyle Buckles, a great guy who scaled to the very pinnacle of success in his chosen profession. His storehouse of love, friendship and all-around genuine service was full and running over."

Giles: APA was "social organization"

Milton C. Giles, publisher of *The Franklin County Times* and APA president when Buckles came to Alabama in 1939, commented that at that time, the Press Association was merely a social organization.

Giles editorialized, "Under Buckles' able leadership and personal guidance in many cases, Alabama today has one of the strongest and most formidable press organizations to be found in the United States, having a membership of almost 150 active and progressive newspapers in the state, following through on a statewide program of great importance in building a better and bigger state in addition to each paper doing a better job in the community it serves."

Another veteran Alabama publisher, George A. Carleton of *The Clarke County Democrat* in Grove Hill, commented that "Having been a member of the Press Association for nearly 40 years, no one knows better than I the struggles and vicissitudes through which it has passed, when it was kept alive by a few faithful souls. Doyle Buckles changed all this. From the moment he took over, he breathed new life into the Association."

Bassett appointed acting field manager

At a Dec. 21 meeting at the McLester Hotel, Buckles' assistant, Norman H. Bassett of Tuscaloosa, was appointed acting field manager and secretary-treasurer. At the 1948 winter convention, Bassett asked to continue serving in the position until a permanent field manager could be selected. Bassett had attended public schools in Dover, N.J., and received his degree in journalism at the University of Alabama in 1940. While at the University as a student, Bassett served on the News Bureau staff, as a student assistant on the journalism faculty and as sports editor of the campus newspaper, *The Crimson White.*

Following graduation, Bassett was telegraph and sports editor of *The Rome* (Ga.) *News Tribune* for 11 months during 1941. He returned to Tuscaloosa in 1942 to work on *The Tuscaloosa News* as telegraph editor and managing editor.

S I D E L I G H T S
MARKING 125 YEARS OF HISTORY

"Would you marry your wife again?"
    Weldon Payne, staff writer for *The Huntsville Times,* conducted a man-on-the-street interview in 1958 with the question, "Would you marry your wife again?"
    Answers were "informative, entertaining and well developed into a story," *The Alabama Publisher* reported.

Buckles' death was a shock to the University community and state newspaper profession. The field manager had been extremely popular with APA members and was credited with a revitalization of the association in the 1940s. *AlaPressa* reported that "it was generally agreed that he had worked himself to death during the eight years he was secretary-treasurer, field manager of the association."

Buckles "guiding hand" of Press Association

At the time of Buckles' death, APA president Neil O. Davis of *The Lee County Bulletin* in Auburn said in an article published in *The National Publisher* entitled "Newspapers and People, "'Buck' has been the guiding hand of the Alabama Press Association since 1939. In his nine years as secretary-treasurer and field manager he has unselfishly worked at a killing pace for the newspapers."

Davis added, "Probably his most important single contribution was in making Alabama's weekly newspapers believe in themselves. He was not concerned alone with helping to improve the papers as business enterprises, but he also took the lead in developing among them a clearer vision of their civic responsibilities."

"Doyle Buckles was field manager, News Bureau director, and he was teaching in the journalism department. I don't know what he did in his spare time," William E. (Bill) Brooks Jr., 1953-1954 APA president, reminisced in a 1995 interview on Buckles' contributions to the Press Association. In a 1940s report to Dr. Robert Earl Tidwell, dean of the Extension Division of the University of Alabama, Buckles was listed as director, devoting a "minimum" of two days a week to the News Bureau. He also listed two student reporters, each receiving $10 a month for a minimum of two afternoons' work a week, and one student photographer "subject to call and assignments," at $20 a month, and his supplies.

Acting field manager Norman H. Bassett wrote in the University of Alabama Extension News Bulletin in 1947 that "The volume of work Doyle Buckles turned out as field manager of APA was equalled by the crammed scrapbooks filled with clippings of University news and activities which he carefully and capably compiled during his nearly nine years as head of the News Bureau."

1947 summer convention, Biloxi, Miss.

The 1947 summer convention was at the Buena Vista Hotel in Biloxi, Miss., on July 18-20 with about 100 in attendance. While it was primarily for recreation, the address at the preliminary business session by Easton King, publisher of *The Pascagoula Chronicle-Star* on "Circulation and Local News Coverage" was reported in *AlaPressa* to be one of the highlights.

Among the other addresses at the business session were those by Clarence B. Hanson Jr., publisher of *The Birmingham News* and chairman of the SNPA Committee, on what Alabama's new $30 million newsprint mill at Childersburg would mean to the South and to Alabama publishers.

Ervin Jackson, president of the Birmingham Chamber of Commerce, spoke on "Alabama Trade Ship." Roy Hickman of Birmingham Engraving Co. spoke on the new color process used in the printing of the latest Birmingham promotion folders, and the use of special layouts by *The Mountain Eagle* of Jasper in increasing local advertising.

Hodding Carter Sr., Pulitzer Prize-winning editor of *The Greenville* (Miss.) *Delta Democrat-Times,* was headline speaker at the banquet. Officers and members of the Board of Governors of the Mississippi Press Association were special guests.

A resolution was adopted seeking greater recreational facilities within the state of Alabama in order that future summer conventions of the "Press Association and other state organizations could be held on home shores."

1948

E.H. (Ed) Pierce, *The Mountain Eagle,* Jasper
1948-1949 president

77th annual press convention, Birmingham
Feb. 13-14, 1948
Summer convention, Panama City, Fla.
July 23-24, 1948

"Most of you know about the high cost of living," *AlaPressa* reported in its Jan. 29, 1948, issue edited by acting APA field manager Norman H. Bassett. It was noted that registration to the 1948 winter convention would be $7.50, and the registration price would include one banquet ticket. "Even at this inflated figure, it looks like we'll have to dig down in the endowment fund for a couple hundred bucks to pay for the convention expenses," *AlaPressa* reported. "We hope this registration price will not keep anyone from attending the convention."

The 77th annual convention Feb. 13-14, 1948, at the Tutwiler Hotel in Birmingham featured addresses, panels and roundtable discussions.

SIDELIGHTS
MARKING 125 YEARS OF HISTORY

Ben Tucker likes suspension bill

Ben Tucker, publisher of *The Chilton County News* in Clanton, wrote in an editorial in 1957 that he liked a bill that had been introduced in Congress to permit weekly newspapers to suspend publication for two weeks each year without sacrificing second-class mailing privileges.

J.C. Henderson, publisher of *The Alexander City Outlook,* wrote in his column, the "News Crier," that he favored the bill, however "We at *The Outlook* do not plan to close down for two weeks or even one week, we hope."

The Birmingham News in its Feb. 11 edition reported that "approximately 200 weekly and daily newspaper publishers, and co-workers" were expected for the convention. "Advertising, editorials and promotions will be discussed." Victor Portman, field manager of the Kentucky Press Association, spoke on advertising, and Charles G. Dobbins, editor of *The Montgomery Examiner,* led a panel discussion on "Are Editorials Worth the Space?"

Members of the panel were Milton C. Giles, *The Franklin County Times,* Russellville; Jep Greer, *The Sylacauga News;* Glenn Stanley, *The Greenville Advocate;* and Col. Harry M. Ayers, *The Anniston Star.* Donald H. Hones, associate professor of the School of Journalism at the University of Missouri, addressed the group on "Building Advertising Volume." Harry S. Ashmore, editor of *The Arkansas Gazette* in Little Rock, was banquet speaker. Ashmore later was awarded a Pulitzer Prize.

George H. Watson of *The Shades Valley Sun,* Homewood, was chairman of the arrangements committee for the 1948 convention. Other members of the committee were Neil C. Cady, Western Newspaper Union, Birmingham; Roy Hickman, Alabama Engraving Co.; Martin Smith, Sparrow Advertising Agency; and Bernie Feld, *The Birmingham News* and *Age-Herald.*

Neil Davis appoints financial committee

A discussion of the financial affairs of APA was held at the 1948 convention. During the closing hours of the convention, the financial condition of the Press Association was thoroughly covered. Outgoing president Neil O. Davis of *The Lee County Bulletin* in Auburn appointed a committee to study the matter and report to the general assembly. The committee, after considerable discussion, recommended a small increase in dues, but admitted that the additional revenue the increase would provide was "pitifully inadequate."

On such short notice however, the committee refused to attempt to set up the budget, and recommended a small dues increase to produce the necessary revenue to carry on the much-needed activities.

The convention delegates refused to accept the recommendation of the committee and, after a lengthy discussion voted unanimously to charge the new Executive Committee with the responsibility of preparing a budget to cover the needed activities of the APA for 1948 and increasing the dues to cover the banquet.

Jasper's Ed Pierce reports to members

Incoming president E.H. (Ed) Pierce of *The Mountain Eagle* in Jasper reported to the members that "your Executive Committee was unanimous in the wish that this problem could have been solved in past years or passed on to future years. But the general assembly, realizing the imperative need for a strong APA, now placed the burden of this responsibility on their shoulders. With the able assistance of (acting field director) Norman Bassett they have worked hard. They investigated, discussed at length and discarded many plans and proposals until they finally agreed unanimously on the present budget and assessment."

At an executive meeting held in Birmingham in March, it was decided to increase the dues structure all the way down the line in order to meet a proposed budget of $11,400. The final revision of the dues structure was as follows:

Weeklies: 2.5 cents a subscriber, minimum $12, maximum $50; Associate Members: $25. Dailies under 10,000, $25; 10,000 to 49,000, $35; 50,000 to 149,999, $50; 150,000 and up, $75. The rates were substantially lower than those first recommended by the Executive Committee.

Reasons given for increasing APA dues

Reasons given for increasing the dues were: "(1) The field manager's need to travel the state so he can personally know more publishers and their local problems. (2) The field manager needs to keep abreast of developments in the newspaper and allied fields by attending meetings in other states, the region and the nation. (3) Competent help must be employed to carry on the more or less daily routine business while the field manager is away. (4) District meetings throughout the state should be revived. (5) Offer mechanical short courses and step up training for mechanical personnel. (6) Money was needed to provide funds for getting outstanding speakers for conventions and district meetings. (7) Publish a monthly publication devoted to ideas, techniques, problems and studies. (8) Maintain a library of books, magazines and other publications in the central office. (9) Foster research projects and activities. (10) Establish a strong Legislative Committee. (11) Continue the 'Alabama Unlimited' program. (12) Increase advertising placed through the APA."

S I D E L I G H T S
MARKING 125 YEARS OF HISTORY

Press day also "baby day" in Grove Hill
"Press day at *The Clarke County Democrat* in Grove Hill is also baby day," *The Alabama Publisher* reported in its October 1958 issue. "Babies born to members of the force seem to have an uncanny way of being born on Wednesday."

Democrat editor and publisher George A. Carleton wrote that "Buster Hall, our Linotype operator, has three children, two of whom were born on Wednesday, the other on Tuesday; Mike Williamson, our pressman and ad man, had one born on Wednesday; John McVay, who was with us until recently, had one born on Wednesday; and the writer has two, both born on Wednesday. Now comes our first grandchild, and he shows up on Tuesday morning. At first glance this would appear considerate on the part of the youngster, but the catch is that he is in Mobile, a distance of some 85 miles, and that the proud grandmother (and granddaddy) have to see him before the paper is out. This means a drive down to Mobile late Tuesday afternoon and a drive back to Grove Hill early Wednesday morning. So the timing of the press babies remains perfect — or does it?"

Some negative reactions were reported from the dues increase. Morgan Brassell of *The Etowah News-Journal* in Attalla wrote that when his current membership expired, he did not desire, nor could afford to continue membership.

"We have, like other county weeklies, been a member of the Association, and we have checked the cash register benefits derived therefrom. They have been practically nil," Brassell wrote. "To base Association dues upon the circulation of a newspaper is a very silly gauge line. Revenue from circulation would not pay for the white newsprint, let alone yield a profit. Apparently, Neil Davis, Gould Beech and other politicos holding offices or past officers are attempting to 'freeze out' the weeklies with an assessment increased from $12 to $99.12 annually. We refuse to be a party to it."

Formation of "Ladies of the Press Association" sought

Weekly publisher Mildred White Wallace of *The Shelby County Democrat* in Columbiana declared in part, "I attended one press conference some years ago and the Male Chorus was terrific — no problems confronting the 'Ladies of the Press', at the time numbering 28, were mentioned — and believe you me they have their problems. I advocated, along with other interested parties, the formation of a Ladies of the Press Association, but Mr. (Doyle) Buckles at that time did not see it so nothing was done about it. The overall program advocated by the Alabama Press as I see it pertains mostly to a larger field of operations than we cover out here."

Committee seeks successor to Buckles

APA president Neil Davis also appointed a committee to represent APA in finding a permanent successor to Doyle Buckles as field manager, secretary-treasurer of APA, instructor in the Department of Journalism, and director of the University News Bureau. Committee members included Davis, incoming APA president E.H. (Ed) Pierce of *The Mountain Eagle* in Jasper, Milton C. Giles of *The Franklin County Times* in Russellville, and James H. (Jimmy) Faulkner Sr. of *The Baldwin Times* in Bay Minette.

On April 9, 1948, the APA and the Associated Industries of Alabama held a joint luncheon at the Tutwiler Hotel in Birmingham. It was one of a series of conferences held by Associated Industries in its statewide public relations campaign of "Cooperation Through Understanding." The speaker was Kenneth Krawer, executive editor of *Business Week* magazine. Following the luncheon, editors and publishers were guests of the Birmingham Barons at an exhibition game between the Barons and the Boston Red Sox at Rickwood Field.

Heitman named APA field manager in 1948

First announcement to editors and publishers of the state that J. Russell Heitman of Lake Forest, Ill., would become field manager of APA was made in the confidential bulletin of the association, *AlaPressa*, on May 14, 1948. Heitman was completing requirements for his master's degree at Northwestern University, and he would begin work on July 1, 1948, *AlaPressa* reported.

AlaPressa described the new manager: "Russ has 20 years of bedrock background in the newspaper and publishing business which eminently qualifies him for the job and the work we believe can be done for our members. As a former owner and manager of a printing company, Russ knows the headaches and the angles of the production end of the business. He is a printer and has been successful in operating and publishing newspapers. He will be able to talk your language."

Through the cooperative agreement established by the University and APA in 1939, Heitman also was director of the News Bureau. But Heitman's work at the University was, for the most part, with APA. A request of long standing, that a full-time assistant be employed whose primary duties would be with the News Bureau, was fulfilled with the hiring of Heitman, when Norman H. Bassett was named associate director of the News Bureau in 1948. Bassett's appointment gave the News Bureau its first full-time assistant in its 20-year history.

S I D E L I G H T S
MARKING 125 YEARS OF HISTORY

Gov. Folsom buys interest in **Arab Journal**

Gov. James E. "Big Jim" Folsom purchased one-third interest in *The Arab Journal* in 1957, publisher Glenn Hewett announced in September.

Folsom's new interest was purchased from former owner Harry E. Black of Arab.

Heitman, Bassett visit newspapers in 1948

Shortly after Heitman joined APA in 1948, both he and Bassett visited daily and weekly newspaper offices in the pattern set years earlier by Buckles. By December 1948 they had visited eight daily newspapers and 43 weeklies in the state.

Clyde C. Lyon succeeded Neil C. Cady as manager of the Birmingham office of Western Newspaper Union in August 1948.

At least 127 newspapers, many of them small dailies and weeklies, were listed as stockholders in Coosa River Newsprint Co., which was building a mill near Childersburg. Clarence B. Hanson Jr., publisher of *The Birmingham News*, was chairman of the newsprint company of Southern Newspaper Publishers Association in charge of the project.

Alabama stockholders included *The Birmingham News*, Gadsden General Newspapers Inc., *The Mountain Eagle* in Jasper, *The Southern Farmer* in Montgomery, *The Tuscaloosa News*, Decatur Tennessee Valley Printing Co. Inc., Consolidated Publishing Co. in Anniston, Scripps Howard Supply Co. of Birmingham, Florence Tri-Cities Publishing Co., *The Dothan Eagle, The Huntsville Times, The Montgomery Examiner, The Selma Times-Journal,* and *The Montgomery Advertiser*.

Press Institute is revived in 1948 at UA

The APA Press Institute, last held at the University of Alabama in 1941, was revived in 1948.

Held at the University on May 21-22 in cooperation with the Department of Journalism and Extension Division, the institute was called the Doyle L. Buckles Memorial Press Institute in honor of APA's popular field manager who died the previous year. Students in the journalism department at the University prepared and edited a special University supplement edition of *The Tuscaloosa News* in honor of Buckles and the Press Institute.

The program included a welcome address by Dr. John M. Gallalee, University president; response by APA president E.H. (Ed) Pierce of *The Mountain Eagle* in Jasper; "Photo-engraving," by M.R. Ashworth of *The Columbus* (Ga.) *Ledger-Enquirer;* "Offset," by Rigby Owen of *The Opelousas* (La.) *Daily World;* "Alabama Unlimited," by John B. Turner, president of Associated Industries of Alabama in Birmingham; "Circulation, How to Build and Hold It," by Howe V. Morgan, publisher of *The Sparta* (Ill.) *News-Plaindealer* and James E. Pope, managing editor of *The Louisville* (Ky.) *Courier-Journal*.

"While we were a bit disappointed in the attendance for our first annual Doyle L. Buckles Press Institute last week, we feel that the program presented will do much to increase the crowd next year," *AlaPressa* reported in its May 27, 1948, issue. "The talks on the new printing methods were interesting and informative as was the session on circulation. We hope we can improve and expand the institute next year."

The Press Institute was not held again until spring 1950.

1948 summer convention, Panama City

The 1948 summer convention was at the Cove Hotel in Panama City July 23-24, with 55 delegates in attendance. Although most activities of the convention were recreational, Clarence B. Hanson Jr., publisher of *The Birmingham News*, reported that "the new $30 million Coosa River Paper Mill, now under construction at Childersburg, Alabama, is proceeding on schedule that officers saw no reason to deviate from their earlier forecast that the first newsprint would roll from the mill by January 1950."

The program, which APA president E.H. (Ed) Pierce of *The Mountain Eagle* in Jasper called a "grand success," included a moonlight cruise on the Gulf aboard a vessel furnished by Avondale Mills of Alabama. Members went deep sea fishing on Saturday.

1949
J.C. Henderson, *The Alexander City Outlook*
1949-1950 president

78th annual press convention, Birmingham
Jan. 21-22, 1949
Summer convention, Point Clear
Sept. 9-10, 1949

A group insurance plan for the weekly newspapers of the state was adopted at the 78th annual press convention, held at the Tutwiler Hotel in Birmingham Jan. 21-22, 1949. APA entered into an agreement with Employers Life Insurance Company, 2112 First Avenue North, Birmingham, by which individual members who wished a group insurance plan could participate in the program.

The official action of APA was that "Employers Life Insurance Company, through F.C. Moore, handle the program for individual publishers according to the plan and agreement signed by the insurance company and the Alabama Press Association. This official action is a recommendation and is not compulsory for all members of the Association."

1949 summer field trip

This photograph was made during a 1949 summer field trip to Lake Martin, according to J.C. Henderson, retired publisher of *The Alexander City Outlook*. From left, are Bonnie Hand, *The LaFayette Sun;* Ed Blair, *The Pell City News, The Leeds News* and *The Southern Aegis* at Ashville; Milton C. Giles, *The Franklin County Times,* Russellville; Bill Jones, who later served as press secretary to Gov. George C. Wallace; Steele McGrew, *The Alabama Courier* and *The Limestone Democrat,* Athens; Ed Pierce, *The Mountain Eagle,* Jasper; Russ Heitman, APA field manager from July 1, 1948, to September 1950; and J.C. Henderson, *The Alexander City Outlook.* (Photograph courtesy of J.C. Henderson)

Highlights of 1949 winter convention

Highlights of the 1949 winter convention included "Welcome to the Convention," by outgoing APA president E.H. (Ed) Pierce, editor of *The Mountain Eagle*, Jasper; "The New South," by Dr. James L. Brakefield, manager of the industrial division of the Birmingham Chamber of Commerce; "The Vari-Typed Newspaper" demonstration and explanation of the Vari-Typer machine by representatives of the Ralph C. Coxhead Corp.; "Rural Journalism — The Hope of the South," by James D. Arrington, publisher of "Mississippi's Most Quoted Newspaper," *The Collins News-Commercial* in Collins, Miss., and president of the Mississippi Press Association; "What Readers Want in News," by Victor R. Portmann, secretary-manager of the Kentucky Press Association; and "Alabama Press and Industry — A Winning Team," by Warren Whitney, vice president of James B. Clow and Sons, Birmingham, and director of the Associated Industries of Alabama.

Hal Boyle, Associated Press columnist from New York City, spoke at the winter convention. *AlaPressa* reported that Boyle would remain in Alabama a few days after the convention "gathering material and writing activities about the state."

The Necrology Committee reported that "only one death occurred among the newspaper fraternity in 1948, Frank Nunnelee, founder and former publisher of *The Montgomery Weekly.*"

Luncheon tickets to the 1949 winter convention were $1.75, and banquet tickets were $3.50, *AlaPressa* reported.

An open house and machinery exhibit was held at Western Newspaper Union in Birmingham. All members and spouses attending the 1949 convention were issued special guest cards by the Down Town Club, Birmingham's newspaper and radio organization.

The Alabama Publisher established in 1949

Early in 1949 a new publication, *The Alabama Publisher*, was established by field manager J. Russell Heitman. In 1996 *The Alabama Publisher* was published twice each year as a winter and summer press convention tabloid newspaper. Three 16-page issues of *The Alabama Publisher* were published in 1949. Heitman also edited and issued 45 issues of *AlaPressa* in 1949. In the first issue of *The Alabama Publisher*, Heitman answered those who had complained about the dues increase in a succinct statement of the advantages of being a member of the Alabama Press Association:

"The Alabama Press Association serves the newspapers of this state, members and non-members alike, in many other ways. Some of these services are apparent and directly beneficial — others are not apparent, and their benefits are indirect. During 1949, the Alabama Press Association will continue to function as a general advertising representative for all weekly newspapers in the state that desire this service.

"The Association through its secretary's office and special committees, aids many publishers each year with their problems, pertaining to legal matters, employment, circulation, advertising, equipment, and office methods. And there are other reasons why the Alabama publisher will benefit by membership in the Alabama Press Association:

"In union there is strength.

"You need the help of a strong state press association during these times to help you meet the rapid changes taking place in America.

"Anti-newspaper legislation is a threat to the liberty not only of the press, but to all free Americans. Only strong state press associations can represent the newspaper industry in opposing this threat.

"Pride in one's profession should incline him to support his professional organization.

"Friendship with fellow editors and publishers, promoted through your state press association, is worth more than dollars can measure.

"Actually, the Alabama Press Association operates on a very small budget, and yet, without the Association, many thousands of dollars would be lost to the newspapers of the state."

Heitman also pointed out the value of the information to be gained at the APA conventions and workshops, and the value of *AlaPressa*.

S I D E L I G H T S
MARKING 125 YEARS OF HISTORY

Newspaper gives away new Buick

The *South Alabamian* in Jackson gave away a new 1957 Buick as a climax of a seven-week circulation campaign.

Publisher Fred Nall commented, "The addition of several hundred names to our mailing list extends our service to a much larger number of people in the Jackson trade area, and we will be able to have a much improved *South Alabamian* as a result." Second prize was a $750 check.

Three district meetings were held during 1949. William M. (Bill) Stewart of *The Monroe Journal* in Monroeville and James H. (Jimmy) Faulkner Sr. of *The Baldwin Times* in Bay Minette were hosts to a meeting at Monroeville Saturday, July 30. The press group met at the office of *The Monroe Journal*, visited the newspaper plant, had a fried chicken dinner at the Williams Cafe, and were guests of Bill Stewart and Jimmy Faulkner at a watermelon cutting. APA president J.C. Henderson of *The Alexander City Outlook* presided.

APA tours *Mountain Eagle* plant in Jasper

Past APA president E.H. (Ed) Pierce gave 32 editors and publishers a tour of his plant at *The Mountain Eagle* in Jasper, and APA president J.C. Henderson of *The Alexander City Outlook* presided at a roundtable discussion. The publishers had dinner at the Jasper Hotel.

L.O. Brackeen, director of publicity at Alabama Polytechnic Institute, Auburn, and Neil O. Davis, publisher of *The Lee County Bulletin*, Auburn, were hosts to a district meeting at Auburn after a tour of the plant at *The Lee County Bulletin*. The discussion sessions were held on the Auburn campus. A luncheon was held at the Women's Quadrangle

on the Alabama Polytechnic Institute campus, and APA members were guests at the Auburn-Alabama freshman football game in the afternoon.

Ed Bounds represents APA at annual meeting

Professor C.E. (Ed) Bounds of the University of Alabama Department of Journalism represented APA at the annual meeting of the Missouri Press Association at the University of Missouri in May 1949.

The Alabama Tuberculosis Association in 1949 cited members of the APA for their participation in the campaign against tuberculosis and support of the Christmas Seal campaign for 40 years. On Nov. 16, 1949, the Tuberculosis Association paid tribute to Alabama newspapers in the following resolution presented to past APA president E.H. (Ed) Pierce, publisher of *The Mountain Eagle* in Jasper, by Roy Hickman, president of the Tuberculosis Association:

"To the newspapers of Alabama, participants in the founding of the campaign against tuberculosis in this state; generous always through these forty years in their gifts of time and space and talent to the support of the Christmas Seal Sale; to the people of Alabama in their efforts to leave better more abundant health for their children; the greater appreciation of the Alabama Tuberculosis Association, its affiliation associations, and all those they have served, is extended this 16th day of November, 1949."

Alabamians attend NEA convention in Chicago

Three Alabama publishers, one associate member of the APA, and the APA field manager attended the annual National Editorial Association's fall convention in Chicago. The Alabama delegates were Mr. and Mrs. J.C. Henderson, *The Alexander City Outlook;* Mr. and Mrs. E.H. (Ed) Pierce, *The Mountain Eagle*, Jasper; and William G. Jones Jr., *The Valley Tribune* and *Chattahoochee Valley Times*, Lanett; L.O. Brackeen, director of publicity, Alabama Polytechnic Institute, Auburn; and J. Russell Heitman, APA secretary-field manager.

Meeting in Montgomery on Saturday, April 9, 1949, the Executive Committee set Nov. 18 and 19, 1949, as the dates for the second annual Doyle L. Buckles Memorial Press Institute, but at the summer outing at Grand Hotel, Point Clear, the institute was postponed until May 19-20, 1950.

The Executive Committee went on record in 1949 as favoring continuation of the Division of Records and Reports of the state administration, "inasmuch as it is performing a worthwhile information service for the press, particularly the weekly press, of the state."

S I D E L I G H T S
MARKING 125 YEARS OF HISTORY

Cox: "Difficult to obtain newspaper help"

Former APA president George M. Cox of The Mobile Press Register addressed the 21st annual conference of the Alabama High School Press Association at the University of Alabama in 1958 and noted that it had become "difficult to obtain competent newspaper help."

"Of all the crafts and the arts, the newspaper industry has failed most miserably in that it has neglected in the past to sell itself as a stable and successful area of employment for the youth of the nation," Cox told the students. "Never in many years have editors noticed such a scarcity of competent help. At its lowest point, the situation was such that we were ready to hire as a reporter any able-bodied person who could distinguish night from day, speak the English language and make change for a quarter."

1949 summer convention, Point Clear

AlaPressa reported that 99 delegates attended the 1949 summer convention Sept. 9-10, 1949, at the Grand Hotel at Point Clear in Baldwin County. The agenda included a tour of the Mobile waterfront in a boat provided by Waterman Steamship Co., which also was host to a cocktail party and seafood dinner. The delegates toured Bellingrath Gardens, where they were guests of Walter B. Bellingrath.

The summer convention was "all play and no work," according to *AlaPressa*. "Those present were pleased with the facilities and service of the Grand Hotel, and many have expressed a desire to return to Point Clear for the 1950 summer meeting."

APA moves from
Union Building to Clark Hall

APA and the News Bureau were located in the Union Building when the University of Alabama began the cooperative agreement with the Press Association in 1939. Approximately three times the space held in the Union Building was made available in 1949 to APA and the News Bureau. University of Alabama president Dr. John M. Gallalee had notified field manager Russ Heitman on Oct. 9, 1948, that the request for new quarters had been granted

and Fred R. Maxwell Jr., consulting engineer, had informed Heitman that the new APA-News Bureau quarters would be ready for occupancy in Clark Hall sometime about March 1, 1949.

Clark Hall was being renovated in the fall of 1948. When that work was completed, offices were moved from the Union Building to the fourth floor of Clark Hall. In Clark Hall, APA occupied Room 403 and part of Room 402. The News Bureau occupied Room 401 and part of Room 402.

APA later moved to Manly Hall, where it was located in 1973 when the Press Association moved off the University of Alabama campus.

1950
Edmund R. (Ed) Blair, *The Pell City News* and *Southern Aegis*, Ashville
1950-1951 president

79th annual press convention, Montgomery
Feb. 9-11, 1950
Summer convention, Biloxi, Miss.
Aug. 4-5, 1950

The Lee County Bulletin in Auburn won a national award in 1950 for the best editorial in a weekly newspaper. The contest was sponsored by the National Editorial Association.

Pearl and Bonnie Hand
Lafayette Sun publisher Bonnie D. Hand and his wife Pearl were extremely involved in APA activities. This photograph of the Hands was probably taken in the early 1940s, according to their son, Mike Hand. At that time, *The Sun* was located across the street from its 1996 location. (Photograph courtesy of Mike Hand, *The LaFayette Sun*)

Judges said of the winning editorial: *"The Lee County Bulletin* of Auburn, Ala., deserved to win for the clear and well written editorial campaign which it carried on to repeal the poll tax and to break down the restrictions used to keep Negroes from voting. In its intelligent approach to working out better community understanding of the Negro in its midst, it did not resort to polemics, but placed its approval on the basis of American justice." The National Editorial Association presented a trophy to Neil and Henrietta Davis.

250 delegates attend 1950 convention

The 79th annual convention at the Whitley Hotel and Jefferson Davis Hotel in Montgomery Feb. 9-11, 1950, was attended by 250 APA delegates. Registration to the convention was $3.50, according to *AlaPressa.* Luncheon tickets were $1.75, and banquet tickets were $3.75.

Featured speaker was Oveta Culp Hobby, executive vice president of *The Houston* (Texas) *Post* and chairman of the board of Southern Newspaper Publishers Association. Mrs. Hobby was wife of W.P. Hobby, former governor of Texas.

Other speakers included:

W. Frank Aycock Jr., advertising director of *The Birmingham News* and *Age-Herald;* Ralph W. Callahan, business manager of *The Anniston Star;* the Honorable Robert B. Carr of the Court of Appeals, state of Alabama; Neil O. Davis, *The Lee County Bulletin,* Auburn; Mayor John L. Goodwyn of Montgomery; Jep V. Greer, *The Sylacauga News;* Floyd L. Hockenhull, publisher of *Circulation Management Magazine;* R.F. Hudson Jr., *The Montgomery Advertiser* and *Alabama Journal;* Glenn Jones, *The Troy Messenger-Herald;* Bob Kyle, *The Tuscaloosa News;* Jack Langhorne, *The Huntsville Times;* Dorothy Marr, *The Moulton Advertiser;* William Stephenson Jr., *The Valley Tribune* and *Chattahoochee Valley Times,* Lanett; Bill Stewart, *The Monroe Journal,* Monroeville; Joseph G. Terry, Wolf and Company, Certified Public Accounts and Management Consultants; and Alex Thomson, *The Talladega News.*

S I D E L I G H T S
MARKING 125 YEARS OF HISTORY

The Elba Clipper *began publication in 1897*

The Elba Clipper published a story in November 1958 detailing the newspaper's early beginning with a hand press which was lugged across a newly built bridge. The story was told by E.G. Peacock, a 72-year-old resident of Coffee County, who said he heard the tale from a Confederate veteran named Green Fowler at a veterans reunion.

According to Peacock, the paper began publication in 1897 when a new bridge was being built across the Pea River on the present Highway 84. The bridge was not yet ready for horses and wagons, but the scaffolding had been built and a walkway was erected for pedestrians. This apparently did not deter Malcolm Carmichael who walked across carrying a hand-operated press and a suitcase with all the other type and material he needed. The first issue, according to the Confederate veteran, was printed on red paper.

Coffee County had a number of newspapers published through the years in Enterprise and Elba. *The Coffee County News,* a weekly, was being published in Elba in 1890, but its date of first publication is not known. The first newspaper in Enterprise was *The Weekly Enterprise,* first printed by Sam Powell, followed by Ed M. Johnson and G.W. Carlisle. After Johnson purchased *The Weekly Enterprise,* its name was changed to *The People's Ledger.*

The Enterprise Ledger was founded in 1898. Owners included J.A. Carnley, R.H. Arrington, Grover C. Hall Sr., Lane Amman, J.H. Singleton, Carnegie Thomas, Clark Edwards, Carmage Walls, Manny Segall, and Walls Newspapers Inc. *The Enterprise Ledger* was a weekly from 1898 until Sept. 12, 1961, when it became a semiweekly.

At one time before World War I, Enterprise had a daily newspaper. A "Dr. Harrison" started *The Enterprise Journal,* a weekly, in competition with *The Enterprise Ledger.* I.B. Hilson purchased *The Enterprise Journal* from Harrison and converted the newspaper into a daily which discontinued publication after about four months.

Delegates tour *Advertiser-Journal* editorial rooms

All daytime sessions of the winter convention were at the Jefferson Davis Hotel, and the annual banquet was at the Whitley Hotel. In addition to the formal convention program, delegates visited *The Montgomery Advertiser* and *Alabama Journal* editorial rooms, the Agricultural Coliseum, W. "Camelia" Stokes Nursery, and Maxwell Air Force Base. They were guests of Gov. and Mrs. James E. Folsom for a buffet luncheon and reception at the executive mansion.

In charge of the 1950 convention were Charles G. Dobbins, *The Montgomery Examiner*, chairman; Bonnie D. Hand, *The LaFayette Sun;* Hunter H. Golson, *The Wetumpka Herald;* APA president J.C. Henderson, *The Alexander City Outlook;* and APA secretary-field manager J. Russell Heitman.

A resolution at the 1950 convention recommended to the president and board of trustees of the University of Alabama that the "present department of journalism at the school be designated and organized as a separate and autonomous school of journalism and that the secretary-manager of the Press Association be appointed a member of the staff of the school of journalism and that he divide his time between Press Association duties and instruction of journalism students."

Doyle Buckles Memorial Press Institute held in 1950

The theme of the Doyle L. Buckles Memorial Press Institute at the University of Alabama, May 19-20, 1950, was "Building Alabama." Four speakers appeared on the program.

Channing Cope, agricultural writer for *The Atlanta Constitution*, discussed the role of agriculture in the South; John M. Ward, executive vice president of the Alabama State Chamber of Commerce, stressed the need of improvement and promotion of tourist facilities in Alabama; Hugh P. Bigler, past president of the Associated Industries of Alabama, discussed the role of industry; and H.R. Long, former secretary-manager of the Missouri Press Association and newly appointed dean of the University of South Carolina School of Journalism, discussed the role of newspapers in building a state.

Alabama newspaper men were welcomed by University of Alabama president Dr. John M. Gallalee, Extension Division dean R.E. Tidwell, and Martin ten Hoor, dean of the College of Arts and Sciences. Professor C.E. (Ed) Bounds, head of the University of Alabama's Department of Journalism, conducted the Press Institute sessions and

---

> **S I D E L I G H T S**
> MARKING 125 YEARS OF HISTORY
>
> ***Ayers: Saw my first "printer's louse" at age 10***
> Col. Harry M. Ayers, editor and publisher of *The Anniston Star*, was featured in the April 19, 1958, issue of *Publishers' Auxiliary.* "I saw my first 'printer's louse' in the office of *The Jacksonville* (Ala.) *Republican* when I was ten years old," Ayers said.
> "My father sold that old pre-War-Between-the States weekly and moved to Anniston, where he bought *The Daily Hot Blast,* so named by Henry Grady as being symbolical of a furnace town," Ayers told *Publishers' Auxiliary.*

explained details of the Alabama Industry Days Promotion on June 15-17, 1950.

The Press Institute apparently was not held after 1950.

Two district meetings held in 1950

Two district meetings were held in 1950, one at Gadsden and one in Huntsville. The first district meeting was on Saturday, April 22, at Gadsden.

Weekly and daily publishers met at 11 a.m. in the editorial department on the second floor of *The Gadsden Times* for an informal inspection of *The Times* plant, guided by Curtis Delamar, publisher, and Carl Hofferbert, editor. A dutch treat dinner at the Reich Hotel was held at 1 p.m., followed by an afternoon roundtable discussion. The group then inspected the printing department of the Alabama School of Trades in Gadsden, under the guidance of John E. Fortin, director of the school, and W.G. (Chief) Galloway, in charge of printing instruction.

The second district meeting was in Huntsville on Oct. 20 with 24 editors and publishers in attendance. The day's activities started with a tour of *The Huntsville Times* printing department, inspection of the Fairchild engraver in operation, and close inspection of the teletype setters in operation. *The Huntsville Times* sponsored a luncheon at Russel Erskine Hotel. In the afternoon the APA members toured Redstone Arsenal.

The 1950 summer convention was Friday and Saturday, Aug. 4-5, at the Buena Vista Hotel in

Biloxi, Miss. It was a "play and recreation" session, with no formal program and no scheduled meeting with the exception of a Friday night banquet at the Buena Vista, *AlaPressa* reported. Room rates for the convention, for two persons per room, were $6, $6.50, $7.50, $8 and $9. "All rates are based on the European plan — meals are extra and may be taken in the Buena Vista dining room or elsewhere," according to *AlaPressa*.

Heitman resigns as field manager in 1950

Besides directing increased activity in the APA during 1948-1949 and 1949-1950 as indicated in annual reports to Dr. R.E. Tidwell, dean of the Extension Division at the University of Alabama, field manager Russ Heitman was also teaching courses in the Department of Journalism in newspaper production and business management of newspapers.

Heitman decided in spring 1950 to take an appointment as director of the Department of Journalism at Texas Technological College in Lubbock, Texas, effective Sept. 1, 1950. Duties of the replacement for Heitman were set forth by Tidwell.

Besides having "overall supervision of the publicity staff" of the University of Alabama, the field manager was to "assist in general counseling and planning long range public relations programs of the institution." A second duty outlined was that of assistant professor in the Department of Journalism, teaching one three-hour course each semester. The course was designed for graduating seniors and was to deal with "business management, sources of revenue, circulation areas served, mechanics, physical problems, state and federal laws and regulations, and any other factors affecting the publishing of weekly newspapers."

Tidwell outlined broadly the duties of the APA field manager: "General advisement and guidance for the state papers, with special attention to the weekly field; maintenance of office records of the Alabama Press Association; planning and directing quarterly regional workshops in advertising, management, circulation for APA members; planning and organizing an annual mid-winter business meeting of APA members; planning and or-

---

S I D E L I G H T S
MARKING 125 YEARS OF HISTORY

Hands announce birth of daughter
Publisher and Mrs. Bonnie D. Hand of *The LaFayette Sun* announced the birth of a daughter, Bonnie Bronwyn, on June 24, 1950, at Wheeler Hospital in LaFayette.

---

ganizing an annual mid-summer recreational meeting for members."

Jack Beisner named field manager in 1950

A faculty committee as well as the APA board of directors interviewed applicants during the summer of 1950 and voted to employ Ernest Bronwin (Jack) Beisner. Announcement was made at the 1950 summer convention in Biloxi of the appointment of Beisner, editor of *The Custer County Chief* at Broken Bow, Neb., as the new secretary-field manager.

Beisner, 29, was a native of Illinois. An experienced newspaper man, Beisner had been involved in journalism as a teenager when he worked as a junior high school stringer for *The St. Louis Post-Dispatch*. Beisner earned a double major in political science and journalism from the University of Illinois and had edited two weeklies in Wyoming, Ill., *The Princeville Telegraph* and *The Wyoming Herald*.

Beisner taught journalism and instituted agricultural journalism and community newspaper programs at the University of Nebraska in Lincoln before joining the paper in Broken Bow.

Norman Bassett resigned in September 1950, shortly after Beisner arrived at APA. Bassett had received a favorable offer from *The Tuscaloosa News* as its news editor at an increased salary. Two recent University of Alabama graduates were hired to replace Bassett. John Hamner on Oct. 1, 1950, came from Anniston where he had been acting managing editor of *The Anniston Star*, and William Bates, a Tuscaloosa native, returned to Tuscaloosa Sept. 15, 1950, from a position as editor of *The Troy Messenger*. Both served as assistant directors of the News Bureau.

CHAPTER 6

More Involvement by Daily Newspapers

1951-1970

"No one would attempt to publish any kind of newspaper now without a Linotype, but it was done for many years before Mr. Mergenthaler invented this type-setting and type-casting machine.

Glenn Stanley
The Greenville Advocate

"In my lifetime I have seen the office change from a hand-operated printing shop to a mechanized shop. We now have individual motors for everything in the shop, from the adding machine to the big press. There is even a motor in the water cooler, and electrical energy to operate the timer in the darkroom and the clock on the wall.

"There are electric heaters to melt metal in the Linotype machine and the stereotype caster, the mat caster, and the stylus in the engraving machine. There are electric motors in the butane heaters. There are at least 15 motors, not counting the 10 in the electric fans and the two in the heaters.

"The world has come a long way since this newspaper came out with its first edition, but we seriously doubt that this Number 1 of Volume 90 is an improvement over Number 1 of Volume 1.

"It employs modern methods, but it's the printed word that makes the difference, not how it is produced."

–J. Glenn Stanley, 1894-1967
Editor, The Greenville Advocate
APA president, 1963-1964
(From an editorial written on the 90th anniversary of
The Greenville Advocate, *November 1954)*

SOME MAJOR ISSUES THAT OTHER STATE newspaper associations struggled with for years were largely settled and set aside during the first convention in Montgomery in 1872 of the Alabama Press Association.

From its founding, APA was an organization that represented interests of both the news-editorial function of a newspaper as well as the business function. Both editors and publishers participated in the Press Association, and both were represented in the leadership. APA was an organization of both dailies and weeklies from the start, although daily newspaper membership and participation waned in the 1920s and 1930s. Daily newspaper involvement in APA grew with the hiring of a full-time field manager and establishment of a central office in 1939 — particularly in the late 1940s and early 1950s.

Comparing the APA of the 1990s with the Press Association of the 1930s, 1941-1942 APA president James H. (Jimmy) Faulkner, Sr., retired publisher of *The Baldwin Times* in Bay Minette, recalled in 1995: "It is no comparison. The association was small and most of the publishers were poor. We didn't even have a secretary. The Western Newspaper Union out of Birmingham kind of sponsored it and kept it together," Faulkner, 79, said.

J.C. Henderson, 91, retired publisher of *The Alexander City Outlook,* recalled in 1995 that the Press Association was "pretty small" when he was president in 1949-1950. "It was more or less a struggle in those days," Henderson said. "We were just getting over the war and all that. Most of the papers were small and not as lucrative as in the

1990s. You couldn't get the money that you can now for advertising." Henderson, who was still attending APA conventions in 1996, said he has seen the Press Association grow and the quality of the state's papers improve since those days.

Ben G. George, publisher of *The Demopolis Times* and APA president in 1956-1957, recalled in a 1991 interview in *The Alabama Publisher* that the APA in the 1950s was "below what it is now. We had a time keeping folks together," the 85-year-old George recalled. "I don't think our dues were but a dollar a month. Even so, we didn't have many members." George died in 1993.

More participation in APA by daily papers

Starting with the election of Clarence B. Hanson Jr. of *The Birmingham News* as APA president, and establishment of Alabama Newspaper Advertising Service in 1951, followed by the Clipping Bureau, the 1950s saw increased participation by daily newspapers. APA represented the interests of the full range of paid-circulation newspapers in Alabama from the largest metropolitan daily to the smallest-circulation weekly. The APA presidency was rotated each year between weeklies and dailies.

As APA became more professional, convention programs dealt with both the news and business functions.

Ayers editorializes on APA's changing nature

Col. Harry M. Ayers, publisher of *The Anniston Star,* editorialized in 1949 on the changing nature of the Press Association after attending the winter convention that year. Ayers served two terms as president of APA, in 1915-1916 and 1916-1917.

"To an old timer who has been connected with the Alabama Press Association, which is composed primarily of editors and publishers of weekly newspapers, for more years than he is willing to admit, the state convention that was held in Birmingham last week was most reassuring," Ayers wrote in the 1949 editorial. "In the old days, the APA met primarily for the purpose of fellowship. And the prevailing note in the conventions was one of mutual commiseration. But not so today, for now the weekly editor evinces a pride in his profession and is thereby able to command respect from the clientele which he serves."

Ayers also noted that "It is a pleasure to note that Clarence Hanson of *The Birmingham News* is first vice president this year."

Veteran APA leaders recalled in 1995 interviews that Clarence B. Hanson Jr., publisher of *The Birmingham News,* definitely helped change the Press Association's membership makeup in the 1950s as it evolved to become an organization of both daily and weekly newspapers. It was in 1951 while Hanson was APA president that Alabama Newspaper Advertising Service Inc., was inaugurated. ANAS in

Clarence B. Hanson Jr.
The Birmingham News

1951 and the Clipping Bureau in 1952 were steps forward in the growth and financial strength of the Press Association.

James H. (Jimmy) Faulkner Sr. of Bay Minette, was 24 when he served as APA president in 1941-1942 and is thought to be the youngest president in the history of the Press Association. Faulkner served on the 1939 committee that established the field manager system with headquarters on the University of Alabama campus.

Faulkner: Hanson involvement changed APA image

In a 1995 interview, Faulkner, 79, said that Hanson's serving as president in 1951-1952 and *The Birmingham News'* involvement in APA did much to change the image of the Press Association. "I insisted that Clarence Hanson serve on the APA board of directors," Faulkner recalled. "That got the dailies involved in APA. Jimmy Mills (editor of the *Birmingham Post-Herald* and 1960-1961 president) became active too; he was one of the few big editors involved. Largely due to Mills and

Hanson, all the dailies got interested in the Press Association."

William E. (Bill) Brooks Jr., former managing editor of the weekly *Brewton Standard,* headed APA's Legislative Committee during much of the early 1950s. Brooks, APA president in 1953-1954, recalled his presidency and legislative involvement in 1995 interviews, and noted two personal contributions "which do not show up on the legislative record."

"I convinced Clarence Hanson that it was in the interest of *The Birmingham News* to take an active part in the Press Association," the 73-year-old Brooks recalled in 1995. "And I refused to alter the succession to the presidency when the more politically-active liberal publishers wanted to bounce Ben George (of *The Demopolis Times*) in favor of someone who would be more in tune with Gov. Jim Folsom during his second reign."

For years, the Alabama Press Association represented weekly newspapers of the state, while daily newspapers primarily participated in the Alabama Associated Press.

Brooks: Large dailies "kind of kissed off the APA"

Before Hanson's and *The Birmingham News'* involvement in APA in the early 1950s, the larger dailies "kind of kissed off the APA," Brooks recalled in the 1995 interview. "They were too big for us. To them, APA was just a bunch of country weeklies. Daily newspapers for a long time said we were country printers, not big-time newspaper folks. They didn't want to be bothered with APA."

"Education of the weekly editors and involvement of the dailies and the money they provided is what really changed the APA," 89-year-old Ralph W. Callahan of Consolidated Publishing Co. in Anniston said in a 1995 interview. Callahan, still actively working at Consolidated Publishing in 1996, was APA president in 1965-1966.

"I've been a member of the APA since 1967, and I can honestly say that the quality of the APA and every newspaper in the state has improved," Pat McCauley, retired editor of *The Huntsville Times,* said in 1990 at APA's winter convention in Auburn. "The Press Association should take full credit on the improvement of all the Alabama newspapers. The APA has transformed from a trade organization to a professional organization who wants quality in all their work."

Davis: APA focus began broadening in late 1940s

The Lee County Bulletin's Neil O. Davis, APA president in 1947-1948, recalled in a 1995 interview that the focus of the Press Association broadened in the late 1940s to include more emphasis on the editorial product. "Too few of the community newspapers in the state even had editorial pages in the 1930s," Davis said. "The editors, many of whom were printers first, were more interested in finding out how to sell ads and how to sell subscriptions. There was not much attention given to the news and editorial side," Davis, 81, recalled.

Alabama's community newspapers in the early 1930s "had no sense of leading, of leadership," Davis said. "They didn't want to offend anybody with opinions, and most newspapers didn't even have editorial pages. It was only in about the mid-1930s that it came into vogue to be bold enough to take sides on an issue or to suggest something be done in the community."

Davis said he worked at getting the daily newspapers more active in the Press Association during his year as president in 1947-1948. Hodding Carter Sr., Pulitzer Prize-winning editor of *The Greenville* (Miss.) *Delta Democrat-Times,* was headline speaker at the 1947 summer convention banquet.

"That drew a number of daily editors who wanted to be associated with a Pulitzer Prize-winning editor," Davis recalled.

S I D E L I G H T S
MARKING 125 YEARS OF HISTORY

Kitten causes commotion at Times-Journal

"A blue-eyed little beauty with a yellow crown" wandered into the office at *The Selma Times-Journal* in October 1958 and created quite a bit of concern until staff members began to devise ways of caring for the tiny kitten.

A drawer was cleaned out of the "lost and found" desk, and it was padded with old newspapers for a bed. Soon, by remarkable coincidence, along came the kitten's owners, Mrs. Frank Rosser and her 13-year-old son, who stopped at the lost and found desk to advertise.

The grateful owners named the kitten "Type" in recognition of the hometown press.

1951
Clarence B. Hanson Jr., *The Birmingham News*
1951-1952 president

80th annual press convention, Birmingham
Jan. 26-27, 1951
Summer convention, Mobile
June 21-23, 1951

Delegates attending the 80th annual APA convention Jan. 26-27, 1951, at the Tutwiler Hotel in Birmingham approved two measures designed to put the Press Association on a modern basis and allow it to increase its benefits to members. The first step was approval of a revised constitution.

The second step was approval of a recommendation from the Executive Committee to establish a three-person committee to take whatever steps were necessary to incorporate a profit-making business affiliate to handle intrastate advertising for APA members. Glenn McNeil, manager of the Tennessee Press Association and Tennessee Press Service Inc., explained to convention delegates how the business affiliate had worked successfully in that state, and he answered questions on the workings of the business affiliate and the manner in which it handled advertising orders for the state's newspapers.

Upon motion of E.H. (Ed) Pierce, *The Mountain Eagle,* Jasper, and seconded by Bonnie D. Hand, *The LaFayette Sun,* the following resolution was adopted: "The Executive Committee recommends to the Convention that it authorize the president to appoint a committee of three to take such steps as may be necessary to organize and incorporate a business affiliate."

On the final day of the 1951 winter convention, incoming APA president Clarence B. Hanson

---

SIDELIGHTS
MARKING 125 YEARS OF HISTORY

Newspapers support Stevenson in 1952
Alabama newspapers gave Adlai Stevenson and the Democratic ticket slightly heavier editorial support than they gave Republican Dwight Eisenhower in the 1952 presidential election. Twenty one weeklies and seven dailies supported Stevenson, and 14 weeklies and eight dailies supported Eisenhower.

Jr., publisher of *The Birmingham News,* named a committee to establish a business affiliate for APA. Members of the committee as incorporators for the affiliate, Alabama Newspaper Advertising Service Inc. (ANAS), were E.H. (Ed) Pierce, *The Mountain Eagle,* Jasper, president; Bonnie D. Hand, *The LaFayette Sun,* vice president; and Edmund R. (Ed) Blair, *The Pell City News-Aegis,* secretary-treasurer.

ANAS officers entered an agreement with field manager Jack Beisner to serve as ANAS manager and assistant secretary-treasurer. ANAS has been in operation since it was incorporated Feb. 12, 1951.

ANAS begins operation in spring 1951
Alabama Newspaper Advertising Service went into operation in the spring of 1951. *AlaPressa* reported that objectives of the new affiliate of APA were to "make it advantageous and attractive to advertisers to use Alabama newspapers; to service advertising from these advertisers in such a manner as to cut down servicing costs to the newspapers receiving such advertising; to assist advertisers using Alabama newspapers in getting better results from their advertising and to increase that advertising; and finally and most important, to give an operating basis upon which efforts could be made to help originate new advertising for Alabama newspapers."

ANAS began handling newspaper advertising service orders on April 1, 1951. ANAS started with the small business that was already being serviced by the Press Association. ANAS started out slowly handling existing NEA accounts and originating only two small new accounts, but building up operating capital by handling NEA business. "Advertisers and agencies were leery of ANAS because the Press Association had let them down before," *AlaPressa* reported.

Officers approve incorporation of APA
Following a board of directors meeting, officers were authorized to incorporate APA as a non-profit association under the laws of the state of Alabama. The application for incorporation was filed by field manager Jack Beisner in the Tuscaloosa County probate office on Feb. 26, 1951, one month after the action was authorized by APA members at their 80th annual convention in Birmingham.

Outgoing APA president Edmund R. (Ed) Blair of *The Pell City News-Aegis* at Ashville announced to winter convention delegates that the Executive Committee had approved a new contract between APA and the University of Alabama.

He explained that the new contract would allow the manager more free time for APA work and eliminate his teaching duties.

Blair extended congratulations from the Press Association to Neil O. Davis, *The Lee County Bulletin,* Auburn, and Charles G. Dobbins, *The Montgomery Examiner,* on their appointments to state boards and their confirmation by the Senate. Davis was appointed to the state Board of Pardons and Paroles, and Dobbins was named to the state Board of Education.

At a closed session, the use-tax was discussed. It was generally agreed that APA should do all it could to help the situation and have its action dependent upon circumstances surrounding the case already in court.

Birmingham Mayor Cooper Green welcomed APA delegates to the city and offered them the services and facilities of Birmingham during their stay.

Knighton conducts session on machinery care

William Knighton, production manager of *The Birmingham News,* conducted a session on "Machinery Procurement, Care and Outlook." Representatives of the supply organizations were given the opportunity to give reports.

"Reports of suppliers were similar in that they all urged Alabama newspapers to take good care of the equipment they had in view of possible wartime shortages, to have repair and replacement parts handy, and invited them to order if necessary, but not to accumulate surplus stocks of equipment," *AlaPressa* reported. "Proper care of existing equipment was stressed."

Edmund R. (Ed) Blair of *The Pell City News-Aegis* gave programs on "Revised Association Constitution" and "Home Training of Mechanical Employees." W.W. Cross, sales manager of Coosa River Newsprint Co. at Coosa Pines, Ala., gave a report on the newsprint supplies over the country and described the Coosa operation. Atomic energy and the implications of atomic warfare was the topic of a talk by Dr. M.D. Peterson of Vanderbilt University titled, "What is Atomic Energy?"

Dr. Eric Rodgers of the University of Alabama and Dr. Fred Allison of Alabama Polytechnic Institute, Auburn, discussed "Problems Likely to be Encountered by Civilian Population in Atomic Energy."

A panel on "Necessity for Extensive, Careful News Coverage, Local, State, National, International, In Emergency Period" included Bill Stewart, *The Monroe Journal,* Monroeville, moderator; Robert C. Miller, United Press International correspondent; Howe V. Morgan, editor and publisher of *The Sparta* (Ill.) *News-Plain Dealer;* George M. Cox, executive editor of *The Mobile Press Register;* and John Hill, reporter, *The Monroe Journal* in Monroeville and *The Frisco City Sun.*

During 1951 *The Alabama Publisher* was changed from a quarterly to a monthly publication.

Brundidge Sentinel sold to Glenn Jones in 1951

The Brundidge Sentinel, published by R.L.S. (Bob) Bickford, was sold to Glenn Jones, publisher of *The Troy Messenger,* in 1951.

The first issue of the new publication, *The Pike County Sentinel,* appeared March 8, 1951. Bickford said he would continue to publish *The Crenshaw County Banner* in Luverne from the Brundidge plant, as well as *The Hobby Sentinel,* a stamp paper of national circulation.

Bickford said his stamp paper had been growing, but local circulation had declined, hence his decision to retire from publishing *The Brundidge Sentinel.*

Jones said *The Pike County Sentinel* would be published from the plant of *The Troy Messenger.*

Glenn Jones
The Troy Messenger

L.O. Brackeen to write history of APA

The July 5, 1951, issue of *AlaPressa* announced that an agreement had been reached between the APA board of directors and L.O. Brackeen, director of publicity at Alabama Polytechnic Institute, Auburn, for compilation and preparation of a history of the APA from 1871 to 1951.

"It is the desire of the board of directors that this history be as complete as possible, so, at the risk of having many duplications, we are urging all members of the association to communicate their historical information to Mr. Brackeen," *AlaPressa* reported. "Please don't assume that the information you have is a duplication of information already available. If everyone does that, the writer of the history will never find out about it. So give! Give! Information is needed on the history of the Alabama Press Association."

APA participated in two statewide promotions in 1951, Alabama Industry Days and the Keep Alabama Forests Green campaign.

Legislative Committee active in 1951

The Legislative Committee, headed by William E. (Bill) Brooks Jr. of *The Brewton Standard*, was particularly active in 1951. Brooks and field manager Jack Beisner, as well as other committee members and Alabama publishers, spent a great deal of time in Montgomery.

The Legislative Committee was successful in obtaining an increase in the legal advertising rate and helping kill bills that would have set the rates

---

SIDELIGHTS
MARKING 125 YEARS OF HISTORY

Editorial salaries were $400 a month in 1957

Newspaper publishers in 1957 were hearing more and more of the need to increase salaries of editorial employees in order to attract young people to journalism.

Salaries offered college graduates in journalism showed improvement, but still trailed other fields. A 1957 editorial in *Publishers' Auxiliary* reported that business and industry would be offering beginning salaries of about $400 a month to 1957 college graduates. The average starting salary for entry-level male reporters was $73 per week. The starting salary for female reporters was $61, according to the fall 1956 issue of *Journalism Quarterly*.

---

for political ads, restricted the reporting of sex offenses, and allowed libel suits in any county where a paper circulated.

In his legislative report at the 1952 convention, Brooks commented on the power which could be

Beisner attends meeting in Atlanta

Jack Beisner, APA field manager from 1950 to 1956, attended a meeting in Atlanta in August 1951 of press association managers and other press representatives. From left are Guy Easterly, Tennessee Press Association; Harry Porte, Mergenthaler Linotype Co.; Stanford Smith, manager of the Georgia Press Association; Beisner; and Glenn McNeil, manager of the Tennessee Press Association. (Photograph courtesy of Mary-Lou Beisner)

exerted in Montgomery by Alabama newspapers working together. "I learned in Montgomery that the expression the 'power of the press' is not an idle phrase," Brooks reported. "The sound of an automatic press turning out 5,000 impressions makes sweet music in the shop and even prettier music in the cash register."

Brooks continued, "All of us enjoy making money and at times some of us are prone to feel that the newspaper is a necessary evil to the operation of a good printing establishment. Your legislators frankly don't care whether you can print envelopes for five dollars a thousand or fifty dollars a thousand. What they do care about is what you print in the paper that goes in the mail each week. With a beat up Babcock drum cylinder, an old Linotype, some type, two or three stones and a casting box, you can put together a weapon which no politician enjoys opposing. You and your newspaper carry the weight in Montgomery."

A Dues Revision Committee did extensive study on the need to increase dues during 1951. The dues increase was unanimously approved by APA membership during the annual convention in January 1952.

1951 summer convention, Mobile

Legislation affecting newspapers was the principal topic at the 1951 summer convention at the Admiral Semmes Hotel in Mobile, June 21-23. William E. (Bill) Brooks Jr., managing editor of *The Brewton Standard* and chairman of the APA's Legislative Committee, gave a summary of bills before the Legislature affecting freedom of the press. "Some of the bills before the Legislature which affect the press are vicious," Brooks said. "They were introduced with mean intent to abridge freedom of the press."

Brooks' report led APA president Clarence B. Hanson Jr., publisher of *The Birmingham News*, to warn delegates that "newspaper executives are not waging this fight solely to protect their own interests, but they are doing it to protect the interests of the people as well."

In the only official action of the convention, delegates adopted a resolution urging all editors and publishers to "continue to bear the moral obligation of conscientious editors and publishers to abstain from printing the names of juvenile victims of sex crimes." A bill had been introduced in 1951 by Rep. Paul Meeks of Jefferson County to make it unlawful for a publication to give the names of victims of sex crimes.

S I D E L I G H T S
MARKING 125 YEARS OF HISTORY

Star-News *employed oldest printer in 1958*

The Andalusia Star-News employed the oldest printer in Covington County in 1958. Eugene Grant, 74, had been working for almost 60 years.

Grant began his career with *The New Era* in 1900. He also worked for *The Florala News*, *The Covington News*, had once owned an Andalusia job shop and newspaper, and managed an Enterprise newspaper. He also worked for an Oklahoma newspaper.

1952
Cecil H. Hornady, *The Talladega News*
1952-1953 president

81st annual press convention, Montgomery
Jan. 17-19, 1952
Summer convention, Panama City, Fla.
July 10-12, 1952

The 81st annual convention at the Jefferson Davis Hotel and Whitley Hotel in Montgomery Jan. 17-19, 1952, was restricted to newspapers only, and featured detailed financial and activity reports on the first year of Alabama Newspaper Advertising Service Inc.

The reports were given by E.H. (Ed) Pierce, publisher of *The Mountain Eagle* in Jasper, who was ANAS president for 1951. Earl L. Britt of *The Mobile Press* gave a report on legal advertising, and William E. (Bill) Brooks Jr., managing editor of *The Brewton Standard*, gave a Legislative Committee report. Brooks was chairman of APA's Legislative Committee.

Other convention highlights included a discussion by Walter C. Johnson, secretary-manager of Southern Newspaper Publishers Association, on the value of a press association to its members, and a report on the newsprint situation.

A panel discussion on community service was led by Neil O. Davis of *The Lee County Bulletin* in Auburn. Participants on the community service panel were J.J. Benford of *The Albertville Herald* who explained the successful county improvement council plan used in Marshall County; Vincent H. Townsend of *The Birmingham News* discussed the

---

community service aspects of his newspaper's annual public affairs forum; J. W. (Jim) Oakley Sr. of *The Centreville Press* discussed the press' public service function as shown in reporting governmental news; and Roberta Morgan of the Jefferson County Coordinating Council discussed the press' community service as viewed by the public.

Political debate held at winter convention

Other activities included a significant and timely political debate suggesting "A Political Course for Alabama" that featured the chairmen of Alabama's Democratic and Republican parties and a leading States Rights Democrat.

"Follow the straight Democratic party line," said Ben F. Ray, Alabama Democratic Executive Committee chairman. "Use the sensible two-party system," said Claud O. Vardamann, Alabama Republican Executive Committee chairman. "The independent voting was following the dictates of one's conscience and reasoning," said Tom Abernathy, editor of *The* (Talladega) *Daily Home.* Moderator was Dr. Douglas Hunt of *The Birmingham News.*

Luncheon speaker on Friday was Edgar S. Bayol, press counsel for Coca-Cola Co. in New York City. He spoke on "What Keeps the Free

Committees of Freedom on Information

"There is an urgent need for citizens of Alabama and this country to become acutely aware that suppression of public information is a wrong against the people rather than against the newspapers, agreed members of the Committees on Freedom of Information of the Alabama Press Association and the Alabama Associated Press in a joint meeting April 17, 1953, at Alabama Polytechnic Institute (API) in Auburn.

Attending the Committees on Freedom of Information at Auburn are, seated from left, Sam Brewster, director of Buildings and Grounds, API; Leroy Simms, AP bureau chief, Birmingham; Neil O. Davis, publisher, *The Lee County Bulletin,* Auburn; Charles Fell, *The Birmingham News;* Dr. Ralph B. Draughon, president of API; Norman Bassett, *The Tuscaloosa News;* Robert G. Bozeman Jr., *The Evergreen Courant;* J.J. Benford, *The Albertville Herald;* and Rex Thomas, AP bureau chief, Montgomery.

Standing from left, are Kenneth Roy, API agricultural editor; Walter Everidge, incoming editor of *The Auburn Plainsman;* Max Hall, *The Plainsman;* L.O. Brackeen, director of publicity at API; M.C. Huntley, dean of Faculties, API; W.T. Ingram, business manager, API; P.O. Davis, Extension director, API; E.V. Smith, director of Agricultural Research, API; Jack Beisner, APA secretary-manager; T.D. Faulkner, executive secretary, *Future Farmers of Alabama;* and Louis Eckl, *The Florence Times.*

Press Free?" State 4-H leader Hanchey E. Logue of Alabama Polytechnic Institute, Auburn, presented an illustrated talk on Alabama 4-H activities.

Mimeographed APA history distributed

A mimeographed copy of "History of the Alabama Press Association, 1871-1951," by L.O. Brackeen, director of publicity at Alabama Polytechnic Institute in Auburn, was distributed to the APA members. Brackeen asked that members make suggestions, corrections or additions to the APA history.

Webb Stanley, business manager of *The Greenville Advocate,* and APA president in 1926-1927 and 1935-1936, reviewed the history for Brackeen and wrote that "It is a monumental work and deserves the high praise with which it will be received. You have embodied the salient points of the whole history of the Press of Alabama since 1871 and while doing it you have shown the changing viewpoints of the people of the State through their newspapers relative to local, state and national questions.

"The whole is a perfect thing and should be a storehouse of information about the men and women who now edit Alabama's newspapers about what those who preceded them thought, did and said," Stanley continued. "Certainly it was a nostalgic treat for me to read it, for my first active association with the Association was when my father and I visited the St. Louis Exposition in 1904, nearly a half century ago. I really didn't realize I was getting to be quite so old as that would indicate, but I was big enough to have had a swell time at that Exposition, and reading the history brings

to mind so many faces and memories from that time on. I certainly think it should be printed, by all means, and added to as the years go on."

Highlighting the Saturday luncheon at the 1952 winter convention was a talk by Seymour Topping, Associated Press foreign correspondent, on the Far East and international relations of the United States in general.

An organizational meeting for an Alabama Mechanical Conference had been scheduled, but when only five newspapers were represented at the meeting it was agreed by those present that the interest shown in a mechanical conference plan was not sufficient to warrant organization of such a group.

Alabama Clipping Bureau established in 1952

ANAS made several significant advances during 1952. First, *The Alabama Publisher* was put on a paying basis. Second, the Alabama Clipping Bureau, which became a profitable sideline to ANAS, was established.

APA officers in 1952 took as their goal making membership the highest in the Press Association's history. Despite the increase in dues, they succeeded.

Important committee work was done in 1952. The Better Newspaper Contest Committee, headed by George H. Watson of *The Shades Valley Sun,* Homewood, made a study of contests conducted in other states to prepare for such a contest in Alabama.

The Legislative Committee, with Ralph W. Callahan of *The Anniston Star* as chairman, and the Legislative Sub-Committee, with James H. (Jimmy) Faulkner Sr. of *The Baldwin County Times* as chairman, did a great deal of study preparing for the 1953 legislative session. A revision of the booklet of Alabama laws relating to publishing was prepared. Legislation to be presented during the 1953 session was planned.

The Journalism and Printing Schools Committee, headed by Col. Harry M. Ayers of *The Anniston Star,* studied the journalism course offerings in the colleges and trade schools of Alabama and examined journalism programs and facilities at some Southern universities.

Mills heads Freedom of Information Committee in 1952

A new committee in 1952 was the Freedom of Information Committee. Led by chairman James E. (Jimmy) Mills of the *Birmingham Post-Herald,* the committee publicized attempts to suppress information in the state, inspiring many

---

S I D E L I G H T S
MARKING 125 YEARS OF HISTORY

Onlooker *publishes without column rule*

The Foley Onlooker published issues in 1959 using no column rule on the front page for the first time in its 50-year history. At the same time, the text type was changed and more horizontal makeup was used. Other improvements included insertion of half column cuts of each correspondent who wrote regularly for the paper and "more attention on make-up of the society and farm pages."

E.M. (Sparky) Howell was publisher, and Doris Rich was news editor.

UA's Carmichael meets with APA officials
The University of Alabama's president, Dr. O.C. Carmichael, held his first meeting with officials of the Alabama Press Association and Alabama Newspaper Advertising Service during a luncheon on Nov. 7, 1953, on the Tuscaloosa campus. The newsmen later were guests at the University of Alabama-Chattanooga football game. Attending the luncheon are, seated from left, Dr. Carmichael; APA president William E. (Bill) Brooks Jr., *The Brewton Standard;* Buford Boone, *The Tuscaloosa News;* Bill Stewart, *The Monroe Journal,* Monroeville; Paul Cunningham, *The Elba Clipper;* and Jack Beisner, APA-ANAS manager.
    Standing from left, are George H. Watson, *The Shades Valley Sun,* Homewood; Ben G. George, *The Demopolis Times;* Jay Thornton, *The Haleyville Advertiser;* Steele E. McGrew, *The Limestone Democrat* and *The Alabama Courier,* Athens; John B. Stevenson, *The Roanoke Leader;* E.H. (Ed) Pierce Sr., *The Mountain Eagle,* Jasper; Jones W. Giles, APA-ANAS assistant manager; Dr. R.E. Tidwell, dean, Extension Division, University of Alabama; Professor John Luskin, Department of Journalism, University of Alabama; and ANAS president Bonnie D. Hand, *The LaFayette Sun.*

editorials in Alabama papers, and prepared legislation to make more effective the laws providing for open meetings of public bodies. At the time the Freedom of Information Committee was appointed, Gov. Gordon Persons offered his full cooperation. Persons pledged to act on any complaint of suppression of information in any state department under his control.

The Cove Hotel in Panama City, Fla., was headquarters for the July 10-12, 1952, summer convention. *AlaPressa* reported that for the banquet, "a whole stuffed chicken each, will be served, plus the trimmings. Total cost to you, including tax and tips, $4.00. You won't have trouble finding something to do to enjoy yourself. The usual group 'chorales' (including our well-known whiskey tenors) will be held each evening."

Twin bed rooms on the Gulf side of the hotel were $8 per night. Meals at the Cove Hotel were 45 cents to 85 cents for breakfast; 85 cents and up for lunch; and $1.40 and up for dinner.

History and recreation were highlights of the 1952 summer convention. Attendance reached a record high for these recreational meetings; delegates registering totaled 91. A record high in newspaper membership for the Press Association was announced by president Cecil H. Hornady of *The Talladega News.*

Former APA presidents recognized

Of the 22 living past APA presidents, 11 were present and received Past President lapel pins by the master of ceremonies, Jep V. Greer of *The Sylacauga News*. Cash M. Stanley of *The Alabama Journal* in Montgomery, APA historian and program chairman, gave a review of Alabama newspaper history since his arrival in Alabama.

Other activities of the delegates included being guests of *The Panama City* (Fla.) *News-Herald* at a reception. Officers and those who were Rotarians were guests of the Panama City Rotary Club at a luncheon. Available for use by the delegates were the "Gomol," Avondale Mills yacht, a fishing boat from Avondale Mills, and a fishing boat provided by Western Newspaper Union.

The APA board of directors met and establishment of an Executive Committee to act in the name of the board was authorized. The committee was composed of Clarence B. Hanson Jr., *The Birm-*

1953 convention dinner dance
        Dinner dances were a popular tradition with APA delegates who attended conventions in the earlier years. Mary-Lou Beisner, wife of deceased APA field manager Jack Beisner, provided this photograph taken at the 1953 summer convention at the Admiral Semmes Hotel in Mobile. Even children of the delegates participated in this dance. Pictured here are Beth Beisner, age 10, daughter of the Beisners, and Dickie McGrew, son of Steele and Ellen McGrew of *The Limestone Democrat* and *Alabama Courier* in Athens. (Photograph courtesy of Mary-Lou Beisner)

ingham News, chairman; William E. (Bill) Brooks Jr., *The Brewton Standard*, first vice president; and Steele E. McGrew, *The Alabama Courier*, Athens, second vice president. APA president Cecil H. Hornady of *The Talladega News* was an ex-officio member of the committee.

Following a report recommending re-establishment of the Better Newspaper Contest, board of directors voted on July 11, 1952, in Panama City to establish a committee to draw up contest plans and present them to the 1953 winter convention delegates for approval. The recommendation was made to the board of directors by a committee headed by Herve Charest Jr. of *The Tallassee Tribune*, which polled Alabama publishers for their reactions to renewing the contest that had been discontinued in 1947.

1953
William E. (Bill) Brooks Jr., *The Brewton Standard*
1953-1954 president

82nd annual press convention, Birmingham
Jan. 22-24, 1953
Summer convention, Mobile
July 16-18, 1953

Problems of publishers and editors were discussed at the work sessions during the 82nd an-

APA visits steam plant in 1953
Delegates to the 1953 summer convention in Mobile toured Alabama Power Company's new Barry Steam Plant and the new Courtlands plant north of Mobile. The two little girls in shorts on the front row are Beverly and Beth Beisner, daughters of APA field manager Jack Beisner. Others in the photograph include Ellen and Steele McGrew and son Dickie of *The Alabama Courier* in Athens; Ben George, *The Demopolis Times;* Pearl and Bonnie Hand,*The LaFayette Sun;* J.C. and Nellie Mae Henderson, *The Alexander City Outlook;* Bill Putman; Mrs. George Watson, *The Shades Valley Sun* in Homewood; Ed Brooks, wife of 1953 APA president Bill Brooks, *The Brewton Standard;* and Herve Charest, *The Tallassee Tribune.* (Photograph courtesy of Mary-Lou Beisner)

nual press convention at the Thomas Jefferson Hotel in Birmingham Jan. 22-24, 1953.

Dailies and weeklies met separately for talks and panel discussions with Steele E. McGrew, publisher of *The Alabama Courier* in Athens, presiding over the weekly session, and Carl Hofferbert, general manager of *The Gadsden Times,* presiding over the dailies. At the weekly session, Bonnie D. Hand of *The LaFayette Sun* urged weekly publishers to increase printing and office supply sales by taking advantage of their local markets. Porter Harvey of *The Advertiser-Gleam* in Guntersville discussed circulation problems.

News and editorial policies for weekly newspapers were discussed by John B. Stevenson of *The Roanoke Leader,* with delegates participating in a general discussion. Carl Wolsoncroft, *The Alexander City Outlook,* and Roy Hickman, Alabama Engraving Co., Birmingham, outlined plans for increasing printing and engraving sales.

Cox discusses editorial policy

George M. Cox, executive editor of *The Mobile Press Register,* began the daily newspaper session with a discussion of editorial policy. Ralph W. Callahan, business manager of *The Anniston Star,* discussed advertising. Circulation methods were reviewed in a discussion led by J.T. Lane, business manager of *The Dothan Eagle.* Bernard D. Feld Jr., promotion director of *The Birmingham News,* led a discussion on newspaper promotions.

The news and editing session was opened with a talk by Buford Boone, editor and publisher of *The Tuscaloosa News,* who urged APA members to give more time to their editorial pages. "The editorial page is a window to the soul of your newspaper," Boone said. Four years later, in 1957, Boone was awarded the Pulitzer Prize for his editorials written during integration at the University of Alabama. Boone followed Grover C. Hall Sr., editor of *The Montgomery Advertiser,* as the second Alabamian to win a Pulitzer.

Problems of the editorial page discussed

Reese T. Amis, editor of *The Huntsville Times,* and Henry F. Arnbold, editor of *The Cullman Tribune,* discussed problems of the editorial page. Norman H. Bassett of *The Tuscaloosa News* discussed the growing demand for interpretation of news. He stressed the need for clarity in news writing.

James E. (Jimmy) Mills of the *Birmingham Post-Herald* presented two specific programs requiring editorial backing. He expressed hope that a well-planned program to help Alabama mental institutions would be supported by APA members. Mills also cited the needs of state mental hospitals and called for support of legislation necessary to meet those needs. J.J. Benford of *The Albertville Herald*, outlined a four-point program calling for collective support of conservation, good government, safety promotion and Americanism.

Guest speakers were Bob Considine, INS reporter, and Bert Struby, executive editor of *The Macon* (Ga.) *Telegraph* and *The Macon News.*

Considine gave an inside look at President Eisenhower, in a speech titled "This Man Eisenhower." Considine was selected to accompany Eisenhower on his Korean tour.

Bert Struby called for a better working relationship between the press and judiciary. In his speech, Struby urged the editors and publishers to examine their relationship with the judiciary and "frankly analyze the course of action which better understanding demands."

1953 APA luncheon featured $2.25 seafood platter

AlaPressa printed a pre-registration form for the 1953 convention, announcing that a seafood platter would be served at the Friday luncheon for $2.25. "Fresh seafood will be served. Do you prefer pompano, red snapper or lobster tail?" Broiled filet mignon was served at the Friday banquet, at $4.75 per plate, and braised Swiss steak, at $2.50 per plate, was served at the Saturday luncheon. Registration to the convention was $5.

1953 was a year of consolidation after several years of rapid advances. Membership remained high, although it did not quite reach the record of the previous year. During the year the Journalism and Printing Schools Committee continued to stress improvement of journalism education in the state, particularly in encouraging the University of Alabama to upgrade its journalism program.

Legislative activities occupied the time of APA officers, the secretary-field manager and the Legislative Committee during the 1953 legislative session.

Statement of legislative policy

The following statement of legislative policy was adopted at the annual convention in 1953 as a guide to legislative activities:

S I D E L I G H T S
MARKING 125 YEARS OF HISTORY

Herald *publishes 50th anniversary edition*
W. H. Golson and his staff produced a 48-page 50th Anniversary Edition of *The Wetumpka Herald* on July 1, 1948. The issue, printed in six sections, contained historical material on Wetumpka and *The Herald.*

The late Howell Rose Golson established *The Herald* in 1898 and was its editor until his death in 1916. The late Hunter Howell Golson and Frances Golson later edited the newspaper. Mrs. Howell Hunter Golson was business manager in 1948, and her son, William Howell Golson, was editor.

Commenting editorially on "A Wetumpka Birthday," *The Alabama Journal* remarked in its July 3, 1948, issue:

"The 50th anniversary edition of *The Wetumpka Herald* issued this week is a credit to Wetumpka and to the newspaper's young and aggressive editor, William Howell Golson, who took over on the death of his late lamented father, Sen. Hunter H. Golson. The entire press of the state of Alabama joins the Montgomery paper in congratulating *The Wetumpka Herald* for its excellent anniversary edition and for its 50 years of inspired leadership in its community."

"1. The Alabama Press Association will never advocate or seek passage of any legislation which (a) will give special privilege to the newspaper industry or its members, or (b) will produce revenue for newspapers without rendering a distinct and beneficial public service.

"2. The Alabama Press Association will oppose any restrictions, other than those contained in the Alabama Code concerning false or misleading advertising, proposed by legislative or other governmental actions on advertising the sale of goods, services or materials which may be legally sold or offered to the public.

"3. The Alabama Press Association will strongly oppose any privilege license on newspaper publishing as being contrary to the guarantee of freedom of the press.

"4. The Alabama Press Association will favor and support good measures designed to maintain, strengthen or increase freedom of information of public affairs."

APA secretary-field manager Jack Beisner commented on the success of the legislative efforts:

"1. It established the APA as a representative of a group definitely to be considered when any legislation affecting newspapers in any fashion was to be presented.

"2. It indicated to those in public office that the newspapers are determined to protect their rights and those of the public.

"3. It established APA as a group which would not take a stand on legislation not affecting it, its members or its legislative policies."

AlaPressa reported that the most outstanding accomplishments of the Legislative Committee in 1953 were passage of bills requiring more adequate and extended financial reports from city and county school districts, an increase in the legal advertising rate, and publication of a booklet, "Alabama Laws Relating to Publications and Notices."

ANAS has good year in 1953

Although the Clipping Bureau had not yet developed into a strong revenue producer, ANAS had a good year in 1953. The volume of advertising handled more than doubled from the previous year, and at the end of the year a full-time assistant manager was hired to spend the majority of the time in sales.

Both the Legislative and the Freedom of Information Committees were instrumental in seeing that a bill was defeated by the Legislature which would have permitted multiple suits against news media in counties in which the newspaper was circulated. The Freedom of Information Committees of APA and Alabama Associated Press were instrumental in opening up meetings of the University of Alabama board of trustees in 1953.

Delegates to the 1953 winter convention approved re-establishment of the Better Newspaper Contest which had been discontinued in 1947. The first winners were announced at the 1954 summer convention in Biloxi.

1953 summer meeting, Mobile

Highlights of the 1953 meeting at the Admiral Semmes Hotel in Mobile, July 16-18, 1953, were tours of the Mobile River and bay on the Alabama State Docks yacht and a visit to Alabama Power Co.'s new Barry Steam Plant and the new Courtaulds plant north of Mobile.

Delegates enjoyed a combination buffet, reception and dance at the Admiral Semmes Hotel at a cost of $3.75 per person. The reception and orchestra for dancing were courtesy of *The Mobile Press Register*. A fish fry "with all the trimmings will be at the Mobile Police Relief Association Club on Chickasabogue," *AlaPressa* reported. "Cost to delegates — nothing, admission by convention identification card pinned to coat, or shirt."

1954
Steele E. McGrew, *The Limestone Democrat* and *Alabama Courier,* Athens
1954-1955 president

83rd annual press convention, Montgomery
Jan. 21-23, 1954
Summer convention, Biloxi, Miss.
July 22-24, 1954

Highlights of the 83rd annual convention in Montgomery, Jan. 21-23, 1954, were five-minute talks by seven prospective candidates for governor of Alabama and addresses by John Saxon Childers, editor of *The Atlanta Journal;* Russ Brines, Associated Press correspondent; Ira Harkey, editor and publisher of *The Pascagoula* (Miss.) *Chronicle Star;* and Earl L. Tucker of *The Thomasville Times.*

"It is my faith that the editorial page is literally the heart of the newspaper," Childers said. "Unless you believe this, you have no right to be fooling with the editorial page. Unless a man has something of the teacher and preacher about him, he will not write good editorials."

Veteran AP correspondent Brines discussed what he termed the government's "new look" in military plan-

Earl L. Tucker
The Thomasville Times

ning and Far East policy and made this observation: "Let us be sure we know what we are looking at and what this 'new look' and policy must fit into."

Tucker, editor of *The Thomasville Times,* gave a humorous talk on "A Way to Happiness" at the luncheon program on the closing day.

Harkey discussed "How to Make Our Newspapers More Interesting." Harkey told delegates, "The easiest way to make a weekly newspaper interesting is to make it look and read like a daily newspaper."

Gubernatorial candidates at the 1954 convention included Lt. Gov. James B. Allen of Gadsden;

1954 APA officers and managers

1954 APA officers and managers are, from left, William E. (Bill) Brooks Jr., *The Brewton Standard*, immediate past president; Ben G. George, *The Demopolis Times*, second vice president; Jack Beisner, APA manager; Jones W. Giles, assistant manager; and George H. Watson, *The Shades Valley Sun*, Homewood, first vice president. Seated is 1954 president Steele E. McGrew, *The Limestone Democrat* and *The Alabama Courier*, Athens.

Judge Elbert Boozer of Gadsden; James H. (Jimmy) Faulkner Sr. of Bay Minette; Winston Gullatte of Selma; J. Bruce Henderson of Millers Ferry; C.C. (Jack) Owen of Montgomery; and Henry W. Sweet of Bessemer.

Participating in a panel discussion on improving Alabama newspapers were Horace Hall, *The Dothan Eagle;* Bill Jones, *The Mountain Eagle,* Jasper; Mickey Clem, *The Mountain Eagle,* Jasper; George H. Watson, *The Shades Valley Sun,* Homewood; J. Martin Smith, Sparrow Advertising Agency; and Billy Lavender, *The Mobile Press Register.*

For first time, program held for spouses

APA minutes reflected that "for the first time, the members made special plans for their wives. In appreciation of the many wonderful ladies who attend the conventions and help in so many ways to make the Association what it is today, the APA awarded prizes for their attendance."

Upon recommendation of the Necrology Committee, the convention delegates officially expressed regret over the passing of the following during 1953: Roy Elliott Neal, *The Huntsville Times;* Atticus Mullin, *The Montgomery Advertiser;* Joe Thornton, *The Gadsden Times;* Price L. Foster, *The Onlooker* in Foley;

Perkins J. Prewitt, *The Montgomery Advertiser;* R.M. Ussery, editor and publisher, *The Ashland Progress;* Edgar Harris, founder, *The West Point* (Miss.) *Daily Times* Leader; Hattye P. Collier, *The Tuscaloosa News;*

S I D E L I G H T S
MARKING 125 YEARS OF HISTORY

Standard *raises subscription rate to $3 yearly*
The Brewton Standard raised its annual subscription rate in 1950 — to $3 a year. "We hate to do this — BUT the subscription price of *The Brewton Standard* will be $3.00 a year beginning Nov. 1, 1950, *The Standard* announced.

Brewton Standard managing editor William E. (Bill) Brooks Jr. justified the increase because of "cost of ink, postage, newsprint and other ingredients of newspapers." Single copy price was raised to seven cents with the note, "With the price of a cup of coffee up to eight cents, we figure *The Standard* is still a good buy."

Louis P. Dumas, *The Mobile Press Register;* and W.J. Knighton, *The Birmingham News.*

Better Newspaper Contest reinstituted in 1954

The Better Newspaper Contest, discontinued in 1947, was reinstituted in 1954 with the awards presented at the summer convention. In the General Excellence division for weeklies published in municipalities under 3,500, *The Monroe Journal* in Monroeville won the first-place award. In the division for weeklies in municipalities over 3,500, *The Mountain Eagle* in Jasper won the first-place award.

ANAS had by far its most successful year to date in 1954. With a 64 percent gross increase in receipts over the previous year. ANAS was still spending more than it took in, but bought a corporate car and other equipment during the year.

A joint committee of APA and the University of Alabama held its first meetings during the year and discussed means of cooperation between the Press Association and the University in recruiting journalism students and establishing a summer internship program for journalism students.

> ## S I D E L I G H T S
> MARKING 125 YEARS OF HISTORY
>
> **Muscle Shoals Sun** *published in 1957*
> A new five-day-a-week morning newspaper was published in Sheffield in 1957. Leroy Gore, former weekly publisher in Saul City, Wis., was editor of *The Muscle Shoals Morning Sun.*
> Gore led the "Joe Must Go" campaign seeking the ouster of Republican Sen. Joseph McCarthy.

The Journalism and Printing Schools Committee continued to seek additional support from University administrators for the journalism department at the University of Alabama. The committee was instrumental in financing expenses so that Professor C.E. (Ed) Bounds, head of the Department of Journalism, could attend national meetings of the Association for

Newsroom of *The Birmingham News*, circa 1950. (Copyright *The Birmingham News*. All rights reserved. Reprinted by permission)

Education in Journalism, the Association of Accredited Schools and Departments of Journalism, and the American Society of Journalism School Administrators.

An expense fund was also established to allow Bounds to travel around Alabama recruiting students for the University of Alabama's journalism program. Equipment was supplied to the Department of Journalism to assist in instruction and production work.

1954 summer convention at Buena Vista Hotel

The 1954 summer convention was July 22-24 at Buena Vista Hotel in Biloxi, Miss. *The Alabama Publisher* reported that the Buena Vista had been "completely air conditioned and other improvements in the hotel and beach facilities made since the last time the APA met there for a summer session."

More than 100 APA delegates attended the annual banquet on July 23. Highlights included announcement of winners of the Better Newspaper Contest and the opportunity to hear Tom Sims, noted newspaper man and writer of the comic strip "Popeye." The banquet program explained that Sims "also carries on a successful career as a farmer at his Ohatchee, Alabama, farm."

AlaPressa reported that the convention was an "informal affair of fun and fellowship for the entire family." A tour of Keesler Air Force Base was given, as well as a boat trip with the APA delegates as guests of the Mississippi Press Association.

1955
George H. Watson, *The Shades Valley Sun,* Homewood
1955-1956 president

84th annual press convention, Huntsville
Jan. 20-22, 1955
Summer convention, Fairhope
July 21-23, 1955

APA surpassed all previous membership figures in 1955. The increase included a substantial jump in the number of weekly newspapers that were members — from 78 in 1954 to 112 in 1955.

The year started with a well-attended 84th annual convention, held Jan. 20-22, 1955, at the Hotel Russel Erskine in Huntsville. The December 1954 issue of *The Alabama Publisher* noted that it was APA's first convention in Huntsville in 59 years. "In Huntsville, 1955 delegates will find that while lying in the heart of an industrially expanding region, it still retains the beauty and charm of the

---

SIDELIGHTS
MARKING 125 YEARS OF HISTORY

The Prattville Progress *listed for sale in 1963*
AlaPressa listed the following newspaper for sale in 1963: "For sale: Unopposed, 78-year-old weekly newspaper, *The Prattville Progress* (Alabama's second fastest growing town). Price slightly over 1962 gross. Please don't waste your time or mine unless you have substantial down payment — Mrs. H.M. Doster."

'old South' that impressed the convention of 1896," *AlaPressa* reported.

Speakers at the convention addressed delegates on "Alabama, Its Resources and Its Future." Speakers included Frank H. Higgins, assistant secretary of Army; Jim Lucas, Scripps Howard correspondent; John Scott, assistant to the publisher of *Time* magazine; Brig. Gen. H.N. Toftoy, commanding general of Redstone Arsenal in Huntsville; Dr. J.L. Brakefield, director of public relations for Liberty National Life Insurance Co.; Fred A. Kummer, head of the department of agricultural engineering at Alabama Polytechnic Institute, Auburn; and Carl T. Jones, consulting engineer, Huntsville.

"Located in Alabama, from Theodore in the south to Huntsville in the north, the Army has seven installations, comprising more than 170,000 acres, at a real property cost of over $291 million," Higgins said. "In Army installations and activities in Alabama, there are over 13,000 civilian personnel employed and over 9,100 military personnel, with a payroll of $85 million a year. So the importance of Alabama in the Army's plan is pretty obvious," Higgins told APA delegates.

Pulitzer Prize winner speaks at convention

"Cynicism and disillusionment are luxuries we can't afford," said Lucas, 1954 Pulitzer Prize winner for international reporting. Lucas warned that "it would be fatal to let down our guard even a moment against communism. Indo-China, Asia, is a dark picture. The mainland of China is Communist-controlled, and their religion is to hate America. They practice it. Korea is divided. Thailand and the Philippines think they are next on the list by the commies. It's a grim and unpleasant picture. However, 99 percent of the people I have met

and known over there don't want to fall behind
the iron curtain."

A belief that a billion people in the Middle
East and North Africa would decide if the world
pendulum would swing toward the United States
or Russia was spelled out to delegates by John
Scott, assistant to the publisher of *Time* magazine. Scott, who had recently returned from a trip
to North Africa, said the French there were faced
with a situation paralleling Indo-China. "Communism is not a factor in French North Africa
now," Scott said, also predicting "it would become
so, should the natives be foiled in their drive for
independence."

Gen. Toftoy addresses delegates

Gen. Toftoy addressed the convention delegates
on "Rockets and Guided Missiles Today and In
Our Future," while Dr. Brakefield spoke on "The
Position of Alabama in Southern Economy." One
of Alabama's most serious problems was aired by
Kummer in his talk on "Progress and Problems in
Irrigation in Alabama." Jones spoke on "Alabama's
Industrial Expansion."

"National Advertising and the Weekly Newspaper" was the title of an address by C.B. Brown,
publisher of *The Oconomowoc Enterprise* in Wisconsin. A full afternoon was devoted to an advertising clinic led by Ben G. George of *The Demopolis
Times,* and a morning session was devoted to a
business clinic led by J.C. Henderson of *The
Alexander City Outlook.*

Dannelly topic leader for advertising panel discussion

Ed Dannelly, editor of *The Andalusia Star-News,*
was topic leader of a panel discussion on selling
retail advertising. Panel members were Arthur
Cook, local advertising manager of *The Birmingham News;* Glenn Jones, publisher of *The Troy
Messenger and Herald;* and Dale Smith, business
manager of *The Progressive Age* in Scottsboro and
The Jackson County Sentinel.

The film "Lexington, U.S.A." was part of the
presentation on "Selling General Advertising,"
along with a talk by C.S. Brown, past president of
Weekly Newspaper Representatives (WNR), who
spoke on "Selling General Advertising for Weekly
Newspapers."

Topics covered during the business clinic were
"Gearing Your Mechanical Facilities and Employ-
ees for Efficient Production" by Jay Thornton of
The Haleyville Advertiser; "How the New Laws
Affect your Business" by George D. King, certi-
fied public accountant from Gadsden; "Maintain-
ing a High Circulation" by E.M. (Sparky) Howell,
The Onlooker in Foley; "Newspaper Public Rela-
tions and Promotion" by John Hamner, *The
Tuscaloosa News;* and "Newspaper Insurance —
How Much and What Kind" by A.D. Harris,
Pritchett-Moore Inc., Tuscaloosa.

Legislative Committee busy in 1955

The legislative tasks of the Legislative Committee and the field manager Jack Beisner were
arduous in 1955 as the governor called three special sessions in addition to the regular session of
the Alabama Legislature.

Legislative Committee chairman Harold S.
May of *The Florence Herald* reported that "the committee had been faced with more anti-newspaper
legislation than had ever been considered by the
Legislature previously, with unique success. All
measures the APA Legislative Committee desired
to have amended were so amended, and anti-newspaper measures the APA wished to defeat were
defeated, and almost all legislation the APA committee favored was passed," May said.

A "school of journalism seminar" sponsored by
the University of Alabama and *The Mobile Press
Register* was held in Mobile in April 1955. Such
seminars had been recommended by the APA Journalism and Printing Schools Committee.

Eight veteran Alabama newsmen participated
in a journalism convocation sponsored by the University of Alabama and APA in October 1955. Those
giving talks and answering questions from students

were Fallon Trotter, *The Mobile Press Register;* Fred Eiland, *The Cleburne News,* Heflin; Bill Lindley, the *Birmingham Post-Herald;* Louis Eckl, *The Florence Times;* George H. Watson, *The Shades Valley Sun,* Homewood; Buford Boone, *The Tuscaloosa News;* J.W. (Jim) Oakley Sr., *The Centreville Press;* and Nat C. Faulk, *The Dothan Eagle.*

Reporter becomes first offset newspaper

In 1955, *The Sand Mountain Reporter* in Albertville became the first offset press operation in Alabama, and only the third offset operation in the United States. "We muddled and fuddled through the first few months," retired publisher Pat Courington recalled in a 1990 interview in *The Alabama Publisher.* "We 'borrowed' a platemaker and pressman for a few months from *The Opelousas World* in Louisiana, the first offset newspaper in the country. The ink companies didn't know anything about offset, and the newsprint companies didn't know anything about offset newsprint."

The fledgling *Sand Mountain Reporter,* which had started in 1955 as a five-day daily, "nearly went broke getting started" in its offset venture, but Courington said he was convinced that offset printing was the wave of the future. "Offset printing began to catch on," Courington said. "Ours was a new trick — shoot a picture today, have it in the paper tomorrow. Other newspapers were taking pictures, sending them to a lithographer and printing the picture in the newspaper a week later."

Graphic one of the first offset weeklies

Karl and Camille Elebash established *The Graphic* in Tuscaloosa as one of the first offset weekly newspapers in the state in 1957. The paper emphasized the quality of photo reproduction and local news. "I had studied offset printing and had seen it done in various places," Elebash recalled in a 1990 interview in *The Alabama Publisher.* "One of the papers in the state, *The Sand Mountain Reporter,* was offset. I knew of one in Louisiana, and there was a weekly down in Florida. They had such great pictures. They made letterpress look awful."

1955 summer convention, Fairhope

V.M. (Rod) Newton, managing editor of *The Tampa Morning Tribune* and vice president of the Associated Press Editors Association, addressed editors and publishers at the 1955 summer convention, held July 21-23 in Fairhope. Freedom of information and freedom of the press was the theme of one program.

S I D E L I G H T S
MARKING 125 YEARS OF HISTORY

Gadsden man finds 98-year-old paper

I.H. Oden of Gadsden found a 98-year-old newspaper in 1961 that carried considerable news of the Civil War. Oden removed the mirror from an old "hall tree" he was refinishing for a customer and found the old paper which had been cut in circular shape. It was a copy of the July 24, 1862, edition of *The Selma Daily Reporter.* Most of the news space was devoted to coverage of the war and even the ads showed intense interest.

One ad read: "Regiment of Mounted Rangers. I am authorized by the Secretary of War to enlist and muster into the service for the war a Regiment of Cavalry to act as Partizan Rangers. I will accept companies of not less than sixty privates, provided the men are mounted. All the officers below the grade of Colonel are to be elected. Guns and Equipments are to be furnished by the men as far as possible, for which they will be paid by the Government. Double barreled shot guns, pistols and Bowie Knives are the best arms to commence with. Persons of every age are at liberty to enlist in this Regiment if they are fit for service. My address is Cahaba, Ala. Jno. T. Morgan, Colonel."

A story of the finding and contents of the old newspaper was written by Clyde Bolton for *The Gadsden Times.*

"Got a favorite comic strip character? Old or new? Dress up like 'em, you could win a prize," *AlaPressa* announced. A costume party was held at the summer convention and a prize was given for the oldest comic strip character. "You too can be the life of the party and have fun yourself," said *AlaPressa.* "So come in costume Friday night. Be sure and tell the wife."

In promoting the convention in its June 1955 issue, *The Alabama Publisher* reported that "Fairhope, overlooking beautiful Mobile bay, is a progressive, friendly small city with as cosmopolitan and gifted a population as you will find in this country."

"Fairhope enjoys a progressive paper for progressive people, *The Fairhope Courier. The Courier* was established in 1894 by Ernest B. Gaston and has stayed in the family down through the years. Mrs. Frances Gaston Crawford is editor and Arthur F. Gaston is business manager," *The Alabama Publisher* continued.

Twenty-three weekly newspapers entered the Better Newspaper Contest, and winners were announced at the 1955 summer convention. *The Alexander City Outlook* was selected for the General Excellence award in Division A, and *The Enterprise Ledger* was General Excellence recipient in Division B.

Birmingham News, Huntsville Times sold in 1955

Sale of *The Birmingham News* and all of its subsidiaries, including *The Huntsville Times,* was announced "in a record $18.7 million deal" on Dec. 1, 1955, *The Alabama Publisher* reported in its December 1955 issue. "Publisher S.I. Newhouse also acquired a television station and three radio stations in the transaction. The Birmingham and Huntsville newspapers became the 12th and 13th newspapers in Samuel I. Newhouse's group."

Editor and Publisher newspaper trade magazine termed the sale "the biggest such transaction in American newspaper history." *Editor and Publisher* reported that the previous high was an $18 million deal in which *The Philadelphia Inquirer* was sold to Cyrus Curtis in 1930. Newhouse signed a managerial contract with Clarence B. Hanson Jr., who would remain as president and publisher of *The Birmingham News.*

The Birmingham News, Alabama's largest newspaper, was founded in 1888, when Birmingham was a city of about 25,000. Rufus N. Rhodes launched *The Evening News* on March 14, 1888. Subscriptions were 10 cents a week or $5 per year. The name of the paper was changed to *The Daily News* in 1889, and in 1894 it became *The Birmingham News.*

S I D E L I G H T S
MARKING 125 YEARS OF HISTORY

1962 salaries range from $60 to $165

June 1962 journalism graduates went to work for salaries ranging from $60 to $165 a week, according to a survey by The Newspaper Fund, supported by grants from *The Wall Street Journal.* The average beginning paycheck for 1,555 graduates in the 41-school study was $89.60.

A year after joining the paper, Victor H. Hanson and an associate purchased *The Birmingham News* in 1910 from Rhodes' widow. In 1920, Franklin P. Glass retired as editor of *The News* and sold his interest to Hanson. In 1945, Clarence B. Hanson Jr. became publisher after the death of Victor H. Hanson. In 1955, *The News* had an afternoon circulation of 187,000, and a Sunday circulation of 230,000. *The Huntsville Times* had a circulation of 20,000 in 1955. In 1983, Clarence B. Hanson Jr. was succeeded as publisher by Victor H. Hanson II.

1956
Ben G. George, *The Demopolis Times*
1956-1957 president

85th annual press convention, Birmingham
Jan. 19-21, 1956
Summer convention, Mobile
July 19-21, 1956

The 85th annual APA convention was at the Tutwiler Hotel in Birmingham Jan. 19-21, 1956, with sessions for the more than 200 delegates ranging from talks by advertising office personnel on "How to Make More Money Out of My Newspaper" to "What I Expect From My Newspaper" conducted by a panel of speakers from non-journalistic fields.

One of the more lively sessions was a discussion of revision of the Wage and Hour law and Child Labor laws and regulations. Presiding over a panel of governmental representatives in these fields was Newell Brown, administrator of the U.S. Labor Department's Wage and Hour Division. Other panelists included Homer E. Krog, regional director of the Labor Department's Wage and Hour Division in the Southeast; Mamie B. Ham, chief of the Child Labor Division, Alabama Department of Industrial Relations; and R.F. Hudson Jr., executive editor and assistant to the publisher of *The Montgomery Advertiser* and *Alabama Journal.*

Panel discusses making more money

Serving on the panel on "How to Make More Money Out of My Newspaper" which touched all aspects of the business side of the newspaper were APA president Ben G. George, publisher of *The Demopolis Times;* Ellen LaCour, national advertising manager of *The Tuscaloosa News;* Clarke Edwards, retail advertising manager of *The Enterprise Ledger;* Gordon J. McPherson of Ralston Purina Co., who discussed cooperative advertising and

---

S I D E L I G H T S

MARKING 125 YEARS OF HISTORY

Star-News *supports sales tax*
Educators in Andalusia paid tribute in 1962 to *The Andalusia Star-News* for the role the newspaper played in supporting an added 1-cent sales tax in October 1961. The occasion was a student assembly at Andalusia High School on Sept. 12, 1962.
The Star-News won the first-place award for best service to education in the 1962 APA Better Newspaper Contest. Byron Vickery, Arthur G. Jones and Ed Dannelly of *The Star-News* had places of honor reserved on the auditorium stage.

---

building local volume; E.M. (Sparky) Howell, classified advertising manager of *The Onlooker* in Foley; Bernard Feld, promotion manager of *The Birmingham News;* and Tommy Alewine of *The Brandon* (Miss.) *News,* who discussed using existing machinery and facilities to develop increased revenue.

George Cox of *Mobile Press Register* presides over panel

George M. Cox, executive editor of *The Mobile Press Register,* presided over the panel on "What I Expect From My Newspaper." Other panelists were C.E. "Tip" Mathews, editorial writer for *The Mobile Press Register;* Wilfred Galbraith, associate editor of *The Anniston Star;* Bonnie D. Hand, publisher of *The LaFayette Sun;* Glenn Jones, publisher of *The Troy Messenger;* Professor C.E. (Ed) Bounds, head of the University of Alabama Department of Journalism; Mrs. Buist Swaim of Birmingham, housewife; Coley Baker Jr. of Alexander City, businessman; J.B. Thompson of Alexander City, farmer; and William Spoor, publicity director of Loveman, Joseph and Loeb, Birmingham.

APA honored two state legislators who were voted most outstanding members of Alabama House and Senate during the 1955 session: Rep. George C. Hawkins of Gadsden and Sen. James S. Coleman Jr. of Eutaw.

APA past presidents receive gavels in 1956

All APA past presidents who had not already received them were presented gavels by L.O. Brackeen, director of publicity at Alabama Polytechnic Institute, Auburn.

Gavels were presented to Col. Harry M. Ayers, *The Anniston Star,* 1915-1916 and 1916-1917 APA president; Webb Stanley, *The Greenville Advocate,* 1926-1927 and 1935-1936 president; W. Emmett Brooks, *The Brewton Standard,* 1929-1930 president; Marcy B. Darnall, *The Florence Herald,* 1930-1931 president; Jack M. Pratt, *The Pickens County Herald,* Carrollton, 1931-1932 president; Robert Gaston Bozeman, *The Evergreen Courant,* 1936-1937 president; Milton C. Giles, *The Franklin County Times,* Russellville, 1939-1940 president; James H. (Jimmy) Faulkner, *The Baldwin Times,* Bay Minette, 1941-1942 president; Charles G. Dobbins, *The Anniston Times,* 1942-1943 president; Parker W. Campbell, *The Progressive-Age,* Scottsboro, 1944-1945 president; George A. Carleton, *The Clarke County Democrat,* Grove Hill, 1945-1946 president; Bonnie D. Hand, *The LaFayette Sun,* 1946-1947 president; Neil O. Davis, *The Lee County Bulletin,* Auburn, 1947-1948 president; E.H. (Ed) Pierce, *The Mountain Eagle,* Jasper, 1948-1949 president; and George H. Watson, *The Shades Valley Sun,* Homewood, 1955-1956 president.

Presidents from 1949-1954 who had already received their gavels included J.C. Henderson, *The Alexander City Outlook,* 1949-1950 president; Edmund R. (Ed) Blair, *The St. Clair News-Aegis,* Pell City, 1950-1951 president; Clarence B. Hanson Jr., *The Birmingham News,* 1951-1952 president; Cecil H. Hornady, *The Talladega News,* 1952-1953 president; William E. (Bill) Brooks Jr., *The Brewton Standard,* 1953-1954 president; and Steele E. McGrew, *The Limestone Democrat* and *The Alabama Courier,* Athens, 1954-1955 president.

A legislative success during the year was the successful fight against bills which would have enforced a 3 percent tax on advertising revenue and a measure designed to prohibit advertising of alcoholic beverages in newspapers.

Jack Beisner resigns in October 1956

Jack Beisner resigned as APA secretary-field manager effective Oct. 31, 1956, to accept an appointment as press officer for overseas duty with the U.S. Information Agency. Beisner, field manager since September 1950, had served as director of the University News Bureau, member of the UA journalism faculty, secretary-treasurer for APA, and manager of Alabama Newspaper Advertising Service. Before coming to Alabama, Beisner was editor of *The Custer County Chief* in Broken Bow, Neb.

Jones W. Giles, assistant manager, was appointed acting field manager. Giles, a native Alabamian, bought his first newspaper, *The Red Bay News* in Franklin County, while still a student. He also edited and published *The Franklin County Times* in Russellville with his father, former APA president Milton C. Giles, from 1945 to 1953.

Earlier in 1956, the University of Alabama separated the APA and News Bureau for the first time since 1939, and Edward Owen (Ed) Brown III became News Bureau director on Feb. 1, 1956, the day Autherine Lucy, the first black student in the University's 125-year history, began attending classes on the Alabama campus.

A statewide chapter of Sigma Delta Chi, national journalism fraternity, was organized in Birmingham in October 1956. Col. Harry M. Ayers, publisher of *The Anniston Star*, presided at the organizational meeting. Charles A. Fell, editor-in-chief of *The Birmingham News*, was elected president; Grover C. Hall Jr., editor of *The Montgomery Advertiser*, was elected vice president; Larry Hamilton of the Chamber of Commerce was elected secretary; and Leroy Simms, Alabama bureau chief, Associated Press, was elected treasurer.

1956 summer convention, Mobile

Journalism excellence awards were presented to 25 Alabama weekly newspapers for their entries in the Better Newspaper Contest awards that were presented at the 1956 summer convention in Mobile, July 19-21 at the Battle House Hotel. In Division A, *The Haleyville Advertiser* was named first place recipient, and in Division B, *The Tallassee Tribune* was first place winner.

The only business session of the three-day meeting was held during the Friday night banquet. Other activities centered on Dauphin Island, "the newly created vacation spot on Mobile County's Gulf coast."

1957
George M. Cox, *The Mobile Press Register*
1957-1958 president

86th annual press convention, Montgomery
Jan. 10-12, 1957
Summer convention, Edgewater Park, Miss.
Aug. 8-10, 1957

"Community Promotion" was the theme of the 86th annual press convention at the Whitley Hotel in Montgomery Jan. 10-12, 1957.

Serving on a panel on "Community Promotion" were outgoing APA president George M. Cox, executive editor of *The Mobile Press Register;* Libba Cornish George, *The Demopolis Times;* Jay Thornton, *The Haleyville Advertiser;* E.R. (Bob) Morrissette Jr., *The Baldwin Times,* Bay Minette; and Fred Eiland, *The Cleburne News,* Heflin. *The Alabama Publisher*

Sharing a laugh
   APA field manager Jack Beisner, right, shares a laugh with Guy Easterly of the Tennessee Press Association. The photograph is believed to have been made in the summer of 1956. Beisner was field manager from 1950 to 1956. (Photograph courtesy of Mary-Lou Beisner)

gave an account of the convention in its Volume 9, Number 1 (January 1957) issue.

"A newspaper man can engage in no greater community project than helping attract industry to his town," said incoming APA president George Cox, panel moderator. Fred Eiland opened his part of the discussion by pointing out that "no newspaper is good without a good town, and no town is good without a good newspaper." Eiland described the work of his newspaper in encouraging the development of Cleburne County and in attracting new industry.

Jay Thornton told APA delegates of his newspaper's campaign against mishandling of Winston County's road funds. The campaign was successful, he said, in correcting fiscal abuses and in increasing the newspaper's circulation. Libba Cornish George discussed the efforts of *The Demopolis Times* on its 50th anniversary issue and

the effect the edition had on local merchants and citizens. Bob Morrissette observed that "anything that benefits merchants benefits the town." He told of several advertising campaigns that *The Baldwin Times* had sponsored.

Thomason conducts session, "Looking at Ourselves"

C.G. Thomason, publisher of *The Industrial Press* at Ensley, conducted a session on "Looking at Ourselves." Each delegate at the session took part in the exchange of ideas and suggestions. Professor C.E. (Ed) Bounds of the University of Alabama Department of Journalism ended the session with a talk on "11,000 Crying Needs for Better Newspapers."

At Friday's luncheon meeting, Dr. Emmett Kilpatrick of Troy State Teachers College assailed the U.S. foreign policy in a talk on "Hungary and the Middle East." Kilpatrick said that "the optimistic policy" of John Foster Dulles, secretary of state, had annoyed him "beyond annoyance. We cannot let the United Nations form our foreign policy," Kilpatrick told delegates. He said the United States should have backed England and France in the Suez Canal controversy. Kilpatrick was introduced by Glenn Jones of *The Troy Messenger*.

In a Friday night speech, FBI director J. Edgar Hoover's assistant appealed to the "law abiding people of Alabama for a crystallization and determination on their part to solve peacefully the civil rights issue." Louis B. Nichols, formerly stationed in Alabama with the FBI, made the appeal as featured speaker at the annual banquet.

Judge Walter B. Jones honored at 1957 convention

Circuit Judge Walter B. Jones of Montgomery was honored at the banquet with an honorary membership in APA and a plaque commending his "vigilant fight for freedom of the press." Bonnie D. Hand of *The LaFayette Sun* hailed Jones as a "friend of the freedom of the press." Jones commented that he had long believed in the right of the people to know, and he likened the press and the bar as "partners in serving human welfare." Jones wrote a weekly column, "Off The Bench," for *The Montgomery Advertiser* and was a champion of freedom of information in the courts.

In addition to the annual business meeting, Saturday's agenda included a meeting conducted by ANAS officers. The program featured Gene

Alleman, director of Research and Information, Weekly Newspaper Representatives; ANAS president Bill Stewart of *The Monroe Journal*, Monroeville; and directors Jay Thornton, *The Haleyville Advertiser;* J.C. Henderson, *The Alexander City Outlook;* and Porter Harvey, *The Advertiser-Gleam*, Guntersville.

Cornish addresses luncheon session

"Daily and weekly newspapers have continued to thrive despite competition from radio and television," said George A. Cornish, executive editor of *The New York Herald Tribune.* Cornish addressed the luncheon session shortly after George M. Cox of *The Mobile Press Register* took over as APA president. Libba Cornish George, wife of outgoing president Ben G. George of *The Demopolis Times,* introduced her brother, George Cornish.

On the legislative front, 1957 was a trying year for the APA. According to president George M. Cox, "We were shot at from all directions, but the Legislative Committee again came through."

A special committee set up by the Alabama Milk Control Board studied possible revision of the board's controls on milk advertising in 1957 after APA charged that advertising of milk distributors was being censored. APA asked for reversal of the Milk Control Board policy. APA president George M. Cox made the censorship charge in a six-page statement.

A $150,000 libel suit against *The Montgomery Advertiser* by Birmingham segregationist Asa E. Carter was dismissed in Montgomery County Circuit Court when Carter failed to appear for the trial. The suit alleged that an *Advertiser* editorial was "falsely and maliciously" published "with intent to defame."

Buford Boone awarded Pulitzer Prize in 1957

An active APA member, *Tuscaloosa News* publisher and editor Buford Boone, was recognized during 1957 for his editorials written during integration at the Uni-

Buford Boone
The Tuscaloosa News

versity of Alabama. Boone followed Grover C. Hall Sr., editor of *The Montgomery Advertiser,* as the second Alabamian to win the highest award in American journalism. Boone won the Pulitzer Prize for his editorials, "In a Community Inflamed by the Segregation Issue." Cited as an outstanding example was his Feb. 7, 1956, editorial, "What A Price for Peace," concerning the efforts of Autherine Lucy to gain admission to the University of Alabama.

"Boone's editorials demonstrated courage"

"Mr. Boone's editorials demonstrated courage and independence in the face of excited and almost hysterical opposition," judges wrote. "At the same time they gave evidence of the willingness of a community to follow sober and enlightened leadership dedicated to the maintenance of order and individual rights, challenged by mob impulses."

The unrelenting fight that Grover C. Hall Sr. carried on against the Klan, flogging, and racial and religious intolerance had brought him national attention in 1928, when he won the Pulitzer for best editorial writing.

Membership again reached a new high in 1957, but 100 percent of the state's newspapers still were not represented. ANAS did not do as well in 1957 as in 1956, primarily because of a decline in Weekly Newspaper Representatives (WNR) automobile advertising business.

Jones Giles named APA manager in 1957

Jones W. Giles was named secretary-field manager of APA in 1957, and an assistant manager was hired to work primarily with the Department of Journalism and the Extension Division in the journalism field. This was done to meet the University's Alabama's requirement that the secretary-field manager have the academic requirements to teach journalism courses. Giles had been acting field manager since the resignation of Jack Beisner in October 1956.

John Edward Weems, a former Texas newspaper man and journalism teacher, was appointed assistant APA manager and assistant professor in the University of Alabama Department of Journalism in 1957. Weems' duties included editorship of *The Alabama Publisher,* which he assumed with the September 1957 issue.

S I D E L I G H T S
MARKING 125 YEARS OF HISTORY

Bertie Gammell Parish plays organ at tea
Bertie Gammell Parish, editor and publisher of *The Clayton Record,* played the organ during the inaugural tea at the Governor's Mansion following George C. Wallace's inauguration on Jan. 14, 1963.

1957 summer convention, Edgewater Park, Miss.

The 1957 summer convention was at Edgewater Gulf Hotel, Edgewater Park, Miss., on Aug. 8-10. More than 130 delegates registered for the three-day event. The majority of the publishers, editors and other newspaper representatives took advantage of the brevity of the official program and enjoyed swimming, golfing, sailing and just plain relaxing.

Highlighting the program was the annual awards banquet in the form of a "plantation dinner." President George M. Cox, executive editor of *The Mobile Press Register,* presented awards to 30 weekly newspaper winners. *The Monroe Journal* in Monroeville was named General Excellence recipient in Division A, and *The Shades Valley Sun* received the General Excellence award in Division B.

Entertainment was provided by the "Circle X Wranglers," a Fort McPherson Army band. Delegates were treated to a visit to Marine Life, a seafood jamboree, a boat trip on the Gulf, and an APA breakfast. Associate members of the Press Association were hosts to two receptions.

1958
C.G. Thomason, *The Industrial Press,* Ensley
1958-1959 president

87th annual press convention, Tuscaloosa
Feb. 6-8, 1958
Summer convention, on top of Lookout Mountain, Tenn.
June 26-28, 1958

"More Profits From Better Service" was the theme of the 87th annual press convention Feb. 6-8, 1958, at the new Hotel Stafford in Tuscaloosa.

C.G. Thomason, publisher of *The Industrial Press* in Ensley, was inducted 1958-1959 president. Thomason, who had been in the newspaper business since 1915, established *The Industrial Press* in April 1931. In 1919 he worked for *The Atlanta Georgian.* From there he went to *The Memphis Press* as managing editor. In 1921 he worked in the promotion department of *The Birmingham Post.*

When Thomason was 19, he was publisher of *The Shelby County Revue. The Alabama Publisher* reported that Thomason laughingly recalled, "The paper folded after I left. I guess I left it in bad shape." Thomason recalled putting out an "Extra" in 1917 when Czar Nicholas abdicated the throne in Russia. "The business has changed a lot since then, but I'll never tire of it," Thomason said.

Mayors of three Alabama cities, along with several newspaper editors, served on a panel at the 1958 winter convention to discuss the complexities of a state population shifting from rural to urban characteristics. They also cited the need for a partnership between local government and the press. Joining the panel was Judge Winston Stewart, representing the Association of County Commissioners in Montgomery.

Participating on the panel were Barrett C. Shelton Jr., *The Decatur Daily;* Mobile Mayor Joseph Langon; Judge Stewart; Ed E. Reid, executive director of the Alabama League of Municipalities; outgoing APA president George M. Cox, *The Mobile Press Register;* Gadsden Mayor Hugh Patterson; and Andalusia Mayor Leland Enzor.

Rose, Arrowsmith featured speakers

Dr. Frank A. Rose, president of the University of Alabama, and Marvin Arrowsmith, White House reporter for the Associated Press, were featured speakers at the Feb. 8 banquet in the ballroom of the Stafford Hotel. Plaques were presented to Jefferson County Sen. Albert Boutwell and Montgomery County Rep. Joseph M. Dawkins as outstanding members of the 1957 Legislature. Plaques were presented by Bonnie D. Hand of *The LaFayette Sun,* chairman of the Legislative Committee.

Tracing the "struggle of mankind to lift itself from the 'valley of ignorance'," Rose cited the invention of the printing press as the event that made possible the democratic way of life.

"With the discovery of the printing press, oppression was to pass away," Rose said. "The rulers and oppressors cannot stand before enlightenment and knowledge. As eyes turned toward newly discovered America we found people dying for their beliefs in the democratic experiment. But today we are living the most glorious life ever accorded the human race. We are living a life that belonged only to kings and queens of yesterday."

Pointing to the scientific achievements of Russia, Rose said education was facing its greatest crisis. "I pledge every ounce of my strength and energy to the challenge of preparing our youth not only for leadership of Alabama, but the nation and world. I ask you to join me in that effort."

Problems of covering nation's Capitol

Guest speaker at the Saturday luncheon was Marvin Arrowsmith, White House reporter for the Associated Press. Arrowsmith told the delegates of the problems and excitement of covering the nation's Capitol, and he discussed at length the three major illnesses of President Eisenhower during a two-year period.

A meeting of Alabama Newspaper Advertising Service featured Joe T. Cook, president of Weekly Newspaper Representatives Inc. (WNR), and publisher of *The Mission* (Texas) *Times*. Cook reviewed the operation of Weekly Newspaper Representatives and the national advertising situation and answered questions from publishers on advertising. ANAS president J.C. Henderson of *The Alexander City Outlook* presided at the meeting.

Field manager Jones W. Giles reported a marked increase in APA functions in 1958. Along with the usual support and cooperation in worthwhile projects such as the High School Press Conference, National Newspaper Week, Alabama Industry Days, and Career Days, more personal inquiries and special requests from members were handled than ever before, Giles said.

Resolutions Committee makes report

The February 1958 issue of *The Alabama Publisher* (Volume 10, Number 2) reported that J.C. Henderson of *The Alexander City Outlook*, Fred Eiland of *The Cleburne News* in Heflin and Ben G. George of *The Demopolis Times* served on the Resolutions Committee which made its report on Feb. 8, the closing day of the convention. The committee reported that "Whereas: We leave our Winter Convention with renewed interest and enthusiasm for our work, we do therefore — Be it resolved that this convention express its sincerest appreciation and confidence through a standing vote, and hereby order that these resolutions be published in full in *The Alabama Publisher* for posterity."

Jo Ann Flirt, a reporter with *The Montgomery Advertiser*, was named assistant manager of APA in September 1958. The announcement was made by APA manager Jones W. Giles. Before moving to Montgomery, Flirt was associate editor of *The Onlooker* in Foley. According to Giles, one of her main duties with APA would be editing *The Alabama Publisher*.

1958 summer convention, Lookout Mountain, Tenn.

"Reaching for a new high in APA summer conventions, the committee this year settled on a site 2,400 feet above sea level, atop famed Lookout Mountain, Tennessee, the resort hotel, Castle in the Clouds," *The Alabama Publisher* reported in its May 1958 issue. The 1958 summer convention was June 26-28. "The only decision you will have to make for a few days will be what to enjoy next," *The Publisher* reported. "Swimming, golf, riding, tennis, loafing or just drinking in the cool mountain air — a variety of pleasures all for you and your family."

<hr>

S I D E L I G H T S
MARKING 125 YEARS OF HISTORY

Porter Harvey elected constable

Porter Harvey, editor of *The Advertiser-Gleam* in Guntersville, used an 8x10 advertisement in January 1964 to proclaim the fact that he once was elected a constable in Dodge City, Kan.

Harvey said he was working for *The Dodge City Daily Globe* at the time and that no one had offered as a candidate for the post. He said several friends, as a gag, wrote in his name when they went to the polls. Harvey was elected.

He resigned immediately. After Dodge City became famous for its lawmen, Harvey said he got out his certificate of election and hung it on the wall of his office at *The Advertiser-Gleam*. "That was several years ago," Harvey said. "Thousands of people have been in the office since then, but only two or three of them have ever noticed the certificate hanging on the wall."

The ad would serve two purposes, Harvey said. "First it will build up the editor's pride by letting people know what a great honor was once bestowed on him. And second, it will demonstrate that although something may go unnoticed even if posted in the most conspicuous place, you can bring it to the people's attention promptly by advertising it in the paper."

<hr>

1959
Bill Stewart, *The Monroe Journal*, Monroeville
1959-1960 president

88th annual press convention, Birmingham
Jan. 22-24, 1959
Summer convention, Dauphin Island
June 11-13, 1959

"We Sell Better Now" was the theme of the 88th annual press convention Jan. 22-24, 1959, at the Tutwiler Hotel in Birmingham. Nearly 200 editors, publishers, key newspaper executives and associate members attended the convention.

Workshop sessions at the convention included an opening address by Robert Luckie, president of Luckie and Co., Alabama's largest advertising agency, who spoke on "Creative Mass Selling" and illustrated with slides and tape the newest approaches to advertising by radio and television.

Besides workshops and speeches, the convention featured a panel discussion by three of Alabama's leading political figures who reported on "The State of the State." Appearing on the panel were Lt. Gov. Albert Boutwell, state Superintendent of Education Frank R. Stewart, and Rep. Charles C. Adams, speaker of the Alabama House of Representatives.

Boutwell told delegates of plans for a legislative committee to spearhead the state's rights battle in Alabama. According to Boutwell, the move could lead to a similar "southwide organization" to set up plans to forestall integration and to put into motion a campaign to "educate the nation on the South's problems."

Adams spoke briefly about the problems facing the Legislature and said that the top problem was that of finding money for highway construction. "Alabama has $370 million in federal money available the next four years, but the state must provide $115 million in matching money to get it," Adams told APA delegates. Adams said most of the money would go for paving primary and secondary roads with only a small part for the federal interstate highway system.

Stewart: Office records open for public inspection

Stewart assured members of the Alabama press that records in the Department of Education office were always available for public inspection, and he invited newspapers to send reporters to his office to "gather facts on the present situation in Alabama."

Stewart asked the support of newspapers in his efforts to get a 20 percent pay raise for schoolteachers. He said the boost would cost $29 million. According to Stewart, Alabama's teacher pay was lower than any other state in the South except Arkansas and Mississippi. Average pay in Alabama in 1959 was $3,372 a year.

Frank Kilcheski of the Bureau of Advertising in New York told of a massive program of total selling and what the newspaper industry was at-

tempting to do to sell itself as an advertising medium competing with television and radio.

Luncheon speaker was W.D. (Pete) Moore, director of advertising and sales promotion of the Dodge division of Chrysler Corporation, who explained Dodge's approach to advertising and advertising media.

Two receptions, one by *The Birmingham News* and the *Post-Herald* at Vestavia Country Club and another by APA associate members, were additional highlights of the 88th annual convention, as were the transistor radios given as door prizes.

Resolution blasts Washington, D.C. newspaper

A resolution introduced by Col. Harry M. Ayers of *The Anniston Star* was adopted that blasted a Washington, D.C., newspaper for refusing to print a pro-segregation letter as paid advertising. The resolution condemned *The Washington Post* for refusing to carry the Putnam letter as paid advertising. The "Putnam letter" was a letter to President Dwight D. Eisenhower by Carleton Putnam, a retired Washington executive, criticizing the U.S. Supreme Court decisions requiring racial integration of public schools.

A committee of prominent Alabamians launched a fund-raising drive to get the letter published as a paid advertisement in Northern and Western newspapers. Already printed in *The New York Times* and *The Washington Star*, the letter was refused by *The Washington Post*.

The resolution adopted by APA said it "does deplore and condemn the betrayal of the press and of the right of the people to know all sides of a public issue." The Press Association decided to sponsor efforts to have the Putnam letter reprinted in Alabama newspapers. Mats of the letter were distributed by the APA office which urged editors

---

S I D E L I G H T S
MARKING 125 YEARS OF HISTORY

Tribune *lists "whole shebang" for $175*

The following classified advertisement was published in the March 11, 1964, issue of *AlaPressa*: "For Sale: 16 full page used chases for Goss Cox-O-Type press, side sticks and footsticks included, $15 each or the whole shebang at one time for $175, as is, where is. *The Tallassee Tribune*. Dial 283-3030."

to run the letter either as a public service or to secure sponsors for it and run it as an advertisement.

Resolution in 1959 calls for "Hall of Fame"

A resolution calling for an "Alabama Newspaper Hall of Fame" was introduced in 1959 by L.O. Brackeen, director of publicity at Alabama Polytechnic Institute, Auburn, and Webb Stanley, business manager of *The Greenville Advocate*. "Alabama has had some outstanding newspaper publishers and editors whose lives and memories should be preserved," stated the resolution which was unanimously adopted.

The resolution suggested that a committee work with the Department of Archives and History in Montgomery to establish a permanent "Hall of Fame," or some other suitable method of honoring Alabama newspapers.

Chatting with the governor
   This photograph was taken sometime in the late 1950s and was provided by J.C. Henderson, retired publisher of *The Alexander City Outlook*. From left are Gov. John Patterson, Public Safety Director Floyd Mann, J. C. Henderson, and Alexander City Mayor W.L. Radley.

Popular with delegates to the 1959 convention was the new format which included a smorgasbord and fashion show on the opening night, and a late "good morning breakfast" on Saturday morning. Entertainment by leading Birmingham entertainers from the Town and Gown Theatre group and others replaced the customary banquet speech Friday night. Mistress of ceremonies at what proved to be one of the convention's most popular programs was Toni Moore, alternate Miss America.

APA sponsors advertising and photo workshop

Sixty newspaper photographers and advertising sales representatives attended a two-day advertising and photography workshop in September 1959 sponsored by APA and the Extension Division of the University of Alabama.

The Legislative Committee and field manager Jones Giles worked hard in Montgomery in 1959 with mixed results. The exemption of newspapers from the state sales tax was removed, but other legislation opposed by the APA was defeated.

1959 summer convention, Dauphin Island

In addition to announcing the winners in the Better Newspaper Contest, delegates attending the 1959 summer outing on Dauphin Island June 11-13 approved plans for the Alabama Newspaper Hall of Honor and discussed legislation adversely affecting newspapers and made plans for combating this type legislation. Under Hall of Honor plans, four outstanding editors would be honored at the annual convention in 1960, and two each future year.

APA, through its officers and Hall of Honor Committee, also agreed to encourage Alabama newspapers to write and prepare in pamphlet form histories of their newspapers. Copies of the histories were to be placed in the Hall of Honor as they became available.

It was announced that the "History of the Alabama Press Association" was being revised by L.O. Brackeen, director of publicity at Alabama Polytechnic Institute, and would be distributed to members at the 1960 convention. The revised history would cover APA history from its start in 1871 to 1959. Brackeen also wrote the original "History of the Alabama Press Association" (1871-1951), that was issued Dec. 22, 1952.

Hall of Honor Committee named

Members of the committee submitting the Hall of Honor plans for approval were L.O. Brackeen, chairman, Alabama Polytechnic Institute, Auburn; Webb Stanley, *The Greenville Advocate;* Cecil H. Hornady, *The Talladega News;* Bonnie D. Hand, *The LaFayette Sun;* and George A. Carleton, *The Clarke County Democrat,* Grove Hill.

Before the summer meeting, APA president Bill Stewart of *The Monroe Journal* in Monroeville, named a six-member committee to nominate those to be voted upon for the Hall of Honor. They included L.O. Brackeen, Alabama Polytechnic Institute, chairman; Cecil H. Hornady, *The Talladega News;* Bonnie D. Hand, *The LaFayette Sun;* Glenn Jones, *The Troy Messenger;* Walter F. Miller, *The Colbert County Reporter,* Tuscumbia; and George A. Carleton, *The Clarke County Democrat,* Grove Hill.

The committee met at Dauphin Island and recommended four individuals to be honored at the 1960 convention: Hunter Howell Golson, publisher of *The Wetumpka Herald* until his death in 1946; Frazier Titus Raiford, editor and publisher of *The Selma Times-Journal* who died in 1937; Maj. William Wallace Screws, editor of *The Montgomery Advertiser* until his death in 1913; and Gen. James Berney Stanley, editor of *The Greenville Advocate* for 70 years who died in 1934. Upon recommendation of the committee, the four deceased editors were approved for induction to the first Alabama Newspaper Hall of Honor.

Brackeen, APA historian, also announced a project to acquire and preserve histories of Ala-

---

---

bama newspapers and called on editors to submit their histories to him.

Grover Hall Jr. speaks in New York

A leading editor and political commentator, Grover C. Hall Jr. of *The Montgomery Advertiser,* presented an Alabama view of school integration and its likely consequences when he spoke in New York in January 1959.

"There is a clear danger that Northern politicians and the federal cops will unleash the violent element in the South," Hall told a New York

Grover C. Hall Jr.
Editor, The Montgomery Advertiser

audience. Hall was guest speaker before the Bronxville Community Forum. According to Hall, the "thug element exists in every city, county and state in this country. The South's thug element is now largely held in restraint by public opinion," Hall said. "But if these Southern expeditionary forces from Washington continue to grind down, I'm afraid that public opinion in the South will become less forbidding towards violence than it is now."

Hall told the New York audience that "Montgomery is presently a peaceful place — never as dangerous as Central Park. And when we did have some bombing, the authorities went after the suspects with so much zeal that the force-fulness of their investigative methods was used in court in behalf of the defendants." Hall was introduced by Alabama native Edward W. Barrett Jr., dean of the Columbia University School of Journalism.

(Barrett's father, Edward W. Barrett Sr., was editor and publisher of *The Birmingham Age-Herald,* one of the newspapers that was a forerunner of the *Birmingham Post-Herald.*)

Mary Howard Raiford dies in 1959

Mary Howard Raiford, 83, co-founder and sole owner of *The Selma Times-Journal* and the only woman editor of a daily newspaper in Alabama, died in her sleep on July 11, 1959.

The widow of Frazier Titus Raiford, publisher of *The Selma Times-Journal* until his death on April 19, 1937, Mrs. Raiford had served the paper as general manager since 1921 and as publisher since the death of her husband. Shortly after her death, the will of Mrs. Raiford was probated and she made provisions for the sale of the historic paper to five veteran employees.

Mary Howard Raiford
The Selma Times-Journal

Steps to purchase *The Times-Journal* were taken by Frank Ford, advertising manager; Ed Field, editor; Mrs. C.W. Wynn, former city editor; Roswell Falkenberry, assistant advertising manager; and W.C. Calhoun, mechanical superintendent. A spokesman for the group said a five-member corporation of the buyers would be formed. The price and terms of the sale were agreed upon by Mrs. Raiford before her death and were not revealed in the will. The new owners elected Frank Ford, advertising manager of *The Selma Times-Journal,* as president of the corporation.

Frazier Titus Raiford
The Selma Times-Journal
One of the first four Hall of Honor inductees

Mrs. Raiford entered the newspaper field in 1914 with her husband when they purchased *The Selma Times,* then operating as a morning newspaper. From this start with a single Linotype machine, a flat-bed, hand operated press and a circulation of 500, the Raifords built a successful and widely influential newspaper. *The Times* was con-

solidated in 1920 with *The Selma Journal* which was purchased by the Raifords.

Times-Journal celebrated centennial in 1927

The Times-Journal was established in 1827 as *The Selma Courier.* When the newspaper celebrated its centennial in 1927, it was reported to be the second oldest newspaper in Alabama, the 10th oldest in the South and 42nd oldest in the nation.

An avid sports fan, Mrs. Raiford followed the Selma Cloverleafs through the years, occupying a box seat which she reserved for each season. She planned to attend the opening game of the 1959 season. Until three years before her death, Mrs. Raiford attended most Alabama and Auburn football games played in the state. Mrs. Raiford was inducted into the Alabama Newspaper Hall of Honor in 1968.

1960

James E. (Jimmy) Mills, the *Birmingham Post-Herald*
1960-1961 president

89th annual press convention, Montgomery
Feb. 9-11, 1960
Summer convention, Dauphin Island
June 14-16, 1960

The 89th annual press convention Feb. 9-11, 1960, in Montgomery topped all others both in number of newspapers represented and in attendance. Attendance by political leaders added to the interest of the 1960 convention as Alabama Gov. John Patterson and Tennessee Gov. Buford Ellington addressed the delegates.

Patterson urged the editors and publishers to "keep the spotlight of publicity focused on state government and to report the people's business" to their readers. "We might not always like what you say," Patterson said, "but we want you to keep reporting and commenting on state affairs. It's good for us, and I learn some things through your newspaper that I don't know myself." Ellington discussed the work and importance of the Southern Regional Education Board, an organization of 16 Southern states which encouraged cooperation in providing specialized college-level training.

"State of the State" panel

A panel discussion called "The State of the State" featured Attorney MacDonald Gallion, Superintendent of Education Frank R. Stewart, Agriculture Commissioner R.C. (Red) Bamberg, State Docks Director Earl McGowin, and Revenue Commissioner Harry Haden. Workshop sessions included "Special Promotions" by Mack Smythe, advertising director of *The Jackson* (Miss.) *Daily News* and "The Case of the Coverage That Wasn't" by Warren Grieb of Weekly Newspaper Representatives (WNR), New York.

Bonnie D. Hand, publisher of *The LaFayette Sun* and chairman of the APA Legislative Committee, presented "Outstanding Legislator" awards to Rep. Joseph W. Smith of Phenix City and Sen. Ryan DeGraffenried Sr. of Tuscaloosa.

Brackeen officiates at first Hall of Honor in 1960

L.O. Brackeen, director of publicity at Auburn University (formerly Alabama Polytechnic Institute) officiated during ceremonies in 1960 installing the first members of the Alabama Newspaper Hall of Honor. The Press Association had adopted a resolution in 1959 establishing the Hall of Honor. When the Hall of Honor Committee made its recommendation to APA, the idea was to locate the Hall of Honor in the Alabama Department of Archives and History in Montgomery.

At that time, in 1959, space was not available in Alabama Archives, and the Hall of Honor remained homeless for at least four years. Its materials were kept at APA headquarters in Tuscaloosa and in the Department of University Relations on the Auburn University campus.

Auburn University officials offered space to house the Hall of Honor in Ralph Brown Draughon Library in 1964. APA accepted the offer, and on Oct. 10, 1964, the dedicatory ceremony took place. The Press Association has met in Auburn each fall since 1964 for the Hall of Honor ceremonies at Draughon Library.

Four inducted into Hall of Honor

In 1960, the first Alabama journalists to be honored at the Hall of Honor ceremonies were Gen. James Berney Stanley, editor and publisher of *The Greenville Advocate;* Maj. William Wallace Screws, editor of *The Montgomery Advertiser;* Frazier Titus Raiford, editor and publisher of *The Selma Times-Journal;* and Hunter Howell Golson, editor and publisher of *The Wetumpka Herald.* The four newspaper men were approved for induction in 1959 and were honored at the 1960 annual convention in Montgomery.

APA received two citations in 1960. Floyd Mann, state director of Public Safety, presented a

---

citation which commended Alabama newspapers for their promotion of public safety, particularly motor vehicle safety. A plaque was presented Alabama newspapers by representatives of the 1960 March of Dimes commending editors and publishers for their interpretive reporting of the new program of the March of Dimes.

APA members were guests in 1960 of the Air Force for a tour of the Semi-Automatic Ground Environment (SAGE) operations at Gunter Air Force Base. SAGE involved a gigantic system of computers which analyzed flight information received from many sources and detected suspicious aircraft.

Delegation attends NEA meeting in Atlanta

In 1960 an APA delegation attended the annual meeting of the National Editorial Association in Atlanta. ANAS went all-out in the area of political advertising, contacting almost all state and district candidates to attract political advertising to Alabama weekly newspapers.

The Alabama Association of Mental Health presented a citation to APA in 1960. Presenting the award to James E. (Jimmy) Mills, editor of the *Birmingham Post-Herald,* on behalf of the APA, was attorney Charles Morgan, state legislative chairman of the Mental Health Association. The citation stated, "During the last 18 months the indifference, apathy and lack of information on the part of citizens regarding the care and treatment of the mentally ill has to a great extent been dispelled. The work of publishers, editors and reporters contributed in a far-reaching constructive way in bringing about this accomplishment."

UA, APA sponsor News-Photo Clinic

The University of Alabama and APA sponsored a News-Photo Clinic at the Tuscaloosa campus in October 1960. On the program were Alabama native Jack Nelson, prize-winning writer for *The Atlanta Constitution;* Wilfred D. Auquin of *The New Orleans States Item;* Ed Strickland, special assistant to the Alabama attorney general, who discussed "The Photographer and the Law;" E.E. Blackburn, photo editor of *The Memphis Commercial-Appeal,* who discussed "Making the Picture Tell the Story;" Stanley Parkman of *The Carroll County Georgian* in Carrollton; and Don Brookhard of *The Crossville* (Tenn.) *Chronicle.*

Alabama newspaper representatives participating as speakers and discussion leaders were James Couey, *The Birmingham News;* Harold S. May, *The Florence Herald;* John Hamner, *The Alabama Journal;* Howell Talley, *The Gadsden Times;* Miriam G.

Hill, University of Alabama Department of Journalism; Karol R.L. Fleming, *The Geneva County Reaper* in Geneva; Dan Dowe, *The Alabama Journal;* Clarke Stallworth, the *Birmingham Post-Herald;* Karl Elebash Jr., *The Graphic,* Tuscaloosa; Fred Eiland, *The Cleburne News,* Heflin; Charles Moore, *The Montgomery Advertiser* and *Alabama Journal;* Bob Adams, *The Birmingham News;* and Calvin Hannah, *The Tuscaloosa News.*

1960 summer convention, Dauphin Island

Dauphin Island again was the site of the 1960 annual summer APA convention, July 14-16. It was the second consecutive year that APA met at Dauphin Island, and the third time in recent years that delegates visited there for their summer meeting.

Convention headquarters was the "spacious, modern Holiday Inn Riviera on Dauphin Island, one of the state's newest and most attractive playgrounds," *The Alabama Publisher* reported. The Dauphin Island Businessmen's Association was host to a seafood dinner on the opening night of the convention. On Friday night, the Alabama Division of U.S. Brewers sponsored a beach party around the Holiday Inn pool.

1961
Harold S. May, *The Florence Herald*
1961-1962 president

90th annual press convention, Huntsville
Feb. 9-11, 1961
Summer convention, Dauphin Island
July 13-15, 1961

Approximately 200 people attended the 90th annual convention at the Russel Erskine Hotel in Huntsville Feb. 9-11, 1961. Delegates received a full-scale, first-hand report on the nation's missile and space program and an inspection of one of the latest installations in the world at Redstone Arsenal.

Presentation of awards shared the limelight with election of officers at the business meeting. Three daily and three weekly newspapers were named winners in the U.S. Savings Bond promotion contest. *The Birmingham News* was presented a trophy as runner-up in the previous year's National Newspaper Week promotion contest, and APA was given a certificate by the Savings Bond Division of the Department of the Treasury for its cooperation in a special sales drive.

First-place winners in the Savings Bond promotion contest were Herve Charest Jr., *The Tallassee Tribune*, and Ed Fields, *The Selma Times-Journal*. Other winners were *The Aliceville Informer*, *The Daily Mountain Eagle* in Jasper, *The Enterprise Ledger* and *The Dothan Eagle*.

The convention featured a day-long tour of Redstone Arsenal and George Marshall Space Flight Center, a debate on reapportionment, discussions of the "State of the State" by three state officials, and several dinners and hospitality hours, according to a report by *Birmingham News* staff writer Tommy Hill in the Feb. 12, 1961, edition.

Sen. E.B. Haltom Jr. of Florence and Rep. McDowell Lee of Barbour County debated reapportionment of the Alabama Legislature. Reporting on the "State of the State" were Attorney General MacDonald Gallion, Superintendent of Education Frank Stewart, and Revenue Commissioner Harry Harden.

Legislative Committee succeeds in helping kill bill

During the 1961 legislative session, the APA Legislative Committee was successful in helping kill a bill in the Legislature which would have prohibited advertising of alcoholic beverages in daily or weekly newspapers.

"Your Newspaper — A Business, A Product, A Public Service" was the theme of a fall workshop in 1961. Featured speakers were Ted Serrill, executive vice president of National Editorial Association in Washington, D.C.; Joe Cook, publisher of *The Winston County Journal* in Louisville, Miss.; Edmund C. Arnold, consultant for Mergenthaler Linotype Co. and journalism professor at Syracuse University, Syracuse, N.Y.; John Luskin, journal-

---

> ## S I D E L I G H T S
> ### MARKING 125 YEARS OF HISTORY
>
> ### *An early encounter with Gen. J.B. Stanley*
> Roger W. Pride Sr., publisher of *The Butler County News* in Georgiana, recalled in 1957 an early encounter with Gen. James Berney Stanley, founder of *The Greenville Advocate:*
>
> "A few days after we published the first edition of *The Butler County News,* we caught the train one morning and went up to Greenville to pass out a few sample copies, and about halfway up to the courthouse, Gen. Stanley came up and introduced himself. After we told him what we were doing he went along and introduced us to every business place in Greenville after which he got his horse and buggy and rode us all over the town showing where people lived and giving a history of the place.
>
> "Mr. Stanley gave us many helpful suggestions and helped us in many ways through the years. He was indeed a gentleman of the old school, and his illustrious son, Glenn, is following in his father's footsteps and giving Greenville one of the best county seat papers in the South."

---

ism professor at the University of Alabama; Harvey Walters, manager of the Georgia Press Association in Atlanta; and Howard R. Long, dean of the School of Journalism at Southern Illinois University in Carbondale, Ill.

APA members on the program were Arthur F. Slaton, publisher of *The Moulton Advertiser;* Donald White, publisher of *The Daily Mountain Eagle* in Jasper; and Karol R.L. Fleming, associate editor of *The Geneva County Reaper,* Geneva.

Archie N. Colby, product development manager at Gulf States Paper Corp., spoke at the opening banquet on "Industrial Considerations for a Community Newspaper."

The Alabama Textile Manufacturers Association saluted APA at a public relations workshop in fall 1961.

Bill Stewart of *The Monroe Journal* in Monroeville, former president of the APA and ANAS, was elected president of Weekly Newspaper Representatives Inc. (WNR).

McClellan Van der Veer dies in 1961

McClellan (Ted) Van der Veer, 66, former editorial page editor of *The Birmingham News*, died June 28, 1961, in a New York hotel. He and his wife had arrived there from a visit of several months in Europe. Van der Veer retired from *The News* Jan. 1, 1960, and had been devoting his time to writing since then.

McClellan Van der Veer
The Birmingham News

His editorials were recognized for their high faith in humankind and for a marked spiritual quality.

In his farewell editorial from *The Birmingham News*, Van der Veer sought to sum up his efforts as an editor:

"To heighten interest and concern as to the problems and opportunities of people — of all people everywhere.

"To increase understanding of those problems and opportunities.

"To help find solutions and realizations.

"To stand fast for the right.

"To evoke and strengthen the appeal and power of the good."

Benjamin McGowan Bloodworth, *The Decatur Daily*, Isaac Grant, *The Clarke County Democrat* in Grove Hill, and Charles Herd Greer of *The Sylacauga News* were selected for induction into the Alabama Newspaper Hall of Honor in 1960 and were inducted during the 1961 annual convention in Huntsville.

Isaac Grant
The Clarke County Democrat,
Grove Hill

1961 summer convention, Dauphin Island

A welcoming reception, with 20 APA associate members as hosts, opened the 90th annual summer meeting at Dauphin Island July 13-15, 1961. The reception was followed by a seafood jamboree in the new Dauphin Island auditorium with the Dauphin Island Businessmen's Association as host.

Benjamin McGowan Bloodworth
The Decatur Daily

Friday's luncheon included a shrimp luncheon for adults, and hamburger and hotdog cookout for children around the pool of the Holiday Inn Riviera. An awards breakfast on Saturday morning climaxed the meeting. At that time, awards were presented to winners in the 1961 APA Better Newspaper Contest.

1962
Glenn Stanley, *The Greenville Advocate*
1962-1963 president

91st annual press convention, Birmingham
Feb. 8-10, 1962
Summer convention, Florence
July 12-14, 1962

Delegates to the 91st annual press convention Feb. 8-10, 1962, at the Tutwiler Hotel in Birmingham, adopted a plan to secure a salesman, with headquarters in Birmingham, to sell advertisers of Alabama and adjoining states on Alabama newspapers. APA incoming president Glenn Stanley of *The Greenville Advocate* commented on the plan, "It is going to cost money. But that money is an investment. It is not a donation, not a gamble, but an investment which should pay a big dividend."

Two workshop sessions were held at the 1962 convention. A workshop on the legisla-

---

S I D E L I G H T S
MARKING 125 YEARS OF HISTORY

Faulkner: "Watch out for 'press haters'"

Baldwin Times publisher Jimmy Faulkner, runner-up for the Democratic nomination for governor in 1954, urged the Alabama public to watch out for "press haters."

"Almost invariably," Faulkner told the Birmingham Junior Chamber of Commerce audience, "Press haters are people who are trying to hide something from the public. We have crooks and racketeers, whether they be gamblers or whether they be politicians — whether they live in Phenix City or Montgomery — they hate the press."

Faulkner continued, "It's amusing how many politicians have claimed they cleaned up Phenix City. Actually, it was the people of Alabama who cleaned up Phenix City because the press let them know what was going on. The politicians were no more than stumbling blocks most of the time."

tive program of state newspapers included discussions on such problems as closed committee meetings by state legislators and anti-newspaper bills. Leading the workshop were Bonnie D. Hand, *The LaFayette Sun;* Clarke Stallworth, *The Birmingham News;* and Fred Taylor, *The Birmingham News.*

A program on promotion of the print media was led by Ed Templin of *The Lexington* (Ky.) *Herald Leader*, and Tom Harper and Bernard D. Feld of *The Birmingham News.* Guest speakers were John N. Popham, general manager of *The Chattanooga* (Tenn.) *Times*, and Jenkin Lloyd Jones of *The Tulsa* (Okla.) *Tribune.*

Doster, Hooper inducted into Hall of Honor in 1961

Harry Martin Doster and Johnson Jones Hooper, who were approved for recognition in 1961, were inducted into the Alabama Newspaper Hall of Honor in 1962 at the Feb. 8-10 annual convention in Birmingham. Doster had been associated with *The Prattville Progress* for 36 years as employee, editor and publisher. Hooper was associated with *The East Alabamian, The Chambers County Tribune* and other Alabama newspapers.

Harry Martin Doster
The Prattville Progress

High school journalism workshops conducted by the University of Alabama Department of Journalism were endorsed by APA. Members were encouraged to sponsor a high school editor for one of the two-week summer sessions in concentrated journalism education.

Johnson Jones Hooper
The Chambers County Tribune,
The East Alabamian

Auburn's L.O. Brackeen dies in 1962

L.O. Brackeen, director of public information at Auburn University since 1948, died Jan. 21, 1962. Brackeen, APA historian, was an active member of the Press Association and had headed the Alabama Newspaper Hall of Honor Committee since its beginning in 1959. Brackeen was author of the "History of the Alabama Press Association, 1871-1951," and the revised edition in 1959. A permanent site for the Newspaper Hall of Honor was established at the Au-

burn University Ralph B. Draughon Library in 1964 as a memorial to Brackeen.

Brackeen believed in state's newspapers

"L.O. Brackeen believed in Alabama newspapers more than some of the rest of us," 1953-1954 APA president William E. (Bill) Brooks said in a 1995 interview. Brooks, retired and living in Gulf Breeze, Fla., was managing editor of *The Brewton Standard* when he served as APA president. "If Mr. Brackeen was not totally disinterested, neither were we. I can remember getting the hand-outs from the state Extension Service, and the way Mr. Brackeen forced local county agents to make regular contributions to their newspapers," the 73-year-old Brooks recalled. Brooks' family once owned *The Brewton Standard.*

Edwin M. Crawford, executive associate with Southern Regional Education Board in Atlanta since 1958, assumed duties June 1, 1962, as director of University Relations at Auburn University. Auburn president Dr. Ralph B. Draughon said the new position would not replace that of director of public information held by the late L.O. Brackeen, "but will be one of broader responsibility and authority."

APA enters Mills court case in 1962

In 1962 the APA entered the court case in which James E. (Jimmy) Mills, editor of the *Birmingham Post-Herald*, was charged with violating Alabama's election law by electioneering on election day. APA submitted an "amicus curiae" brief maintaining that Mills should be acquitted.

A hearing was held Nov. 27, 1962, in Jefferson County Criminal Court for Mills, who was charged

The Clarke County Democrat *begins 100th year in 1955*

The following article by editor and publisher George A. Carleton appeared in the April 7, 1955, issue of *The Clarke County Democrat:*

Enters 100th Year of Operations Service —
Only Two Men Edit

"This week's issue (April 7, 1955) of *The Clarke County Democrat* is Number One of Volume 100. This means that we are beginning the hundredth year of publication, which will not be completed for another twelve months. However *The Democrat* will reach the hundredth anniversary of its founding on Jan. 31, 1956.

"Publication was suspended for a time during the War Between the States, which explains why we do not reach No. 52 of Volume 100 on the date of its founding.

"Ninety-nine years is a considerable period for two men to edit a newspaper. Isaac Grant, the founder, published it from January 1856 to Dec. 4, 1907. There is an overlap of a year there, as the writer and present editor worked with him during the last year of his life. The nearly 52 years that Mr. Grant was editor seemed extremely long to us at the time, but the more than 48 years that we have been on the job seem rather brief.

"This period has seen transportation develop from the horse and buggy and the steamboat and sailing ship to ocean liners, jet planes and railroads and automobiles that offer the utmost in luxury and comfort. it has seen communication developed from the first crude telegraph systems to wireless telephone and telegraph. it has seen the living conditions of the common man raised to an undreamed of plane. And it has seen the printing industry keep pace with all the other marvelous developments. It has seen this newspaper evolve from a sheet in which two pages were set by hand and laboriously printed on a Washington hand press (the paper had 'patent' inside), into a plant in which the type is mechanically set, the presses are driven by electricity and some of them are automatic. It has seen the general equipment of the county newspaper plant develop to the extent that should an old-time printer step into the plant, he wouldn't know which way to turn nor what to do.

"The list might be continued indefinitely, but these are a few of the multitude of wonders which have been developed since the founding of *The Democrat*. We hope to be at the helm when No. 52, Volume 100 is printed, and we furthermore hope to make a good start on the second century of publication."

---

with violation of Alabama's Corrupt Practices Act. The warrant was served Nov. 13 after a Hayes Aircraft mechanic swore out a complaint charging that Mills "did electioneer or solicit for and in support of a proposition that was being voted on" on Nov. 6. Mills signed his own bond of $100.

An editorial, which appeared in the *Post-Herald* Nov. 6, disagreed with a policy of a "news blackout" by Birmingham Mayor Arthur J. Hanes and urged citizens to vote for the mayor-council form of government. (The mayor-council system of government was approved by Birmingham citizens by a margin of 777 votes over the other two alternatives, commission and council-manager).

"In our judgment we have violated no law," Mills said. "The editorial complained of was fair comment on a question of vital public interest. Had we failed to make it we would have been guilty of defaulting on our responsibility as a newspaper to the people of Birmingham and the area surrounding it."

The Alabama law, Title 17, Section 285, of the Code of Alabama of 1940 said in part, "It is a corrupt practice for any person on any election day... to do any electioneering or to solicit any vote...on the day on which the election...is being held." A conviction for a violation of the law carried a maximum fine of $500 or a prison term of six months.

Following hearings in Jefferson County Criminal Court Nov. 27-30, the case was continued until Dec. 28.

Interest shown throughout state

Interest in the case was shown throughout the state. The Alabama professional chapter of Sigma Delta Chi (Society of Professional Journalists), in a meeting Nov. 29, affirmed its faith in the "journalistic standards" of Birmingham newsmen following the "news blackout policy" invoked by the mayor. The resolution said in part:

"One or more officials of Birmingham have publicly declared intent to refrain from discussing certain matters with newsgatherers...and said official or officials have implied other than high professional conduct on the part of the press."

1962 summer convention, Florence

A tour of industrial sites in the Tri-Cities area, recreation at locations along the Tennessee River, presentation of awards in the Better Newspaper Contest, and parties galore highlighted the 1962 summer convention July 12-14 at the Holiday Inn in Florence. The decision to have the summer convention in the Tennessee Valley area came after three successive summer conventions at Dauphin Island.

APA associate members were hosts to a welcoming reception Thursday, followed by a luau party around the Holiday Inn pool, courtesy of *The Florence Times* and *Tri-Cities Daily*. Friday's schedule included a tour of Ford Motor Co., Reynolds Metals Co., and Tennessee Valley Authority, and a buffet banquet at the new Turtle Point Yacht and Country Club. Elmer Hinton, columnist for *The Nashville Tennessean*, was banquet speaker.

1963
Herve Charest Jr., *The Tallassee Tribune*
1963-1964 president

92nd annual press convention, Montgomery
Feb. 21-23, 1963
Summer convention, Dauphin Island
July 18-20, 1963

Gov. George C. Wallace's address at the 92nd annual APA convention in 1963 "apparently alleviated fears the chief executive is too defiant about the race issue," United Press International writer Donald F. Martin reported in the Monday, Feb. 25, 1963, issue of the *Birmingham Post-Herald*.

Martin reported that "many of the newspaper editors and publishers commented after the speech they were surprised at how temperate it was. They were also impressed by the governor's sincerity in trying to eliminate waste in government spending, his program to attract industry to the state, and his pledge to keep administration records open to in-

quiring reporters."

Wallace addressed APA delegates during the winter convention at the Whitley Hotel in Montgomery Feb. 21-23, 1963.

"I was most pleased with his speech," James E. (Jimmy) Mills, editor of the *Birmingham Post-Herald*, told UPI. "It was much more temperate than I had expected. Perhaps we have been over-exaggerating the governor's attitude on the race issue."

Ed Dannelly, editor of *The Andalusia Star-News*, told UPI that he agreed with Wallace when the governor "pegged the problem on economics." Dannelly said he also was convinced that Northerners were trying to exploit the South because of the "recent business boom in Dixie."

Wallace mentions "stand in schoolhouse door"

Wallace made only one mention of standing in the schoolhouse door, and that was in friendly reply to his introduction by Grover C. Hall Jr., editor of *The Montgomery Advertiser* and *The Alabama Journal*, who speculated the "Little Judge" may spend some of the next four years in prison. Wallace invited Hall to "stand with me in the schoolhouse door."

S I D E L I G H T S
MARKING 125 YEARS OF HISTORY

Florala News *publishes tribute to "Old Betsy"*

The Florala News published a tribute to its old Country Campbell cylinder press on June 17, 1954:

Old Betsy prints history, now gone

"Old Betsy is the old Country Campbell cylinder press that has groaned and moaned every week since the days of the ancients, giving birth for the last fifty years or so of *The Florala News*, and before her day in Florala, a considerable portion of a half century in Andalusia brought forth *The Andalusia Star* each week. Many and varied has been the recording of events in the progress of this region told in the printed word of Old Betsy.

"Now comes one to take up where Old Betsy has left off. In her room and stead is now a larger, faster and more modern press in a Miehle Two Revolution press which the editor christens 'Lady Lucille'."

The governor's only comment on the race issue came near the end of his talk when he said "Alabama has the ability, wisdom and courage to maintain stable social relationships."

Wallace received a hearty laugh when he mentioned there were "too many lights burning at the mansion. I never have seen so many lights," he said while discussing the finance committee's recommended cuts in the governor's operating funds.

Wallace: "I have healthy respect for press"

Wallace told the editors and publishers, "I have a healthy respect for the press in this state. A free press is necessary for the rights and freedom of the people. I'm not a monarch. I'm a servant of the people. The free press should have open access to every record. And I shall see to it that every record is made available to you."

A resolution was passed commending Wallace for his announced intention to see that the records of the various departments of Alabama government were made available to the news media.

Along with a report on ANAS, an advertising workshop session was held at the 1963 winter convention in response to concern on the part of many Alabama publishers about loss of advertising to other media. Participating on the advertising panel were Arthur Cook, The Sun Papers, Birmingham; Ralph W. Callahan, *The Anniston Star;* J.C. Henderson, *The Alexander City Outlook;* Bill Stewart, *The Monroe Journal* in Monroeville; and W.H. (Bill) Metz, the *Birmingham Post-Herald.*

ANAS manager is introduced

Delegates attending the 1963 winter convention saw the ANAS sales program, which had been outlined at the 1962 convention, become a reality. The new ANAS manager, Charles I. Reynolds, was officially introduced to the Press Association at the Friday morning session in the State Room of the

---

Whitley Hotel. Every newspaper in the state, with the exception of three small weeklies, pledged support to the sales program designed to bring new advertising for ANAS newspapers. Reynolds was former manager of general advertising for the old *Birmingham Post* and later assistant general manager of *The Birmingham News* and *Age-Herald.* In 1947-1948, Reynolds was publisher of *The Daily Banner* in Cleveland, Tenn. He returned to Birmingham from Cleveland to join *The Birmingham Post.*

The convention also featured a panel that included Lt. Gov. James B. Allen, Highway Director Ed Rodgers, Attorney General Richmond Flowers and Finance Director Seymore Trammel.

R.F. Hudson Sr. sells *Advertiser/Journal*

Announcement had been made Jan. 31, 1963, of the sale of *The Montgomery Advertiser* and *The Alabama Journal* to Carmage Walls. Sale was completed March 7, 1963.

Richard F. Hudson Sr., 78, had been associated with The Advertiser Company for 60 years. Hudson made the following statement following sale of the newspapers: "Since Dick (Hudson's son, R.F. Hudson Jr. who died in 1959 at age 43) died,

R. F. Hudson Sr.
The Montgomery Advertiser

I have had many offers to sell *The Advertiser* and *Journal,* though I did not offer them for sale. I accepted Mr. Walls' offer because he is worthy to control these institutions."

Hudson was made a lifetime member of APA at the 1963 winter convention. Cash M. Stanley, editor of *The Alabama Journal,* paid tribute to Hudson, saying that "He has been a constant inspiration to the massive group of men and women who helped him in building his newspapers to greatness in the Southern newspaper field."

Harold E. Martin was named associate publisher of *The Advertiser* and *Alabama Journal,* effective May 10, 1963.

APA delegation attends luncheon with Kennedy in 1963

Invitations to a luncheon at the White House with President John F. Kennedy went out to all Alabama daily newspaper publishers, six weekly publishers, and officers of the APA in 1963. The luncheon was one in a series of luncheons that the president held with leaders of the press from various states.

As racial outbreaks occurred in Birmingham between the time the invitations were received and the time of the luncheon, the racial situation dominated "at least 99 percent" of the discussion with President Kennedy. "Summing up the luncheon, our impression is that no one's mind was changed, but that the exchange of views was beneficial to all concerned," said APA president Herve Charest Jr. of *The Tallassee Tribune*.

"The racial outbreak hit Birmingham after the luncheon was scheduled, and the golden opportunity to advance the interests of Alabama and the region of which it is a part was lost," commented Louis A. Eckl, executive editor of *The Florence Times* and *Tri-Cities Daily*.

Charles I. Reynolds resigned as ANAS manager following a meeting in Birmingham on May 3, 1963. Reynolds, who had been ANAS manager since Feb. 15, resigned "due to personal reasons." Directors of APA and ANAS met in Birmingham May 3 to hear a detailed report from Reynolds regarding his resignation.

The sales committee, comprised of Ralph W. Callahan, *The Anniston Star;* W.H. (Bill) Metz, the *Birmingham Post-Herald;* J.C. Henderson, *The Alexander City Outlook;* Bill Stewart, *The Monroe Journal* in Monroeville; and Arthur P. Cook, The Sun Papers in Birmingham, expressed the opinion that the salary paid Reynolds and the expense incurred during his two and a half months with the APA were "the best investment" that ANAS and APA could have made. In September 1963, E. Hal Davidson joined the Press Association staff as ANAS salesman.

The 1963 ANAS Rate and Data Guide listed 104 weekly newspapers and 22 dailies.

Area workshops which challenged every Alabama newspaper to put out a better product were held during the fall of 1963 in Mobile, Birmingham, Huntsville and Montgomery.

A new system was introduced for selection of inductees to the Alabama Newspaper Hall of Honor. Two individuals were to be nominated each year, one who served before 1920, and one who served after that year.

Three individuals, selected in 1962, were inducted into the Hall of Honor in 1963 at the winter convention in Montgomery: William Lee Gammell of *The Clayton Record*, Franklin Potts Glass of *The Montgomery Advertiser* and Grover Cleveland Hall Sr. of *The Montgomery Advertiser*.

1963 summer convention, Dauphin Island

Dauphin Island was site of the 1963 summer convention, held July 18-20 at the Holiday Inn Riviera. Highlight of the convention was presentation of awards in the Better Newspaper Contest. APA president Herve Charest Jr. of *The Tallassee Tribune* presented the awards at a Sunday brunch.

Other activities included a seafood jamboree, shrimp and beer luncheon, cookouts for children "with adult supervision," associates' luncheon, and buffet dinner at the Isle Dauphine Club, *AlaPressa* reported.

"If fishing is your idea of getting away from it all, you may either fish from the new 'Free Fishing Pier' which extends 300 feet out into the Gulf of Mexico and offers fighting fish to land lubbers," *The Alabama Publisher* reported. "But if you want the feel of the rolling deck under your feet, charter boats from the Dauphin Island Marina are available."

1964
E.M. (Sparky) Howell, *The Onlooker*, Foley
1964-1965 president

93rd annual press convention, Tuscaloosa
Feb. 6-8, 1964
Summer convention, Decatur
July 23-25, 1964

Selling methods and production were stressed at the 93rd annual press convention at the Hotel Stafford in Tuscaloosa Feb. 6-8, 1964.

Earl English, dean of the University of Missouri School of Journalism, led a discussion on principles of makeup and production. Glenn E. McNeil, manager of the Tennessee Press Association, and E. Hal Davidson, Alabama Newspaper Advertising Service sales director, led a panel discussion on "Making It Easier to Spend Money With You."

Jim Creamer, account executive with Robert Luckie & Associates, Birmingham advertising agency, spoke on "How You, the Practitioners of the Newspaper Business, Can Get More Business From Us."

"Outstanding Legislators of 1963," Sen. Pete Matthews and Rep. Albert Brewer, were presented plaques at the 1964 convention.

Resolution urges return of "USS Alabama"

Delegates adopted a resolution at the Tuscaloosa convention endorsing the fund-raising campaign to bring the Battleship "USS Alabama" back to a permanent home in the Port of Mobile.

APA secretary-field manager Jones W. Giles missed the convention when he came down with a severe case of pneumonia the opening day. In the March 11, 1964, issue of *AlaPressa*, it was reported that Giles had been seriously ill since Feb. 4 and had been granted a leave of absence by the APA board of directors. "Jones is reported to be improving daily, but will not be able to return to his official duties for some time."

An achievement of the APA Legislative Committee led by Bonnie D. Hand of *The LaFayette Sun* in 1964 was securing passage of an increase in legal advertising rates. Rep. Jack Hawkins, publisher of *The Lamar Democrat* in Vernon, introduced the bill in the House.

Huntsville had a new weekly newspaper in 1964, *The Huntsville News*, which began publication Jan. 8. Charles Jackson of Tullahoma, Tenn., was editor of *The News*, according to an announcement by general manager John Higdon.

Permanent home for Hall of Honor established

A permanent site for the Alabama Newspaper Hall of Honor was established at Auburn University's Ralph B. Draughon Library in the fall of 1964 as a memorial to the late L.O. Brackeen, long-time APA historian and Auburn University news bureau director who earlier held the title of director of publicity at Alabama Polytechnic Institute. Inductees to the Hall of Honor in 1964 were Jesse B. Adams of *The Southern Star* in Ozark and Olin Hampton Stevenson of *The Roanoke Leader*.

U.S. Steel Corp. initiated the presentation of Alabama "Journalist of the Year" awards at the 1964 convention. Two awards were presented, one to a representative of the daily press and another to a weekly newspaper representative. Nominations for the awards were made by chambers of commerce and civic organizations. Only APA-member newspaper representatives were eligible for the awards.

Visit made to NORAD headquarters

Some 14 Alabama newspaper representatives joined reporters from Louisiana for a trip to North American Air Defense Command (NORAD) headquarters in Colorado Springs, Colo., in 1964. The group included Rex Thomas, the Associated Press; L.P. Patterson, *The Montgomery Advertiser;* Don Martin, United Press International; Dan Dowe, *The Birmingham News;* James H. (Jimmy) Faulkner Sr., *The Baldwin Times;* Vivian Cannon, *The Mobile Press Register;* Joel P. Smith, *The Eufaula Tribune;* Ewell Reed, *The Arab Tribune;* Jesse Culp,

The Sand Mountain Reporter, Albertville; Brandt Ayers, *The Anniston Star;* Steele E. McGrew, *The Alabama Courier* and *The Limestone Democrat,* Athens; Dickey Bozeman, *The Thomasville Times;* Ben Davis, *The Tuscaloosa News;* and E.M. (Sparky) Howell, *The Onlooker,* Foley.

1965
Ralph W. Callahan, *The Anniston Star*
1965-1966 president

94th annual convention, Birmingham
Feb. 11-13, 1965
Summer convention, Decatur
July 22-24, 1965

The first "Journalist of the Year" awards were presented to Alyce Billings Walker, associate editor of women of *The Birmingham News,* and Edmund R. (Ed) Blair, publisher of *The St. Clair News-Aegis* in Pell City during the 94th annual convention Feb. 11-13, 1965, in Birmingham. The awards were presented by Fred LePell, director of public relations for U.S. Steel Corp.

APA field manager Jones W. Giles reported at the convention that membership fell from 152 to 148 in 1964 because of mergers and discontinuance of some publications. The membership included 20 daily newspapers and 90 weeklies.

Guest speakers at the 1965 convention included Gov. George C. Wallace and nationally syndicated columnist Ann Landers. A panel discussion on Alabama politics and government featured Lt. Gov. Jim Allen, Sen. Pete Mathews and Rep. Albert Brewer.

J.P. Kauffman, executive vice president of the American Newspaper Publishers Association bureau of advertising, spoke on the work of his association.

Dailies, weeklies hold separate workshop sessions

Daily and weekly publishers held separate workshop sessions. Daily members heard discussions of common problems by Robert Bryan, *The Cullman Times;* Frank Helderman Jr., *The Gadsden Times;* George M. Cox, *The Mobile Press Register;* Roswell Falkenberry, *The Selma Times-Journal;* Richard Hammell, *The Florence Times* and *Tri-Cities Daily;* and Harold E. Martin, *The Montgomery Advertiser* and *Alabama Journal.*

Weekly members saw a slide presentation on Weekly Newspaper Representatives and heard

Wallace signs proclamation in 1965

APA officers gathered in the office of Gov. George Wallace for the signing of a proclamation in recognition of National Newspaper Week in 1965 when Ralph W. Callahan was APA president. From left are long-time APA Legislative Committee chairman Bonnie D. Hand, *The LaFayette Sun;* Wallace; Ralph Callahan, *The Anniston Star;* Bob Bryan, *The Cullman Times;* Herve Charest Jr., *The Tallassee Tribune;* and J.C. Henderson, *The Alexander City Outlook.* (Photograph courtesy of J.C. Henderson)

comments from WNR executive vice president Warren Grieb and Kay Aldous of the public relations department.

In a mock sales presentation, Grieb and Aldous posed as agency space buyers, and three publishers acted as sales representatives. The three "actors" were Bertie Gammell Parish, *The Clayton Record;* Joel P. Smith, *The Eufaula Tribune;* and Ben G. George, *The Demopolis Times.*

A voluntary program of employee insurance which would be made available to APA members by American Fidelity Assurance Co. was outlined to members at the convention.

Resolution on journalism education

A resolution on journalism education, introduced by Norman Bassett of *The Tuscaloosa News,* was adopted by convention delegates. The resolution pledged the APA and Sigma Delta Chi (later renamed The Society of Professional Journalists) to promote recruitment of young Alabamians for careers in journalism. The resolution urged offi-

cials of state institutions of higher learning to improve and expand their programs in journalism.

APA president Ralph W. Callahan, executive vice president of *The Anniston Star,* appointed a committee to study and recommend improvements in both APA and ANAS. The committee was composed of Ed Dannelly, *The Andalusia Star-News;* Graham McTeer, *The Lee County Bulletin,* Auburn; Harold E. Martin, *The Montgomery Advertiser* and *Alabama Journal;* Bill Stewart, *The Monroe Journal* in Monroeville; and W.H. (Bill) Metz, the *Birmingham Post-Herald.*

Jones W. Giles resigns in 1965

APA secretary-field manager Jones W. Giles resigned effective April 30, 1965, and was succeeded by assistant manager John Burton who served as acting manager. Giles had been field manager since 1957.

A proposed bill which would forbid communists from speaking at Alabama colleges and universities was opposed by the APA in 1965. "The Alabama Press Association is firmly and positively opposed to the communist ideology," APA president Ralph W. Callahan said. "But we cannot condone any attempt to curb free speech and free expression in Alabama."

Two north Alabama publishers, Marcy B. Darnall Sr. of *The Florence Herald* and Milton C. Giles of *The Franklin County Times* in Russellville and *The Red Bay News*, were inducted into the Alabama Newspaper Hall of Honor in 1965.

SIDELIGHTS
MARKING 125 YEARS OF HISTORY

Advocate *celebrated 90th year in 1954*

The Greenville Advocate began its 90th year of publication in October 1954.

In a 1954 speech, editor J. Glenn Stanley said the newspaper was established by his father, the late Gen. James Berney Stanley, a 20-year-old Confederate veteran, who had a $5 gold piece and a patched uniform when the War Between the States ended:

"To establish *The Advocate,* the founder borrowed $100 (from a bartender, promising to pay it back Saturday night)," Glenn Stanley said. "He did, by borrowing $5 here and $5 there.

"In my lifetime I have seen the office change from a hand-operated printing shop to a mechanized shop," Stanley continued. "We now have individual motors for everything in the shop, from the adding machine to the big press. There is even a motor in the water cooler, and electrical energy to operate the timer in the darkroom and the clock on the wall. There are electric heaters to melt metal in the Linotype machine and the stereotypecaster, the mat caster, and the stylus in the engraving machine; there are electric motors in the butane heaters. There are at least 15 motors, not counting the 10 in the electric fans and the two in the heaters.

"The world has come a long way since this newspaper came out with its first edition, but we seriously doubt if this Number 1 of Volume 90 is an improvement over Number 1 of Volume 1. It employs modern methods, but it's the printed word that makes the difference, not how it's produced."

1966
Ed Dannelly, *The Andalusia Star-News*
1966-1967 president

95th annual press convention, Birmingham
Feb. 10-12, 1966
Summer convention, Kowaliga Beach
(near Alexander City)
July 14-16, 1966

Services to APA members lapsed somewhat during the latter part of 1965 and early 1966 as the Press Association had no secretary-manager. But one activity that wasn't sacrificed was the 95th annual convention.

Guest speakers at the 1966 press convention Feb. 10-12 at the Parliament House in Birmingham were Frank Kilcheski of the Bureau of Advertising, Dr. Frank A. Rose, president of the University of Alabama, and Phil Newsom of United Press International.

Kilcheski reported on the latest in advertising research. Rose appealed for more money for education in Alabama and hinted that a large, new department, embracing radio and television as well as journalism, might be in the making at the University of Alabama. Rose said that within the next few months, the University would be in a position to "move in the area of journalism."

Workshop sessions included a panel discussion led by incoming APA president Ed Dannelly, *The Andalusia Star-News,* Barrett C. Shelton Jr., *The Decatur Daily,* and Cliff Wear, *The Opelika Daily News,* who told of their own experiences in converting to offset printing and giving their opinions about the process.

Weekly newspaper session held

Taking part in a weekly newspaper session were Porter Harvey, *The Advertiser-Gleam,* Guntersville; Bill Stewart, *The Monroe Journal,* Monroeville; Harold S. May, *The Florence Herald;* Joseph H. (Joe) Adams, *The Southern Star,* Ozark; John A. Burgess, *The Opp News;* Claude E. Sparks, *The Franklin County Times,* Russellville; Camille Elebash, *The Graphic,* Tuscaloosa; J. Fred Nall, *The Monroe Journal,* Monroeville; Phil Sokol, *The Atmore Advance;* Cliff Knight; James H. (Jimmy) Faulkner Jr., *The Baldwin Times,* Bay Minette; Jesse Culp, *The Sand Mountain Reporter,* Albertville; Alvin Bland, *The Luverne Journal and News;* Dick Smith, *The Sumter County Journal,* York; and John B. Stephenson, *The Roanoke Leader.*

The daily panel included Roswell Falkenberry, *The Selma Times-Journal,* Bill Ennis, *The Huntsville Times;* George M. Cox, *The Mobile Press Register,* Ben Davis, *The Tuscaloosa News;* and Les Daughtry, *The Montgomery Advertiser.*

During the business session, ANAS president W.H. (Bill) Metz of the *Birmingham Post-Herald* announced the hiring of a salesman during the Alabama election campaign year and said that ANAS was in good financial shape. Outgoing APA president Ralph W. Callahan of *The Anniston Star* reviewed APA's accomplishments at a President's Breakfast on Saturday. Callahan said one of the major problems facing the APA was hiring a secretary-manager to replace Jones W. Giles, who resigned in 1965, *The Birmingham News* reported in its Sunday, Feb. 13, 1966, edition.

Callahan makes five recommendations

Callahan made five recommendations for APA goals in 1966: "One, work with Dr. (Frank) Rose (University of Alabama president) to get a new journalism building; two, try to work out a joint summer meeting with the Alabama Associated Press Association; three, effect immediate improvement in the APA quarters at the University; four, meet with the APA auditor to work out more detailed and comprehensive financial reports; five, continue to search for a qualified (APA) manager."

Hall named APA field manager in 1966

A new secretary-manager began work on May 2, 1966. James W. Hall Jr., a graduate of the University of Alabama, had been in public relations work in New Orleans. With the hiring of Hall, the executive's title was changed from "secretary-field manager" to "secretary-manager."

Hall, 34, who had been serving as public relations manager in Southern Bell Telephone Company's headquarters office, graduated from the University of Alabama with a bachelor's degree in journalism. Hall succeeded Jones W. Giles, who resigned April 30, 1965. Assistant manager John Burton had been serving as acting manager.

Hall was paid $12,000 annually, plus retirement and medical benefits, one-half of which was paid by the University of Alabama. Among Hall's responsibilities, in addition to his duties managing APA, was to obtain a master's degree in journalism with the goal of teaching a course in the Department of Journalism at the University of Alabama. (Hall earned a master's degree in 1968.)

Supreme Court rules on Mills case in 1966

Former APA president James E. (Jimmy) Mills, editor of the *Birmingham Post-Herald,* made national headlines in 1966 with a legal triumph before the U.S. Supreme Court. In 1966 the U.S. Supreme Court ruled on the Mills case in which the APA had participated. The court ruled to strike the Alabama law forbidding the state's newspapers from publishing election day editorials.

Justice Hugo L. Black, who wrote the opinion, said, "The Alabama Corrupt Practices Act by providing criminal penalties for publishing editorials such as the one here silences the press at a time when it can be most effective."

In a 1990 interview with *Birmingham News* staff writer Bill Plott, Mills recalled that Birmingham had been in the middle of a bitter change-of-government election in 1962 when the editorial was published in the *Post-Herald.* Birmingham Mayor Arthur Hanes was irritated over press coverage and had declared that no city employee was to give information to a reporter unless it came through him and his office first, Mills recalled.

"I pointed out in an editorial that if anyone needed any other reason for why they should be thrown out on their fannies, that was it," Mills said in 1990. "The editorial ran in the paper on the morning of the election. A sheriff's deputy came up with a warrant for my arrest for violating the Alabama Corrupt Practices Act. Under that legislative act, no electioneering or politicking, or political advertising or other things could

S I D E L I G H T S
MARKING 125 YEARS OF HISTORY

Dothan Eagle's *Josie Hall dies in 1954*

Josie C. Hall, 80, wife of pioneer Houston County newspaper man W.T. Hall, died Feb. 18, 1954. Mrs. Hall was the mother of Horace Hall, publisher of *The Dothan Eagle*.

The following editorial was published in *The Dothan Eagle*:

"One of *The Eagles* was stilled Friday afternoon when death came to Mrs. Josie C. Hall, widow of the editor who converted it from a weekly into a daily and mother of its two subsequent editors.

"More than any person now associated with this newspaper, Mrs. Hall was responsible for what it is today, perhaps its very existence. As the wife of W.T. Hall, she shared in the decision to buy *The Eagle* when it was a struggling weekly in 1905. She shared his faith when he turned it into a daily in 1908.

"It was she who, on the death of Editor Hall in 1924, made another vital decision and made it alone, when counseled by one adviser to sell the paper lest her boys 'run it into the ground or bankruptcy.'

"'Those boys,' she replied with unshakable faith, 'were raised in the business. If the paper is run into the ground or bankruptcy, they'll just have to do it.'

"For many years she was president of the W.T. Hall Co., owners of *The Eagle,* but to 'the boys,' Julian and Horace, she gave free reign over the paper's management. She never interfered. Not only did they have her complete confidence, but to them she was an inspiration and, like all good mothers, a well of faith that never ran dry.

"She saw her sons, working as a team, make *The Eagle* into an institution. She saw Horace, after the death of Julian in 1939, carry on the tradition of the Hall family — a newspaper tradition.

"With such devotion and the faith she had in her husband and sons, she could only be proud of their craftsmanship achieved. And she was. She saw her dream, and theirs, come true. Her heart too, belonged to *The Eagle.*"

be done on election day. Under that law you couldn't even tell your wife how to vote if they found out about it."

Mills: "It was a landmark case"

Mills continued, "I was acquitted in the first trial. They took it down to the (Alabama) Supreme Court. The Supreme Court upheld the prosecution. We appealed to the Supreme Court of the United States and we won the case there. That law had never been tested and it affected the whole country because several other states had similar laws and they were invalidated, too. It was a landmark case."

Ironically, despite the *Post-Herald's* reputation for crusading, the editorial was not a deliberate challenge of the state law, Mills said. "I hadn't even thought about it. I was just writing an editorial so people would know what was going on," Mills recalled. "Hugo Black was the justice who wrote the decision, and he gave a ringing decision upholding a free press and the Constitution."

1966 summer convention at Lake Kowaliga

The 1966 summer convention was July 14-16 at Lake Kowaliga near Alexander City. Gov. George C. Wallace was keynote speaker. Convention host was past president J.C. Henderson, publisher of *The Alexander City Outlook.* Delegates stayed in private cottages located around the lake. Some of the functions were dampened by rain downpours, but spirits remained high. Former APA executive director Jim Hall recalled in a 1996 interview that a highlight of the summer convention was "the arrival of APA president Ed Dannelly in an antique Rolls Royce borrowed for the occasion from one of his friends."

With the appointment of a new secretary-manager in 1966, the Press Association began a process of revitalization that was not fully realized until the next year. The new spirit, however, was exemplified by the surpassing of the old "record membership" by November 1966.

Among the promises the University of Alabama made to APA when Hall was appointed secretary-manager in 1966 was to remodel the Press Association's quarters in Manly Hall. The offices were in ill-repair when Hall was named to the post. In the reception area and in the manager's office, floors were open to the ground, and in the business offices, the Clipping Bureau was using "27 syrup cans to separate clippings before sending them to customers," Hall's wife, Martha, recalled in a 1996 interview.

Open house held in 1966

In fulfilling its promise, the University began work on the remodeling project early after Hall's arrival, and it was completed in the fall of 1966. An open house for APA members was held in the refurbished quarters in October 1966.

Martha Hall joined the APA staff later in 1966 as manager of the Clipping Bureau. The number of subscribers to the service increased to more than 120, and the Clipping Bureau became profitable for the Press Association.

Oscar M. Dugger Sr. of *The Andalusia Star-News* and Julian O. Hall of *The Dothan Eagle* were inducted into the Alabama Newspaper Hall of Honor Oct. 8, 1966, on the Auburn University campus.

Dr. William E. Winter was named head of the University of Alabama Department of Journalism on Sept. 1, 1966. Winter came to the University from the University of South Carolina where he was a professor of journalism. Winter succeeded C.E. (Ed) Bounds, who had been head of the Department of Journalism since 1946.

1967
Porter Harvey, *The Advertiser-Gleam,* Guntersville
1967-1968 president

96th annual press convention, Mobile
Jan. 26-28, 1967
Summer convention, Florence
July 13-15, 1967

1967 was a year that began with a well-attended 96th annual convention Jan. 26-28 at the Admiral Semmes Hotel in Mobile. Featured speakers were Howard Benedict, Associated Press space reporter from Cape Kennedy, Fla., and Judge Walter P. Gewin, U.S. Court of Appeals, 5th Circuit, who spoke about the federal judiciary.

Various suppliers presented a panel discussion on offset printing. The panel discussion for weekly publishers was moderated by incoming APA president Porter Harvey of *The Advertiser-Gleam* in Guntersville. Participating on the weekly panel were Bill Stewart, *The Monroe Journal,* Monroeville; Jesse Culp, *The Sand Mountain Reporter,* Albertville; and Orsen B. Spivey, *The Geneva County Reaper,* Geneva.

Barrett C. Shelton Jr. of *The Decatur Daily* moderated a panel discussion for daily newspapers on "Automation" assisted by Russ Arnold, *The Pensacola* (Fla.) *News-Journal;* Leo Ring, *The Bir-*

mingham News; and Cliff Hendrickson, *The Mobile Press Register.*

Resolution urges fair trial, fair press

James E. (Jimmy) Mills, recently retired as editor of the *Birmingham Post-Herald,* was chiefly responsible for a resolution adopted at the APA convention which stated the group's determination that both the fair trial and free press be protected. In March, Mills was scheduled to address the International Academy of Trial Lawyers on press coverage of trials at the trial lawyers' convention in Mexico City.

Mills said the bar and the press sought the same goals in the 1967 controversy over trial coverage — because a fair trial and a free press were dependent on each other. "The press does not take the attitude of antagonism toward the bench on this matter," Mills said in a interview with UPI reporter James Felder. "It stands ready to cooperate to protect the right of a fair trial. Without a free press to check on all phases of the judicial process and report to the public, there can be no fair trial," Mills said. "A muzzled press and news censored at its source are the first steps toward a police state."

Mills said erroneous conclusions were reached from the Supreme Court decision on a retrial for Dr. Sam Sheppard. He said the order was never intended to be a restriction on the press or a license for lower courts to impose their own restric-

---

S I D E L I G H T S
MARKING 125 YEARS OF HISTORY

Henderson seeks House seat in 1969

APA past president J.C. Henderson, editor and publisher of *The Alexander City Outlook* for 25 years, announced in 1969 plans to seek a seat in the House of Representatives in the 1970 elections. Henderson ran for the post held by Owen Harper of Tallassee.

The Alabama Publisher noted that during the past sessions of the state Legislature, a newspaper owner served in both the House and Senate. W.E. (Gene) Hardin, editor of *The Greenville Advocate,* was a state representative, and C.C. (Bo) Torbert Jr., one of the partners at *The Opelika-Auburn Daily News,* was a state senator.

tions on free flow of news.

The three-day winter convention was marked by a declaration of APA's intention to protect the constitutional rights of both a fair trial and a free press — establishing the APA's position in the controversy.

Mills, Faulkner named "Journalists of the Year"

At the awards banquet Friday night, James E. (Jimmy) Mills was named "Journalist of the Year" in the daily division, and James H. (Jimmy) Faulkner Sr., publisher of *The Baldwin Times* in Bay Minette, received the award in the weekly division. In addition, Mills received a silver gift as a tribute from APA for his years of service in journalism. He was editor of the old *Post* and the *Post-Herald* for 35 years when he retired Jan. 1, 1967.

During 1967, the board of directors and various committees did extensive planning work on the Code of Ethics for the Press Association and the setting up of an APA Journalism Foundation to assist journalism education in the state.

W.C. Bryant of *The Alexander City Outlook* planned a third District Workshop which was held in June 1967. The meeting was so successful that members voted to meet at least once each six months and study further the problems and challenges of the newspaper profession at both the weekly and daily field.

Bonnie Hand dies in 1967

Bonnie Duncan Hand, veteran newspaper man with 38 years experience, died in Emory University Hospital of a heart ailment on May 27, 1967. A native of Autauga County, Hand began his newspaper career at *The Chilton County News* in Clanton, and he later became editor and publisher of *The LaFayette Sun* where he remained until his death.

Hand was active in the APA and served as president in 1946. For 20 years he served on APA's Legislative Committee.

Four Alabama newsmen became telecasters during National Newspaper Week in 1967. John W. Bloomer, managing editor of *The Birmingham News;* H. Brandt Ayers, managing editor of *The Anniston Star;* James H. (Jimmy) Faulkner Sr., publisher of *The Baldwin Times,* Bay Minette; and Hollis Curl, publisher of *The Choctaw Advocate.* Butler, participated in an educational television program, "A Free Press in a Free Society," with Dr. William E. Winter and Dr. James Jensen of the University of Alabama. The program was sponsored by APA and the University of Alabama Department of Journalism.

Past APA presidents honored in 1967

APA past presidents were honored in 1967 with the unveiling of the "Past Presidents Gallery" in the central office on the University of Alabama campus. The collection was incomplete, with pictures available of only 27 of the 72 past presidents.

Some 64 newspeople and interested observers participated in the University of Alabama-Alabama Press Association Newspaper Design Workshop in Tuscaloosa. Principal speakers were George Gill, man-

---

S I D E L I G H T S
MARKING 125 YEARS OF HISTORY

Austin Johnson featured in **Anniston Star**

The Anniston Star published a feature story in 1957 on Austin Johnson, editor and publisher of *The Piedmont Journal:*

"Austin Johnson of Piedmont has held the same post office box for 50 years, hasn't missed a meeting of the Lions Club in 18 years, has missed only one meeting of the official board of his church in 20 years, and has never had full week vacation in his life," *The Star* reported. "While setting these records, Johnson — with the help of his wife and one or two other helpers — has edited, published and distributed *The Piedmont Journal* every week for the past 50 years. Johnson was born in Cherokee County, only a few miles north of Piedmont. In 1897 he obtained his first job, in a Piedmont cotton mill. After a short stay in the cotton mill, Johnson launched his long newspaper career in the print shop of *The Piedmont Inquirer* about 1900.

"There he learned to hand-set type. In 1902 he moved to Anniston where he took a part-time job with *The Anniston Hot Blast* and worked at Woodstock Cotton Mill. In 1906 Johnson decided to establish a newspaper in Piedmont. He bought equipment from *The Anniston Hot Blast* for $650, hauled it to Piedmont in two horse-drawn wagon, and launched his new enterprise in January 1906. 'My wife, Ora Davis, had been my right arm from the first,' Johnson recalled. 'Many times, in the absence of an operator, she took over the machine and set the type for a coming edition'."

aging editor of *The Louisville* (Ky.) *Courier-Journal* and Edmund C. Arnold, chairman of the graphic arts department at Syracuse University in New York State.

Summer convention held in Florence

The 1967 summer convention was July 13-15 in Florence. *The Alabama Publisher* reported that E.M. (Sparky) Howell of *The Onlooker* in Foley and Hollis Curl of *The Choctaw Advocate* in Butler competed in a hula contest at the Thursday night luau, and that "judges decided on Hollis as the fastest shaker in the South."

At the Saturday morning awards breakfast, David Stewart, son of Bill Stewart of *The Monroe Journal* in Monroeville "treated members to a circulation collection idea. The young lad, editor of his own newspaper, was reported to have written in his newspaper a notice informing all subscribers to notify the paper that they were subscribers or their subscription would be canceled," *The Alabama Publisher* reported.

Victor Henry Hanson, *The Birmingham News*, and William E.W. Yerby, *The Greensboro Watchman*, were inducted into the Alabama Newspaper Hall of Honor on Oct. 7, 1967.

1968

W.H. (Bill) Metz, the *Birmingham Post-Herald* 1968-1969 president

97th annual press convention, Montgomery
Feb. 8-11, 1968
Summer convention, Nassau, the Bahama Islands
July 11-14, 1968

Two proposals affecting the profession of journalism were approved at the 97th annual convention of the APA. One was establishment of a foundation to support journalism in the state. A Code of Ethics, the first in the history of the APA, was cited by officers as being a statement of professional ideals and objectives.

More than 250 APA members and associate members attended the 97th annual convention Feb. 8-11, 1968, at the Jefferson Davis Hotel in Montgomery in what was one of the Press Association's most historic conventions. Delegates stated in writing their dedication to fair and impartial news coverage, editorial writing, and to integrity in advertising practices.

Arguments of some delegates attending the winter convention that a Code of Ethics was unnecessary were overridden by the majority. Expressions on the floor and final vote indicated

that most newspaper officials favored adopting the written code.

AlaPressa: "Something different about 97th meeting"

AlaPressa commented about the convention: "There was something different about the 97th annual meeting of the Alabama Press Association. Yes, there was a record crowd in attendance. There was a good program, too. But there was also something else. There was an attitude of accomplishment. There was a feeling that something really worthwhile was going on. The members sensed it. So did the visitors. Several said that they had never seen a press group so friendly, so unified, so eager to learn and to get things done. One of the members pointed out he had been attending Association meetings in two states for 25 years, but he had never been to any as enjoyable and as beneficial as the Montgomery meeting."

Approval of a dues increase at the 1968 convention enabled the members to receive more services from their association and to keep up with the rising costs.

W.H. (Bill) Metz, vice president of the *Birmingham Post-Herald,* was installed as president at the 97th annual convention, succeeding Porter Harvey, publisher of *The Advertiser-Gleam* in Guntersville. Other officers included Joel P. Smith, publisher of *The Eufaula Tribune,* first vice president, and Karl Elebash Jr., publisher of *The Graphic* in Tuscaloosa, second vice president.

Code of Ethics approved by 1968 convention delegates

The Code of Ethics was among the final items given approval at the convention. Co-chairmen of the committee drafting the code were Norman Bassett, executive editor of *The Tuscaloosa News,* and Jo Ann Flirt of Mobile, president of the Public Relations Council.

The Code of Ethics called for upgrading the profession of journalism and newspaper content. James E. (Jimmy) Mills, retired editor of the *Birmingham Post-Herald,* objected to the code on the grounds that "every editor and publisher in the business has his code of ethics," and "I don't think we need a code to say we are honest men of integrity. I don't think we need to apologize for what the newspapers have stood for all these years," according to a Feb. 11, 1969 capital bureau report in *The Birmingham News.*

Outgoing APA president Porter Harvey of *The Advertiser-Gleam* in Guntersville said the code "should not be interpreted as an apology, but merely as a written statement of beliefs."

The Press Association refused to adopt a companion resolution which would have created a five-member committee to administer the Code of Ethics and to set up procedures for handling complaints.

Advertising also part of Code

The Code of Ethics dealt with advertising as well as editorial and news content, and stated, "The freedom of all citizens to enjoy and expect fair and impartial treatment at the hands of newspapers is as precious as the freedom of the press to operate without censorship." Other sections of the code called for newspapers not to accept or prepare any advertising that is false or misleading or, "suggestive or offensive to public taste."

"Accurate statements of circulation figures should be made available to the public indicating the numbers of paid subscribers, single-copy sales, percentage of local circulation and other pertinent information," the code read.

Portions of the code were as follows:

Alabama Press Association Code of Ethics

"We, as members of the Alabama Press Association, do hereby pledge our efforts to uphold the principles of journalism hereafter described in order that we may serve the best interest of the people of Alabama and our profession; and to protect and defend the rights and privileges provided for all in The Constitutions of the State of Alabama and the United States of America.

"We hereby affirm that the people's right to know is a sacred trust that we shall guard zealously agaInst encroachment or infringement by government restraint or censorship.

"We do hereby recognize that to uphold and preserve the right to know and the guarantee of freedom of expression there are obligations and responsibilities which we, as newspaper editors and publishers, must assume and maintain.

"We pledge that in all business transactions, honesty and integrity will be prime requisites for our operations and practices.

"We also subscribe to the theory that the right to know embraces a continuing process of learning for ourselves and our readers in order that we be better informed. Through our Alabama Press Association, we seek constantly to improve and upgrade the profession of journalism."

News and editorial content

"The right of each individual who may be the subject of a news story or editorial comment is as basic as the right of the individual newspaper, and the freedom of all citizens to enjoy and expect fair and impartial treatment at the hands of newspapers is as precious as the freedom of the press to operate without censorship.

"A newspaper, in its news and editorial coverage and policies, should strive always to reflect the truth.

"The tests of accuracy, truth and impartiality must be added to all elements of news coverage, including

---

S I D E L I G H T S
MARKING 125 YEARS OF HISTORY

B'ham papers blacked out by printer's strike
The Birmingham Post, Birmingham News and Age-Herald, blacked out by a printer's strike during the last month of World War II, issued four-page photo engraved editions detailing Japan's surrender and followed up with an announcement that the newspaper strike had also ended.

The strike proved to subscribers and members of the staff how essential their daily newspapers were to "our American way of life," AlaPressa reported.

news stories, headlines photographs, cutlines, and typographical display.

"Editorial comment, syndicated columns, cartoons, and illustrations all should reflect dedication to the highest principles of journalism.

"The public figure, as well as the private citizen, deserves fair and impartial treatment at the hands of the press even though he may expect a greater degree of interest in all areas of his life.

"The right of the accused to a fair trial before an impartial jury of his peers is as inherent a part of American democracy as is freedom of the press. Newspapers, therefore, are obligated to exercise their own freedom in such a manner that they do not jeopardize the rights of others.

"Our problems as a free society are increasingly difficult and demand more knowledgeable and sophisticated solutions. It is the responsibility of the press to inform and educate the public so that it can more rationally and effectively solve these problems. The press should strive always to bring light and knowledge, to dispel ignorance and rumor.

"A newspaper has within its editorial complex the capacity to create or destroy the reputations of people, organizations and institutions; to determine the fate of the accused; to affect the decisions of our elected officials and governing bodies; to promote progress or cling to the past; to lead or to follow. This capacity to do good or evil is so great that the newspaper bears an unusual burden to conduct itself in its news coverage as a responsible member of the free press and as a good public citizen.

"The newspapers of America owe their existence to the United States Constitution which guarantees freedom of the press; this is affirmed in our Alabama Bill of Rights. Because we are a state and nation dedicated to preserving government processes, it is the responsibility of the press, through its editorial content, to insure the continued existence of the democratic form of government at all levels, to advocate orderly processes for maintaining our cherished democratic institutions, and to extend the privilege of our free American society to all its people."

Jim Hall subpoenaed in lawsuit

Shortly after it was adopted, the Code of Ethics was to play an important role in a suit being brought by Robert M. Shelton of Tuscaloosa, grand dragon of the Ku Klux Klan, against *The Tuscaloosa News*. APA secretary-manager Jim Hall was subpoenaed by Shelton and testified to the existence of the code and how it affected a story in *The Tuscaloosa News*. "When the court was told, in response to a question by Shelton's attorney that Norman Bassett (executive editor of *The Tuscaloosa News*) was co-chairman of a committee to draft the code, I was dismissed from the courtroom and *The Tuscaloosa News* subsequently prevailed in the case," Hall said in a 1996 interview.

Exhibits by suppliers featured in 1968

For the first time in a number of years, APA allowed exhibits by suppliers at the 1968 convention. The exhibits were enjoyed by the publishers who were eager to look at new equipment. Another first at the convention was a meeting of the associate members who formed their own organization.

Program participants at the Montgomery convention included J. Montgomery Curtis, vice president of Knight Newspapers in Miami; Marion Krehbiel, newspaper broker of Norton, Kan.; Eddie Ryan, "the father of offset printing," of New York; Billy Thomasson, publisher of *The Newnan* (Ga.) *Times-Herald*; and Grant Dillman of United Press International in Washington, D.C.

Delegates to the 1968 winter convention voted to take steps to form a Journalism Foundation to improve the quality and quantity of young men and women going into the newspaper field. The setting up of the corporation to establish a Journalism Foundation to benefit and encourage journalism education in Alabama was approved at the convention.

Committee to establish Journalism Foundation

A committee headed by H. Brandt Ayers, editor of *The Anniston Star*, initiated proceedings for establishing the Journalism Foundation in 1966. The foundation was chartered in July 1968.

Ayers was named foundation president. Victor H. Hanson II, vice president and general manager of *The Birmingham News*, was named vice president, and APA secretary-manager Jim Hall was named secretary. Treasurer was Bill Stewart of *The Monroe Journal*. Directors included Jesse Culp, *The Sand Mountain Reporter* in Albertville; Neil O. Davis, *The Auburn Bulletin;* and Richard N. Hammell, *The Florence Times* and *Tri-Cities Daily.*

The purposes of the foundation were: "To sponsor, promote, encourage, support and assist, financially and otherwise, the advancement of education in the field of journalism, by encouraging and assisting in making provision for the greatest possible educational opportunities and advantages for students of journalism;

"By promoting and making possible educational opportunities and advantages for students of journalism; by promoting and making scholarships, fellowships, loans, and other means of financial assistance for worthy, qualified students of journalism;

"By promoting, creating, and assisting in the creation of Chairs of Journalism for the teaching of any or all phases of journalism and in paying in full or in supplementing the salary or salaries of persons engaged in any phase of journalism;

"By donating or otherwise providing all or any part of the buildings, equipment, materials or facilities necessary, or useful in such education in the field of journalism."

Five additional members were added to the Journalism Foundation board of directors in late 1968, including Barrett C. Shelton Jr., *The Decatur Daily;* Roswell Falkenberry, *The Selma Times-Journal;* James H. (Jimmy) Faulkner Sr., *The Baldwin Times,* Bay

1968 summer convention in Nassau
The 1968 summer convention was held July 11-14 at the Sheraton-British Colonial Hotel in Nassau, Bahamas. *The Alabama Publisher* reported that "cost for the fun-filled vacation will be $200 per person." Relaxing at the summer convention are W.H. (Bill) Metz, left, the *Birmingham Post-Herald* (1969 president) and James E. (Jimmy) Mills, the *Birmingham Post-Herald* (1960 president). (Photograph courtesy of Jim Hall)

Minette; James B. Boone Jr., *The Tuscaloosa News;* and Mirl Crosby, *The Dothan Eagle.*

1968 summer convention, Nassau

The 1968 summer convention was July 11-14, 1968, at the Sheraton-British Colonial Hotel, Nassau, Bahamas. *The Alabama Publisher* reported that "cost for the fun-filled vacation will be $200 per person." Delegates departed on chartered planes from Huntsville/Decatur, Montgomery, Birmingham and Mobile. A rum punch party was featured on Friday night, followed by the Better Newspaper Contest awards banquet. Saturday's activities included golf, sailing, deep sea fishing, diving and sight-seeing.

In October 1968, the board of directors voted to "strongly support" Dr. Frank A. Rose, president of the University of Alabama, in his decision to deny permission for the Democratic Student Organization to invite four controversial speakers to speak at the Tuscaloosa campus.

APA supports UA president

The vote of the board was expressed in a telegram to Rose from APA president W.H. (Bill) Metz. In the telegram, Metz noted that APA had on several previous occasions joined with the University and other institutions of higher learning in defending the right of academic communities to hear anyone they please. "We feel that the current Democratic Student Organization request is an entirely different matter, however," Metz stated in the telegram.

The telegram concluded that Rose had acted in the best interest of the University and the state in "reserving the right of the University to say who shall and who shall not use its facilities."

Edward Seymour Cornish of *The Demopolis Times* and Mary H. Raiford of *The Selma Times-Journal* were inducted into the Alabama Newspaper Hall of Honor on Sept. 21, 1968.

1969
Joel P. Smith, *The Eufaula Tribune*
1969-1970 president

98th annual press convention, Huntsville
Feb. 13-15, 1969
Summer convention, Point Clear
July 17-19, 1969

"It's Fine in '69" was the theme of the 98th annual press convention at the Carriage Inn Motor

Hotel in Huntsville, Feb. 13-15, 1969.

APA Journalism Foundation president H. Brandt Ayers of *The Anniston Star* announced at the Huntsville convention the establishment of the Journalism Foundation and the start of its first public fund solicitation campaign. Ayers reported that the Journalism Foundation had already received $66,000 in pledges from the state newspapers. Ayers' report was received so enthusiastically that several publishers and editors interrupted the program to present their checks on the spot.

In a show of strong support for the Press Association, APA associate members overwhelmingly endorsed a $25 a year dues increase. The $25 increase was placed in a reserve to be used only by the associate members in APA programs and activities for their group.

The increase was recommended by outgoing chairman Clinton R. Milstead of U.S. Steel

Gov. Brewer addresses 1969 winter convention
Gov. Albert Brewer, at podium, is welcomed by, from left, APA president Bill Metz of the *Birmingham Post-Herald*; chairman of the board Porter Harvey of *The Advertiser-Gleam* in Guntersville; first vice president Joel P. Smith of *The Eufaula Tribune*; board member E.R. (Bob) Morrissette Jr. of *The Atmore Advance*; and past president Jimmy Mills of the *Birmingham Post-Herald* during the 98th annual APA winter convention in Huntsville Feb. 13-15, 1969. Governors and other political leaders often speak at APA conventions.

Corp. Milstead was honored by being presented with a silver tray by the APA "in deep and great appreciation." Milstead served as the first chairman of the associate members and repeatedly planned the annual associates receptions. George Smith of Samford University was elected new chairman of the associate members.

Joel P. Smith, editor and publisher of *The Eufaula Tribune,* was installed as president at the winter convention. Featured speakers at the 1969 convention were Gov. Albert P. Brewer and UPI Washington correspondent Merriman Smith.

Conducting professional sessions were Roy Sheridan of the U.S. Post Office Department who discussed second class mailing regulations; Tom Jones, instructor in the University of Alabama Department of Journalism, who discussed press photography; and Leo Franconeri, ANPA Research Institute, who conducted a seminar for dailies.

Harold S. May, *The Florence Herald;* Karl Elebash Jr., *The Graphic* in Tuscaloosa; and Jim

McKay, *The Demopolis Times,* discussed the pros and cons of publishing a twice-weekly newspaper.

Martin named *Advertiser/Journal* publisher in 1969

Harold E. Martin was named publisher of *The Montgomery Advertiser* and *Alabama Journal* in January 1969. Carmage Walls, president of The Advertiser Co., relinquished the title of publisher to Martin, who had been editor and co-publisher of the two newspapers since 1963. Martin, a native of Birmingham, graduated from Samford University and received a master's degree in journalism from Syracuse University. He began his career as a newspaper executive in Syracuse and held management positions with several newspapers before joining The Advertiser Co.

In March 1969, Multimedia Inc., a South Carolina-based firm headed by J. Kelly Sisk, purchased The Advertiser Co. Harold E. Martin, editor and publisher of *The Montgomery Advertiser* and *Alabama Journal,* newspapers, continued in his position as chief executive officer of The Advertiser Co.

The Advertiser Co. sold to Multimedia

The Advertiser Co. was sold to Multimedia Inc. by Southern Newspapers Inc., and Bristol (Tenn.) Independent Publishing Co. Carmage Walls, president of Southern Newspapers Inc., and T. Eugene Worrell, president of Bristol Independent Publish-

---

---

ing Co., announced the effective date of the sale as March 1, 1969.

Sisk, a Livingston native and graduate of the University of Alabama, said he was "happy to have the privilege of being a part of the company assuming the operation of Montgomery's excellent newspapers." Multimedia was formed in January 1968 and had interests in several South Carolina newspapers, as well as radio and television stations.

Anniston Star seeks access to city records

In 1969, APA along with Southern Newspaper Publishers Association (SNPA), entered as a friend of the court a suit by *The Anniston Star* against various Anniston city officials.

The suit brought by *The Anniston Star* sought access to city records. Action to bar *The Star* from access to city records originally was taken, city officials said, on the basis "That the publication in question deals mainly in speculation or seeks such records from mere idle curiosity and that the reporters and staff of *The Anniston Star* have often interfered with and hindered the discharge of the official duties of city employees by excessive demands and rude and offensive behavior."

The suit was settled in favor of *The Anniston Star.* The city was ordered to open its records to the newspaper and to pay court costs.

APA book service starts in 1969

In addition to her duties with the APA Clipping Bureau and ANAS, Martha Hall began a new service for the Press Association in 1969 that offered books at a discount. Through the service, members could buy best sellers at a 15 percent discount.

APA waged a legislative battle against attempts to pass local laws doing away with the necessity of publishing voter lists and some types of local legislation.

A joint University of Alabama-APA committee began to study ways and means of preserving the history of Alabama journalism. Plans were begun for a museum and reference room of Alabama journalism, a journalism collection in the library at the University of Alabama, microfilming of all Alabama newspapers, and a booklet tracing the genealogy of Alabama newspapers and magazines.

Members of the board of directors of the APA Journalism Foundation studied and inaugurated new ideas and programs with increased vigor in September 1969. A total of $94,000 was pledged to its operation. An all-day campaign for support was held Aug. 21, and editors were surveyed on what projects they would like the Journalism Foundation to undertake.

Offset printing seminar held in 1969

An offset printing seminar was held in May with the cooperation of equipment suppliers. More than 60 APA members and their guests attended the sessions in the plant of *The Cullman Times.*

During the legislative session, APA objected to the method used by a House committee in approving a series of bills which would allow cities to adopt proposed building and zoning codes without publishing them in full in a newspaper.

APA Legislative Committee chairman Barrett C. Shelton Jr. of *The Decatur Daily* said, "In effect, what the House committee has done is approve a set of bills which would make it much harder for the people to find out what their own city hall is doing, and have done it in a manner that attempts to prevent the people from knowing what they did."

The Executive Committee of the Press Association unanimously adopted a resolution praising *The Montgomery Advertiser* and staff writer Milo Dakin for conducting "themselves as courageous and responsible members of the press." *The Advertiser* and Dakin were instrumental in exposing wrongdoing by at least one member of the Alabama Senate. Dakin's articles resulted in investigations by a grand jury and the Senate, and spurred a drive for a code of ethics in the Alabama Legislature.

Editor's Hot Line new feature in *Alabama Publisher*

During 1969 *The Alabama Publisher* was expanded and made more meaningful. A new feature was the Editor's Hot Line which answered tough questions from newspaper reporters. The largest Rate and Data Book in the history of the APA was published in 1969. The Clipping Bureau set a record for the number of clippings mailed, which contributed substantially to the Alabama Newspaper Advertising Service budget.

Converting to offset printing in 1969 were *The Tallassee Tribune, The Fairhope Courier, The Wetumpka Herald* and *The Clayton Record. The Gadsden Times* launched a $750,000 modernization program in 1969 and set November as the date for conversion to offset. *The Moulton Advertiser* began using Compugraphic phototypesetting machines in 1969, and *The Franklin County Times* in Russellville installed a new Cottrell V-15A web offset press. More than 60 APA members attended a Cottrell offset seminar at *The Cullman Times* in 1969.

> ### S I D E L I G H T S
> #### MARKING 125 YEARS OF HISTORY
>
> #### *Reporters write book on Phenix City*
> "Many reporters and editors have said it, few ever do it — 'I'm going to write a book about this big story I'm working on'," *The Alabama Publisher* reported in its July 1955 issue.
>
> "Edwin Strickland, *The Birmingham News,* and Gene Wortsman, the *Birmingham Post-Herald,* did it! They wrote the book about their big story — Phenix City."
>
> "Phenix City" was published June 24, 1955, by Vulcan Press of Birmingham. "If you, like most Alabamians, doubted the stories that came out of Phenix City last year, doubted that such conditions existed, you'll find them repeated in more detail with references," *The Alabama Publisher* reported. "Ed and Gene name names, they name and describe places and actions, they pull no punches on conditions they found in the city. 'Phenix City' tells what happens when an average Alabama town becomes 'the wickedest city in America'."

Bob Plowden's *The Sun* of Prattville joined APA in 1969, bringing the membership to 105 weeklies and 21 dailies. *The Mobile Beacon* became the 126th member of the APA in 1969.

The 1969 summer convention was July 17-19 at the Grand Hotel at Point Clear.

Hall elected SDX president

In December 1969, APA secretary-manager Jim Hall was elected president of the Alabama professional chapter of Sigma Delta Chi (later renamed the Society of Professional Journalists) in Birmingham. Hall succeeded O.B. Copeland, assistant to the president of Progressive Farmer Company. Elected to the board of directors at the same time were Cody Hall Jr., executive editor of *The Anniston Star,* W.H. (Bill) Metz, vice president of the *Birmingham Post-Herald,* Dr. William E. Winter, head of the Department of Journalism at the University of Alabama, and Hoyt Harwell, correspondent with the Associated Press in Birmingham.

News Bureau moves to Administration Building

AlaPressa reported in its Dec. 3, 1969, issue that APA was losing a "much-valued friend," Ed Brown,

---

S I D E L I G H T S
MARKING 125 YEARS OF HISTORY

Hugh Sparrow honored at 1957 luncheon
Political writer Hugh Sparrow of *The Birmingham News* was honored at a luncheon
in 1957 in Montgomery given by members of
the Legislature and friends.
    Attending were Lt. Gov. Guy Hardwick, At-
torney General John Patterson and Alabama
Supreme Court Justice J. Ed Livingston.

---

director of the University of Alabama News Bureau. "Not that he's going away or anything,"
AlaPressa continued. "It's just that he's moving his
offices.

"Ed Brown, for so many years a sympathetic
listener to Alabama Press Association managers,
will move himself and his staff into bright new
quarters in the new University Administration
Building," *AlaPressa* reported. "That's across the
quadrangle from the location in Manly Hall the
University News Bureau has occupied for so long.
There really is no way to list all the ways Ed has
helped APA down through time. Certainly, besides
his personal friendship, the use of his equipment
must be ranked high in importance. We'll miss Ed,
Gillis Morgan and Betty West and all the other
folks in the News Bureau. This corner of Manly
Hall just won't be the same without them."

Col. Harry Mell Ayers, editor and publisher of
The Anniston Star, and Charles Glenn Jones, edi-
tor and publisher of *The Troy Messenger, The Troy
Herald* and *The Pike Sentinel* in Brundidge were
inducted into the Alabama Newspaper Hall of
Honor on Oct. 4, 1969.

1970
**Karl Elebash Jr., *The Graphic*, Tuscaloosa
1970-1971 president**

**99th annual press convention, Tuscaloosa
Feb. 12-14, 1970
Summer convention, Gulf Shores
July 23-25, 1970**

Abraham Lincoln's birthday, Friday the 13th,
and Valentine's Day were the dates for the 99th
annual press convention at the Stafford Hotel in
Tuscaloosa, Feb. 12-14, 1970.

Gay Talese, a graduate of the University of Alabama and the author of the best-selling "The Kingdom and the Power," addressed a combined APA
and University of Alabama Journalism Day banquet.

William E. Branen, president and publisher of
The Burlington (Wis.) *Standard Press*, talked about
central printing plants. Alabama native Carroll
Kilpatrick, White House correspondent for *The
Washington Post*, addressed a luncheon meeting.
Kilpatrick, a native of Montgomery, edited the
University of Alabama's campus newspaper, *The
Crimson White*, while a student. He was president
of the Overseas Writers Association and president
of the White House Correspondents Association.
Before moving to Washington, Kilpatrick worked
at *The Montgomery Advertiser, The Birmingham
News* and *The Birmingham Age-Herald*.

Dr. Warren Agee, dean of the Henry W. Grady
School of Journalism at the University of Georgia,
directed a session on "A Long Range Analysis of
the Effect of Current Attacks on the Press."

Press conferences were held with the numerous candidates for governor and lieutenant governor. A new feature at the 1970 convention was a
"$1.00 Half Hour" at which Herve Charest Jr. of
The Tallassee Tribune and Ed Dannelly of *The
Andalusia Star-News* passed out dollar bills for every idea that could be used by other publishers.

Journalism accreditation being sought
Dr. David Mathews, president of the University of Alabama, spoke to the convention audience
at a luncheon on Feb. 12, saying that two objectives of his administration would be to "seek accreditation of the journalism program as an immediate goal" and to "try to save Woods Hall for
another 100 years."

In a resolution, the APA delegates received "with
appreciation and pleasure the report of President
David Mathews of improvements which have been
made and are being planned in faculty number, cur-
riculum, and teaching techniques in the University
of Alabama Department of Journalism," but stated
that "anxiety and concern on the part of the members
of the Alabama Press Association will remain unrelieved until such time as the Department is fully accredited by ACEJ and is housed in quarters encouraging the most effective projection of the discipline."

1970 delegates "unrelieved concern"
"Unrelieved concern" for the lack of accreditation and the poor housing of the University's Department of Journalism in Woods Hall was ex-

pressed by APA members attending the convention in Tuscaloosa. Woods Hall, 102 years old, was completed in April 1868 as the first major campus building of the Reconstruction era. The fourth floor of the building had been condemned. Journalism occupied the second floor and part of the third floor.

In a unanimous resolution, delegates said they were pleased with the report of President Mathews concerning the department, but they urged "strongly that definite long-range plans be incorporated into the institution's programming for construction of a new building for the Department of Journalism and for equipping it in a manner to encourage the most effective instructional procedure."

At the 1970 winter convention, the APA board of directors voted to change Jim Hall's title from secretary-manager to executive director.

Support sought for journalism education

Several meetings were held by the APA Journalism and Printing Schools Committee with University of Alabama officials during 1970, seeking more University support for journalism education. The drive by APA was supported editorially by several Alabama newspapers and by *The Crimson White*, student newspaper at the University of Alabama.

Another resolution adopted at the 1970 convention renewed and rededicated the members to

---

continued responsible exercise of freedom of the press and urged that newspapers make a special effort to "acquaint and educate their readers, including public officials, as to the basic, vibrant meaning of the First Amendment and the guarantees contained therein...and to convey to their readers the extent to which the other freedoms — religion, speech, assembly and dissent — depend upon a free press to make them a reality."

Offset seminar held at *Tuscaloosa News* in 1970

A Goss Offset seminar was held at *The Tuscaloosa News* in March 1970. As part of the seminar, a demonstration newspaper was published featuring articles on offset and photos of the seminar.

The Anniston Star turned out its first fully offset editions on newly installed press units in November 1970. The first run of the new press represented a milestone in the daily newspaper's continued conversion from letterpress to offset methods. Newspaper officials said advantage of the new system included a reduction in long-term costs, improved printing quality of both photographs and news copy, better color capability, and increased production speed.

Martin awarded Pulitzer Prize in 1970

The Pulitzer Prize was presented to Harold E. Martin, editor and publisher of *The Montgomery Advertiser* and *Alabama Journal,* in 1970. The Pulitzer was in recognition of Martin's reporting which exposed and brought to a halt a commercial scheme using Alabama prisoners for drug experimentation.

Martin, 46, wrote a series of articles exposing the drug-testing program conducted by Southern Food and Drug Research Inc. The stories pointed out that the program subjected prison inmates to drug tests by unqualified technicians in poorly equipped laboratories without the supervision of trained medical personnel.

The Pulitzer Prize in 1970 was the third ever awarded an Alabama newspaper man and the first ever awarded for outstanding reporting. In 1928, Grover C. Hall Sr., editor of *The Montgomery Advertiser,* won a Pulitzer Prize for editorials, and in 1957 Buford Boone, publisher of *The Tuscaloosa News,* was awarded a Pulitzer, also in the field of editorial writing.

Illegal postal strike concerns APA

The illegal strike of postal workers early in 1970 worried the APA board of directors, both as citi-

---

SIDELIGHTS
MARKING 125 YEARS OF HISTORY

Cohen was sports writer for B'ham Ledger

Octavus Roy Cohen, 67, a former Birmingham newspaper man who wrote more than 1,000 short stories, died Jan. 6, 1959, in Los Angeles. Cohen was a prolific writer who turned out 66 novels, six plays and numerous radio and motion picture scripts, in addition to his short stories.

Cohen told an interviewer not long before his death that he earned between $30,000 and $100,000 a year for 35 years from writing. Cohen was a former sports writer for the old *Birmingham Ledger.* Many of his stories used Birmingham's 18th Street as a setting. Along with Birmingham newspaper writers and other prominent men, he founded the Loafers, a group interested in writing.

zens and as mail users. The directors sent the following statement to President Nixon, Postmaster General Winton Blount, a Montgomery native, and to the state's congressional delegation:

"The breakdown in postal service is intolerable. The illegal strike by postal workers and their defiance of court injunctions threaten the nation's stability, economy and security. Never before in our nation's proud history have we had a postal strike and we strongly urge you to take every means necessary to stop it and get the mails moving again. It is unthinkable that such should be allowed in the world's greatest and most powerful nation. Our Congress and President should initiate moves now that will prevent any such occurrence in the future. First, as citizens of the United States and second, as mail users vitally dependent upon uninterrupted postal service, we urge prompt and forceful action to restore normal mail service throughout our country."

Distinguished Lecture Series gets support

In the summer of 1970, the APA Journalism Foundation approved a grant to the University of Alabama's Department of Journalism for a Distinguished Lecture Series during the spring semester of 1971. Dr. Frank Deaver, associate professor of journalism, made the proposal to the Journalism Foundation board of directors. The Distinguished Lecture Series would bring to the Tuscaloosa campus every three weeks an outstanding individual in a journalism-related field.

Senior and graduate students in journalism participating in the seminar would receive course credit and do supervised reading before a lecturer's arrival. APA members would be invited to attend the lectures, and a fellowship would be granted to one APA member in each congressional district to participate in each seminar.

The Journalism Foundation expressed the intent of allowing funds to accumulate to a certain level before expending them on any project. However, members of the Journalism Foundation board of directors felt that more interest and enthusiasm in the foundation and its projects could be generated by its functioning quickly and meaningfully on some projects.

Former APA manager Jones W. Giles dies in 1970

Former APA manager Jones W. Giles died in July 1970 at Druid City Hospital in Tuscaloosa. Giles, 49, was executive secretary and field manager from 1957 to 1965. He resigned and later

became assistant director of the University of Alabama Press. Giles, a Tuscaloosa native, had edited and published several weekly newspapers in Alabama before joining APA. He bought his first newspaper, *The Red Bay News* in Franklin County, while still a student. He also edited and published *The Franklin County Times* in Russellville in partnership with his father, former APA president Milton Giles, from 1945 to 1953.

APA president Karl Elebash Jr., publisher of *The Graphic* in Tuscaloosa, issued the following statement: "The newspaper fraternity of our state is deeply grieved by the death of Jones Giles. As an editor and publisher and later as executive secretary and field manager of the Alabama Press Association, he served the cause of journalism well and with honor. He loved his work and his associates respected him because of it."

1970 summer convention, Gulf Shores

Guest speaker for the 1970 summer convention in Gulf Shores was Grover C. Hall Jr., nationally known Washington columnist for Publishers-Hall Newspaper Syndicate and former editor of *The Montgomery Advertiser*. The summer convention was July 23-25, 1970, at the Holiday Inn in Gulf Shores. APA president Karl Elebash Jr., publisher of *The Graphic* in Tuscaloosa, said the first item on the convention agenda was a seafood banquet featuring deep sea delicacies caught from the Gulf. Orsen B. Spivey, publisher of *The Geneva County Reaper* in Geneva, coordinated the APA-sponsored golf tournament at the Gulf Shores Golf Club.

On Sept. 26, 1970, Grover C. Hall Jr. was listed in "satisfactory condition" at University Hospital in Birmingham where he was undergoing tests for a possible brain tumor. Hall was flown to Birmingham by air ambulance from a Charlotte, N.C., hospital where he had been listed in unsatisfactory condition. The 55-year-old newspaper man had been missing since Sept. 9. Hall had left Washington that day by car, and friends said he had planned to arrive in Alabama the next day.

But he was in Meckleberg County Jail in Charlotte, N.C., on Sept. 18 until a Charlotte reporter, who knew Hall, had him admitted to a hospital. The jail supervisor said Hall was picked up by officers on suspicion of driving while under the influence of alcohol. Hall had no belongings with him when he was arrested, "except for a press card that looked like it might get him into the White House," the jail supervisor said.

SIDELIGHTS
MARKING 125 YEARS OF HISTORY

Brandt Ayers returns to Anniston

H. Brandt Ayers returned to Anniston in October 1963 to become assistant to his father, Col. Harry M. Ayers, publisher of *The Anniston Star.* He assumed the title of assistant to the publisher and was responsible for the newspaper's editorial page.

Ayers had served as a capital and legislative reporter for *The Raleigh* (N.C.) *Times* and was Washington correspondent in a news bureau serving Southern and Southwestern newspapers.

Ayers later was named editor and publisher of *The Anniston Star,* which *Time* magazine called "one of the two best small newspapers in the United States." He was principal stockholder of a family newspaper group, which included two daily newspapers and two weeklies.

Ayers wrote a weekly syndicated column titled "Out Here," which was distributed to some 30 newspapers. He had also written for *The New York Times, The International Herald Tribune, The Boston Globe, The Philadelphia Inquirer, The Atlanta Constitution, The St. Petersburg Times, Newsday, Southern Living* and *The Washington Post/Los Angeles Times* Service.

Ayers was the recipient of the National Headliner Award for an expose of corruption in Anniston city government. During 1967-1968, he was a Nieman Fellow at Harvard University and was named Distinguished Journalism Graduate of the University of Alabama. In 1985 he received the Green Eyeshade Award, The Society of Professional Journalists' award for Best Commentary in the Southeast.

In 1989 Ayers was awarded a senior fellowship at the Gannett Center for Media Studies at Columbia University, where he focused on a project titled: "Heartland Editors and Their Coverage of the Third World."

Ayers was founding president of the Alabama Press Association Journalism Foundation.

His lectures on foreign and domestic affairs included visits to Harvard University, Princeton University, the University of Capetown, the University of Nairobi, and several others.

His wife, the former Josephine Peoples Ehringhaus of Raleigh, was a theater producer and director who had managed community theatre, a professional regional theater and had international credits, including the Soviet premiere of "Driving Miss Daisy."

Ayers was featured in a story in the *Birmingham Post-Herald* titled "Ayers: His *Star* Shines," in which staff writer Sam Hodges noted that "Reporters who worked for Ayers — and moved on to bigger papers — remember him as an extraordinarily good steward of the newspaper he inherited. They don't all like his style, which some describe as pompous, but they agree on his virtues as a newspaper owner:

"He hires talented, ambitious reporters and editors, he spends money relatively freely on the news operation, and he encourages aggressive reporting and fearless editorial writing, even when it gets him in trouble with friends and advertisers.

"As for hiring, Ayers wants bright young people with liberal arts backgrounds. Though he speaks eloquently about how Southerners are looked down upon, he likes to hire Ivy Leaguers from the North," the *Post-Herald* continued. "He mentions with pride that the editor of *The Harvard Crimson* recently interviewed for a job with *The Star.*"

" 'When I was there Brandy really did pull together a diverse group of people,' says Patricia Greene, now an associate city editor of *The Capital City Times* in Madison, Wis. 'The Star brought people down from the North for what we laughingly referred to as their 'Southern experience.' "

Memorial to Grover C. Hall Jr.

Hall died Sept. 24, 1971, at age 56. The APA Journalism Foundation established a memorial fund honoring him. "We can think of no better way to recognize the work this great newspaper man did than to establish a fund in his name in an organization that has as its sole purpose the encouragement of young people to consider newspaper work as a career," said APA president Robert Bryan of *The Cullman Times.*

Edmond Cody Hall Sr., editor and publisher of *The Alexander City Outlook,* and R.H. (Harry) Walker Sr., editor and publisher of *The Limestone Democrat* of Athens, were inducted into the Alabama Newspaper Hall of Honor Oct. 17, 1970.

Boone purchases *The Natchez Democrat* in 1970

Natchez Newspapers, a corporation whose stock was owned by Tuscaloosa Newspapers Inc., purchased *The Natchez Democrat* in 1970. Tuscaloosa Newspapers Inc. was principally owned by James B. Boone Jr., publisher of *The Tuscaloosa News.* Warren Koon, former managing editor of *The Tuscaloosa News,* was named editor and general manager of *The Natchez Democrat.* Koon was succeeded in Tuscaloosa as managing editor by Charles Land, sports editor of *The News* since 1955. *The Natchez Democrat* was operated for 105 years by the Lambert family. James K. Lambert, president and publisher since 1931, announced the sale.

SDX accepts women in 1970

The Alabama professional chapter of Sigma Delta Chi, journalism society with headquarters in Birmingham, accepted six women for membership in 1970. The chapter vote was the first since the national organization approved women membership in 1969. The six women, all staff members of *The Birmingham News,* were Martha Hood, women's editor; Jo Ellen O'Hara, food editor; Carol Nunnelly, Barbara Ann Thomas and Cynthia Anita Smith, news reporters; and Anna Davis, copy editor.

CHAPTER 7

APA Moves from the University of Alabama Campus

1971-1985

"It takes more spunk and involves more sacrifice for a country editor to retain his self-respect than for the editor of a national magazine or a metropolitan daily. The whole set-up is nicely arranged to strip him of dignity. Though he knows better, he must pretend that the ignoramuses who run the local schools are educators; that the vulgar gossip-mongers constitute 'society'; that the hole-in-the-mud where he's stuck is a significant community."

Julian O. Hall
The Dothan Eagle

— *Julian O. Hall (1900-1939)*
Editor, The Dothan Eagle
(From a personal column in The Dothan Eagle)

THE TUSCALOOSA NEWS EDITORIALIZED IN its Sept. 9, 1972, issue that *Montgomery Advertiser* editor and publisher Harold E. Martin had "rendered a service to all" by calling attention to a contract under which the University of Alabama paid $8,500 of the APA executive secretary's salary and provided office space to the Press Association valued at $7,000 annually.

"The 'contract,' which actually amounts to a 'subsidy,' should be terminated," *The Tuscaloosa News* commented. "Until then, there should be and are red faces in the trade association and educational institution alike."

"Taxpayers Subsidize Alabama Press Association" was the 8-column, banner headline above the

nameplate of the Sept. 8, 1972, issue of *The Montgomery Advertiser.* "It's a situation that developed over the years, but any way you look at it the state is subsidizing the Alabama Press Association," a University of Alabama spokesman told *The Montgomery Advertiser* and *Alabama Journal.*

The Montgomery Advertiser reported that APA executive director Jim Hall helped the University in organizing the journalism department's summer high school journalism clinic. A University official was quoted as saying Hall delivered "an occasional lecture." President Dr. David Mathews' office declined comment on the University's contract with APA.

Less than four months after publication of the story in *The Montgomery Advertiser,* the Alabama Press Association officially ended ties with the University of Alabama, on Jan. 1, 1973. APA agreed to pay rent to the University for the space it occupied in Manly Hall on the campus, but only until sufficient quarters were found elsewhere in Tuscaloosa. In May 1973, APA moved to an office location at 1925 Queen City Avenue in Tuscaloosa.

Cooperative agreement began Sept. 1, 1939

The Alabama Press Association and the University of Alabama had entered a cooperative agreement on Sept. 1, 1939. A field manager, Doyle L. Buckles, was hired to devote half his time to APA and the other half to the University News Bureau, as well as serve on the faculty of the Department of Journalism.

Under a new contract negotiated between APA and the University of Alabama in 1950, the University continued to pay half the field manager's salary and expanded the office space, but the new agreement "would allow the secretary-manager more free time for association work," the contract stated.

In 1968, a new contract had been drawn up by University president Dr. Frank Rose and APA president W.H. (Bill) Metz of the *Birmingham Post-Herald,* making the secretary-manager a consultant to the University and calling for his participation in seminars and programs conducted by the University for high school journalism students. The journalism department and Extension Division duties were eliminated.

Officials of *The Montgomery Advertiser* and *Alabama Journal* resigned from the Press Association when they learned that the executive director no longer taught classes at the University. Publisher Harold E. Martin also objected to the subsidy arrangement between APA and the University of Alabama.

The Tuscaloosa News pointed out in its Sept. 9, 1972, editorial that even in 1939 when the first contract was signed between the University and the Press Association, a minority group from APA protested the arrangement on subsidy grounds and its relationship to a free press.

News: Subsidy exists because of outdated contract

"The subsidy occurs because of an outdated contract that does not fit the current situation — if it ever fit," *The Tuscaloosa News* commented. "Thus (Harold) Martin charges, taxpayers are subsidizing the trade association. We agree."

The Tuscaloosa News reported that in about 1970, top officials of *The News* had urged Press Association officials to consider the contract a subsidy, and to eliminate it. "The urgings were made twice in 1972," *The Tuscaloosa News* continued. "Similar sentiments were expressed to University officials. We know of no mutual effort between the two to eliminate the contract."

The Tuscaloosa News added, "We hope, and expect that *The Advertiser* will join with *The News* and a number of other Alabama newspapers in urging the Press Association and the University to terminate the subsidy."

APA president W.E. (Gene) Hardin, editor of *The Greenville Advocate* and state representative for Butler, Crenshaw and Pike counties, told *The Tuscaloosa News* that the allegations in *The Montgomery Advertiser* had "caught us all a little off balance. There's a lot of background to this that hasn't come out yet," Hardin said. "I expect our board of directors will be getting together in a few days and we'll come up with an answer to this whole thing. I think our response should come that way."

APA releases formal statement

A formal, written statement prepared by Hall as executive director and Hardin as APA president described the relationship between the University and Press Association as "a long and mutually profitable one. We feel that our efforts for the University and for the people of the state of Alabama are much more valuable than the price tab placed on the occupancy of space on the campus or on that portion of the salary paid to the Association's executive director by the school," the statement said.

APA's reaction to *The Montgomery Advertiser* report was as follows:

"The subject about which Harold Martin wrote in The Montgomery Advertiser *today is nothing new. Facts in his story are a matter of public record and there is nothing in his report which merits an apology from the members of the Alabama Press Association or from its staff. The contractual relationship between the Alabama Press Association and the University of Alabama has been a long and mutually profitable one. The vigorous growth in services provided its members by the Association during the past few years, however, has created a need for the organization's board of directors to study changes in the arrangement which will result in the organization more adequately meeting the demands both of the University and of the Association.*

"We are disappointed, of course, that certain members of the Administration and of the University are not aware of the terms of the institution's contract with the Association or with the work that the members and

the staff of APA perform for the students and for the journalism faculty," the APA statement continued. "We feel that our efforts for the University and for the people of the state of Alabama are much more valuable than the price tag placed on the occupancy of space on the campus or on that portion of the salary paid to the Association's Executive Director by the school."

Editorial: "Dog Days In The Press"

Tom Johnson, editor and publisher of *The Montgomery Independent,* commented in a Sept. 14, 1972, editorial titled "Dog Days In The Press" that every Alabama editor "who is at least six months old or has the equivalent intelligence thereof is well aware that an alliance, a misalliance, a liaison — take your pick — has existed between the University of Alabama and the Alabama Press Association."

Johnson wrote that *The Independent* had suggested to an APA official years earlier that the Press Association "get the hell off the U of A campus and run away to sea if that was the only alternative."

"It was left to (Harold) Martin to take the lid off the pot, finally committing to print that the APA's office space in Tuscaloosa is furnished by the University of Alabama and that part of the APA executive director's salary is paid by the University. That is, by the state," Johnson wrote. "…the story

of the APA-University courtship needed to be printed. Any editor who objects to Martin's having printed it first had better re-examine his credentials as an editor.

"The APA is flatly the recipient of gratuities furnished from the public treasury," Johnson continued. "Why does the U of A furnish money and office space to the APA but not to associations representing plumbers, electricians and chiropractors? The bad news, papa, is that we editors have been caught in a compromising position and the gal's folks (the taxpayers in this case) are going to be watching to see whether we do the honorable thing about it."

Martin unpopular with some weekly editors

Martin's calling attention to the contract between the University of Alabama and APA did not make *The Montgomery Advertiser* editor and publisher popular with some newspaper editors and publishers, particularly in the weekly field.

The Opp News editorialized on Sept. 14, 1972: "The University of Alabama pays $8,500 per year on the salary of the Press Association's secretary-manager. The Press Association pays the director an additional $8,500. We consider this a just and reasonable salary for a qualified man who is a press encyclopedia for all the newspapers in Alabama. We believe that Editor Martin is a little reckless in assuming *The Advertiser-Journal* is operating in a glass house, through which no subsidized tax rocks could penetrate. The taxpayers are subsidizing his newspaper 365 days a year. Each day he places his newspaper in the mails, the taxpayers are paying a substantial percentage of the postage based on his second-class permit that he enjoys partly at the expense of the taxpayers."

Spivey: *Advertiser* story "didn't expose anything"

Orsen B. Spivey, editor and publisher of *The Geneva County Reaper* in Geneva commented that "Those of us who are members of the 'fourth estate' in Alabama, and especially those of us who are members and officers of the Alabama Press Association, find it impossible to understand what is behind the recent story written by Harold Martin, editor and publisher of *The Montgomery Advertiser.* It certainly didn't expose anything. Was he trying to say that Dr. David Mathews and the University trustees are stupid, or crooks? As a member of the board of directors of the Alabama Press Association, this writer certainly feels no guilt about the arrangement with the University. In fact, we

---

SIDELIGHTS
MARKING 125 YEARS OF HISTORY

Mills honored at 30th anniversary dinner

James E. (Jimmy) Mills, editor of the *Birmingham Post-Herald,* was honored Sept. 16, 1961, at a 30th anniversary surprise dinner staged by employees of the newspaper.

Mills became editor of the old *Birmingham Post* on Sept. 16, 1930, when the newspaper was little more than 10 years old. Some 70 persons attended the dinner. Attorney Francis Hare, long-time friend of Mills, was featured speaker and cited four editorial campaigns waged by Mills in *The Post* and later in the *Post-Herald,* which had lasting effect in Birmingham and in Alabama.

Hare referred to the newspapers' drives for lower power rates, a good small loan law, the cleanup of Phenix City, and for keeping the Jefferson congressional district intact.

are one of the board members who feel that the Association would be better served if the office was moved to Montgomery. And, as an alumnus of the University, and as a taxpayer of Alabama, we will be happy to accept the apology of Mr. Martin for any disservice he has done to the institution and the state. We would even be happy to vote for his return to membership in the Alabama Press Association," Spivey concluded.

Elebash: Contract renewed in 1968

"For the record, the contract between the Press Association and the University of Alabama was re-evaluated and renewed as recently as 1968," editor and publisher Karl Elebash Jr. wrote in *The Graphic* of Tuscaloosa. "It provided that the University would continue to provide one-half of the secretary's salary; it would continue to provide retirement, medical, and other fringe benefits for the secretary; it would continue to provide office space for the APA in Manly Hall," Elebash, 1970-1971 APA president, wrote. "Furthermore the new agreement relieved the secretary of any requirement for regular classroom teaching.

"The APA executive director is highly energetic, capable and conscientious in rendering these services," Elebash continued. "He does all this and

---

SIDELIGHTS
MARKING 125 YEARS OF HISTORY

"Son of Sam" killings sells newspapers

The 1977 "Son of Sam" killings in New York produced significant circulation gains for New York newspapers, especially for *The New York Post, AlaPressa* reported.

"Summer, a traditionally slow time for newspaper sales, has been quite different this year. Sales of *The Post,* which provided front page coverage of the story for weeks, have been up consistently following the July 31 'Son of Sam' murder. Normally 600,000 circulation, *The Post* was selling 100,000 copies daily over that figure, and on the day of the capture circulation was estimated to exceed 1 million. On the same day, *The New York News* sold an additional 350,000 copies and even the reserved *New York Times,* which had not dramatized the killings, printed 35,000 extra copies."

---

more, and the Alabama Press Association's educational activities have been expanded and enriched since this contract through the efforts of its Journalism Foundation."

Hall said he felt "betrayed"

Jim Hall of Troy, APA executive director from 1966 to 1974, recalled in a 1996 interview that he felt "betrayed" when *Montgomery Advertiser* editor Harold E. Martin accused the Press Association of being subsidized by taxpayers. "The Press Association had a good, working relationship with the University of Alabama, with (Department of Journalism chairman) Dr. Bill Winter, and with the journalism department," Hall said. "The University got its money's worth. The Press Association certainly wasn't getting a free ride by being on the campus."

In 1996 Hall headed Jim Hall Media Services in Troy, a newspaper brokerage, appraisal and consulting service.

1971
Robert Bryan, *The Cullman Times*
1971-1972 president

100th annual press convention, Birmingham
Feb. 11-13, 1971
Summer convention, Biloxi, Miss.
July 29-31, 1971

Plans to commemorate the 100th anniversary of the Alabama Press Association began with the signing of a contract with an outside firm to produce a magazine chronicling accomplishments of APA. The magazine, entitled "Century of Challenge," was to be distributed at the Centennial Anniversary Convention.

The 100th annual convention was Feb. 11-13, 1971, at the Parliament House Motor Hotel in Birmingham. APA past president Herve Charest Jr., retired publisher of *The Tallassee Tribune*, was keynote speaker at the centennial convention. Charest discussed what APA meant to Alabama newspapers and what it should strive to mean in years ahead.

Syndicated newspaper columnist Erma Bombeck was featured speaker at one of the luncheon meetings, and Jenkin Lloyd Jones of Tulsa, Okla., was keynote speaker at one of the banquets. A highlight of the convention was a steak and champagne dinner honoring APA outgoing president Karl Elebash Jr., publisher of *The Graphic* in Tuscaloosa.

APA past presidents honored at centennial convention

Past presidents were honored at the banquet, along with newspapers that had been published for more than 100 years. APA came into being on March 17, 1871. It was then that Maj. William Wallace Screws, editor of *The Montgomery Advertiser*, called representatives of the state's newspapers to his office "for the purpose of organizing the press." Only eight editors and publishers responded.

One year later, on June 18, 1872, the first convention of the Alabama Press Association (at that time called the Editors and Publishers Association of the State of Alabama) was held in Montgomery.

In 1971, APA represented 110 weekly newspapers and 24 daily newspapers.

Screws was not first president of Press Association

Ironically, Screws was not the first president of APA. S.J. Saffold, editor of *The Selma Daily*

Times, held the honor. Screws was elected to the top post in 1879 and served four consecutive years.

In the 100 years that followed, some 75 of the state's outstanding newsmen served as APA president. Fully a third of them were living in 1971, and practically all of them were at APA's centennial con-

Past presidents attend 100th convention in 1971
 APA past presidents attending the Nominating Committee meeting during the 100th annual APA winter convention at the Parliament House Motor Hotel in Birmingham Feb. 11-13, 1971, are, front row from left, W. Emmett Brooks, *The Brewton Standard;* George H. Watson, *The Shades Valley Sun,* Homewood; J.C. Henderson, *The Alexander City Outlook;* and Clarence B. Hanson Jr., *The Birmingham News.*
 Back row from left, are Ralph W. Callahan, *The Anniston Star;* Ed Dannelly, *The Andalusia Star-News;* Neil O. Davis, *The Auburn Bulletin;* Porter Harvey, *The Advertiser-Gleam,* Guntersville; Harold S. May, *The Florence Herald;* Charles G. Dobbins, *The Anniston Times;* Herve Charest Jr., *The Tallassee Tribune;* William E. (Bill) Brooks Jr., *The Brewton Standard;* Bill Stewart, *The Monroe Journal;* Jimmy Mills, the *Birmingham Post-Herald;* George M. Cox, *The Mobile Press Register;* Ben George, *The Demopolis Times;* Bill Metz, the *Birmingham Post-Herald;* and Joel P. Smith, *The Eufaula Tribune.*

vention in Birmingham in 1971. Nineteen state newspapers were recognized for service to Alabamians and to the profession of journalism. The dailies and weeklies, each of which had been published for a century or more, were honored by APA at the 100th convention.

Former APA president Bill Stewart, publisher of *The Monroe Journal* in Monroeville, said that "it is fitting on the centennial birthday of the organization that some very special recognition be afforded those newspapers which have served the state so proudly."

19 newspapers recognized at centennial convention

The 19 newspapers recognized and the length of time they were in operation were: *The Mobile Register* (157 years), *The Tuscaloosa News* (153 years), *The Montgomery Advertiser* (144 years), *The Selma Times-Journal* (143 years), *The Moulton Advertiser* (143 years), *The Standard and Times*, Sheffield (140 years), *The Shelby County Reporter*, Columbiana (128 years), *The Pickens County Herald* and *West Alabamian*, Carrollton (118 years), *The Clarke County Democrat*, Grove Hill (115 years), *The Wilcox Progressive Era*, Camden (111 years), *The Greenville Advocate* (106 years), *The Monroe Journal*, Monroeville (105 years), *The Tuskegee News* (105 years), *The Troy Messenger* (105 years), *The Union Springs Herald* (105 years), *The Southern Star*, Ozark (104 years), *The Gadsden Times* (104 years), *The Daily Home*, Talladega (103 years), and *The Florence Times-Tri Cities Daily* (102 years).

Three still in hands of original owners

Three Alabama newspapers of more than 100 years of service were still in the hands of the original owners in 1971: *The Southern Star* of Ozark, owned by the Adams family and published by Joseph H. (Joe) Adams; *The Clarke County Democrat* of Grove Hill, owned by the Carleton family and published by George Carleton; and *The Greenville Advocate*, owned by descendants of founder Gen. James Berney Stanley and edited by W.E. (Gene) Hardin, son-in-law of the late Glenn Stanley.

In recognizing the 19 newspapers, Stewart pointed out that they "are steeped in the tradition of service. They have proven their faith in the principles and aspirations of truth," Stewart said, "and they have reaped the abundant reward of seeing their state and their communities reach the threshold of economic prosperity."

SIDELIGHTS
MARKING 125 YEARS OF HISTORY

Boone Newspapers Inc. buys Georgia papers

Boone Newspapers Inc. and executives associated with the corporation acquired two weekly newspapers in Georgia in 1978, *The Walker County Messenger* of Lafayette, and *The Dade County Sentinel* of Trenton. Alvin Benn, former editor of *The Alexander City Outlook*, became publisher of *The Walker County Messenger*.

Stockholders included Jim Boone; Benn; Charles H. Land, editor and associate publisher of *The Tuscaloosa News;* Randolph C. Tillotson, publisher of *The Oskaloosa* (Iowa) *Herald;* Anne Plott, managing editor of *The Tuscaloosa News;* Warren H. Koon, publisher of *The Natchez* (Miss.) *Democrat;* Paul R. Davis, publisher of *The Auburn Bulletin;* Stanley Voit, publisher of *The Tuskegee News;* and Jimmy Tilley, publisher of *The Dadeville Record.*

Legislature congratulates APA on 100th anniversary

State legislators adopted a resolution congratulating APA on its 100th anniversary and commending state newspapers for their leadership in publishing and disseminating the truth. In approving a resolution introduced by Rep. W.E. (Gene) Hardin of Greenville, editor of *The Greenville Advocate*, the Legislature also praised the 130 daily and weekly newspapers of Alabama for their efforts to secure for the citizens of the state their proper place in the economic and social life of the nation.

Almost from the beginning, the resolution noted, APA became active in "seeking governmental action on matters that would directly benefit the people." Action was sought by the Press Association, the resolution noted, on rewriting the 1875 Constitution, on establishing a fair or exposition where the region's agricultural products could be spotlighted and sold, and on devising means by which public transportation could be improved.

The resolution also noted the "unparalleled leadership" the newspapers of Alabama provided during "two great wars" in "raising millions of dollars in bond revenue and in prompting citizens to participate in the numerous activities which would help the war effort." Also cited by the Legislature was APA's role in the drive to establish the Alabama State Chamber of Commerce.

Commemorative Hall of Honor Ceremony in 1971

At the 1971 Alabama Newspaper Hall of Honor induction ceremony, a special program was published as a commemorative salute by Auburn University to those inducted and to the 100 years of APA. The program that year included pictures and biographical information on the 28 persons who had been inducted into the Hall of Honor. Included in the Oct. 2, 1971, program was a message from APA president Robert Bryan of *The Cullman Times*, and the original resolution that established the Hall of Honor in 1959.

Reese Thomas Amis
The Huntsville Times

Inductees to the 1971 Hall of Honor were two north Alabama journalists, Reese Thomas Amis, editor of *The Huntsville Times*, and William Randolph Shelton, founder of *The Decatur Daily*. The ceremony was at the Ralph B. Draughon Library on the Auburn University campus.

William Randolph Shelton
The Decatur Daily

Journalism established at Troy State

A new journalism department was established at Troy State University in 1971. Dr. Ralph Adams, TSU president, said an initial budget of $150,000 to begin operations would be requested of the Legislature in 1971. Announcement of the establishment of the department was made at the 100th anniversary convention of APA.

In late 1971, Gov. George C. Wallace, in a news conference in his office, announced with Dr. Ralph Adams that TSU's new journalism school would be named in honor of Julian O. Hall, editor of *The Dothan Eagle*, and Grover C. Hall Sr. and Grover C. Hall Jr., former editors of *The Montgomery Advertiser*.

Newspapers may receive advance payment for legals

APA president Robert Bryan announced in April 1971 that J.W. (Jim) Oakley Sr., mayor of Centreville and publisher of *The Centreville Press*, had secured a ruling from Attorney General Bill Baxley that there was nothing in the Alabama Code to prevent state newspapers from requiring payment in advance for legal advertising.

J.W. (Jim) Oakley Sr.
The Centerville Press

The ruling came in two separate letters, one dated March 17 and another dated April 12.

Oakley, acting on the request of APA's Legislative Committee, of which his son, James W. (Jim) Oakley Jr. was chairman, asked Baxley on Feb. 20 if "it would be legal for a newspaper to set up a requirement that all legal notices, regardless of for what purpose, to be paid in advance."

Bryan said APA would strongly oppose a bill introduced in the House of Representatives that would require newspapers to provide equal space to candidates for public office where editorials had appeared about them or about their opponents. Bryan said the legislation was unconstitutional "on its face." The bill was introduced by Jefferson County Rep. Robert C. Gafford.

1971 summer convention, Biloxi

Broadwater Beach Hotel and Golf Club in Biloxi, Miss., was the site of APA's 100th anniversary summer convention July 29-31, 1971. APA president Robert Bryan said Broadwater Beach offered some of the finest accommodations and resort facilities of any major hotel in the South. "It is a real pleasure for us to be returning to Biloxi after so long an absence," Bryan said. APA last met in Biloxi-Gulfport in the summer of 1957.

S I D E L I G H T S
MARKING 125 YEARS OF HISTORY

Cullman Times *selling Compugraphic 7200*
Publisher Bob Bryan of *The Cullman Times* listed a Compugraphic 7200 for sale in the March 1983 issue of *AlaPressa*. "Sets 14 point to 72 point type. Also Nu-Arc Vic-1418 camera. Copy board 20 by 24. Film size 14 by 18. Good condition."

Ed Pepperman was host of a U.S. Brewers Association luncheon. A bar-equipped bus was reserved for a side trip to New Orleans. Cost of bus transportation and refreshments was $10 per person.

Citing an "unprecedented" attack on public notice procedure, delegates to the 1971 summer convention called on lawmakers "to defeat those attempts which are being made in the present session of the Legislature to prevent or to curtail disclosure."

The request for help came at the closing session of the summer convention. Newspaper executives noted that at least 10 bills had been introduced in the Legislature which would alter or curtail publication requirements. Delegates then passed a resolution encouraging members of the Legislature "to rededicate themselves to seeing that government continues to function as openly as possible in every way possible."

Statement on journalism education adopted

Delegates also adopted a statement expressing their expectations for journalism education in institutions of higher learning. APA said the needs of Alabama newspapers could best be met through journalism courses designed to teach students to report, edit and publish the news. Journalism students also should receive a "broad education in liberal arts and sciences," APA commented in the statement.

APA president Robert Bryan said the statement was adopted "to serve as an indication of the deep and abiding interest of the newspapers of Alabama in quality journalism education in the state, and as a pledge by them to support and encourage any institution which will give serious consideration to providing the industry and the people enlightened communicators."

Nixon issues 90-day freeze

On Aug. 15, 1971, President Richard Nixon announced that he had issued an executive order placing a 90-day freeze on wages, prices, rents and salaries. The president's action caught some Alabama newspapers in the middle of rate revisions and others planning them.

John W. Bloomer
The Birmingham News

A group of 27 Alabama newspaper representatives participated in the first state invitational seminar on international understanding in 1971. The seminar was in Guatemala and was convened at the invitation of the Guatemala Press Association and the Guatemala Partners of the Americas. John W. Bloomer, managing editor of *The Birmingham News*, was president of the Alabama Partners.

During the visit to the Latin American country, Alabama editors and publishers were shown small villages, Indian huts, markets and an "almost primitive hospital," according to *AlaPressa.*

1972

W.E. (Gene) Hardin, *The Greenville Advocate*
1972-1973 president

101st annual press convention, Mobile
Feb. 10-12, 1972
Summer convention, Disney World, Orlando, Fla.
July 20-22, 1972

Seminars, politics and a costume ball were featured at the 101st annual press convention Feb. 10-12, 1972, at the Admiral Semmes Hotel in Mobile.

W.E. (Gene) Hardin, editor of *The Greenville Advocate* and a member of the Alabama House of Representatives, was elected APA president at the winter convention. He was the fourth news executive from *The Greenville Advocate* to be elected to the presidency in the association's 101-year history.

The Greenville Advocate had produced more APA presidents than any other newspaper in the state. Serving before Hardin were Gen.

Courant's *Gaston Bozeman dies in 1974*

Robert Gaston Bozeman Sr., a veteran newspaper man who was editor and publisher of *The Evergreen Courant* for 31 years until his retirement in 1957, died Oct. 16, 1974, after a long illness.

The following editorial, reprinted from the Oct. 21 edition of *The Tuscaloosa News,* outlined Bozeman's long record of community and professional service:

"Robert Gaston Bozeman who died last week in Evergreen was one of the foundations of Alabama journalism. He was an inspiration to countless newsmen as to what one man can do as a leader of his community. Most know Mr. Bozeman as editor and publisher of *The Evergreen Courant,* a weekly newspaper he ran for more than 30 years prior to a 1957 retirement.

"But Mr. Bozeman was much more than that.

"He was educated as a teacher, and actually went to Evergreen as a school principal. Some three years after arriving in Evergreen, he became a newspaper man and set a standard for community service that stands as a challenge. Over the years Mr. Bozeman served on the County Board of Education, a number of years as its chairman. He was an Evergreen city councilman. and he was one of several citizens of his area instrumental in founding Conecuh County Hospital, an institution he further served for years through membership on its executive board and as an officer of the board. When something was important for his community, Mr. Bozeman was out front leading.

"His service to his journalistic profession is also a standard. He served two terms as president of the Alabama Press Association. He leaves a legacy to Alabama journalism in three sons who are themselves editors and publishers, R.G. Bozeman Jr., of *The Evergreen Courant,* Clyde Dickey Bozeman of *The Choctaw Advocate,* and Pace W. Bozeman of *The Thomasville Times.*

"Thus, Mr. Bozeman will be long remembered. And, longer than that, his contributions to his community, his state and his profession will continue to serve others."

James Berney Stanley, 1882-1886 (four terms), and his sons, Foster Webb Stanley, 1926-1927 and 1935-1936 (two terms), and John Glenn Stanley, 1962-1963. Hardin was son-in-law of Glenn Stanley.

Hardin had been editor of *The Greenville Advocate* since 1967. He first joined the newspaper's staff in 1951. A native of Bessemer, Hardin graduated from Andalusia High School and attended Mercer University and the University of Alabama. Before his election to the Alabama House, Hardin was a member of the Greenville City Council for eight years.

Legislation changes definition of legal newspaper

A milestone in newspaper legislation was passed by the Alabama Legislature and signed into law by Gov. George C. Wallace in 1972. The legislation changed the definition of a legal newspaper and threw out decades-old stipulations regarding the qualifications newspapers must have for publishing public notice advertising. Introduction of the measure was approved by the Press Association's board of directors and had the encouragement and backing of APA president W. E. (Gene) Hardin and many of the members of both the Senate and House.

Specifically, the legislation allowed a newspaper to be printed anywhere and still qualify for legal advertising — so long as certain other requirements were met. Those requirements were that the newspaper be printed in the English language, have a general circulation in the county in which it was published, have its principal editorial office in the county in which it was published, and be mailed under a second class mailing permit from the post office where it was published.

The law also made it possible for a newspaper to close down one week a year and still qualify for legals. The provision was included to allow publishers to give their employees a week off and not put out an edition. The legislation was needed for several reasons — the most pressing of which was the relief needed by newspapers which printed in central plants.

Hotel rooms at Disney World $30 a day in 1972

APA officers and members of the board of directors received a memo in April 1972 from APA president W.E. (Gene) Hardin on the upcoming summer convention to Disney World. "The Disney World convention will be full of new sights and sounds, but it will be very expensive," the memo noted. "Rooms will cost $30 a day. Registration at a hotel only allows visitors unlimited free use of the transportation system. Each admission to the theme park will cost anywhere from $3 to $5. As best we can determine, a minimum 'on the premises' cost for a family of four to attend the convention will be in the neighborhood of $200.

"In view of the above, we need to know as quickly as possible if you think we should continue with our plans to hold the summer meeting at Disney World. A ballot and return envelope are enclosed for your convenience."

APA members elected to hold the 1972 summer convention at Disney World.

APA terminates relationship with UA

In September 1972, *The Montgomery Advertiser* reported that the Alabama Press Association was being subsidized by taxpayers of the state. *The Advertiser* reported that the University was not only paying half of the salary for APA manager Jim Hall, but also was providing free office space.

At one time, the APA manager-secretary

taught classes in journalism. When Hall was hired in 1966, his duties were arranged so that approximately one-fourth of his time would be devoted to the Department of Journalism, one-fourth to the University Extension Division, and one-half to APA activities.

In 1968, a new contract was drawn up, making the manager-secretary a consultant to the University and calling for his participation in seminars and programs conducted by the University for high school journalism students. The journalism department and Extension Division duties were eliminated.

After Harold E. Martin, editor and publisher of *The Montgomery Advertiser,* wrote that the University was subsidizing APA, the Press Association terminated its relationship with the University and began a rental arrangement for the space it occupied in Manly Hall. APA also assumed full responsibility for Hall's salary.

Earl Lee Tucker, editor and publisher of *The Thomasville Times,* and George Robert Cather, editor and publisher of *The Ashville Southern-Aegis,* were inducted into the Alabama Newspaper Hall of Honor Oct. 21, 1972, at Ralph B. Draughon Library on the Auburn University campus.

1973
Ewell H. Reed, *The Arab Tribune*
1973-1974 president

102nd annual press convention, Montgomery
Feb. 8-10, 1973
Summer convention, Decatur
July 26-28, 1973

The Alabama Press Association officially ended ties with the University of Alabama, effective Jan. 1, 1973.

Outgoing APA president W.E. (Gene) Hardin of *The Greenville Advocate* announced to APA membership that after that date the Press Association would be dependent only upon the membership for financial support. APA members, upon recommendation of the board of directors, voted to double membership dues, to assume responsibility for all of the manager's salary, and to move off the University campus.

University of Alabama administrators were notified of APA's intentions prior to the Jan. 1, 1973, cutoff. Negotiations were entered into for APA to remain on campus only until suitable quarters were found off-campus.

A lease was signed by APA and University of-

Past presidents gather in 1973

Past APA presidents gathered for a photograph during the 102nd winter convention at the Downtowner Motor Hotel in Montgomery Feb. 8-10, 1973. Seated from left are Ben G. George, *The Demopolis Times* (1956); Ed Dannelly, *The Andalusia Star-News* (1966); James E. (Jimmy) Mills, the *Birmingham Post-Herald* (1960); Herve Charest Jr., *The Tallassee Tribune* (1963); and J.C. Henderson, *The Alexander City Outlook* (1949).

Standing from left are Karl Elebash Jr., *The* (Tuscaloosa) *Graphic* (1970); W.H. (Bill) Metz, the *Birmingham Post-Herald* (1968); Joel P. Smith, *The Eufaula Tribune* (1969); Robert Bryan, *The Cullman Times* (1971); Bill Stewart, *The Monroe Journal* (1959); and Ralph W. Callahan, *The Anniston Star* (1965). (Photograph courtesy of Jim Hall).

ficials in which the Press Association agreed to pay $200 a month rent on the quarters it occupied on campus. APA also assumed responsibility for all of the executive director's salary. Previously, the University paid half the salary in return for services performed for the University.

The 102nd annual APA convention was Feb. 8-10, 1973, at the Downtowner Motor Hotel in Montgomery. Among the guest speakers were Gov. George C. Wallace and Lt. Gov. Jere Beasley. Sessions at the winter convention were concerned almost entirely with relocation and reorganization of APA. Delegates voted to move the headquarters from the University of Alabama campus to an off-campus site.

Tuscaloosa remained choice location

Tuscaloosa remained the choice location, and after lengthy searching by the site selection com-

Elebash addresses 1973 convention delegates

Past president Karl Elebash Jr. of *The* (Tuscaloosa) *Graphic* addresses delegates at the 1973 winter convention in Montgomery. Seated from left, are Ben G. George, *The Demopolis Times* (1956 president); Nonnie Hardin, *The Greenville Advocate;* and Jim Hall, APA executive director. The 102nd annual convention was held Feb. 18-19, 1973, at the Downtowner Motor Hotel in Montgomery. (Photograph courtesy of Jim Hall)

mittee, a location on Queen City Avenue was picked. Rent was $225 a month for the 2,000-square-foot office building. The move took place in May 1973.

APA offices on the University campus had been in Manly Hall, a Civil War structure with a porch connecting the various rooms. APA was located in the Union Building when the cooperative agreement with the University of Alabama was established in 1939.

AlaPressa reported in its May 1973 issue that APA headquarters were "quieter, more efficient, and easier to get to." The new address was 1925 Queen City Avenue in Tuscaloosa, telephone 345-5611.

Other press associations also move off campus

Four press associations in the South moved from university campuses in the early 1970s. The Florida Press Association moved first. The Kentucky Press Association followed. They were later joined by the Alabama Press Association and the Louisiana Press Association. In 1973, the Tennessee Press Association and South Carolina Press Association were the only Southern press associations still on university campuses.

"The move into quarters of their own is the culmination of a lot of dreams for APA members," APA executive director Jim Hall wrote in *AlaPressa* at the time. "Our organization has experienced rapid growth during the past few years, and it needed new room in which to operate and to expand."

S I D E L I G H T S
MARKING 125 YEARS OF HISTORY

Lowry buys **Greensboro Watchman** *in 1969*

Edward E. Lowry Jr., a native of Greensboro who learned to set type at *The Greensboro Watchman* during his high school days, became new owner of *The Watchman* on Jan. 1, 1969, after negotiations were concluded with the estate of N. Hamner Cobbs, who died June 27, 1968.

Lowry graduated from Auburn University with a bachelor of science degree in science and literature, and a minor in journalism. While attending Auburn University, he ran a printing business at *The Lee County Bulletin*. After graduation he accepted a job with Mergenthaler Linotype Co. in Atlanta where he helped install Linotype machines in Southern states.

The 92-year-old *Greensboro Watchman* had been purchased by N. Hamner Cobbs in 1942 from the estate of William E.W. Yerby. In announcing the sale of *The Greensboro Watchman* to Lowry, the Cobbs family expressed pleasure that the newspaper would be operated by one who had "cut his teeth" in the office of *The Watchman*.

Chatting at 1971 convention
Chatting at the 1973 winter convention are from left, past president Robert Bryan, *The Cullman Times*; outgoing president W.E. (Gene) Hardin, *The Greenville Advocate*; and incoming president Ewell Reed, *The Arab Tribune*. (Photograph courtesy of Robert Bryan)

Delegates to the 1973 winter convention had voted unanimously to double membership dues and ordered that billing for the increase be mailed July 1973. APA president Gene Hardin said additional money was necessary to finance independence of the Press Association. "As a result of the dues increase and the move of the Press Association from the University, not one single member was lost," Hall said in a 1996 interview.

Newspapers increase rates in 1973

Several Alabama newspapers adjusted subscription and advertising rates in 1973 to compensate for sharp increases in newsprint and production costs. *The*

Gov. Wallace addresses 1973 delegates
   Gov. George C. Wallace addresses delegates at the 102nd annual APA convention in Montgomery Feb. 8-10, 1973. Seated to Wallace's left is APA past president Robert Bryan of *The Cullman Times*. Sessions at the 1973 winter convention were concerned almost entirely with relocation and reorganization of APA. Delegates voted to move the headquarters from the University of Alabama to an off-campus site. (Photograph courtesy of Robert Bryan)

1973 summer convention, Decatur

The 1973 summer convention was July 26-28 at Decatur Inn in Decatur. U.S. Brewers Association sponsored a luncheon in the back yard of *Decatur Daily* general manager Barrett C. Shelton Jr.'s home. The summer convention also featured an afternoon bus trip to Nashville and Opryland.

Newly appointed dean of the School of Public Communication at the University of Alabama, Dr. Mort Stern, was featured speaker at the Thursday night banquet. Stern, former editorial page editor of *The Denver Post*, was appointed dean at Alabama effective July 1, 1973. With it came consolidation of the Departments of Journalism and Broadcast and Film Communications. Formerly, the two departments were part of

Birmingham News and the *Post-Herald* raised their prices to distributors and franchised dealers on Oct. 1. The retail price suggested was 60 cents a week for daily delivery and 90 cents a week for daily and Sunday delivery.

In south Alabama, all three Baldwin County newspapers, *The Baldwin Times, The Fairhope Courier* and *The Onlooker in Foley,* raised single copy prices from 10 cents to 15 cents. New annual subscription rates were also instituted. At *The Onlooker,* in-county subscription rates were $5.50; in state, $7.50; and out of state, $8.50.

Critical shortage of newsprint in 1973

In Gadsden, the critical shortage of newsprint forced *The Gadsden Times* to limit the number of newspapers allocated to single copy sales through newsracks and news dealers.

Bowater Corp., with major newsprint production facilities in Canada and the United States, asked U.S. price controllers for permission to increase newsprint prices $15 a ton effective Jan. 1, 1974. Newsprint was $210 a ton in 1973.

AlaPressa reported in 1973 that with *The Clarke County Democrat's* upcoming conversion to offset printing, Alabama would have only four weekly newspapers still printing letterpress — *The Alabama Messenger, The Marion Times-Standard, The Lamar Democrat* at Vernon and *The Clanton Union Banner.*

the College of Arts and Sciences.

Tribute paid to Kenneth Bell

APA delegates also paid tribute to retiring University of Alabama professor Kenneth Bell whose career in teaching and journalism spanned four decades. Bell was editor of *The Alexander City Outlook* from 1941 to 1944 when he was succeeded by J.C. Henderson. "We were one of the first weeklies in the state to use color," Bell said while looking over a copy of the Sept. 9, 1943, edition of *The*

Outlook. The edition featured a red "V" superimposed on the front page with a banner headline: "Carry The Blitz to Berlin."

Rufus Napoleon Rhodes, editor and publisher of *The Birmingham News,* and John Henry Singleton, editor and publisher of *The Enterprise Ledger,* were inducted into the Alabama Newspaper Hall of Honor on Oct. 6, 1973, at Ralph B. Draughon Library on the Auburn University campus. An advertising seminar was held in conjunction with the 1973 Hall of Honor ceremony. On Friday, professor Edmund C. Arnold, nationally known newspaper design authority and chairman of the graphics department at Syracuse University in New York, conducted the ad workshop.

Police search for clues in slaying of editor

Mobile police were searching for clues in the shotgun slaying in 1973 of *The Mobile Press Register's* Sunday editor, Arch McKay. McKay's body was found in the front seat of his car, parked in a lot on Government Street across from the newspaper building in downtown Mobile. Medical examiners said the editor had been shot in the right side of the head at close range. Police did not rule out the possibility that McKay was killed in a robbery attempt. *The Press Register* offered a $5,000 reward for information leading to the arrest and conviction of the killer.

Sears represents APA at PSC hearing

Marcia M. Sears, editor of *The Shelby County Reporter* in Columbiana, represented APA at a hearing before the Alabama Public Service Commission Oct. 4, 1973. The commission met to consider whether Alabama Power Company's advertising budget was "unnecessary and exorbitant" as charged by consumer advocate Jim Zeigler. Mrs. Sears' testimony was in defense of utility advertising. Zeigler was an employee of *The Daily Home* in Talladega.

S I D E L I G H T S
MARKING 125 YEARS OF HISTORY

Ed Lowry also commercial catfish farmer
Ed Lowry Jr., editor and publisher of *The Greensboro Watchman* "is also a commercial catfish farmer and has received a federal patent on a floating fish feeder," *AlaPressa* reported in 1983.

Zeigler filed a seven-part complaint against Alabama Power Company's rates that questioned the firm's earnings, advertising and promotional expenses and "other matters." His complaint was filed "as an individual and as president of the Alabama League of Young Voters." Zeigler alleged that net earnings for the power company for the first five months of 1973 were up 63.9 percent over the same period in 1972.

1974
Barrett C. Shelton Jr., *The Decatur Daily*
1974-1975 president

103rd annual press convention, Huntsville
Feb. 7-9, 1974
1974 summer convention, Gulf Shores
July 18-20, 1974

Gov. George C. Wallace delivered the keynote address at the 103rd annual winter convention at the Carriage Inn in Huntsville Feb. 7-9, 1974. Other speakers included Jules Whitcover of *The Washington Post* and Clarence Kelly, director of the FBI.

In a resolution passed unanimously at the closing session of the 1974 winter convention, delegates voted to "use their individual and collective influence to support efforts of those members of the Legislature who seek compliance with the provisions of the Alabama Constitution." APA members asked state senators and representatives to publish local bills as required by law.

Newspaper executives expressed concern over past practices of legislators introducing and passing general bills of local application. Such tactics bypassed the constitutional requirement that local bills be published four times prior to the time they were introduced.

Top female politicians attended

Alabama's three top female politicians, Mabel Amos, candidate for treasurer; Agnes Baggett, candidate for secretary of state; and Melba Till Allen, candidate for treasurer, were guests at the convention. "Seeing all three ladies in the same room and on the same platform is an opportunity newsmen won't want to miss!" *AlaPressa* reported.

The convention delegates took side trips to the Space Center and Jack Daniel's distillery in Lynchburg, Tenn., and traveled to Nashville for a performance at the Grand Ole Opry. "Here's just the trip you've been waiting for!" *AlaPressa* reported in its January 1974 issue. "It starts out from the Carriage Inn in Huntsville at noon Saturday, Feb. 9. Good old Kentucky Fried Chicken and ice cold refreshments will be served to get the party off to a fine start. First stop on the tour is Lynchburg. That's where the finest bourbon in the country is made."

Hardin blasts Shell Oil Co. in 1974

APA past president W.E. (Gene) Hardin, editor of *The Greenville Advocate*, blasted Shell Oil Co. in 1974 for sending him a news release about the energy shortage instead of an ad. In a letter to public relations officials, Hardin pointed out that Shell published full-page advertisements in daily newspapers and yet sent press releases to weeklies. "I find it difficult to publish your news releases when other newspapers publish your paid advertisements," Hardin wrote.

Dr. William E. Winter, head of the Department of Journalism at the University of Alabama, died of a heart attack in March 1974. Professor John Luskin of the University of Alabama Department of Journalism announced his retirement at the end of the spring semester. Luskin was honored at the School of Communication's first Communications Banquet on Honors Day at the University on April 3, 1974. Robert Bryan, publisher of *The*

Cullman Times, received the Distinguished Alumni Award at the banquet.

Hall resigns as APA executive in April 1974

APA executive director James W. Hall resigned from his post, effective April 1, 1974. In doing so he wrote, "Martha and I have served the newspapers of this state with dedication and to the best of our abilities. It is with a great deal of love for the newspapers of Alabama and for the people who produce them that this resignation is tendered."

Hall had succeeded Jones W. Giles as secretary-manager on May 1, 1966.

APA president Barrett C. Shelton Jr. of *The Decatur Daily* appointed Juanita Smith, a long-time APA employee, as interim manager. Mrs. Smith, who had served as supervisor of ANAS, would serve until the board of directors completed its search for a new executive director, Shelton said. Norman H. Bassett, executive editor of *The Tuscaloosa News,* was appointed consultant to the board of directors on APA matters. Bassett, acting manager of APA in 1947-1948 following the death of field manager Doyle L. Buckles, was familiar with Press Association programs, Shelton said.

Shelton asked that applications be forwarded to him at *The Decatur Daily.* The Executive Committee, consisting of Shelton, Orsen B. Spivey, *The Geneva County Reaper* in Geneva, and Claude E. Sparks, *The Franklin County Times* in Russellville, would review the applications and recommend a group of them to the screening committee.

Hall joined the administrative staff of Troy State University later in 1974. Details of his appointment as an assistant to TSU president Dr. Ralph Adams were carried by the dailies during the week of May 27. Martha Hall became editor of Troy State University Press, the book printing arm of TSU.

Bradley named APA executive in July 1974

Stephen E. Bradley became executive director of APA, effective July 1, 1974. Bradley, 30, was chosen from a field of applicants by screening committee members composed of APA president Barrett C. Shelton Jr. of *The Decatur Daily,* immediate past president Ewell H. Reed of *The Arab Tribune,* and vice presidents Orsen B. Spivey, *The Geneva County Reaper,* and Claude E. Sparks, *The Franklin County Times,* Russellville. Bradley was interviewed by the board of directors at a meeting in Tuscaloosa, and his selection was the unanimous choice of the directors.

A native Alabamian, Bradley grew up in Florence and worked for *The Florence Times-Tri Cities
Daily* in the circulation and editorial departments.
Since 1971, he had been with Shell Oil in the
company's public relations department handling a
variety of assignments, including editing and producing the company's monthly magazine. Bradley
held bachelor's and master's degrees from the University of Alabama.

Shelton: "Bradley will be fine asset"

"I have a great deal of confidence in this young
man, and given time to learn the job, I believe he
will be a fine asset for the association," APA president Barrett Shelton Jr. wrote in the June 19, 1974,
issue of *AlaPressa*. "Stephen comes to us knowing
the value of keeping things out in the open, and I
hope you will be as open with him as possible.

"Changes are going to be made in accounting
procedures which will enable you to know much
more about your organization than you ever have
before," Shelton continued. "He (Bradley) will be
dedicated to keeping you informed. He's a fine man.
Get to know him, be open with him, and let him
know when you disagree. There may be something
there for both of you to learn."

The 1974 summer convention was July 18-20
at Gulf State Lodge and Convention Center in
Gulf Shores.

Thomas Eastin, editor and publisher of *The
Halcyon* at St. Stephens, and Glenn Stanley, editor
and publisher of *The Greenville Advocate*, were inducted into the Alabama Newspaper Hall of Honor

on Oct. 12, 1974, at Ralph B. Draughon Library
on the Auburn University campus.

1975

**Orsen B. Spivey, *The Geneva County Reaper*, Geneva
1975-1976 president**

**104th annual press convention, Birmingham
Feb. 27-28, March 1, 1975
Summer convention, Point Aquarius
July 17-19, 1975**

A preview of the upcoming session of the Alabama Legislature was a highlight of the 1975 winter convention Feb. 27-28 and March 1, 1975, at
the Kahler Plaza Hotel in Birmingham. The legislative preview came during a Friday afternoon
session at a "two-way" press conference between a
panel of legislators and reporters. It was preceded
by opening remarks from Lt. Gov. Jere Beasley and
House Speaker Joe McCorquodale.

Not only did reporters ask legislators questions
about what could be expected in Montgomery, but
legislators fired questions back at reporters on their
views of potential problems facing the lawmakers.

Gov. George C. Wallace addressed APA delegates following Friday's luncheon. The first
speaker at the opening session on Thursday was
Jesse Lewis, publisher of *The Birmingham Times*,
and the first black to serve in a governor's Cabinet
since Reconstruction.

At the Thursday night banquet, Vic Gold, a
native Alabamian and former press secretary to
Vice President Spiro Agnew, was the speaker. Gold
was a syndicated columnist whose column appeared
regularly in *The Birmingham News*.

Instead of a formal banquet on Friday night,
delegates attended a special performance of the
Broadway play, "The Seven-Year Itch."

Kellee Reinhart, APA assistant manager, resigned effective April 30, 1975. "Due to the necessity to reduce operating costs as much as possible
during this period of rising inflation, applications
for the position of assistant manager will not be
considered at this time," *AlaPressa* reported.

APA moves to new quarters in Tuscaloosa

Effective May 5, 1975, the APA central office was located in new quarters in Tuscaloosa.
The board of directors approved the move at its
1975 winter convention in Birmingham. "The
present facilities are undesirable for several reasons and are not suited to the association's needs,"

AlaPressa reported in its March 25, 1975, issue. "The new quarters are more suited to the daily operation of the association office and will provide better working conditions and facilities for the office staff at a cost comparable with our current rental agreement."

The new address was Professional Plaza East, 921 Third Avenue East, Tuscaloosa. The old address was 1925 Queen City Avenue, Tuscaloosa.

AlaPressa reported in its May 12, 1975, issue that the vice president for sales for Bowater Co., John C. Davis, had forecast that newsprint would cost $450 a ton by 1985. Speaking at a meeting of the Kentucky Press Association, Davis predicted that demand for newsprint in the United States would increase slightly by more than two million tons in the next decade, and that the growth of large dailies would slow down while small dailies and weeklies would experience only "moderate" growth.

Davis said that profits in 1975 were too low to encourage the investment required for substantial expansion of capacity. He said that Bowater required that any new investment project return a "minimum profit, before taxes and interest charges, of 20 percent per year on the total capital employed in that project over its useful life. In order to achieve that return on an investment in additional newsprint capacity, the price of newsprint would have to rise to about $320 a ton for 30-pound paper."

1975 summer convention, Point Aquarius

The Better Newspaper Contest and a special performance by the Alabama Shakespeare Festival players highlighted the 1975 summer convention July 17-19 at Point Aquarius Lodge and Country Club near Pell City. The Shakespeare players presented a special performance of "The Tempest" on Thursday in Anniston to begin convention activities. Delegates also attended a reception at the home of *Anniston Star* editor and publisher Brandt Ayers.

While at Point Aquarius, convention delegates had the opportunity to tour the nearby Kimberly-Clark paper plant. A Saturday morning general business meeting concluded convention activities. Registration was $12.50 per person.

Sid McDonald speaks at banquet

Speaking at the Friday night banquet was state Sen. Sid MacDonald of Arab who told the delegates, "I don't know what we're going to celebrate in 1976, our bicentennial year, if we don't

change our attitudes about a lot of things." MacDonald also acknowledged the strong contribution made by newspapers to Alabama through their support of the 1973 Ethics Act. He added that newspapers must marshal public opinion again in order to save the Ethics Act which "needs minor surgery but doesn't deserve the gutting that is being threatened."

APA had scheduled Guntersville Lodge and Convention Center as the site of the 1975 summer convention, but facilities at Guntersville were not completed in time for the 1975 convention.

John C. Burruss
The Universalist Herald,
Notasulga and Montgomery

John Crenshaw Burruss, editor and publisher of *The Universalist Herald* in Notasulga and Montgomery, and Robert B. Vail, editor and publisher of *The Baldwin Times* and *The Atmore Record*, were inducted into the Alabama Newspaper Hall of Honor at the 12th annual induction program Oct. 4, 1975, at the Ralph B. Draughon Library on the Auburn University campus.

1976
Claude E. Sparks,
***The Franklin County Times,* Russellville**
1976-1977 president

105th annual press convention, Mobile
Feb. 5-7, 1976
Summer convention, Gulf Shores
July 15-17, 1976

APA concluded its 105th annual winter convention and three days of meetings and activities in Mobile Feb. 5-7, 1976, with the election of Claude E. Sparks of Russellville as president. Sparks had been publisher of *The Franklin County Times* in Russellville and *The Red Bay News* since 1953.

Elected first vice president was Phillip A. Sanguinetti, president of The Anniston Star Publishing Corp., and publisher of *The Jacksonville News*. E.R. (Bob) Morrissette Jr., publisher of the weekly *Atmore Advance*, was elected second vice president.

Convention highlights included addresses to delegates by Joe C. McCorquodale, speaker of the Alabama House of Representatives, and state Mental Health Commissioner Taylor Hardin.

Delegates and guests toured several Mobile attractions including historic Mobile sights and the "USS Alabama."

Rep. Walter Owens of Centreville was recipient of the first "Thomas Jefferson Award" to be presented annually to the Alabama public official who best demonstrated his or her belief in freedom of the press in Alabama.

Wilcox American, News-Record can't print voting lists

Newspapers must have published 51 weeks with a Second Class mailing permit before they may be eligible to print lucrative county voting lists, Circuit Judge Edgar Russell ruled in Selma in April 1976. In an informal hearing, Russell said *The Wilcox American* in Camden could not print voting lists in Wilcox County, and *The Selma News-Record* could not do likewise in Dallas County, because the two papers were not old enough to meet state requirements for circulating voting lists.

The cases were heard because two older newspapers, *The Wilcox Progressive Era* in Wilcox County, and *The Selma Times-Journal* in Dallas County, protested awarding of the voting lists to the younger papers after they under-bid the older

---

SIDELIGHTS
MARKING 125 YEARS OF HISTORY

Grimes elected Georgia Press president

Former APA vice president Millard Grimes of Opelika was elected president of the Georgia Press Association in 1985.

Grimes, president of Grimes Publications based in Opelika, was former publisher of *The Opelika-Auburn News*. He wrote a book, "The Last Linotype: The Story of Georgia and its Newspapers Since World War II."

---

papers for publishing the lists. The circuit judge ruled that the bidding wasn't relevant since the younger papers were not qualified to bid. Concerning the ruling, APA executive director Steve Bradley said that without the 51-week requirement, someone could start a newspaper just to publish the voting lists, and "the best interest of the public would not be served."

Bradley told *The Montgomery Advertiser* that "APA strongly opposes any attempt to place publications required by law in any newspaper not qualified to accept those notices" and that the APA would "fight any attempt to place those notices in an unqualified publication."

Melson named dean of UA School of Communication

Dr. William H. Melson was named dean of the University of Alabama School of Communication in 1976. Melson had been chairman of the Department of Radio, Television and Motion Pictures at the University of North Carolina at Chapel Hill. The School of Communication had been without a dean since the resignation of Dr. Mort Stern in 1975.

Resolution in 1976 condemns PSC action

A resolution condemning action of the Alabama Public Service Commission was passed unanimously in the closing session of the 1976 summer convention in Gulf Shores July 15-17. The main thrust of the resolution protested the Public Service Commission's commitment "to a course designed to ultimately prevent Alabama Power Company from its constitutionally guaranteed right to advertise."

The resolution also condemned those actions designed "to deny organizations under the Public Service Commission's jurisdiction their constitutionally guaranteed right to advertise information to customers and to the general public in the most cost effective manner possible."

"We are very concerned. We are not going to let this matter drop until we can guarantee that people will have the right to advertise," APA executive director Steve Bradley told the Associated Press. The resolution pointed out that free expression was guaranteed by the first amendment to the U.S. Constitution and that free expression of a business organization or business enterprise was just as strongly guaranteed as the rights of an individual.

1976 summer convention was largest attended ever

AlaPressa reported that the 1976 summer convention was the largest attended convention

Billy Jack Jones
Appointed APA historian in 1976

Before the annual Hall of Honor induction ceremony on Saturday morning, APA members and guests attended a Friday night banquet. Speaker for the event was Howard Simons, managing editor of *The Washington Post.* A $5,000 grant from the APA Journalism Foundation and matching Auburn University funds made it possible to convert a little-used library classroom into a Newspaper Hall of Honor-Reading Room.

"By combining the Hall of Honor and Reading Room, both will be better served," AU University president Dr. Harry M. Philpott said in announcing the project. "Not only will the room be an attractive showplace for the Hall of Honor, but it will be a multipurpose room available to students and faculty."

"Such an area will serve as a newspaper reading room, as a reserve reading room and a study area, and as an attraction to visitors," said Dr. William Highfill, director of Ralph B. Draughon Library. "It will provide an opportunity for a more formal recognition of the outstanding leaders in the state's newspaper industry, as well as an opportunity for more people to participate in the history of Alabama newspapering."

Billy Jack Jones appointed APA historian

Billy Jack Jones, well-known Auburn historian and collector of Alabama newspapers, was appointed historian of the Alabama Press Association and curator for the new APA Hall of Honor reading room. Jones, typesetting coordi-

ever, with more than 340 separate registrations. "The APA conventions have grown so popular and have become so well-attended during the last several years that Gulf Shores is the only area in Alabama able to meet our room needs," *AlaPressa* noted. "And that is fortunate because Gulf Shores, with the beautiful Gulf State Park Lodge and Convention Center, just happens to be one of the most pleasant places to have a summer meeting." Rooms at the convention were $28 per day for single occupancy and $34 for double occupancy.

A buffet lunch with refreshments on Friday was sponsored by the U.S. Brewers Association and Ed Pepperman of the Brewers Association. The buffet lunch on Saturday was sponsored by the Alabama Petroleum Council and Johnny Johnson of the Petroleum Council.

Tucker, Hand inducted into Hall of Honor

Mark L. Tucker of *The Chilton County News* and Bonnie D. Hand of *The LaFayette Sun* were inducted into the Alabama Newspaper Hall of Honor on the Auburn University campus on Oct. 16, 1976, in a special ceremony that included dedication of a permanent newspaper Hall of Honor room at Ralph B. Draughon Library.

S I D E L I G H T S
MARKING 125 YEARS OF HISTORY

Curl tangles with Fish and Wildlife Service
Hollis Curl, publisher of *The Wilcox Progressive Era* in Camden, was featured in an Oct. 21, 1985, issue of *The Washington Post.* The article, dealing with federal bureaucracy, reported Curl's tangle with the U.S. Fish and Wildlife Service over a dead alligator.

Curl cooked and ate part of the tail of an alligator a reader killed and brought to the newspaper office. The man who shot the gator claimed it was threatening some children. Curl appealed the verdict of a federal administration law judge who found him guilty of violating the Endangered Species Act.

nator for the Auburn University Printing Service, was earlier presented the Alabama Historical Commission citation for his interest in newspapers. Jones studied and collected newspapers, particularly Alabama newspapers, as a hobby. He compiled a "Clips from Alabama Papers" column published by *The Auburn Bulletin,* and also compiled the "This Week in Alabama History" column for *The Alabama Encyclopedia.*

Nine dailies endorse Gerald Ford in 1976

Nine Alabama dailies endorsed President Gerald Ford in the 1976 presidential election while seven papers gave their approval to Democrat Jimmy Carter. *The Daily Mountain Eagle* of Jasper said in an editorial, "Those who would endorse Gov. Carter because he is a Southerner had better take a long look at his tendencies, and those who endorse his ideals should look at the realities." Other newspapers endorsing Ford were *The Tuscaloosa News, The Mobile Press and Register, The Birmingham News, The Troy Messenger, The Dothan Eagle, The Selma Times-Journal,* and the *Birmingham Post-Herald.*

Giving the nod to Carter were *The Anniston Star, The Huntsville News, The Huntsville Times, The Montgomery Advertiser, The Alabama Journal, The Decatur Daily* and *The Athens News Courier. The Montgomery Advertiser* and *Alabama Journal,* both supporters of former President Richard M. Nixon in 1968 and 1972, noted that they were "not swayed too much" by Carter's Southern heritage and that the former Georgia governor would "make an excellent president at a time when a restoration of trust in Washington is needed."

News cameras allowed inside courtroom

For the first time in the history of the Alabama Supreme Court, still and television news cameras were allowed inside the courtroom in 1976 to record a part of that day's proceedings. News cameras were allowed inside Alabama's courtrooms under the new Canons of Judicial Ethics that had been recently adopted by the Alabama Supreme Court. In an interview following the historic use of news cameras in the Supreme Court, Chief Justice Howell Heflin said that he thought the use of cameras in the courtroom caused no disruption whatever and remarked that he was not aware when the cameras were being used.

1977
Phillip A. Sanguinetti, *The Anniston Star*
1977-1978 president

106th annual press convention, Huntsville
March 11-13, 1977
Summer convention, Gulf Shores
Aug. 4-6, 1977

"According to that old adage, 'if at first you don't succeed you should try again' and that is exactly what we're going to do about our 1977 winter meeting," *AlaPressa* reported in its Jan 27, 1977, issue.

The 106th annual winter convention, scheduled Jan. 20-22, 1977, in Huntsville had to be rescheduled because of weather and road conditions. "We were very fortunate in securing March 11-13, 1977, at the Hilton Inn in Huntsville for our rescheduled 1977 meeting," *AlaPressa* reported. "We hope to have an identical program in March."

Phillip A. Sanguinetti, president of *The Anniston Star,* was elected APA president at the Sunday business meeting of the Huntsville convention. Sanguinetti succeeded Claude E. Sparks of *The Franklin County Times* in Russellville. Elected first vice president was E.R. (Bob) Morrissette Jr., publisher of *The Atmore Advance.* Also at the convention, Rep. Hugh Merrill of Anniston was honored as "Most Effective Member" of the Alabama House for 1976. The award was based on a vote of reporters who regularly covered the Alabama Legislature. Saturday night APA members presented the Thomas Jefferson

---

S I D E L I G H T S
MARKING 125 YEARS OF HISTORY

"Spirit of the Age" presented to J.E. Dodd
A copy of one of Abbeville's earliest newspapers, *The Spirit of the Age,* dated Tuesday, April 6, 1886, was presented to J.E. Dodd, publisher of *The Abbeville Herald,* in 1954. The contents reflected a great change in times of two periods, Dodd noted.

The newspaper was published by James H. Laborus, and publication date was Tuesday. "Only two inside pages were printed on the old hand press, with all the type laboriously set by hand. The two outside pages, the front and back, were printed weeks ahead by an out-of-town concern," Dodd wrote.

Newspaper Week observed in 1977
        Gov. George C. Wallace proclaimed Oct. 9-15, 1977, as "Newspaper Week in Alabama." APA officers attending the signing of the official proclamation were from left, first vice president E.R. (Bob) Morrissette Jr., *The Atmore Advance;* president Phillip A. Sanguinetti, *The Anniston Star;* APA executive director Steve Bradley; and second vice president James W. (Jim) Oakley Jr., *The Centreville Press.* Newspaper Week was sponsored each year by the Newspaper Association Managers of America to pay tribute to the newspaper industry. In 1977, APA represented 114 weekly and 22 daily newspapers.

Award to Sen. Bill King of Huntsville. King was recognized for his significant contributions to freedom of the press and freedom of information in Alabama.

King was sponsor of a bill calling for a constitutional convention to draft a new Alabama Constitution. The constitutional convention was also endorsed by two other speakers at the 1977 winter convention, Lt. Gov. Jere Beasley and former Gov. Albert P. Brewer. In his speech, Brewer said the "voice of the press has been a strong voice for a better Alabama." Brewer said that the Constitutional Revisions Commission was created during his term as governor and he felt that it was the best approach to rewrite the antiquated basic document of state government.

Papers raise single-copy prices to 15 cents

The Birmingham News and the *Birmingham Post-Herald* announced in January 1977 that single

copy costs would be increased from 10 cents to 15 cents. The Sunday *Birmingham News* increased from 30 cents to 35 cents. The newspapers cited increased costs, especially the increased cost of newsprint which had more than doubled in the past several years. "We sincerely regret the necessity of this price increase," Clarence B. Hanson Jr., publisher of *The Birmingham News,* said. "We have held the line for many years, long after most other daily newspapers raised their price to 15 cents daily and many of them to 50 cents on Sunday. Our last single copy price increase, from 5 to 10 cents, came 12 years ago in 1964."

"Meanwhile, costs have skyrocketed, particularly in the past few years," Hanson continued. "Newsprint prices alone, which increased only $33 a ton, from $140 to $173, in the six years between 1967 and 1973, jumped four times in 1974, twice more in 1975 and

1976, and now will rise again to $300 a ton effective March 1, 1977."

AlaPressa reported that of the 24 daily newspapers in Alabama, 10 newspapers charged 10 cents for single copies, while 14, including *The Birmingham News* and the *Birmingham Post-Herald*, would begin charging 15 cents for single copies.

There were 16 Sunday editions of Alabama daily newspapers — eight charged 35 cents for their Sunday editions; four charged 30 cents; three charged 25 cents; and one Sunday newspaper charged 20 cents for its Sunday edition. "However, the cost of daily and Sunday newspapers in Alabama is generally less than some of the major eastern, western and mid-western metropolitan dailies," *AlaPressa* noted. "Some of those newspapers are charging 25 cents per single copy and as much as 50 cents for Sunday editions."

News raises single copy price

In May 1977, *The Tuscaloosa News* became the first daily in Alabama to increase its single copy price to 25 cents and its Sunday price to 50 cents. Of the 24 daily newspapers published in Alabama in 1977, 10 were priced at 10 cents per copy; 13 at 15 cents per copy; and one at 25 cents per copy.

In another business area, one out of three daily newspapers in the United States had adopted either a nine- or six-column advertising format in 1977. The Newspaper Advertising Bureau reported that a study of 1,347 newspapers showed that 246 (18.3 percent) based their advertising makeup dimensions on a six-column page. Another 189 (14 percent) had adopted nine-column formats. The remaining newspapers "still hold to the traditional eight-column format."

$3,000 grant presented in 1977

The APA Journalism Foundation presented a $3,000 grant in 1974 to the University of Alabama School of Communication to support the community journalism program at the University. Participating in the grant presentation are from left, Shelton Prince Jr., publisher of *The Daily Mountain Eagle* in Jasper and APA Journalism Foundation president; Barrett C. Shelton Jr., general manager of *The Decatur Daily* and APA president; Dr. David Mathews, University of Alabama president; and Dr. Roger Sayers, acting dean of the UA School of Communication.

Provisional accreditation granted UA journalism program

The American Council on Education for Journalism granted the University of Alabama School of Communication provisional accreditation in 1977 for the news-editorial sequence of the journalism program. Dr. William H. Melson, dean, said the designation marked the first step in returning full accreditation to the journalism program. Dr. Charles Arrendell was chairman of the news-editorial sequence.

The summer convention was Aug. 4-6, 1977, at Gulf State Lodge in Gulf Shores.

Monroe Journal files suit for open meetings

A circuit judge in October 1977 ordered the Conecuh-Monroe Counties Gas District to hold open meetings and give the public notice of all scheduled and regular city council meetings. *The Monroe Journal* had been refused access to meetings of the gas district, which was created and owned by the cities of Monroeville and Evergreen. Steve Stewart, editor, filed suit in August 1976.

APA's proposed revision to the Alabama open meetings law was pre-filed Dec. 5, 1977, by Rep. Walter Owens of Centreville. "Editorial and news coverage of our bill has been significant and response from around the state has been outstanding," *AlaPressa* reported. "The bill would extensively revise Alabama's current open meetings law which is severely restricted by the 'character or good name' clause. The Owens/APA bill is a unique solution to this decades-old problem in Alabama." The bill had the support of Gov. George Wallace, House Speaker Joe McCorquodale and Lt. Gov. Jere Beasley.

The Alabama Newspaper Hall of Honor ceremony was at Ralph B. Draughon Library on the Auburn University campus on Oct. 8, 1977. Inductees were James W. (Jim) Oakley Sr., *The Centreville Press*, and Pearle Ennis Gammell, *The Clayton Record*.

1978

E.R. (Bob) Morrissette Jr., *The Atmore Advance*
1978-1979 president

107th annual press convention, Birmingham
Feb. 24-26, 1978
Summer convention, Gulf Shores
July 14-16, 1978

Presentation of the APA Thomas Jefferson Award to *The Monroe Journal* highlighted the 1978 winter convention Feb. 24-26, 1978, at the Kahler Plaza Hotel in Birmingham.

It was the first time that the award, made annually by the Press Association, had been given to an APA-member newspaper. However, the Press Association felt that the outstanding contribution made by *The Monroe Journal* to upholding Alabama's open meetings law deserved special attention. *The Monroe Journal* went to court and won a judgment in 1977 that forced the Conecuh-Monroe Counties Gas District to give public notice of all scheduled and regular meetings.

At the Saturday luncheon, James McNair of American Fidelity announced the annual "Mr. X"

S I D E L I G H T S
MARKING 125 YEARS OF HISTORY

"Daily Hot Blast" returned to **Star** *masthead*

A name that was dropped as a source of embarrassment 71 years earlier was returned as a source of pride to *The Anniston Star* in a 1983 Sunday edition recognizing the newspaper's 100th anniversary.

Star publisher H. Brandt Ayers said the name of the newspaper's forerunner, *The Daily Hot Blast,* would begin appearing daily on the paper's editorial pages beginning with the first centennial edition, along with the name of *The Anniston Star.*

Ayers' father, the late Col. Harry M. Ayers, bought and merged *The Daily Hot Blast* and *The Evening Star* in 1912 and gave the newspaper its current name. The founder of the city, Samuel Nobel, began publishing *The Hot Blast* on Aug. 18, 1883, the same year Nobel's "Model City" was opened to the public.

Anniston had been a privately owned, planned city, founded by Nobel, a northern industrial developer.

A copy of the first newspaper was reproduced and distributed to *Star* readers, along with an 80-page tabloid celebrating the paper's and the city's centennial. In a letter in the centennial edition, Ayers said he was "proud and pleased" to see the name of *The Daily Hot Blast* return to the editorial page, "the soul and character of a newspaper."

Ayers said his father, who had dropped the name of the paper because it was undignified, later had regretted the decision.

---

award, a popular feature of APA winter conventions for years.

Elected president was E.R. (Bob) Morrissette Jr., publisher of *The Atmore Advance.* James W. (Jim) Oakley Jr., publisher of *The Centreville Press,* was elected first vice president, and Shelton Prince Jr., publisher of *The Daily Mountain Eagle* in Jasper, was elected second vice president.

Open meetings bill dies in session

Even though the APA-backed open meetings bill died in the 1978 legislative session, APA said it would continue to push for passage of the legislation. The Press Association sent each candidate for the Alabama House and Senate a questionnaire concerning the open meetings bill.

"We intend to find out how each candidate for the Alabama Legislature feels about the bill — for or against," said APA executive director Steve Bradley. "We think that during this important election year the people have a right to know if a candidate will support a much-needed open meetings law during the 1979 legislative session." The bill that died during the spring session, sponsored by Rep. Walter Owens, would have made secret or "executive" sessions of public bodies more difficult. Many tax-supported, public bodies, used the "character or good name" loophole in Alabama's law to avoid meeting in public.

Advertiser/Journal, Prattville Progress return to APA

APA welcomed three new members to the Press Association in August 1978, *The Montgomery Advertiser* and *Alabama Journal*, James G. (Jim) Martin, publisher, and *The Prattville Progress*, Norman Ridenhour publisher. Officials at the newspapers, owned by Multimedia of Greenville, S.C., had resigned from the Press Association in the late 1960s after the editor and publisher, Harold E. Martin, learned that the APA executive director no longer was teaching classes at the University. Martin also objected to the subsidy arrangement between APA and the University of Alabama.

The three newspapers' return to the Press Association came following Harold E. Martin's res-

ignation from *The Montgomery Advertiser* and *Alabama Journal* on June 21, 1978. Martin was succeeded by his brother, James G. (Jim) Martin, 46, who had been president and co-publisher of the two newspapers. Ray Jenkins, 47, editorial page editor of *The Montgomery Advertiser*, became vice president and editor of both Montgomery newspapers.

Harold Martin announces retirement in 1978

Harold Martin, 54, who served as publisher of the Montgomery publications for 15 years, announced his retirement, saying he was leaving the newspaper management field for personal reasons. "I want to have more time with my family and would like to devote the remaining productive years of my life to writing and teaching journalism and newspaper management in some college," Martin said.

Martin, who was awarded the Pulitzer Prize in 1970 for local reporting in exposing drug experiments in Alabama prisons, began his newspaper career with Newhouse Newspapers in 1957. He worked for *The Syracuse Herald Journal*, *The St. Louis Globe-Democrat* and *The Birmingham News*.

Jim Martin was a 30-year veteran of the newspaper business. He entered the industry in Birmingham in 1949 as a printer. He later was vice president and general manager for Southern Publications, then based in Cedartown, Ga. He was president of *Alabama Sunday Magazine*, and when Southern Publications moved to Montgomery, he became president. After serving as vice president and general manager of *The Gadsden Times*, Jim Martin returned to Montgomery in 1970 as personnel manager and purchasing director for *The Advertiser/Journal*.

Jenkins joined *Alabama Journal* in 1959

Ray Jenkins joined *The Alabama Journal* in 1959. He was managing editor of *The Journal* before being named editorial page editor of the paper, and he became editorial page editor of *The Advertiser* in 1976. In 1954 Jenkins was a staff writer for *The Columbus* (Ga.) *Ledger*, and team coverage of the Phenix City cleanup led to the paper's winning of a Pulitzer Prize for meritorious and distinguished journalism.

The summer convention was July 14-16, 1978, at Gulf State Lodge in Gulf Shores. Room rates were $30.50 per day for a single and $33.50 for a double. A Friday night luau featured roast pig, Hawaiian steak, scallops, clams, oysters, fried trout, pork fried rice, corn on the cob and Ha-

---

S I D E L I G H T S
MARKING 125 YEARS OF HISTORY

Citronelle's "Mr. Tilly" dies of heart attack

William Wirt Tillotson, known as "Mr. Tilly" by the family and friends of *The Citronelle Call*, died of a heart attack on Dec. 27, 1951.

Mrs. N.B. Stallworth, in reporting the death in a front page story, presented an autobiographical sketch that "Mr. Tilly had prepared just several weeks before his death."

In his sketch, the 84-year-old editor/printer/operator told of 67 years spent with newspapers in Mississippi, Arkansas and Alabama.

Stan Atkins worked for AP for 35 years

After 22 years of telling the rest of the world what was happening in and around Mobile, Stan Atkins, the Associated Press' bureau chief in the Port City, retired June 30, 1976.

One of the deans of the Mobile press corps, Atkins was employed by the AP for 35 years, the first 13 of which were spent in the Birmingham bureau.

During his career, Atkins covered the infamous Selma civil rights march in the 1960s, and he was on the story when Murphy High School became the first Mobile public school to be integrated under federal court order.

Atkins also reported the sensational trial of three men accused of the murder of Albert L. Patterson on June 18, 1954, in Phenix City. At the time of his gangland slaying, Patterson was the Democratic nominee for Alabama attorney general.

Atkins began his career in the news business in the mail room of *The Birmingham News* in 1931. He then moved to the position of sportswriter for *The News* and later moved to the copy desk of the old *Birmingham Age-Herald*. Atkins was succeeded in the Mobile bureau by Kendall Weaver, previously assigned to the AP Montgomery bureau.

waiian fruit hash. Alabama Petroleum Council served a complimentary breakfast on Sunday. The U.S. Brewers Association sponsored a Saturday buffet luncheon.

Bradley resigns, O'Connor named APA executive in 1978

APA executive director Steve Bradley resigned effective July 21, 1978 to become assistant vice president-public information with Alabama Power Company. Bradley assumed the new position July 24. He was to be responsible for the company's entire public information program, including advertising, educational services, news media relations and company publications.

The board of directors met in special session on June 22 in Tuscaloosa and accepted Bradley's resignation. The board voted unanimously to em-

ploy William F. (Bill) O'Connor Jr. as executive director. O'Connor, a Tuscaloosa native, was director of communications for the state Department of Mental Health in Montgomery. O'Connor was a graduate of the University of Alabama with a bachelor's degree in journalism and a master's degree in public relations.

O'Connor assumed his new position July 24, 1978. Before joining the Mental Health Department in 1976, O'Connor was director of field services for the School of Communication for the University of Alabama.

Native Alabamian leads Hoosier Press Association

William E. (Bill) Brooks Jr., became the only Alabamian to serve as president of two press associations when he was inducted president of the Hoosier State (Indiana) Press Association in 1978.

Brooks was managing editor of *The Brewton Standard* when he served as APA president in 1953-1954. He was editor and publisher of *The Vincennes Sun-Commercial* when he was president of the Hoosier State Press Association in 1978-1979. Brooks' father, W. Emmett Brooks, was APA president in 1929-1930 and was inducted into the Alabama Newspaper Hall of Honor in 1983.

"As a matter of community pride, I insisted on having the 1978 annual Indiana press convention in Vincennes," Bill Brooks recalled in 1995. "(*USA Today* founder) Al Neuharth was head of ANPA that year, and he came to Vincennes because he was visiting as many state organizations as possible. We had worked our way into full-color spot news coverage by that time. Our photographer got an early morning shot of Al after he had finished jogging."

Brooks continued, "We ran it in the same-day PM edition and delivered it to the convention about three that afternoon. Many of the publishers tried to argue that we had faked the photo, or had it set up somewhere else. They couldn't believe that sweet little old Vincennes could turn out that kind of work. We could, and did, all the time. That, of course is an Indiana story, but I was pleased that an Alabama native could show the Hoosiers the possibilities of spot color news coverage."

Forney Gilmore Stephens, founder of *The Southern Democrat* in Oneonta, and Grover Cleveland Hall Jr., editor of *The Montgomery Advertiser* and *Alabama Journal*, were inducted into the Alabama Newspaper Hall of Honor during ceremonies Oct. 21, 1978, at Ralph B. Draughon Library on the Auburn University campus.

1979

James W. (Jim) Oakley Jr., *The Centreville Press*
1979-1980 president

l08th annual press convention, Mobile
Feb. 16-18, 1979
Summer convention, Gulf Shores
July 26-28, 1979

A bill was introduced in the Alabama Legislature in 1979 to strengthen the state's open meetings law. Sens. Ryan deGraffenried Jr. of Tuscaloosa, Charles Martin of Decatur and Hinton Mitchem of Albertville introduced the bill in the Senate, and Rep. Phil Kelley of Guntersville introduced it in the House.

According to the legislators, new open meetings legislation was needed because the current law, which had been on the books since 1915, was difficult to enforce.

The proposed bill included in its definition of "governing body" any board or commission charged with the duty of disbursing any funds belonging to the state, county or municipality. In addition, a governing body would include boards or commissions that had been delegated legislative or judicial functions, except petit and grand jury proceedings.

While the APA-backed open meetings bill was favorably reported out of both the Senate Judiciary Committee and the House State Administration Committee, the bill was never brought up for a vote in either chamber.

O'Connor reports in Green Sheet

"But we do feel progress was made toward eventual passage of this important legislation," APA executive director Bill O'Connor reported in APA's Legislative Green Sheet, a confidential report of legislative activities mailed to APA members. "The Tennessee Open Meetings Law, on which our proposed legislation is based, took four years of intensive lobbying to pass," O'Connor continued. "We will be contacting key legislators during the next few months seeking to gain their support for the bill, and I sincerely believe we have a good chance of passing it during the 1980 regular session."

Two out of three daily newspapers in the United States sold for 15 cents or less in 1979, but the trend toward the 20-cent newspaper was growing, according to an annual survey by the American Newspaper Publishers Association.

Winter convention held in Mobile

More than 230 APA members and guests attended the 108th annual winter convention Feb. 16-18, 1979, at the Sheraton Inn in Mobile. Delegates heard banquet speeches by Gov. Fob James, Sen. Howell Heflin and newspaper executive Rhea Eskew. They attended panel discussions on circulation, "Newspapers in Education," and advertising.

James W. (Jim) Oakley Jr., editor and publisher of *The Centreville Press,* was elected APA president. Other officers elected for 1979 were Shelton Prince Jr., publisher of *The Daily Mountain Eagle* in Jasper, first vice president, and Marcia M. Sears, editor of *The Shelby County Reporter* in Columbiana, second vice president.

1979 summer convention, Gulf Shores

Following 20 consecutive days of rain, sunny skies greeted the more than 325 APA active and associate members and guests at the summer convention. The convention was at Gulf State Lodge in Gulf Shores, July 26-28, 1979. One of the most enjoyable convention sessions was the Friday luncheon where Jeanne Swanner Robertson spared no one, including herself. For 45 minutes, she poked fun at her height (6-foot-2) and her experiences as a contestant in the Miss America Pageant. She ended her performance by staging the first (and last) APA male beauty contest.

Woodward named advertising manager

The first full-time advertising manager was hired in 1979. Craig Woodward was named advertising manager for the Alabama Newspaper Advertising Service, effective April 30, 1979. Carolyn West, who had been handling advertising for ANAS, graduated from the University of Alabama in May and planned to return to her hometown of Hackleburg, Ala.

George Alexander Carleton, owner, editor and publisher of *The Clarke County Democrat* in Grove Hill for 65 years, and Ralph Bradford Chandler, founder and first publisher of *The Mobile Press* and *The Birmingham Post*, were inducted into the Alabama Newspaper Hall of Honor Oct. 6, 1979, at the Ralph B. Draughon Library on the Auburn University campus.

1980

**Shelton Prince Jr., *The Daily Mountain Eagle,* Jasper and *The Selma Times-Journal*
1980-1981 president**

**109th annual press convention, Huntsville
Feb. 22-24, 1980
Summer convention, Destin, Fla.
July 18-20, 1980**

Legislation to strengthen the state's open meetings law was passed May 1, 1980, by the Alabama Senate and sent to the House. The Senate-passed bill, approved by a vote of 32-0, provided "more precise language on what types of public boards and agencies are covered by the law and conditions that must be met in order to conduct a public and secret meeting," said APA executive director Bill O'Connor.

The 109th annual press convention was Feb. 22-24, 1980, at the Huntsville Hilton. Featured speakers included Jody Powell, press secretary and adviser to President Carter, U.S. Sen. Donald Stewart, and Bob Burke, director of readership and training programs for the American Newspaper Publishers Association.

Shelton Prince Jr., publisher of *The Daily Mountain Eagle* in Jasper, was elected APA president at the winter convention. Other officers included Marcia M. Sears, editor of *The Shelby County Reporter* in Columbiana, first vice president, and Don Woodward, general manager of *The Advertiser-Gleam* in Guntersville, second vice president.

S I D E L I G H T S
MARKING 125 YEARS OF HISTORY

Mobile maritime reporter honored in 1976

Harry McDonnell, 70, veteran maritime reporter for *The Mobile Press Register* whose news career began in Mobile in 1929, was honored in July 1976 on his retirement.

McDonnell, who was known for wearing a beret, came to *The Mobile Press* at age 23, two weeks after its founding in an old former church building at the northeast corner of St. Michael and Jackson streets.

McDonnell wrote the following farewell column on July 14, 1976:

"To write '30' — the old newspaper symbol signifying the end of a story — to a career of journalism and kindred pursuits covering a period of approximately 35 years isn't easy. So today I am retiring from service of the morning *Mobile Register* and afternoon *Mobile Press* that stretched over a total of more than 27 years, 1929-42 and 1962 to the present. Gone is the cry of the newsboy, shouting 'Extra!' to herald the verdict of a sensational murder trial, a catastrophic fire, the death of a statesman or a disaster at sea, such as the sinking of the Titanic with heavy loss of life after ramming an iceberg in the North Atlantic. Instant electronic reporting ended an era in which the newspaper was the supreme and only media for reaching the masses. But for the whole panorama of daily news on the national, state and local level, there is no substitute for the printed word in conveying meaning and understanding to the people."

McDonnell offered these words of parting advice to his younger contemporaries: "For Pete's sake, get it right, tell it like it is. Give both sides of an issue and don't let bias or personal prejudices creep into your account."

Prince named *Times-Journal* publisher

In April 1980, Shelton Prince Jr. was named publisher of *The Selma Times-Journal*, succeeding Bruce Morrison. Prince, who had been publisher of *The Daily Mountain Eagle* since 1970, assumed his new post on April 14. *AlaPressa* reported that Morrison, publisher of *The Selma Times-Journal* since 1973, had resigned and was considering offers from other publishing firms.

Doug Pearson of Chillicothe, Mo., was named publisher of *The Daily Mountain Eagle* in Jasper. Pearson had been editor and publisher of *The Chillicothe Constitution* since 1972. A Tuscaloosa native, Pearson had been associated with *The Tuscaloosa News* and *The Montgomery Advertiser* and *Alabama Journal* earlier in his newspaper career.

1980 summer convention, Destin, Fla.

The 1980 summer convention July 18-20 was moved to Sandestin in Destin, Fla. *AlaPressa* said all 88 rooms and more than 50 villas were reserved for the convention. "Following extensive discussions with state officials and those working at Gulf State Lodge, it was decided to move our convention from Gulf Shores because of the uncertainty over whether the state complex would be open in time for our summer convention program," *AlaPressa* reported. Gulf State Lodge was damaged by Hurricane Frederic.

A record crowd of 320 APA members and guests attended the summer convention. The delegates heard a speech by Pulitzer Prize-winning publisher Joe Murray and enjoyed entertainment provided by the "Mayor and Buford" and Shearen Elebash of Montgomery.

The 1980 Alabama Newspaper Hall of Honor was Oct. 18 at the Ralph B. Draughon Library on the Auburn University campus. Inductees were Robert Gaston Bozeman Sr., editor and publisher of *The Evergreen Courant*, and McClellan Van der Veer, editor of *The Birmingham News*.

1981

Marcia M. Sears,
***The Shelby County Reporter,* Columbiana**
1981-1982 president

110th annual convention, Montgomery
Feb. 27-March 1, 1981
Summer convention, Gulf Shores
July 24-26, 1981

The winter convention was at the Governor's House Motel in Montgomery Feb. 27-28 and March 1, 1981.

Banquet speakers included Gov. Fob James, nationally syndicated columnist Lewis Grizzard and Robert Wussler, executive vice president of Turner Broadcasting System.

The first woman APA president was elected in 1981. Marcia M. Sears, editor of *The Shelby County*

Reporter in Columbiana, was elected president at the winter convention. Other officers elected for 1981 included Don Woodward, general manager of *The Advertiser-Gleam* in Guntersville, first vice president, and Millard Grimes, president of *The Enterprise Ledger,* second vice president.

More than 30 years of operation of *The Tuscaloosa News* by the Boone family ended with expiration of a lease on the newspaper property held by Tuscaloosa Newspapers Inc., a Boone-owned corporation. James B. Boone Jr., controlling stockholder of the corporation that operated *The News* and publisher for 10 of the past 12 years, moved to Natchez, Miss., and established his offices there. Boone had succeeded his father, Buford Boone, who had headed the newspaper in Tuscaloosa since 1947.

Early in 1980, Boone gave notice that he did not want to lease *The News* after Dec. 31, 1980.

APA moves to new location in Tuscaloosa

Effective May 1, 1981, APA moved to a new location in Tuscaloosa, #4 Office Park, 2615 Sixth Street. The new location included 275 more square feet than the previous office. APA's previous address was Suite 100, 921 Third Avenue East.

Louis A. Eckl
The Florence Times,
Tri-Cities Courier

The 1981 summer convention was July 24-26 at Gulf State Lodge in Gulf Shores.

Louis A. Eckl, executive editor of *The Florence Times and Tri-Cities Daily*, and Robert M. Tucker, editor and publisher of *The Chilton County News* in Clanton, were inducted into the Alabama Newspaper Hall of Honor on Oct. 10, 1981, at Ralph B. Draughon Library on the Auburn University campus.

Robert M. Tucker
The Chilton County News, Clanton

1982

Don Woodward, *The Advertiser-Gleam,* Guntersville
1982-1983 president

111th annual press convention, Birmingham
Feb. 19-21, 1982
Summer convention, Gulf Shores
July 23-25, 1982

The winter convention was Feb. 19-21, 1982, in Birmingham. Don Woodward, general manager of *The Advertiser-Gleam* in Guntersville, was elected

---

S I D E L I G H T S
MARKING 125 YEARS OF HISTORY

Montgomery Advertiser's *Buster MacGuire buys country store in 1977*

After 15 years with *The Montgomery Advertiser,* Colin H. (Buster) MacGuire left in June 1977 to go into private business.

After writing many stories about country stores during his tenure at *The Advertiser,* MacGuire decided to get some firsthand experience in a country store. MacGuire purchased Hartley's Store on U.S. Highway 31 south of Greenville.

A native of Montgomery, MacGuire first joined *The Advertiser* staff in 1946 after serving in World War II. He was a police reporter and general assignment reporter for *The Advertiser* while his sister, Jeffie MacGuire, was covering city hall for *The Alabama Journal.* After two years, MacGuire left to work for *The Chattahoochee Valley Times* in Lanett and *The West Point* (Ga.) *News.* After one year there, he joined the old *Birmingham Age-Herald* as a general assignment reporter. Then for three years he covered the waterfront for *The Newport News* (Va.) *Times-Herald* before returning to Montgomery to run an insurance business.

MacGuire later worked for *The Atmore Advance* and was self-employed in a garment manufacturing business in Greenville before returning to *The Advertiser* in 1963 as assistant city editor. MacGuire was soon promoted to city editor, and upon the retirement of Stuart X. Stephenson as state editor, MacGuire took over "The Passing Throng" column, which had

been a feature of *The Advertiser* for half a century.

During his stay at *The Advertiser,* MacGuire noted that he worked for three different publishers, R.F. Hudson, Carmage Walls, and Harold E. Martin. And during that time, the newspaper business changed drastically, he recalled. The clatter of Linotype machines, which once set type for the newspaper, had been replaced by the hum of computers. "The clack of the Linotype is gone forever from the composing room now, and folks can actually converse in whispers there, if such be their want," MacGuire wrote in a farewell column. "Things have changed mightily over three decades, some for the better and some not, but the people there for the most part have remained just plain good folks."

The Advertiser newsroom, 30 years earlier, was a crowded jumble of desks and a litter-strewn floor. "Now it looks like an executive office," he chuckled. Another major change that MacGuire noted was in newspapers' use of photographs. Once, wire service photos were sent by mail, and the use of photos was rare because it was a time-consuming, complicated task. In 1977 wire service photos arrived by telephone and lasers, and the photography staff of *The Advertiser-Journal* had tripled in size since MacGuire first began work at the newspaper.

Bryan featured in **Business Alabama Monthly**

In an article titled "Media Moguls" featuring "profitable tales from Alabama's family-owned Fourth Estate," *Business Alabama Monthly* reported in its June 1992 issue that Robert Bryan's daily and weekly newspapers filled a niche between Birmingham and Huntsville:

"At one time, Bob Bryan had a number of counterparts, but today more and more small publications are selling to chains because of rising costs, and the days are past when a young person could simply enter a small town and buy a newspaper," Gadsden free-lance writer Joyce Davis wrote for *Business Alabama Monthly.*

" 'Nobody can afford my newspapers,' says Bryan, referring to *The Cullman Times* and his other holdings, *The Athens News Courier, The St. Clair News-Aegis* in Pell City, *The North Jefferson News* in Gardendale and *The Leeds News.* He won't disclose their price tags.

"When he began his media career in the early 1950s, however, it was possible to buy into a newspaper operation. After he graduated from the University of Alabama in 1951, Bryan went to work for *The Talladega News,* then was hired by a Cullman newspaper, *The Banner.* In a few months he became part owner of *The Banner.* With his partners, he bought out two other weeklies, *The Cullman Democrat* and *The Cullman Times,* and began daily publication under the name *Times-Democrat.* In 1961, with Bryan as sole owner, *The Times-Democrat* became *The Cullman Times.*

"Bryan acquired *The News Courier* in 1968 and the weekly newspapers during the 1970s, for an undisclosed price. *The Times* leads circulation, at just over 11,000, while the daily *Courier* boasts an 8,500 circulation, and the rest, all weeklies, stand at 5,000 each. Together, they employ 120.

"Bryan's management style is low-key, but active. From his office on the second floor of the red brick *Times* building in Cullman, he meets by phone with the editors of the various publications daily and encourages them to call him about problems. He has also boosted the careers of former employees Terry Abbott, Gov. Guy Hunt's press secretary; Joey Kennedy, an award-winning writer for *The Birmingham News;* and Don Snead, a flamboyant former editor who is now chairman of the Department of Journalism at the University of Mississippi.

"At one time or another, Bryan's whole family has been involved with the newspaper — but not all at the same time nor on the same newspaper. 'We'd split the sides of the building if we tried that,' he says. 'My family are all free-thinkers.'

"Bryan's wife, Betty, wrote a popular weekly column, and only recently retired after a number of years as society editor of *The Cullman Times.* Bryan's daughter Kelly edited *The News-Aegis* for several years, and her sister, Kerry, worked at *The Leeds News.* The Bryan sons, Robert and Bruce, both worked for *The Cullman Times.* Robert, who is managing editor for a Gannett publication, *The Battle Creek* (Mich.) *Inquirer,* continues the family tradition, but the other Bryans have changed careers. Although family members own stock, Bryan said he probably will bring in someone outside the family as his successor when he decides to retire.

"In addition to the publications, Bryan owns an office supply store, an electronic equipment store, a camera shop, a 24-hour film lab and a commercial print shop, all located in the Times building.

"Bryan has a reputation as a shrewd, uncompromising businessman, and at the same time a generous supporter of community and philanthropic causes. 'I have always tried to do my share of civic work,' he says, 'and to be a builder in the community.' "

president. Other officers for 1982 included William J. (Bill) Hearin, publisher of *The Mobile Press* and *Mobile Register,* first vice president, and Luke Slaton, editor of *The Moulton Advertiser,* second vice president.

The summer convention was July 23-25, 1982, at Gulf State Lodge in Gulf Shores.

Baldwin voter's list causes dispute

A dispute over publication of the voter's list in Baldwin County resulted in legal action in October 1982 between Gulf Coast Media Inc. and The Mobile Press Register Inc. A declaratory judgment was being sought by Gulf Coast Media in Baldwin County Circuit Court to determine whether *The Baldwin Press Register* met all the requirements necessary to carry legal advertising. Publication of the voters list was ultimately awarded to Gulf Coast Media, publishers of *The Baldwin Times, The Independent, The Onlooker* and *The Eastern Shore Courier.* The four papers were permitted to publish the voters list under the stipulation that the list be published at no cost to the county unless the declaratory judgment ruling favored Gulf Coast Media.

Section 6-8-60, Code of Alabama (1975) set forth the following requirements a newspaper must meet to be eligible to publish legal notices:

"...all publications required by any law, mortgage or other contract to be published in a newspaper must be published in any newspaper printed in the English language which has a general circulation in the county, regardless of where the paper is printed, if the principal editorial office of the newspaper is within the county and which newspaper shall have been mailed under second class mailing privilege of the United States postal service from the post office where it is published for at least 51 weeks a year."

Gulf Coast Media, in its written complaint, stated "that the defendant, The Mobile Press Register Inc., is a corporation organized under the laws of the State of Alabama with its principal place of business in Mobile, Mobile County, Alabama." A date for hearing the case was not set.

O'Connor resigns as executive director in 1982

In 1982, APA executive director Bill O'Connor was named assistant to the chancellor for University Relations, Dr. Thomas Bartlett, chancellor of the University of Alabama System announced. O'Connor assumed his new post Dec. 15, 1982. "Bill O'Connor has an excellent professional and academic background and we are looking forward to having him join us as a key member of the

system's staff," Bartlett said.

O'Connor had served as executive director since July 24, 1978, when he succeeded Steve Bradley. Before joining APA, O'Connor worked for the state Department of Mental Health in Montgomery as director of communications, a position he held more than two years. During 1974 and 1975, O'Connor served as director of field services for the School of Communication at the University of Alabama.

Keller assumes APA post in January 1983

William B. (Bill) Keller, director of information services for the University of Montevallo, succeeded O'Connor as executive director. Keller, assumed the APA post Jan. 3, 1983. Keller joined the University of Montevallo in February 1977. He previously worked as a reporter for *The Tuscaloosa News* and as a reporter-photographer, news editor and managing editor of *The Sand Mountain Reporter* in Albertville.

Keller received his bachelor's and master's degrees from the University of Alabama where he was named Outstanding Graduate Student in Journalism. He had also completed work toward a doctorate in higher education administration from the University of Alabama.

Veteran newspaper man H. Doyle Harvill was named publisher of *The Montgomery Advertiser* and *Alabama Journal* in September 1983. Harvill succeeded James G. Martin who said he resigned for health and personal reasons. Martin had been publisher of *The Advertiser* and *Alabama Journal* since June 21, 1978, when he succeeded his brother, former publisher and editor Harold E. Martin.

Roanoke Leader, Randolph Press merge in 1982

In 1982, John B. Stevenson, publisher of *The Roanoke Leader* and *The Randolph Press* in Wedowee, announced plans to merge both papers into a county-wide weekly called *The Randolph Leader.*

The original name of the Roanoke paper, which began publication in 1892, was *The Randolph Leader.* The merger and return to the original name took place Sept. 14, 1982, *The Leader's* 90th birthday.

Only two men had served as editor of *The Leader* — Olin H. Stevenson for 45 years, and his son, John B. Stevenson, for 45 years.

John B. Stevenson also announced the appointment of his son, John W. Stevenson, as editor of the paper and younger son, David S. Stevenson, as publisher. Alabama newspaper people and the public were invited to attend an open house birthday celebration in *The Leader's* new plant on Sunday, Oct. 10, 1982.

Webb Stanley of *The Greenville Advocate* and G. Whatley Carlisle Sr. of *The People's Ledger,* Enterprise, were inducted into the Alabama Newspaper Hall of Honor on Oct. 16, 1982, at Ralph B. Draughon Library on the Auburn University campus.

G. Whatley Carlisle Sr.
The People's Ledger, Enterprise

1983

William J. (Bill) Hearin, *The Mobile Press Register*
1983-1984 president

112th annual press convention, Mobile
Feb. 25-27, 1983
Summer convention, Gulf Shores
July 15-17, 1983

Outstanding speakers, informative panel discussions, seminars and entertainment highlighted the 112th annual APA convention Feb. 25-27, 1983, at the Mobile Hilton.

The publisher of *The Mobile Press* and *The Mobile Register,* William J. (Bill) Hearin, was elected APA president during the Mobile convention. Hearin succeeded Don Woodward of Guntersville, general manager of *The Advertiser-Gleam.* Other officers elected included Luke Slaton, editor and publisher of *The Moulton Advertiser,* first vice president; and Mike Breedlove

---

S I D E L I G H T S
MARKING 125 YEARS OF HISTORY

Roanoke *abandons two-edition experiment*
The Roanoke Leader began publishing two editions each week in November 1948, but abandoned the experiment within a year. John B. Stevenson was publisher of *The Leader.* The newspaper was published on Wednesday most of its life, but on Thursday during World War II and several years thereafter.

---

of Jackson, publisher of *The South Alabamian,* second vice president.

A circuit judge ordered the Montgomery County Commission to meet openly instead of secretly, if it wanted to discuss the racial makeup of potential construction contractors. Circuit Judge Randall Thomas ruled in a lawsuit filed by The Advertiser Co., which published *The* (Montgomery) *Advertiser* and *The Alabama Journal.* Birmingham attorney David Olive represented the newspapers. (Note: Publisher H. Doyle Harvill dropped "Montgomery" from *The Advertiser's* nameplate in an effort to give the newspaper a more statewide appeal.)

Former jail inmate files lawsuits

Lawsuits totaling $125 million were filed against *The Selma Times-Journal* by a former Dallas County Jail inmate in March 1983. The suits claimed that the paper libeled and slandered the inmate when it printed his obituary in January. The man's obituary was telephoned to *The Times-Journal* by a caller who gave information on death, burial and survivors. The lawsuits were dismissed in May 1983. Circuit Judge J.C. Norton's order dismissing the suit stated that the "…alleged publication is not defamatory…" and that the inmate's complaint failed to state a claim upon which relief could be granted.

Morgan begins contributing column

Gillis Morgan, journalism professor at Auburn University, began contributing a column, "Words and Heads" to *AlaPressa* in April 1983. "With all due respect to my articulate colleagues on the APA Resolutions Committee, I intend for this column to be a scholarly effort on the subject of words," Morgan wrote in his first column. The column remained a regular feature in *AlaPressa* in 1996 and was also published in *The Lee County Eagle* in Auburn, *The Greensboro Watchman,* and *The Wilcox Progressive Era* in Camden.

The Coalition for the Preservation of Alabama Newspapers received a $10,000 grant to develop a statewide plan to preserve Alabama's newspaper files. Concern over potential loss of Alabama's unique newspaper records led scholars, librarians, newspaper executives and archivists as well as leaders of colleges and universities to form a cooperative venture to preserve the old copies. Work on the project began July 15, 1983, with a survey to determine newspaper files held in Alabama.

APA joins *The Abbeville Herald* in complaint against judge

APA and *The Abbeville Herald* filed a complaint in 1983 against a Henry County circuit judge who cited an Abbeville woman with contempt of court for writing a Letter to the Editor critical of the judge. APA filed the complaint with the Alabama Judicial Inquiry Commission. Although Judge Billy Joe Sheffield withdrew his contempt order, he implied in his recision order that he could use the power of his office to stifle criticism.

APA officials said the judge's actions themselves were contemptuous — contemptuous of two of the basic freedoms underpinning the American system of constitutional democracy: freedom of expression and the right to petition government for redress of grievances.

In March 1984, the judge was suspended for two months without pay. Sheffield was charged with 12 alleged violations of the canons of judicial ethics. In a case which was publicized nationally, he was found guilty of four of the charges. Stories about Sheffield's actions were carried by newspapers all over the country, and *Abbeville Herald* editor Eddie Dodd received dozens of Letters to the Editor from all over Alabama and the nation protesting the judge's action.

Sen. Ernest F. Hollins of South Carolina spoke at the summer convention at Gulf State Park in Gulf Shores July 15-17, 1983. The Saturday luncheon included a performance by "The Mayor and Buford," a comedy team that was the hit of the 1980 summer convention in Sandestin.

First black inducted into Hall of Honor

The Alabama Newspaper Hall of Honor inducted its first black newspaper executive and a Brewton publisher during ceremonies at Auburn University Saturday, Oct. 22, 1983.

Families of Frank P. Thomas Jr., *The Mobile Beacon,* and W. Emmett Brooks, *The Brewton Standard,* were recognized during ceremonies at Auburn's Ralph B. Draughon Library, site of the Newspaper Hall of Honor.

The University of Alabama School of Communication moved to the renovated Old Union Building during the Christmas break — after more than five years of planning and renovation, said Dr. Ed Mullins, dean. "The move itself was just like Christmas for us," Mullins said. "We've been recruiting faculty and stu-

dents for years, saying we were going to have a new building."

1984
Luke Slaton, *The Moulton Advertiser*
1984-1985 president

113th annual convention, Huntsville
Feb. 24-26, 1984
Summer convention, Gulf Shores
July 20-22, 1984

Activities at the 113th annual convention at the Huntsville Hilton Feb. 24-26, 1984, included a buffet reception and tour of the Alabama Space and Rocket Center, an update on politics by Lt. Gov. Bill Baxley, a mock libel trial conducted by Cumberland School of Law, and a newspaper promotion and marketing program.

The editor and publisher of the oldest continuously published weekly newspaper in Alabama became one of the youngest presidents ever elected to lead the APA in 1984. Luke Slaton, 33, of *The Moulton Advertiser,* was elected president during the 113th annual convention. He succeeded William J. (Bill) Hearin, publisher of *The Mobile Press Register.*

Slaton had been active in APA since beginning full-time newspaper work at *The Moulton Advertiser* in 1971. He became general manager of the weekly when his father, the late Arthur F. Slaton, retired in 1976. The elder Slaton had published the newspaper since 1946. Luke Slaton became publisher after his father's death in 1982.

Other officers elected included Mike Breedlove, publisher of *The South Alabamian* in Jackson, first vice president; Jay Thornton, general manager of *The Daily Home* in Talladega, second vice president; Ben Shurett, publisher of *The Troy Messenger,* president of ANAS; and

James E. Jacobson, editor of *The Birmingham News*, president of the APA Journalism Foundation.

Tradition continues with "Mr. X" at convention

Tradition continued with "Mr. X" being the most popular person at the winter convention. Years earlier, American Fidelity Assurance Co. established the tradition of "Mr. X" to promote goodwill and interaction among APA members and guests attending the winter convention.

American Fidelity would select someone as "Mr. X" before the convention and would swear the appointee to secrecy. When he (or she) arrived at the convention, he simply went about his business as any convention guest would, greeting old friends, mingling and introducing himself to new folks.

But unlike other convention delegates, "X" would count each person who shook his hand, and the 50th person who pressed his flesh would receive a $50 prize. The lucky winner would be announced at the Saturday luncheon when the identity of "Mr. (Mrs., Miss or Ms.) X" would be revealed.

Judge rules in favor of Mobile Press Register Inc.

In March 1984 Baldwin County Circuit Judge Henry J. Wilters Jr. ruled in favor of The Mobile Press Register Inc., over Gulf Coast Media in a case involving publication of Baldwin County legal advertising. Gulf Coast Media, publishers of the four weekly newspapers in Baldwin County, had asked for a declaratory judgment concerning publication of legal advertising from Baldwin County in *The Baldwin People*, distributed each week in Baldwin County by *The Press Register*.

Gulf Coast Media maintained that *The Baldwin People* did not qualify to carry legal ads from Baldwin County because it did not meet all requirements of state law, Alabama Code, section 6-8-60. The dispute began in 1982, when *The Press Register* bid for publication of the Baldwin County voters list to run in *The People*, formerly *The Baldwin Press Register*.

Board files neutral brief

The APA board of directors in April 1984 voted to ask the Alabama Supreme Court to help clear the confusion over which newspapers were eligible to publish legal advertising in particular counties. In a called meeting, the board unanimously approved a motion asking legal counsel David Olive to prepare a friend-of-the-court brief to submit in

---

---

the dispute between Gulf Coast Media and *The Mobile Press Register*.

The Mobile Press Register, William J. (Bill) Hearin, publisher and APA chairman of the board, dropped the newspaper's Press Association membership in 1984 after the APA board decided to file a neutral brief in the case. The brief asked the Alabama Supreme Court to clarify the law.

The Gadsden Times filed suit in March 1984 against two local school systems to obtain a school-by-school breakdown of scores from a state competency test administered to high school juniors. The suit sought a court order to force the city and county boards of education to provide records showing the pass-fail ratio of each school in their system on the Alabama High School Graduation Examination.

Ryland joins APA staff in June 1984

The June 1984 issue of *AlaPressa* announced that the former publisher of a prize-winning Alabama weekly had been named ANAS manager. Mike Ryland, formerly of *The Independent* in Robertsdale, joined the APA staff on June 11. During Ryland's first week he worked with former manager Craig Woodward, who joined the firm of Gillis, Townsend and Riley Advertising in Birmingham as an account executive.

Ryland, a Brewton native, graduated Phi Beta Kappa from the University of Alabama in 1978, before becoming managing editor of *The Atmore Advance*.

The 1984 summer convention at Gulf State Park Lodge in Gulf Shores, held July 20-22, featured a poolside seafood buffet, complete with freshly shucked oysters, boiled shrimp and draft beer, children's programs, a Saturday afternoon cruise around the Orange Beach and Ono Island area, and "Three On a String," one of the state's most popular bluegrass groups.

Duard M. Le Grand Jr.
Birmingham Post-Herald

Auburn University archivist Dr. Allen W. Jones gave a program on Alabama newspaper history.

Two Birmingham newspaper executives were inducted into the Alabama Newspaper Hall of Honor in 1984. Duard M. Le Grand Jr., editor of the *Birmingham Post-Herald* from 1967 to 1978, and S. Vincent Townsend, a 52-year veteran of *The Birmingham News*, were inducted during ceremonies on Oct. 20, 1984, at the Ralph B. Draughon Library on the Auburn University campus.

S. Vincent Townsend
The Birmingham News

State classified ad network gets tentative approval

A program to produce revenue for Alabama newspapers and provide a new service to newspaper readers was tentatively approved by board members of the Alabama Newspaper Advertising Service. At a Nov. 30, 1984, meeting ANAS board members directed ANAS to survey member newspapers to determine how many papers were interested in participating in a statewide classified advertising network. The board agreed to discuss the program again at its meeting during the APA winter convention in February 1985.

1985
Mike Breedlove, *The South Alabamian*, Jackson
1985-1986 president

114th annual press convention, Montgomery
Feb. 22-24, 1985
Summer convention, Gulf Shores
July 12-14, 1985

Columnist James J. Kilpatrick and Defense Department whistle-blower Ernest Fitzgerald, a native of Birmingham, were guest speakers at the 114th annual winter convention Feb. 22-

24, 1985, at Montgomery's Governor's House motor lodge.

Buses took delegates to nearby Victoryland dogtrack for a reception and banquet Friday night. At a Sunday morning session, a panel of APA publishers discussed how they were meeting direct-mail competition.

Mike Breedlove, publisher of *The South Alabamian* in Jackson, was elected president during the 114th annual winter convention. Other officers elected were Jay Thornton, general manager of *The Daily Home in Talladega*, first vice president; Steve Stewart, editor of *The Monroe Journal* in Monroeville, second vice president; and Luke Slaton, publisher of *The Moulton Advertiser*, chairman of the board.

Breedlove and his wife, Linda Breedlove, the associate publisher, purchased *The South Alabamian* in 1974 and moved to Jackson from Fairhope. Breedlove had been editor of *The Fairhope Courier*, later named *The Eastern Shore Courier*, since 1971. From 1968 to 1971, Breedlove worked at *The Prattville Progress*. He started his newspaper career at *The Montgomery Advertiser* in 1966.

Weekly newspaper jobs held by 1985 journalism graduates paid a median salary of $10,660, according to a Dow Jones Newspaper Fund survey. At the dailies, the median salary was $13,520. The survey also found that public relations jobs paid 1985 graduates a median salary of $14,560.

Court rules in Baldwin County dispute

The Alabama Supreme Court unanimously ruled that a weekly supplement to *The Mobile Press*

S I D E L I G H T S
MARKING 125 YEARS OF HISTORY

Jack Smith returns to **Decatur Daily**
Jack Smith, Moulton native and former reporter for *The Decatur Daily*, returned to that position Dec. 17, 1958. Smith had been attending Alabama Polytechnic Institute at Auburn to complete classroom work toward a master's degree in government. Smith was in charge of the county news desk, a position he held before returning to college. Barrett C. Shelton Jr., who had served as county editor, assumed responsibility for the city news beat, replacing Doug Norman.

Register could not publish legal notice advertisements from Baldwin County because it was not a separate newspaper. The court's opinion in May 1985 overturned a March 1984 ruling by a Baldwin County circuit judge that said the supplement, *The Baldwin People,* qualified to publish legal advertisements under Alabama law. Gulf Coast Media Inc., which owned four newspapers based in Baldwin County, had appealed the lower court ruling.

APA successfully lobbied the Alabama Legislature in 1985 to allow qualified newspapers to publish legal notices at a rate no higher than their published classified rates. The state no longer set a maximum word rate.

ALA-SCAN begins operation in 1985

Daily and weekly newspapers in Alabama began a new statewide classified advertising service the week of June 16, 1985. A total of 94 newspapers joined the Alabama Statewide Classified Advertising Network (ALA-SCAN). The network enabled an advertiser to purchase a classified ad in all 94 newspapers with one buy, by contacting any participating newspaper or the ANAS office. ANAS is the business affiliate of APA. Alabama joined many other state press associations already offering the service.

ANAS manager Mike Ryland reported that the number of customers taking advantage of ALA-SCAN the first six weeks of the program had far surpassed expectations. "We really expected that we'd be handling about five ads a week during the first few months," Ryland reported in *AlaPressa.* "Instead, we're placing an average of 10 a week, and that number is growing."

Harold S. May
The Florence Herald

The APA summer convention was held July 12-14, 1985, at Gulf State Park Lodge.

Weekly newspaper publishers-editors from north and south Alabama were inducted into the Alabama Newspaper Hall of Honor in 1985. Families of Harold S. May, editor and co-publisher of *The Florence Herald,* and John S. Graham,

John S. Graham
The South Alabamian, Jackson

publisher and editor of *The South Alabamian* in Jackson, were honored during ceremonies at Auburn University's Ralph B. Draughon Library on Oct. 5, 1985.

CHAPTER 8

APA Moves to Birmingham

1986-1996

Bill Stewart
The Monroe Journal, Monroeville

THREE HISTORIC DECISIONS WERE MADE in the decade 1986 - 1996 that strengthened the Alabama Press Association. In 1987 the board of directors of both APA and its for-profit affiliate, the Alabama Newspaper Advertising Service, approved sale of the Clipping Bureau. Press Association headquarters were moved from Tuscaloosa to Birmingham in 1987. In 1994 the Press Association purchased its own office building.

APA was first based in Tuscaloosa in 1939, when it was housed on the University of Alabama campus. Under a cooperative agreement, the University paid half the salary of APA's executive director, then called the field manager, and provided office space. Like many trade associations, APA had been managed by its elected officers until 1939. Similar relationships between state universities and newspaper trade associations were found in a number of states, and in 1987 some press association offices were still on state university campuses.

APA headquarters remained on the Tuscaloosa campus until 1973, when some newspapers began questioning the Press Association's ties to an arm of state government. In Alabama, other association offices formerly on the University campus were the Alabama Broadcasters Association, which moved to Birmingham, and the Alabama Association of School Boards, which moved to Montgomery.

Clarence B. Hanson Jr. led in establishment of ANAS

In 1951, APA officers and directors led by president Clarence B. Hanson Jr., publisher of *The Birmingham News,* established Alabama Newspaper Advertising Service as a for-profit corporation to operate a clipping service and a one-order, one-bill newspaper advertising placement service. The Clipping Bureau started in 1952. APA established the service affiliate to supplement dues income and to help advertisers place multi-newspaper ad buys. The additional income was needed to pay a professional staff and to support new member services.

When APA moved from the University of Alabama campus in 1973, the board of directors discussed relocating the headquarters to either Birmingham or Montgomery. Past APA president Jay Thornton, publisher of *The Daily Home* in Talladega, said the Press Association office remained in Tuscaloosa largely because of the difficulties involved in moving the Clipping Bureau.

Thornton, 1986-1987 president, said he wanted to do two things during his term. One was to move to Birmingham to help sell more advertising for newspapers, and the other was to sell the Clipping Bureau so the Press Association could devote its time and attention to member-related matters.

Thornton: Move to Birmingham would strengthen APA

Thornton, who had been involved in APA activities since the 1930s, said the move to Birmingham would provide the opportunity to strengthen and promote the Press Association, the advertising service's one-order, one-check advertising placement service, and the new statewide classified service, ALA-SCAN. Thornton also said the move to Birmingham rather than to Montgomery would not lessen APA's commitment to legislative lobbying, a major member service, and other government relations responsibilities. ALA-SCAN, less than two years old in 1987, already was providing almost three times the net income of the 35-year-old Clipping Bureau.

APA executive director Bill Keller wrote in the 1987 winter convention edition of *The Alabama Publisher* that sale of the Clipping Bureau to Magnolia Clipping Service of Jackson, Miss., would continue to provide income to APA for three years based on a percentage of gross income it earned on accounts purchased from APA. In addition, for at least 10 years Magnolia would pay the Press Asso-

ciation 75 percent of the value of two copies of each member newspaper.

"The Clipping Bureau provided cash flow, but at a low profit margin in a labor-intensive operation with no direct benefit to members," Keller wrote. "It would have to be revamped to be more profitable, but we felt that in the long run, it would be more efficiently operated by an organization whose only business is its clipping services."

1986
Jay Thornton, *The Daily Home,* Talladega
1986-1987 president

115th annual press convention, Birmingham
Feb. 28-March 2, 1986
Summer convention, Gulf Shores
July 18-20, 1986

Delegates to the 115th annual convention in Birmingham Feb. 28-March 2, 1986, heard candidates for governor and lieutenant governor. They also heard about developments at the federal level that affected newspapers — developments such as forecasts of even higher postal rates and the new hazardous substance labeling requirements.

Politics was the focus of a Saturday program that involved a discussion of Alabama's past and future, and a discussion about the roles of political parties in the state's development.

Veteran newspaper publisher Jay Thornton of *The Daily Home* in Talladega was elected president during the winter convention. Thornton, 68, publisher, general manager and editor of *The Daily Home,* had worked continuously for 58 years in the newspaper business, starting as a carrier for *The Birmingham Post* at age 10 in his hometown of Tuscaloosa.

Thornton was sports editor of *The Tuscaloosa News* for four years while attending the University of Alabama, where he graduated in 1938. In 1939 Thornton bought a weekly newspaper in Haleyville, converting it to a daily in 1962 and selling it in 1965 before moving to Talladega.

Also elected were Steve Stewart, editor of *The Monroe Journal* in Monroeville, first vice president, and Jack Venable, publisher of *The Tallassee Tribune,* second vice president.

Monument to honor Justice Hugo L. Black

APA adopted a resolution in 1986 endorsing a monument to the late Supreme Court Justice Hugo L. Black. The resolution noted that Black was the state's only native to become a member of the U.S. Supreme Court. Black was a staunch defender of freedom of the press. The APA resolution urged newspapers to support efforts to erect a memorial to the Clay County native "editorially and otherwise as they see fit."

Black wrote the opinion in 1966 when the Supreme Court ruled to strike the Alabama law forbidding the state's newspapers from publishing election day editorials. Former APA president James E. (Jimmy) Mills, editor of the *Birmingham Post-Herald*, had written an election-day editorial commenting on a bitter change-of-government election in 1962. Black wrote in the opinion, "The Alabama Corrupt Practices Act by providing criminal penalties for publishing editorials such as the one here silences the press at a time when it can be most effective."

Birmingham was in middle of bitter election

In a 1990 interview with Bill Plott of *The Birmingham News*, Mills recalled that Birmingham had been in the middle of a bitter change-of-government election in 1962 when the editorial was published in the *Post-Herald*. Birmingham Mayor Arthur Hanes was irritated over press coverage and had declared that no city employee was to give information to a reporter unless it came through him and his office first, Mills recalled.

"I pointed out in an editorial that if anyone needed any other reason for why they should be thrown out on their fannies, that was it," Mills said in 1990. "The editorial ran in the paper on the morning of the election. A sheriff's deputy came up with a warrant for my arrest for violating the Alabama Corrupt Practices Act. Under that legislative act, no electioneering or politicking, or political advertising or other things could be done on election day. Under that law you couldn't even tell your wife how to vote if they found out about it."

Jimmy Mills acquitted in first trial

Mills continued, "I was acquitted in the first trial. They took it down to the (Alabama) Supreme Court. The Supreme Court upheld the prosecution. We appealed to the Supreme Court of the United States, and we won the case there. That law had never been tested, and it affected the whole country because several other states had similar laws and they were invalidated, too. It was a landmark case."

Ironically, despite the *Post-Herald's* reputation for crusading, the editorial was not a deliberate challenge of the state law, Mills said. "I hadn't even thought about it. I was just writing an editorial so people would know what was going on," Mills recalled. "Hugo Black was the justice who wrote the decision, and he gave a ringing decision upholding a free press and the Constitution."

1986 summer convention held at Gulf State Park

"Come back to the coast with the APA family." That's what APA office staffers wrote to APA active and associate members in the 1986 summer convention announcement. APA gathered for its 115th annual summer convention July 18-20, 1986, at Gulf State Park Resort. Speakers included a popular Alabama-based comedian, Andy Andrews, and David Lawrence Jr., publisher and chairman of *The Detroit Free Press.*

The Birmingham News, The Daily Mountain Eagle in Jasper, *The Prattville Progress* and *The Leeds News* won first place General Excellence awards in APA's Better Newspaper Contest. Winners were announced at the Saturday night banquet during the summer convention.

Breedlove wins first political race

Mike Breedlove, publisher and editor of *The South Alabamian* in Jackson, won the 1986 Democratic primary runoff election for the House of Representatives in his first political race. Jack Venable, publisher and editor of *The Tallassee Tribune,* won the primary election June 3 and was being mentioned as a contender for a top leadership post in the House, possibly speaker. Neither faced Republican opposition.

Venable was a former aide to Congressman Bill Nichols and a former television newsman at WSFA-TV in Montgomery. He purchased *The Tallassee Tribune* from former APA president Herve Charest Jr.

Breedlove, immediate past president of APA, purchased *The South Alabamian* from another Alabama newspaper man involved in politics, James

H. (Jimmy) Faulkner Sr., a strong contender for governor in 1954 and 1958, and APA president in 1941-1942.

Daily Home in Talladega first to charge 50 cents

The Daily Home in Talladega became the first Alabama daily in 1986 to increase the newsrack single copy price to 50 cents. Publisher Jay Thornton said the increase in August 1986 was intended to combat the cost of stolen papers and to fight inflation. "We feel that a copy of this newspaper, with the efforts of 11 reporters, is worth as much as a cup of coffee or a soft drink," Thornton said. Later in 1986, *AlaPressa* reported that Thornton had "taken some ribbing about selling 50-cent newspapers," but that Thornton "doesn't understand why other dailies don't increase their prices."

"We've been taking in more money from day one," Thornton said, adding that his monthly rack sales totals increased from $17,000 in July, the month before the price increase, to $25,000 by the end of the year. "It doesn't make sense to sell it for 25 cents."

Thornton said publishers of other small dailies had called to discuss the price increase with him. Several Alabama weeklies had already announced single-copy price increases to 50 cents in 1986.

Newspapers continue conversion to laser typesetting

Alabama newspapers continued their conversion to laser typesetting in 1986. *The Troy Messenger,* a daily, and two weeklies, *The Shelby County Reporter* in Columbiana and *The Atmore Advance,* began using Apple laserwriters in the fall of 1986. Newspapers already using laser typesetting were *The Daily Mountain Eagle* in Jasper, *The Monroe Journal* in Monroeville, and *The Clarke County Democrat* in Grove Hill. *The Daily Mountain Eagle* in Jasper was one of the first newspapers in the state to convert to laser typesetting.

S I D E L I G H T S
MARKING 125 YEARS OF HISTORY

Tiner: **Register** *no longer "out of register"*
When *The Mobile Press Register* installed new equipment in 1993 to improve color printing, the newspaper could no longer be called the Mobile "out of register," editor Stan Tiner wrote in a column.

Daily Mountain Eagle publisher Doug Pearson said that in early 1985 it became obvious to him and his staff that they needed to replace their front-end system in the newsroom and the typesetting equipment in the composing room. "This led to talks with publishers, editors, and production people at other newspapers who had recently installed new equipment or were contemplating such a move soon," Pearson said. After months of discussions with equipment salesmen, Pearson and his staff had almost decided on new phototypesetting equipment, but had begun to read more about laser technology.

"Here and there an article would crop up where a weekly publisher had decided to install a laser system and was pleased with the results," Pearson said. Laser technology made sense, Pearson said, and it appeared to be the direction for the industry.

Three Boone weeklies plan conversion

Officials of Boone Newspapers Inc., said three of its Alabama weeklies, *The Brewton Standard, The Franklin County Times* in Russellville and *The Demopolis Times,* would convert soon. Laser typesetters already were purchased for *The Alexander City Outlook* and *The Selma Times-Journal,* but the systems could not be fully utilized until existing computers could be linked to them.

Terry Everett, president of Gulf Coast Media, said he planned to purchase laserprinting units for each of the Baldwin County group's four weeklies and one of its two shoppers. By late 1986, two more Alabama newspapers, *The Daily Home* in Talladega and *The Cherokee-Colbert News,* had converted to laser typesetting.

Wiregrass Today begins publication on Nov. 2, 1986

Wiregrass Today, the first new Alabama daily in a number of years, published its first copy on Sunday, Nov. 2, 1986. Although seven dailies in Alabama converted from weekly or twice-weekly publication since 1970, *Wiregrass Today* was the first new Alabama newspaper to start as a daily in recent memory.

Already in place in Dothan, in the southeast corner of Alabama known as the Wiregrass, were a daily, the 83-year-old *Dothan Eagle* owned by Thomson Newspapers with a daily paid circulation of 22,600 and 26,000 Sunday, and a weekly, *The Dothan Progress,* with some 26,000 free circulation. In 1986 Dothan's population was approximately 50,000.

For publisher Wayne Chancey, it was the fourth newspaper he started in the area. The first, *The Headland Observer*, a paid-circulation weekly, was founded in 1966. In 1980, Chancey sold three newspapers, *The Headland Observer, The Dothan Progress* which he founded in 1970, and *The Ashford Power*, a free-circulation weekly he started in 1974, to Freedom Newspapers Inc., a group based in California. Financial backers of *Wiregrass Today* included 17 other Dothan-area based business leaders, and the new daily was printed in a new 16,000 square foot building with a 10-unit offset press.

At *The Clarke County Democrat* in Grove Hill, publisher and editor Jim Cox showed his newly renovated office to the public with an open house in 1986. He showed visitors equipment ranging from a Linotype machine still in operation to the latest in small newspaper technology, laser typesetting and graphics equipment.

Shelton, Chappell inducted into Hall of Honor

Two of the dominant figures in Alabama journalism in the 20th century were inducted into the Newspaper Hall of Honor in 1986. W. Bruce Shelton, editor and publisher of *The Tuscaloosa News*, and James E. (Jim) Chappell, editor, president and general manager of *The Birmingham News*, were inducted during ceremonies at Ralph B. Draughon Library on the Auburn University campus Oct. 28, 1986.

W. Bruce Shelton
The Tuscaloosa News

H. Doyle Harvill, publisher of *The Montgomery Advertiser* and *Alabama Journal* since September 1983, resigned in 1986 and was succeeded by Richard H. (Dick) Amberg Jr.

Amberg became publisher of the two Montgomery newspapers on Dec. 1, 1986. Amberg was also responsible for two subsidiaries, Southern Publications, a printing firm, and *The Prattville Progress*, a 3-times a week paper. Amberg previously was general manager and executive editor of *The St. Louis Globe-Democrat*.

"Grandma" returns to *The Montgomery Advertiser*

In a Dec. 25, 1986, page 1 personal column titled "A letter to our readers," Amberg announced the return of "Montgomery" to the newspaper's nameplate and the resurrection of "Grandma," for years an affectionate nickname for *The Montgomery Advertiser*. Amberg wrote that he had received "unanimous advice from staff and readers alike to return to the name that the morning paper had boasted from 1829 until earlier this decade: *The Montgomery Advertiser*."

Amberg added, "We are delighted to give back to our readers the name '*Montgomery Advertiser*' as our Christmas present to you. The change will be made on the 'flag,' or nameplate, at the start of the new year if the logo can be redesigned by then." Indeed, on Jan. 1, 1987, the capital city newspaper was sporting a redesigned nameplate displaying "*The Montgomery Advertiser*." Amberg said changing the name of the newspaper to "*The Advertiser*" several years earlier by management at the time apparently was intended to give the newspaper, which circulated in central and south Alabama, "more of a statewide appeal."

"Grandma" had been an affectionate nickname for *The Montgomery Advertiser* since 1892. In 1983, "Grandma" vanished from the editorial page and was replaced with a "letters to the editor" logo. "I don't know who Grandma was, but everyone used to write her here at *The Advertiser*," Amberg wrote. "It turns out that Grandma didn't die after all; she just took an extended vacation. I'm pleased to announce that Grandma lives…write her!"

Former APA manager Jack Beisner dies in 1986

Jack Beisner, APA field manager from 1950-1956, died Jan. 22, 1986, at age 64 in Arkansas where he published a weekly newspaper. Beisner and his wife, Mary-Louise, had published *The Times of Northeast Benton County* in Pea Ridge, Ark., since 1978. Mary-Lou Beisner continued to publish *The Times of Northeast Benton County* until 1988 when she sold the paper to former Alabama newspaper man Mike Freeman, former managing editor of *The Alabama Journal* and *The Selma Times-*

S I D E L I G H T S
MARKING 125 YEARS OF HISTORY

Mobile Press Register *on "Jeopardy!"*
The Mobile Press Register was the answer to a question posed on the television quiz show, "Jeopardy!" in 1995. The answer: "*The Mobile Press Register* is the oldest newspaper in this state.*"

Journal. Mary-Lou Beisner continued to live in Pea Ridge in 1996.

Jack Beisner's full name was Ernest Bronwin Beisner, "though he's been known as 'Jack' since childhood," Mrs. Beisner wrote in a 1995 letter. "Funny story: the name resulted from a 'draw' fistfight with a cousin during the heyday of prize fighter Jack Dempsey," Mrs. Beisner continued. "After cleaning the youngsters up, the two dads dubbed them 'Jack' and 'Dempsey,' and so they remained almost exclusively for the rest of their lives."

APA hired Beisner in 1950

Beisner was editing *The Custer County Chief* at Broken Bow, Neb., when he was hired by APA directors in 1950. "Among the major challenges were getting ANAS on a secure footing, building the Clipping Service, persuading the dailies that they needed APA, and representing newspaper interests in the Legislature in Montgomery," Mrs. Beisner wrote in 1995.

"Another challenge in this period, which perhaps did not involve APA directly — though it did, in some ways — came when Autherine Lucy became the first black student to enroll at the University of Alabama" in 1956, Mrs. Beisner wrote. "It was a major event in the turmoil and unrest of this time, and life got pretty hectic. Reporters flooded the campus from all over the country, and from Reuters and other foreign press services. There were riots and threats, some of those threats directed at Jack. Things were not pleasant. At one point, he did not leave the office for a couple of days. How strange that all seems now, so many years later."

Beisner left APA in 1956 for overseas duty

Beisner left APA effective Oct. 31, 1956, to accept an appointment as press officer for overseas duty with the U.S. Information Agency. Beisner was posted to Calcutta, India, until 1959 when he returned to the United States and edited two weekly newspapers in Owego, N.Y. He was associated with the Los Angeles office of California Newspapers Publishers Association and Western Newspaper Foundation from 1966 to 1978 when he purchased *The Times of Northeast Benton County* in Pea Ridge, Ark.

"In 1977 we began our search for a little paper of our own," Mary-Lou Beisner wrote in 1995. "Our last child would soon finish college, and it was time. Thus we came to beautiful Northwest Arkansas. Jack had done his homework in our search, and predicted this area would soon boom. How right he was! It reminds me of how Orange

County, Calif., was when we first moved there in 1966: Livestock and crops one day, new subdivisions and industry the next."

Mrs. Beisner concluded, "I wish Jack were here to see how right he was, though the process had already begun well before his death in 1986. I continued to operate the paper until 1988, when I sold it to Mike Freeman, whose father was a publisher in Tennessee. I believe Mike is known to many Alabamians, as well."

Lafayette Sun still using Linotype

AlaPressa reported in 1986 that *The LaFayette Sun* had one of an estimated 130 Mergenthaler Linotype machines still being used in the United States. First produced in the 1880s, the machine helped newspaper circulation jump from 3.6 million to 33 million in the late 1800s. Some 70,000 were produced in the United States alone.

In a 1986 story in *The Columbus* (Ga.) *Enquirer,* Pearl H. Hand said her husband, the late Bonnie D. Hand, bought the Linotype just after World War II. *The LaFayette Sun* still used the Linotype for job printing in 1986, but the newspaper, like all other weeklies in Alabama, was printed on an offset press. Mrs. Hand, 68, died Nov. 26, 1989. Her son, Michael Hand, who had worked at the newspaper since 1970, became publisher and editor.

In a 1996 interview, Mike Hand said his father, Bonnie D. Hand, bought the Linotype machine in 1947 at a cost of approximately $8,000. "At that time, that sum of money probably would have purchased three automobiles," Mike Hand said. "The Linotype's days are definitely numbered because of the parts replacement problem."

In 1996, the Linotype operator at *The LaFayette Sun* was 60-year-old George Parker, a deaf man who was trained to run the Linotype at the School for the Deaf in Talladega. "Since commercial printing was less than one percent of our gross last year, when Parker decides to retire we'll get out of the commercial printing business," Hand said in the 1996 interview.

Operating the Linotype
George Parker, a deaf man, operates the Linotype machine at *The LaFayette Sun* in Chambers County. The Linotype, purchased by publisher Bonnie D. Hand in 1947, was still being operated by Parker in 1996. (Photograph courtesy of Mike Hand, editor and publisher, *The LaFayette Sun*)

1987
Steve Stewart, *The Monroe Journal*, Monroeville
1987-1988 president

116th annual press convention, Mobile
Feb. 20-22, 1987
Summer convention, Perdido Beach
July 17-19, 1987

AlaPressa reported that the 116th annual winter convention would be Feb. 20-22, 1987, in Mobile at the city's "Four-Star, Three-Diamond hotel, Stouffer's Riverview Plaza. Many association executives consider it the best convention hotel in the state."

"Publishers can look forward to at least two programs that can more than pay for their trip to the convention," according to the October 1986, issue of *AlaPressa* promoting the upcoming convention. Jim

---

LINOTYPING

Push a key, the matrix plops;
Press again, the spacer drops:

Hear the rattle of the rig
Chewing up another pig

Lift the bar and hear the clatter,
Tiny bits of metal chatter
Forth a tittle or a jot
Stamped in hot goo from the pot

Load the magazine or change it,
Flub a line and re-arrange it,
Un-transpose a transposed letter,
Space the space a little better.

Scan the galley for correction,
Wrong font — make a new selection;
Indent, paragraph or stet it:
That's a hair line? Yep, re-set it.

Think now of the operator,
Keyboard-banging perpetrator
Of it all; through endless days
His typo temp music plays.

Nimble bending, flying fingers
Dance as deadline ever lingers
But his goal's the vital one:
All the copy must be done.

When relief comes into sight
No overtime to face tonight.
He tears his hair and rips his shirt
Because, you see, he's got a squirt.

— W.C. Bryant
The Alexander City Outlook

Boone, president of Boone Newspapers Inc., head-quartered in Tuscaloosa, led a panel on cost-saving and revenue-generating techniques. "Inflation, as we've known it since 1946, is over," Boone told publishers. "Newspapers can no longer expect an 8- to 10-percent gain in revenue simply by existing."

Boone told publishers that "if you want to do better in 1987, you're going to have to work harder, work smarter, and practice ingenuity, imagination and innovation."

Mike Pippin, vice president of Boone Newspapers Inc., noted that newspapers had entered a new age with laser typesetting. Pippin said Boone Newspapers, a group of weekly and small daily newspapers, had installed laserprinters at 16 of its newspapers in 1986. "Laserprinting is cleaner and cheaper, it saves space, and it's quieter in operation," Pippin said.

Kelley: "Evaluate your highest-paid employee"

Mike Kelley, publisher of *The Independent Advertiser* in Clanton, suggested to publishers that they "evaluate the strengths and weaknesses of each of your employees, their main responsibilities and how they perform." Kelley added, "You do yourself a favor by beginning an evaluation of your highest-paid employee — yourself."

Former *New York Times* attorney Barbara Dill gave a half-day libel prevention program at the winter convention, and Wisconsin publisher Bill Branen discussed postal and newspaper circulation. Gov.-elect Guy Hunt spoke on his plans to lead Alabama into the 1990s during a Saturday luncheon. U.S. Circuit Judge John C. Godbold of Montgomery spoke on the bicentennial of the U.S. Constitution.

Delegates attended a Mardi Gras party Saturday night, complete with Mobile's "The Original Flash in the Pan" jazz band. Mobile was site of the oldest Mardi Gras celebration in the nation.

Steve Stewart elected APA president

Steve Stewart, editor of *The Monroe Journal* in Monroeville, was elected president at the 116th annual convention. Elected first vice president was Jack Venable, publisher of *The Tallassee Tribune*. James E. Jacobson, editor of *The Birmingham News*, was elected second vice president.

Stewart, 36, became editor of *The Monroe Journal* in 1973, when he returned to his hometown from Atlanta, where he had been a reporter at *The Atlanta Constitution. The Monroe Journal* was a family-owned weekly of 6,500 circulation in southwest Alabama. Steve's father, past APA president Bill Stewart, was publisher. Steve's wife Patrice was managing editor. Steve grew up in Monroeville and earned a bachelor's degree in journalism from the University of Georgia, where he was editor of the student newspaper, *The Red and Black.*

S I D E L I G H T S
MARKING 125 YEARS OF HISTORY

Reporters trade war stories in Selma

Reporters who covered the voting rights movement in Selma 30 years earlier got together in 1995 to exchange journalistic war stories. They recalled events that put their stories on front pages around the world.

John Herbers and Ben Franklin worked for *The New York Times;* Tony Hefferman was with United Press International; Jack Hopper and Gillis Morgan spent weeks in Selma for *The Birmingham News;* and Jamie Wallace worked at *The Selma Times-Journal.* Brandt Ayers of *The Anniston Star* helped lead the discussion.

Most of the reporters said they didn't realize the story they were covering in Selma would be as significant as it turned out to be, and none saved their notes, *Montgomery Advertiser* reporter Alvin Benn wrote. Jamie Wallace, who was directing the Selma Chamber of Commerce in 1995, brought laughs when he recalled in 1995 how some subscribers and advertisers urged him and his editors to "just ignore" what was happening "because they felt it would go away if we did."

APA moves to Birmingham in 1987

Two historic decisions were made by APA in 1987: The boards of directors of both the Press Association and its for-profit affiliate, the Alabama Newspaper Advertising Service, approved sale of the Clipping Bureau, and moving of the Press Association office from Tuscaloosa to Birmingham. The decisions, which were made at a Dec. 5, 1986, board meeting, ended discussions that began as early as 1973, when the APA office left the University of Alabama campus, but remained in Tuscaloosa.

APA moved to new quarters in the Commerce Center on First Avenue North in Birmingham the weekend of May 29, 1987. Commerce Center was a 14-story building between 20th Street, Birmingham's main street, and 21st Street. APA occupied space on the 11th floor. The building was owned by the Birmingham Area Chamber of Commerce.

When the Press Association office moved from the UA campus in 1973, the APA board discussed relocating it to either Birmingham or Montgomery.

APA president Jay Thornton of *The Daily Home* in Talladega said the office remained in Tuscaloosa largely because of the difficulties involved in moving the Clipping Bureau. Thornton said the move to Birmingham would strengthen the APA's ability to sell and place newspaper advertising. Thornton also said the move to Birmingham rather than to Montgomery would not lessen the APA's commitment to legislative lobbying, a major member service, and other government relations responsibilities.

Clipping Bureau sold in 1987

APA sold its clipping service to Magnolia Clipping Service of Jackson, Miss., on Jan. 1, 1987. Magnolia, which opened an office in Tuscaloosa on Jan. 2, hired most of the APA Clipping Bureau's full-time and part-time employees. APA announced that the Press Association headquarters would move to Birmingham "sometime around May 31, 1987, when the lease on the Tuscaloosa office expires."

ANAS was established in 1951

In 1951, APA officers led by president Clarence B. Hanson Jr., publisher of *The Birmingham News*,

established ANAS as a for-profit corporation to operate a clipping service and a one-order, one-bill newspaper advertising placement service, following the lead of other state newspaper trade associations around the country. The Clipping Bureau started in 1952. APA established the service affiliate to supplement dues income and to help make it easy for advertisers to place multi-newspaper ad buys. The additional income was needed to pay a professional staff and to support new member services.

ALA-SCAN began operation in 1985

In June 1985 APA/ANAS added another service and a new income source when it started the statewide classified advertising service, ALA-SCAN. The Alabama Press Association had joined another national trend among state press associations when it offered the new service. Using ALA-SCAN, advertisers could buy a 25-word classified ad for $125. ANAS placed the ad in 100 newspapers, ranging from the largest metro dailies to some of the smallest weeklies in the state. The selling newspaper would keep a third of the sale price. ANAS received the other two-thirds of the sale price and divided half of its share evenly with all participating newspapers.

In 1986, advertisers bought almost $175,000 in ALA-SCAN ads. ANAS earned most of its income from its newspaper advertising placement service, which in 1986 placed advertising valued at almost $1.6 million. ANAS collected a commission from the newspapers where the ads were placed.

APA Legal Hotline established in 1987

Beginning in the winter of 1987, executives of Alabama newspapers were able to phone a law office in Montgomery for free legal advice. APA attorney Dennis Bailey and two other attorneys from the Montgomery firm of Rushton, Stakely, Johnston and Garrett were on hand during normal business hours weekdays to answer questions on routine media law matters. Subjects ranged from open meetings and public records laws to shield laws, city business license or tax questions, access to courts, postal regulations, libel, political advertising, copyright law and legal advertising. The APA office distributed information about the new legal hotline and included stick-on labels to apply to telephones.

Alabama newspapers, particularly weeklies that included *The Cleburne News* in Heflin and *The Pickens County Herald* in Carrollton, contin-

---

S I D E L I G H T S
MARKING 125 YEARS OF HISTORY

K.A. Turner: Public journalism nothing new

Public journalism, the main focus of the APA's 1995 winter convention in Birmingham, and the focus of many journalism programs around the country, is and has been practiced at a number of newspapers for a long time, *Alexander City Outlook* managing editor K.A. Turner wrote in a column after the convention.

"It's getting toward what we at this newspaper and many other small papers have been practicing for years," she wrote. "I've always called it community journalism — journalism inexorably linked to the people we live and work among."

She reminded readers that community journalism "is not about keeping bad things or dissenting opinions out of the newspaper. Community journalism, in my book," she wrote, "is not about limiting your exposure to the world around us. It is about challenging us all to make that world a little better."

ued to convert from phototypesetting to laserprinting in 1986.

In April Auburn University journalism professor Ed Williams, a former weekly and small daily editor, led a newspaper design workshop on the Auburn campus with funding by a grant from the APA Journalism Foundation. Jim Morgan, publisher of *The Alexander City Outlook,* Steve Stewart, editor of *The Monroe Journal,* and Jim Cox, publisher and editor of *The Clarke County Democrat* in Grove Hill, joined Williams in a workshop on how to implement laserprinting using Macintosh computers. In 1986 many newspapers were switching from phototypesetting using Compugraphic systems to Apple Macintoshes for laserprinting output of text.

Jay Black was named chairman of the University of Alabama Department of Journalism in 1987 after a lengthy search. Black, who had been assistant chairman of the communications department at Utah State University, assumed his new duties in the fall of 1987.

Jack Nelson 1987 summer convention speaker

Alabama native Jack Nelson, Washington bureau chief for *The Los Angeles Times,* was guest speaker at the annual Better Newspaper Contest Banquet during the summer convention July 17-19, 1987, at the new Perdido Beach Hilton. APA was one of the first organizations to meet at the Perdido Beach Hilton, the newest resort hotel.

A Pulitzer Prize winner, Nelson was the third nationally known journalist to speak during the annual series sponsored by the Better Newspaper Contest. The other speakers were former presiden-

---

tial press secretary Jody Powell and *Detroit Free Press* publisher David Lawrence. *AlaPressa* reported that the summer convention would include "speeches by newsmakers, entertainers and newspaper executives as well as good food, good times and plenty of Gulf Coast sun and sand."

Felicia Mason joins APA/ANAS staff in 1987

APA/ANAS added a new full-time sales rep, Felicia Mason, to its staff Sept. 1, 1987. Mason, retail sales manager for the University of Alabama student newspaper, *The Crimson White,* graduated in August.

Alabama native Hazel Brannon Smith, a 1964 Pulitzer Prize-winning editor and publisher in Mississippi, was inducted into the Mississippi Journalism Hall of Fame in 1987. She was known for her weekly column in which she expressed views on civil rights and other state and national issues — views that often were opposed by her readers. Smith got her newspaper start in Alabama with *The Etowah Observer* in Alabama City, Etowah County.

Arthur F. Slaton Jr.
The Moulton Advertiser

William Dorsey Jelks of *The Eufaula Times and News* and a former Alabama governor, and Arthur F. Slaton Jr., publisher of *The Moulton Advertiser,* were inducted into the Alabama Newspaper Hall of Honor during ceremonies at Ralph B. Draughon Library on the Auburn University campus Oct. 10, 1987.

Wiregrass Today ceases publication in 1987

Less than three weeks after the new Dothan daily celebrated its first anniversary, *Wiregrass Today* ceased publication. Publisher Wayne Chancey announced that the stockholders of the new daily made the decision to publish the last edition on Nov. 19, 1987. Chancey several years earlier had developed the twice-weekly *Dothan Progress* and weekly *Headland Observer* and had sold them to Freedom Newspapers.

In October 1987, *Wiregrass Today's* stockholders, all local businessmen, had hired Jim Perry of Arkansas-based Phillips Media Inc. as chief operating officer. He was to have spearheaded a subscription campaign involving local high school bands and to organize other efforts to revitalize the newspaper. The effort was to have centered on the first anniversary in early November.

Original plans called for substantial coverage of the broad 12-county Wiregrass area, six counties in Alabama, three in Florida, and three in Georgia. Almost 7,000 subscribers were receiving *Wiregrass Today.*

Wiregrass Today had shifted its publication from morning to afternoon since the established daily, *The Dothan Eagle,* was a morning publication. The paper began by distributing its Sunday edition free to more than 50,000 households and selling 5,000 copies in newsracks weekdays. *The Dothan Eagle,* owned by Thomson Newspapers, had 22,600 paid circulation on weekdays and more than 26,000 on Sunday.

Wiregrass Today was printed in a new 16,000 square foot building with a 10-unit offset press. The original news staff included 11 full-time personnel and several part-time writers. The original advertising staff included nine full-time employees.

1988
Jack Venable, *The Tallassee Tribune*
1988-1989 president

117th annual press convention, Huntsville
Feb. 26-28, 1988
Summer convention, Perdido Beach
July 15-17, 1988

The 117th annual winter APA convention at the new Huntsville Marriott, next to the Alabama Space and Rocket Center in Huntsville Feb. 26-28, 1988, featured two presidential candidates and marked the Press Association's first trade show in memory.

The Rev. Pat Robertson, Republican, attended the Saturday night reception at the Alabama Space and Rocket Center and spoke briefly, and Rep. Richard Gephart, D-Mo., spoke for 30 minutes after the Sunday morning membership meeting.

The trade show featured 22 booths and attracted such vendors as Ray Davis and Co. of Selma, Apple Macintosh desktop publishing systems, and SFS Desktop Publishing Systems of Montgomery.

Convention programs included an address by Michael Zinser of the Nashville law firm, King and Ballow, who discussed efficiency in management of employees and the avoidance of antitrust problems. Bill Rinehart, vice president of technology for American Newspaper Publishers Association, led a discussion on how changes in technology were altering the newspaper industry.

S I D E L I G H T S
MARKING 125 YEARS OF HISTORY

Takes three to write Jasper editorial
It took three people to write an editorial at *The Daily Mountain Eagle* in Jasper in 1986. "Two were so angry they couldn't write," said Doug Pearson, publisher and editor.

The editorial was written in response to a resolution by the Walker county Commission calling for *The Daily Mountain Eagle* to submit stories about county matters to a commissioner before publication. It said that the newspaper "had routinely and consistently and incorrectly and untruthfully reported certain county commissioners and employees of Walker County."

Venable elected APA president

Jack Venable, editor and publisher of *The Tallassee Tribune* since 1970 and a four-term member of the Alabama House of Representatives, was elected APA president at the winter convention. A native of Wetumpka in Elmore County, Venable returned to his home county to purchase *The Tallassee Tribune* from Herve Charest Jr., APA president in 1963-1964. From 1967 to 1970, Venable had been administrative assistant to Congressman Bill Nichols.

From 1963 to 1967, Venable was on the news staff of WSFA-TV, the award-winning NBC affiliate in Montgomery, and was news director the last two years. Also elected at the Huntsville convention were James E. Jacobson, editor of *The Birmingham News,* first vice president, and Paul R. Davis, publisher of *The Auburn Bulletin,* second vice president.

Survey: 89 percent of voters are newspaper subscribers

Alabama newspaper advertising executives in 1988 received the first in a series of ad slicks and promotional pieces showing strong voter-newspaper readership ties. Based on research conducted after the 1986 elections for APA by Dr. Jack Hamilton, 89 percent of voters surveyed in Alabama were newspaper subscribers or regular readers. Hamilton, a political science professor and pollster at the University of Montevallo, also found strong readership of newspaper political advertising and solid rela-

S I D E L I G H T S

MARKING 125 YEARS OF HISTORY

Ann Landers publishes Thornton's letter
A letter from Jay Thornton, publisher of *The Daily Home* in Talladega, appeared in a 1986 Ann Landers column. In the letter, Thornton said the biggest problem he had with newsracks was vandalism — "like toothpicks and matches shoved in the coin slots. Sometimes people haul off the machines and knock them to pieces with an axe just to get a few quarters. Twenty-five years ago we had 'honor racks.' Customers could put a nickel in the slot and take as many papers as they wanted. We didn't lose nearly as much money then as we lose now. This certainly says something about how times have changed, doesn't it, Annie?" Thornton wrote.
Ann Landers' answer was, "Dear J.T.: You'd better believe it, Mister."

tionships between educational levels, voting and newspaper readership.

Workshops held at UA, Auburn

APA sponsored two Journalism Foundation-supported workshops in spring 1988. Jay Black, chairman of the University of Alabama's Department of Journalism, led a workshop in Tuscaloosa on practical decision-making on ethical issues that weekly and daily reporters, editors and publishers face each day. Ed Williams, an assistant professor in the Auburn University Department of Journalism, led a workshop on newspaper and design for small newspapers. Award-winning Alabama newspaper managers who assisted with the hands-on workshop at Auburn included Jim Morgan, publisher of *The Alexander City Outlook,* and David Moore, editor of *The Andalusia Star-News.*

APA donates $10,000 for newspaper preservation project

APA made a $10,000 donation in 1988 to the Alabama Department of Archives and History to catalog and microfilm Alabama's newspapers. APA was part of the Coalition for the Preservation of Alabama Newspapers, which began coordinating the project in 1983. By 1988, more than 17,000 volumes of newspapers in the Alabama Department of Archives and History had been cataloged,

and the information was loaded into the Archives computer system. The next step in the Alabama Newspaper Preservation Project was to complete the newspaper survey in county courthouses, local libraries and newspaper offices, and to compare it to newspaper holdings in the Archives and those in major university and municipal libraries.

Low salaries for beginning journalism graduates

The College Employment Research Institute reported that the average starting salary for beginning journalism graduates in 1988 was the lowest among the occupation category figures. Recent college graduates majoring in journalism earned $15,743 compared to salaries in the following major fields of study: "$29,680, electrical engineering; $23,474, chemistry; $21,037, accounting; $19,643, general business administration; $19,267, personnel administration; $18,184, geology; $17,873, education; and $16,975, liberal arts."

The Alabama Journal wins Pulitzer Prize in 1988

It was high fives, hugs, champagne and cigars in *The Alabama Journal* newsroom on Thursday, March 31, 1988, when news staff members learned the paper won a Pulitzer Prize. The Pulitzer was the second major national award given to the 20,000 circulation afternoon daily for its coverage of the state's high infant mortality rate.

The prize was the fourth Pulitzer won by an Alabama newspaper and was *The Journal's* first. Two others earlier came to *The Journal's* sister newspaper, *The Montgomery Advertiser.* The other Pulitzer was awarded to *The Tuscaloosa News.*

Series: "A Death in the Family"

The series, "A Death in the Family," which ran in September 1987, was cited by judges for being a "compelling investigation of the state's unusually high infant mortality rate, which prompted legislation to combat the problem." Alabama, along with a number of other Southern states, had rates exceeding 12 deaths per thousand births. In 1986, the state's rate of more than 13 deaths per thousand was the highest of the 50 states. Officials said the series had an impact on efforts to improve health care for indigent mothers. *Alabama Journal* managing editor Jim Tharpe said he hoped the articles would have a lasting impact on the state's infant death rate.

"It's nice to win the Pulitzer Prize, but as journalists, our biggest accomplishment would be to have the state do something about this tragic problem," Tharpe said. Publisher Richard H. (Dick) Amberg Jr. said that the $3,000 prize would be donated to the Gift of Life Foundation, a local group dedicated to fighting the state's infant death rate. Multimedia Inc., the paper's parent company, matched the donation.

Despite rain Saturday afternoon, the 1988 summer convention held July 15-17 at the Perdido Beach Hilton, was an enjoyable, informative and restful weekend for delegates. At the Saturday night banquet, the hotel staff served 332 meals, the largest meal count in recent years.

Gov. Hunt addresses 1988 summer convention delegates

Delegates heard Gov. Guy Hunt talk about the upcoming session of the Legislature and the need for cooperation between the House and Senate. Robert Bryan, publisher of *The Cullman Times*, one of Hunt's hometown newspapers, distributed a copy of a special edition his newspaper had published on Hunt.

In his speech Saturday night, *Baltimore Sun* editorial page editor Ray Jenkins, former editor of *The Montgomery Advertiser* and former special

Alabama Journal wins Pulitzer in 1988

It was high fives, hugs, champagne and cigars in *The Alabama Journal* newsroom on Thursday, March 31, 1988, when news staff members learned the paper won a Pulitzer Prize. The Pulitzer for the series, "A Death in the Family" on infant mortality, was the fourth Pulitzer won by an Alabama newspaper and was *The Journal's* first. Joining in the celebration in the newsroom are from left, are assistant copy editor Nancy Dennis, editorial page editor Jim Earnhardt, executive editor Bill Brown, reporter Frank Bass, and city editor Ann Green. (Photograph courtesy of Bill Brown, *The Montgomery Advertiser*)

assistant to President Jimmy Carter, praised the professionalism of a number of present and past Alabama newspaper leaders, including the Stanleys of *The Greenville Advocate*, the Halls of *The Montgomery Advertiser* and *The Dothan Eagle*, Hamner Cobbs of *The Greensboro Watchman*, Neil Davis of *The Lee County Bulletin* in Auburn, and the Stewarts of *The Monroe Journal* in Monroeville.

Weeklies, small dailies raise single copy price

A number of weeklies and small dailies increased their single copy price from 25 cents to 50 cents in 1988. "The days of 25-cent cups of coffee and 25-cent candy bars have passed, and so have the days of 25-cent newspapers," *The West Alabama Gazette* of Millport reported in a story announcing the price increase. Another weekly that increased its single-copy price to 50 cents was *The Greensboro Watchman*. The twice-weekly *Brewton Standard* raised its single copy price to 50 cents. *The Union Springs Herald* and *The Call-News Dispatch* in Chatom raised their single copy prices from 25 cents to 35 cents.

The South Alabamian in Jackson raised its single copy price to 50 cents. *The Clarke County Democrat* in Grove Hill raised its price from 25 cents to 35 cents. "Even at 35 cents, the price is cheaper than a soft drink, cup of coffee or candy bar, and a lot more filling," said publisher and editor Jim Cox.

The Selma Times-Journal raised the price of weekday single copies to 50 cents in 1988. The single copy price on Sunday was $1.

APA considers move from downtown in 1988

The August 1988 issue of *AlaPressa* reported that a committee of APA officers and the presi-

dents of Alabama Newspaper Advertising Service and APA Journalism Foundation, APA's affiliate organizations, were exploring options to buy or build office space for the Press Association. APA and ANAS, with a staff of four full-time employees and one part-time employee, were renting a 1,200 square foot office in downtown Birmingham. APA had moved from Tuscaloosa to Birmingham in June 1987.

APA president Jack Venable of *The Tallassee Tribune*, who appointed the committee during the 1988 summer convention, said the committee was seeking expert opinion on the advantages and disadvantages of ownership. The APA staff began working with the committee to collect information on financing, ownership, space needs and other factors from other state press associations, as well as from other in-state trade associations.

Newspaper layout expert Edmund C. Arnold led a design workshop at the University of Alabama Oct. 14, 1988, at the new Bryant Conference Center. The workshop was sponsored by the APA Journalism Foundation.

Alabama newspapers participating in ALA-SCAN, APA's statewide classified service, began receiving the statewide classifieds already typeset in 1988. The staff announced plans to begin electronic transmission of ads to participating newspapers, computer to computer. ANAS set a record in 1988 with 52 ads placed in one week.

Courtesy titles added at *Advertiser/Journal*

The switch in 1988 to using "Mr.," "Mrs.," "Miss," and "Ms." in second and subsequent references in news stories drew little response from readers, said Bill Brown, executive editor of *The Montgomery Advertiser* and *Alabama Journal*. Brown said he received four phone calls from readers, with three favoring the change and one against it. A number of his staff writers opposed the change, Brown said, because they thought it was sexist, others because it added "just one more thing to get right."

Brown said *The Advertiser-Journal* decided to start using the courtesy titles after he and other executives at the newspaper thought about it for a long time. "Experts have been suggesting it for some time," Brown said. "They've been suggesting that a return to some degree of civility was called for." Brown said the newspapers tried to keep the new style rule simple. On all second references, a courtesy title was used for adults and older youths in general news stories and editorials. In sports, last names only were used in second references.

Birmingham News refuses ads for controversial movie

The Birmingham News refused to accept advertisements in 1988 for the controversial movie, "The Last Temptation of Christ." The film was criticized by some religious leaders who said it was a blasphemous depiction of Jesus. *The News* had a policy of not running advertisements of X-rated movies, and on occasion it did not accept advertising for other films and other businesses.

Newspapers that accepted advertising for the movie included the *Birmingham Post-Herald* and *The Tuscaloosa News. Decatur Daily* publisher Barrett C. Shelton Jr. said *The Decatur Daily* would publish ads for the movie if purchased, but he said that theatre owners in Decatur had said they would not show the movie.

The Birmingham News successfully sued the state in 1988 to review phone use records by legislators, who used assigned codes to gain access to the state long distance lines.

The Cullman Times filed suit against law enforcement officers in Cullman to gain access to police incident reports. State law said that records were open unless closed by specific statutes. The state Supreme Court, though, ruled in 1983 that some unnamed law enforcement documents may be withheld from inspection.

Boone Publishing buys Michigan newspapers

Boone-Narragansett Publishing of Michigan, a limited partnership largely of Selma and Tuscaloosa newspaper executives, purchased two dailies, two weeklies and a shopper in southwest Michigan in 1988. Key associates in the new ownership were Shelton Prince Jr., publisher, Mike Pippin, associate publisher, and Jay Davis, business manager, all of *The Selma Times-Journal;* James B. Boone, chairman and president, and Wilson Koeppel, vice president, Boone Newspapers; Bob Tanner, a Tuscaloosa attorney; and John Mathew, publisher of *The Natchez* (Miss.) *Democrat.*

Alabama weeklies update equipment

Several Alabama weeklies updated their equipment in 1988. *The Cherokee County Herald* in Centre purchased a new Itek typesetting computer connected to a Linotronic 100 laser printer. *The Arab Tribune, The Journal-Record* in Hamilton and *The Northwest Alabamian* in Haleyville began using Apple Macintosh equipment. Compugraphic announced in 1988 that consultation was no longer available on some older Compugraphic equipment. Effective July 6, 1988, Compugraphic no longer accepted trouble-shooting calls on older models. Parts and service were still available, however.

Alabama newspapers in 1988 began finding that facsimile machines would pay for themselves in a short time. For example, *Selma Times-Journal* publisher Shelton Prince Jr. said his advertising staff saved time and car use for trips to local car dealers to proof ads. They simply faxed the ads. *The Times-Journal* and other Boone newspapers all used fax machines. Publishers of the Boone weeklies and dailies found that the machines brought an efficient new way to communicate with other newspapers, advertisers, suppliers, and the group office in Tuscaloosa.

UA professor John Luskin dies in 1988

John Luskin, longtime journalism professor at the University of Alabama, died Sept. 11, 1988, at age 80. Luskin taught generations of Alabama journalists from 1938 until his retirement in 1974.

David Moore, editor of *The Andalusia Star-News,* was one of five journalists from around the nation chosen in 1988 to participate in an expense-paid trip to Egypt. Sponsored by the National Newspaper Association and an American-Egyptian cooperation organization, Moore represented APA on the trip. "While I'm a firm believer in the local news product we publish at *The Andalusia Star-News,* I also realize the world gets smaller every day," Moore wrote when he returned from Egypt. "Egypt may be on the other side of the planet, but events happening there could affect our lives here: Middle East war could cut our supply of petroleum; Egypt could provide a market for our cotton farmers; Egyptian-made garments could (or could not) be a threat to Alabama jobs."

First Metz Scholarship awarded in 1988

A senior journalism major at the University of Alabama was named winner of the first W.H. Metz

---

S I D E L I G H T S
MARKING 125 YEARS OF HISTORY

Ed Reed wins first place in Irish golf tourney
Ed Reed, publisher of *The Arab Tribune* and an accomplished amateur golfer, was on a four-man team that won first place in a golf tournament in Ireland in 1987.

Scholarship in 1988. Christi Parsons, who was also a part-time staff writer for *The Tuscaloosa News* and a former intern at *The Birmingham News,* was selected from a field of four candidates. W.H. (Bill) Metz, former president of the *Birmingham Post-Herald,* was APA president in 1968-1969 and helped establish the APA Journalism Foundation. The foundation for a number of years made grants to support college journalism programs. The scholarship sought to encourage upper level under-

W. H. (Bill) Metz
Birmingham Post-Herald

graduate and graduate students who were interested in newspaper management.

APA's business affiliate, Alabama Newspaper Advertising Service, placed more than $260,000 in political advertising in 1988, a year without major statewide races. ANAS manager Mike Ryland said a combination of competitive primary races in June and the growing strength of the two-party system in Alabama encouraged candidates from both major parties to purchase more newspaper advertising than expected.

The Cullman Times and *Athens News Courier* dropped the comic strip "Cathy" after publisher Robert Bryan said the strip became a pro-Dukakis political cartoon.

APA contributes to Newspaper Preservation Project

APA, ANAS and APA Journalism Foundation donated $15,000 during 1988 to the State Department of Archives and History to help the agency receive federal matching funds for the Newspaper Preservation Project. Archives director Dr. Ed

Bridges said the project to catalog a list of existing newspaper files held around the state in libraries and courthouses was almost complete, and the microfilming portion of the project was well under way. Using the information gleaned in the title-gathering project should lead to the publication of a catalog that would include a brief history and description of each newspapers. Although the Archives staff was microfilming some 50,000 pages a month, they were not to complete the microfilming project for 20 to 30 years, Bridges said.

A Pulitzer Prize-winning editor-publisher and a business leader of Birmingham's daily newspapers were inducted into the Alabama Newspaper Hall of Honor Oct. 1, 1988. Families of James Buford Boone, publisher and president of *The Tuscaloosa News,* and John W. Frierson, president of The Birmingham Post Co. and assistant general manager of The Birmingham News Co., were guests during the annual ceremony on the Auburn University campus. The ceremony was held at Ralph B. Draughon Library.

Charles Gordon Dobbins, a former Alabama journalist and national higher education leader, died Nov. 6, 1988, in Washington, D.C. Born in Greensboro, Dobbins' newspaper career included positions as a reporter at *The Birmingham Age-Herald,* editor and publisher of

John W. Frierson
The Birmingham Post, News Co.

The Anniston Times, editor of *The Montgomery Advertiser,* and editor and publisher of *The Examiner,* another daily in Montgomery. He was APA president in 1942-1943.

1989
James E. (Jim) Jacobson, *The Birmingham News* 1989-1990 president

**118th annual press convention, Grand Hotel
Feb. 17-18, 1989
Summer convention, Perdido Beach
July 21-23, 1989**

The 118th annual press convention Feb. 17-18, 1989, featured buying and selling newspapers, a program on postal savings, and a session on environmental workplace issues. The convention featured APA's second trade show and was the first APA convention at the historic Grand Hotel on Mobile Bay since the early 1970s.

Tuscaloosa attorney Robert C. Tanner joined APA accountant Mike Echols of Tuscaloosa to lead the newspaper buy-sell program Saturday morning and roundtable discussion Saturday afternoon.

Alabama-born comedienne, actress and author, Fannie Flagg spoke at the Saturday luncheon. Her two Southern novels, "Coming Attractions" and "Fried Green Tomatoes at the Whistle Stop Cafe," were drawing rave reviews from critics around the nation in 1989. "Fried Green Tomatoes," which became a movie, used a small town newspaper column format to tell some of the goings on in a fictional railroad crossroads town just outside Birmingham.

Jacobson elected 1989 APA president

James E. Jacobson, editor of *The Birmingham News* and long-time leader in Alabama journalism professional activities, was elected APA president during the convention. Moving up to APA first vice president was Paul R. Davis, publisher of *The Auburn Bulletin, The Lee County Eagle* in Auburn and *The Tuskegee News.* Terry Everett, publisher of *The Union Springs Herald,* moved up to second vice president.

Jacobson, who started at *The Birmingham News* in 1959 as an editorial writer, moved up to editorial page editor and managing editor before being named editor in 1978.

S I D E L I G H T S
MARKING 125 YEARS OF HISTORY

Western Star *housed in restored 1890s house*
AlaPressa reported in 1987 that *The Western Star* in Bessemer, APA's newest active member newspaper "probably has one of the most attractive offices in the state. It is housed in a restored 1890s Charleston-style house a block from downtown."

AlaPressa continued, "*Greensboro Watchman* Ed Lowry has a full range of equipment in his plant from a flat-bed press and Linotype machine to an Apple Macintosh and laserwriter. Lowry, a former salesman for the Mergenthaler Linotype, keeps the old Linotype machine in working order as a hobby."

Huntsville News celebrates 25th anniversary

The Huntsville News, the morning daily in Alabama's Rocket City, celebrated its 25th anniversary on Jan. 8, 1989. The banner headline on the first edition said, "New Communications Capsule Blasts Off." The group that launched the newspaper had just sold their shares of a local television station and "were looking for an interesting investment," *Huntsville News* staff writer David Bowman wrote. It started as a weekly in January, went to semi-weekly in February, and went to a six-day daily in August. At the time, it was the Tennessee Valley's only morning daily. Lee Woodward, who had been with the paper since 1972, became editor in January 1977.

Harvey: "First it was our grammar"

"A few weeks ago it was our grammar," Sam Harvey wrote in a 1989 *Advertiser-Gleam* column. "Now it's the way we look." Harvey wrote about newspaper designer Edmund C. Arnold's critique of *The Gleam's* page design in *Publishers' Auxiliary.* Harvey reported Arnold's criticism of its one-column heads, one small photo on the front page, the front-page ads. "By having all the headlines the same size, Arnold says, we're shirking one of our obligations to our readers," Harvey wrote.

The Advertiser-Gleam was known for its loyal and large readership, unusual design, and thorough coverage of local news.

Seigenthaler speaks at 1989 summer convention

John Seigenthaler, editor and publisher of *The Nashville Tennessean* and editorial director of *USA Today,* was guest speaker at the summer convention July 21-23, 1989, at the Perdido Beach Hilton at Orange Beach. Speaking at the Saturday luncheon was Rheta Grimsley Johnson, an Auburn University graduate and former staff writer for *The Monroe Journal, The Lee County Eagle* in Auburn and *The Opelika-Auburn News.*

Delegates heard how newspapers were responding to declining readership from Susan Miller, director of editorial development for Scripps Howard. Miller discussed how the prevalence of two-income families had led to a substantial decline in newspaper readership by women.

Alabama newspapers that raised newsrack prices from 25 cents to 50 cents in 1989 included *The Alexander City Outlook, The Dadeville Record, The Monroe Journal* in Monroeville, *The Tri-City Ledger* in Flomaton, and *The Andalusia Star-News.* Jim Morgan, publisher of *The Alexander City Out-*

look and *The Dadeville Record,* cited newsprint and production cost increases. *The Call-News Dispatch* in Chatom raised its single copy price from 35 cents to 50 cents.

Demopolis native George Anthony Cornish dies in 1989

George Anthony Cornish, retired editor-in-chief of Encyclopedia Americana and a former Alabama and New York newspaper man, died in 1989 at age 87. He was a Demopolis native. Cornish, who also was executive editor of the old *New York Herald-Tribune,* began his newspaper career working at his father's newspaper, *The Demopolis Times.* His father,

George Anthony Cornish
The New York Herald-Tribune

the late Edward Seymour Cornish, was editor and publisher of *The Times* from 1910 to 1936, when it was sold to Ben G. George. Cornish worked in the shop and wrote editorials and feature stories as well, while in high school and later at the University of Alabama.

After graduation, Cornish went to work at the old *Birmingham Age-Herald,* before becoming an Associated Press correspondent. After two

Edward Seymour Cornish
The Demopolis Times

years, he went to New York, where he found a job at *The New York Tribune,* which later merged with *The Herald.* He was at *The Herald-Tribune* for 37 years and became its highest ranking editor. He retired six years before the newspaper ceased publication.

Survivors included his sister, Elizabeth Cornish (Mrs. Ben) George of Demopolis.

Boone Newspapers buys Texas-based group of papers

A partnership including Boone Newspapers Inc. of Tuscaloosa bought a Texas-based group of six daily and seven weekly newspapers in 1989. Boone/Narragansett Publishing of the Southwest, a new partnership, acquired Woodson Newspapers Inc. of Brownwood, Texas, on July 26, 1989. At the time of the purchase, Boone Newspapers owned 11 newspapers in Alabama, three in Mississippi, one in New Mexico, and one in Ohio.

The new purchase included five dailies in Texas and one in Oklahoma, as well as six weeklies in Texas and one weekly in Kansas. With the new purchase, Boone Newspapers Inc. and the partnerships owned approximately 33 newspapers and a number of shoppers. Boone, who worked some 12 years with another Texas-based newspaper organization headed by Carmage Walls, succeeded his father, the late Buford Boone, as publisher of *The Tuscaloosa News* in 1968. He was at *The News* until 1980.

Shelton Prince Jr., publisher of *The Selma Times-Journal* since 1980, moved to Brownwood, where he became editor and publisher of *The Brownwood Bulletin,* a six-day daily. He also had management responsibilities with the other newly purchased papers. Prince was APA president in 1980-1981.

Pippin succeeds Prince at *Selma Times-Journal*

Succeeding Prince at *The Selma Times-Journal* was Mike Pippin, who had been associate publisher for the past year. Pippin continued as a vice president and group manager of Boone Newspapers. Pippin, who had been publisher of three newspapers, began his career at *The Oak Ridger* in Oak Ridge, Tenn., as an ad salesman. In Alabama, he helped found *The Marion Messenger* in 1973, which was purchased by Boone in 1975. Pippin lived briefly in Selma as a management trainee at *The Times-Journal* during the mid-1970s. He was publisher of *The Auburn Bulletin* and *The Brewton Standard.* Before moving to Selma in 1988, Pippin worked in Boone Newspapers' corporate headquarters in Tuscaloosa.

Morgan becomes publisher in Waxahachie

Jim Morgan, publisher of *The Alexander City Outlook* and *The Dadeville Record,* became publisher of a daily in Waxahachie, just south of Dallas. Succeeding Morgan at *The Outlook* and *Record* was Kenneth Boone, managing editor of *The Selma Times-Journal.* Kenneth Boone, son of Jim Boone, was at *The Times-Journal* three years, first as a reporter, then as associate editor and finally as managing editor for the last two years.

E. Wilson Koeppel, vice president of Boone Newspapers, became publisher of *The Stephenville* (Texas) *Empire-Tribune.* Koeppel also continued as a vice president and group manager of some of the Boone newspapers.

UA's Charles Arrendell dies in 1989

Dr. Charles Arrendell, 52, former chairman of the Department of Journalism at the University of Alabama, died July 4, 1989, in Arlington, Texas. Arrendell joined the UA faculty in 1969 and became department chairman in 1974. He filled that post until 1981, when he joined the faculty at the University of Texas in Arlington. "He came here when the place was in the dumps, and restored confidence and morale," said Dr. Ed Mullins, dean of the UA School of Communication. "And he treated journalism as a serious subject in its own right, worthy of careful study by students and professionals alike."

Burruss featured in column

An 1857 report by an APA Hall of Honor member was featured in a 1989 historical column in *The Opelika-Auburn News.* John Crenshaw Burruss was editor/publisher of *The Universal Her-ald* and a minister who lived in Notasulga, wrote *Opelika-Auburn News* correspondent Martha Swann. Burruss was a 1975 inductee to the Alabama Newspaper Hall of Honor.

Swann recounted an 1857 story written by Burruss about "laying the corner stone of the East Alabama Male College." Burruss wrote: "Bishop Pierce arose and delighted the audience with a most pertinent, chaste, and eloquent speech. 'Education,' he said, 'is mining itself down through the strata of ignorance, and percolating its influence even through the ore of superstition'."

APA delegation goes to Washington

Eleven daily and weekly Alabama newspaper executives from Alabama went to Washington, D.C. in 1989 in the APA's first group trip to visit the state's congressional delegation. The publishers went to the Capitol to discuss HR 2140, a bill that would lift restrictions on the regional Bell phone companies. They explained that they supported the Bell companies' efforts to convince Congress to take the lead in setting policy on the emerging issue. The Alabama newspaper executives also urged the congressmen to encourage the Bell companies to go ahead and set up new computer phone-access gateway systems to help create a demand and market for computer-available information.

Newspapers opposed lifting the restrictions that kept the phone companies from owning or controlling any of the information that flowed through their own local lines. To do so, they said, would be the same as letting the U.S. Postal Service print and sell newspapers and magazines, when they have a government-licensed monopoly to deliver them — except that newspapers at least had the option of relying on carriers for local delivery.

Hanson, Shelton inducted into Hall of Honor

Two giants in Alabama's newspaper industry in the 20th century were inducted into the Alabama Newspaper Hall of Honor on Nov. 11, 1989. Clarence Bloodworth Hanson Jr., publisher of *The Birmingham News,* and Barrett Clinton Shelton Sr., publisher of *The Decatur Daily,* were inducted during ceremonies on the Auburn University campus. The ceremony was held at Ralph B. Draughon Library.

Alabama native Edward W. Barrett Jr., dean of the Columbia Graduate School of Journalism from 1956 to 1968, died Oct. 23, 1989.

S I D E L I G H T S
MARKING 125 YEARS OF HISTORY

Cullman Times *publishes tornado tabloid*

The Cullman Times sold a special 16-page tabloid two Sundays after a tornado wrecked a large section of the city on Tuesday, Jan. 19, 1988.

Copies of the special edition, which contained no advertising, sold for $3 each, and publisher Bob Bryan donated all proceeds, $4,408, to the county United Way to be used for storm relief.

Barrett was a leading figure in American journal-
ism for more than three decades. In 1962, he founded
*The Columbia Journalism
Review,* one of the earliest
national magazines de-
voted to criticism of the
news media. His father,
Edward W. Barrett Sr., was
editor and publisher of *The*
Birmingham Age-Herald,
one of the newspapers that was a forerunner of
the *Birmingham Post-Herald.* The elder Barrett
also was involved in APA activities.

Barrett Clinton Shelton Sr.
The Decatur Daily

1990
Paul R. Davis, *The Auburn Bulletin,*
***The Lee County Eagle,* Auburn,**
and *The Tuskegee News*
1990-1991 president

119th annual press convention, Auburn
Feb. 23-25, 1990
Summer convention, Perdido Beach
July 13-15, 1990

The 119th annual winter convention of the
Alabama Press Association was Feb. 23-25, 1990,
at the Auburn University Hotel and Conference
Center. The convention began a two-year celebration of APA's 120th year.

The Alabama Publisher, APA's convention tabloid newspaper, featured stories on some of the
member newspapers' senior publishers and editors
as well as some retired publishers.

At the Saturday luncheon, Southern history
writer Dr. Wayne Flynt of the Auburn University history department discussed Alabama his-

tory and his view of the future of the state.
Flynt also discussed the role of Alabama newspapers in the state's history and the role newspapers could play in guiding the state's future
development.

Auburn University journalism students covered
the convention and prepared a post-convention
newspaper, *APA Convention News,* that was mailed
to delegates following the convention.

The editor, publisher and president of *The Auburn Bulletin* and *The Tuskegee News,* Paul R. Davis,
was elected president of the APA during the 119th
annual convention in Auburn. Davis, an award-
winning journalist at both daily and weekly newspapers, had been at the Auburn twice-weekly since
1983, and he was publisher there from 1975 to
1978. Elected first vice president was Terry Everett,
publisher of *The Union Springs Herald,* while
Charles Land, publisher of *The Tuscaloosa News,*
was elected second vice president.

The Elba Clipper published on time; office under water

When flood water roaring down the Pea River
and Whitewater Creek first poured over the levee
at 6 a.m. Saturday, March 17, 1990, *Elba Clipper*
publisher Ferrin Cox was there with a camera.
When the water broke through and began to flood
the adjacent school ground, he shot another photo.
"By the time the third photograph was snapped,
he was concerned about getting out of the water's
path," the cutline said below a blurred photograph.

"People here have had a good time kidding me
about that photograph," Cox said.

Cox and his family saved cameras, computers,
printers, waxer, subscription plates and other basic
equipment and records from his downtown office
and set up shop in an empty doctor's office. Friends
installed new locks on the doors of the temporary
office, put up signs, and even helped deliver the
papers since the mail didn't run. Others prepared
food for the staff.

Other Alabama newspapers offer help

Cox said the National Guard lent furniture, *The
Troy Messenger* loaned its darkroom, and other
newspapers around Alabama offered help. Cox normally printed the paper at *The Dothan Progress,* and
The Progress didn't charge him that week, he said.
A Specht family weekly in Chipley, Fla., let him
use its old Addressograph machine. A number of
newspapers phoned the APA office to offer help
to *The Clipper.* They couldn't phone Elba because
the phone system was down for more than a week.

"We were about to convert our circulation records to computer," Cox said, "and now we'll do it." Cox credited having his typesetting and business records on desktop computers with being able to stay in business after such a devastating flood. Water and mud damaged *The Clipper's* downtown office all the way to the ceiling, and on March 25, his family and staff were still cleaning the mud out of the office.

Flood destroys *Clipper* bound copies

The flood destroyed all of the bound copies of *The Clipper* going back to the 1929 flood. That was the paper's largest loss, but Cox didn't dwell on damage to the newspaper office in his columns and news stories. Cox said it wasn't just simple water damage, but destruction caused by the motion of the rushing flood water. Water pouring through the building tore down shelving and destroyed the old newspapers as though they were in a washing machine, he said.

The good news was that the Alabama Department of Archives and History had finished microfilming *The Elba Clipper* only two months earlier. Because of the Alabama Newspaper Preservation Project, copies of that newspaper since 1901 had been preserved. APA, ANAS, APA Journalism Foundation and Alabama newspapers contributed more than $40,000 to the microfilming and newspaper inventory project over the last seven years, said Dr. Ed Bridges, director of Archives.

Aerial photo shows water-covered downtown area

The Clipper's March 22, 1990, edition featured pictures of the flooded courthouse over the top of the front page fold. Other front page photos showed a team of volunteers helping a family evacuate, and another photo, an aerial photo, showed the water-covered downtown area. Television viewers around the country saw similar scenes of a town submerged in flood so deep that only the top two

Past presidents gather in 1990

The 119th annual winter convention, held at the Auburn University Hotel and Conference Center on Feb. 23-25, 1990, began a two-year celebration of APA's 120th year. APA past presidents who attended the convention are, seated from left, W.E. (Gene) Hardin, *The Greenville Advocate* (1972); Neil O. Davis, *The Lee County Bulletin*, Auburn (1947); Marcia M. Sears, *The Shelby County Reporter*, Columbiana (1981); Porter Harvey, *The Advertiser-Gleam*, Guntersville (1967); Bill Stewart, *The Monroe Journal*, Monroeville (1959); and Jay Thornton, *The Daily Home*, Talladega (1986).

Standing from left, are Barrett C. Shelton Jr., *The Decatur Daily* (1974); Luke Slaton, *The Moulton Advertiser* (1984); Mike Breedlove, *The South Alabamian*, Jackson (1985); James E. Jacobson, *The Birmingham News* (1989); Steve Stewart, *The Monroe Journal*, Monroeville, (1987); and James W. (Jim) Oakley Jr., *The Centreville Press* (1979).

Marcia Sears was the first woman to be elected president of APA. Neil Davis is the only weekly publisher from Alabama to have received a Nieman Fellowship to Harvard University.

or three rows of the high school football stadium were above the water. They saw only the roofs of the town's schools.

Front page stories in *The Clipper* included a general story about the extent of the flood damage and households that were displaced. Another story listed businesses that had reopened, and other stories discussed security and a detailed account of the vigil that Cox and other city leaders held to watch the flood waters rise and to prepare for the evacuation.

Inside stories included clean-up priorities, garbage collection schedules, warnings to remove dead animals, recommendations to take tetanus shots, and a piece on being alert about rats and snakes.

Geneva County Reaper publisher's house flooded

Geneva County Reaper publisher Jim Specht's house was flooded to the second floor when the high water from the Pea and Choctawhatchee rivers met in the flood plain there, some 30 miles down-river from Elba. The levee around Geneva held and protected that city's downtown area. Specht evacuated his house when friends came by in a boat. He then joined them to help evacuate other families whose houses were on the flood plain outside the levee. "It was scary," Specht said.

Both the Elba and Geneva levees were built after a flood in 1929. More than 12 inches of rain fell in the area on Friday, March 16, and almost 17 inches fell at the headwaters of several south Alabama rivers. Floods damaged farms and houses from Eufaula on the Georgia line to Brewton in south Alabama.

When the flood water in Elba reached the point at which it crested in the most recent serious flood,

SIDELIGHTS
MARKING 125 YEARS OF HISTORY

Johnson: **Plainsman, Journal** *best in state*
Nationally syndicated columnist Rheta Grimsley Johnson said in a 1988 column that Auburn University's student newspaper, *The Auburn Plainsman,* and *The Monroe Journal* of Monroeville were the best two newspapers she and her husband, cartoonist Jimmy Johnson, ever worked on.

Johnson's cartoon, "Arlo and Janis," was also nationally syndicated. Both graduated from Auburn University.

the 1975 flood, city officials began to consider ordering an evacuation. That was at 5 a.m., and Cox was there with other city leaders. That's when he phoned home to ask his wife, Heddy, his son, Eric, and his daughter, Michelle, to remove the office equipment and records.

Michelle Cox, editor of *The Franklin County Times* in Russellville, was home for a wedding, and "she took over," Cox said. "I became a 'gofer'," he said, as Michelle Cox organized the staff to cover the stories that needed to be written. Michelle Cox, who stayed home a few more days to help put out the paper, was named editor and publisher of *The Atmore Advance* in June 1990, succeeding Mike Scogin, who was named editor and publisher of *The Alice* (Texas) *Echo News.*

Elba Clipper publishes despite flooding of office

Of Elba's 130 retail establishments, 120 suffered severe flood damage. In his page 2 column the week after the flood, Cox wrote, "We are publishing a paper this week in spite of the major interruption to our office routine Saturday morning. The flood has put many of us on our knees in more ways than one. But the important thing is that we are alive and capable of rebuilding. A newspaper must publish on a 52-week schedule to be a legal newspaper, and we fully intend to maintain this established position of 93 years at *The Clipper.* The hometown paper was bigger than the flood of 1929, and by George, it has more stickability than the flood of 1990."

Cox continued, "We also feel that the spirit and determination of a community is reflected in the local newspaper, especially a small town newspaper. Therefore, to continue accurately showing the heart of Elba, it has a mandate that publication continue on the schedule established by those who toiled to maintain the publication for those 93 years."

Clanton newspaper changes name

He never believed that changing the name and flag could cause such commotion, but Mike Kelley, publisher of *The Clanton Advertiser,* said that when he dropped *"Independent"* from the name and added *"Clanton,"* in 1990 he even had people phoning him from rural communities worrying that news from their communities would no longer be covered. The name change and flag redesign were part of a front page redesign project. Kelley said the new flag design included a peach, which showed off Chilton County's famous farm products. The name change, he said, caused more problems "than a late freeze on the peach crop."

Seymour Topping, director of editorial development for *The New York Times* Regional Newspapers, and Sam Griffin, editor and publisher of *The Post-Searchlight* in Bainbridge, Ga., were among the guest speakers at the 1990 APA summer convention at the Perdido Beach Hilton July 13-15.

The summer convention also featured Ferrin Cox of *The Elba Clipper* and Lee Woodward of *The Huntsville News.* The editors recommended steps that newspaper publishers could take to minimize the effects of natural disasters on their newspapers. *The Clipper* office was severely damaged by a flood in the spring of 1990, and a tornado that struck Huntsville in December 1989 left *The Huntsville News* without power — but both papers published on time.

Cullman Times' Shelton named best sports columnist

The remarkable story of nursing home-bound *Cullman Times* executive sports editor Bill Shelton made newspapers across the South when the Associated Press learned of an APA award the sportswriter had received. Shelton was named best sports columnist in

Picnicking at Old Live Oak Cemetery
Alabama journalist, author and story-teller Kathryn Tucker Windham relaxes in Selma's Old Live Oak Cemetery where she had a picnic lunch with Ed Williams, author of APA's 125th anniversary history, on April 3, 1996. Mrs. Windham, a former staff writer for *The Selma Times-Journal* and other Alabama newspapers, was widely known for her books on Southern ghosts and for her story-telling skills. She was keynote speaker for the 125th anniversary convention of APA in Montgomery in February 1996. While at Old Live Oak Cemetery, Mrs. Windham and Williams swapped stories about Alabama newspaper personalities and visited the graves of husband and wife Alabama Newspaper Hall of Honor inductees Mary and Frazier Raiford of *The Selma Times-Journal.* (Photograph by Ed Williams)

the small daily division of the APA Better Newspaper Contest in 1990. Shelton, who had lived in a nursing home since 1985, wrote a column two times a week for *The Cullman Times.* He lived in the nursing home because of breathing problems, and he suffered ill health most of his life.

Despite these handicaps, Shelton covered local sports events from T-ball to college for more than 19 years, never missing a day of work. "My column keeps me alive," Shelton said. "I guess if they didn't allow me to write my sports column, I would not have much to live for."

Kathryn Tucker Windham writes "Odd-Egg Editor"

Alabama journalists enjoyed reading a new book in 1990 by Kathryn Tucker Windham, "Odd-Egg Editor." Mrs. Windham, a former journalist who was widely known for her books on Southern ghosts and for her story-telling skills, described in the book her career in journalism that took her from her hometown paper, *The Thomasville Times,* to *The Alabama Journal, The Birmingham News* and *The Selma Times-Journal.* As a woman reporter, she had the position as "odd-egg editor," the person responsible for measuring prize-winning squashes and writing about the

Williams fills in at **The Atmore Advance**

Mike Scogin, publisher of *The Atmore Advance,* left for his honeymoon in February 1989 assured that his paper would still get out on time with plenty of news.

Auburn University journalism professor Ed Williams, a former weekly and daily editor, took a week's leave from the classroom to fill in. Williams said the week's work reinforced what he told his students about community newspaper work, that it is varied and exciting. One day, he investigated a story about an elementary school youngster who gave away his parent's prescription drugs in school; another day he covered a drug bust.

strangely shaped produce brought to the office by proud farmers.

In the book, Mrs. Windham told readers about memorable news events in Alabama and about the colorful characters in Alabama newsrooms and politics. Mentioned in the book were several former newspaper people, including Vincent Townsend, Grover C. Hall Jr., Leroy Simms, Lily Mae Caldwell, Hugh Sparrow, Alyce Bilings Walker, and cartoonist Hubert Harper. Mrs. Windham's son, Ben Windham, was managing editor of *The Tuscaloosa News.*

300 years of newspaper history celebrated

Journalists from New England and around the country celebrated 300 years of American newspaper history in September 1990 with a week-long series of activities in Boston, Mass. A copy of the first newspaper, *Publick Occurrences Both Foreign and Domestick,* was on display in Boston Sept. 25-29 — 300 years after it was printed, and 300 years from the day it was banned by the colonial governor and his council.

AlaPressa reported in its September 1990 issue, "With the 300th anniversary of the first newspaper in America, Alabama newspaper executives should remember that the first newspaper published in Alabama was *The Mobile Centinel,* which was issued at Fort Stoddard. The fort was an American outpost in the Mississippi Territory on the Mobile River about 32 miles north of Mobile near Mt. Vernon. The fort was on an important

site near where the Tombigbee and Alabama rivers merge to form the Mobile River. *The Centinel* was published May 23, 1811, when the city of Mobile itself was still part of the Spanish colony of West Florida. The lower two-thirds of what became Mobile and Baldwin counties were Spanish at the time. Alabama became a state in 1819."

It was a long tradition in Mobile for carriers to sell copies of *The Mobile Press Register* on street corners and in the medians of major streets as cars stopped at red lights. Former Mayor Arthur Outlaw had stopped the practice, but after a federal court in Florida approved similar street-side sales in 1990, *Press Register* carriers began selling the papers again.

Alabama editors, reporters visit Cuba in 1990

On Oct. 19, 1990, a group of Alabama editors and reporters flew from Miami to Havana, Cuba, to start a week-long APA Study Tour. The trip marked the fourth visit to Cuba in the history of the APA. University of Alabama journalism professor Dr. Frank Deaver coordinated the tour, which included a visit to Havana newspapers. It wasn't on the travel agenda, but the 10 newspaper editors saw Fidel Castro.

They saw the Cuban leader during a dedication ceremony for a new school for the blind. In a story in *The Decatur Daily,* state editor Regina Wright said, "It was a real unexpected thing. We didn't think we were going to be able to see him. It was something we were invited to by the foreign minister."

The seven-day trip included a visit to the journalism school at the University of Havana and a visit to the offices of Cuba's largest newspaper, *Granma.* APA president Paul Davis of *The Auburn Bulletin,* one of the 10 on the trip, said some 400 staffers in a 12-story building produced the eight-page daily newspaper. The paper's size was small because of a shortage of newsprint, which was supplied by Cuba's old trade partner, the Soviet Union. In addition, the newsprint shortage had forced former provincial dailies to become weeklies.

When *Eufaula Tribune* publisher Joel P. Smith asked Cuban journalists if they printed Letters to the Editor, they said they did only if the letters agreed with the goals of the revolution.

Group dines at Hemingway's favorite restaurant

In a trip to author Ernest Hemingway's favorite restaurant and bar, most of the members of the APA group conspired to convince Betty Bryan of *The Cullman Times* to order the house specialty.

They didn't tell her it was horse meat until she had eaten half of it, when they began to sing, "The old grey mare, she ain't what she used to be."

In addition to Mrs. Bryan, Frank Deaver, Joel Smith, Regina Wright and Paul R. Davis, others on the study tour included Ron Casey of *The Birmingham News*, Terry Everett of *The Union Springs Herald*, Ken Hare of *The Montgomery Advertiser*, Lee Roop of *The Huntsville Times*, and Peter O'Connell, a student reporter with *The Crimson White* student newspaper at the University of Alabama.

1990 wasn't first APA trip to Cuba

It wasn't the first trip to Cuba by an APA delegation. More than 400 Alabama newspaper executives, their families and friends went to Cuba in June 1936 for the 65th annual APA convention. They traveled to Havana from Tampa, Fla., via steamer. Once in Cuba they were treated to four days of welcomes, dinners, dances, cocktail parties, sightseeing tours, sports events, receptions and shopping trips. A story in the 1950 issue of *AlaPressa* recalled the trip, but the story was mistaken when it said the 1936 trip was the first such trip — because in April 1928 the APA met in Havana for the 57th annual convention and even earlier, in January 1895, on the eve of the island nation's revolution against Spain.

Participating in the 1928 trip to Havana were 108 delegates who boarded a train in Dothan bound for Tampa, Fla. The delegates toured sugar, pineapple and tobacco plantations, and the sponge and fish-packing industries. They enjoyed the trip so much that 1927-1928 APA president Robert B. Vail of *The Baldwin Times* in Bay Minette named a committee to buy and place a marble plaque in the Reporters' Building in Havana.

Wilbur H. (Bill) Metz of the *Birmingham Post-Herald* and Edgar Hughleigh (Ed) Pierce of *The Daily Mountain Eagle* in Jasper, leaders in the Alabama newspaper industry, were inducted into the Alabama Newspaper Hall of Honor Oct. 13, 1990. The ceremony was held at Ralph B. Draughon Library on the Auburn University campus.

Keller joins Consolidated Publishing

Bill Keller, executive director of APA since January 1983, joined the staff of Consolidated Publishing Co. in Anniston on Nov. 12, 1990, as associate publisher of *The Daily Home* in Talladega and assistant to the publisher of *The Anniston Star*. Paul R. Davis, publisher of *The Auburn Bulletin* and APA president,

---

SIDELIGHTS
MARKING 125 YEARS OF HISTORY

Oakley family featured in 1969 article

The Oakley family of Centreville was featured in a 1969 article in *The Tuscaloosa News*. The article noted that J.W. (Jim) Oakley Sr., 57, editor and publisher of *The Centreville Press* since 1927, was mayor of Centreville and his son, Jim Oakley Jr., 33, was tax collector:

Days of Nail Kegs 'N' Sorghum Behind

"It's been quite some time since city business in Centreville has been done while sitting on nail kegs in a shoe shop.

"But that's the way it was when Jim Oakley Sr., editor and publisher of *The Centreville Press* since 1927, became an alderman in 1939.

"While the younger Oakley is out paving pavement to rustle up advertising for the weekly edition, his father can be found sitting at a Linotype machine writing editorials, for which the paper is known throughout Alabama.

"After completing Linotype school, Jim Oakley Sr. jumped into the newspaper business feet first, picking the Depression years to build a newspaper, although it wasn't done by choice. Taking over the paper with only 700 or 800 subscribers at the age of 17 years was quite an accomplishment. Oakley's father, O.C. Oakley, a railroad agent at Centreville, bought the paper. Two years later Jim Oakley paid his father for the $1,000 down payment and assumed the mortgage of $5,000.

"He was faced with the battle of circulation for survival during the Depression years. Many of the subscribers on the mailing list, when the paper was purchased, were already two or three years in arrears. So, to get things started, Oakley accepted two gallons of sorghum syrup for one-year paid subscriptions, but he wound up with 3,000 gallons of the sticky stuff, some of it two to three years old. 'We cleaned the county,' Oakley commented.

"However, the federal government took the syrup and shipped two carloads to Oklahoma City, Okla. Thus the circulation of *The Centreville Press* braved the Depression on sorghum syrup for which Oakley realized very little profit when he resold it."

said the association's Executive Committee would meet with the presidents of ANAS and the APA Journalism Foundation, APA's two subsidiary organizations, to begin a search for Keller's successor.

Mike Ryland was named acting director during an Oct. 11, 1990, meeting of the APA Executive Committee. Ryland was manager of the Alabama Newspaper Advertising Service, APA's for-profit subsidiary. Ryland became acting APA director effective Nov. 9, 1990.

"We hate to lose Bill," Davis said. "He's done a fine job for us at APA, but I see this as a great opportunity for him to work with a fine newspaper company." *Anniston Star* publisher Brandt Ayers said he would encourage Keller to remain active in APA activities. "Before the members form a lynch mob and come after me, I want you all to know that Bill is not deserting APA," Ayers said. "We will encourage Bill to be very active in the affairs of the association for years to come. I'm just glad we were able to keep this talented couple, Bill and Jeanetta, in Alabama."

Keller's wife, Jeanetta, was director of public relations for Southern Progress Corp., the Birmingham-based magazine and book publisher.

Keller joined APA in 1983 from Montevallo

Keller came to APA in 1983 from the University of Montevallo, where he had been on its public relations staff for seven years. Before joining the Montevallo staff, Keller had been a reporter at *The Tuscaloosa News*, his first job after he earned a master's degree in journalism at UA in 1976. He began his newspaper career in 1971 as a reporter at his hometown newspaper, *The Sand Mountain Reporter* in Albertville. He became managing editor before he left in 1975 to go to graduate school. From 1967 to 1971, Keller served in the U.S. Air Force as an aircraft maintenance officer. He was awarded a bachelor's degree from UA in 1967 and a doctorate in higher education administration from UA in 1983.

Mike Ryland, a Brewton native, joined the APA staff in June 1984, succeeding former ad manager Craig Woodward. Ryland had worked a year as a part-time newswriting instructor at the University of Alabama and correspondent for *The Birmingham News* before joining APA.

From 1979 to 1983, Ryland worked for *The Independent* in Robertsdale as a reporter, editor and publisher. He was publisher of *The Independent* when it won first place in General Excellence in the 1983 Better Newspaper Contest. He gradu-

ated from the University of Alabama in 1978 with a degree in journalism and was managing editor of *The Atmore Advance* before joining *The* (Robertsdale) *Independent* in Baldwin County.

Montgomery Advertiser issues front-page apology

AlaPressa reported that a Montgomery newspaper issued a front-page apology in 1990 for stories that misinterpreted the financial disclosure forms that Gov. Guy Hunt filed with the Alabama Ethics Commission. *The Montgomery Advertiser* reported that Hunt began his term as governor with at least $750,000 in personal and property-related debt and had reduced the debt by at least $650,000 by April 1989. In its correction, *The Advertiser* said that because of the broad ranges allowed by law on the ethics forms, there was no way to make valid year-by-year comparisons of an individual's debt.

Alabama native Howell Raines, who criticized Alabama politics in a 1990 *New York Times* Sunday magazine article, said later that the state's newspapers did not adequately criticize state and local politics. Some political leaders, including Gov. Guy Hunt, did not like the article. Hunt told *The Huntsville Times* that Raines "displayed the prejudice of a warped mind." While Raines would not respond to Hunt's criticism, he did comment on the state's press.

S I D E L I G H T S
MARKING 125 YEARS OF HISTORY

Choctaw Advocate *celebrates 100th birthday*
The Choctaw Advocate in Butler celebrated its 100th anniversary on Saturday, June 2, 1990. A crowd estimated at more than 1,200 visited the offices of The Advocate to help celebrate the newspaper's centennial.

Editor Tommy Campbell and the staff also published an 80-page special edition, with special historical information written by a student intern, who researched old copies.

Attending the open house were past staff members, as well as descendants of founder C.C. McCall, including Judge Dan T. McCall, a retired associate justice of the Alabama Supreme Court. Newspaper design critic Edmund C. Arnold featured The Choctaw Advocate's centennial edition in his column in Publishers' Auxiliary.

Raines said he sympathized with people of Alabama who reacted negatively or personally to journalism that was critical of the state, in part because they had little exposure to such reporting, *The Huntsville Times* reported. "Alabama doesn't have the tradition you have in other states of this kind of open discussion and criticism of the state's shortcomings," Raines said. "We've never had, except in isolated cases…, an indigenous press that was encouraging deep-reaching discussion of political issues."

Raines: Alabama lacks aggressive journalism tradition

Raines said the lack of an aggressive journalism tradition in the state "is almost entirely a function of outside ownership." He said the acquisition of Alabama newspapers by corporations in other states makes for "disinterested ownership."

"I hope I don't come across as beating up on Alabama newspapers, because that's where I got my start, but the lack of a consistently vigorous press has been a detriment to the state, and it helps explain why people respond so sharply in some cases to what a so-called outside journalist" may write, Raines told *The Huntsville Times.*

Raines, a graduate of Birmingham-Southern College, and the University of Alabama where he received a master's degree in English, had been a reporter for the *Birmingham Post-Herald* and *The Tuscaloosa News.*

Ryland named APA executive director

Effective on Jan. 1, 1991, Mike Ryland, an APA staff member since 1984, became executive director of the Alabama Press Association, replacing Bill Keller, who left APA in November 1990 to join Consolidated Publishing Co. of Anniston. Since Keller's departure, Ryland had served as acting executive director.

A search committee led by APA president Paul Davis selected Ryland after interviewing finalists for the job in December 1990. The vacancy had been advertised nationwide. Ryland was manager of the APA's business affiliate, the Alabama Newspaper Advertising Service. As ANAS manager, he had participated in the development of the Alabama Statewide Classified Ad Network, the expansion of display advertising accounts, the move of the APA's office from Tuscaloosa to Birmingham, the hiring of a full-time account executive to represent newspapers, and increased advertising education and training activities. His wife, Julie Spafford, was manager of investor relations for Energen Corp. in Birmingham.

Felicia Mason was promoted to manager of the Alabama Newspaper Advertising Service, APA's advertising arm that promoted and sold newspaper advertising. She succeeded Mike Ryland when he was named APA executive director. Mason had served as ANAS's sales/marketing representative since 1987.

1991
Terry Everett, *The Union Springs Herald*
1991-1992 president

120th annual press convention, Riverchase Galleria, Wynfrey Hotel, Hoover
Feb. 23-25, 1991
Summer convention, Perdido Beach
July 12-14, 1991

The 120th annual APA convention was Feb. 23-25, 1991, at the Wynfrey Hotel in the Riverchase Galleria, a large shopping center complex on U.S. 31 in the Birmingham suburb of Hoover. Convention programs included a new technology session, future newspaper prototypes, a report from Washington on postage and other matters, tax reform efforts in Alabama, a libel loss prevention program and discussions with political leaders.

Keynote speaker at the Saturday night banquet was Howell Raines, Washington editor for *The New York Times*. A native Alabamian, Raines began his journalism career in Alabama. In 1990, his *New York Times* article about his home state generated a wave of controversy.

Proctor dies after attending Lineville game

C. Lester Proctor, 75, the owner, editor and publisher of *The Clay Times-Journal*, collapsed Friday, Oct. 9, 1992, and died at a local hospital after "doing what he enjoyed best — watching the Lineville Aggies play football," his son David Proctor wrote.

Lester Proctor had been a star high school player himself at nearby Ashland and had missed few games since he returned home from World War II.

Before the war, Proctor had studied commercial printing. After the war, he became a Linotype operator at *The Lineville Tribune*, which he bought in 1948. Three years later he bought *The Ashland Progress*. In 1990, he combined the two weeklies into *The Times-Journal*.

In the early years, Proctor often worked 16 to 18 hours a day, six days a week. Despite his training in Linotype and letterpress printing, he changed with the times, converting to offset printing in the 1970s. In 1989, he bought the latest in computers and laserprinters. In recent years, his health had declined, but he still worked 30 hours a week.

A story in *The Anniston Star* reported that Proctor avoided the headlines himself, but over the years he had exerted community leadership in a variety of ways. In Lineville, he had been on the City Council, was vice chairman of the county school board, member of the Lineville Housing Authority, church board member, and Sunday School teacher.

Behind the scenes, Proctor helped a number of local youngsters get college scholarships, and he helped several local young people by giving them jobs, "not because he needed help, but to help them," David Proctor wrote. That list of people included the editor of a nationally distributed magazine, a teacher, a lawyer, and a top Hollywood movie producer.

"I suppose this is one of his greatest attributes," David Proctor wrote of his father, "that he could be a leader without being loud or outspoken — because his actions spoke louder than his words. But when he did speak, people listened."

In addition APA's fourth annual trade show featured a variety of booths.

William E. (Bill) Brooks Jr., whose family once owned *The Brewton Standard*, led a Saturday morning program on pagination and other newspaper technology topics. Brooks gained a national reputation as editor and publisher with *The Vincennes* (Ind.) *Sun-Commercial*. The only Alabamian to serve as president of two state press associations, Brooks was APA president in 1953-1954 and president of the Hoosiers State Press Association in Indiana in 1978-1979.

Terry Everett elected APA president

Terry Everett, president of *The Union Springs Herald*, was elected APA president during the 1991 winter convention. Charles Land, publisher of *The Tuscaloosa News*, was elected first vice president, and Sam Harvey, editor of *The Advertiser-Gleam* in Guntersville, was elected second vice president.

Everett founded, owned and sold a number of newspapers during a career that began as a police reporter at *The Dothan Eagle* in 1959. In the 1960s, he was editor and publisher of *The Graceville* (Fla.) *News* and *The Hartford News-Herald*, and he worked at *The Montgomery Advertiser* and again at *The Dothan Eagle*. He founded weekly newspapers in Dothan and Daleville in the early 1970s and bought *The Enterpriser* in Enterprise and *The Union Springs Herald* in 1976. Everett became publisher of *The Enterprise Ledger* in 1977 and later bought newspapers in Aurora and Festus, Mo. In 1979, he purchased the six community newspapers in Baldwin County.

Gov. Guy Hunt spoke at the Sunday morning breakfast, which was followed by a one-hour session of delegates' best ideas for raising revenue and cutting costs.

Reception in 1991 honors Thornton

More than 600 people attended a reception in Talladega Feb. 3, 1991, to honor Jay Thornton, retiring publisher of *The Daily Home*. Thornton, 73, joined *The Daily Home* in 1965 as general manager and was named publisher in 1986. His newspaper career began at age 10 as a youth carrier in Birmingham. During college at the University of Alabama, Thornton served as sports editor of *The Tuscaloosa News*. He graduated in 1938 and bought a weekly newspaper in Haleyville in 1939.

In 1962, he converted it to a regional daily, *The Northwest Alabamian*. He also owned weekly newspapers in several neighboring counties. Thornton sold the Haleyville paper in 1965 and moved to Talladega. *The Daily Home* grew from a circulation of 1,000 to approximately 10,000. The paper expanded its coverage to include the Sylacauga-Childersburg area. During Thornton's years at *The Daily Home*, it absorbed *The Sylacauga Advance, The Sylacauga News, The Childersburg Star* and *The Coosa Press* in Goodwater.

The Birmingham News went from no pagination in March 1991 to almost full pagination by September 1991. The system combined Macintosh-produced art, graphs and television grids into a Harris system. Executive editor Tom Scarritt said pagination allowed editors more control and freedom to become designers and not just layout people.

Newspaper design consultant Edmund C. Arnold gave a one-day seminar on advertising design at Auburn University in May 1991. The program was coordinated by the Auburn journalism department, with grant support from ALA-SCAN.

Birmingham News wins Pulitzer in 1991

The Birmingham News in 1991 became the second Alabama newspaper in three years to win a Pulitzer Prize. A trio of *News* editorial writers, Ron Casey, Harold Jackson and Joey Kennedy, was awarded the 1991 Pulitzer Prize for a series of editorials on tax reform in Alabama. *The Alabama Journal* in Montgomery won a Pulitzer for public service in 1988 for its series on infant mortality.

Two other Alabama newspapers previously were awarded Pulitzers, *The Montgomery Advertiser*, two, and *The Tuscaloosa News*, one.

The News ran nine editorials in August and September 1990 examining inequities in the state's tax system. The series titled "What They Won't Tell You About Your Taxes" said that the crucial link in providing a higher standard of living in Alabama was reforming a tax structure that robbed the poor of state services and education of adequate support while giving millions of dollars in tax breaks to special interests.

Hanson praises editorial writers

Birmingham News publisher Victor Hanson II praised the editorial writers for their work. "They're doing what editorial writers are supposed to do — taking complex issues and making the public understand them and then making suggestions on how to improve things." Added editor James E. Jacobson: "I'm proud of the work the editorial page staff did. I believe it is journalism that makes a difference. That's what we ought to be about."

C.C. (Bo) Torbert Jr., former Alabama Supreme Court chief justice and chairman of the Alabama Commission on Tax and Fiscal Policy Reform, said *The News'* series was "very helpful."

"When the thing started, I told Casey, 'Keep the fire burning, keep writing those articles.' And it really made a great difference."

E. Clark Richardson, president of the Business Council of Alabama, said, "We firmly believe that *The News* and other newspapers across Alabama played a key role in promoting legislation that established the Alabama Commission on Tax and Fiscal Policy Reform."

State Rep. Jim Campbell, speaker pro-tem of the House, said, "I've taken all (the editorials) the newspaper has done on tax reform and given them to a lot of folks and said this is about as good an exposition as there is on what's wrong with our tax system and what we need to fix it. But we got in this shape over a 50-year period and we are not going to get out of it overnight."

The Pulitzer Prize in editorial writing was given for "distinguished editorial writing, the test of excellence being clearness of style, moral purpose, sound reasoning and power to influence public opinion in what the writer conceives to be the right direction."

The News printed a booklet containing the series of editorials.

Woodhall speaks at summer convention

Former Gannett newspaper executive Nancy Woodhull was banquet speaker during the APA's 1991 summer convention July 12-14 at the Perdido Beach Hilton. Woodhull was a founding editor of *USA Today* and later became editor-in-chief of Southern Progress magazines.

Other events during the convention included programs on newspapers' handling of election coverage and advertising; how the media covered the Alabama Legislature; how to become a better manager and decision-maker; and an update on recycling and solid waste management in Alabama.

English named APA sales representative

Brad English was named new sales and marketing advertising representative for the Alabama Newspaper Advertising Service, business affiliate of APA, in 1991. The University of Alabama marketing graduate filled the vacancy created when Felicia Mason was named ANAS manager.

A publisher and editor from the Wiregrass and one from the Tennessee Valley were the 1991 inductees into the Alabama Newspaper Hall of Honor. Karol Ruth Latimer Fleming of *The Geneva County Reaper* and Steele E. McGrew of *The Alabama Courier* and *The Limestone Democrat* in Athens were inducted into the Hall of Honor on Oct. 5, 1991, during ceremonies at Auburn University. The induction ceremony was held at the Ralph B. Draughon Library.

Karol R. L. Fleming
The Geneva County Reaper, Geneva

Steele E. McGrew
The Alabama Courier,
The Limestone Democrat

Auburn coach critical of *Montgomery Advertiser*

Alabama news organizations became the subject of media attention in 1991 when Auburn University coach Pat Dye and Gov. Guy Hunt blasted press coverage of controversies surrounding them. Dye spoke out against *The Montgomery Advertiser,* the newspaper which broke the Eric Ramsey story. *The Advertiser* reported in 1991 that former football player Ramsey had been given cash by Auburn boosters and coaches in violation of NCAA regulations.

On his weekly radio show Oct. 24, 1991, Dye appeared to urge Auburn supporters to boycott *The Advertiser* and merchants who advertised in the newspaper. On his radio show, Dye told listeners that he planned "to do everything I can do to let them dry up on the vine. I don't buy *The Montgomery Advertiser.* If I knew where I was shopping in Montgomery advertised in *The Advertiser,* I wouldn't do one thing that would help *The Montgomery Advertiser* make a dime."

While *The Advertiser* was the target of Dye's criticism, Hunt blasted the Associated Press, which reported on Hunt's use of state airplanes and security guards. Taking questions from reporters at a Huntsville event, Hunt called the Associated Press "the *National Enquirer* of Alabama."

AP: "We're just reporting on our government officials"

Kendall Weaver of AP's Alabama bureau said he did not know if Hunt's comment was serious or said in jest. "When you do your job, you expect that kind of response," Weaver said. "We're just reporting on our government officials. We're not saying what's right or what's wrong. We're just putting the news out there for the people."

Rex Thomas, whose reporting career with AP included 34 years in Montgomery, died in 1991 at age 77. Thomas' byline was well known in Alabama. Thomas, who retired in 1979, covered politicians such as Jim Folsom and George Wallace and the civil rights movement. Born in Missouri, Thomas was a copy boy for *The St. Joseph News Press-Gazette* for six years before he joined *The Birmingham News* in 1937. He went to the AP in Atlanta in 1942, and then arrived in Montgomery, to stay, in 1944.

1992
Charles Land, *The Tuscaloosa News*
1992-1993 president

121st annual press convention, Tuscaloosa
Feb. 21-23, 1992
Summer convention, Perdido Beach
July 10-12, 1992

The APA winter convention returned to Tuscaloosa in 1992 for the first time in 22 years. Speakers Hodding Carter III and U.S. Sen. Howell Heflin highlighted the Feb. 21-23 event at the Paul (Bear) Bryant Conference Center and Hotel on the University of Alabama campus. Carter, former Mississippi newspaper man, served as State Department spokesman during President Jimmy Carter's administration.

Media broker Jim Hall of Troy, executive director of APA from 1966 to 1974, discussed newspaper properties and buying and selling at a Sunday morning breakfast meeting.

Charles Land, publisher of *The Tuscaloosa News*, was elected APA president during the membership meeting at the winter convention in Tuscaloosa. Land, publisher of *The News* since 1978, had been associated with the newspaper for most of the past 36 years. Other APA presidents from *The Tuscaloosa News* included Edward Doty, 1917-1918; Bruce Shelton, 1935 (who served two months before resigning to be succeeded by Webb Stanley of *The Greenville Advocate*); and Ben A. Green, 1943-1944. Green purchased *The Tallassee Tribune* and moved to Tallassee during his presidency.

Joining Land as APA officers for 1992 were first vice president Sam Harvey, editor of *The Ad-*

---

vertiser-Gleam in Guntersville, and second vice president Linda H. Breedlove, associate publisher of *The South Alabamian* in Jackson.

Harvey's father, *Advertiser-Gleam* publisher Porter Harvey, was president of APA in 1967, and his brother-in-law, general manager Don Woodward, was president in 1982.

Mrs. Breedlove's husband, Mike Breedlove, was APA president in 1985. She became the second woman to be elected APA president. Marcia M. Sears, former editor of *The Shelby County Reporter* in Columbiana, was the first woman APA president in 1981.

Mike Ryland dies March 5, 1992

Friends and colleagues of the late Mike Ryland remembered him in columns, news stories, resolutions and editorials after his death March 5, 1992, at age 34. Ryland collapsed at about 11 a.m. while sitting in the House gallery at the State House in Montgomery during a debate about taxes. He was taken to Jackson Hospital, where attempts to revive him were unsuccessful. The House adjourned for an hour in his memory, and the Senate paused for silent prayer.

The APA board of directors established the Michael T. Ryland Family Trust and made a $12,500 donation to get it started. Ryland's widow, Julie, was expecting their first child in August. The board of directors agreed that the trust fund would be established with Julie Ryland as the trustee.

In news stories, APA president Charles Land said, "We're all shocked and saddened by Mike's death, and our hearts go out to the family."

Land: "Mike was highly intelligent, able, hard-working"

"Mike was highly intelligent, able and hard-working," Land added. "He had a genuine understanding of and appreciation for newspapers. Most of his adult life was devoted to working with newspapers, either directly or indirectly. A lot of us have worked with him for a good many years and we're really going to miss him."

APA past president Terry Everett said, "He was probably the most intellectually honest person I've ever met." Ryland worked for Everett as publisher of *The Independent* in Robertsdale. Ryland, a 1979 Phi Beta Kappa graduate of the University of Alabama Department of Journalism, began his newspaper career as a reporter at *The Atmore Advance*. Former *Advance* publisher E.R. (Bob) Morrissette Jr. said Ryland came to him highly recommended, "and I interviewed him and was highly impressed."

Ryland called compassionate, committed

John Cameron, editor of *The Selma Times-Journal*, taught Ryland at the University of Alabama and later hired him at *The Independent* in Robertsdale. In a column, "Saying 'goodbye' has never been more difficult," Cameron said. "Back at the University of Alabama it was easy to see that Mike Ryland would be an outstanding journalist because he was an outstanding person. He was real. He was compassionate. He was committed."

Cameron said that when he went by *The Advance* office to ask Ryland about working for him at his new newspaper, he found Mike stuffing newspapers. "That was the way Mike treated his duties at the newspaper," Cameron said. "He could always be found doing things to help out, never giving a second thought to whose job it was. To him 'getting the paper out' was everybody's job."

"Newspapers have lost great leader"

"The state's newspapers have lost a great leader in Mike Ryland," Cameron said. "He extended integrity to everything he touched, including APA. He was a rare individual with a heart as big as all outdoors. Newspapering in Alabama is better for his contributions of unusual commitment and compassion."

Cameron named Ryland editor of *The Independent,* and Everett named him publisher after he bought it. While Ryland was there, *The Independent* won a number of major APA awards, including the General Excellence award.

Ryland first became interested in newspapers in Brewton

Ryland first became interested in newspaper work when he wrote stories for *The Brewton Stan-*

S I D E L I G H T S
Marking 125 Years of History

First publisher of Tribune *inducted into Hall*

The first publisher of the 113-year-old *Cullman Tribune*, Johann G. Kullmann, a native of Bavaria, was inducted into the Alabama Business Hall of Fame in 1987. Kullmann was responsible for the large German immigration into the area in the 1870s and for the area's substantial business growth. It was estimated that Kullmann brought 20,000 to 100,000 immigrants to the United States.

dard in high school, where he was an honor student and star athlete. After he left *The Independent,* he worked a year as a correspondent for *The Birmingham News* and instructor at the University of Alabama before joining APA as advertising manager in 1984.

At the APA/ANAS office, he was instrumental in starting ALA-SCAN, one of the most successful statewide classified advertising programs in the nation. He became acting APA executive director in November 1990 and executive director in early 1991. Ryland was working on his master's degree at Birmingham-Southern College at the time of his death.

Arab Tribune editor David Moore said in a column, "Julie and Mike were to sell their small home in Edgewood this week and close on a new house. Mike was excited. It was to have been their first home in which they wouldn't have to paint all the rooms, where doors and windows would work, and plumbing was new. Mike was already in love with the child Julie will have in August."

Moore said Ryland's love for life was "probably why more than 500 people packed into the church for the funeral. That's why the motorcade to the cemetery was probably several miles long."

Keller returns as executive director

Bill Keller returned to the APA office March 30, 1992, to begin his work as executive director again.

Keller was APA executive director from 1983 until November 1990, when he resigned to join Consolidated Publishing Co., as associate publisher of *The Daily Home* in Talladega and assistant to the publisher of *The Anniston Star.* He became publisher of *The Daily Home* in February 1991, succeeding Jay Thornton, a former APA president.

"Bill Keller did an excellent job for APA for many years, including help develop Mike Ryland as a highly capable successor," APA president Charles Land said. "Mike's death was tragic, but we're fortunate to be able to again get the benefit of Bill's knowledge and experience with APA as well as the experience he has gained as a newspaper executive," he added.

"I regret the circumstances that led to this change," Keller said in a story in *The Daily Home.* "Mike was a good friend and a trusted colleague, and I look forward to working with Charlie Land and the rest of the APA membership to carry out some of the ideas that Mike was developing for the association."

Press Register returns to APA in 1992

The new chief executive officer, president and publisher of *The Mobile Press Register,* William Howard Bronson Jr., brought the Mobile dailies back into the APA in 1992. Bronson, former president and publisher of *The Shreveport* (La.) *Times,* a Gannett newspaper, succeeded William J. (Bill) Hearin, president and publisher of *The Mobile Press Register* for 22 years. Hearin assumed the new post of chairman of the board Feb. 1, 1992.

Hearin was APA president in 1983. *The Press Register* dropped its membership in 1984 after the APA board filed a neutral brief in a case involving the qualification of newspapers to publish legal notices. The brief asked the Alabama Supreme Court to clarify the law.

Hearin, 82, began his newspaper career at *The Press Register* in 1927 as a classified advertising salesman. He rose through the ranks to become publisher in 1970.

Harvey named Citizen of the Year

Former APA president Porter Harvey, 88, publisher of *The Advertiser-Gleam* in Guntersville, was named Citizen of the Year in 1992 by the Chamber of Commerce. Harvey, called "a legend in his own time," celebrated his 50th year at *The Gleam* on May 1, 1991, and his 65th year as a journalist. "His down-home reporting has helped keep alive in Guntersville the wonderful flavor of living in a small Southern town," said Jeannie Wallace, who introduced Harvey.

"*The Gleam* as it is published today follows the same unwritten guidelines with which it began some 50 years ago," Wallace continued. "Those guidelines included local news; telling about things

Land: Two separate APA corporations inefficient

Having two corporations, a non-profit association and a for-profit affiliate, seemed inefficient, APA president and *Tuscaloosa News* publisher Charles Land said during an APA board meeting in 1992. ANAS president Jim Cox, publisher of *The Clarke County Democrat,* agreed.

ANAS was established by APA in 1951 after the Press Association had started making more income from its one-bill, one check ad placement service. ANAS earned income for APA by paying a proportionate share of rent, salaries and other expenses. While expenses charged to ANAS reduced its taxable income, ANAS paid substantial state and federal income taxes. The third affiliated corporation, the Journalism Foundation, maintained a strict separation from the other corporations. Land asked APA accountant Mike Echols and APA legal counsel Dennis Bailey to study the tax-related issues, and he asked APA executive director Bill Keller to talk with other state press association managers.

UA's Bill Melson retires in 1992

Dr. William H. (Bill) Melson, former dean of the University of Alabama School of Communication, retired in spring 1992, ending a career of 24 years in education, including 16 years at the University. Melson came to Alabama in 1976 as dean. His first year at UA, the journalism program received provisional accreditation for the first time in about six years. In 1977, the journalism department received full reaccreditation. Melson also led the school's move from Carmichael Hall to the old Union Building in 1983.

Melson stepped down as dean in 1983, when he became a professor of advertising and public relations. Melson was succeeded by Dr. Ed Mullins.

Everett runs for Congress in 1992

When long-time newspaper man Terry Everett decided to run for Congress in 1992, he made the same mental leap that some other journalists had made. He moved from reporting and criticizing government to direct participation.

Everett, owner of *The Union Springs Herald,* owned the Gulf Coast Media group of newspapers in Baldwin County from 1983 to 1988. In Alabama, one weekly newspaper publisher in the Legislature was Jack Venable, publisher of *The Tallassee Tribune.* Like Everett, Venable was a past APA president. Venable also served on the Auburn University board of trustees.

people are interested in; trying to tell it in a readable, entertaining way; not playing favorites; and trying to make the paper for everybody and not just some people."

Other weekly publishers who had served in the Legislature included Mike Breedlove of *The South Alabamian* in Jackson and W.E. (Gene) Hardin, editor of *The Greenville Advocate,* both former APA presidents. In local politics, Barbara Bobo, editor of *The West Alabama Gazette,* was mayor of Millport. City councilmen included Thomas May, editor and publisher of *The Union Springs Herald,* and Ed Lowry, editor and publisher of *The Greensboro Watchman.* Local school board members included Larry Beasley, publisher of *The Hartselle Enquirer.* Another former APA president, Luke Slaton, president of *The Moulton Advertiser,* was chairman of the local hospital board and vice chairman of the statewide organization of local hospital boards.

Other Alabama journalists have served in public office
In the Alabama Legislature, Sen. Jim Bennett of Birmingham was a former reporter for the *Birmingham Post-Herald* where he once covered the Legislature. Rep. Jane Gullatt of Phenix City was a former reporter at a number of newspapers, including *The Tuscaloosa News.* She also was editor of *The Phenix Citizen* in Phenix City.

In Georgia, the late Marvin Griffin, a weekly newspaper publisher from Bainbridge, became governor. In Alabama, a former newspaper publisher and businessman from Barbour County, William Dorsey Jelks, was governor of Alabama from 1901 to 1907. Interestingly, Terry and Barbara Everett owned Gov. Jelks' bedroom furniture. Like Everett, Jelks owned *The Union Springs Herald* at

Gov. William Dorsey Jelks
The Eufaula Times,
The Union Springs Herald

one time. Jelks, an APA officer in the 1880s and 1890s, also owned *The Eufaula Times and News.* Everett won the Republican nomination for the U.S. House of Representatives from Alabama's 2nd Congressional District on June 2, 1992, defeating veteran state Sen. Larry Dixon of Montgomery. He received 57 percent of the vote and carried 12 of 15 counties in the district.

Auburn's Jack Simms retires in 1992
The first and only head of the Auburn University journalism department, Jack Simms, announced he would retire in September 1992. Simms, 65, said he was retiring as Auburn's first journalism department head because of "old age," an AP story said. Simms had been head of the Department of Journalism since 1974.

"Newspapers in the state will definitely miss the services of one of the hardest-working journalism teachers ever when Auburn University's Jack Simms retired in September," an editorial in *The Selma Times-Journal* said. "He has had a dramatic and positive impact on journalism in the state and has turned out many outstanding newspaper professionals."

The editorial compared Simms to the late Charles Scarritt who taught at Alabama Polytechnic Institute (Auburn University) and the University of Alabama, both of whom "seemed to share the conviction that college journalists should 'learn by doing' and were never afraid to be out front as teachers putting their reputations on the line for the sake of the young people and the newspaper community."

Simms directed Olympic sports coverage
Simms grew up in Auburn and received a bachelor's degree in English-journalism from Auburn in 1949. He came back to his alma mater to head the fledgling journalism program after 23 years at the Associated Press. After he came to Auburn, Simms continued to take leaves of absence to work with the AP on special projects. He supervised sports coverage at the Montreal Olympics in 1976, directed the news pool coverage of the Moscow Olympics in 1980, and supervised a multinational staff of AP writers at the Seoul Olympics in 1988.

Simms was honored during APA's 1992 summer convention luncheon. Joel P. Smith of *The Eufaula Tribune,* president of the APA Journalism Foundation, gave Simms a framed resolution from the Foundation board. The resolution cited Simms'

S I D E L I G H T S
MARKING 125 YEARS OF HISTORY

Room named in honor of Claude Sparks
A conference room in the newly remodeled offices of *The Franklin County Times* in Russellville was named after Claude E. Sparks, former owner of *The Times,* in 1991. The newsroom was named for former *Times* news staff writer and columnist Mae Streit, who wrote a weekly column, "Mae's Maze."

contributions to Alabama journalism as a teacher and adviser to hundreds of students. Boone Newspapers Inc. announced plans to give a one-year tuition scholarship at Auburn University in honor of Simms. An article about Simms' retirement was entered into the Congressional Record by Sen. Howell Heflin, who also gave a tribute to Simms on the floor of the Senate.

Brown named acting head of department

Dr. Jerry E. Brown, a professor in the Department of Journalism, became acting head. Brown said he and other faculty members planned to work to uphold the department's reputation. "There'll be no changes in the philosophy of the department," Brown said.

Brown said the Auburn faculty tried to prepare students for newspaper work with a sound grounding in practical classes and a strong dose of liberal arts. Brown said the department, which was exploring the process of accreditation, would conduct a search for a permanent successor to Simms. Before his retirement, Simms said the department had begun to consider applying for accreditation because of potential private grant money available to accredited programs. The Auburn program offered a bachelor's degree in journalism and had not ventured into graduate level programs.

Mills: Newspaper business hasn't changed

James E. (Jimmy) Mills, 91, said in 1992 that the newspaper business hadn't change much, despite the technology. Mills was editor of the *Birmingham Post-Herald* for 35 years and APA president in 1960-1961. Mills was profiled in "Current Communication Studies," a lab newspaper at the University of Alabama at Birmingham. "I think journalists should feel an obligation to the people and to the country — an obligation to keep the First Amendment intact," Mills said. "You want to paint pictures with words," said Mills, who studied oil painting after his retirement. "You would like to be able to write a damn good story that people like to read and get a kick out of."

Construction starts on newspaper recycling plant

Construction started in July 1992 on a newspaper recycling facility near the Alabama River Newsprint plant at Claiborne, near Monroeville. It was the second plant in Alabama to manufacture recycled newsprint. It joined Kimberly-Clark's Coosa River newsprint

---

S I D E L I G H T S
MARKING 125 YEARS OF HISTORY

Moulton returns to weekly publication

The *Moulton Advertiser* once again became a weekly newspaper in 1994 after trying twice-weekly publication for six months. Publisher Luke Slaton said the second edition had not found the advertiser and single-copy sales support he had hoped to find.

"We had rather put out a very good weekly newspaper than a mediocre bi-weekly," Slaton said.

---

plant near Childersburg, which began manufacturing newsprint with 11 percent recycled pulp in 1991. The newsprint mill at Claiborne, which began manufacturing newsprint in 1990, was capable of making 220,000 tons of recycled newsprint each year when the de-inking plant was finished in 1993. The plant was a joint project of Parsons & Whittemore Inc. and Abitibi-Price Inc.

With completion of the recycling plant in Monroe County, Abitibi-Price would supply almost 660,000 tons of recycled newsprint to the market from that plant and another it owned in Augusta, Ga.

Decatur Daily editor Tom Wright wrote in a 1992 column that a caller criticized the newspaper for running a photograph of two men kissing. The caller said he felt the photo might have an adverse effect on impressionable children. The photo, Wright said, gave impact to an important story about homosexual rights, an important issue in the 1990s.

Howell Raines wins Pulitzer Prize in 1992

Alabama native Howell Raines won a Pulitzer Prize in feature writing in 1992 for "Grady's Gift," an account of the childhood friendship between the writer, who was white, and his family's black housekeeper in Birmingham. The story appeared in *The New York Times* Sunday Magazine.

Former APA president Shelton Prince Jr., publisher of *The Brownwood* (Texas) *Bulletin*, completed a round of chemotherapy and radiation treatments for a second bout with cancer in 1992. Prince was former publisher of *The Daily Mountain Eagle* in Jasper and *The Selma Times-Journal*.

When Bill Hardin of *The Greenville Advocate* was elected to the APA board of directors in 1992, he became the fourth generation of his family on the board. His great-grandfather, Gen. James Berney Stanley; his grandfather, Glenn Stanley; his great uncle, Webb Stanley, and his father, W.E. (Gene) Hardin, were all APA presidents. That's the most from one family and one newspaper in Alabama.

AlaPressa: Darkroom "may go the way of hot metal"

AlaPressa reported in 1992 that the darkroom "may go the way of hot metal and phototypesetters." The cost of new video technology dropped from about $35,000 in 1987 to about $3,500 in 1992, and some small papers were starting to experiment with video technology. The video still cameras used a two-inch disk that could store 25 photos, and the disk could be reused. The disk went into the drive that loaded the photos into computers. The image was sent to laserprinters after cropping and sizing on the computer screen. No chemicals, print paper or PMT paper was used.

"Someone covering an away football game will be able to send pictures to a computer over a telephone," *AlaPressa* reported. "Production quality still isn't up to par, but it's getting close, some say."

Retired *Alexander City Outlook* publisher J.C. Henderson at dedication of Henderson Conference Room in 1992. *The Outlook* celebrated its 100th anniversary in 1992 with dedication of the room in Henderson's honor. (Photograph by K.A. Turner, *The Alexander City Outlook*)

Alexander City Outlook celebrates anniversary

To celebrate its 100th anniversary in 1992, *The Alexander City Outlook* printed a multi-section special edition with pages reproduced from old editions, collected old photographs from readers, and dedicated a conference room to former publisher J.C. Henderson. Henderson's "Town Crier" column had appeared in the paper for 48 years. Henderson, APA president in 1949-1950, was owner and publisher of the paper for almost half of its 100 years. A cast-bronze plaque bearing the words, "Henderson Conference Room" was mounted on the wall leading into the room. Henderson, 88, remarked that he'd never had his name in bronze before, and publisher Kenneth Boone said that anyone who had worked at *The Outlook* for 48 years deserved his own room.

The Outlook began as a weekly and went twice-weekly in 1945, and thrice-weekly in 1976. It became a five-day daily in 1978, publishing Monday through Friday. In 1979 it began publishing Tuesday through Friday and Sunday. During an open house, souvenir coffee mugs, printed with *The Outlook's* logo, were given to visitors. In addition, old-time tea cakes and fried apple and peach pies were served with lemonade. A correspondent displayed old-fashioned quilts.

Flynt speaks at 1992 summer convention

The 1992 APA summer convention, July 10-12 at the Perdido Beach Hilton in Orange Beach, would be a mixture of relaxation, "food for thought," and good times, said APA president Charles Land of *The Tuscaloosa News.*

Speakers included Dr. Wayne Flynt of Auburn University's history department, whose speech at the

1990 winter convention in Auburn caused more comment than any APA convention speech in recent memory. Flynt played a key role in leading statewide discussions about education reform and tax reform.

Jim Boone, chairman of Boone Newspapers Inc., led a discussion on the state of the newspaper industry. He was joined by Boone Newspapers executives John Mathew of Natchez, Miss., and Ed Darling of *The Natchez Democrat.*

ANAS bylaws change approved at summer convention

APA members approved a change in ANAS bylaws during the summer convention. Effective February 1993 after the APA winter convention, membership of the board of directors of Alabama Newspaper Advertising Service would be the same as the APA board. It was a governance structure already used by most state press associations and their business affiliates.

APA and ANAS leaders said the change would mean clearer management of the association's income from ANAS services to help the association meet member needs. In recent years, with two different boards, the APA board had to go to the ANAS board to request money to support association programs.

During the membership meeting at the summer convention, Julie Ryland, wife of Mike Ryland, and Helen Ryland, mother of the former APA executive director, received framed memorial resolutions from APA. Mike's brother, Scott, and sister, Cindy, also attended the membership meeting. Ryland, 34, died March 5, 1992.

APA sponsors trip to Russia in 1992

Russian journalists and ordinary Russians supported the reforms and appreciated the new freedoms they enjoyed, but they were concerned about

the future, *Gadsden Times* publisher Frank Helderman Jr. found during the APA-sponsored trip to Russia Aug. 23-31, 1992. "From centralized planning down to water heaters in hotels, the system doesn't work," Helderman said.

Helderman said the Russian people, despite their hardships, were open and friendly. "Frankly, I felt more welcome in Moscow and St. Petersburg than in many cities in my own country," Helderman said. Terry Everett, chairman of the board of APA and the Republican nominee for Congress, led the group that also included Everett's wife, Barbara; Helderman's wife, Jennie; Barrett C. Shelton Jr., publisher of *The Decatur Daily,* and his wife Tolly, and several other people from the Decatur area.

One of the state's most colorful newspaper editors, Edward A. (Ed) Dannelly Jr., publisher of *The Andalusia Star-News,* and one of the South's best-known daily editors, John W. Bloomer of *The Birmingham News,* were inducted into the Alabama Newspaper Hall of Honor on Sept. 26, 1992. The ceremony was held at Ralph B. Draughon Library on the Auburn University campus.

Delaney named chairman of UA journalism department

Alabama native Paul Delaney, a senior editor at *The New York Times,* was appointed chairman of the University of Alabama Department of Journalism, effective Oct. 1, 1992. He was the first black chairman and the first full-time black faculty member. Delaney had been a correspondent and editor at *The Times* since 1969. Delaney succeeded Jay Black, who resigned in 1991 to teach and conduct research.

"Paul Delaney is a talented and distinguished journalist on perhaps the world's greatest newspaper," said Dr. Ed Mullins, dean of the UA College of Communication. "We are pleased to have him as chairman of our 66-year-old Department of Journalism. He covered the civil rights story in the South for leading publications, and his reports have been hailed as among the best, fairest and most authoritative," Mullins said.

Southern Star celebrates 125th anniversary

The Southern Star in Ozark celebrated its 125th year of publication in 1992. For the occasion, *The Star* reprinted news stories from the special edition that was published in 1967 on the newspaper's 100th birthday. The edition included photographs of APA vice president W.H. (Bill) Metz of the *Birmingham Post-Herald* presenting a plaque from the APA to Vivian Adams, senior member of the publishing family.

S I D E L I G H T S
MARKING 125 YEARS OF HISTORY

Porter Harvey buys **Guntersville Advertiser**
Porter Harvey, publisher of *The Guntersville Gleam,* purchased *The Guntersville Advertiser* from the Yancy Burke estate in August 1944.

"Both papers will be continued, giving semi-weekly service to this fine community," *AlaPressa* reported in its Sept. 9, 1944, issue.

Mrs. Adams was the grandmother of editor and publisher Joseph H. (Joe) Adams. Mrs. Adams' husband, John Q. Adams, was Joe Adams' grandfather. Mrs. Adams worked at the paper from 1925 to 1969, and she worked until three weeks before she died. Joseph A. Adams, Joe Adams' great grandfather, established the paper in 1867.

Terry Everett defeated Alabama Treasurer George C. Wallace Jr., the Democratic candidate, in the Nov. 4, 1992, general election to represent the state's 2nd Congressional District. Wallace, son of former Gov. George Wallace, won the Democratic Party nomination in June. Everett, the new 2nd District congressman, was owner of *The Union Springs Herald* and was APA president in 1991-1992.

Times vs. Sullivan program held

The First Amendment was strengthened by a 1960 Supreme Court decision involving Alabama, but press and speech freedoms were weakened gradually by later court rulings. That's what panelists at an Auburn University program agreed upon during a program on *The New York Times* vs. Sullivan case, the Montgomery-based case that overthrew a libel judgment against *The New York Times*.

The Times had been sued by a number of people, including Montgomery Police Commissioner L.B. Sullivan after an advertisement in *The Times* asked for help for Dr. Martin Luther King. The civil rights leader had been sued in Alabama for income tax evasion. The famous ruling said that libel suits against public officials could win only if a publication printed false information knowingly and with actual malice — a callous disregard for the truth.

Times-Sullivan ruling added extra layer of protection

The ruling added that extra layer of protection — the actual malice test. In Alabama even before Sullivan, the plaintiff had to prove the defa-

mation was false. In many other states before Sullivan, the burden of proof was on the newspaper to prove the statement in question was false.

Panelist Ray Jenkins, former editorial page editor of *The Montgomery Advertiser,* said that there had been a "steady erosion" of press freedoms since the Sullivan case. Montgomery attorney Rod Nachman who represented Sullivan in the case, was an attorney for *The Montgomery Advertiser* in 1992. Nachman told an Advertiser reporter jokingly, "Your employer and my client think the greatest thing I ever did was lose that case."

Clayton Record featured in column

In a column for National Newspaper Week in 1992, *The Clayton Record* recalled that the paper had been printed by the Gammell family and its descendants since 1915. William Lee Gammell was editor until 1954, when his widow, Pearle Ennis Gammell, became editor. At her death in 1960, the Gammells' daughter, Bertie Gammell Parish, became editor.

William Lee Gammell
The Clayton Record

Elise Austin Mills, 90, wife of former *Birmingham Post-Herald* editor Jimmy Mills, died Nov. 5, 1992. She was known among APA members over the years for her vibrant participation in conventions and other programs with her husband. Known as "Mimi" to friends, she and Jimmy Mills would have celebrated their 71st anniversary in November 1992. Mills, 92, was editor at

Pearle Ennis Gammell
The Clayton Record

the *Post-Herald* and its predecessor newspaper, *The Birmingham Post,* from 1930 to 1966.

APA studies office space options

In December 1992, James H. Denley, editor of the *Birmingham Post-Herald,* was named to head a committee to study office space options for the APA office. Denley, who also was vice president of the APA Journalism Foundation, said the committee's first meeting would be in Tuscaloosa on Saturday, Jan. 16, 1993, just before the UA-APA Day Program. The committee would study other rental options as well as possible building ownership. It would

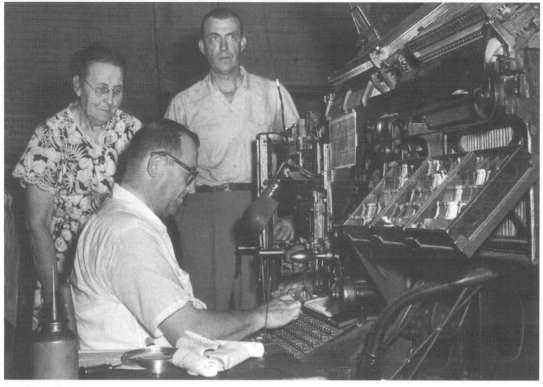

Operating the Linotype

Editor Jesse B. Adams was photographed in 1950 operating the Linotype machine at *The Southern Star* in Ozark with his mother, Vivian B. Adams, and brother, John Q. Adams, looking on. Jesse Adams' mother joined him upon the death of his father, John Q. Adams Sr., and remained with the newspaper until her death in 1969. John Q. Adams was editor-publisher from 1952 until 1957 and subsequently was in charge of advertising and commercial printing. *The Southern Star* and editor-publisher Joseph H. (Joe) Adams were recognized at the 125th anniversary APA winter convention as the oldest family-owned newspaper in Alabama. *The Southern Star* was founded by Joe Adams' great-grandfather, Joseph A. Adams, in 1867. (Photograph courtesy of Joe Adams, *The Southern Star*)

also study how the office space could be used for member services. In 1992 the APA was located on the 11th floor of a downtown office building.

Julie Ryland was promoted to director of investor relations at Energen in Birmingham in December 1992. *AlaPressa* reported that Mrs. Ryland and her son, Evan Braxton Ryland, almost 5 months old, were doing well and that she planned to return to full-time work after the New Year. Mrs. Ryland was the widow of Mike Ryland, APA executive director from November 1990 to March 1992 and APA/ANAS advertising manager from 1984 to 1990.

"Auld Lang Syne" played at Adams' funeral

John Quincy Adams Jr., 83, former publisher of *The Southern Star* in Ozark, died Dec. 30, 1992. Joseph H. Adams, his son and publisher of the newspaper, said in a column about his father's death, "He always told Mama and us, 'When they take me out of the church, I want Auld Lang Syne played.' He got his wish. Ironically, his funeral was

held on New Year's Day." John Q. Adams Jr. had been associated with the family paper longer than any other member during its 125 years of Adams family ownership. "He literally grew up in the newspaper and printing shop," Joe Adams said.

John Q. Adams Jr. had lost his father, John Quincy Adams Sr., in 1925, and he had worked

---

S I D E L I G H T S
MARKING 125 YEARS OF HISTORY

Gov. Folsom buys stock in **Arab Journal**

Gov. James E. "Big Jim" Folsom purchased one-third stock in *The Arab Journal* in 1957, publisher Glenn Hewett announced in September.

Folsom's stock was purchased from former owner Harry E. Black of Arab.

with his older brother, Jesse B. Adams, who died in 1952, as associate publisher. He became publisher after his brother's death. While older brother Jesse was the "front man," John Q. backed him "as a person who was as steady and constant as the humming and thumping rhythm of the sheet-fed newspaper and job printing presses of the day," Joe Adams wrote in his column.

Adams: "You're not in the damned Army"

In 1957, Joe Adams came home to be editor after a stint as an Army officer, he said in the column. When he tried to tell his father how to run the business, his father settled the issue. "He listened without saying anything for about three weeks. Then one day when I was bearing down pretty hard, he slammed his fist down on the desk and said, 'You're not in the damned Army any more. You're working for me'." Joe Adams said his father and grandmother (Vivian B. Adams) weren't too impressed with Lt. Adams.

John Q. Adams Jr. attended Alabama Polytechnic Institute at Auburn, and he studied graphic arts at the Chicago Art Institute. He was an accomplished artist and took a great interest in advertising layout and design. During World War II, in addition to publishing *The Southern Star*, he led crews that worked around the clock several days each week to put out publications for nearby Camp Rucker and Napier Field, an Army Air Corps base in Dale County. Adams was survived by his wife, Elizabeth Holman Adams; and three sons, Joseph H. Adams of Ozark; John Q. Adams III of Thomasville; and Jesse D. Adams of Montgomery.

Strong newspaper circulation in Marshall County

Strong circulation was noted among Marshall County newspapers in 1992. The three papers in Marshall County were *The Advertiser-Gleam* in Guntersville, *The Sand Mountain Reporter* in Albertville, and *The Arab Tribune*. Postal statements in 1992 showed that *The Advertiser-Gleam* was the largest circulation non-daily in the state. Circulation was 12,034 in a city of about 7,000 people. Publisher Porter Harvey established *The Advertiser-Gleam* in the 1940s. *The Gleam's* circulation surpassed that of its neighbor paper, *The Sand Mountain Reporter*, which had a circulation of 11,965. Pat Courington Sr. established *The Reporter* in 1954 as a five-day daily. It later became a weekly and merged with another weekly, *The Albertville Herald*. *The Reporter* later became a thrice-weekly paper, and it also bought out the

weekly in Boaz. Pat Courington Jr. was president of the company in 1992.

Reed second generation to publish *Arab Tribune*

The *Arab Tribune* had an average paid circulation of 6,177 in a town of 6,900. *Tribune* publisher Ed Reed was the second generation of his family to publish *The Tribune*. His uncle, the late Ralph Reed, died shortly after starting the paper in 1958. Ed Reed's father, Ewell Reed, a co-owner with Ralph Reed's wife, Martha Jean, took over the paper, and Ewell Reed became publisher. Ed Reed came to the paper in the early 1970s and took over the management.

Boone purchases Minnesota dailies

Subsidiaries of Boone Newspapers Inc. bought three dailies in Minnesota Dec. 22, 1992, from Thomson Newspapers Inc. of Toronto. Jim Morgan, publisher of *The Alexander City Outlook* before he went to *The Waxahachie* (Texas) *Daily Light*, a Boone newspaper, became publisher of *The Daily Journal* of Fergus Falls, Minn. Jeff Stumb, publisher of *The Brewton Standard*, became publisher in Waxahachie.

Cody Hall Jr. retires from *Anniston Star* in 1992

An editor who influenced the lives of hundreds of reporters, Cody Hall Jr., retired in 1992 after working at *The Anniston Star* for 43 years. At last count, 358 staffers had started work at *The Star* during the years Hall worked there. Hall retired as

S I D E L I G H T S
MARKING 125 YEARS OF HISTORY

Alice Harvey retires after 28 years at **Gleam**

Alice Harvey retired in 1973 after working 28 years at *The Advertiser-Gleam* in Guntersville. "Make that 32 years if you count the years she got up at 4 a.m. every Thursday morning to cook the flour paste for the mailing labels," a story in *The Advertiser-Gleam* noted.

The story also pointed out that Mrs. Harvey's title was circulation manager, but her job included writing news, taking ads, making out tax reports and handling the payroll.

Mrs. Harvey's husband, Porter, was publisher of *The Advertiser-Gleam* and an APA past president.

editor-in-chief, but said he would continue to offer his services as editor of the Sunday book page. He also continued to write his popular column for the Saturday edition. Hall, 69, said he was "well beyond the minimum retirement age."

Publisher and editor Brandt Ayers said, "Generations of journalists all over the country who began their careers here remember *The Star* not as an institution but as a person, Cody Hall — a teacher, a friend and elder brother. I will always think of him that way." Hall was the son of the late E. Cody Hall Sr., who was editor of *The Alexander City Outlook.* Cody Hall Jr. said he spent his boyhood in the backshop of the Alexander City paper. Joe Distelheim, executive editor of *The Star* since July 1990, moved up as the chief operating officer.

1993

Sam Harvey, *The Advertiser-Gleam,* Guntersville
1993-1994 president

122nd annual press convention, Huntsville
Feb. 19-21, 1993
Summer convention, Perdido Beach
July 16-18, 1993

The 1993 winter convention was Feb. 19-21 at the Huntsville Marriott.

A 30-minute panel on attracting readers was led by Tom Wright, editor of *The Decatur Daily.* The new president of the National Newspaper Association, Tonda Rush, gave a "state-of-the industry" speech during the Saturday night banquet. On Friday night, delegates attended a reception and dinner at the Space and Rocket Center next door to the Huntsville Marriott.

When Sam Harvey became president of the APA in 1993, he became the third member of his family to head the Press Association — and all were still active in the business in 1993. Harvey, editor of *The Advertiser-Gleam* in Guntersville, was elected at the close of the APA winter convention Feb. 21 in Huntsville. His father, publisher Porter Harvey, was president in 1967-1968. *Advertiser-Gleam* general manager Don Woodward, Sam Harvey's brother-in-law, was president in 1982-1983.

As *The Gleam* reported in a page one story with 14-point headline and a mug shot (the same way any other local person elected president of an organization was treated in the paper), it was the first time in the Press Association's 122-year history that three APA presidents had been working on the same newspaper at the same time. *The Gleam* said

that although Sam Harvey had the title of editor and Porter Harvey had the title of publisher, both were mostly reporters. Woodward, the story said, was in charge of advertising.

Sam Harvey born in Dodge City, Kan.

Sam Harvey, 62, had been editor of *The Gleam* since 1967. He was born in Dodge City, Kan., and grew up in Guntersville. He graduated with a journalism degree from the University of Alabama in 1951. At UA, Harvey was editor of *The Crimson White* after the elected editor was called up during the Korean War. As a youth, Harvey worked as a newspaper delivery boy and worked in the print shop. Feeding the flatbed newspaper press was his main job. After graduating from UA, he spent two years in the Air Force before returning to the University to work on a master's degree.

Harvey worked for 13 years for dailies in Columbus, Ohio, and Louisville, Ky., before returning home to the newspaper his father established in 1941.

During the membership meeting, Linda Breedlove of *The South Alabamian* in Jackson was elected first vice president, and Pat McCauley of *The Huntsville Times* was elected second vice president.

Heavy snow stops, delays presses in March 1993

For the first time in the memory of most publishers, the weather stopped or delayed the presses at several north Alabama newspapers the weekend of March 13-14, 1993. An AP story also reported that some newspapers couldn't deliver papers because of the late season heavy snow — from 12 to 20 inches in a belt from Marengo County into northwest Georgia with high winds blowing drifts up to 6 feet and with temperatures plunging almost to zero. Gale-force winds, glaze ice and snow pulled down thousands of trees and power lines. The storm also delayed delivery for some semi-weeklies and tri-weeklies. Snow was also reported all over the state, from the Gulf

Past presidents gather in 1993

Past presidents attending the Nominations Committee meeting on Friday, Feb. 19, 1993, at the 122nd annual winter convention in Huntsville are, front row from left, Ralph W. Callahan, *The Anniston Star* and *The Daily Home*, Talladega; Jimmy Mills, former editor, the *Birmingham Post-Herald;* J.C. Henderson, former publisher, *The Alexander City Outlook;* Claude Sparks, former publisher, *The Franklin County Times;* Jay Thornton, former publisher, *The Daily Home*, Talladega; Porter Harvey, publisher, *The Advertiser-Gleam*, Guntersville; Steve Stewart, publisher, *The Monroe Journal,* Monroeville; and Marcia Sears, former publisher, *The Shelby County Reporter,* Columbiana.

Back row from left, are Joel P. Smith, editor-publisher, *The Eufaula Tribune;* Don Woodward, general manager, *The Advertiser-Gleam*, Guntersville; Jim Oakley, Jr., former publisher, *The Centreville Press;* Barrett Shelton Jr., publisher, *The Decatur Daily;* Bill Brooks, former managing editor, *The Brewton Standard;* Phil Sanguinetti, president, Consolidated Publishing Co. *(The Anniston Star);* Paul Davis, publisher, *The Auburn Bulletin;* Mike Breedlove, publisher, *The South Alabamian,* Jackson; Luke Slaton, president, *The Moulton Advertiser;* and Jim Jacobson, editor, *The Birmingham News.*

Coast, with two inches in Mobile, all the way to the Tennessee line. Even Selma, Dothan and Montgomery, whose residents might see snow every three or four years, had two to four inches of snow. In southwest Alabama, Marengo County, the snowfall exceeded 12 inches.

The Anniston Star canceled its Sunday paper after being unable to deliver the Saturday paper. It was the first time the paper had missed an edition since another snowstorm in 1961. *The Star* published a special Sunday-Monday snow edition. The special edition flag was a photo of its snow-covered nameplate on *The Star* building.

Post office unable to deliver *Sand Mountain Reporter*

The Sand Mountain Reporter's edition on Friday, March 12, 1993, was printed, but the post office couldn't deliver it until Tuesday. Publisher Mike Hudgins said that *The Reporter's* news and advertising staff put together their Monday paper, but the press crew couldn't get in to print it.

Henry Jackson, publisher of *The Cleburne News* in Heflin, said he got stuck in a 35-mile traffic jam on Interstate 20 while trying to deliver a shopper to nearby Tallapoosa, Ga.

At *The Daily Home* in Talladega, general manager Ed Fowler said he canceled the Monday paper because it was still too dangerous for employees to get to work and for carriers to deliver the papers. At *The Gadsden Times*, the staff got out a Saturday paper and stacked it in the press room. Only a few thousand issues of the Sunday paper made it to racks.

The Birmingham News was printed Saturday and Sunday, but carriers couldn't deliver them. Carriers delivered back issues of *The News* and the *Birmingham Post-Herald* on Tuesday to many subscribers. In Selma, publisher Mike Pippin said the snow forced them to publish the Sunday paper earlier so they could get it out before the roads iced over again Saturday night.

AP's Hoyt Harwell retires in 1993

Hoyt Harwell, Associated Press correspondent since 1966, retired in March 1993. Harwell, who had been with the AP for 41 years, started in Birmingham when he was a student at Howard College, now Samford University. He also worked for the AP in Mobile, as well as in Atlanta. In 1988, Harwell found himself in the middle of a national news story in Tuscaloosa, where a gunman held students hostage at a school. The gunman demanded that an AP reporter listen to his complaints in exchange for releasing some of the students. Harwell went into the school to listen to the gunman's complaints and, eventually, all of the students were released unharmed.

Harwell said he planned to do some freelance writing and to teach journalism in the Birmingham area.

Alabama Journal merges with Advertiser

The Alabama Journal executive editor Bill Brown said he went in early on Friday, April 16, 1993, to see the last issue printed with the headline, "Thanks for the Memories." The final issue reproduced a photograph of newsroom staff members taken when they learned they won the Pulitzer Prize in 1988. *The Alabama Journal,* Montgomery's 104-year-old, Pulitzer Prize-winning afternoon daily, merged with its sister morning publication, *The Montgomery Advertiser,* on April 19, 1993.

On Monday, April 19, the first day without an afternoon paper, Brown said he missed looking over first copies brought up from the newsroom. Publisher Richard H. (Dick) Amberg Jr. said the merger reflected national trends to strong morning newspapers. *The Journal's* circulation had withered to about 11,800, and it was distributed almost exclusively in the Montgomery area. *The Advertiser* had seen its circulation grow to about 59,000 with readership extending from Clanton down into the Florida Panhandle.

The combined newspaper was called *Montgomery Advertiser,* or more completely, *"Montgomery Advertiser Incorporating The Alabama Journal."* The

incorporated newspaper reflected not only most features of both newspapers, but many new ones as well, Amberg said.

Long-time political commentator Bob Ingram returned to *The Montgomery Advertiser* as a regular columnist. Ingram, formerly with *The Advertiser, Alabama* magazine, and successively with state government as finance director in the Albert Brewer Administration, and most recently as editorial director of WSFA-TV, began writing a regular political column. Editor Bill Brown said Ingram would provide a strong sense of history to the newsroom. Bob Ingram's son, Ragan Ingram, began writing a daily man-about-town column, somewhat like the casual columns that Joe Azbell once wrote in *The Montgomery Independent.*

Sound-off columns become trend in 1993

The Advertiser also became the sixth Alabama newspaper to offer an anonymous phone-in response column, "Soapbox." The "Sound-Off" type columns were started first at *The Mobile Press Register* and *The Arab Tribune.* The phone-in response columns became a trend among Alabama newspapers in 1993. *The Choctaw Advocate* got more than 100 phone calls for its first "Sound Off" column. Editor Tommy Campbell said *The Advocate* staff got the idea from the nearby *Clarke County Democrat* in Grove Hill, which started a column a couple of weeks after the program was discussed at the APA winter convention.

The Sand Mountain Reporter in Albertville began running a response column, and two more papers, *The Selma Times-Journal* and *The Monroe Journal* in Monroeville, advertised plans to start the columns. Publisher Jim Cox of *The Clarke County Democrat* said he was proud that his "Sound Off" column had allowed some people to offer legitimate criticism when they couldn't do it publicly without fear of, say, being fired.

Auburn's Mickey Logue retires in 1993

Journalism professor Mickey Logue, who taught at Auburn University for 29 years, announced that he would retire July 1, 1993. Logue, a veteran newspaper man who came to Auburn to teach in the Department of Journalism and serve as faculty adviser of *The Auburn Plainsman* student newspaper, was known for his teaching skills and for developing Auburn's respected internship program. Before joining the Auburn faculty, Logue was a reporter at *The Montgomery Advertiser* from

---

S I D E L I G H T S
Marking 125 Years of History

Publication of Frisco City Sun *suspended*

Bill Stewart, publisher of *The Monroe Journal* in Monroeville, reported that publication of *The Frisco City Sun* had been suspended Sept. 1, 1951, "simply for a lack of sufficient advertising."

The Sun had begun publication June 6, 1950.

1954 to 1955, sportswriter and assistant sports editor of *The Atlanta Constitution* from 1955 to 1960, publications editor for TCI steel in Birmingham in 1960, and reporter for *The Birmingham News* from 1962 to 1964.

Retired journalism professor Paul C. Burnett, who headed the Auburn University journalism program when Logue came to Auburn as adviser of *The Auburn Plainsman*, said the weekly newspaper won the Pacemaker award so many times after Logue became adviser that one of the Associated Collegiate Press officials said *The Plainsman's* nameplate would be engraved on an award before the judging began. Neil O. Davis, retired editor and publisher of *The Auburn Bulletin*, said, "Mickey represents the best and finest in character, personality and professionalism that is in the Auburn journalism department."

Tri-City Ledger mails bills with Elvis stamps

The Tri-City Ledger in Flomaton caused a stir in town when it mailed its monthly bills with Elvis Presley stamps. "Everybody in town was talking about it," said editor Joe Thomas, who thought of the idea. "Some people even came in to buy a classified ad so they would get a bill next month." Thomas said they asked the local postmaster to set aside 400 Elvis stamps in the local post office's second shipment.

An April Fools' Day edition of *The Clarke County Democrat* in 1993 got more comment than the paper's regular news, said editor and publisher Jim Cox.

Cox said he had fun making up the seven front-page stories, and he wrote them in about an hour. The lead story detailed plans to construct a six-lane expressway through the county, how to raise armadillos and dandelions for extra income, and renaming of nearby Thomasville as Waltonville in honor of the successful new Walmart there.

Montgomery Advertiser publishes "Extra" edition

The Montgomery Advertiser staff was quick to respond on April 22, 1993, when former Gov. Guy Hunt was found guilty of ethics charges. Within minutes of the verdict at 9:45 a.m., *Advertiser* executives made the decision to put out the first "Extra" since the death of Alabama Coach Paul (Bear) Bryant in 1983.

Although timing was off-cycle for the morning *Advertiser*, executive editor Bill Brown assembled a team of editors and reporters to write stories and analysis pieces and to conduct man-on-the-street interviews. What emerged was a 10-page "Extra" of fresh copy with "Hunt Guilty" bannered across the front page in what was thought to be the largest type in the paper's history. Even on short notice, the retail ad staff brought in ads from about 25 advertisers. At 2 p.m., the first copies left the building for newsstands in the three-county area, and a hurriedly formed team of eight hawkers took up station near the Capitol complex and at other major office buildings. Within a few hours, they sold 8,000 copies and were asking for more.

Rep. June Bugg, 73, the legislator who led the fight in the 1980s and 1990s for stronger open meetings, died May 18, 1993. Mrs. Bugg sponsored several bills to strengthen the state open meetings law, including two that passed the House of Representatives — bills that died in the Senate. *Birmingham News* staff writer Dave White wrote in a commentary about her death that Mrs. Bugg, of Gadsden, fought year after year to strengthen the state's open meetings law.

More page 1 ads in newspapers in 1993

More ads were showing up in newspapers on the front page in 1993, a trend that design experts said was expected to increase. Mario Garcia, director of design and graphics at the Poynter Institute in St. Petersburg, Fla., said the 1990s would bring an increase in front page ads. Tradition held that page one ads took away from news content, but proponents said readers were just as concerned with ads as they were with news. In Alabama, *The Lee County Bulletin* in Auburn sold "sticker" ads on the flag. Publisher Paul R. Davis called them "bullets" and sold them for $275 each. *The Advertiser-Gleam* in Guntersville had been selling small ads across the bottom of the front page for years.

Front-page space in *The Gleam* cost almost three times the regular rate. A number of Alabama newspapers sold "ears" beside the front-page flag at a premium rate.

Johnson: *Monroe Journal* best weekly in state

Syndicated columnist Rheta Grimsley Johnson described in a column seeing her old bosses, Steve and Patrice Stewart of *The Monroe Journal,* at a Mobile gathering in 1993. She called *The Journal* Alabama's best weekly newspaper. "I worked for the Stewarts for one year and got, as reporters do, an immersion course in their beloved Monroe County," Johnson wrote. "In Monroeville, I learned the importance of the first cotton bloom, bluegrass tunes from generous fiddler George Frye, and how to fashion a wedding write-up that would please even the mother of the bride." Monroeville was already on her mind, Johnson wrote, when she saw publicity-shy Nell Harper Lee at the University of Alabama a week earlier at a celebration marking 100 years since the University admitted women. Miss Lee, a native of Monroeville, won the Pulitzer Prize for "To Kill a Mockingbird," which Johnson called the "finest, certainly the most gentle, song of the South ever written."

The Arab Tribune picked best large weekly in state

For *Arab Tribune* publisher Ed Reed, being picked the best large weekly in the state in 1993 was "icing on the cake." It was the first time *The Tribune* had ranked so high. "Next time you wrap your fish in a copy of *The Arab Tribune,* you can do so with the assurance that you are using the very best newspaper wrapping available in Alabama," was the lead in the story announcing *The Tribune's* contest showing.

The 1993 summer convention July 16-18 at the Perdido Beach Hilton featured a new "Editors and Publishers Bright Idea Roundtable" during the Sunday morning breakfast. Syndicated columnist Cynthia Tucker, editorial page editor of *The Atlanta Constitution* and a native of Monroe County, spoke at the Saturday night banquet. Gov. Jim Folsom Jr. spoke at the Saturday luncheon.

Porter Harvey, 90, bungee jumps

Advertiser-Gleam publisher Porter Harvey of Guntersville, who celebrated his 90th birthday in May 1993, made national news that summer — for bungee jumping. Jumping from a 176-foot tower with an elastic cord attached to his back merely ranked as the latest adventure in 1993 for

Harvey, a past APA president. All the television accounts and national wire accounts of Harvey's bungee-jumping adventure missed that point.

Harvey had challenged other family members to join him in Chattanooga Aug. 28, 1993, and 30 members of the family came. They represented four generations and came from six states. Of the group, 16 jumped, and five more rode the bungee launch, where a stretched elastic cord propelled the rider into the air from the ground.

Other family members who jumped included Harvey's son, *Advertiser-Gleam* editor Sam Harvey (1993 APA president), and grandson Craig Woodward (a past APA advertising manager). Sam Harvey's sister, Mary Woodward, wife of *Advertiser-Gleam* general manager Don Woodward (another APA past president) rode the bungee launch. Don Woodward said there was a reason why he didn't bungee jump.

Woodward: "Someone had to say behind"

"Someone had to stay behind to look after the estate," Woodward said.

Porter Harvey said he was surprised by all the attention and the national news coverage. "It never occurred to him it would land him in the news across the U.S.," a story in *The Gleam* said. Cable News Network showed Harvey bungee jumping during hourly newscasts on Sunday after the jump, and Sam and Porter Harvey were interviewed on NBC's "Today" show.

Fifteen or 20 radio station announcers from New York to California called Porter Harvey the Monday after the jump "He couldn't get his obituaries checked out (Monday morning) for all the phone calls," Sam Harvey said. *(The Gleam* was known for its detailed obituaries).

AP photo of Harvey published around the world

AP carried *The Huntsville Times'* photograph by Dave Dieter of Harvey bouncing at the end of the cord. The photograph was published around the world. *The Times* sent a reporter and photographer, as did newspapers in Chattanooga.

Sam Harvey told Katie Couric of the NBC "Today" show that his father's risk-taking began at an early age and continued when he came to Guntersville in 1941 to start a weekly newspaper. Porter Harvey turned down a trip to New York to appear on the morning television show.

Friends said that the television news segments that showed him falling and bouncing several times missed the main story. True, it was a television event — visual. But they did miss the larger story, a story that a reporter making a phone call and asking a few questions could have developed. None of the news accounts told about Harvey's electrical engi-

neering degree from Emory University or his year at Harvard. Or his early days as a reporter for dailies in New York, Nashville and Indianapolis and his nine years at a daily in Dodge City, Kan., where he met his wife, Alice.

Harvey had other adventures

Reporters didn't tell readers about Harvey's three long-distance multi-day rides down the Tennessee River to the Mississippi River in a 12-foot fishing boat or about his climbing up on Tennessee River bridge support structures high above the river in Guntersville to get a better photograph of a wedding. Reporters also didn't tell about the two family trips he organized to raft down the Ocoee River in southeast Tennessee. And they didn't mention Harvey's determination to work hard, to push himself all his life. They didn't talk about the exercises he did to keep his strength.

A leg weakened by polio never slowed Harvey down. "He learned young not to let it bother him," Sam Harvey said. "He grew up thinking he would do things other kids would do." Before planning the bungee jump, Porter said he studied the odds of serious injury and decided he could survive it. The only side effects, he said, were some leg pains the next few days.

His next adventure might be hang-gliding, he said. Meanwhile, he would go on working almost full time at *The Advertiser-Gleam* as the oldest newspaper executive in Alabama and one of the oldest in the nation.

Advertiser-Gleam publisher Porter Harvey celebrates his 90th birthday in 1993 by making national news — bungee-jumping. It merely ranked in 1993 as the latest adventure for Harvey, an APA past president. (Photograph courtesy of Dave Dieter, *The Huntsville Times*)

The story about Harvey's jump and photographs made the front page of the Sunday, Aug. 29, 1993, edition of *The Huntsville Times.* It made a section front in *The Birmingham News* on Monday, Aug. 30, 1993.

It made the last page of *The Advertiser-Gleam* on Sept. 1, 1993.

Mobile Beacon inspiration to other papers

It's hard enough to publish a newspaper anywhere, but the challenges experienced during *The Mobile Beacon's* 50 years of service to the black community stood as inspiration to all newspapers in 1993. "Many obstacles faced the newspaper from the beginning," wrote *Beacon* editor Cleretta Thomas Blackmon. "There have been numerous threats for publishing 'news facts' that were untold."

The paper and its staff faced mobs, fires, hurricanes "and, of course, less revenue, but we never missed an issue," Mrs. Blackmon said. "That in itself is outstanding history." Mrs. Blackmon wrote the introduction, "50 Years of History Celebrated Inside," in a special anniversary edition published in the summer of 1993. The special issue featured personal glimpses by Mrs. Blackmon and other staff members, including publisher Lancie Thomas. It also featured articles on local leaders, and it reprinted stories and pages from the past.

Beacon was founded in Tuscaloosa

The Mobile Beacon was founded first in Tuscaloosa as *The Alabama Citizen* by Mrs. Blackmon's father, the late Frank P. Thomas Jr. and Mrs. Thomas.

Frank Thomas
The Mobile Beacon

Thomas' newspaper work began at age 8 when he began delivering the *Birmingham Post-Herald,* not just as a newsboy, but as a district agent. He had a profitable route for himself and supervised two other carriers. During high school in Tuscaloosa, Thomas not only was editor of the student newspaper, but he also was a correspondent for *The Atlanta Daily World* and *The Birmingham World.* He became editor of *The Tuscaloosa World* in 1943.

Thomas forced to leave Tuscaloosa

But the threat of mob violence forced Thomas to leave Tuscaloosa while he was in college. *The World* had written stories about the shooting of three young black men accused of raping a white woman. Sheriff's deputies allegedly shot them, and one survived. Thomas and an associate, Robert Mallard, were convinced the three were innocent, and they tried to use their newspaper to see that justice was done in the case.

Local racists mounted an attack on the newspaper and its staff, but they escaped injury. Mallard was the victim of a lynch mob in Georgia several years later, a story in *The Beacon* reported.

Thomas continued his newspaper work while attending Alabama State University. He worked on the staff of ASU's student newspaper staff and *The Montgomery World.* After his service in the Navy in World War II, he returned to Tuscaloosa to launch *The Alabama Citizen* with a $150 bank loan that he and Mrs. Thomas borrowed. Soon he expanded the newspaper to cover Alabama's western Black Belt, and he opened another office in Selma.

When Thomas went to Lincoln University to study journalism and to the Mergenthaler Linotype School in New York, Mrs. Thomas managed the newspaper. Before Thomas left to join the Navy, he had started a newspaper in Mobile, *The Mobile Weekly Review.* That was the Thomases' first business venture in Mobile.

Thomases started *Mobile Beacon* in 1954

The Thomases started another weekly in Mobile, *The Beacon,* in 1954, and for more than a year they commuted between Tuscaloosa and Mobile, publishing both *The Citizen* and *The Beacon.* The two papers were combined in 1964.

In 1956, when Autherine Lucy registered as the first black student at the University of Alabama, Mrs. Thomas and another staff member were there to be with her. Thomas was in Mobile while Mrs. Thomas was in Tuscaloosa. Each day, Miss Lucy ate lunch at *The Citizen* office with some friends. Whites threatened to burn the building and attack Miss Lucy and the staff. When a mob marched on *The Citizen's* office, they found it protected by several hundred blacks, who turned them back.

S I D E L I G H T S
MARKING 125 YEARS OF HISTORY

City editor John Williams dies in 1983

John B. Williams, 57, city editor of *The Montgomery Advertiser* since 1968, died Feb. 9, 1983, at a local hospital where he was undergoing treatment for cancer.

A native of Montgomery, Williams later moved to Kansas and took his first newspaper job with *The Topeka Daily Capital*. He later became editorial page editor of *The Topeka State Journal*. Williams returned to Montgomery, joining *The Advertiser* in 1962 as a state desk reporter, eventually becoming city editor.

"He was a professional to all of those who worked with him," said publisher H. Doyle Harvill. "He knew quality journalism when he saw it in his people and his peers and he responded positively."

Williams once told a reporter that his father, who was an agent for the Louisville and Nashville Railroad, had always wanted to be a newspaper reporter himself, but was unable to pursue his dream when the Depression put college out of reach. Scores of reporters learned the basics of reporting and writing style from what former *Advertiser* city editor and state editor Colin H. (Buster) MacGuire called Williams' "exacting editing."

"John Williams demanded and got the best out of everyone who worked from him," MacGuire said. "Williams' penchant for accuracy and fairness in reporting and writing any story, whether a purse-snatching or a governor's clash with the courts, set the standard which *Advertiser* city desk reporters sought to observe."

Frank Thomas lived to see significant changes in race relations in Tuscaloosa and Alabama before he died in 1974. He saw Gov. George C. Wallace crown a black homecoming queen at the University of Alabama.

Thomas inducted into Hall of Honor in 1983

Thomas was inducted into the Newspaper Hall of Honor in 1983, and the National Newspaper Publishers Association enshrined him in the Gallery of Distinguished Newspaper Publishers in 1988. NNPA was the national organization of black community newspapers.

Mrs. Thomas, 76, a past member of the APA board of directors, and Mrs. Blackmon was a member of the APA board and past president of the ANAS board of directors.

Mrs. Thomas attended Tuskegee Institute (now Tuskegee University) and Alabama State University, where she received a degree in home economics. In Mobile, she and her husband spent what little time they had away from work starting and supporting a Presbyterian church to serve the black community. In 1993, the newspaper was still a family enterprise with Mrs. Thomas as publisher and Mrs. Blackmon as editor. Mrs. Thomas' grandson, Hjordis Blackmon, was production manager, and granddaughter Merina Blackmon was on the staff.

Mrs. Blackmon grew up working at the newspaper. She majored in business and minored in journalism at Wayne State University in Detroit before returning home to Mobile. In a story about Mrs. Thomas reprinted in a special edition of *The Monroe Journal*, Mrs. Thomas said *The Beacon's* purpose had been "to serve the black communities and make better relationships between the races and let everybody have an opportunity to express their opinions and their ideas, which they were not able to do in the white papers." Mrs. Thomas grew up in Beatrice, near Monroeville. In addition to publishing the special edition, *The Beacon* staff and local leaders celebrated the paper's anniversary with a banquet.

Mobile Press Register tells news of Amtrak accident

The Mobile Press Register's reporters, photographers and editors played a major role in telling news to the world about the tragic Amtrak accident Sept. 22, 1993. Editor Stan Tiner called the staff's response "their finest effort," an effort that even included the paper's first "Extra" edition since 1945. "The story was to be told in words and pictures and as comprehensively as possible," Tiner wrote in his Sunday column Sept. 26, 1993. Two *Press Register* photographers, Victor Calhoun and Glenn Andrews, became part of the Coast Guard unit at the scene, site of Amtrak's deadliest accident. One hitched a ride to the remote location on the Coast Guard boat, and the other climbed aboard a Coast Guard helicopter.

The paper's government editor, David Holloway, became a field force editor at the Scott Paper Co. plant near the derailment site. The paper's outdoor editor, David Rainer, launched the newspaper's fishing boat at the Mobile Bay causeway, and he and another photographer headed up river to the site. Tiner said readers praised the paper's effort, although some complained about the paper's photograph of a barge where bodies were placed before being taken to a morgue. The photograph, he said, didn't show any closeup shots of the victims' bodies, and most were covered with sheets. "This was clearly a strong photograph," Tiner wrote, "which perhaps told the ultimate price of this tragedy better than any other."

McTeer, Prewitt inducted into Hall of Honor
The long-time managing editor of *The Lee County Bulletin* in Auburn, Graham M. McTeer, was known for dealing in facts, for dealing objectively and fairly. Perkins J. Prewitt, whose versatile career took him to several points across the South, including *The Mobile Register* and *The Birmingham News*, even published his own newspaper aimed at young

people. Both were inducted into the Alabama Newspaper Hall of Honor Oct. 9, 1993, in annual ceremonies at Auburn University's Ralph B. Draughon Library.

Perkins J. Prewitt
The Mobile Register
The Birmingham News

APA to purchase its own building
AlaPressa reported in its October 1993 issue that the APA office might move to its own building in 1994, "if the right building at the right price goes on the market." The APA and ANAS Executive Committees, meeting with the building-facilities committee, agreed in principal that APA should buy its own building. The vote was unanimous. Committee members said the building should contain about 3,000 square feet of space. In addition, it should contain a multi-purpose room large enough for board and committee meetings, advertising presentations, and small workshops. APA accountant Mike Echols said the Press Association and its affiliates had the resources to pay for and furnish a building. ANAS could be the primary owner, and in years when earnings from ANAS's ad placements were large enough, a loan could be paid down early, he said.

Since June 1987, APA had occupied an 1,800 square foot office in the Commerce Center in downtown Birmingham, a 14-story office building owned by the Birmingham Chamber of Commerce. APA and ANAS paid $13,200 a year rent in 1993, and a $19 monthly parking fee for each of the office's five full-time employees and one part-time employee.

The Press Association moved from Tuscaloosa to Birmingham in 1987 to be located in the financial and business center of the state.

UA, AU campus papers celebrate anniversaries
At the University of Alabama, former *Crimson White* staffers, including novelist Gay Talese and journalists from across the country, gathered for a three-day meeting at homecoming. At Auburn University, *Plainsman* staffers prepared a 100th anniversary edition, with interviews with former editors and stories about changes in campus life.

The Auburn Plainsman started as *The Orange and Blue* during the 1893-1894 school year. *The Plainsman* anniversary edition included columns by former staffers Neil O. Davis, editor in 1934, who retired as publisher of *The Lee County Bulletin;* Bob Ingram, sports editor in 1947 and columnist for *The Mont-*

gomery *Advertiser;* Jerry E. Brown, editor in 1966-1967 and head of the Auburn journalism department; and Rheta Grimsley Johnson, editor in 1974-1975 and a syndicated columnist. Jack Simms, *Plainsman* editor in 1948-1949, the only *Plainsman* editor fired, was the focus of a staff story. Simms retired in 1992 as head of the journalism department.

Former staffers of *The Crimson White* who attended a homecoming program at the University of Alabama included Talese; Sam Harvey, editor of *The Advertiser-Gleam* in Guntersville and 1993-1994 APA president; author Rick McCammon of Birmingham; *Mobile Press Register* associate editor Bailey Thomson; *Birmingham News* editorial page editor Ron Casey; 1953-1954 APA president Bill Brooks Jr.; *Birmingham News* editor James E. Jacobson, 1989-1990 APA president; *Mobile Press Register* assistant managing editor for sports John Cameron; (Ozark) *Southern Star* publisher Joe Adams; *Atmore Advance* publisher Michele Cox Gerlach; and *Huntsville Times* managing editor Bob Ward.

Flomaton man arrested for stealing papers

A Flomaton man was arrested in October 1993 for stealing 14 copies of *The Tri-City Ledger* from a news rack at a fast food restaurant. Publisher Bo Bolton told police that the rack had come up short on money several times. The arrested man had been taking several copies and paying only 50 cents. The man apparently had been stealing them as revenge for something it had printed. Bolton and the police chief waited in Bolton's car to observe the rack, and they saw the man deposit 50 cents and take the copies of the paper.

1994
Linda Hayes Breedlove, *The South Alabamian,* Jackson
1994-1995 president

123rd annual press convention, Mobile
Feb. 25-27, 1994
Summer convention, Perdido Beach
July 22-24, 1994

Publishers and editors heard about the latest trends in newspaper ties to electronic information delivery during the 123rd annual APA convention at the Adam's Mark Hotel in Mobile Feb. 25-27, 1994.

Speakers discussed how newspapers would be affected by the changes in the information selling business, especially selling information by tele-phone. A gubernatorial candidates' forum was held on Saturday morning.

New National Newspaper Association president Sam Griffin of *The Post-Searchlight* in Bainbridge, Ga., was the Friday night banquet speaker. On Saturday night, delegates attended a reception at historic Fort Conde and then attended an all-you-can-eat seafood buffet at Roussos Restaurant. Later that night, delegates toured the new Mobile Convention Center. On Thursday night before the convention, delegates attended an optional pre-convention bus trip to a casino in Biloxi, Miss.

Linda H. Breedlove elected APA president

The associate publisher of *The South Alabamian* in Jackson, Linda H. Breedlove, became the second woman to be elected president of the APA in 1994. She was elected to a one-year term during the 123rd annual convention in Mobile, succeeding Sam Harvey, editor of *The Advertiser-Gleam* in Guntersville.

The first woman to serve as president of APA was Marcia M. Sears, former publisher of *The Shelby County Reporter.* Mrs. Sears was president in 1981-1982. Other new officers included Doug Pearson, publisher and editor of *The Daily Mountain Eagle* in Jasper, first vice president; Mike Kelley, publisher and editor of *The Clanton Advertiser,* second vice president; and Harvey, chairman of the board.

APA's new president, Linda Breedlove, took the same career path that many women took in the

---

S I D E L I G H T S
MARKING 125 YEARS OF HISTORY

Ed Blair: "Aegis" means "a period of time"
Publisher and editor Edmund R. (Ed) Blair of *The St. Clair News-Aegis* gave an explanation in 1955 for the name of his paper.

"Aegis," said Blair, means "a period of time." And in older dictionaries, he added, there was another meaning given the word: "A shield, or protection." Blair said he suspected the latter meaning was what printer George R. Cather meant when he founded the newspaper back in Reconstruction days of 1873. "Either meaning honors a weekly, or any other newspaper," Blair wrote.

"Aegis is pronounced 'E-gis'."

newspaper business. Moreover, with her steady career climb, she often found herself the only woman or the first woman in many leadership roles. She began as an office manager at *The Prattville Progress* in 1966. Like other office managers, she not only took classified ads, sold subscriptions and did everything else that a front office staffer does at small newspapers, but she also wrote social news and became a photographer for the newspaper.

Her responsibilities grew.

Mrs. Breedlove began working at newspapers before her husband, Mike, did. Mike Breedlove's newspaper career began in advertising sales at *The Montgomery Advertiser*, after he decided not to take an out-of-state job transfer. He later joined Linda at *The Progress*. There he sold ads and covered sports. Both continued to develop their writing and editing skills and their business skills. They worked as a team.

Breedloves moved to Fairhope in 1971

In 1971, Mike and Linda Breedlove moved to Fairhope to manage *The Eastern Shore Courier*. Linda worked as bookkeeper and wrote features and church news. Mike was the editor and publisher. In 1974, they made their move to Jackson, when they bought *The South Alabamian* from J. Fred Nall Sr. At *The South Alabamian*, the Breedloves produced a prize-winning weekly paper, and they became deeply involved in the community life of the Clarke County town. They not only became local opinion leaders, they became community leaders.

Mrs. Breedlove was often the first or only woman in certain jobs. She was the first woman to be elected president of the local Chamber of Commerce, and she was the only woman on the board of directors of a local bank in 1994. She was also past president of the Woman's Club, member of the administrative board of the First United Methodist Church, and president of the Pine City Community Concert Association. In 1991, the local Civitan Club named her Jackson's Citizen of the Year.

APA considers purchase of building in Homewood

AlaPressa reported in its January 1994 issue that if inspections, legal reviews and other details went as expected, the APA Journalism Foundation would soon own a 22-year-old building in Homewood. The APA/ANAS staff would rent the second floor of the 5,100 square foot building on U.S. 31 from the Journalism Foundation, and a real estate company would rent the first floor.

"Grover" opens at Shakespeare Festival

"Grover," a fictionalized look at a few tense days in the life of Pulitzer Prize-winning editor Grover C. Hall Sr., editor of *The Montgomery Advertiser*, opened in 1994 at the Alabama Shakespeare Festival in Montgomery. The play, by Randy Hall, assistant news editor of *The Anniston Star*, took place during 1926, when Hall's editorials opposing the Ku Klux Klan appeared — editorials that won him the Pulitzer Prize. Randy Hall was great nephew of Grover Hall. The actor who played Hall in the production was Stuart Culpepper, a former newspaper man. Culpepper even worked for Grover C. Hall Jr. when Hall was editor of *The Montgomery Advertiser*.

Culpepper covered the civil rights movement and was nominated for a Pulitzer Prize himself. As a cub reporter, he covered Martin Luther King's first speech as a civil rights leader, in Tuskegee during the downtown merchants boycott. Culpepper himself was later run out of Montgomery by Klan elements and started writing about entertainment and theatre for *The Atlanta Constitution*, moving eventually into acting.

S I D E L I G H T S
MARKING 125 YEARS OF HISTORY

Page of **Democratic Watchtower** *reproduced*

Readers of *The Talladega News* were given a rare treat in the summer of 1952 when publisher Cecil H. Hornady reproduced a page from a 108-year-old newspaper published in Talladega June 12, 1844.

For many years the musty, discolored and faded publication had been kept in a safety deposit box at a local bank. Called *The Democratic Watchtower*, the newspaper was published every Wednesday by J.J. Woodward and Company, a firm operated by John J. Woodward and James G.L. Huey.

The slogan of the newspaper was "Principles — Not Men." Apparently the newspaper was founded in 1839 since the nameplate carried the inscription, Volume V, Number 18.

The old issue of the newspaper had been kept in the family of the late Maj. G.A. Joiner, who owned and operated *The Democratic Watchtower* in the 1850s.

Past presidents gather in 1994

Attending the past president's luncheon on Feb. 25, 1994, at the 123rd annual winter convention in Mobile are, seated from left, W.E. (Gene) Hardin, *The Greenville Advocate*; Barrett C. Shelton Jr., *The Decatur Daily*; Jimmy Mills, retired editor, the *Birmingham Post-Herald*; Marcia Sears, former publisher, *The Shelby County Reporter*, Columbiana; Ralph W. Callahan, *The Anniston Star* and *The Daily Home*, Talladega; J.C. Henderson, retired publisher, *The Alexander City Outlook*; Mike Breedlove, publisher, *The South Alabamian*, Jackson; and Steve Stewart, publisher, *The Monroe Journal*, Monroeville.

Standing from left, are Joel P. Smith, *The Eufaula Tribune*; Don Woodward, general manager, *The Advertiser-Gleam*, Guntersville; Jim Oakley, former publisher, *The Centreville Press*; Jimmy Faulkner, former publisher, *The Baldwin Times*, Bay Minette; Bob Bryan, president, Bryan Publications, Cullman; Bill Brooks, former managing editor, *The Brewton Standard*; E.R. (Bob) Morrissette Jr., former publisher, *The Atmore Advance*; Luke Slaton, publisher, *The Moulton Advertiser*; Charles Land, publisher, *The Tuscaloosa News*; and Jim Jacobson, editor, *The Birmingham News*.

Birmingham Joint Operating Agreement amended

Managers at *The Birmingham News* and the *Birmingham Post-Herald* surprised readers when they announced Feb. 24, 1994, that they had amended their Joint Operating Agreement to postpone the swap in publishing cycles. The change had been scheduled for Jan. 1, 1995. "A change in publishing cycles would not be in the best interest of the community or of the newspapers at this time," said *News* publisher Victor Hanson II.

The Birmingham News, the state's largest daily with almost 179,000 circulation weekdays and 230,000 on Sunday, would have switched its weekday publication cycle from afternoon to morning. The *Birmingham Post-Herald* would have become the city's afternoon paper. The switch would have forced publishers at some other afternoon dailies in north Alabama to consider shifting to mornings, industry observers had speculated.

Morning dailies around the nation were usually the largest newspapers except in Birmingham and a few other markets. Circulation at Birmingham's morning paper, the *Post-Herald*, had been slowly increasing since the mid-1980s, from about 61,000 in 1986 to almost 64,000 in 1994.

The two Birmingham dailies were separately owned and editorially independent newspapers. *The News* was a Newhouse newspaper, and the *Post-Herald* was owned by Scripps Howard. The Birmingham News Co. acted as business agent for both papers, selling advertising and managing circulation for both. The papers had operated under the Joint Operating Agreement since 1950. The

congressionally approved agreements were enacted to preserve two separately owned daily newspapers in a number of cities, including Birmingham.

Documentary aired on Buford Boone

When Buford Boone, publisher of *The Tuscaloosa News*, won the Pulitzer Prize for editorial writing in 1957, he didn't dare tell anyone about one of his congratulatory letters. "Ever since I read your editorial, I have had an unspeakable admiration for you," it read. "The moral courage and profound dignity you have evidenced in so many situations will be long remembered."

The letter was from Martin Luther King Jr.

And while Buford Boone knew it was futile to resist integration, most people in Tuscaloosa — his readers, advertisers and neighbors — were ready to fight. A documentary on Alabama Public Television which aired March 3, 1994, told how Boone made a courageous stand for an unpopular cause, the integration of the University of Alabama. "A Voice of Justice and Reason: Buford Boone's *Tuscaloosa News*," focused on Boone and his reaction to the unsuccessful attempt to integrate the University in 1956, two years after Brown vs. the Board of Education, the Supreme Court ruling that outlawed racial segregation in public schools.

Autherine Lucy first black to register at UA in 1956

In 1956, Autherine Lucy became the first black student to register at the University of Alabama. The Tuscaloosa campus was the first institution ordered to desegregate after the Brown ruling.

"Grover" opens in 1994 at Shakespeare Festival
    Stuart Culpepper played Grover C. Hall Sr. in the 1994 Alabama Shakespeare Festival production of "Grover," a fictionalized look at a few tense days in the life of the Pulitzer Prize-winning editor of *The Montgomery Advertiser.* Culpepper, a former newspaper man, even worked for Grover C. Hall Jr. at *The Advertiser.* (Photograph by Phil Scarsbrook)

Stevenson said national news organizations from CNN and all the television networks to large metro radio stations to *The New York Times* called him for local background on the issue. *The Randolph Leader's* objective treatment of the controversy was praised, but criticized by some people in nearby Wedowee. After Stevenson wrote an editorial calling for the resignation of the principal, his paper could no longer get news from the school. CNN's Larry King asked Stevenson to appear on his program, but Stevenson declined: "I have a weekly newspaper to put out."

Angry crowds, stirred on by members of the Ku Klux Klan, met Ms. Lucy and pelted her with rocks and eggs. After three days of discord, the UA trustees decided to suspend Ms. Lucy for her own safety. Court-ordered desegregation had been resisted.

Boone was livid that a mob had bullied public officials and had showed more might than those with the Constitution on their side. "What does it mean today at the University of Alabama, and here in Tuscaloosa, to have the law on your side," he wrote. "The answer had to be: Nothing — that is, if the mob disagrees with you and the courts."

His editorial was widely reprinted in the North, and he won the Pulitzer Prize the next year. The APT program showed that Boone kept up his call for equal opportunities for all Americans. He attacked Gov. George C. Wallace, writing that he was the architect of racial violence in the state. The program aired as part of the series, "The Alabama Experience," narrated by E. Culpepper Clark, author of "The Stand in the Schoolhouse Door." *The Anniston Star* and the Ayers family were the focus on "The Alabama Experience" series on May 18, 1994.

Leader headquarters for national media

The Randolph Leader office in Roanoke became official headquarters for national news coverage of the Wedowee High School principal and the controversy tied to his comments about interracial dating by students. Publisher and editor John W.

APA moves to new location on Independence Drive

On Saturday, April 25, 1994, movers loaded boxes and furniture in the old downtown Birmingham office of the APA and moved them to the Press Association's new suburban location on U.S. 31 in Homewood on Independence Drive. The APA staff occupied the second floor of the two-floor building, and a real estate company continued to occupy the first floor.

The move was the culmination of more than six years of on-again, off-again studies about the pros and cons of owning a building. Work on the moving project was coordinated with the APA building committee and approved by the Journalism Foundation board. Committee chairman James H. Denley of the *Birmingham Post-Herald* helped select the building. APA and ANAS pay rent to the Journalism Foundation, as does the first-floor tenant.

APA did not have a permanent office of any kind until 1939, when the University of Alabama offered space. The University also offered to pay half the salary of the Press Association's field manager, Doyle L. Buckles.

The office stayed on campus even after ANAS was established in 1951. APA created ANAS when it established an ad placement service and a clipping service. The office remained on the University campus until 1973, when some newspapers began questioning the newspaper association's ties to an arm of state government.

Permanent home culminates five years of study

The purchase of a permanent home in 1994 culminated about five years of study, first in 1989, again in 1991, and the most recent two-year effort.

In fall 1993, the committee and staff leaned toward constructing a new building about 15 miles southeast of downtown Birmingham on U.S. 280 in Shelby County. The committee had not been able to find a suitable building for sale in southern Jefferson County.

Former APA executive director Steve Bradley said in 1994 that Jim Boone, then publisher of *The Tuscaloosa News,* had suggested the same financial structure almost 20 years earlier — that the Journalism Foundation should own a building and rent space to APA and ANAS. The new APA location included about 1,700 square feet of space for the five full-time and one part-time employees. The office also included a multi-use room large enough to conduct board and committee meetings, contest judgings, and small workshops.

The Birmingham News named Pulitzer finalist

Three years after winning its first Pulitzer Prize, *The Birmingham News* was named a finalist for a 1994 Pulitzer Prize. *The News'* series of editorials on education reform earned it the honor. It was one of three finalists for the editorial award. The series on school reform, published in April 1993, was written by editorial page editor Ron Casey and writers Harold Jackson and Joey Kennedy, the same three who won the 1991 Pulitzer.

Mullins to step down as UA dean

Dr. Ed Mullins, dean of the University of Alabama College of Communication since 1983, announced in 1994 that he would step down effective summer 1995. Mullins said he would stay un-

---

S I D E L I G H T S
Marking 125 Years of History

Wrights profiled in **The Birmingham News**

Tom and Regina Wright of *The Daily Home* in Talladega were profiled in the July 4, 1977, issue of *The Birmingham News*.

"For more than a dozen years, journalists Tom and Regina Wright have been making waves, friends and a top-notch paper in this town of 18,000," *The News* reported in the article headlined "Married to a small newspaper."

"When state Sen. Robert Weaver was accused of financial wrongdoing that led to his conviction and imprisonment on charges of false pretense, it was *The Talladega Daily Home that* first revealed much of the damaging information," *The News* continued.

Though the Wrights were low-key about their roles as crusading journalists, they told *The News* they were proud that their brand of vigorous reporting had brought *The Daily Home* three major community service awards in two years — two from the Alabama Associated Press Association and one from the APA. Tom Wright was managing editor of *The Daily Home,* and Regina Wright was chief investigative reporter.

The News asked the Wrights if they ever considered moving to a larger newspaper in a larger town. "I've thought it would be nice," Wright said. "But we have an awful lot of freedom here, something that's getting rare. For now, we're just working on making *The Daily Home* the best small paper in Alabama."

til the college found a replacement and that he planned to remain on the journalism faculty. Mullins helped oversee major building renovations and improvements after the college moved to the Old Union Building. He also worked to improve the academic profiles of students, cultivated alumni and industry support, and developed a research center and a doctoral program. In addition, all mass communications programs earned national accreditation in 1985 and were reaccredited in 1991.

Brown to head Auburn program

Dr. Jerry E. Brown, who had been acting head of Auburn University's Department of Journalism since the retirement of Jack Simms in 1992, was

named head of the department in 1994. Brown said he wanted the 150 journalism majors at Auburn and their successors to concentrate on the discipline of writing, and writing under deadline pressure. "Fewer of our students want to go into newspapering these days," Brown said, "but we offer a strong foundation in general, clear and concise communication."

Auburn University journalism students began attending classes in the newly renovated Tichenor Hall in fall 1994, moving from the eighth floor of Haley Center, Auburn's main liberal arts classroom building. Brown said the new offices and classrooms would give the department a separate identity. The new space included the Logue Library, which would allow students access to newspapers, a database, television, basic reference books and study tables. The new space also included an office for retired professors Mickey Logue, Jack Simms and Paul Burnett.

Provisional accreditation awarded to AU journalism dept.

Provisional accreditation was awarded to Auburn University's Department of Journalism by the Accrediting Council on Education in Journalism and Mass Communications in 1994. It was the department's first attempt at achieving national accreditation. Department head Dr. Jerry E. Brown said the Department of Journalism would seek full accreditation in 1995 after answering what the visiting team saw as weaknesses: Lack of minority enrollment and faculty, and insufficient involvement in outreach.

Rheta Grimsley Johnson named Atlanta columnist

Syndicated columnist Rheta Grimsley Johnson became the new human interest columnist for *The Atlanta Constitution* in 1994. Mrs. Johnson, who once worked for *The Monroe Journal, The Auburn Bulletin* and *The Opelika-Auburn News,* had been with *The Memphis Commercial Appeal* and Scripps Howard News Service for 14 years. Johnson filled the vacancy left by the death of legendary Southern columnist Lewis Grizzard. "My politics are a 180 degree style from Grizzard's," Johnson wrote. "I don't know how you can write a column from the heart and change your style to suit what paper you're writing for. You just have to write what you feel and what you believe and do the best you can."

Hazel Brannon Smith dies in 1994

Hazel Brannon Smith, 80, former editor and publisher of *The Lexington* (Miss.) *Advertiser,* died

---

S I D E L I G H T S

MARKING 125 YEARS OF HISTORY

Henderson featured in "The Passing Throng"
Alexander City Outlook publisher J.C. Henderson was featured in a 1955 column, "The Passing Throng," in *The Montgomery Advertiser* by Stuart X. Stephenson, *Advertiser* state editor.

"Lean and always hungry for work, the popular publisher of the fine weekly, *The Alexander City Outlook,* has parlayed his publications into something of an empire," Stephenson reported. In 1946 Henderson bought *The Opelika Eagle* and operated it five years until the sale of those holdings to *The Opelika Daily News.*

"Then in sort of a big lump he obtained *The Dadeville Record, The Goodwater Enterprise Chronicle* and *The Camp Hill News,*" the article continued.

"Then he bought *The Chambers County News* at Lanett and continued to snowball his newspapers, taking on *The Chattahoochee Valley Times* and *The West Point News* in 1949. One year later he combined *The Chambers County News, The Valley Times* and *The West Point News* and operated these as *The Valley Daily Times-News,* published in West Point."

Soon after publication of *The Montgomery Advertiser* feature story, Henderson announced the sale of *The Valley Daily Times-News* to Davis Haines.

APA Building Open House in 1994
    APA advertising manager Felicia Mason holds Evan Ryland, age 2 years and 4 months, during the new APA Building Open House in late November 1994. His mother, Julie Ryland, is far left, and APA president Linda Breedlove of *The South Alabamian* is far right with APA classified advertising specialist Leigh Leigh Tortorici. Former APA advertising manager and executive director Mike Ryland died in March 1992 before Evan, his and Julie's first child, was born. APA moved into a building owned by the APA Journalism Foundation in April 1994.

S I D E L I G H T S
MARKING 125 YEARS OF HISTORY

The Graphic *begins publication in 1957*
    The first issue of a new Tuscaloosa newspaper, the weekly *Graphic,* was distributed Sept. 26, 1957. The paper, edited and published by Karl Elebash Jr., was circulated on Thursdays. Associate editor was his wife, Camille Maxwell Elebash.
    Both were Tuscaloosa County natives who graduated from Tuscaloosa High School and the University of Alabama.
    The Alabama Publisher reported that *The Graphic,* a tabloid newspaper, was "printed by the offset process." Elebash, 37, had been on the staff of *South* magazine. Previously he had been a staff writer for *The Wall Street Journal* in New York and editorial writer for *The Mobile Press.*
    Camille Elebash had been on *The New York Times* staff and later was editor of the University of Alabama *Alumni News.*

May 14, 1994. Mrs. Smith, who won the Pulitzer Prize in 1964 for editorials speaking out against racism, was a graduate of the University of Alabama and grew up in Gadsden. She got her start in the newspaper business at *The Etowah Observer* in Alabama City.
    Former Mississippi publisher Hodding Carter III said of Mrs. Smith, "What she did in Holmes County, Mississippi, was the definition of everything American journalism is supposed to be about and usually isn't." Because of her stands against bigotry, her newspaper became the target of an economic boycott, yet she stayed in business another 10 years and continued to speak out against injustice. A television movie, "A Passion for Justice," detailed Mrs. Smith's career shortly before she died.
    The APA 1994 summer convention was July 22-24 at the Perdido Beach Resort at Orange Beach.
    Alabama's first fax-delivered or computer-delivered news package went on line Aug. 1, 1994 as a joint project of some of the state's largest newspapers. *The Alabama Hotline* was a five-day-a-week newsletter sent each morning to subscribers. The eight-page publication was a cooperative effort of *The Birmingham News, The Huntsville Times,* and *The Mobile Press Register.*

APA plans 125th anniversary for 1996

Members of the 125th Anniversary Committee to plan the Press Association's 125th anniversary in 1996 included Ann Sutton Smith, chairman, Ralph W. Callahan, Nonnie Stanley Hardin, Mike Breedlove, Linda Breedlove, Joe Adams, Bertie Gammell Parish, Lancie Thomas, Jim Cox, Barrett C. Shelton Jr., Luke Slaton, Jay Thornton, Nell Metz, J.C. Henderson, Jimmy Mills and Jim Oakley Jr. APA president Linda Hayes Breedlove encouraged other retired and active members of APA to volunteer to serve on the committee.

Hall of Honor ceremony held Nov. 5, 1994

Two Alabama newspaper men, both born in small Black Belt towns, both of whom moved on, one to New York, the other to Washington, D.C. were inducted into the Alabama Newspaper Hall of Honor Nov. 5, 1994.

George Anthony Cornish first smeared ink on his hands working in his father's pressroom at *The Demopolis Times.* While in high school, he worked there at the shop. In high school, he also wrote his first editorials and features for the Marengo County weekly. His father, Edward Seymour Cornish, editor and publisher of *The Times* from 1910 to 1936, was inducted into the Alabama Newspaper Hall of Honor in 1968. Cornish was also the brother of Elizabeth Cornish George, widow of Ben George, who was publisher of *The Times* from 1936 to 1968.

Charles Dobbins
The Montgomery Examiner

Born in Greensboro, Ala., Charles Dobbins was a graduate of Samford University. He received his master's degree from Columbia University and doctorates from Jamestown College and the College of St. Francis. In 1939, he worked as a reporter for the old *Birmingham Age-Herald* and later became editor and publisher of the weekly *Anniston Times.* In 1942, he entered active duty with the U.S. Navy, serving in Chungking and Calcutta before being discharged in 1946 as a lieutenant commander. After World War II, he worked as editor of *The Montgomery Advertiser.* In 1947 he established a new daily newspaper in Montgomery, *The Examiner,* where he served as editor and publisher until the paper closed in 1955. During President Franklin Roosevelt's first administration, Dobbins

served as Alabama director of the Federal Emergency Relief Administration and the National Youth Administration. For three years, he was assistant to the president of Alabama College in Montevallo.

For 17 years, Dobbins was with the American Council on Education in Washington, D.C., 10 years of which he spent as executive secretary. He served as APA president in 1942-1943, executive director of the National Home Library Foundation, director of the Office of Price Stabilization for Alabama, member of the Alabama Board of Education, and trustee of Eckerd, Judson and Alderson Broaddus colleges.

Press-Register featured in AJR

American Journalism Review's November 1994 issue featured a cover story on Newhouse Newspapers and on the group's new emphasis on stronger news coverage in recent years — an emphasis that owners said wasn't new. The article also focused on the dramatic changes at *The Mobile Press Register* that were led by publisher Howard Bronson and editor Stan Tiner over the last two years. The article mentioned *The Press Register's* newly aggressive local news coverage and community involvement as well as its earning both Most Improved and first place in the large daily General Excellence competition in the APA Better Newspaper Contest in 1993.

Dr. Hudson Baggett, 71, editor of *The Alabama Baptist* for 28 years, died Nov. 17, 1994, in Point

Clear. With 123,000 subscribers, *The Alabama Baptist* was the second-largest circulation newspaper in Alabama. *The Alabama Baptist* was a long-time associate member of the APA.

The Greenville Advocate sold to Boone Newspapers

The Greenville Advocate, the oldest newspaper in Alabama owned by the same family, was sold to Boone Newspapers in December 1994. *The Advocate* was founded by the late Gen. James Berney Stanley, one of the founding fathers of APA in 1872. With sale of *The Advocate*, designation of oldest newspaper owned by the same family went to *The Southern Star* in Ozark, where members of the Adams family had published the weekly since 1867.

The Greenville Advocate and all assets used in its publication were sold to a holding company owned by Boone Newspapers, Greenville Newspapers LLC. The new publisher was Todd H. Carpenter, 25, a Tuscaloosa native who had been at *The Andalusia Star-News*, where he was regional circulation manager for the Boone organization.

Sellers of *The Advocate* were heirs of the Glenn Stanley family of Greenville. W.E. (Gene) Hardin, who had been editor and publisher, was only the third editor of the paper in its 129-year history. Stockholders at the time of the sale included Hardin and his wife, Nonnie, and Mrs. Hardin's sister, Virginia Plummer, and her son, McDonald Plummer Jr.

The sisters were granddaughters of Gen. James Berney Stanley, who came home from the Civil War to establish the paper in 1865. He was editor and publisher of *The Advocate* until 1934, when he died at age 90 — 60 years ago the same week that the newspaper was sold.

Stanley: "Dean of American newspaper editors"

As editor of the same newspaper for 69 years, Gen. James B. Stanley became nationally known. In 1924, *The New York Times* designated him the "dean of American newspaper editors." After Stanley's death, his son Glenn Stanley, became editor, and Glenn's brother, Webb Stanley, was named business manager.

All three Stanleys served as APA president. Moreover, all three were inducted into the Alabama Newspaper Hall of Honor at Auburn University's Ralph B. Draughon Library.

Hardin was APA president in 1972-1973. *The Advocate* was sold Dec. 12. Troy broker Jim Hall, former APA executive director, represented Boone Newspapers in the sale.

1995
Doug Pearson, *The Daily Mountain Eagle,* Jasper
1995-1996 president

124th annual press convention,
Riverchase Galleria, Wynfrey Hotel, Hoover
Feb. 24-26, 1995
Summer convention, Perdido Beach
July 14-16, 1995

With postal regulations and rates changing in 1995, newspaper publishers had the opportunity to learn new postal information at the 124th annual convention in Birmingham in 1995.

Max Heath of Landmark Newspapers in Elizabethton, Ky., led a Saturday afternoon program. Heath, who last spoke to an APA program in 1989, also consulted with individual newspaper executives during the convention. Running parallel to Heath's program, which focused on issues for weekly newspapers, was a discussion about newspapers as community reformers and leaders.

On Saturday morning, Gov.-elect Fob James led a discussion about the next four years of state government in Alabama. A panel of legislative leaders also participated. "This is a watershed year in politics here in Alabama," said outgoing APA president Linda Breedlove of *The South Alabamian* in Jackson, "and we think that all of our members will want to hear about the agenda for this first year of the new administration's four-year term."

Events planned for APA's 125th anniversary

APA winter convention delegates got a chance to look over photographs and publications from APA's past. A special 125th Anniversary Committee manned a table near the convention registration desk to display artifacts and historic documents about APA. The committee, headed by Ann Smith of *The Eufaula Tribune*, began planning a number of events for the 125th anniversary convention in 1996.

As part of the 125th commemoration, Auburn University journalism professor Ed Williams was writing an updated history of APA. Two earlier histories of APA (1871-1951 and 1871-1959) were written by a former director of public relations at Auburn, the late L.O. Brackeen, when Auburn University was called Alabama Polytechnic Institute. Brackeen's files about APA were housed in the Archives of the Auburn University Ralph B. Draughon Library.

Doug Pearson elected APA president in 1995

Doug Pearson became either the second or the third president of the APA from a newspaper in Jasper in 1995 — depending on how it is counted. Pearson, editor and publisher of *The Daily Mountain Eagle,* succeeded Linda Breedlove, associate publisher of *The South Alabamian* in Jackson, who became chairman of the board. Mrs. Breedlove and her husband, Mike, were the first married couple to both be elected APA president. Mike Breedlove was president in 1985.

Other publishers from Jasper to be elected APA president were E.H. (Ed) Pierce of *The Mountain Eagle* in 1948 and Shelton Prince Jr. of *The Daily Mountain Eagle* in 1980. Prince, however, moved on to *The Selma Times-Journal* the year he was president.

Pearson, 57, was elected during APA's 124th annual winter convention. He was also elected president of APA's business affiliate, the Alabama Newspaper Advertising Service. Pearson had been active in APA since he returned to his home state and to Jasper in 1980. He served on the APA/ANAS and APA Journalism Foundation Boards and as chairman of the Better Newspaper Contest.

Pearson came to Jasper from *The Chillicothe* (Mo.) *Constitution-Tribune,* where he had been editor and publisher since 1972. In 1959, he graduated from the University of Alabama where he earned a degree in journalism. At UA, he began his newspaper career in his hometown, Tuscaloosa, as a part-time ad salesman for *The Graphic,* a weekly, and later at *The Tuscaloosa News.*

After graduating, Pearson began full-time sales work at *The Maryville-Alcoa* (Tenn.) *Daily News.* Later, he was general advertising manager at *The Montgomery Advertiser* and *Alabama Journal* from 1963 to 1965. In 1965 he became editor and publisher of *The Cedartown* (Ga.) *Standard.*

Newsprint prices is 1994 convention topic

Newsprint companies discounted their prices in 1989 and 1990 when demand fell as newspapers slumped into their worst recession since World War II. Manufacturers were forced to reduce production at a time when many were investing millions of dollars in new equipment to process pulp from old newspapers back into usable pulp. The effects of newsprint price increases was the topic of a program at the 1994 winter convention. Business analysts said they expected newspaper prices to increase as much as 40 percent in 1995 over contract prices in 1994 with the price more than the $635 per ton record.

Most weekly and daily newspapers started cost-cutting measures to offset the sharp increases in newsprint prices. Newsprint was the second largest item in a newspaper's budget after employee pay and benefits. Newsprint purchases represented about 20 percent of a newspaper's total expenses. Some newspapers reduced staff size, page-width and news space, and took other steps to lower newsprint consumption. Newsprint usually accounts for 15-20 percent of a newspaper's expenses. Many newspapers also raised subscription rates, single copy prices and advertising rates to pay for the newsprint price increases.

APA convention quilt
   Holding a quilt of APA convention ribbons made by the family of APA's sixth president, Gen. James Berney Stanley of *The Greenville Advocate,* are, from left, Bill Keller, APA executive director; Mike Parta, chairman of the National Newspaper Association and publisher of *The New York Mills* (Minn.) *Herald;* and Joel P. Smith, APA's long-time NNA chairman, past APA president, and editor and publisher of *The Eufaula Tribune.* The quilt was displayed during APA's 124th annual winter convention Feb. 24-26, 1995, in Birmingham. Gen. Stanley was one of the founders of APA at the first convention in 1872 in Montgomery.

80 percent more for newsprint

By June 1995, newspapers were paying about 80 percent more for newsprint than in January 1994 — which included a 10 percent price increase announced for September 1995. Publishers were expecting to pay another 5 percent increase in January 1996 and even higher prices later in 1996.

The head of Media General's Garden State Paper Co. told newspaper executives in 1995 that he expected price increases in 1996 because newsprint mills were operating near capacity and because foreign demand for newsprint was strong. Champion International Corp announced in June 1995 that it would raise the price of newsprint to about $743.85 a metric ton, which nearly doubled the prevailing price in early 1994.

Newsprint increases shock newspapers

The sudden increases were a shock to newspapers, which for the past several years had enjoyed low newsprint prices because of the early 1990s recession. Newspapers from late 1990 to 1993 experienced their worst economic conditions since World War II, with 1991 the bottom. Papers became smaller because they ran fewer advertisements, and other papers folded or merged during the downturn. All of that contributed to cutbacks in newsprint mill production. Demand and prices plummeted.

In a May 1995 column, *Alexander City Outlook* publisher Kenneth Boone said he was paying $632 a ton for newsprint, some $200 more than the same time in 1994. Boone said he had already received a

---

S I D E L I G H T S
MARKING 125 YEARS OF HISTORY

Kyle wrote "Fiddlin' Around" column

Bob Kyle, 80, prize-winning columnist for *The Tuscaloosa News* for more than 50 years, died March 1, 1990. He was known for his humorous column, "Fiddlin' Around," and for leading political rallies around Tuscaloosa County.

Paul R. Davis, former associate editor of *The News*, paid tribute to Kyle: "He was one of the most colorful characters I've ever known, with a corncob pipe that he fired up with those long kitchen matches. He took every cub reporter in the world under his wing, teaching and training them."

---

letter announcing price increases not only for September 1995, but also for January 1996.

Newsprint producers warned newspaper publishers to expect another round of price increases in early 1996, but analysts said prices might level or actually decline later in 1996. Stone Container of Chicago announced in November 1995 that it was raising its list price of newsprint to $905 a ton, a 9.7 percent increase. Weyerhauser said it would raise its list price by $40 to $840 a metric ton. Fletcher Challenge Canada Ltd. announced a similar increase to $857.

After staffing, newsprint constituted a newspaper's second-largest cost category.

Two papers increase single copies to 75 cents

The price of a small soda at a hamburger joint may become one measure of the price of a newspaper, *Clanton Advertiser* editor-publisher Mike Kelley said in 1995. "You can't get a Coke for 50 cents any more," he said. "And what's the price of a pack of cigarettes now?"

The Clanton Advertiser, a thrice-weekly, and a sister Boone newspaper, *The Greenville Advocate*, a weekly, both raised their single copy prices to 75 cents on June 1, 1995. Both papers raised prices as a response to increasing printing and delivery costs. They were the first newspapers in Alabama to sell nonweekend newspapers for more than 50 cents. As a result, income was up at both papers. Moreover, with 40 additional newsracks placed around the Greenville area, *The Advocate's* circulation numbers even inched up slightly, editor-publisher Todd Carpenter said.

Carpenter: "A tribute to the loyal readership"

"It's a tribute to the loyal readership this newspaper gained over the years," Carpenter said of *The Advocate*, which Boone Newspapers purchased from the Stanley family, including former editor Gene Hardin, in late 1994.

"It's working very well," Carpenter said. "We hear about some grumbling, but no one has said anything to us yet." Most of the complaints were tied to readers having to fumble around for more change, Carpenter said. In addition, newsracks could not hold all of the change, unless circulation managers unload the money during the peak sales days. One double rack in Greenville wouldn't work because it was so full of quarters.

Both Kelley and Carpenter said that theft was up at first, but then only marginally.

A number of Alabama dailies and weeklies increased single copy prices to 50 cents over the past eight years. In the mid-1980s, when the prices began to move to 50 cents, it wasn't the price of a soft drink that was used as a comparison price. It was the price of a cup of coffee. Kelley said he thought many other newspapers would increase their single-copy prices to 75 cents soon.

The Montgomery Advertiser to build satellite plant

The Montgomery Advertiser announced in January 1995 that it would build a $15 million satellite plant in an old railroad yard by the city's old depot, near the banks of the Alabama River. Publisher Richard H. (Dick) Amberg Jr. called it "a most significant investment in our future and in serving our readers and advertisers better, at a time when many newspapers are backing away from investment due to skyrocketing newsprint costs and concerns about the future of the newspaper industry."

The Advertiser announced it would install a larger, faster press and a Harris SP-21 Newsmaker computer editing and composing system and would become the second largest newspaper in the nation with total pagination. Production was expected to begin at the new plant in June 1996, Amberg said.

The $1 million Harris system would allow the staff to lay out the paper with true total pagination. Many newspapers, including *The Advertiser,* had used computers for partial page composition, but staff members still had to strip halftone negatives into the plate negatives. The new plant housed an eight-unit, four-color-deck Goss Metroliner offset press that *The Advertiser* bought from *The Boston* (Mass.) *Globe.*

Amberg said the new *Advertiser* building would be the first building in Montgomery that travelers would see when they drove south over the Interstate 65 bridge and headed toward downtown. A globe would sit atop the building, a classic daily newspaper building design element. While the non-production departments remained in the main office, the new plant design also included an adjacent office tower as a later option.

Monroe Journal's Bill Stewart dies in 1995

The minister who led Bill Stewart's funeral said Stewart was a man whose quiet and calm leadership had helped lead Monroeville through the social changes of the past 35 years. Stewart, owner of *The Monroe Journal* and radio station WMFC, died Jan. 21, 1995, from complications of Parkinson's disease. He was 74.

Stewart and James H. (Jimmy) Faulkner Sr., both former APA presidents, bought *The Monroe*

Journal in 1947 and started the radio station in 1952. They also founded a radio station in Bay Minette. Stewart was, at times, an owner or partner in *The Baldwin Times* in Bay Minette, *The South Alabamian* in Jackson, *The Wilcox Progressive Era* in Camden, and *The Brewton Standard.* Stewart owned *The Monroe Journal* longer than any other individual since the paper's founding in 1866.

Stewart was APA president in 1959-1960. Survivors included his wife, Carolyn Stewart; sons, Steve Stewart and David Stewart of Monroeville; daughter, Orpah Travis of Fort Myers, Fla., and five grandchildren. His son, Steve, APA president in 1987-1988, had been publisher of *The Monroe Journal* since 1989. His daughter-in-law, Patrice Stewart, was associate publisher of the paper.

Stewart "was a real gentleman"

In an editorial in *The Wilcox Progressive Era* in Camden, editor and publisher Hollis Curl said that Stewart was "atypical of the hard-drinking, smoking, joke-telling, don't-give-a-damn newspaper men personified in popular fiction. We suppose it would be accurate to say of Bill Stewart that he and his newspaper became somewhat of a yardstick by which those in our profession measure ourselves."

An editorial in *The South Alabamian* in Jackson by publisher Mike Breedlove, 1985-1986 APA

---

president, said that "Mr. Bill was a real gentleman, a patriot, a solid citizen, a family man, and most of all to us, a friend."

The Arab Tribune damaged by tornado in 1995

The front of *The Arab Tribune* building was a tangle of steel, wires, bricks, insulation, computers and broken glass when publisher Ed Reed, editor David Moore and other staff members tried to probe their way through the wreckage on the morning of Feb. 16, 1995. A tornado struck the town in the early morning hours. "The damage was too weird to be real," Moore wrote in a column. "It was too dangerous to enter, but the beam of the flashlight picked up the face of the clock, blown dead at 5:02."

Despite the damage, the news and ad staff went to work the morning that the tornado hit. When news editor and advertising manager Phil Baker stopped by the local phone company to use a phone, the manager offered the newspaper a spare room and ran the paper's phone lines to the room. By the next morning, they were working on computers loaned by Ray Davis and Co.

Shortly after the tornado hit, reporter Stephanie Reed Chisum found a laptop computer under one of the damaged desks, and Moore found some batteries. By 10 a.m., he was typing stories while sitting in his car. Pressmen were able to clean the press, which was housed in the back of the building. The storm didn't damage the structure of the pressroom.

When local electric co-op linemen strung new electric lines early the next week, the pressmen cranked up the press and printed *The Tribune's* special tornado edition Feb. 22. They also printed *The Blount Countian* in Oneonta on time. The staff was able to salvage subscription records and other business records, but they lost photo negatives from the past two or three years. They also lost stories they had been developing for a special section.

Alabama publishers offer help to *Arab Tribune*

Reed and Moore said a number of newspaper publishers from around the state called to offer help. They offered supplies, equipment, press time, even staffers to help. Reed said he appreciated the offers and was touched by the generosity.

Many of the publishers around the state said they learned about the storm damage to *The Tribune* building while watching television news the morning of the storm. CNN's coverage of the north Alabama storm showed the damaged building.

During the APA winter convention, Sam Harvey, editor of *The Advertiser-Gleam* in neighboring Guntersville, praised Reed, Moore, Baker

---

S I D E L I G H T S
MARKING 125 YEARS OF HISTORY

Boone purchases Bulletin, Tuskegee News

The Auburn Bulletin and *The Tuskegee News* were purchased in 1975 by companies whose controlling stock was owned by James B. Boone Jr., publisher of *The Tuscaloosa News* and president of Tuscaloosa Newspapers Inc.

Announcement of the purchase was made by Neil O. Davis, editor, publisher and majority owner of both newspapers. Davis retired from the newspaper business and began teaching classes in the Auburn University Department of Journalism.

Paul R. Davis, editor and general manager of *The Selma Times-Journal,* became editor and publisher of the Auburn and Tuskegee newspapers on June 30, 1975, and was a major stockholder in both newspapers.

Stockholders included several of Boone's associates at *The Tuscaloosa News* — Charles H. Land, James M. Ward, T. Wayne Townsend, William M. Bonner Jr., Edgar L. Fowler Jr., W.J. LaFoy, C.E. McCracken, Charles J. Reck and H. Brooks Ward, and former Tuscaloosan Stanley C. Voit, a member of *The Selma Times-Journal* staff.

Among stockholders in the newly formed Auburn Newspapers Inc. were Bruce G. Morrison, publisher of *The Selma Times-Journal.* Morrison was a stockholder in the newly formed Tuskegee Newspapers Inc., along with Paul Anderson, editor and publisher of The Dadeville Record; Tony Manuel, publisher of *The Alexander City Outlook;* James W. Lambert Jr., editor and publisher of *The Andalusia Star-News;* and Mike Kelley, editor of *The Alexander City Outlook.* All were associates of James B. Boone Jr., publisher of *The Tuscaloosa News* and controlling stockholder of the new Auburn and Tuskegee companies.

The new companies owned and published *The Auburn Bulletin* and *The Tuskegee News* after June 30, 1975, closing date on sale of the newspapers.

and other staff members for the job they did publishing the edition on time and for publishing such a complete edition.

In the 30-page, three-section edition, the staff published photos and a feature on the six residents killed in the storm. They also published many other photographs as well as lists of injured from local hospitals, interviews with Gov. Fob James and U.S. Rep. Tom Bevill, a story about the lack of warning, relief efforts, pet stories and several other stories.

The special edition even had large house ads. "We're just a little windblown!" The ads apologized for lost photos, stories and ads.

Ed Arnold features *Tribune*

The Arab Tribune was featured in Ed Arnold's *Publishers' Auxiliary* column, "Page of the Week," in June 1995 for its special tornado edition. "There is nothing about this issue that would suggest the conditions under which it was produced," Arnold wrote. "Stories are excellent. Layout is crisp. Presswork is excellent." And in "Arnold's Ancient Axiom," he said, "Memo to the Pulitzer Prize committee: Be sure to look at *The Arab Tribune* for Feb. 22, 1995, and you've got a winner here."

Arnold said that editor David Moore's personal account "was just one gripping story in an absolutely admirable edition of the weekly."

Porter Harvey, 91 eulogized in 1995

When family members and friends drove up to the Guntersville First United Methodist Church for *Advertiser-Gleam* publisher Porter Harvey's funeral March 12, they saw a crew from Channel 31 in Huntsville.

Associated Press reporter Jay Reeves wrote a story about Harvey's death and sent out a photograph to AP subscribers around the South. The file photo showed Mr. Harvey and his wife, Alice, shortly after he had made his much publicized bungee jump in August 1993 to celebrate his 90th birthday.

Reporters at *The Birmingham News*, *The Huntsville Times* and several other area newspapers wrote their own stories about him.

Even his obituary was longer than he would have wanted, *Gleam* editor Sam Harvey said. "Daddy would have been embarrassed about all the attention," Sam Harvey said. The obituary, however, was on the back page with the other obituaries, as he would have insisted.

Three weeks before his death, Harvey was described by *Birmingham News* editor James E.

Jacobson as one of the most written-about weekly newspaper publishers in the nation. Jacobson wrote an editorial page column about the gathering of Alabama's "newspaper family" at the APA winter convention.

Bungee jumping made Harvey known around nation

The bungee-jumping project that he organized for his children and grandchildren and an AP story about *The Gleam's* detailed obituaries had made Porter Harvey and *The Advertiser-Gleam* known around the nation.

The Gleam's layout style of 14-point heads, its non-traditional design and its large circulation had been described in stories in NNA's *Publishers' Auxiliary* and other national trade publications. In 1994, AP sent out a story about the detailed obituaries that Porter Harvey wrote, and the story was carried around the world.

NAA's *Presstime* magazine ran a small piece and photo about *The Gleam's* continued use of manual typewriters and its use of old black-and-white Polaroid cameras.

Harvey died March 10, 1995, at Guntersville-Arab Hospital. At 91, he was the oldest active newspaper publisher in Alabama. Harvey had worked at newspapers for 68 years.

News, Post-Herald sponsor information phone line

With little fanfare, *The Birmingham News* and the *Birmingham Post-Herald* became the first newspapers in Alabama in 1995 to sponsor a N11 information phone line. The service was also one of only a handful of such three-digit information services in the nation. The new service at *The News* and *Post-Herald* was followed closely by similar services at *The Huntsville Times* and *Huntsville News* and at *The Mobile Press Register*. The Birmingham papers began offering the new service March 5.

Internship program honors Mike Ryland

A new advertising internship program was announced in 1995 to honor the late Mike Ryland, former executive director and advertising manager of APA. Underwritten with income from ALASCAN, the statewide classified advertising program, two new $2,500 Michael T. Ryland Internships were offered in the summer of 1995.

Advertising manager Felicia Mason said the internship grants would be given to two newspapers to pay an intern $250 for 10 weeks. Ms. Mason, who suggested the new internships to the APA Advertising Committee and ANAS board of di-

SIDELIGHTS
MARKING 125 YEARS OF HISTORY

That's Where You'll Find the Readers of The Advertiser-Gleam

From the point of Preston island
  To the mouth of Parches Cove,
From Swearengin to Horton,
  From the Mobbs to Cedar Grove;
By Town Creek's quiet waters,
  By Shoal Creek's rushing stream —
That's where you'll find the readers
  Of the Advertiser-Gleam

You can ask them in Click Hollow,
  Snug Harbor, Rayburn Switch,
On Minkie Creek or Mink Creek,
  It makes no difference which;
At the Painted Bluff, at Langston,
  High Point, Clear Spring, Fairview,
In Bucksnort beat, or Ringold Street —
  They read it through and through.

Around the dam and Hebron
  Where the cedar thickets grow,
At Alder Springs and Grassy,
  At Feemsters Gap, Shiloh;
In Polecat Hollow, Friendship,
  On Mayo Mountain's peak,
On Holiness Point, at Guntersville,
  At Douglas and Beech Creek;

Where Wyeth Rock rears toward the sky,
  Where Short Creek Falls plunge down,
At Pine Grove, Big Spring Valley,
  Bonds Chapel, Kirbytown,
Ney-A-Ti, John R. Hollow,
  Rockdale and Lattiwood,
Old Union, Rabbits Cross Roads,
  At Thompson Falls, Haygood;

Cathedral Caverns, Bethel,
  Suck Egg Road from end to end,
At Nixon Chapel, Wakefield,
  Hopewell and Horseshoe Bend;
On the slopes above South Sauty,
  Where the wildcats used to scream —
reedbrake, East Lake — that's where they take
  The Advertiser-Gleam

At all the pleasant places —
  Pleasant Hill and Pleasant View,
Mountain Pleasant, Pleasant Valley,
  Pleasant Grove — they read it too.
And at all the homey places —
  Free home and Happy Home,
At Welcome Home and Sweet Home,
  New Home and Honeycomb;

On Simpson Point, on Pea Ridge,
  Half Acres, Valley View
At Claysville, Little New York,
  On O'Brig Avenue;
Morrow Acres, Mirror Lake,
  New Prospect, Chigger Hill,
Lane Switch and Bakers Chapel,
  Oak Grove and Meltonsville;

At Warrenton, and Solitude
  On Sunset Drive, Redhill,
Star Point, Columbus City,
  Kings Hollow, Butlers Mill;
On the short steep curve at Lucas Gap,
  Where brakes and tires scream —
That's where you'll find the readers
  Of the Advertiser-Gleam

All through Short Creek Canyon,
  Where the cliffs are steep and rough
In Sherwood Forest, Corinth,
  At Dogant, and Streets Bluff;
At Haneys Chapel, Grove Oak,
  Mount Tabor and Mount high,
At Cottonville, at Bakers Gap,
  At Browns Creek and the Y;

On all the various Mountains —
  On Brindlee, Gunter, Sand,
On Georgia, Grassy, Center Point,
  On Merrill, Lewis, and
McCorkle, Bishop, Wyeth,
  Little Mountain, Taylor too,
On Lang and Long and at Mount Shade,
  Grant Mountain, Mountain View;

At Mountain Gap, Mount Olive,
  Mount Moriah, Mount Oak,
Rocky Mount, Mount Carmel —
  They read it — that's no joke.
At Mount High and Mount Pleasant,
  Blacks Mountain, Mountain Crest —
That's where they read our paper —
  They say it is the best.

Buck Island and Pine Island
  Where the big boat houses are,
Asbury, Lindsey Hollow,
  Browns Valley, DAR;
Anderson Ridge, Rehobeth,
  Where the pulpwood barges load,
Long Hollow, Sorters Cross Roads,
  Along the Fish Trap Road.

At Poplar Springs, at Five Points
  Near the big Monsanto plant,
At Rock Springs, Pisgah, Ebell,
  At Meadowwood and Grant;
'Mid the State Park's fabled spleandor,
  Where it all seems like a dream—
That's where you'll find the readers
  Of the Advertiser-Gleam

Buck's Pocket, where defeated
  Politicians used to meet,
Jugshandle Hollow, martling,
  Wrights Cove and Henry Street;
At hyatt and at Liberty Hill,
  Which aren't very far apart,
Holiday Shores and Diamond,
  Scant City and Boshart;

At Brashiers Chapel (Brindlee),
  At Brashers Chapel (Sand),
On Paint Rock, where the river
  Sometimes gets out of hand;
Hog Jaw and Hide-Away Acres,
  Snow Point and Kennamer Cove,
On Lakeview Hill, at Henryville,
  Manchester, Union Grove;

And when the end of earth shall come
  And time shall cease to me,
When Carlisle Park and Wesson Branch
  Are swallowed by the sea,
When Signal Point and Sims behold
  The dying sun's last beam —
They'll believe it when they read it
  In the Advertiser-Gleam.

— By Porter Harvey

rectors, said that the Ad Committee would award the internships to two newspapers on a first-come, first-serve basis.

Ryland was APA/ANAS advertising manager from 1984 to 1990, and he was APA executive director from the fall of 1990 until he died at age 34 in March 1992. Ryland led the effort to develop ALA-SCAN in 1985.

Anniston's Ralph Callahan named Citizen of Year

Ralph W. Callahan was named Citizen of the Year by *The Anniston Star* in 1995. He received the award during the Chamber of Commerce's annual meeting. When he received the award, he said he was "flabbergasted" to be named, because in years past, he, himself, had helped pick the award recipient. Callahan had worked at *The Star* and its parent company, Consolidated Publishing Co., since 1927. But it was for a lifetime of community service, notably a quarter-century as chairman of the chamber's Military Affairs Committee, that he was honored.

The Star had never chosen one of its own for the annual award, but this year, *The Star* broke its own rules, publisher and editor Brandt Ayers said.

Callahan was born in Anniston on April 18, 1906, and he worked as a sportswriter at *The Star* in 1922 before attending Howard College in Birmingham. He later worked at *The Nashville Ten-* *nessean,* but returned to *The Star* in 1927 and worked his way up to managing editor, business manager and president. He remained a consultant and president of *The Daily Home* in Talladega, which was owned by Consolidated.

He was still coming to *The Star* every day in 1996. Asked why he was still so active at the age of 90, Callahan replied, "Because I'm still young. I enjoy participating. I enjoy decision-making. I enjoy helping. The older you get, the greatest pleasure out of life is helping someone else."

Callahan was APA president in 1965-1966, and when he was president he led an effort to update the elections and nominations process and other sections of the APA bylaws. He also was past president of the Southern Newspapers Publishers Association.

Two Alabama dailies named Pulitzer finalists

Two Alabama dailies, *The Montgomery Advertiser* and *The Mobile Press Register,* were finalists in Pulitzer Prize competition in 1995, and both won National Headliner Awards.

The Press Register was one of three finalists in the Pulitzer's editorial writing category, which was won by *The St. Petersburg* (Fla.) *Times.* The paper's entry was a nine-part editorial series on the need to update the 1901 Alabama Constitution.

The Advertiser was one of three finalists in the Pulitzer's explanatory journalism category for its probe of the Southern Poverty Law Center. *The Washington Post* won the category.

The Advertiser also won two National Headliner Awards in 1995, a first place for its three-year probe of the SPLC, and a second place award in the Public Service category for its continuing series, "Doctors Watching Doctors."

1995 was the first year *The Press Register* had been named a Pulitzer finalist. *The Advertiser* and its sister publication, *The Alabama Journal* which was no longer published, had previously won two Pulitzers.

The Alabama Journal and *The Birmingham News* were the last two Alabama

Advertiser-Gleam publisher Porter Harvey used a manual typewriter until his death in 1995 at age 91. Harvey was the oldest active newspaper publisher in Alabama. (Photograph courtesy of Sam Harvey, *The Advertiser-Gleam*)

Ralph W. Callahan, relaxes in his office at *The Anniston Star* on July 28. 1995. Callahan, 89 at the time, had worked at *The Star* and its parent company, Consolidated Publishing Co., since 1927. He was named Anniston's Citizen of the Year in 1995. Callahan was born April 18, 1906 (Photograph by Alex Pippin)

Foundation grants had gone to journalism professors for summer work projects at a newspaper. Foundation president Lee Woodward said the new foundation-backed program encouraged college faculty members to experience the day-to-day challenges of gathering, writing and editing news at a newspaper. The real world experience should help professors do a better job teaching, Woodward added.

At the same time, the newspapers would benefit because the newspapers to win the Pulitzer, the nation's top journalism award.

Auburn journalism department receives accreditation

Called a model program, the Auburn University Department of Journalism received national accreditation in its first attempt in 1995. The department received unanimous approval for a six-year accreditation period by the Accrediting Council on Education in Journalism and Mass Communications, said Doug Anderson, director of the Walter Cronkite School of Journalism and Telecommunications at Arizona State University. "I told the council that in many respects Auburn's department was a model small- to medium-size program," Anderson said.

Dr. Jerry E. Brown, head of the Auburn department since 1992, credited Auburn's quality program to the department's first head, Jack Simms, who served from 1974 to 1992, former faculty members Paul Burnett and Mickey Logue, and long-time Lee County newspaper editor and publisher and part-time faculty member, Neil Davis.

Journalism Foundation starts college grant program

Journalism professors from five colleges and universities in Alabama experienced some real-world newspaper work in the summer of 1995 with $2,000 grants from the APA Journalism Foundation. This was the first year that APA Journalism

professors used their skills to help editors. The faculty members did a variety of work from substituting for editors-publishers who were on vacation to working on an editorial page staff, to helping to redesign a newspaper. They studied the newspapers before visiting, and they and their host editors both evaluated the summer program afterward.

The Cullman Times started charging $7.50 for birth announcement photos and for birthday photos in 1995. Citing increased costs, a number of other small dailies around Alabama started charging for photos in recent years. Most larger Alabama dailies started charging for obituaries and wedding and engagement stories in the last two years.

Miss Alabama sings at convention

When his neighbor's daughter was named "Miss Alabama" in 1995, APA president Doug Pearson had an idea. That idea led to an invitation. The new Miss Alabama, Leigh Sherer of Jasper, sang during the 1995 summer convention's Better Newspaper Contest banquet on Saturday, July 15. Pearson, editor and publisher of *The Daily Mountain Eagle* in Jasper, invited Miss Sherer, whose parents lived across the street from the Pearson, to appear.

Featured speaker during the banquet was Alabama's 2nd District congressman, Terry Everett of Enterprise. Everett, owner of *The Union Springs Herald*, was APA president in 1991-1992 and was elected to Congress in 1992.

The 1995 summer convention was July 14-16 at the Perdido Beach Resort.

Gannett makes move into Alabama

When Gannett announced plans to buy Multimedia on July 24, 1995, it meant that the nation's largest newspaper group was buying its first newspapers in Alabama. In addition to *The Montgomery Advertiser*, Multimedia subsidiaries also owned *The Prattville Progress* and *The Community News* in Millbrook.

The announcement ended a five-month search by Multimedia for a new way to boost its stagnant stock price. Multimedia was based in Greenville, S.C., and Gannett was based in Arlington, Va.

The Advertiser Co. also operated three military newspapers, *The Redstone Rocket* in Huntsville, *The Maxwell-Gunter Dispatch* in Montgomery, and *The Bayonet* at Fort Benning, Ga.

Gannett, which published 82 newspapers including *USA Today*, announced that it would buy Multimedia Inc. for some $1.7 billion. Gannett was the largest newspaper group in the nation in 1995.

The Advertiser became the third capital city daily in the south central states owned by Gannett. Gannett already owned *The Jackson* (Miss.) *Clarion-Ledger* and *The Nashville Tennessean*. Gannett had owned *The Arkansas Gazette* in Little Rock, Ark., which had been one of the nation's most respected newspapers, but later sold it to *The Arkansas Democrat*.

Gannett outbid a number of suitors

Gannett outbid a number of suitors including a team with financing from the Retirement Systems of Alabama. RSA did not seek to own Multimedia, but rather to finance the deal. The Multimedia bid was not RSA's first attempt to buy news media or to finance their purchase.

Several years earlier, RSA had announced its intent to buy WSFA-TV in Montgomery, but backed off the plan after several organizations including APA had concerns about an arm of the state owning a television station in the state capital. In 1994, RSA helped finance the purchase of Park Communications Inc., which owned a number of newspapers.

Montgomery Advertiser publisher Richard H. (Dick) Amberg Jr., publisher of the newspaper since 1986, said he told the newspaper staff about the sale the morning of the announcement. "It was well received," Amberg told a *Birmingham News* reporter. "Nobody expressed any concern. Everybody feels pretty positive about it."

The Advertiser had a weekday circulation of about 53,000 and a Sunday circulation of 81,500. *The Progress*, a twice-weekly paper, had a paid circulation of about 5,800, and *The Community Press*, a weekly, had a paid circulation of about 2,000.

Consolidated buys *Cleburne News* in 1995

The Cleburne News, a weekly in Heflin, and its free-circulation publication, *Total*, were sold to Consolidated Publishing Co. of Anniston in 1995. Henry and Minnie Ree Jackson, former owners of *The Cleburne News*, and Phil Sanguinetti, president of Consolidated, made the announcement on Aug. 1, 1995.

With the purchase of *The Cleburne News*, Consolidated owned two weeklies as well as two dailies: *The Anniston Star* and *The Daily Home* in Talladega, both dailies, and *The Jacksonville News*, a weekly, and *The Cleburne News*.

Henry Jackson said he felt he was leaving *The Cleburne News* in good hands. "We have had a good relationship with Ralph Callahan over the years, and we felt like he and his staff would continue what he had built in the past 20 years," Jackson said.

Callahan was president of *The Daily Home* and a member of Consolidated's board of directors and former general manager of *The Anniston Star*. Sanguinetti said Consolidated Publishing planned to "publish a quality newspaper for the people of Cleburne County." Brandt Ayers, editor and publisher of *The Anniston Star*, said he appreciated the Jacksons "entrusting their newspaper to us."

Foundation report: Work to retain minority staffers

A big part of the problem with recruiting black newspaper staff members was the image of news-

---

S I D E L I G H T S
MARKING 125 YEARS OF HISTORY

Cross sells Wilcox Progressive Era *to Curl*

Cecil Cross Jr., owner and publisher of *The Wilcox Progressive Era* in Camden, sold the 96-year-old newspaper to M. Hollis Curl in 1969.

Before purchasing *The Progressive Era*, Curl had been owner of *The Choctaw Advocate* in Butler for seven years. Curl was also a major stockholder in *The Demopolis Times*.

papers, a new report said in 1995, and with 25 percent of Alabama's population represented by minorities, newspapers leaders in the state must work harder to hire and retain minority staffers. The report, prepared by a committee of the APA Journalism Foundation board of directors, said that newspapers needed to work with young people as early as elementary school to begin improving the newspaper industry's image.

"It makes good business sense," said APA president Doug Pearson of *The Daily Mountain Eagle* in Jasper, who attended the Journalism Foundation board of directors meeting when the committee presented the report. "I'd like to see the Alabama Press Association become a national leader in recruiting minority reporters and other staff members," Pearson said. "We all need to do a better job."

Few minority journalists in newsrooms

Most young black youths viewed most newspaper stories as bad news stories about the black community, the report said. In addition, there were few minority journalists working in the state's newsrooms to set an example for other youths. Foundation president Lee Woodward, editor of *The Huntsville News*, said the Journalism Foundation board of directors planned to gather information in the fall of 1995 about minority employees in the state's newspapers. Members of the committee included Mike Smelley,

---

S I D E L I G H T S
MARKING 125 YEARS OF HISTORY

Most Foundation grants support college journalism education

In some states the foundations set up by newspaper associations are used to shelter income and to hire an employee or two to manage workshops. They also raise money with golf tournaments, auctions, special shows and other ways.

Newspapers in Alabama contributed the endowment to create the APA Journalism Foundations' endowment. The APA Journalism Foundation began with a 10-year, $100,000 fund drive in 1968.

One reason to start the Foundation was to show industry support for the University of Alabama Department of Journalism to help it regain national accreditation.

In Alabama, most of the income on the APA Journalism Foundation's endowment has provided small grants to support innovative programs in college journalism classes in Alabama.

The Foundation's first grants went to UA to support a lecture series and to support a community journalism class.

From the start, too, grants also went to Auburn University and Troy State University. Later grants went to journalism programs at other colleges and universities, including Alabama State University, Miles College, University of Alabama at Birmingham, University of South Alabama and Samford University.

Foundation grants also supported programs to help high school newspaper advisers and editors.

After the Foundation launched a second $100,000 fund drive in 1984, the Foundation board began offering a new scholarship to honor the memory of W.H. Metz of the *Birmingham Post-Herald*, who was president of APA when the Foundation began.

In 1994, the Foundation purchased a building in the Birmingham suburb of Homewood, a building to house the offices of APA and the Alabama Newspaper Advertising Service. Both APA and ANAS pay rent to the Foundation as does a first-floor tenant.

In 1995, the Foundation also began offering $2,000 grants to encourage journalism professors to return to newspapers for a short course in real-world journalism.

The Foundation board planned to launch a new student internship program in the summer of 1997.

The Foundation board also sees itself as the primary connection between the newspaper industry and journalism education in Alabama. It meets two or three times a year with college journalism faculty and students.

By 1996, the Foundation's endowment, including the value of its building, exceeded $400,000.

editor and associate publisher of *The Tuskegee News,* chairman; Deangelo McDaniel, managing editor of *The Moulton Advertiser;* and Joe Distelheim, editor of *The Huntsville Times.*

Alabama newspapers hitch ride on World Wide Web

The Huntsville Times, the *Birmingham Post-Herald* and *The Mobile Press-Register* all hitched a ride on the growing world-wide computer link, Internet's World Wide Web, in 1995.

And at least one weekly in Alabama, *The Madison Globe,* was moving toward creating a web page on the Internet.

In Huntsville, Alabama's technology center where one out of two homes was equipped with a personal computer, *"The Huntsville Times OnLine"* officially started July 12, 1995. "We're getting some very positive feedback," said Cooper Green, general manager of *The Huntsville Times.* "It reflects well not only on *The Times,* but also on Huntsville and on the state as well."

At *The Mobile Press Register,* John Sellers said staffers already had sold its first home page to a local exporter of farm implements, and the staff expected to sell more advertising. *The Mobile Register's* web page gave information about every department at the newspaper as well as a history of the paper.

"Having a home page on the internet is like having a billboard alongside the interstate highway," a story in *The Press Register* said. "Internet travelers from around the world can find a particular home page in a dictionary, in an online mall or in hypertext on someone else's home page."

Post-Herald first Alabama newspaper on-line

The *Birmingham Post-Herald,* which may have been the first Alabama newspaper on-line, provided all the paper's local news, sports, editorials, business stories and features to readers via Internet's World Wide Web.

The web gave users access to almost every Internet service, a story in the *Post-Herald* said. It connected its documents with hyperlinks, which allowed users to go from one part of the web to another with a point and click of their computer's mouse.

Post-Herald editor James H. Denley said the newspaper's service only included text in 1995, but that photos might be added later. "The extent of the web page will depend a lot on the response we get and on the evolution of society over the next five to 10 years," Denley said. "We've got to wait and see if this is a fad or an ingrained part of every household."

Joel Smith: 40 years of columns

In 1995, Joel P. Smith, editor and publisher of *The Eufaula Tribune,* marked his 40th year writing columns, including the first three and half years at *The Geneva County Reaper* at Geneva. Looking back, Smith said he had written more than 2,090 columns.

Meredith White, the new publisher of Gulf Coast Newspapers' six newspapers in Baldwin County, took the helm in mid-July 1995. Ms. White, 35, came to Gulf Coast Newspapers from *The News & Advance* in Lynchburg, Va., where she was advertising director. Both were owned by Worrell Newspapers.

Ms. White succeeded Stephanie Pressly, who accepted a management position with Phoenix Newspapers Inc., in Phoenix, Ariz., where she became business manager of a business weekly. Ms. Pressly had been at Gulf Coast Newspapers for six months.

Long-time newspaper man Edward T. (Buster) Hall Jr., 86, of Grove Hill, died in Northport on July 8, 1995. Hall had a lengthy career in journalism, including work at *The Thomasville Times,* the old *Hale County News* in Moundville, *The Tuskegee News* and *The Clarke County Democrat.* Hall was a skilled Linotype operator and printer and was general manager of *The Democrat* when he retired in the 1970s. After his retirement, he wrote columns for *The Thomasville Times* and the "Friends and Adventures of Yesteryear" column for *The Clarke County Democrat.*

Thomson buys *Lee County Eagle/Auburn Bulletin* in 1995

Two Alabama newspapers with deep roots in Auburn and Opelika began sharing common ownership in 1995. Thomson Newspapers, which owned *The Opelika-Auburn News* and two other Alabama daily newspapers, purchased *The Auburn Bulletin,* effective Sept. 1, 1995.

The purchase included *The Lee County Eagle* and *The Auburn Bulletin.* Former *Eagle/Bulletin* owner Paul R. Davis continued to own and publish *The Tuskegee News.*

Purchase price was not disclosed. Paul Seveska, president and chief executive officer of Thomson's Alabama Group, was named interim publisher, and Davis' son, Alan Davis, continued as associate publisher of *The Eagle* and *Bulletin.*

"The Lee County Eagle and *Auburn Bulletin* will continue to be autonomous, locally managed community newspapers," Seveska said. "This purchase strengthens Thomson's commitment to serving readers and advertisers in Lee County. The newspapers, their readers and advertiser will be well served by our committee management team, lo-

cated in the community, close to our customers."

The Opelika-Auburn News, circulation 14,000, was first published in 1870 as *The Opelika Observer.* It became *The Opelika Daily News* in 1904 and *The Opelika Auburn Daily News* in about 1965. Millard Grimes, who sold *The Opelika-Auburn News* to Thomson in 1977, had bought it in 1968. Grimes was publishing a business magazine, *Georgia Trend,* in 1995 and had published newspapers in Georgia. Grimes was a vice president of APA when he left Alabama, and later became president of the Georgia Press Association.

Neil Davis founded newspaper in 1937

The Lee County Bulletin was first published in February 1937. The founding publisher was Neil O. Davis. At the time, Davis was a 21-year-old student at Alabama Polytechnic Institute.

When *The Daily News* expanded into Auburn, Neil Davis changed his newspaper's name to *The*

Auburn Bulletin. For years, *The Bulletin* won the APA's top honor, General Excellence, in the Better Newspaper Contest. Neil Davis, 81 in 1995, said his lifeblood was local news. "We sold more than 4,000 papers in Auburn alone 25 years ago, and the population couldn't have been more than 13,000, Davis said. "It's because *The Bulletin* is newsy. It sold on the basis of its news content. I never kidded myself that it was my writing that sold it."

While Neil Davis was publisher, *The Bulletin* gained a national reputation for its courageous editorial stances and its community leadership. Davis was one of the first weekly newspaper publishers to be named a Nieman Fellow.

Graham McTeer served 22 years as managing editor

Graham McTeer
The Lee County Bulletin, Auburn

Under Neil Davis' ownership, Graham McTeer served 22 years as managing editor, helping drive the local news coverage that won the newspaper honors. "He was a great newspaper man, in the true sense of the tradition," Davis said. McTeer died of cancer in 1975. McTeer Park in Auburn was named for him, and he was inducted into the Alabama Newspaper Hall of Honor in 1993.

On June 30, 1975, Neil Davis sold *The Bulletin* to Boone Newspapers. During Boone's ownership, staff members included Rheta Grimsley Johnson, who in 1995 was a syndicated columnist for *The Atlanta Journal* and Atlanta Constitution; and Jimmy Johnson, the syndicated cartoonist of Arlo & Janis.

Boone later sold *The Bulletin* to local investor Andy Gentry, who in 1981 sold it to Paul R. Davis. During Paul Davis' tenure, the newspaper's name was changed to *The Lee County Eagle,* and *The Bulletin* became a shopper. Paul Davis, 57, said his tenure as *Eagle-Bulletin* publisher was "an honor and a privilege."

Alan Davis to remain at *Lee County Eagle*

Paul Davis added, "I am pleased that my son Alan will continue in a leadership role with the paper and that Thomson is planning to maintain the unique role of *The Bulletin* as a community newspaper."

Purchase by Thomson Newspapers of *The Lee County Eagle* marked the second time in four months that Thomson had bought newspapers in the same Alabama markets served by its dailies. Thomson also owned *The Dothan Eagle, The Enterprise Ledger,* and

---

SIDELIGHTS

MARKING 125 YEARS OF HISTORY

Daily Northwest Alabamian *formed in 1962*

Newspapers of Winston, Fayette and Marion counties combined to form *The Daily Northwest Alabamian* on Feb. 1, 1962.

Announcement of the daily was made by Jay Thornton, publisher. The five-morning daily was formed by consolidation of *The Haleyville Advertiser, The Marion County News-Journal,* and *The Fayette County Times.*

W.D. Smith Jr., publisher of *The Fayette County Times,* was editor and general manger of the daily and Oscar Roden of Winfield was Marion County editor.

Establishment of a daily in northwest Alabama culminated 22 years of building up newspapers in Winston, Marion and Fayette counties by Thornton. He took over *The Advertiser-Journal* in Haleyville in 1939, and *The Winston Herald* of Double Springs in 1945.

Thornton and Roden bought *The Marion County News* in 1957 and combined it with *The Winfield Journal* to become *The Marion County News-Journal.* Thornton and Smith bought *The Fayette County Times* in 1961. He also published *The Hackelburo Sentinel* in Marion County, which in 1955 had a circulation of 125 weekly.

The Jackson County Floridian in Marianna, Fla., just across the state line from Dothan.

In June 1995, Thomson announced that it planned to buy *The Dothan Progress*, a free-circulation weekly, and its two sister newspapers, *The Headland Observer* and *The Ashford Power*, from Freedom Communications Inc. Sale was finalized on Oct. 3, 1995.

Specht purchases *The Washington County News*

Jim Specht, publisher of three weeklies in Geneva County, purchased *The Washington County News* in Chatom on Sept. 1, 1995, from long-time owners Dalton and Pauline Jackson.

Specht, publisher of *The Geneva Reaper, The News Herald* in Hartford and *The Samson Ledger*, announced that he would move to Chatom as sole owner and publisher of *The Washington County News*. Specht's wife, Shirley Helms Specht, became advertising manager of the Chatom paper, and Frank Harwell continued as editor.

Specht was succeeded as publisher in Geneva by Maurice Pujol, who had been publisher of the Specht group's Florida weeklies. Pujol had been publisher in Chipley, Fla., since 1979 and had worked for dailies in Florida and Louisiana.

Specht's family bought the three papers in Geneva County in 1984 from Orsen B. Spivey, and Specht Newspapers continued to own them in 1995. Specht continued to be part-owner of Specht Newspapers, which also owned two weeklies in Florida and a daily in Louisiana. Interestingly, the Specht newspaper in Chipley, Fla., also was called *The Washington County News.*

Specht: *Washington County News* has strong support

Specht said *The Washington County News* had strong local support from Chatom advertisers and readers. Circulation topped 3,700, including about 2,200 paid subscriptions and strong rack sales, he said. Total population of the county was less than 17,000, and population of the town was about 1,500. "I see an enormous amount of potential in news, advertising and circulation," Specht said. Specht added that he planned to hire another reporter to help Frank Harwell, who had worked at the paper more than 20 years.

Dalton Jackson bought *The Washington County News* in April 1961 from N.B. Stallworth. In 1963, he merged it with *The Citronelle Call*, a weekly that had been based in nearby northern Mobile County. The merged papers became *The Call News-Dispatch*. In 1993, Jackson sold the "Call" part of the paper, which became *"The Citronelle Call."* After the sale, the Chatom-based paper again became *The Washington County News.*

The Jacksons, both of whom grew up in Centreville, first moved south to Chatom to work for Stallworth in 1953.

The Washington County News was established at St. Stephens in 1892 by William Mosley. Washington County was older than the state of Alabama. When it was named, it was much larger and was part of the Mississippi Territory. The site of St. Stephens, Alabama's territorial capital, was in the northeastern part of the county, alongside the Tombigbee River.

The Gadsden Times converts to morning delivery

The Gadsden Times staff had been planning to convert to morning delivery the first part of 1996, but they made the change in August 1995 because of the summer's extreme heat. The conversion change was made with only four days notice.

Concerns for the health of carriers caused the earlier change, said publisher Roger Hawkins. High temperatures from mid-July to late-August regularly hit 100 degrees, and lows often barely dropped below 80 degrees. *The Gadsden Times* became a morning paper on Monday, Aug. 21, 1995. It joined its sister New York Times paper, *The TimesDaily* in Florence, as a morning paper. *The TimesDaily* made the conversion to a morning paper in the 1980s.

With the change to a morning newspaper, *The Gadsden Times* joined most other dailies around the country. The shift from afternoon to morning distribution started in the 1960s and continued in 1995. The conversion to morning circulation was the third major change at *The Gadsden Times* in recent months. Earlier the newspaper moved to pagination and a redesign.

Tiner: "Forgiving nature of people of Vietnam"

The forgiving nature of the people of Vietnam touched *Mobile Press Register* editor Stan Tiner, who traveled as part of a tour sponsored by the American Society of Newspaper Editors. Tiner, who wrote an article about the trip for ASNE's *The American Editor*, and Brandt and Josie Ayers of *The Anniston Star* joined 15 other editors from around the nation on the tour.

"It is amazing how time heals the wounds of war," Tiner said. "There is little evidence that there was ever a war here." In Vietnam, the group noticed development differences between the north and the south, with Ho Chi Minh City, formerly

Saigon, clearly ahead of Hanoi. "While Hanoi has a shabby charm (and some classic French buildings in need of repair), Ho Chi Minh City whirs with energy," Tiner said.

Thirty years earlier, Tiner was a Marine who fought in the war there. "I was one of those fortunate boys who came home in one piece," Tiner wrote. "I got married. Went to college. Became a father. Got a job." Tiner wrote that the return to Vietnam in 1995 was akin to returning home.

"To say that I have come home to Vietnam may sound strange, but it is my truest sense of moment," he wrote. "I had come to Vietnam in search of my youth, and those I had known there. I discovered a new Vietnam that is trying to survive and is willing to employ the tools of capitalism to advance the lives of the people."

Joe Azbell dies in 1995

Veteran newspaper man Joe Azbell died in September 1995 after a long bout with lung cancer. Azbell was a columnist for *The Montgomery Independent* at the time of his death. *Montgomery Advertiser* columnist Bob Ingram paid tribute to Azbell in his column on Oct. 3, 1995:

"I owe a huge debt to Joe Azbell," Ingram wrote. "In the summer of 1953 the management at *The Gadsden Times* did some major housecleaning. A half-dozen or more heads rolled, mine included. I was able to take some consolation from the fact that when I was given the boot, I was in pretty good company. Some of the other victims included Al Fox, Frank Bruer and Don Wasson, all of whom, like me, eventually ended up as Capitol reporters in Montgomery. But back to my Azbell story."

Ingram continued, "A reporter who had been fired a few weeks earlier from *The Gadsden Times* had landed a copy desk job with *The Advertiser.* When he heard that I was unemployed, he mentioned my name to Azbell, who was city editor of *The Advertiser.* Azbell called and we set up an interview at a most unlikely place — Willie's Sports Center, or some name similar to that, on Montgomery Street next to the Empire Theater. Willie's was a combination pool hall-sandwich shop. Some of you old-timers will remember it. Against the din of colliding pool balls and players shouting 'rack,' Azbell hired me as a reporter for *The Advertiser* at a salary of $75 a week."

Ingram concluded, "Montgomery has been exceptionally good to me and my family since that day at Willie's, and for that I will always be grateful to Joe." Ingram, a veteran political writer, served as finance director in the Albert P. Brewer administration.

Sutton, Sheehan, inducted into Newspaper Hall of Honor

Weekly editor-publisher Robert E. Sutton Sr. of *The Democrat-Reporter* in Linden lived the classic tale of the youngster who went to work in a print shop and stayed enthralled with the newspaper business until he died at age 97. Daily editor William T. Sheehan moved quickly in his career to become editor of *The Montgomery Advertiser* before his death at age 54.

Robert E. Sutton Sr.
The Democrat-Reporter, Linden

Both men influenced their communities and their states, and both were inducted into the Alabama Newspaper Hall of Honor on Oct. 21, 1995, at the Auburn University Ralph B. Draughon Library.

Sutton, the son of a schoolteacher in Moss Point, Miss., was so well educated that he was certified to teach at age 11. Instead of becoming a teacher, he worked in a print shop and never got the printer's ink out of his blood. Early on, Sutton became an able hand typesetter, yet was always interested in new equipment. He installed one of the first Linotype machines in Marengo County, and he was one of the first newspaper publishers in the state to change to offset printing.

Sutton bought *The South Alabamian* in Jackson in 1910. In 1917, he sold it and bought *The Democrat-Reporter* in Linden and remained its editor and publisher until 1965. He was the newspaper's editor and publisher emeritus until his death in 1986. In 1982, he sold the paper to his son, Goodloe Sutton. In service to the community, Sutton was mayor of Linden and was elected to the House of Representatives. He was also involved in a variety of other local and state organizations, including the Chamber of Commerce and APA.

Sheehan entered journalism business in 1898

Sheehan entered the journalism business in 1898 and gained a reputation as an outstanding reporter for *The Birmingham Age-Herald, The Montgomery Journal* and *The Montgomery Advertiser.* Before his newspaper career began, he had been a teacher and principal in Eufaula, his hometown.

After Sheehan bought one-fourth interest in *The Advertiser,* he directed changes in typography and outreach, devoting new sections to religion, education, children and women. He sought to make

The Advertiser "the clearing-house of political information in Alabama."

Sheehan's career was cut short when he suffered a stroke.

Outside the newspaper, Sheehan served on the State Normal School Board for eight years, helped organize the Montgomery Press Club and helped organize a "lunch house" for the needy. He was APA president in 1922-1923.

William T. Sheehan
The Montgomery Advertiser

Sheehan led a number of civic and political leadership posts, including service as tax collector in Montgomery County, delegate to the Democratic National Convention, chairman of the governor's inauguration, and leader of a variety of other local projects. He became a sought-after speaker for efforts to bolster support for the nation's effort in World War I.

The 1995 Hall of Honor program was tied to Auburn University's Media Day and an outdoor barbecue lunch before the afternoon football game between Auburn and Western Michigan University.

New category added to Better Newspaper Contest

A new sports category was added to the 1996 Better Newspaper Contest. The BNC Contest Committee, led by Rusty Starr of *The Gadsden Times,* added Best Sports Single Event Story to the contest. Judges from Florida suggested the new category to give newspapers the opportunity to show off how they cover a sports event.

Hurricane Opal uprooted trees and cut off electricity all over Alabama in October 1995 in one of the most widely destructive storms in Alabama's history. Alabama's weekly and daily newspapers responded by serving readers with special sections and hard work by newspaper staffers.

Alabama's newspapers also lent a hand to papers in Florida. *The Montgomery Advertiser's* newsroom became *The Pensacola* (Fla.) *News-Journal* newsroom for a day, but the Florida paper's storm edition was printed on its own press.

Advertiser publishes hurricane "Extra" edition

The Montgomery Advertiser also published a special "Extra" edition Thursday after the hurricane hit. "People bought them from staffers trying to put them in racks," said publisher Richard H. (Dick) Amberg Jr.

The Birmingham News printed *The Destin* (Fla.) *Log,* and staffers from the *Birmingham Post-Herald* helped write and assemble the news for *The Log,* the *Post-Herald's* sister Scripps Howard newspaper.

APA president Doug Pearson of *The Daily Mountain Eagle* in Jasper said he was proud of the help that newspaper executives offered each other. "Helping one another is part of being a newspaper man or woman," Pearson said. "We tend to chip in and help even a rival newspaper when they need it."

Photographers try out new camera

One week before Hurricane Opal hit the Florida and Alabama coast, *Birmingham Post-Herald* photographers tried out their new camera. The day after the hurricane hit the coast, a *Post-Herald* photographer was on the Florida coast with his NC2000 electronic video camera that the paper bought from the Associated Press.

"The quality really held up," *Post-Herald* editor James H. Denley said. After shooting the photo, the photographer pulled a small disk out of the camera and inserted it into a Macintosh Powerbook. He sent it back to the paper by modem.

Denley said the *Post-Herald* staff still used traditional photography, but would use the camera for breaking news such as the 1995 Birmingham mayoral election. The *Birmingham Post-Herald* was thought to be the first newspaper in Alabama to use the more sophisticated electronic video cameras. Some Alabama newspapers were already using the small Apple video still cameras for real estate and auto ad photographs.

Tribune's Trib Talk gets workout

At *The Eufaula Tribune,* the paper's new audiotex system, Trib Talk, got a workout, as callers relied on *The Tribune* to keep them posted about school and business closings. The local radio station was knocked off the air. Even before the hurricane, Eufaula area residents had called *The Eufaula Tribune's* Trib Talk audiotex system much more than the paper's staff had expected.

"It's really going great," Jack Smith said. Smith, a journalism graduate student at the University of Alabama and son of *Tribune* publisher Joel P. Smith and associate publisher Ann Smith, said the 24-hour service offered local news, weather, time, sports, obituaries and other information free.

Managing editor Tom Davis said the new service complimented and promoted *The Tribune's* twice-weekly publication of local news. "*The Tri-*

bune and our local news consumers are now on the Information Superhighway and not under it," Davis said. Moreover, the new system almost paid for itself already, Smith said. Local advertisers were buying 20-second spots for the 90-second news items. During the first month, callers made 3,688 calls to the service. That didn't include the hundreds of calls during Hurricane Opal.

The Tuscaloosa News converts to morning publication

Friday the 13th (Oct. 13, 1995). That was the day *The Tuscaloosa News* published its last afternoon weekday edition. "Momentous" was how editor Donald Brown described the schedule change. "Momentous, certainly, for we've been doing it this way for a lot of years, since the founding of this community's first newspaper, *The Afternoon Mirror*, in 1818," Brown wrote in a column.

Publisher Ron Sawyer said copies were in newsracks by 6 a.m. from the start of the change, but carriers continued to deliver to subscribers in the afternoon for two more weeks.

The two-week shakedown period gave the staff time to smooth out the production cycle before Oct. 30, when the paper was first delivered to homes by 6 a.m. weekdays and 7 a.m. on weekends.

"We're going with the flow, you might say, as the number of morning newspaper readers nationally is almost triple that of afternoon readers — 42.8 million to 16.2 million in 1994, according to the Newspaper Association of America," Brown wrote.

With the morning shift at *The Tuscaloosa News,* all three dailies owned by The New York Times Co. in Alabama were morning publications. *The Gadsden Times* changed in August 1995, and *The TimesDaily* in Florence converted several years earlier.

Lamar Democrat enters 100th year of publication

The Lamar Democrat in Vernon entered its 100th year of publication in 1995. Editor Howard Reeves had been with the paper since 1952, and publisher Rex Rainwater had been there since 1950.

According to a story in the paper, they said *The Democrat* had been printed weekly since 1886, including some weeks when it seemed doubtful. In one instance, the hand-set type had not been locked into place and as the printing press started up, the type scattered and flew across the room. Staffers reassembled the forms and the paper came out. In another scare, the paper came out after a weekend fire in the office. "We still managed to get things in order so we could print a paper that week," they said in the story.

Former owner of *South Alabamian* dies

J. Fred Nall Sr. of Jackson, former owner of *The South Alabamian,* died Oct. 30, 1995, in a Baldwin County health care facility. Nall bought *The South Alabamian* from the late Bill Stewart and James H. (Jimmy) Faulkner Sr. in 1955 and after four years of struggling to make it profitable, he turned it back to the original owners. In 1969, Nall again purchased the newspaper and succeeded in making the paper and associated print shop and office supply store profitable.

Nall sold the paper to Mike and Linda Breedlove in 1974.

Nall was a newspaper man from the time he was 16, first going to work as a printer's devil at *The Atmore Advance.* Later, he was production manager of *The Baldwin Times* in Bay Minette and editor of *The Monroe Journal* in Monroeville. He owned and managed Nall Printing in Spanish Fort from 1976 to the mid-1980s.

"Fred Nall witnessed the tremendous change in newspapering and printing since the early part of this century," Mike Breedlove wrote in a personal column. Breedlove praised Nall's courage, honesty, generosity and calming influence. (Thelma Ritchy Nall, 83, widow of Fred Nall, died eight months later, on June 7, 1996, in Mobile.)

Evelyn Faulkner dies in 1995

Evelyn Irwin Faulkner, 85, the wife of former newspaper executive James H. (Jimmy) Faulkner Sr., died Oct. 28, 1995, after a long illness. In a story in *The Mobile Press Register,* friends remembered her as "very witty, lots of fun and very musical." Her husband, who was APA president in 1941-1942, owned weeklies in Baldwin County and other southwest Alabama counties. Mrs. Faulkner worked at *The Baldwin Times* in Bay Minette.

Williamson honored for 40 years' service

Mike Williamson, 65, long-time production chief at *The Clarke County Democrat* in Grove Hill, was honored in 1995 at the paper's Thanksgiving dinner for his 40 years of service at the newspaper. Williamson was hired by the late George Carleton. Publisher and editor Jim Cox presented Williamson with a plaque and camcorder.

Andy Gentry, 54, former co-owner of *The Auburn Bulletin,* died in early November 1995. Gentry, a long-time civic leader in Auburn, was also a former municipal court judge and former president of Auburn radio station WAUD.

Dunnavant was local historian

A well-known reporter in the Tennessee Valley, Robert Dunnavant Jr., died at age 48 on Dec. 7, 1995. Dunnavant grew up in the Athens area and had worked for a number of newspapers. He began his newspaper career with *The Athens Courier/Limestone Democrat* as editor. Dunnavant was also a reporter for *The Decatur Daily,* a correspondent for the *Birmingham Post-Herald,* and he was a reporter for *The Birmingham News* at the time of his death. Dunnavant, who was also a local historian, wrote at least three Civil War books and printed them through his own company, Pea Ridge Press. He also taught Civil War history at the University of Alabama in Huntsville.

Messenger no longer using Linotype

The Dec. 9, 1995, issue of *The Alabama Messenger,* a legal-notice weekly in Birmingham, was the last edition of the paper to use the Linotype machine. Since 1919, the paper had been printed on a No. 3 Miehle flatbed letterpress by A.H. Cather Publishing Co., in Birmingham. Editor Karen Abercrombie said the staff had no choice but to convert, because their typesetter became disabled, "and it takes six years to learn to use a Linotype machine."

S I D E L I G H T S

MARKING 125 YEARS OF HISTORY

Advertiser *unveils plaque honoring Hall*

A bronze plaque, in memory of the late Grover Cleveland Hall Sr., 10th editor of *The Montgomery Advertiser,* was unveiled Thursday, Nov. 4, 1948, in *The Advertiser* office.

The plaque was the fourth to commemorate great American journalists and was placed at *The Advertiser* by Sigma Delta Chi, professional journalistic fraternity. The other three plaques were presented in honor of Joseph Pulitzer of *The St. Louis Post-Dispatch,* Anthony Haswell of *The Vermont Gazette,* and James King of *The San Francisco Bulletin.*

The marker honoring Hall stated, "He was a Tribune of the Southern States. He bravely fought tyrannies over men's minds. Awarded the 1929 Pulitzer Prize for his editorial onslaughts 'Against Gangsterism, Floggings, Racial and Religious Intolerance'," Hall was editor of *The Montgomery Advertiser* from 1926 to 1941.

"There's not many of those gentlemen left who can do this anymore," said Traci Abercrombie Smeraglia, who published the paper with her mother, Karen Abercrombie, and grandmother, Eleanor Abercrombie Foster.

FTC approves Gannett's purchase of Multimedia

The Federal Trade Commission gave final approval to Gannett's purchase of Multimedia Inc. on Dec. 4, 1995. The purchase included *The Montgomery Advertiser* and its two sister weeklies in Alabama, *The Prattville Progress* and *The Community Press* in Millbrook.

At *The Advertiser,* Richard H. (Dick) Amberg Jr. remained as publisher and reported to a former executive at Multimedia, Bern Mebene. Mebene headed a new division for Gannett, Piedmont Newspaper Group, which included most of the old Multimedia dailies and a few other Gannett newspapers. In addition, executive editor Bill Brown remained at *The Advertiser,* as did editorial page editor Ken Hare and managing editor Jim Tharpe. Lamar Smitherman remained as publisher of *The Progress* and *The Community Press,* as well as vice president of special products and acquisitions for The Advertiser Co.

The Arab Tribune featured in *Editor & Publisher*

The Arab Tribune and editor David Moore were the focus of a feature in the "Weekly Editor" series of *Editor & Publisher's* Dec. 16, 1995, edition. The article quoted publisher Ed Reed praising Moore for bringing new energy to the weekly paper. "Moore's arrival five years ago helped push reporting, writing, photography and typography to new heights," the article by Tom Riordan said.

The article also mentioned *The Tribune* staff's reporting on the deadly tornado that destroyed the newspaper's front office in February 1995.

Smith started career in Jasper

H.E. "Buddy" Smith Jr., 70, of Baldwin County died Christmas Day 1995 of cancer. He was a former editor, columnist and reporter.

Smith began his newspaper career at *The Daily Mountain Eagle* in Jasper after World War II and moved to *The South Alabamian* in Jackson in 1952. He had moved back to southwest Alabama, nearer his hometown of Stockton. While in Jackson, he began writing his column, "Passing Comment," a column he later wrote for *The Onlooker* in Foley, and *The Mobile Press Register* for more than 30 years. He was known as an outdoorsman and a conservation advocate.

"He could shoot dove, hunt deer, call turkeys, shuck oysters and talk college football with the best of the 'good old boys' in the Foley Coffee Shop," John Cameron wrote in a *Press Register* column. Smith was survived by his wife, Hattie Smith, who was head of the Foley Chamber of Commerce.

1996
Mike Kelley, *The Clanton Advertiser*
1996-1997 president

125th annual press convention, Montgomery
Feb. 23-25, 1996
Summer convention, Perdido Beach
July 12-14, 1996

History and the future of the newspaper industry were the focus of APA's 125th Anniversary Convention Feb. 23-25, 1996, in Montgomery. Convention delegates gathered in the same city where the Press Association was founded in 1872 as the Editors and Publishers Association of Alabama.

The convention began on Friday, Feb. 23, 1996, with a reception at the Montgomery Museum of Art sponsored by *The Montgomery Advertiser.*

Past presidents met for a luncheon at noon on Friday, and committees met that afternoon.

Saturday morning, two workshops studied the history of the APA. Historians and political scientists discussed the role that newspapers played in the state's history. In the second program, delegates reviewed some leading newspaper law cases that started in Alabama and affected the entire country.

Archives Department displays historic newspapers

All day Saturday, the Alabama Department of Archives and History displayed several historic newspapers from Alabama in the foyer outside the meeting area.

At Saturday's luncheon, delegates heard several of the state's senior members discuss how the business had changed over the years. The oldest participant was Jimmy Mills, 95, retired editor of the *Birmingham Post-Herald,* and J.C. Henderson, 91, retired editor and publisher of *The Alexander City Outlook.*

Auburn University journalism professor Ed Williams, who was writing a new history of APA for the 125th anniversary in 1996, interviewed the senior members. The book, to be published later in 1996, was a major project of the 125th Anniversary Committee, headed by Ann S. Smith, associate publisher of *The Eufaula Tribune.*

A keepsake edition of *The Alabama Publisher* was published after the winter 1996 convention. The special edition featured photographs and stories about the 1996 convention.

Afternoon program focused on future

Saturday afternoon's program at the 1996 winter convention focused on the future, the emerging electronic technology, and other topics — programs that concluded with roundtable discussions.

The afternoon programs' focus on the future started with a discussion led by Jack Fishman, chairman of the National Newspaper Association. That program was followed by roundtable discussions including: Daily publishers led by Frank Helderman of *The Times-Daily* in Florence, weekly publishers led by Mike Hudgins of *The Sand Mountain Reporter* in Albertville, daily editors led by Joe Distelheim of *The Huntsville Times,* weekly editors led by Joe Thomas of *The Tri-City Ledger* in Flomaton, and a special roundtable on new media technology, such as Internet and audiotex, led by James H. Denley of the *Birmingham Post-Herald* and Jack Smith of *The Eufaula Tribune.*

Late in the afternoon. delegates toured *The Montgomery Advertiser's* new plant, which was being constructed behind the convention hotel, the new Embassy Suites in downtown Montgomery.

Kathryn Tucker Windham is guest speaker

Saturday night, delegates attended a reception and banquet in the hotel. Kathryn Tucker Windham, a former newspaper reporter at *The Thomasville Times, The Alabama Journal, The Birmingham News* and *The Selma Times-Journal,* was guest speaker.

Joseph H. (Joe) Adams, editor and publisher of *The Southern Star* in Ozark, was recognized by APA as having the oldest newspaper owned by the same family in the state. Joseph A. Adams, Joe Adams' great grandfather, established the paper in 1867. APA also recognized the oldest member newspapers, the oldest active editors and publishers, multi-generation newspaper families and past presidents.

Delegates attending the convention received commemorative paper weights and lapel pins.

Sunday morning, the convention continued with a breakfast and Senate candidates forum. Election of officers and the membership meeting concluded the winter convention.

When Kenneth Boone called the APA office the Monday after APA's 125th Anniversary Convention had ended, he said, "I have some bad news and some good news."

Boone named publisher of *The Natchez Democrat*

Boone, editor and publisher of *The Alexander City Outlook,* said he was moving to Natchez, Miss., to become publisher of *The Natchez Democrat.* Boone said he did not make up his mind until the

Sunday night after the convention closed.

Boone, publisher of *The Outlook* since 1989, began work in Natchez on March 4. Boone said he would continue to own *The Alexander City Outlook*, a five-day daily, and the weekly *Dadeville Record*, and he said he expected to spend one day a week in Alexander City.

As publisher of *The Natchez Democrat*, Boone was publisher of Boone Newspaper Inc.'s flagship newspaper. "I'll also be more involved with the company," he said. "This is the right decision for me, my family and the future of our business," Boone wrote in *The Outlook*.

Succeeding Boone at *The Alexander City Outlook* was Bruce Wallace, who came to Alexander City from Alice, Texas, where he had been publisher of *The Alice News-Echo*, a daily newspaper managed by Boone Newspapers Inc.

K.A. Turner, managing editor of *The Outlook* since 1992, was promoted to editor. Turner, a 1981 graduate of the University of Montevallo, held a number of newspaper staff and management jobs. Before joining *The Outlook*, she was corporate relations director for the Harbert Corp. in Birmingham.

Coosa News established in 1992

The Coosa County News in Rockford and *The Birmingham Business Journal* became APA's newest active members when the board of directors approved their membership at the 1996 winter convention.

The News was established in 1992 by Lewis Scarbrough and Carlton Jones, and Scarbrough eventually became sole owner.

The Coosa River News was the first newspaper published in Coosa County since *The Coosa Press* in Goodwater ceased publication in the early 1980s.

Coosa County had been the only county in the state without a newspaper with a second-class permit until 1994.

The Birmingham Business Journal applied for its active membership a year after it began publishing weekly with a second-class postal permit. *The Journal* was established in 1982 by Tina Savas, publisher. The publication began as a monthly tabloid and was published every two weeks in 1994. It became a weekly in January 1995.

TSU's Merrill Bankester retires in 1996

Merrill Bankester, dean of Troy State University's Hall School of Journalism since 1981, announced that he would retire on Sept. 1, 1996. During Bankester's tenure, the program's print, public relations and broadcast students won a number of state and national

awards, and while he was the local SPJ chapter adviser, the chapter was recognized as one of the nation's best. Bankester received his bachelor's and master's degrees at the University of Alabama.

Bankester was a native of Robertsdale, and he worked at newspapers in the area: *The Baldwin Times* at Bay Minette, *The Monroe Journal* in Monroeville, *The Pensacola* (Fla.) *News-Journal*, and *The Atmore Advance*. He went to Troy State after 10 years at Memphis State University. Bankester was appointed dean at TSU in 1981 after serving as acting dean for one year.

Dr. Steve Padgett was named acting dean of the School of Journalism. Padgett, whose specialty was broadcast journalism, came to TSU in 1991.

The Huntsville News closes on March 15, 1996

Alabama lost a daily newspaper in 1996. *The Huntsville News* announced that it would shut down on March 15. In most larger cities, the afternoon papers had either closed or merged with morning papers.

"It's been sad around here, like losing a member of the family," editor Lee Woodward said, "but morale is good because of the company's fairness and generosity." Publisher Bob Ludwig offered the 20 full-time employees of *The News* two choices. They could receive a buyout of one and half times salary plus credit for longevity, or they could work at *The News'* sister paper, *The Huntsville Times*.

Woodward said he had heard of shutdowns at other dailies where the owner walked in and told staff members to clean out their desks that day, with no warning or severance pay.

Woodward said that other area editors and publishers, including Tom Wright, editor of *The Decatur Daily*, and Robert Bryan, publisher of *The Cullman Times* and *The Athens News-Courier*, had called to ask about hiring some of the staff.

Woodward, editor since 1977, had already planned to retire in March 1996.

Ludwig blamed the decision on newsprint price increases of 60 percent in the past 18 months. "Regretfully, it is not economically viable to publish two daily newspapers in a population area the size of Huntsville and Madison County," Ludwig said.

The Huntsville News published its first edition on Jan. 8, 1964. It introduced itself to its Rocket City readers with this headline: "New Communications Capsule Blasts Off."

The original owners were James Cleary, a Huntsville attorney; John Higdon, former man-

Past presidents attend 125th convention in 1996

Past presidents attending the Nominating Committee meeting during APA's 125th anniversary convention Feb. 23, 1996, in Montgomery are, front row from left, Jay Thornton, retired, *The Daily Home*, Talladega; Barrett Shelton Jr., *The Decatur Daily;* Linda Breedlove, *The South Alabamian*, Jackson; Jimmy Mills, retired, the *Birmingham Post-Herald;* Luke Slaton, T*he Moulton Advertiser;* and Bob Bryan, *The Cullman Times*.

Back row from left, Sam Harvey, *The Advertiser-Gleam*, Guntersville; Jack Venable, *The Tallassee Tribune;* Phil Sanguinetti, *The Anniston Star;* J.C. Henderson, retired, *The Alexander City Outlook;* Ralph W. Callahan, Consolidated Publishing Co.; Bill Brooks Jr., retired, *The Brewton Standard* and *The Vincennes* (Ind.) *Sun-Commercial;* Steve Stewart, *The Monroe Journal;* W.E. (Gene) Hardin, former editor, *The Greenville Advocate;* Jim Jacobson, *The Birmingham News;* Jim Oakley Jr., former publisher, *The Centreville Press;* Don Woodward, *The Advertiser-Gleam*, Guntersville; Joel P. Smith, *The Eufaula Tribune;* and Mike Breedlove, *The South Alabamian*, Jackson.

The Breedloves are the only married couple to both have been elected president. In the photo, Harvey, Brooks and Stewart were the only second generation of their families to be elected APA presidents. Three of the past presidents, Henderson, Callahan and Mills, were age 90 or above, with Mills topping the list at age 96 on July 28, 1996. Venable was the only newspaper publisher in the Alabama Legislature in 1996, and both Mike Breedlove and Hardin had served in the Legislature. Brooks was president of both the APA and the Hoosier State Press Association in Indiana. Callahan had also been president of the Southern Newspaper Publishers Association.

ager of a local television station; and Thomas A. Barr, an electrical engineer.

Huntsville News began as weekly

The paper began as a weekly printed on its own press, a three-unit Vanguard offset press. The Fotomatic typesetter the staff used was one of the most modern in the business. Less than two months after starting, it became a twice-weekly paper, and by August 1964 it was a six-day daily, publishing every day but Sunday.

Stoney Jackson was the paper's first editor, but Sid Thomas, a former city editor with *The Huntsville Times*, became editor less than two months after the paper began publication. Other editors included Hollice Smith, Dave Langford, Tom Lankford and Woodward. Woodward first began work at the paper in 1972.

The News had a paid circulation of about 18,500. *The Times* had a circulation of about 65,000 and a Sunday circulation of about 86,000. Newhouse, which also owned *The Times*, bought *The News* in 1964.

News, Post-Herald exchange publishing cycles

In 1988, when *The Birmingham News* and the *Birmingham Post-Herald* renegotiated their Joint Operating Agreement through 2015, they agreed to exchange publication cycles.

January 1994 was the first target date for the conversion, but that was delayed after an announcement in 1993. In January 1996, a firm change date was set.

The News, owned by Newhouse, would become Birmingham's morning paper on Aug. 5, and the *Post-Herald*, owned by Scripps Howard, would become the afternoon paper.

The News distributed some 162,000 copies on weekday afternoons and 205,000 Sundays, while circulation of the *Post-Herald* was approximately 60,500. The two papers jointly produced a Saturday morning edition.

The *Birmingham Post-Herald* had been a morning paper since May 15, 1950, when the old *Birmingham Post*, afternoon paper, merged with *The Birmingham Age-Herald*, a morning paper owned by *The Birmingham News. The Post* was founded in 1921 by Edward W. Scripps. The Joint Operating Agreement was also established in 1950.

The News was established in 1888, and Newhouse purchased it in 1955.

"The time is now right for this change, which should help us serve our community even better," said Victor H. Hanson II, publisher of *The News*.

"Birmingham will continue to have two distinct editorial voices," said James H. Denley, editor and president of the *Post-Herald*. "We will continue to strive to give our readers the best possible newspaper each day."

Under the JOA, the two newspapers were served by combined advertising, circulation and production departments, all managed by The Birmingham News Co. The editorial departments, including all news-gathering functions, were separate and independent.

The two dailies in a JOA in Knoxville, Tenn., were the only other morning and afternoon papers to swap cycles, and the afternoon newspaper there folded.

Denley: *Post-Herald* will maintain niche

Denley said he was confident that the *Post-Herald* would maintain its niche in the Birmingham area.

The publication change reflected changes in readership from afternoon to morning around the country in most markets. Although there were still more afternoon dailies, 928 afternoon papers to 621 morning papers in 1995, morning papers had steadily increased their share of readers in the past four decades. Morning readership first exceeded afternoon readership in the early 1980s, according to the Newspaper Association of America.

Demographic changes encouraged *The News* and *Post-Herald* cycle change, Victor Hanson II told members of the Rotary Club in 1996.

Reading from Congressional Record in 1996

U.S. Rep. Terry Everett reads from *The Congressional Record* what he said about APA's 125th anniversary. Everett read from *The Congressional Record* during the past presidents meeting at the APA winter convention Feb. 23, 1996, in Montgomery. Everett, APA president in 1991-1992, is president of *The Union Springs Herald*. Linda Breedlove, chairman of the board and associate publisher of *The South Alabamian* in Jackson, accepted the proclamation on behalf of APA.

Rep. Everett's *Congressional Record* entry joined a letter from President Bill Clinton, a *Congressional Record* entry from U.S. Sen. Howell Heflin, and a resolution from the Alabama Legislature commemorating the Press Association's 125th anniversary. Everett may be the only newspaper publisher from Alabama to be elected to Congress. The resolutions, letter and Congressional Record entries are framed and hanging in the APA office in Birmingham.

News editor Jim Jacobson and *Post-Herald* editor Jimmy Denley brought a similar message to the Kiwanis Club of Birmingham. The Birmingham area's economy had changed from a mine and factory emphasis to a diverse service economy over the past 15 years, an economy with better educated readers who had higher incomes.

Harvey writes history of family, *Advertiser-Gleam*

Sam Harvey, editor of *The Advertiser-Gleam* in Guntersville, was writing a history of his parents and the newspaper in 1996. Harvey undertook the project after his father's death in 1995 at age 91. Harvey's mother and other relatives were helping with the research. Sam's wife, Valerie, said that Harvey had written seven chapters so far, and he said he plans "to lobby for a law forcing everybody to forget about being modest and write down in some detail the events of his or her life, so it will be there first-hand for all those who come after."

Joel Smith focus of feature story

Joel P. Smith, publisher of *The Eufaula Tribune,* was the focus of a feature story, "Leadership Spotlight," in *Publishers' Auxiliary* on Jan. 1, 1996. Smith said small-town publishers can't separate their lives from their work. "You're always on duty. But I don't mind it any more. I've learned to live with it. Age has helped," he said.

"The paper is an important part of the community," Smith said. "We can't take ourselves lightly." Smith also said that calls, letters, and visits after his heart surgery in 1995 proved to him that the community "does love me back." Many editors, he said, feel that although they love their communities, they never feel it in return from the community.

Some price relief possible in newsprint prices

The newspaper industry, hard hit by newsprint prices that almost doubled in the last two years, might get some price relief in 1996, *AlaPressa* reported in its March 1996 issue.

"Inventories are up and demand has slowed," *AlaPressa* reported. "Some large newsprint producers may be forced to drop plans for a 7 percent price hike that they had already planned for April 1996."

Newspapers had already factored in higher newsprint prices into their 1996 budgets, and "they may see higher profits as a result of the lower than expected newsprint prices," *AlaPressa* continued.

Distinguished Lecture Series marks 25th year in 1996

The Distinguished Lecture Series, a program to bring top speakers to the University of Alabama's

Newsroom editors at the *Birmingham Post-Herald* put out an edition in the mid 1950's. (*Post-Herald* file photo)

Department of Journalism, marked its 25th year in 1996.

The Lecture Series began in 1971, APA's 100th anniversary. The executive director at the time, Jim Hall, and several APA leaders that included Jim Boone, *The Tuscaloosa News;* Brandt Ayers, *The Anniston Star,* the late Bill Metz, the *Birmingham Post-Herald,* Karl Elebash, *The* (Tuscaloosa) *Graphic,* and the late Norman Bassett, *The Tuscaloosa News.* Ayers was the first president of the Journalism Foundation, and Metz was APA president when the Foundation started. Elebash was APA president in 1970-1971. Boone was chairman of the priorities committee of the Journalism Foundation.

Others involved in the decision were Neil O. Davis of *The Auburn Bulletin,* Jim Oakley Jr. of *The Centreville Press,* and Pat McCauley of *The Huntsville Times.*

The program began as a way to help show local industry support for the Department of Journalism, as it sought to regain national accreditation.

Journalism professor Dr. Frank Deaver proposed the series, and he continued to coordinate the program in 1996. The Lecture Series was launched with a $7,500 grant, which was the first grant from the three-year-old APA Journalism Foundation. The Lecture Series attracted a number of nationally known speakers. In 1983, the name was changed to the Editor-in-Residence Program, which also brought in a number of in-state and regional editors and publishers to visit UA journalism classes.

The Journalism Foundation supported the Lecture Series for its 25 years.

Ayers returned to the University of Alabama April 8 as its Editor-in-Residence to mark the program's 25th year.

Curl appears on "Donahue" show

Hollis Curl, editor and publisher of *The Wilcox Progressive Era* in Camden, appeared on the "Donahue"show in 1996, along with other community leaders in Camden. They discussed the new ferry that connected the Gee's Bend area of the county back to Camden, the county seat. Curl and his wife, Glenda, and the other community leaders spent three days in New York City as guests of the show.

In addition to being local newspaper editor and publisher, Curl was a licensed boat captain, and he was pictured in a wire service photo transporting U.S. Rep. Earl Hilliard and other officials across the Alabama River the day the ferry was opened.

Ralph Sears, Vernon Payne die in 1996

Ralph Sears, 72, former president of *The Shelby County Reporter,* died Feb. 14, 1996, while he and his wife, Marcia Sears, were visiting friends in Fort Walton Beach, Fla.

Sears was mayor of Montevallo for 24 years and had been on the City Council for 16 years. He came to Montevallo in 1948, when he went to work at Alabama College as spokesman for the college and as an instructor in broadcast and speech. He also owned radio station WBYE for many years.

Survivors included his wife, who was the first woman to be president of APA, and three children.

Vernon Payne, 67, of Montgomery died Jan. 19, 1991. Payne, a printer, began his career at *The Chilton County News* and later served there as editor.

Payne moved to *The Montgomery Advertiser* and later became general manager of Southern Publications, the offset printing operation. He later went to *The Gadsden Times* and later to *The Baldwin Times* at Bay Minette where he was publisher. At one time, Payne was active in APA, particularly in Hall of Honor activities.

"Promise me you'll deliver my papers"

"Promise me you'll deliver my papers," *Cullman Times* carrier Jim Hays told his daughter, Jerri, shortly before he died Feb. 13, 1996. Hays, a long-time carrier, suffered a heart attack while getting his papers ready for delivery. "He never missed a day delivering his papers except for two times he was in the hospital," said circulation manager Sam Mazzara.

The daughter delivered the papers even though her father died.

More than $30,000 provided in journalism-related grants

Income from the APA Journalism Foundation's investments provided more than $30,000 in journalism-related grants and a scholarship for the 1996-1997 year.

The Foundation board of directors approved grants for Alabama State University, the University of Alabama, Auburn University, Miles College, Troy State University and Samford University. It also gave provisional approval of a grant to the University of Alabama at Birmingham.

The grants supported a variety of programs from lab newspapers and newsletters to student field trips, high school journalism workshops, and a student Internet news project.

Buck Wilson, left, and Jim Robbins, *Birmingham Post-Herald* photographers, working the newspaper darkroom in the early 1950's. (*Post-Herald* file photo)

In addition, the board approved summer faculty grants for journalism professors to work at newspapers in Alabama: Gillis Morgan, Auburn University, to work at *The Wilcox Progressive Era* at Camden; Judy Sheppard, Auburn University, to work at *The Phenix Citizen* in Phenix City; Marie Parsons, the University of Alabama, to work at *The Huntsville Times;* Michael Hesse, University of South Alabama, to work at *The Monroe Journal;* and Dennis Jones, Samford University, to work at *The Birmingham News.*

Plainsman editor receives Metz Scholarship

When the Journalism Foundation board of directors met in spring 1996, they had to pick the annual Metz Scholarship recipient from among four highly qualified candidates.

They picked Greg Walker of Demopolis, not only because of his experience at his hometown paper, *The Demopolis Times,* his demonstrated interest in the newspaper business, and his leadership at *The Auburn Plainsman,* but also because he stood up to intimidation by Auburn's student government.

Walker was the only candidate for editor of the campus newspaper, after being qualified by the campus Communications Board. When SGA officers asked him to take a test on SGA constitution, budget and finance, a test required of other candidates for campus offices, Walker refused. He said that the Communications Board had already qualified him. He insisted that the newspaper and the SGA should be separate powers.

Although students pick an editor during Auburn's student government elections, the newspaper receives no money from the student activity fees.

Student senate backed down

The student senate then backed down and adopted a resolution excluding editor candidates from the test, thus preparing the way for the Communications Board to appoint Walker.

"His defense of the newspaper as an institution is a remarkable piece of work for one so young," said Dr. Jerry Brown, head of Auburn's Department of Journalism. "He made it clear that principles, not his personal pride, were at state."

Journalism Foundation president David Moore, editor of *The Arab Tribune,* said the board unanimously selected Walker for the $2,000 scholarship.

Walker's goal in 10 years: "I would like to be editing or publishing a daily or semi-weekly local newspaper."

1996 summer convention focuses on the future

While APA's 125th anniversary winter convention focused on the past, the summer convention, held July 12-14, 1996, focused on the future.

The head of Alabama's public employee retirement systems, David Bronner, spoke at Saturday's luncheon. Bronner, whose investment skills were known throughout the country, was a frank and constructive critic of Alabama, his adopted state. Bronner looked at the future of newspapers and how newspapers could play a stronger role in the future.

Dr. Culpepper Clark named UA dean

Dr. E. Culpepper Clark was named dean of the University of Alabama's College of Communication in March 1996, succeeding Dr. Ed Mullins who returned to full-time teaching. Clark earlier had served a executive assistant to the president of the University.

Before joining the president's office, Clark was chairman of the Department of Speech Commu-

nication from 1987 to 1990. Clark was the author of three books, including "The Schoolhouse Door: Segregation's Last Stand at the University of Alabama."

Ralph W. Callahan, president of *The Daily Home* in Talladega and a consultant to *The Anniston Star,* celebrated his 90th birthday on April 18, 1996. *The Star* staff gave a barbecue in his honor.

James Free, long-time Washington correspondent for *The Birmingham News,* died April 3, 1996 at age 87. Born in Gordo, Free graduated from the University of Alabama and earned a master's degree from Columbia University. He was part-owner and editor of a weekly newspaper in Tuscaloosa before he joined *The News* in 1935.

Free questioned McCarthy charges

Free was one of the first reporters to question in print the validity of charges brought against public officials by Sen. Joseph McCarthy.

His wife, Ann Cottrell Free, said he also passed along messages from moderate Alabamians to then-Attorney General Robert Kennedy during the Freedom Rider bus-burning crisis. Free was buried in Arlington National Cemetery with a memorial service in the National Press Club in Washington.

Tom Conner, long-time employee of *The Montgomery Advertiser,* died March 17, 1996, of injuries caused by a car accident on Feb. 28.

Conner joined *The Advertiser* in 1952 and remained on the payroll until 1985. He continued to work part-time, writing a weekly column entitled "Round and About." Conner was best remembered for his "Remember When" columns, which ran in *The Advertiser* on Sundays for about 20 years.

130-year-old *Monroe Journal* sold in 1996

When the family of the late Bill Stewart sold the 130-year-old Monroe Journal to Bo and Jodie Bolton, owners of *The Tri-City Ledger* in Flomaton on May 1, 1996, they sold one of Alabama's top weekly newspapers to the publishers of another top weekly.

The Stewarts also sold the job printing operation and other assets of Southwest Alabama Publishing Co. to the Boltons.

Both *The Monroe Journal* and *The Tri-City Ledger* were consistent winners in APA's Better Newspaper Contest for a number of years.

"I know that I have some big shoes to fill," Bolton said. "I have admired *The Monroe Journal* and the work that the Stewarts have done for years."

Marilyn Handley, *Journal* editor, purchased a minority share of the paper and continued as editor.

Joe Thomas, new publisher of *The Tri-City Ledger,* had been editor of the Flomaton newspaper. Thomas was also a former editor and publisher of *The Brewton Standard,* and he held a minority interest in *The Tri-City Ledger.*

The Stewart family did not sell its two radio stations in Monroeville. David Stewart managed the radio stations.

Stewart to seek daily newspaper work

Steve Stewart, former publisher of *The Monroe Journal,* said he hoped to find work at a daily newspaper as an editorial writer or mid-level editor. Stewart said he also was interested in the emerging possibilities for selling news on the Internet. Under Stewart, *The Journal* was the first weekly in Alabama to set up a Web Page on the Internet. The page featured a daily update of local news.

Stewart joined the staff of *The Decatur Daily* in August 1996 as an editorial writer and mid-level editor.

Stewart said he was glad he sold the paper to an independent owner who would live in Monroeville. He did not use a broker in the sale.

Bo Bolton was also a former editor and publisher of *The Demopolis Times.* Jodie Bolton had been art director at *The Tri-City Ledger* since 1986, and she had done job work for *The Alexander City Outlook,* advertising for *The Andalusia Star-News,* and composing work for *The Demopolis Times.* Mrs. Bolton helped *The Ledger* earn the reputation as one of the most technologically advanced weeklies in the South. Her work helped the paper earn a number of awards for overall design and advertising design.

Thomas' work as editor and editorial writer helped *The Ledger* earn awards in news coverage.

The Stewarts had owned all or part of *The Monroe Journal* since 1947. The newspaper was founded at Claiborne in 1866, but soon moved to Monroeville.

Both Bill Stewart, who died in 1995, and Steve Stewart served as president of APA. Patrice Stewart and Bo Bolton had been on the APA Board of Directors, and Ms. Handley served on the APA Journalism Foundation Board of Directors.

Geneva's "Red" Spivey lived by the Golden Rule

"Everyone who knew Orsen B. Spivey said he was a truly good man who lived by the Golden Rule," reporter Franklin Drumheller said in a story in *The Geneva County Reaper.*

Spivey, former owner and publisher of three weeklies in Geneva County, died May 2, 1996, at

Wiregrass Hospital after a long bout with emphysema. He was 84.

Drumheller wrote that Spivey owned and published *The Geneva County Reaper* at Geneva, *The Samson Ledger* and *The Hartford News-Herald* from 1959 to 1984, when he sold it to the Specht family. He first went to work at *The Reaper* in 1947 when it was owned by the Scott brothers.

After six months, Spivey became editor and manager and worked there until 1954, when he bought *The Graceville* (Fla.) *News* and worked there four years. When the Scott brothers were ready to sell *The Reaper,* they called Spivey.

When Spivey bought *The Reaper,* he also bought *The Samson Ledger* and *The Hartford News-Herald,* also located in Geneva County.

"Mr. Spivey was a unique person"

District Judge Charlie Fleming, whose mother, Karol Fleming, worked for 23 years with Spivey as editor of *The Reaper,* said, "We've just lost an excellent citizen. Mr. Spivey was a unique person, the kind hard to find these days. He was very broad minded. He was at home talking with the governor or the very elite in society, or in having a conversation with a garbage man.

"He was very well read and knowledgeable in politics and sports," Fleming added. "A man for all seasons."

Other friends noted Spivey's work with the Methodist Church and with his family and community. His father, the late A.O. Spivey, was a Methodist minister. Friends also described him as a scholar and a thoughtful community leader, and they talked about his love of the University of Alabama and his political leanings.

"A true Democrat," one called him.

Moe Pujol, publisher of *The Reaper,* said, "Mr. Spivey was one of that generation of community journalists who we would all do well to emulate.

"They worked not just to run a business, but to build their communities," Pujol said.

Spivey graduated in journalism from the University of Alabama in 1938.

Survivors included his wife, Laura, and a son, a sister and two brothers. The Spiveys continued to attend APA conventions for a number of years after he sold his newspapers, and he continued to attend journalism alumni gatherings at the University of Alabama.

At 81, John B. Stevenson active in 1996

John Bluford Stevenson, 81, was still actively working at *The Randolph Leader* in Roanoke in 1996. Stevenson, the father of editor and publisher

John Wyatt Stevenson, APA first vice president, said his responsibilities included editing copy, including engagements and weddings, obituaries and submitted articles, and serving as chief proofreader. Stevenson, the son of Olin Hampton Stevenson, 1964 Newspaper Hall of Honor inductee, also prepared a weekly feature, "Backward Glances," and he wrote occasional articles.

"I am also the fellow who does reports for the post office. On the outside, I make trips to the bank and post office. My favorite task is taking all the money to the bank," he joked.

Stevenson's wife, Gwendolyn Wyatt (Gwen) Stevenson, worked at *The Randolph Leader* until three months and one week before her death on Nov. 21, 1992, at age 76. Mrs. Stevenson was receptionist, bookkeeper, proofreader and occasional writer.

Alyce Billings Walker dies at age 88

Alyce Billings Walker, a pioneering newspaper woman, died April 30, 1996, at age 88. She was the former women's page editor and columnist for *The Birmingham News* and long-time civic leader. *Birmingham News* editor James E. Jacobson said Mrs. Walker was a trailblazer in many ways during a time when women weren't often seen in newsrooms.

Although Mrs. Walker's work required her to cover traditional women's page issues such as fashion shows, she also supported more serious issues facing women such as changing state laws to make women equal to men in the passing of property to heirs.

Shelby County Reporter transmits pages via modem

The Shelby County Reporter in Columbiana became the first newspaper in the state in 1996 to send its pages to a central printer via modem. Kim Price, editor and publisher of *The Shelby County Reporter*, said sending pages via modem to the printing plant at *The Selma Times-Journal* saved time and allowed later deadlines for breaking stories. Price said production staff members at *The Reporter* began copying the pages to SyQuest disks in May 1996.

Old drum cylinder press still around in 1996

The old drum cylinder press used before and after the war by Capt. Arthur Henley Keller to

Gwen and John Stevenson
John Bluford Stevenson and wife Gwen Stevenson at office of *The Randolph Leader* in Roanoke in 1989. Mrs. Stevenson worked at *The Leader* until three months before her death in 1992 at age 76, and Stevenson still worked at the newspaper in 1996. The first issue of *The Randolph Leader* to come off the press in 1892 is on the wall behind Stevenson. (Photograph by Ed Williams)

publish *The Tuscumbia Times* (now *The Standard and Times*), was still in the building that housed the weekly paper, *AlaPressa* reported in 1996. The building, built in 1821, was on the National Register of Historic Places, and the newspaper was the second oldest newspaper still published in the state, according to editor and publisher Jim Crawford.

Capt. Keller was the father of famed deaf-blind Alabamian, Helen Keller.

Crawford said the paper missed publication only once, and it took the Union occupation of Tuscumbia to do it. The old press, which was still intact and in good condition, was brought over piece by piece from North Carolina by wagon, Crawford said. The press was turned by hand. "It's was like a coffee grinder," Crawford said. "It had a big handle, about three feet long."

Lecture series to honor Neil and Henrietta Davis

The Auburn University Department of Journalism started a fund drive in 1996 to launch an annual lecture series honoring two journalists from Auburn, Neil O. Davis and the late Henrietta Worsley Davis.

Davis, a 1935 graduate of Alabama Polytechnic Institute (now Auburn University), founded *The Auburn Bulletin* in 1937 with the assistance of Auburn journalism professor Joseph Roop. Davis served as editor and publisher of *The Bulletin* for 40 years. Mrs. Davis, also a 1935 API graduate, was the paper's associate editor and chief reporter.

Neil O. Davis
The Auburn Bulletin

"*The Bulletin's* editorial voice, calling for citizens to stand strong against racism, provincialism and myopic politicians, was heard across the country," a news release stated.

"Neil Davis' prose was reprinted in papers ranging from *The New York Times* to

Henrietta Worsley Davis
The Auburn Bulletin

The St. Louis Globe-Democrat, and he was nominated for a Pulitzer Prize. Henrietta Davis' precise reporting of local civic and social affairs made their newspaper a staple in Auburn homes," the news release continued. "The two also served as de facto journalism professors, teaching generations of *Auburn Plainsman* staff members how to publish a paper that served the everyday needs of readers and, at the same time, directed their thinking to the most important political issues of the day."

Delaney named editorial page editor of *Our World News*

Paul Delaney, chairman of the Department of Journalism at the University of Alabama, resigned in 1996 to become editorial page editor of a new weekly national newspaper that targeted black readers. Delaney, 63, came to the University in 1992 from *The New York Times,* where he had been a senior editor.

Delaney began working at the new newspaper, *Our World News,* in August 1996. The paper was based in Baltimore and was printed and distributed by Dow Jones & Co, publishers of *The Wall Street Journal.*

An Alabama native, Delaney graduated from high school in Montgomery in 1950 when blacks could not attend the University of Alabama. He became the first black faculty member in the UA Department of Journalism.

The College of Communications dean, Dr. E. Culpepper Clark, said former dean Dr. Ed Mullins would step in as acting department chairman until a new chairman was named.

Bob Morrissette, 73, dies July 21, 1996

E.R. (Bob) Morrissette Jr., 73, former owner, editor and publisher of *The Atmore Advance* and APA president in 1978-1979, died July 21, 1996, at his home. Morrissette spent more than 30 years working as a reporter, editor and publisher before joining U.S. Sen. Howell Heflin's staff at his Mobile office. Morrissette joined Heflin's staff after selling *The Advance* to Morris Newspaper Corp. of Savannah, Ga., in 1979. (Eighteen months later, in 1980, *The Advance* and *The Brewton Standard* were purchased by Boone Newspaper Group).

"Bob Morrissette was not only a close adviser but a good friend," Heflin said. "We met in college at the University of Alabama and had remained friends ever since. He had an outgoing personality and a wonderful sense of humor.

"Bob always considered himself a newspaper man in the traditional sense and saw to it that he knew everything and everybody in his community," Heflin added.

Stanton was *News* state editor

Al Stanton, 70, a veteran journalist and former state editor of *The Birmingham News,* died Aug. 20, 1996. A Tuscaloosa native, Stanton served with the Navy in the Pacific during World War II. He graduated from the University of Alabama in 1950 with a major in journalism.

Stanton worked in the classified advertising department of *The Tuscaloosa News* before becoming a reporter with *The Troy Messenger* and later *The Dothan Eagle.* He joined *The News* in 1955 and covered the city hall and courthouse beats. In 1959, he was assigned to cover state government initially as a reporter and later as chief of the Montgomery bureau.

Stanton became city editor of *The News* in 1963 and state editor in 1967, a position he held for several years. He retired from *The News* in 1984 as a copy editor and had been publications editor for BE&K Inc.

J.C. Henderson marries at age 92

"Henderson finds love is ageless" was the headline in a page 1 feature story in *The Alexander City Outlook* on July 20, 1996. Staff writer Debra Burleson wrote that former *Outlook* publisher J.C. Henderson had married at age 92.

Ann Bozeman was visiting the Biltmore estate in Asheville, N.C., in November 1995 along with an Alexander City tour group when she met Henderson. Ann didn't know that meeting Henderson in North Carolina would begin a relationship that would continue after they returned to Alexander City.

They courted, and according to Henderson, he knew he was in love after a five-day hospital stay, and she stayed with him the entire time.

"After I was in the hospital, we became good friends. I knew I loved her and I wanted to marry her, so I got down on my knees and asked her to marry me," Henderson told Burleson.

Couple married July 17, 1996

The couple married July 17, 1996, at First Methodist Church in Alexander City in a small ceremony with family and friends in attendance. Henderson has "gorgeous big blue eyes," Ann said before the wedding.

In his weekly column in *The Outlook* under the pen name of "The Ole Crier," Henderson wrote that he was having a hard time trying to decide if he was "an old married man, or just an old man who is newly married."

"The Ole Crier is having a time getting accustomed to the many changes that an old fellow has to do," Henderson wrote in *The Outlook* on July 24. "One was to get used to the hair curlers that we have not experienced for the past 10 years while we lived alone except for the company of the Crier's old dog, Daisy."

"It is a wonderful thing to know someone loves you and is willing to spend her life with you. With a new red car and a new bride, what more can you ask for?"

Descendant of Maj. William Wallace Screws dies

A descendant of APA founding father William Wallace Screws died in Florida on Aug. 27, 1996.

Marion Pitts McNutt, 69, was buried in Tampa, Fla., where she lived with her husband of 44 years. A Montgomery native and a 1948 graduate of the University of Alabama, Mrs. McNutt was the great-granddaughter of Maj. William Wallace Screws, editor and publisher of *The Montgomery Advertiser* from 1865 to 1913.

Screws served as APA president from 1878 through 1882. He called the first meeting in his office on March 17, 1871, to consider the possibility of organizing the press of Alabama. Out of that meeting of eight editors came a call for a meeting of all the editors of the state. It was held on June 18, 1872, at which time the Editors and Publishers Association of the State of Alabama, now the Alabama Press Association, was organized.

Mrs. McNutt was a member of the Junior League and did volunteer work in New Orleans and Augusta, Ga. She was survived by her husband, Edwin R. McNutt Jr.; two sons, E. Roland McNutt III of Chica, Calif.; and William Screws McNutt of Tampa.

Linda Breedlove receives prestigious NNA award

Linda Hayes Breedlove, co-owner and associate publisher of *The South Alabamian* in Jackson, was the 1996 recipient of the National Newspaper Association's Emma C. McKinney Memorial Award. She was the 30th recipient of the prestigious award given to a newspaper woman in recognition of distinguished service to her community and profession.

The award was presented by NNA chairman R. Jack Fishman, president of Lakeway Publishers

Mr. and Mrs. J. C. Henderson
Henderson, 92, "finds love is ageless" in 1996

Inc., in Morristown, Tenn., during ceremonies on Sept. 27, 1996, at NNA's 111th annual convention in Nashville.

Mrs. Breedlove, APA president in 1994-1995, was the second woman to rise to president in APA's history. She also served on the Press Association's board of directors for two terms, as well as serving on a variety of committees.

Keller made award nomination

In nominating Mrs. Breedlove for the award, APA executive director Bill Keller noted, "Like many women who have become leaders in the industry today, Linda Breedlove worked her way up from what was considered 'women's work.' In her first newspaper job, she worked as a front-office clerk. She 'took' and wrote classified ads and handled subscriptions and bookkeeping. She also began learning newspaper writing skills by rewriting community announcements. From those beginnings, her career grew and blossomed."

Mrs. Breedlove also served as president of the Jackson Chamber of Commerce. She was a member of the Jackson Sales Team, a local economic development effort. In 1990, she was selected Citizen of the Year by the Jackson Civitan Club.

The McKinney award was created in 1966 to honor the pioneering newspaper woman Emma C. McKinney's 58 years as co-publisher and associate editor of *The Hillsboro* (Ore.) *Argus.*

The Thomasville Times sold to Breedlove and Cox

Two veteran Clarke County newspaper publishers joined in partnership in 1996 to purchase *The Thomasville Times.*

Mike Breedlove, publisher of *The South Alabamian* in Jackson, and Jim Cox, publisher of *The Clarke County Democrat* in Grove Hill, as the principal stockholders of The Thomasville Times Inc., announced the purchase. The change of ownership from Pace Wells Bozeman Jr. of Thomasville and Jackie Bozeman of Fairhope became effective Sept. 1, 1996.

The Times, begun in 1921, had been owned by the Bozeman family for 37 years.

"We appreciate the Bozeman family's confidence and faith in us to continue the significant part *The Thomasville Times* has played in the growth of Thomasville, south Marengo and Wilcox county area," Breedlove said.

"I am delighted that Mike and I were able to work together to buy *The Thomasville Times,*" Cox said. "We plan for the newspaper to continue to be a separate and independent entity with its own voice for the Thomasville area."

Bozemans a newspaper family for three generations

"In 1926, a high school principal decided to purchase the newspaper in Evergreen," *Thomasville Times* editor Dana Dunn wrote in the Sept. 5, 1996, issue of *The Times.*

"The decision would forever change the life of Robert Gaston Bozeman, his children and grandchildren. The family's involvement would continue for 70 years and span three generations."

Robert Gaston Bozeman was principal of Evergreen City School when he decided to enter the newspaper business. He purchased *The Evergreen Courant* in 1926, and owned and operated the newspaper until his retirement in 1957. Bozeman was publisher emeritus until his death in 1974.

During Bozeman's reign at the helm of *The Courant,* he served two terms as APA president (1936-1938), and in 1980 was posthumously inducted into the Alabama Newspaper Hall of Honor.

Printer's ink flowed in Bozeman's blood, it seemed, and he passed that condition to his three sons.

Bob Bozeman bought *Courant* in 1957

Robert G. (Bob) Bozeman Jr. bought the paper from his father in 1957. Bob Bozeman, who spoke to his readers each week in a front page column titled, "The Colyum," was succeeded at *The Courant* by his son, Robert G. Bozeman III, and his widow, Maurice, after his death in 1991. They continued to publish and edit *The Courant* in 1996.

At one time all three of Robert Gaston Bozeman's sons were editors and publishers of weekly newspapers: Robert Gaston Bozeman Jr., the eldest, at *The Evergreen Courant,* Dickey Bozeman at *The Choctaw Advocate* in Butler, and Pace Bozeman at *The Thomasville Times.*

Dickey Bozeman first purchased *The Thomasville Times* from renowned editor and publisher Earl Tucker in 1959. He sold *The Times* in 1964 to his brother Pace after he took a job as postmaster in Thomasville. Pace Bozeman died in 1983.

Wells Bozeman was just 5 when his father, Pace Bozeman, bought *The Thomasville Times.* Pace Bozeman wrote a popular column, "Keeping Pace With The Times," that recounted life around Thomasville and at the Bozeman household.

Who lays the egg, hen or rooster?

"I remember one time when my cousin and I were arguing over which laid the eggs — a hen or a rooster," Wells Bozeman recalled in 1996, recalling his late father's columns in *The Times*. "I said the rooster could, and my cousin just really teased me. I was a little boy."

Young Wells would never concede the argument, and finally told his cousin, "Well, a rooster could lay an egg if he tried hard enough."

His father wrote about the incident in "Keeping Pace With The Times," and he was teased about the comment for years, Wells Bozeman recalled in 1996.

Wells and his cousin, Robert Bozeman, at *The Evergreen Courant*, were third generation newspaper men in 1996. But for Wells, the newspaper had never been his calling.

"It just wasn't my chosen profession, but I have enjoyed doing it," he said. "But it's time to move on."

The Bozeman legacy in Alabama newspapers encompassed six weekly papers. At various times, family members owned, edited and published *The Thomasville Times, The Evergreen Courant, The Choctaw Advocate* in Butler, *The Brewton Standard, The Dadeville Record*, and *The Sumter County Journal* in York.

Long-time *Andalusia Star-News* employee dies at 74

Retired *Andalusia Star-News* employee Paul Jordan, who died Aug. 29, 1996, at age 74, began work at what was then *The Andalusia Star* as a high school student. The ink got in his blood, and he remained there until his retirement in 1985.

During his almost 50 years of newspapering, Jordan saw the revolutionary changes in the industry, from Linotype machines to computers. Jordan started his newspaper career as a Linotype operator, first working half-days for no pay but for school credit. The editor of *The Andalusia Star* was Oscar M. Dugger, and subscriptions were 50 cents a year.

Syrup, sweet potatoes exchanged for subscriptions

Back then, Jordan recalled, traveling sales people would hire on to sell subscriptions. A can of syrup or a bushel of sweet potatoes could pay the annual subscription fee. "I've seen as many as 90 gallons of syrup in Mr. Dugger's office," Jordan recalled to *Star-News* columnist Jan White several months before his death. Dugger, in turn, would sell the syrup to local grocery stores to get the money for the subscriptions.

Jordan said the Linotype machine he worked on had been rebuilt in 1905, so he wasn't sure of its age. But he knew the Linotype, which formed letters from molten metal, was a great improvement over setting type by hand.

In 1956, the newspaper bought a new Linotype

that could produce four sizes of type. Jordan said printing presses changed very little. Sheets of paper were hand-fed into the presses. Printing and folding 5,500 issues of an eight-page paper took 13 hours, he recalled.

Offset printing came in the 1960s

Then came offset printing in the 1960s, and the same number of newspapers could be printed in only 30 minutes. Offset printing also brought about a machine that made a perforated tape. The tape was then fed through a computer that set columns of type that were pasted onto pages.

On Nov. 1, 1948, Jordan saw the merger of *The Andalusia Star* and *The Covington News* to become *The Andalusia Star-News*.

After his retirement in 1985, Jordan spent time as a volunteer at Three-Notch Museum in Andalusia. Like Dick Jones, Joe Jones, Oscar M. Dugger, Ed Dannelly, Oscar Byrd, Byron Vickery and Arthur G. Jones — and many other typesetters, printers, editors and publishers — Paul Jordan played an integral part in the history of newspapers in Andalusia and Covington County.

Kilpatrick, McLendon inducted into Hall

One of the nation's most distinguished political reporters, Carroll Kilpatrick, and a weekly publisher called "a power with a pen in Alabama," Jonathan Cincinnatus McLendon, were inducted into the Alabama Newspaper Hall of Honor on Nov. 9, 1996.

The induction was in the Hall of Honor room in the Ralph B. Draughon Library on the Auburn University campus.

Carroll Kilpatrick, a Montgomery native, began his career on Alabama newspapers and finished it as White House correspondent for *The Washington Post*. For 35 years, from 1940 through 1975, Kilpatrick covered the national government, from the Roosevelt administration through the Watergate scandal, and was praised as much for his courtesy for his integrity and accuracy.

Kilpatrick attended the University of Alabama and was editor of *The Crimson White*. His journalism education continued through his early years as a reporter for two Birmingham dailies, *The Birmingham News* and *The*

Carroll Kilpatrick
The Washington Post

Birmingham Age-Herald, and as associate editor of *The Montgomery Advertiser* under Grover C. Hall Sr.

Grover C. Hall Sr.
The Mongtomery Advertiser

After a year as a Nieman Fellow at Harvard University, he and a colleague began a two-man Washington bureau that served papers in Birmingham, Chicago and San Francisco over a 10-year period.

After one year as an assistant press secretary at the State Department, Kilpatrick began a phase of a career that put him in the forefront of American journalism. His skills were best demonstrated during Watergate when he reported the Nixon administration's denials about its involvement in the 1972 break-in at the Democratic National Headquarters. Bob Woodward later said of Kilpatrick's reporting: "It was one of the hardest jobs in journalism. He did it without compromising his integrity."

In *The Post* obituary, Katherine Graham, chairman of the Washington Post Co., said Kilpatrick was "gentle, fair, tough-minded and skeptical, but never lost his own sense of modest perspective, gentle humor and consideration for others."

Kilpatrick was recipient of the Merriman Smith Award for White House coverage in 1972 and was past president of both the Overseas Writers of Washington and the White House Corespondents Association. Kilpatrick, who died in 1984, spent his final years as a Virginia farmer and part-time public affairs consultant.

Accepting a plaque on behalf of the Kilpatrick family at the Hall of Honor ceremony was a son, former *Birmingham News* and *Birmingham Post-Herald* staff writer Andy Kilpatrick.

McLendon was ordained a Baptist minister

Jonathan Cincinnatus McLendon was educated in a school house near Ramer, Ala., by his father,

James Riley McLendon, who was a scholar, teacher and farmer. He graduated from the Baptist-owned Howard College. His desire was to become a preacher like his paternal grandfather, George Grandberry McLendon. After leaving Howard, he went to the Southern Baptist Theological Seminary in Louisville, Ky., and was ordained a Baptist minister.

Jonathan McLendon
The Luverne Journal

At age 29, McLendon left the ministry and came to Luverne. McLendon, who had a desire to own his own business, not only saw the need for a newspaper in Crenshaw County, he established *The Luverne Journal,* a weekly newspaper he owned and operated for more than 40 years.

During that time writing editorials, McLendon was a power with a pen in Alabama. It was said he could make or break a politician by the power of his words. Many a politician made their way to Luverne to make their peace with McLendon before they announced their candidacy for public office.

Longtime friend O.P. Bentley said of McLendon, "He had stood four-square always for the best interest of his county and had been the unflinching friend of the farmers, merchants, schools, churches and for all things else that would be of well-being to the people of this county. His voice has been heard many times, from the public forum, in defense of his town's and his country's interest. His editorial pen has distributed gallons of ink in an effort to upbuild his people in every laudable way."

On Aug. 9, 1933, after 45 years of publishing *The Luverne Journal,* McLendon, who was APA president in 1925-1926, turned the paper over to his son and junior editor, James Merritt McLendon.

McLendon died in 1946.

CHAPTER 9

Presidents, Officers, Field Managers & Executive Directors

1872-1996

"The yardstick by which a good newspaper must be measured is not popularity. It is integrity, truth and the courage to take a stand and hold fast to its convictions, regardless of the effect upon its subscription list or advertising income.

"We hope we have measured up. To us, our job is more than a living, it is a way of life. And we like it."

Herve Charest Jr.
The Tallasse Tribune

— *Herve Charest Jr. (1900 -1993)*
Editor and Publisher, The Tallassee Tribune
APA president, 1963-1964
(From an editorial in 1955 on The Tallassee Tribune's
55th year of consecutive publishing)

PRESIDENTS

June 18, 1872
Col. Seaborn Jones Saffold, *The Selma Daily Times,* was elected chairman and president of the first official convention, June 18, 1872. He then was elected president for 1872-1873.

1872-1873
Col. Seaborn Jones Saffold, *The Selma Daily Times* (Served three terms)

1873-1874
Col. Seaborn Jones Saffold, *The Selma Daily Times*

1874-1875
Col. Seaborn Jones Saffold, *The Selma Daily Times*

1875-1876
Col. Richard Holmes Powell, *The Union Springs Herald and Times*

1876-1877
James Freeman Grant, *The Jacksonville Republican*

1877-1878
Willis Brewer, *The Hayneville Examiner*

1878-79
Maj. William Wallace Screws, *The Montgomery Advertiser*
(Served four terms)

1879-1880
Maj. William Wallace Screws, *The Montgomery Advertiser*

1880-1881
Maj. William Wallace Screws, *The Montgomery Advertiser*

1881-1882
Maj. William Wallace Screws, *The Montgomery Advertiser*

1882-1883
Gen. James Berney Stanley, *The Greenville Advocate*
(Served four terms)

1883-1884
Gen. James Berney Stanley, *The Greenville Advocate*

1884-1885
Gen. James Berney Stanley, *The Greenville Advocate*

1885-1886
Gen. James Berney Stanley, *The Greenville Advocate*

1886-1887
William M. Meeks, *The Gadsden Times and News*
(Served two terms)

1887-1888
William M. Meeks, *The Gadsden Times and News*

1888-1889
Harry G. McCall, *The Shelby Sentinel*, Columbiana
(Served two terms)

1889-1890
Harry G. McCall, *The Shelby Sentinel*, Columbiana

1890-1891
John C. Williams, *Our Mountain Home*, Talladega
(Served three terms)

1891-1892
John C. Williams, *Our Mountain Home*, Talladega

1892-1893
John C. Williams, *Our Mountain Home*, Talladega

1893-1894
Edward Louis Collen Ward, *The Bridgeport News*

1894-1895
Robert M. Rawls, *The Athens Courier*
(Served two terms)

1895-1896
Robert M. Rawls, *The Athens Courier*

1896-1897
Moncure Woodson Camper, *The Florence Times*
(Served three terms)

1897-1898
Moncure Woodson Camper, *The Florence Times*

1898-1899
Moncure Woodson Camper, *The Florence Times*

1899-1900
Rufus Napoleon Rhodes, *The Birmingham News*
(Served two terms)

1900-1901
Rufus Napoleon Rhodes, *The Birmingham News*

1901-1902
William E.W. Yerby, *The Greensboro Watchman*
(Served three terms)

1902-1903
William E.W. Yerby, *The Greensboro Watchman*

1903-1904
William E.W. Yerby, *The Greensboro Watchman*

1904-1905
Charles Herd Greer, *The Marion Standard*

1905-1906
Robert E. Lee Neil, *The Selma Times*
(Served two terms)

1906-1907
Robert E. Lee Neil, *The Selma Times*

1907-1908
Howard S. Doster, *The Prattville Progress*

1908-1909
J.C. Lawrence, *The Union Springs Breeze*

1909-1910
C.G. Fennell, *The Guntersville Democrat*

1910-1911
McLane Tilton Jr., *The Pell City Progress*

1911-1912
Luman Handley Nunnelee, *The Centreville Press*
(Served three terms)

1912-1913
Luman Handley Nunnelee, *The Centreville Press*

1913-1914
Luman Handley Nunnelee, *The Centreville Press*

1914-1915
Christopher James Hildreth, *The New Decatur Advertiser*

1915-1916
Col. Harry Mell Ayers, *The Anniston Star* (Served two terms)

1916-1917
Col. Harry Mell Ayers, *The Anniston Star*

S I D E L I G H T S
MARKING 125 YEARS OF HISTORY

First woman APA president:
Marcia M. Sears, *The Shelby County Reporter,* Columbiana, 1981-1982

Women APA presidents:
Marcia M. Sears, *The Shelby County Reporter,* Columbiana, 1981-1982
Linda H. Breedlove, *The South Alabamian,* Jackson, 1994-1995

Husband-wife APA presidents:
Mike Breedlove, *The South Alabamian,* Jackson, 1985-1986.
Linda H. Breedlove, *The South Alabamian,* Jackson, 1994-1995.

Father-son APA presidents:
Gen. James Berney Stanley, *The Greenville Advocate,* 1882-1886
Webb Stanley, *The Greenville Advocate,* 1926-1927 and 1934-1935
Glenn Stanley, *The Greenville Advocate,* 1962-1963.

• • •

Bill Stewart, *The Monroe Journal,* Monroeville, 1959-1960
Steve Stewart, *The Monroe Journal,* 1987-1988

• • •

Porter Harvey, *The Advertiser-Gleam,* Guntersville, 1967-1968.
Sam Harvey, *The Advertiser-Gleam,* 1993-1994.

• • •

W. Emmett Brooks, *The Brewton Standard,* 1929-1930.
William E. (Bill) Brooks Jr., *The Brewton Standard,* 1953-1954.

Only individual to serve as president of two state press associations:
William E. (Bill) Brooks Jr., Alabama Press Association, 1953-1954. Hoosier State (Indiana) Press Association, 1978-1979.
(Brooks was managing editor of *The Brewton Standard* when he served as APA president. He was editor and publisher of *The Vincennes Sun-Commercial* when he was president of the Hoosier State Press Association.)

• • •

Other involvement in two state press associations:
Millard Grimes, *The Enterprise Ledger,* was second vice president of the Alabama Press Association in 1981-1982. He was president of the Georgia Press Association in 1985-1986.

Joel P. Smith, *The Eufaula Tribune,* was president of the Alabama Press Association in 1969-1970. He served on the board of directors of the Georgia Press Association from 1989-1992.

• • •

Greatest number of APA presidential terms from one newspaper:
The Greenville Advocate (eight terms)
Gen. James Berney Stanley, *The Greenville Advocate,* was president four terms.
Webb Stanley, son of Gen. James Berney Stanley, served two terms.
Glenn Stanley, son of Gen. James Berney Stanley, served one term.
Glenn Stanley's son-in-law, W.E. (Gene) Hardin, served one term.

1917-1918
Edward Doty, *The Tuscaloosa News*

1918-1919
A.W. McCullock, *The Gadsden Journal*

1919-1920
Oscar M. Dugger Sr., *The Andalusia Star*

1920-1921
Frank N. Julian, *The Sheffield Standard*

1921-1922
William Theodore Hall, *The Dothan Eagle*

1922-1923
Capt. William Thomas (Will) Sheehan,
The Montgomery Advertiser

1923-1924
Forney G. Stephens, *The Southern Democrat*, Oneonta
(Served second term, 1932-1933)

1924-1925
W.R. Jordan, *The Huntsville Morning Star*
(Jordan died while in office and was succeeded by
first vice president James S. Benson, *The Progressive Age*, Scottsboro)

1925-1926
Jonathan Cincinnatus McLendon,
The Luverne Journal

1926-1927
F. Webb Stanley, *The Greenville Advocate*
(Stanley served second term, 1935-1936, after W.
Bruce Shelton, *The Tuscaloosa News*, resigned in
1935 after serving two months as president)

1927-1928
Robert B. Vail, *The Baldwin Times*, Bay Minette

1928-1929
Edmond Cody Hall Sr., *The Alexander City Outlook*

1929-1930
W. Emmett Brooks, *The Brewton Standard*

1930-1931
Marcy B. Darnall Sr., *The Florence Herald*

1931-1932
Jack M. Pratt, *The Pickens County Herald*, Carrollton

1932-1933
Forney G. Stephens, *The Southern Democrat*,
Oneonta

1933-1934
Jesse B. Adams, *The Southern Star*, Ozark
(Served two terms)

1934-1935
Jesse B. Adams, *The Southern Star*, Ozark

1935-1936
W. Bruce Shelton, *The Tuscaloosa News*
(Shelton resigned after two months and was succeeded
by F. Webb Stanley, *The Greenville Advocate*)

1936-1937
Robert Gaston Bozeman Sr., *The Evergreen
Courant*
(Served two terms)

1937-1938
Robert Gaston Bozeman Sr., *The Evergreen
Courant*

1938-1939
Clifford L. (Cliff) Walton, *The LaFayette Sun*

1939-1940
Milton C. Giles, *The Franklin County Times*,
Russellville

1940-1941
Hunter H. Golson, *The Wetumpka Herald*

1941-1942
James H. (Jimmy) Faulkner Sr., *The Baldwin Times*,
Bay Minette

1942-1943
Charles G. Dobbins, *The Anniston Times*

1943-1944
Ben A. Green, *The Tuscaloosa News*,
The Tallassee Tribune

1944-1945
Parker W. Campbell, *The Progressive Age*,
Scottsboro

1945-1946
George A. Carleton, *The Clarke County Democrat*,
Grove Hill

1946-1947
Bonnie D. Hand, *The LaFayette Sun*

1947-1948
Neil O. Davis, *The Lee County Bulletin,* Auburn

1948-1949
E.H. (Ed) Pierce, *The Mountain Eagle,* Jasper

1949-1950
J.C. Henderson, *The Alexander City Outlook*

1950-1951
Edmund R. (Ed) Blair, *The Pell City News and Southern Aegis,* Ashville

1951-1952
Clarence B. Hanson Jr., *The Birmingham News*

1952-1953
Cecil H. Hornady, *The Talladega News*

1953-1954
William E. (Bill) Brooks Jr., *The Brewton Standard*

1954-1955
Steele E. McGrew, *The Limestone Democrat* and *The Alabama Courier,* Athens

1955-1956
George H. Watson, *The Shades Valley Sun,* Homewood

1956-1957
Ben G. George, *The Demopolis Times*

1957-1958
George M. Cox, *The Mobile Press Register*

1958-1959
C.G. Thomason, *The Industrial Press,* Ensley

1959-1960
William M. (Bill) Stewart, *The Monroe Journal,* Monroeville

1960-1961
James E. (Jimmy) Mills, *Birmingham Post-Herald*

1961-1962
Harold S. May, *The Florence Herald*

1962-1963
J. Glenn Stanley, *The Greenville Advocate*

1963-1964
Herve Charest Jr., *The Tallassee Tribune*

1964-1965
E.M. (Sparky) Howell, *The Onlooker,* Foley

1965-1966
Ralph W. Callahan, *The Anniston Star*

1966-1967
Edward A. (Ed) Dannelly Jr., *The Andalusia Star-News*

1967-1968
Porter Harvey, *The Advertiser-Gleam,* Guntersville

1968-1969
W.H. (Bill) Metz, *Birmingham Post-Herald*

1969-1970
Joel P. Smith, *The Eufaula Tribune*

1970-1971
Karl Elebash Jr., *The Graphic,* Tuscaloosa

1971-1972
Robert Bryan, *The Cullman Times*

1972-1973
W.E. (Gene) Hardin, *The Greenville Advocate*

1973-1974
Ewell H. Reed, *The Arab Tribune*

1974-1975
Barrett C. Shelton Jr., *The Decatur Daily*

1975-1976
Orsen B. Spivey, *The Geneva County Reaper,* Geneva

1976-1977
Claude E. Sparks, *The Franklin County Times,* Russellville

1977-1978
Phillip A. Sanguinetti, *The Anniston Star*

1978-1979
E.R. (Bob) Morrissette Jr.,*The Atmore Advance*

1979-1980
James W. (Jim) Oakley Jr., *The Centreville Press*

1980-1981
Shelton Prince Jr., *The Daily Mountain Eagle,* Jasper, and *The Selma Times-Journal*

1981-1982
Marcia M. Sears, *The Shelby County Reporter,* Columbiana

1982-1983
Don Woodward, *The Advertiser-Gleam,* Guntersville

1983-1984
William J. (Bill) Hearin, *The Mobile Press Register*

1984-1985
Luke Slaton, *The Moulton Advertiser*

1985-1986
Mike Breedlove, *The South Alabamian,* Jackson

1986-1987
Jay Thornton, *The Daily Home,* Talladega

1987-1988
Steve Stewart, *The Monroe Journal,* Monroeville

1988-1989
Jack Venable, *The Tallassee Tribune*

1989-1990
James E. Jacobson, *The Birmingham News*

1990-1991
Paul R. Davis, *The Auburn Bulletin, The Lee County Eagle* and *The Tuskegee News*

1991-1992
Terry Everett, *The Union Springs Herald*

1992-1993
Charles Land, *The Tuscaloosa News*

1993-1994
Sam Harvey, *The Advertiser-Gleam,* Guntersville

1994-1995
Linda Hayes Breedlove, *The South Alabamian,* Jackson

1995-1996
Doug Pearson, *The Daily Mountain Eagle,* Jasper

1996-1997
Mike Kelley, *The Clanton Advertiser*

1997-1998
John W. Stevenson, *The Randolph Leader,* Roanoke

1998-1999
James H. Denley, *Birmingham Post-Herald*

"I admire editors who are individualists and non-conformists...men who can think and write; who can roar or caress; who broadly express the sense of their breed, but in head-on dissent find all things a subject for fair comment. Their business is writing editorials that are widely read and argued about. Men who feel theirs is a high calling...doing the Lord's work and safeguarding the public interest."

Grover C. Hall Jr.
The Montgomery Advertiser

— *Grover C. Hall Jr. (1915-1971)*
Editor, The Montgomery Advertiser, *1948-1966*
(From a personal column in The Montgomery Advertiser*)*

OFFICERS

1872

The first official convention of the Alabama Press Association was in Montgomery on June 18, 1872. Col. Seaborn Jones Saffold, *The Selma Daily Times,* was elected chairman of the convention, and J.M. Richards, *The LaFayette Reporter,* was elected secretary. Elected to serve as president at the 1872 convention was Gen. Jones Mitchell Withers of *The Mobile Tribune.* Withers, "for reasons stated, which deemed to be satisfactory by the convention" asked to be excused from serving as president, and Col. Seaborn Jones Saffold, *The Selma Daily Times,* was elected the first president of the Editors and Publishers Association of the State of Alabama.

Maj. William Wallace Screws, *The Montgomery Advertiser,* was elected first vice president, and J.M. Macon, *The Eufaula Daily Times,* was elected second vice president. Others officers were James Freeman Grant, *The Jacksonville Republican,* treasurer; Leonidis (Lon) Grant (son of James Freeman Grant), *The Jacksonville Republican,* recording secretary; and J.H. Francis, *The Montgomery Advance,* corresponding secretary.

These editors and publishers, who served during the first APA convention in 1872, are the first elected officers of APA.

1872-1873

Col. Seaborn Jones Saffold, *The Selma Daily Times,* president.

Vice presidents: Maj. William Wallace Screws, *The Montgomery Advertiser;* J.M. Macon, *The Eufaula Daily Times;* Robert McFarland, *The Florence Journal;* R.D. Osbourne, *The Stevenson New Era;* and Robert Alexander Moseley Jr., *The Talladega News* and *Our Mountain Home.*

James Freeman Grant, *The Jacksonville Republican,* treasurer; Leonidis (Lon) W. Grant, *The Jacksonville Republican,* recording secretary; and J.H. Francis, *The Montgomery Advance,* corresponding secretary.

1873-1874

Col. Seaborn Jones Saffold, *The Selma Daily Times,* president.

Leonidis (Lon) W. Grant, *The Jacksonville Republican,* recording secretary. (Names of other officers are not listed in APA minutes).

1874-1875

Col. Seaborn Jones Saffold, *The Selma Daily Times,* president.

Vice presidents: R. Randolph, *The Tuscaloosa Blade;* Joseph Shackleford, *The Tuscumbia Times;* Willis Brewer, *The Hayneville Examiner;* J.M. Richards, *The Montgomery News;* and L.H. Mathews, *The Birmingham Independent.*

Leonidis (Lon) W. Grant, *The Jacksonville Republican,* recording secretary; J.H. Francis, *The Selma Daily Times,* corresponding secretary; and James Freeman Grant, *The Jacksonville Republican,* treasurer.

Executive committee members: Frank A. Duval, *The Birmingham Iron Age;* Gen. James Berney Stanley, *The Greenville Advocate;* C.C. NeSmith, *The Summerville Free Press;* G.M. Johnson, *The Huntsville Advocate;* and Willis Roberts, *The Columbiana Guide.*

1875-1876

Col. Richard Holmes Powell, *The Union Springs Herald and Times,* president.

Vice presidents: Willis Brewer, *The Hayneville Examiner;* Maj. William Wallace Screws, *The Montgomery Advertiser;* J.R. Rogers, *The Union Springs Herald and Times,* D.W. Hundley, *The Huntsville Democrat;* and William A. Collier, *The Chilton Courier,* Clanton.

F.W. McIver, *The Tuskegee News,* secretary, and J.H. Francis, Jacksonville (newspaper unknown), treasurer.

1876-1877

James Freeman Grant, *The Jacksonville Republican,* president.

A. Snodgrass (newspaper unknown), first vice president; J.M. Macon, *The Eufaula Daily Times,* second vice president; Willis Brewer, *The Hayneville Examiner,* third vice president; William M. Meeks, *The Gadsden Times and News,* fourth vice president; and Gen. James Berney Stanley, *The Greenville Advocate,* fifth vice president.

Benjamin H. Screws (brother of Maj. William Wallace Screws), *The Montgomery Advertiser,* corresponding secretary; F.W. McIver, *The Tuskegee News,* recording secretary; and Francis Mitchell Grace, *The Montevallo Guide,* treasurer.

Executive committee members: Malcolm C. Burke, *The Demopolis News-Journal;* William A. Collier, *The Chilton Courier,* Clanton; W.C. Bledsoe, *The LaFayette Clipper;* D.R. Handley (newspaper unknown); and Leonidis (Lon) W. Grant, *The Jacksonville Republican.*

W.T. Walthall (newspaper unknown), orator, and George Robert Cather, *The Ashville Aegis,* alternate orator.

1877-1878

Willis Brewer, *The Hayneville Examiner,* president; Gen. James Berney Stanley, *The Greenville Advocate,* secretary; and George Robert Cather, *The Ashville Aegis,* orator.

1878-1879

Maj. William Wallace Screws, *The Montgomery Advertiser,* president; Malcolm Clayton Burke, *The Demopolis News-Journal,* and W.D. Wilkinson, *The Prattville Signal,* vice presidents; Gen. James Berney Stanley, *The Greenville Advocate,* secretary; F.W. McIver, *The Tuskegee News,* treasurer; and Ben F. Herr, *The Livingston Journal,* orator.

Executive committee members: W.H. Chambers, *The Farm Journal;* William M. Meeks, *The Gadsden Times and News;* and Willis Roberts, *The Birmingham Iron Age.*

1879-1880
Maj. William Wallace Screws, *The Montgomery Advertiser,* president; Malcolm Clayton Burke, *The Demopolis News-Journal,* and W.D. Wilkinson, *The Prattville Signal,* vice presidents; Gen. James Berney Stanley, *The Greenville Advocate,* secretary; D.W. McIver, *The Tuskegee News,* treasurer; and Ben F. Herr, *The Livingston Journal,* orator.

Executive committee members: W.H. Chambers, *The Farm Journal;* William M. Meeks, *The Gadsden Times and News;* and Willis Roberts, *The Birmingham Iron Age.*

1880-1881
Maj. William Wallace Screws, *The Montgomery Advertiser,* president; Gen. James Berney Stanley, *The Greenville Advocate,* first vice president; William M. Meeks, *The Gadsden Times and News,* second vice president; D.F. McCall, *The Union Springs Herald,* secretary; L. Hensley Grubbs, *The Decatur News,* treasurer; and J.E. Gilbert, *The Tuscumbia Democrat,* orator.

Executive committee members: Stephen Franklin Nunnelee, *The Tuscaloosa Gazette;* O.A. Burnett, *The Opelika Leader;* and Jourd White, *The Moulton Advertiser.*

1881-1882
Maj. William Wallace Screws, *The Montgomery Advertiser,* president; Gen. James Berney Stanley, *The Greenville Advocate,* first vice president; Arthur Henley Keller, *The Tuscumbia North Alabamian,* second vice president; D.F. McCall, *The Union Springs Herald,* secretary; A.H. Thomas, *The Clayton Courier,* orator; and Richard Bauth, *The Birmingham Observer,* alternate orator.

Executive committee members: G.K. Miller (newspaper unknown); L.H. Matthews, *The Birmingham Independent;* and W.D. Wilkinson, *The Prattville Signal.*

1882-1883
Gen. James Berney Stanley, *The Greenville Advocate,* president; H.M. King, (newspaper unknown) first vice president; Stephen Franklin Nunnelee, *The Tuscaloosa Gazette,* second vice president; D.F. McCall, *The Union Springs Herald and Times,* secretary; L. Hensley Grubbs, *The Decatur News,* treasurer; L.J. Walker (newspaper unknown), orator; and H.C. Jones Jr. (newspaper unknown), alternate orator.

Executive committee members: G.K. Miller (newspaper unknown); L.H. Matthews, *The Birmingham Independent;* and W.D. Wilkinson, *The Prattville Signal.*

1883-1884
Gen. James Berney Stanley, *The Greenville Advocate,* president; William M. Meeks, *The Gadsden Times and News,* first vice president; D.F. McCall, *The Union Springs Herald and Times,* second vice president; Thomas Baine, *The Hayneville Examiner,* secretary; L. Hensley Grubbs, *The Decatur News,* treasurer; and Chappell Cory, *The Selma Times,* orator.

1884-1885
Gen. James Berney Stanley, *The Greenville Advocate,* president; William M. Meeks, *The Gadsden Times and News,* first vice president; William Dorsey Jelks, *The Eufaula Times and News,* second vice president; Thomas Baine, *The Hayneville Examiner,* secretary; L. Hensley Grubbs, *The Decatur News,* treasurer; W.D. Wilkinson, *The Prattville Signal,* orator; and W.H. Skeggs (newspaper unknown) and F.B. Lloyd, *The Selma Times,* essayists. Original poems presented by Ina Marie Porter Henry, *The Greenville Advocate;* Julia Shelton (newspaper unknown); and Dr. Seymore Bullock (newspaper unknown).

1885-1886
Gen. James Berney Stanley, *The Greenville Advocate,* president; William M. Meeks, *The Gadsden Times and News,* first vice president; William Dorsey Jelks, *The Eufaula Times and News,* second vice president; L. Hensley Grubbs, *The Decatur News,* treasurer; Thomas Baine, *The Hayneville Examiner,* secretary; and F.B. Lloyd, *The Selma Times,* orator.

1886-1887
William M. Meeks, *The Gadsden Times and News,* president; Thomas Hudson, *The Marion Standard,* first vice president; Harry G. McCall, *The Shelby Sentinel,* Columbiana, second vice president; James Howell Nunnelee, *The Tuscaloosa Gazette,* secretary; Robert M. Rawls, *The Athens Courier,* treasurer; J.L. Burnett, *The Cherokee Advertiser,* orator; and L.H. Matthews, *The Blount County News,* poet.

Executive committee members: Gen. James Berney Stanley, *The Greenville Advocate;* D.W. McIver, *The Tuskegee News;* and J.W. Davison (newspaper unknown).

1887-1888

William M. Meeks, *The Gadsden Times and News,* president.

Tom Hudson, *The Marion Standard,* and Rufus Napoleon Rhodes, *The Birmingham News,* vice presidents; James Armstrong, *The Scottsboro Citizen,* secretary; and Robert M. Rawls, *The Athens Courier,* treasurer.

1888-1889

Harry G. McCall, *The Shelby Sentinel,* Columbiana, president.

H.C. Graham, *The Selma Times,* first vice president; R.E. Pettus, *The Huntsville Independent,* second vice president; Charles Woodroph Hare, *The Alabama Baptist,* secretary; Robert M. Rawls, *The Athens News Courier,* treasurer; J.A. Reynolds (newspaper unknown), orator; Frank H. Gist, *The Bibb Blade,* Centreville, alternate orator; J.W. Dubose, *The Gadsden Times and News,* historian; and Mary Hudson, *The Marion Standard,* essayist.

Executive committee members: Gen. James Berney Stanley, *The Greenville Advocate;* Chappell Cory, *The Selma Times;* W.P. Johnson, *The Gadsden Times and News;* Thomas Hudson, *The Marion Standard;* and Edward S. Cornish, *The Demopolis Times.*

1889-1890

Harry G. McCall, *The Shelby Sentinel,* Columbiana, president.

Chappell Cory, *The Selma Times,* first vice president; John C. Williams, *Our Mountain Home,* Talladega, second vice president; Virginia C. Clay, *The Huntsville Democrat,* secretary; Charles Woodroph Hare, *The Alabama Baptist,* assistant secretary; and Robert M. Rawls, *The Athens News Courier,* treasurer.

Frank H. Gist, *The Bibb Blade,* Centreville orator; Joseph H. Adams, *The Southern Star,* Ozark, poet; and N.A. Graham (newspaper unknown), historian.

Executive committee members: Maj. William Wallace Screws, *The Montgomery Advertiser;* Gen. James Berney Stanley, *The Greenville Advocate;* J. Asa Rountree, *The Hartselle Enquirer;* and Thomas Hudson, *The Marion Standard.*

1890-1891

John C. Williams, *Our Mountain Home,* Talladega, president.

L. Hensley Grubbs, *The Decatur News,* first vice president; Hugh McCalla Wilson, *The Dadeville New Era,* second vice president; Virginia C. Clay, *The Huntsville Democrat,* secretary; Charles Herd Greer, *The Chambers County Democrat,* LaFayette, orator; William J. Blan, *The Troy Messenger,* treasurer; J.H. West, *The Russellville Idea,* essayist; and Professor James Archibald Bradford Lovett, *The Teacher at Work,* Huntsville, poet.

Executive committee members: William M. Meeks, *The Gadsden Times and News;* Edward S. Cornish, *The Demopolis Times;* William Haywood *The Chilton View,* Clanton; and J.E. Graves (newspaper unknown).

1891-1892

John C. Williams, *Our Mountain Home,* Talladega, president.

L. Hensley Grubbs, *The Decatur News,* first vice president; Hugh McCalla Wilson, *The Dadeville New Era,* second vice president; William J. Blan, *The Troy Messenger,* third vice president; Virginia C. Clay, *The Huntsville Democrat,* secretary; Rufus Napoleon Rhodes, *The Birmingham News,* orator; Charles Paul Lane, *The Huntsville Mercury,* poet; L. Hensley Grubbs, *The Decatur News,* historian; and Charles Woodroph Hare, *The Alabama Baptist,* essayist.

1892-1893

John C. Williams, *Our Mountain Home,* Talladega, president.

Joseph H. Adams, *The Southern Star,* Ozark, first vice president; Christopher James Hildreth, *The New Decatur Advertiser,* second vice president; William J. Blan, *The Troy Messenger,* treasurer; J. Asa Rountree, *The Hartselle Enquirer,* secretary; Edward Louis Collen Ward, *The Bridgeport News,* orator; J.S. Barr, *The Florence Gazette,* poet; Fannie V. King (newspaper unknown), essayist; L. Hensley Grubbs, *The Decatur News,* historian.

Executive committee members: Gen. James Berney Stanley, *The Greenville Advocate;* James Howell Nunnelee, *The Selma Times;* and William M. Meeks, *The Gadsden Times and News.*

Official delegates to national press convention: Virginia C. Clay, *The Huntsville Democrat,* and Mrs. James Armstrong, *The Scottsboro Citizen.*

1893-1894

Edward Louis Collen Ward, *The Bridgeport News*, president.

Robert M. Rawls, *The Athens Courier*, first vice president; James B. Simpson, *The Montgomery Journal*, second vice president; J. Asa Rountree, *The Hartselle Enquirer*, secretary; James Armstrong, *The Scottsboro Citizen*, treasurer; Charles Paul Lane, *The Huntsville Tribune*, orator; Virginia C. Clay, *The Huntsville Democrat*, essayist; Col. Ryland Randolph, *The Birmingham Argus*, poet; and Maj. William Wallace Screws, *The Montgomery Advertiser*, historian.

Executive committee members: John C. Williams, *Our Mountain Home*, Talladega; Edward Louis Collen Ward, *The Bridgeport News* (ex-officio); Gen. James Berney Stanley, *The Greenville Advocate*; Edward O. Neely, *The Guntersville Democrat*; and Franklin Potts Glass, *The Montgomery Advertiser*.

1894-1895

Robert M. Rawls, *The Athens Courier*, president.

James B. Simpson, *The Montgomery Journal*, first vice president; Ira Champion, *The Troy Messenger*, second vice president; J. Asa Rountree, *The Hartselle Enquirer*, secretary; William M. Meeks, *The Gadsden Times and News*, treasurer; William H.H. Judson, *The Bessemer Weekly*, essayist; Howard S. Doster, *The Prattville Progress*, poet; Maj. William Wallace Screws, *The Montgomery Advertiser*, historian; and Charles Paul Lane, *The Huntsville Tribune*, orator.

Executive committee members: Gen. James Berney Stanley, *The Greenville Advocate*; John C. Williams, *Our Mountain Home*, Talladega; Franklin Potts Glass, *The Montgomery Advertiser*; and Edward O. Neely, *The Guntersville Democrat*.

1895-1896

Robert M. Rawls, *The Athens Courier*, president.

James B. Simpson, *The Montgomery Journal*, first vice president; Ira Champion, *The Troy Messenger*, second vice president; J. Asa Rountree, *The Hartselle Enquirer*, secretary; William M. Meeks, *The Gadsden Times and News*, treasurer; Moncure Woodson Camper, *The Florence Times*, essayist; Margaret E. O'Brien, *The Birmingham Age-Herald*, poetess; and Maj. William Wallace Screws, *The Montgomery Advertiser*, historian.

1896-1897

Moncure Woodson Camper, *The Florence Times*, president.

James B. Simpson, *The Montgomery Journal*, first vice president; Ira Champion, *The Troy Messenger*, second vice president; J. Asa Rountree, *The Birmingham State-Herald*, secretary; William M. Meeks, *The Gadsden Times and News*, treasurer; Virginia C. Clay, *The Huntsville Democrat*, poetess; P.F. Miles, *The Union Springs Herald*, essayist; and Maj. William Wallace Screws, *The Montgomery Advertiser*, historian.

Executive committee members: Moncure Woodson Camper, *The Florence Times* (ex-officio); Gen. James Berney Stanley, *The Greenville Advocate*; Edward O. Neely, *The Guntersville Democrat*; William H.H. Judson, *The Bessemer Weekly*; and H.S. Shackleford (newspaper unknown).

1897-1898

Moncure Woodson Camper, *The Florence Times*, president.

William Dorsey Jelks, *The Eufaula Times and News*, first vice president; Edward O. Neely, *The Guntersville Democrat*, second vice president; J. Asa Rountree, *The Dixie Home Manufacturer*, secretary; William M. Meeks, *The Gadsden Times and News*, treasurer; William E.W. Yerby, *The Greensboro Watchman*, orator; and Mrs. John C. Lawrence, *The Marion Standard*, essayist.

1898-1899

Moncure Woodson Camper, *The Florence Times*, president.

Edward O. Neely, *The Guntersville Democrat*, first vice president; Hugh McCalla Wilson, *The Opelika Daily News*, second vice president; J. Asa Rountree, *The Dixie Home Manufacturer*, secretary; Thomas Henry Garner, *The Tuscaloosa Gazette*, treasurer; Mrs. Robert M. Rawls, *The Athens Courier*, essayist; Mrs. Robert Alexander Moseley, *The Birmingham Times*, poetess; and Maj. William Wallace Screws, *The Montgomery Advertiser*, historian.

1899-1900

Rufus Napoleon Rhodes, *The Birmingham News*, president.

William E.W. Yerby, *The Greensboro Watchman*, first vice president; Thomas Henry Garner, *The Tuscaloosa Gazette*, second vice president; J. Asa Rountree, *The Dixie Home Manufacturer*, secretary; W.M. Bunting, *The Florence Herald*, treasurer; Isidore A. Levy, *The Eutaw Mirror*, Forkland, orator; Mrs. M.B. Pearce, *The Citronelle Times*, poetess; and Robert M. Rawls, *The Athens Courier*, essayist.

Delegates to the National Editors Association convention: Maj. William Wallace Screws, *The Montgomery Advertiser*; W.M. Bunting, *The Florence Herald*; Gen. James Berney Stanley, *The Greenville Advocate*; J. Asa Rountree, *The Dixie Home Manufacturer*; Isidore A. Levy, *The Eutaw Mirror*, Forkland; Robert M. Rawls, *The Athens Courier*; L. Hensley Grubbs, *The Decatur News*; Mildred B. Pearce, *The Citronelle Times*; William E.W. Yerby, *The Greensboro Watchman*; S.P. West, *The Alabama Christian Advocate*; Moncure Woodson Camper, *The Florence Times*; and Jacob Pepperman, *The Montgomery Advertiser*.

1900-1901

Rufus Napoleon Rhodes, *The Birmingham News*, president.

William E.W. Yerby, *The Greensboro Watchman*, first vice president; Thomas Henry Garner, *The Tuscaloosa Gazette*, second vice president; J. Asa Rountree, *The Dixie Home Manufacturer*, secretary; W.M. Bunting, *The Florence Herald*, treasurer; Howard S. Doster, *The Prattville Progress*, orator; Mrs. C.H. Frye, *The Pratt City Herald*, essayist; Charles Herd Greer, *The Marion Standard*, poet; and Maj. William Wallace Screws, *The Montgomery Advertiser*, historian.

Executive committee members: Rufus Napoleon Rhodes (ex-officio chairman), *The Birmingham News*; William Hayward Lawrence, *Our Southern Home*, Livingston; Maj. William Wallace Screws, *The Montgomery Advertiser*; W.C. Jemison, Tuscaloosa (newspaper unknown); Christopher James Hildreth, *The New Decatur Advertiser*; William H.H. Judson, *The Bessemer Weekly*; and Chappell Cory, *The Selma Times*.

1901-1902

William E.W. Yerby, *The Greensboro Watchman*, president.

Thomas Henry Garner, *The Tuscaloosa Gazette*, first vice president; W.M. Bunting, *The Florence Herald*, second vice president; P.F. Miles, *The Union Springs Herald*, third vice president; S.P. West, *The Alabama Christian Advocate*, Birmingham, fourth vice president; J. Asa Rountree, *The Dixie Home Manufacturer*, secretary; J.C. Orr, *The Alabama Enquirer*, Hartselle, treasurer; Chappell Cory, *The Montgomery Journal*, orator; Mrs. Sidney H. Blan, *The Troy Messenger*, essayist; Rufus Napoleon Rhodes, *The Birmingham News*, poet; and Maj. William Wallace Screws, *The Montgomery Advertiser*, historian.

Executive committee members: William E.W. Yerby (ex-officio chairman), *The Greensboro Watchman*; J. Asa Rountree (ex-officio secretary), *The Dixie Home Manufacturer*; Horace Hood, *The Evening Journal*, Montgomery; H.G. Brenners, *The Alabama Beacon*, Greensboro; Thomas Henry Garner, *The Tuscaloosa Gazette*; Howard S. Doster, *The Prattville Progress*; William Hayward Lawrence, *Our Southern Home*, Livingston; W.M. Bunting, *The Florence Herald*; H.E. Whitaker, *The Montevallo Sentinel*; and S.P. West, *The Alabama Christian Advocate*, Birmingham.

1902-1903

William E.W. Yerby, *The Greensboro Watchman*, president.

Charles Herd Greer, *The Marion Standard*, first vice president; P.F. Miles, *The Union Springs Herald*, second vice president; S.P. West, *The Alabama Christian Advocate*, Birmingham, third vice president; John Franklin Cothran, *The Mobile Item*, fourth vice president; J. Asa Rountree, *The Dixie Home Manufacturer*, secretary; J.C. Orr Jr., *The Alabama Enquirer*, Hartselle, treasurer; Max Hamburger, *The Mobile Herald*, orator; Mildred B. Pearce, *The Citronelle Times*, essayist; R.G. Hiden, *The Birmingham News*, poet; and Maj. William Wallace Screws, *The Montgomery Advertiser*, historian.

Executive committee members: William E.W. Yerby (ex-officio chairman), *The Greensboro Watchman*; J. Asa Rountree (ex-officio secretary), *The Dixie Home Manufacturer*; H.C. Brenners, *The Alabama Beacon*, Greensboro; Thomas Henry Garner, *The Tuscaloosa Gazette*; Howard S. Doster, *The Prattville Progress*; Edward O. Neely, *The Guntersville Democrat;* Christopher James Hildreth, *The New Decatur Advertiser;* H.E. Whitaker, *The Montevallo Sentinel*; Jacob Pepperman, *The Montgomery Advertiser*; Frank Crichton, *The Clanton Banner*; and S.P. West, *The Alabama Christian Advocate*, Birmingham.

1903-1904

William E.W. Yerby, *The Greensboro Watchman*, president.

Charles Herd Greer, *The Marion Standard*, first vice president; S.P. West, *The Alabama Christian Advocate*, Birmingham, second vice president; J.C. Lawrence, *The Union Springs Breeze*, third vice president; J. Asa Rountree, *The Dixie Home Manufacturer*, secretary; S.H. Morris, *The Fayette Banner*, treasurer; H.G. Brenners, *The Alabama Bea-*

con, Greensboro, orator; Lula Judson, *The Bessemer Weekly*, essayist; Thomas Henry Garner, *The Tuscaloosa Gazette*, poet; and Maj. William Wallace Screws, *The Montgomery Advertiser*, historian.

Executive committee members: William E.W. Yerby (ex-officio chairman), *The Greensboro Watchman*; J. Asa Rountree (ex-officio secretary), *The Dixie Home Manufacturer*; Thomas Henry Garner, *The Tuscaloosa Gazette*; Howard S. Doster, *The Prattville Progress*; H.E. Whittaker, *The Montevallo Sentinel*; Jacob Pepperman, *The Montgomery Advertiser*; Frank Crichton, *The Clanton Banner*; John C. Williams, *Our Mountain Home*, Talladega; William H.H. Judson, *The Bessemer* Weekly; and Hugh McCalla Wilson, *The Opelika Daily News*.

1904-1905
Charles Herd Greer, *The Marion Standard*, president.

S.P. West, *The Alabama Christian Advocate*, Birmingham, first vice president; Robert E. Lee Neil, *The Selma Times*, second vice president; Howard S. Doster, *The Prattville Progress*, third vice president; H.Y. Brooke, *The Luverne Journal*, fourth vice president; Jacob Pepperman, *The Montgomery Advertiser*, secretary; S.H. Morris, *The Fayette Banner*, treasurer; Maj. William Wallace Screws, *The Montgomery Advertiser*, historian; Lula Judson, *The Bessemer Weekly*, essayist; and Frank Crichton, *The Clanton Banner*, poet.

Executive committee members: Charles Herd Greer (ex-officio president), *The Marion Standard;* Jacob Pepperman (ex-officio secretary), *The Montgomery Advertiser*; William E.W. Yerby, *The Greensboro Watchman*; Hugh McCalla Wilson, *The Opelika Daily News*; H.E. Whittaker, *The Montevallo Sentinel*; William H.H. Judson, *The Bessemer Weekly*; John C. Williams, *Our Mountain Home*, Talladega; Virginia C. Clay, *The Huntsville Democrat*; M.W. Tucker, *The Tuscaloosa Gazette*; Frank Crichton, *The Clanton Banner*; and Christopher James Hildreth, *The New Decatur Advertiser*.

1905-1906
Robert E. Lee Neil, *The Selma Times*, president.
Howard S. Doster, *The Prattville Progress*, first vice president; J.C. Lawrence, *The Union Springs Breeze*, second vice president; Jacob Pepperman, *The Montgomery Advertiser*, secretary; S.H. Morris, *The Fayette Banner*, treasurer; Maj. William Wallace Screws, *The Montgomery Advertiser*, historian; H.Y. Brooke, *The Luverne Journal*, orator; Virginia C.

Clay, *The Huntsville Democrat*, essayist; and J.C. Lawrence, *The Union Springs Breeze*, poet.

Executive committee members: Charles Herd Greer (ex-officio president), *The Marion Standard*; Jacob Pepperman (ex-officio secretary), *The Montgomery Advertiser*; William E.W. Yerby, *The Greensboro Watchman*; Hugh McCalla Wilson, *The Opelika Daily News*; R.L. O'Neal, *The Huntsville Mercury*; William H.H. Judson, *The Bessemer Weekly*; Frank Crichton, *The Clanton Banner*; John C. Williams, *Our Mountain Home*, Talladega; and M.W. Tucker, *The Tuscaloosa Gazette*.

1906-1907
Robert E. Lee Neil, *The Selma Times*, president.
Howard S. Doster, *The Prattville Progress*, first vice president; J.C. Lawrence, *The Union Springs Breeze*, second vice president; Jacob Pepperman, *The Montgomery Advertiser*, secretary; Frank Crichton, *The Clanton Banner*, treasurer; Maj. William Wallace Screws, *The Montgomery Advertiser*, historian; Olin Hampton Stevenson, *The Roanoke Leader*, orator; Mrs. J. DuBoise M. Rutherford, *The Eutaw Whig and Observer*, poet; and Virginia C. Clay, *The Huntsville Democrat*, essayist.

Executive committee members: Robert E. Lee Neil (ex-officio president), *The Selma Times*; Jacob Pepperman (ex-officio secretary), *The Montgomery Advertiser*; Moncure Woodson Camper, *The Florence Times*; A.B. Kennedy, *The Montgomery Advertiser*; the Rev. Frank Willis Barnett, *The Alabama Baptist*, Birmingham; Hugh McCalla Wilson, *The Opelika Daily News*; F.I. McKenzie, *The Tri-County Weekly*, Tallassee; W.D. Sowell, *The Pine Belt News*, Brewton; and William H.H. Judson, *The Bessemer Weekly*.

1907-1908
Howard S. Doster, *The Prattville Progress*, president.

J.C. Lawrence, *The Union Springs Breeze*, first vice president; C.G. Fennell, *The Guntersville Democrat*, second vice president; Jacob Pepperman, *The Montgomery Advertiser*, secretary; Frank Crichton, *The Clanton Banner*, treasurer; Maj. William Wallace Screws, *The Montgomery Advertiser*, historian; the Rev. Frank Willis Barnett, *The Alabama Baptist*, Birmingham, orator; C.F. Striplin, *The Ashland Standard*, poet; and Helen Meredith (newspaper unknown), Eutaw, essayist.

Executive committee members: Howard S. Doster (ex-officio president), *The Prattville Progress*; Jacob Pepperman (ex-officio secretary),

The Montgomery Advertiser; William E.W. Yerby, *The Greensboro Watchman*; A.B. Kennedy, *The Montgomery Advertiser*; John C. Williams, *Our Mountain Home*, Talladega; Moncure Woodson Camper, *The Florence Times*; William H.H. Judson, *The Bessemer Weekly*; F.L. McKenzie, *The Tri-County Weekly*, Tallassee; J.H. Hand, *The Bessemer Journal*; and W.H. Taylor, *The Uniontown Herald*.

NEA delegates in 1907: Robert Henry (Harry) Walker Sr., *The Limestone Democrat*, Athens; G.H. Ward (newspaper unknown); William E.W Yerby, *The Greensboro Watchman*; Robert E. Lee Neil, *The Selma Times;* C.G. Fennell, *The Guntersville Democrat*; R.L. O'Neal, *The Huntsville Mercury*; Gen. James Berney Stanley, *The Greenville Advocate*; John C. Williams, *Our Mountain Home*, Talladega; Charles Woodroph Hare, *The Tuskegee News*; A.J. O'Keafe, *The Birmingham Republican*; and W.H. Taylor, *The Uniontown Herald*. Past president of the National Editorial Association: Maj. William Wallace Screws, *The Montgomery Advertiser*.

National Editorial Association executive committee member: Jacob Pepperman, *The Montgomery Advertiser*.

William H.H. Judson, *The Bessemer Weekly*, was named a life member of National Editorial Association.

F.L. McKenzie, *The Tri-County Weekly*, Tallassee, was ex-officio delegate to National Editorial Association.

1908-1909

J.C. Lawrence, *The Union Springs Breeze*, president.

C.G. Fennell, *The Guntersville Democrat*, first vice president; Jacob Pepperman, *The Montgomery Advertiser*, secretary; Frank Crichton, *The Clanton Banner*, treasurer; Maj. William Wallace Screws, *The Montgomery Advertiser*, historian; C.F. Striplin, *The Ashland Standard*, orator; Walter S. Smith, *The Lineville Headlight*, essayist; and E.B. McCarty, *The Demopolis Times*, poet.

Executive committee members: J.C. Lawrence (ex-officio president), *The Union Springs Breeze*; C.G. Fennell (ex-officio vice president), *The Guntersville Democrat*; A.B. Kennedy, *The Montgomery Advertiser*, assistant secretary; Jacob Pepperman, *The Montgomery Advertiser*, secretary; Frank Crichton, *The Clanton Banner*, treasurer; Moncure Woodson Camper, *The Florence Times*, group vice president; Olin Hampton Stevenson, *The Roanoke Leader*, group vice president; George Marcus Cruikshank, *The Talladega Reporter*, group

vice president; William Theodore Hall, *The Dothan Eagle*, group vice president; and E.B. McCarty, *The Demopolis Times*, group vice president.

1909-1910

C.G. Fennell, *The Guntersville Democrat*, president.

A.B. Kennedy, *The Montgomery Advertiser*, vice president; Jacob Pepperman, *The Montgomery Advertiser*, secretary; Frank Crichton, *The Clanton Banner*, treasurer; Maj. William Wallace Screws, *The Montgomery Advertiser*, historian; R.C. Williams, *The Wiregrass* Siftings, Dothan, orator; Mrs. Robert E. Lee Neil, *The Selma Times*, essayist; and William Theodore Hall, *The Dothan Eagle*, poet.

Executive committee members: C.J. Fennell, *The Guntersville Democrat*, president; A.B. Kennedy, *The Montgomery Advertiser*, vice president; F.L. McKenzie, *The Tri-County Weekly*, Tallassee, assistant secretary; Frank Crichton, *The Clanton Banner*, treasurer; Moncure Woodson Camper, *The Florence Times*, group vice president; W.S. Gilbert, *The Bessemer Workman*, group vice president, northwestern division; Edward Louis Collen Ward, *The Bridgeport News*, group vice president, northeastern division; Joseph H. Adams, *The Southern Star*, Ozark, group vice president, southeastern division; and E.B. McCarty, *The Demopolis Times*, group vice president, southwestern division.

1910-1911

McLane Tilton Jr., *The Pell City Progress*, president.

A.B. Tucker, *The Thomasville Echo*, vice president; Jacob Pepperman, *The Montgomery Advertiser*, secretary; Frank Crichton, *The Clanton Banner*, treasurer; Maj. William Wallace Screws, *The Montgomery Advertiser*, historian; Webb Stanley, *The Greenville Advocate*, orator; Mrs. Charles Herd Greer, *The Marion Standard*, essayist; and Thomas Henry Garner, *The Tuscaloosa Gazette*, poet.

Executive committee members: McLane Tilton Jr., *The Pell City Progress*, president; A.B. Tucker, *The Thomasville Echo*, vice president; Jacob Pepperman, *The Montgomery Advertiser*, secretary; F.L. McKenzie, *The Tri-County Weekly*, Tallassee, assistant secretary; Frank Crichton, *The Clanton Banner*, treasurer; John W. Davis, *The Alabama Watchman*, Tuscumbia, group vice president, northern division; J.H.F. Moseley, *The Labor Advocate*, Birmingham, group vice president, northwestern division; Edward Louis Collen Ward, *The News Reporter*, Talladega, group vice president, southeastern division; Charles Woodroph Hare, *The Tuskegee News*, group vice president, southeastern division; and David Holt, *The Baldwin Times*, Bay Minette, group vice president, southwestern division.

1911-1912

Luman Handley Nunnelee, *The Centreville Press*, president; A.B. Tucker, *The Thomasville Echo*, vice president; and J.R. Rosson, *The Cullman Democrat*, secretary.

1912-1913

Luman Handley Nunnelee, *The Centreville Press*, president; A.B. Tucker, *The Thomasville Echo*, vice president; and J.R. Rosson, *The Cullman Democrat*, secretary.

1913-1914

Luman Handley Nunnelee, *The Centreville Press*, president; Christopher James Hildreth, *The New Decatur Advertiser*, vice president; and J.R. Rosson, *The Cullman Democrat*, secretary.

1914-1915

Christopher James Hildreth, *The New Decatur Advertiser*, president; Col. Harry Mell Ayers, *The Anniston Star*, vice president; J.R. Rosson, *The Cullman Democrat*, secretary.

Executive committee members: Edward Ware Barrett, *The Birmingham Age-Herald*, chairman; William H.H. Hudson, *The Bessemer Weekly*; J. Asa Rountree, *The Dixie Home Manufacturer*, Birmingham; M.B. Wiggins, Hartselle (newspaper unknown); Webb Stanley, *The Greenville Advocate*; R.L. O'Neil, *The Huntsville Mercury*; and Charles Woodroph Hare, *The Tuskegee News*.

1915-1916

Col. Harry Mell Ayers, *The Anniston Star*, president; C. Earnest Jones, *The Clio Free Press*, first vice president; Hugh McCalla Wilson, *The Opelika Daily News*, second vice president; James H. Hard, Birmingham (newspaper unknown), secretary-treasurer; and Webb Stanley, *The Greenville Advocate*, recording secretary.

Executive committee members: Christopher James Hildreth, *The New Decatur Advertiser*; C.A. Verbeck (newspaper unknown); J. Asa Rountree, *The Dixie Home Manufacturer*, Birmingham; H.H. Smith (newspaper unknown); Horace Hood, *The Montgomery Journal*; and Charles Woodroph Hare, *The Tuskegee News*.

1916-1917

Col. Harry Mell Ayers, *The Anniston Star*, president; A.W. McCullock, *The Gadsden Journal*, first vice president; Webb Stanley, *The Greenville Advocate*, second vice president; James H. Hard, Birmingham (newspaper unknown), secretary-treasurer; S.H. Oliver, *The LaFayette Sun*, corresponding secretary; T.L. Cannon, *The State Sentinel*, orator; and Robert E. Lee Neil, *The Alabama Democrat*, poet laureate.

1917-1918

Edward Doty, *The Tuscaloosa News*, president; Oscar M. Dugger Sr., *The Andalusia Star*, first vice president; Sam H. Oliver, *The LaFayette Sun*, second vice president; James H. Hard, Birmingham (newspaper unknown), secretary-treasurer; Frank H. Julian, *The Sheffield Standard*, recording secretary; Frances Golson, *The Wetumpka Weekly Herald*, essayist; Dolly Dalrymple, *The Birmingham Age-Herald*, poetess; Mrs. C.H. Mathis, Gadsden (newspaper unknown), orator; and John C. Williams, *Our Mountain Home*, Talladega, historian.

Executive committee members: Frank N. Julian, *The Sheffield Standard*; C.A. Verbeck (newspaper unknown); the Rev. Frank Willis Barnett, *The Alabama Baptist*, Birmingham; C.G. Fennell, *The Guntersville Democrat*; and Webb Stanley, *The Greenville Advocate*.

1918-1919

A.W. McCullock, *The Gadsden Journal*, president; Oscar M. Dugger Sr., *The Andalusia Star*, first vice president; Samuel H. Oliver, *The LaFayette Sun*, second vice president; James H. Hard, Birmingham (newspaper unknown), secretary-treasurer; Frank N. Julian, *The Sheffield Standard*, recording secretary; and John C. Williams, *Our Mountain Home*, Talladega, historian.

1919-1920

Oscar M. Dugger Sr., *The Andalusia Star*, president; Frank N. Julian, *The Sheffield Standard*, first vice president; Capt. William Thomas Sheehan, *The Montgomery Advertiser*, second vice president; William Theodore Hall, *The Dothan Eagle*, third vice president; James H. Hard, Birmingham (newspaper unknown), secretary-treasurer; N.J. Lillard, *The Standard Gauge*, Brewton, recording secretary; and John C. Williams, *Our Mountain Home*, Talladega, historian.

1920-1921

Frank N. Julian, *The Sheffield Standard*, president; Capt. William Thomas Sheehan, *The Montgomery Advertiser*, first vice president; William Theodore Hall, *The Dothan Eagle*, second vice president; Forney G. Stephens, *The Southern Democrat*, Oneonta, third vice president; James H. Hard, Birmingham (newspaper unknown), secretary; Fowler Dugger, *The Andalusia Star*, assistant secretary; Frances Golson, *The Wetumpka Weekly Herald*, poetess; Walter Miller, *The Tuscumbia Reporter*, orator; and John C. Williams, *Our Mountain Home*, Talladega, historian.

1921-1922

William Theodore Hall, *The Dothan Eagle*, president; Capt. William Thomas Sheehan, *The Montgomery Advertiser*, first vice president; Forney G. Stephens, *The Southern Democrat*, Oneonta, second vice president; W.R. Jordan, *The Alexander City Outlook*, third vice president; Webb Stanley, *The Greenville Advocate*, secretary-treasurer; Fowler Dugger, *The Andalusia Star*, assistant secretary; James H. Hard, Birmingham (newspaper unknown), historian; Frances Golson, *The Wetumpka Herald*, poetess; and James S. Benson, *The Scottsboro Citizen*, orator.

1922-1923

Capt. William Thomas Sheehan, *The Montgomery Advertiser*, president; Forney G. Stephens, *The Southern Democrat*, Oneonta, first vice president; W.R. Jordan, *The Alexander City Outlook*, second vice president; E.V. O'Connor, Mobile (newspaper unknown), third vice president; Webb Stanley, *The Greenville Advocate*, secretary-treasurer; Mark L. Tucker, Western Newspaper Union, Birmingham, assistant secretary; Frank N. Julian, *The Sheffield Standard*, orator; Mabel Yerby, *The Greensboro Watchman*, poetess; and John C. Williams, *Our Mountain Home*, Talladega, historian.

1923-1924

Forney G. Stephens, *The Southern Democrat*, Oneonta, president; W.R. Jordan, *The Alexander City Outlook*, first vice president; Grover C. Hall Sr., *The Montgomery Advertiser*, second vice president; C.W. Wear, *The Opelika Daily News*, third vice president; Victor H. Hanson, *The Birmingham News*, orator; Frances Golson, *The Wetumpka Herald*, poetess; Webb Stanley, *The Greenville Advocate*, secretary; R.P. Greer, *The Sylacauga News*, editor of *The Ala-Pressa*; C.G. Fennell, *The*

Guntersville Democrat, historian; F.J. Julian, *The Sheffield Standard*, orator; Mabel Yerby, *The Greensboro Watchman*, poetess; and John C. Williams, *Our Mountain Home*, Talladega, historian.

1924-1925

W.R. Jordan, *The Huntsville Morning Star*, president; (Jordan died while in office and was succeeded by first vice president James S. Benson, *The Progressive Age*, Scottsboro); Jonathan Cincinnatus McLendon, *The Luverne Journal*, second vice president; Marcy B. Darnall, *The Florence Herald*, third vice president; R.P. Greer, *The Sylacauga News*, editor of *The Ala-Pressa*; the Rev. Frank Willis Barnett, *The Alabama Baptist*, Birmingham, historian; Howard S. Doster, *The Prattville Progress*, orator; and Frances Golson, *The Wetumpka Herald*, poetess.

1925-1926

Jonathan Cincinnatus McLendon, *The Luverne Journal*, president; Webb Stanley, *The Greenville Advocate*, vice president; Robert B. Vail, *The Baldwin Times*, Bay Minette, secretary-treasurer; R.P. Greer, *The Sylacauga News*, editor, *The Ala-Pressa*; Jack M. Pratt, *The Pickens County Herald*, Carrollton, auditor; Mrs. T.L. (Dixie) Vail, *The South Baldwin News*, poetess; and David Holt, *The Baldwin Times*, Bay Minette, reporter.

1926-1927

F. Webb Stanley, *The Greenville Advocate*, president; Robert B. Vail, *The Baldwin Times*, Bay Minette, first vice president; Horace Hall, *The Dothan Eagle*, secretary-treasurer; John C. Williams, *The Talladega Daily Home*, historian; P.O. Davis, Extension Service, Alabama Polytechnic Institute, Auburn, reporter; Mrs. C.W. Thomas, *The Citronelle Call*, poetess; W. Emmett Brooks, *The Brewton Standard*, editor of *The Ala-Pressa*; and Neil C. Cady, Western Newspaper Union, Birmingham, business manager of *The Ala-Pressa*.

1927-1928

Robert B. Vail, *The Baldwin Times*, Bay Minette, president; Lawrence S. Richardson, *The Mountain Eagle*, Jasper, vice president; Jack M. Pratt, *The Pickens County Herald*, Carrollton, secretary-treasurer; Jack M. Pratt, *The Pickens County Herald*, Carrollton, editor of *The Ala-Pressa*; P.O. Davis, Extension Service, Alabama Polytechnic Institute, Auburn, reporter; Neil C. Cady, Western Newspaper Union, Birmingham, business manager of *The Ala-Pressa*; Gen. James Berney Stanley, *The Greenville Advocate*, historian; and Mrs. C.W. Thomas, *The Citronelle Call*, poetess.

1928-1929

E. Cody Hall Sr., *The Alexander City Outlook*, president; W. Emmett Brooks, *The Brewton Standard*, vice president; Hunter H. Golson, *The Abbeville Herald*, secretary-treasurer; W.A. (Bill) Young, (newspaper unknown) Auburn, reporter; and Mildred Stephens, *The Southern Democrat*, Oneonta, poetess.

Executive committee members: Webb Stanley, *The Greenville Advocate*; Robert B. Vail, *The Baldwin Times*, Bay Minette; Forney G. Stephens, *The Southern Democrat*, Oneonta; Lawrence S. Richardson, *The Mountain Eagle*, Jasper; and R.P. Greer, *The Sylacauga News*.

1929-1930

W. Emmett Brooks, *The Brewton Standard*, president; Marcy B. Darnall, *The Florence Herald*, vice president; Hunter H. Golson, *The Abbeville Herald*, secretary-treasurer; Horace Hall, *The Dothan Eagle*, convention secretary; J.B. Brown, Bridgeport (newspaper unknown), historian; Isabel Moses, *The Phenix-Giruad Journal*, Phenix City, poetess; and J.L. Kimbro, *The Opp News*, reporter.

Executive committee members: Howard S. Doster, *The Prattville Progress*; R.P. Greer, *The Sylacauga Advance*; E. Cody Hall Sr., *The Alexander City Outlook;* Jack M. Pratt, *The Pickens County Herald*, Carrollton; Webb Stanley, *The Greenville Advocate*; Forney G. Stephens, *The Southern Democrat*, Oneonta; and Robert B. Vail, *The Baldwin Times*, Bay Minette.

1930-1931

Marcy B. Darnall, *The Florence Herald*, president; Jack M. Pratt, *The Pickens County Herald*, Carrollton, vice president; E. Cody Hall Sr., *The Alexander City Outlook*, secretary-treasurer; R.P. Greer, *The Sylacauga Advance*, convention secretary; J.W. Norwood, *The Cullman Tribune*, historian; Mrs. Scottie McKenzie Frazier, Dothan (newspaper unknown), poetess; Howard C. Smith, Woman's College, Montgomery, reporter.

Executive committee members: Marcy B. Darnall, *The Florence Herald*; W. Emmett Brooks, *The Brewton Standard*; Webb Stanley, *The Greenville Advocate*; M.S. Hansbrough, (newspaper unknown) Russellville; Forney G. Stephens, *The Southern Democrat*, Oneonta; Robert B. Vail, *The Baldwin Times*, Bay Minette; J.W. Norwood, *The Cullman Tribune*; W.E.P. Lakeman, (newspaper unknown) Haleyville; and E. Cody Hall Sr., *The Alexander City Outlook*.

1931-1932

Jack M. Pratt, *The Pickens County Herald*, Carrollton, president; Forney G. Stephens, *The Southern Democrat*, Oneonta, vice president; E. Cody Hall Sr., *The Alexander City Outlook*, secretary-treasurer; R.P. Greer, *The Sylacauga Advance*, convention secretary; J.W. Norwood, *The Cullman Tribune*, historian; Mrs. Scottie McKenzie Frazier, (newspaper unknown) Dothan, poetess; and Howard C. Smith, Woman's College, Montgomery, reporter.

Executive committee members: Forney G. Stephens, *The Southern Democrat*, Oneonta; Webb Stanley, *The Greenville Advocate*; Billy Smith, *The Chilton County News*, Clanton; Marcy B. Darnall, *The Florence Herald*; Robert E. Sutton Sr., *The Democrat-Reporter*, Linden; and W. Emmett Brooks, *The Brewton Standard*.

1932-1933

Forney G. Stephens, *The Southern Democrat*, Oneonta, president; Jesse B. Adams, *The Southern Star*, Ozark, vice president; R.P. Greer, *The Sylacauga Advance*, historian; Mrs. Scottie McKenzie Frazier, (newspaper unknown) Dothan, poetess; Howard C. Smith, Woman's College, Montgomery, reporter; Webb Stanley, *The Greenville Advocate*, editor of *The Ala-Pressa*; P.O. Davis, Extension Service, Alabama Polytechnic Institute, Auburn, associate editor of *The Ala-Pressa*; and Neil C. Cady, Western Newspaper Union, Birmingham, business manager of *The Ala-Pressa*.

1933-1934

Jesse B. Adams, *The Southern Star*, Ozark, president; W. Bruce Shelton, *The Tuscaloosa News*, vice president; E. Cody Hall Sr., *The Alexander City Outlook*, secretary-treasurer; W. Roy Brown, Montgomery, field manager; Rowe Greer, *The Sylacauga News*, convention secretary; J.W. Norwood, *The Cullman Tribune*, historian; Mrs. Scottie McKenzie Frazier, (newspaper unknown) poetess; and Howard C. Smith, Woman's College, Montgomery, reporter.

1934-1935

Jesse B. Adams, *The Southern Star*, Ozark, president; W. Bruce Shelton, *The Tuscaloosa News*, vice president; E. Cody Hall Sr., *The Alexander City Outlook*, secretary-treasurer; W. Roy Brown, field manager; and W. Emmett Brooks, *The Brewton Standard*, state NEA representative.

1935-1936

W. Bruce Shelton, *The Tuscaloosa News* (Shelton resigned after two months and was succeeded by F. Webb Stanley, *The Greenville Advocate*); Milton C. Giles, *The Sheffield Standard and Times*, first vice president; Robert Gaston Bozeman, *The Evergreen Courant*, second vice president; Billy Smith, *The Chilton County News*, Clanton, secretary-treasurer; R.C. Bryan, *The Elba Clipper*, recording secretary; E. Cody Hall Sr., *The Alexander City Outlook*, convention secretary.

District chairmen: H.H. Murray, *The Winfield Journal*; A.F. Leavitt, *The Etowah Observer*, Alabama City (name later changed to Gadsden); Clifford L. (Cliff) Walton, *The LaFayette Sun*; Cullen Morgan, *The Hale County News*, Moundville; Hunter H. Golson, *The Wetumpka Herald*; George A. Carleton, *The Clarke County Democrat*, Grove Hill; and R.C. Bryan, *The Elba Clipper*.

1936-1937

Robert Gaston Bozeman Sr., *The Evergreen Courant*, president; Clifford L. (Cliff) Walton, *The LaFayette Sun*, vice president; and R.C. Bryan, *The Elba Clipper*, secretary-treasurer.

Executive committee members: Milton C. Giles, *The Sheffield Standard and Times*, chairman; Forney G. Stephens, *The Southern Democrat*, Oneonta; Robert Henry (Harry) Walker, *The Limestone Democrat*, Athens; Webb Stanley, *The Greenville Advocate*; E. Cody Hall Sr., *The Alexander City Outlook*; George A. Carleton, *The Clarke County Democrat*, Grove Hill; and W. Emmett Brooks, *The Brewton Standard*.

1937-1938

Robert Gaston Bozeman Sr., *The Evergreen Courant*, president; Clifford L. (Cliff) Walton, *The LaFayette Sun*, vice president; and R.C. Bryan, *The Elba Clipper*, secretary-treasurer.

Executive committee members: Milton C. Giles, *The Sheffield Standard and Times;* Forney G. Stephens, *The Southern Democrat*, Oneonta; Robert Henry (Harry) Walker, *The Limestone Democrat*, Athens; Webb Stanley, *The Greenville Advocate*; E. Cody Hall Sr., *The Alexander City Outlook*; George A. Carleton, *The Clarke County Democrat*,

Grove Hill; and W. Emmett Brooks, *The Brewton Standard*.

1938-1939

Clifford L. (Cliff) Walton, *The LaFayette Sun*, president; Milton C. Giles, *The Sheffield Standard and Times*, vice president; and R.C. Bryan, *The Elba Clipper*, secretary.

1939-1940

Milton C. Giles, *The Franklin County Times*, Russellville, president; Hunter H. Golson, *The Wetumpka Herald*, vice president; and R.C. Bryan, *The Elba Clipper*, secretary-treasurer.

Executive committee members: E. Cody Hall Sr., *The Alexander City Outlook;* James H. (Jimmy) Faulkner Sr., *The Baldwin Times*, Bay Minette; Mildred White Wallace, *The Columbiana Democrat;* Robert Gaston Bozeman, *The Evergreen Courant;* Marcy B. Darnall, *The Florence Herald*; Webb Stanley, *The Greenville Advocate*; R.W. Bottler, *The Mountain Eagle*, Jasper; James Merritt McLendon, *The Luverne Journal*; Jesse B. Adams, *The Southern Star*, Ozark; Parker W. Campbell, *The Progressive Age*, Scottsboro; Hunter H. Golson, *The Wetumpka Herald*; and R. C. Bryan, *The Elba Clipper*.

1940-1941

Hunter H. Golson, *The Wetumpka Herald*, president; James H. (Jimmy) Faulkner Sr., *The Baldwin Times*, Bay Minette, vice president; and R.C. Bryan, *The Elba Clipper*, secretary-manager.

Executive committee members: E. Cody Hall Sr., *The Alexander City Outlook*; Webb Stanley, *The Greenville Advocate*; Neil O. Davis, *The Lee County Bulletin*, Auburn; Charles G. Dobbins, *The Anniston Times*; Parker W. Campbell, *The Progressive Age*, Scottsboro; Joe Jones, *The Covington County News*, Andalusia; Ralph B. Chandler, *The Mobile Press Register*; H.L. Upshaw, *The Eufaula Tribune*; Robert Henry Walker Jr., *The Limestone Democrat*, Athens; W. Bruce Shelton, *The Tuscaloosa News*; Sam B. Sloane Jr., *The Sumter County Journal*, York; and George A. Carleton, *The Clarke County Democrat*, Grove Hill.

1941-1942

James H. (Jimmy) Faulkner Sr., *The Baldwin Times*, Bay Minette, president; Charles G. Dobbins, *The Anniston Times*, vice president; and R.C. Bryan, *The Elba Clipper*, secretary-treasurer.

Executive committee members: Webb Stanley, *The Greenville Advocate*; Neil O. Davis, *The Lee*

County Bulletin, Auburn; Parker W. Campbell, *The Progressive Age*, Scottsboro, and *The Sentinel*; J. Fisher Rothermel, *The Birmingham News*; Ben A. Green, *The Tuscaloosa News*; George A. Carleton, *The Clarke County Democrat*, Grove Hill; Sam B. Sloane Jr., *The Sumter County Journal*, York; E.H. (Ed) Pierce, *The Mountain Eagle*, Jasper; C.G. Thomason, *The Industrial Press*, Ensley; Horace Hall, *The Dothan Eagle*; and Bonnie D. Hand, *The LaFayette Sun*.

1942-1943

Charles G. Dobbins, *The Anniston Times*, president; Marcy B. Darnall Jr., *The Florence Herald*, first vice president; and Neil O. Davis, *The Lee County Bulletin*, Auburn, second vice president.

Executive committee members: Webb Stanley, *The Greenville Advocate*; Parker W. Campbell, *The Progressive Age*, Scottsboro; Ben A. Green, *The Tuscaloosa News*; Hunter H. Golson, *The Wetumpka Herald*; Henry Arnold, *The Cullman Tribune*; J. Fisher Rothermel, *The Birmingham News*; Milton C. Giles, *The Franklin County Times*, Russellville; Cullen Morgan, *The Moundville News*; E.H. (Ed) Pierce, *The Mountain Eagle*, Jasper; Bonnie D. Hand, *The LaFayette Sun*; Horace Hall, *The Dothan Eagle*; R.C. Bryan, *The Elba Clipper*; George M. Cox, *The Mobile Press Register*; and George A. Carleton, *The Clarke County Democrat*, Grove Hill.

The three top officers of the APA resigned in late 1942 to enter the armed forces.

President Charles G. Dobbins, *The Anniston Times*, was a lieutenant in the Navy; first vice president Marcy B. Darnall Jr., *The Florence Herald*, was a lieutenant and naval aviator; and second vice president Neil O. Davis was a lieutenant in the Army.

Ben A. Green of *The Tuscaloosa News* served as acting president from the time of Dobbins' resignation in November 1942 until the annual convention in 1943.

In 1950 for *The Alabama Publisher*, Green recalled how he had been "drafted" as acting president:

"As I recall it, things first took shape at a barbecue held in Montgomery during July, 1942, at the closing session of a summer meeting of the Association. James H. Faulkner...was president. A war was going on and Jimmy (Faulkner), father of two children and mayor of Bay Minette, was on the verge of enlisting in the U.S. Air Corps.

"Charles Dobbins, then publisher of *The Anniston Star* (sic) *Times*, a weekly, was Associa-

tion vice president. He was on the verge of going into the U.S. Navy. Somebody, probably the irrepressible Hunter Golson of Wetumpka (God bless his memory), suggested that a second vice president would be needed to take over if the other two officers left for military service. It seems that at the barbecue I was elected second vice president. I did not know anything about it until I reached Tuscaloosa late Saturday afternoon, as I left before the barbecue.

"By the time November came around both Jimmy (Faulkner) and Charlie (Dobbins) were wearing Uncle Sam suits and Doyle Buckles (a noble soul) called on me to start functioning. Of course Buck (Doyle Buckles) was responsible for the continued progress of the Association. He was a wonder and a wonder worker."

1943-1944

Ben A. Green, *The Tuscaloosa News* (later of *The Tallassee Tribune*), president; Parker W. Campbell, *The Progressive Age*, Scottsboro, vice president; and George A. Carleton, *The Clarke County Democrat*, second vice president.

Executive committee members: John Henry Singleton, *The Enterprise Ledger*; Walter Miller, *The Tuscumbia Reporter*; Robert D. Burgess, *The Opp News*; Ralph W. Callahan, *The Anniston Star*; Isabel Moses, *The Phenix City Journal*; Cash M. Stanley, *The Montgomery Advertiser*; John B. Stevenson, *The Roanoke Leader*; Edmund R. (Ed) Blair, *The Pell City News*; Henry Arnold, *The Cullman Tribune*; J. Fisher Rothermel, *The Birmingham News*; Cullen Morgan, *The Moundville News*; E.H. (Ed) Pierce, *The Mountain Eagle*, Jasper; Bonnie D. Hand, *The LaFayette Sun*; and George M. Cox, *The Mobile Press Register*.

1944-1945

Parker W. Campbell, *The Progressive Age*, Scottsboro, president; George A. Carleton, *The Clarke County Democrat*, Grove Hill, vice president; and J.A. Downer, *The Fort Payne Times*, second vice president.

Executive committee members: Ben A. Green, *The Tallassee Tribune*; Hunter H. Golson, *The Wetumpka Herald*; Cash M. Stanley, *The Montgomery Advertiser*; J. Fisher Rothermel, *The Birmingham News*; W. Bruce Shelton, *The Tuscaloosa News*; Edmund R. (Ed) Blair, *The Pell City News*; E.H. (Ed) Pierce, *The Mountain Eagle*, Jasper; Bonnie D. Hand, *The LaFayette Sun*; Clark S. Hodgins, *The Moulton Advertiser*; Jay Thornton, *The*

Haleyville Advertiser; Webb Stanley, *The Greenville Advocate*; John B. Stevenson, *The Roanoke Leader*; Jack M. Pratt, *The Pickens County Herald*, Carrollton; and Milton C. Giles, *The Franklin County Times*, Russellville.

1945-1946

George A. Carleton, *The Clarke County Democrat*, Grove Hill, president; Bonnie D. Hand, *The LaFayette Sun*, first vice president; and E.H. (Ed) Pierce, *The Mountain Eagle*, Jasper, second vice president.

Executive committee members: Hunter H. Golson, *The Wetumpka Herald*; Cash M. Stanley, *The Montgomery Advertiser*; J. Fisher Rothermel, *The Birmingham News*; W. Bruce Shelton, *The Tuscaloosa News*; Edmund R. (Ed) Blair, *The Pell City News*; Henry Arnold, *The Cullman Tribune*; J.C. Henderson, *The Alexander City Outlook*; Clark S. Hodgins, *The Moulton Advertiser*; Jay Thornton, *The Haleyville Advertiser*; Webb Stanley, *The Greenville Advocate*; J.A. Downer, *The Fort Payne Times*; Robert D. Burgess, *The Opp News*; Mrs. M.M. Marchard, *The Onlooker*, Foley; and Parker O. Campbell, *The Progressive Age*, Scottsboro.

1946-1947

Bonnie D. Hand, *The LaFayette Sun*, president; Neil O. Davis, *The Lee County Bulletin*, Auburn, first vice president; E.H. (Ed) Pierce, *The Mountain Eagle*, Jasper, second vice president; and field manager Doyle L. Buckles, secretary-treasurer.

Executive committee members: Hunter H. Golson, *The Wetumpka Herald*; Gould Beech, *The Southern Farmer*, Montgomery; Richard F. Hudson Jr., The Montgomery Advertiser Co.; Clarence B. Hanson Jr., *The Birmingham News*; J.C. Henderson, *The Alexander City Outlook;* Henry Arnold, *The Cullman Tribune*; Jay Thornton, *The Haleyville Advertiser;* Cecil H. Hornady, *The Talladega News*; Steele E. McGrew, *The Athens Courier*; Ben G. George, *The Demopolis Times*; Edmund R. (Ed) Blair, *The Pell City News*; Horace Hall, *The Dothan Eagle*; Ralph W. Callahan, *The Anniston Star*; W.L. Foreman, *The Atmore Advance*; and George A. Carleton, *The Clarke County Democrat*, Grove Hill.

1947-1948

Neil O. Davis, *The Lee County Bulletin*, Auburn, president; E.H. (Ed) Pierce, *The Mountain Eagle*, Jasper, first vice president; J.C. Henderson, *The Alexander City Outlook*, second vice president; and field manager Doyle L. Buckles, secretary-treasurer.

Executive committee members: George H. Watson, *The Shades Valley Sun*, Homewood; William E. (Bill) Brooks Jr., *The Brewton Standard*; McClellan Van der Veer, *The Birmingham News*; Jack M. Pratt, *The Pickens County Herald*, Carrollton; Milton C. Giles, *The Franklin County Times*, Russellville; James H. (Jimmy) Faulkner Sr., *The Baldwin County Times*, Bay Minette; Charles G. Dobbins, *The Montgomery Advertiser*; Eugene Thomley, *The Geneva Reaper*; Webb Stanley, *The Greenville Advocate*; R.K. Coffee, *The Jacksonville News*; Bonnie D. Hand, *The LaFayette Sun*; Gould Beech, *The Southern Farmer*, Montgomery; Cecil H. Hornady, *The Talladega News*; Steele E. McGrew, *The Athens Courier*; and Edmund R. (Ed) Blair, *The Pell City News*.

1948-1949

E.H. (Ed) Pierce, *The Mountain Eagle*, Jasper, president; J.C. Henderson, *The Alexander City Outlook*, first vice president; and Clarence B. Hanson Jr., *The Birmingham News*, second vice president.

Executive committee members: Edmund R. (Ed) Blair, *The Pell City News*; William E. (Bill) Brooks Jr., *The Brewton Standard*; R.K. Coffee, *The Jacksonville News*; Neil O. Davis, *The Lee County Bulletin*, Auburn; Bonnie D. Hand, *The LaFayette Sun*; James H. (Jimmy) Faulkner Sr., *The Baldwin Times*, Bay Minette; Ben G. George, *The Demopolis Times*; Eldon J. Hoar, *The Troy Messenger and Herald;* Cecil H. Hornady, *The Talladega News*; Richard F. Hudson Jr., *The Montgomery Advertiser* and *Alabama Journal*; William Irby, *All-Alabama Magazine*, Sylacauga; and George H. Watson, *The Shades Valley Sun*, Homewood.

1949-1950

J.C. Henderson, *The Alexander City Outlook*, president; Clarence B. Hanson Jr., *The Birmingham News*, first vice president; and Edmund R. (Ed) Blair, *The Pell City News*, *The Leeds News* and *The Southern Aegis*, Ashville, second vice president.

Executive committee members: Charles G. Dobbins, *The Montgomery Examiner*; J.A. Downer, *The DeKalb Times*, Fort Payne; Ben G. George, *The Demopolis Times*; Milton C. Giles, *The Franklin County Times*, Russellville; Jep V. Greer, *The Sylacauga News*; Bonnie D. Hand, *The LaFayette Sun*; Cecil H. Hornady, *The Talladega News*; Steele E. McGrew, *The Alabama Courier*, Athens; E.H. (Ed) Pierce, *The Mountain Eagle*, Jasper; Jack M. Pratt, *The Pickens County Herald*, Carrollton; Martin L. Ritchie, *The Atmore Advance*;

Webb Stanley, *The Greenville Advocate*; Bill Stewart, *The Monroe Journal*, Monroeville; and H.L. Upshaw, *The Eufaula Tribune*.

1950-1951

Edmund R. (Ed) Blair, *The Pell City News and Southern Aegis*, Ashville, president; Clarence B. Hanson Jr., *The Birmingham News*, first vice president; and Cecil H. Hornady, *The Talladega News*, second vice president.

Executive committee members: William E. (Bill) Brooks Jr., *The Brewton Standard*; R.K. Coffee, *The Jacksonville News*; Charles G. Dobbins, *The Montgomery Examiner*; Ben G. George, *The Demopolis Times*; Milton C. Giles, *The Franklin County Times*, Russellville; Jep V. Greer, *The Sylacauga News*; Bonnie D. Hand, *The LaFayette Sun*; J.C. Henderson, *The Alexander City Outlook*; Steele E. McGrew, *The Alabama Courier*, Athens; James E. (Jimmy) Mills, *The Birmingham Post*; E.H. (Ed) Pierce, *The Mountain Eagle*, Jasper; Jack M. Pratt, *The Pickens County Herald*, Carrollton; Martin L. Ritchie, *The Atmore Advance*; and Bill Stewart, *The Monroe Journal*, Monroeville.

1951-1952

Clarence B. Hanson Jr., *The Birmingham News*, president; Cecil H. Hornady, *The Talladega News*, first vice president; and field manager Jack Beisner, secretary-treasurer.

Board of trustees for two-year terms: Ben G. George, *The Demopolis Times*; Orsen B. Spivey, *The Geneva County Reaper*, Geneva; J.C. Henderson, *The Alexander City Outlook*; Milton C. Giles, *The Franklin County Times*, Russellville; and George H. Watson, *The Shades Valley Sun*, Homewood.

Board members for one-year terms: Charles G. Dobbins, *The Montgomery Examiner*; Ralph W. Callahan, *The Anniston Star*; J.W. (Jim) Oakley Sr., *The Centreville Press*; and Steele E. McGrew, *The Alabama Courier*, Athens.

1952-1953

Cecil H. Hornady, *The Talladega News*, president; William E. (Bill) Brooks Jr., *The Brewton Standard*, first vice president; and Steele E. McGrew, *The Alabama Courier*, Athens, second vice president.

Board of directors: Clarence B. Hanson Jr., *The Birmingham News*, chairman; Ben G. George, *The Demopolis Times*; Robert D. Burgess, *The Opp News*; Orsen B. Spivey, *The Geneva County Reaper*, Geneva; Herve Charest Jr., *The Tallassee Tribune*;

J.C. Henderson, *The Alexander City Outlook*; Milton C. Giles, *The Franklin County Times*, Russellville; J.W. (Jim) Oakley Sr., *The Centreville Press*; Jack Langhorne, *The Huntsville Times*; and George H. Watson, *The Shades Valley Sun*, Homewood.

1953-1954

William E. (Bill) Brooks Jr., *The Brewton Standard*, president; Steele E. McGrew, *The Alabama Courier*, Athens, first vice president; and George H. Watson, *The Shades Valley Sun*, Homewood, second vice president.

Board of directors: Cecil H. Hornady, *The Talladega News*, chairman; Ben G. George, *The Demopolis Times*; Robert D. Burgess, *The Opp News*; Paul Cunningham, *The Elba Clipper*; Herve Charest Jr., *The Tallassee Tribune*; John B. Stevenson, *The Roanoke Leader*; J.W. (Jim) Oakley Sr., *The Centreville Press*; Jones W. Giles, *The Red Bay News*; Jack Langhorne, *The Huntsville Times*; and James E. (Jimmy) Mills, the *Birmingham Post-Herald*.

1954-1955

Steele E. McGrew, *The Limestone Democrat* and *Alabama Courier*, Athens, president; George H. Watson, *The Shades Valley Sun*, Homewood, first vice president; and Ben G. George, *The Demopolis Times*, second vice president.

Board of directors: William E. (Bill) Brooks Jr., *The Brewton Standard*, chairman; George M. Cox, *The Mobile Press Register*; Ed Dannelly, *The Andalusia Star-News*; Paul Cunningham, *The Elba Clipper*; Cecil H. Hornady, *The Talladega News*; John B. Stevenson, *The Roanoke Leader*; Buford Boone, *The Tuscaloosa News*; Grace Pratt, *The Aliceville Informer*; Harold S. May, *The Florence Herald*; and James E. (Jimmy) Mills, the *Birmingham Post-Herald*.

1955-1956

George H. Watson, *The Shades Valley Sun*, Homewood, president; Ben G. George, *The Demopolis Times*, first vice president; and George M. Cox, *The Mobile Press Register*, second vice president.

APA Board of directors: Steele E. McGrew, *The Alabama Courier*, Athens, chairman; Bill Stewart, *The Monroe Journal*, Monroeville; Ed Dannelly, *The Andalusia Star-News*; Neil O. Davis, *The Lee County Bulletin*, Auburn; Cecil H. Hornady, *The Talladega News*; Fred Eiland, *The Cleburne News*, Heflin; Buford Boone, *The Tuscaloosa News*; Jack M. Pratt,

The Pickens County Herald, Carrollton; James E. (Jimmy) Mills, the *Birmingham Post-Herald*; and Harold S. May, *The Florence Herald*.

1956-1957

Ben G. George, *The Demopolis Times*, president; George M. Cox, *The Mobile Press Register*, first vice president; and C.G. Thomason, *The Industrial Press*, Ensley, second vice president.

Board of directors: George H. Watson, *The Shades Valley Sun*, Homewood, chairman; Bill Stewart, *The Monroe Journal*, Monroeville; Glenn Stanley, *The Greenville Advocate*; Neil O. Davis, *The Lee County Bulletin*, Auburn; Col. Harry Mell Ayers, *The Anniston Star*; Fred Eiland, *The Cleburne News*, Heflin; Buford Boone, *The Tuscaloosa News*; Jack M. Pratt, *The Pickens County Herald*, Carrollton; Harold S. May, *The Florence Herald*; and James E. (Jimmy) Mills, the *Birmingham Post-Herald*.

1957-1958

George M. Cox, *The Mobile Press Register*, president; C.G. Thomason, *The Industrial Press*, Ensley, first vice president; and Bill Stewart, *The Monroe Journal*, Monroeville, second vice president.

Board of directors: Ben G. George, *The Demopolis Times*, chairman of the board; N.B. Stallworth, *The Washington County News*, Chatom; Glenn Stanley, *The Greenville Advocate*; J.E. Dodd, *The Abbeville Herald*; Harry Mell Ayers, *The Anniston Star*; Porter Harvey, *The Advertiser-Gleam*, Guntersville; Buford Boone, *The Tuscaloosa News*; Jack Hankins, *The Lamar Democrat*, Vernon; Harold S. May, *The Florence Herald*; and James E. (Jimmy) Mills, the *Birmingham Post-Herald*.

1958-1959

C.G. Thomason, *The Industrial Press*, Ensley, president; Bill Stewart, *The Monroe Journal*, Monroeville, first vice president; and James E. (Jimmy) Mills, the *Birmingham Post-Herald*, second vice president.

Board of directors: George M. Cox, *The Mobile Press Register*, chairman; N.B. Stallworth, *The Washington County News*, Chatom; Glenn Jones, *The Troy Messenger*; J.E. Dodd, *The Abbeville Herald*; Col. Harry Mell Ayers, *The Anniston Star*; Porter Harvey, *The Advertiser-Gleam*, Guntersville; Buford Boone, *The Tuscaloosa News*; Jack Hankins, *The Lamar Democrat*, Vernon; Harold S. May, *The Florence Herald*; and James E. (Jimmy) Mills, the *Birmingham Post-Herald*.

1959-1960

William M. (Bill) Stewart, *The Monroe Journal*, Monroeville, president; James E. (Jimmy) Mills, the *Birmingham Post-Herald*, first vice president; and Harold S. May, *The Florence Herald*, second vice president.

Board of directors: C.G. Thomason, *The Industrial Press*, Ensley; Tip Mathews, *The Mobile Press Register*; Glenn Jones, *The Troy Messenger*; Joel P. Smith, *The Eufaula Tribune*; Col. Harry Mell Ayers, *The Anniston Star*; Porter Harvey, *The Advertiser-Gleam*, Guntersville; Buford Boone, *The Tuscaloosa News*; Jay Thornton, *The Haleyville Advertiser*; Arthur F. Slaton Jr., *The Moulton Advertiser*; and Arthur Cook, *The Shades Valley Sun*, Homewood.

1960-1961

James E. (Jimmy) Mills, the *Birmingham Post-Herald*, president; Harold S. May, *The Florence Herald*, first vice president; and Glenn Stanley, *The Greenville Advocate*, second vice president.

Board of directors: Bill Stewart, *The Monroe Journal*, Monroeville, chairman; George A. Carleton, *The Clarke County Democrat*, Grove Hill; Ed Dannelly, *The Andalusia Star-News*; Joel P. Smith, *The Eufaula Tribune*; Herve Charest Jr., *The Tallassee Tribune*; Porter Harvey, *The Advertiser-Gleam*, Guntersville; Buford Boone, *The Tuscaloosa News*; Jay Thornton, *The Haleyville Advertiser*; Will C. Mickle, *The Huntsville Times*; and Arthur Cook, *The Shades Valley Sun*, Homewood.

1961-1962

Harold S. May, *The Florence Herald*, president; Glenn Stanley, *The Greenville Advocate*, first vice president; and Herve Charest Jr., *The Tallassee Tribune*, second vice president.

Board of directors: James E. (Jimmy) Mills, the *Birmingham Post-Herald*, chairman; George M. Cox, *The Mobile Press Register*; Ed Dannelly, *The Andalusia Star-News*; Joel P. Smith, *The Eufaula Tribune*; Edward B. Field, *The Selma Times-Journal*; Jesse Culp, *The Sand Mountain Reporter*, Albertville; Buford Boone, *The Tuscaloosa News*; Robert Bryan, *The Cullman Times*; Jack Langhorne, *The Huntsville Times*; and James Thomason, *The Industrial Press*, Ensley.

1962-1963

J. Glenn Stanley, *The Greenville Advocate*, president; Herve Charest Jr., *The Tallassee Tribune*, first vice president; and Buford Boone, *The Tuscaloosa News*, second vice president.

Board of directors: Harold S. May, *The Florence Herald*, chairman; George M. Cox, *The Mobile Press Register*; E.M. (Sparky) Howell, *The Onlooker*, Foley; Joel P. Smith, *The Eufaula Tribune*; Ralph W. Callahan, *The Anniston Star*; Jesse Culp, *The Sand Mountain Reporter*, Albertville; J. W. (Jim) Oakley Sr., *The Centreville Press*; Robert Bryan, *The Cullman Times*; Luther Baker, *The Florence Times and Tri-Cities Daily*; and James Thomason, *The Industrial Press*, Ensley.

1963-1964

Herve Charest Jr., *The Tallassee Tribune*, president; Buford Boone, *The Tuscaloosa News*, first vice president; and E.M. (Sparky) Howell, *The Onlooker*, Foley, second vice president.

Board of directors: Glenn Stanley, *The Greenville Advocate*, chairman; George M. Cox, *The Mobile Press Register*; Ed Dannelly, *The Andalusia Star-News*; Graham M. McTeer, *The Lee County Bulletin*, Auburn; Ralph W. Callahan, *The Anniston Star*; Ewell H. Reed, *The Arab Tribune*; J.W. (Jim) Oakley Sr., *The Centreville Press*; Robert Bryan, *The Cullman Times*; Luther Baker, *The Florence Times and Tri-Cities Daily*; and Victor H. Hanson II, *The Birmingham News*.

1964-1965

E.M. (Sparky) Howell, *The Onlooker*, Foley, president; Ralph W. Callahan, *The Anniston Star*, first vice president; and Ed Dannelly, *The Andalusia Star-News*, second vice president.

Board of directors: Herve Charest Jr., *The Tallassee Tribune*, chairman; George M. Cox, *The Mobile Press Register*; E.R. (Bob) Morrissette Jr., *The Atmore Advance*; Graham M. McTeer, *The Lee County Bulletin*, Auburn; Bruce Jetton, *The Wetumpka Herald*; Ewell H. Reed, *The Arab Tribune*; Karl Elebash Jr., *The Graphic*, Tuscaloosa; Robert Bryan, *The Cullman Times*; Leroy Simms, *The Huntsville Times*; and Victor H. Hanson II, *The Birmingham News*.

1965-1966

Ralph W. Callahan, *The Anniston Star*, president; Ed Dannelly, *The Andalusia Star-News*, first vice president; and Porter Harvey, *The Advertiser-Gleam*, Guntersville, second vice president.

Board of directors: E.M. (Sparky) Howell, *The Onlooker*, Foley, chairman; George M. Cox, *The Mobile Press Register*; E.R. (Bob) Morrissette Jr., *The Atmore Advance*; Joseph H. (Joe) Adams, *The Southern Star*, Ozark; Herve Charest Jr., *The Tallassee Tribune*; Ewell H. Reed, *The Arab Tribune*; Karl Elebash Jr., *The Graphic*, Tuscaloosa; Robert Bryan, *The Cullman Times*; Leroy Simms, *The Huntsville Times*; and James Thomason, *The Industrial Press*, Ensley.

1966-1967

Edward A. (Ed) Dannelly Jr., *The Andalusia Star-News*, president; Porter Harvey, *The Advertiser-Gleam*, Guntersville, first vice president; and W.H. (Bill) Metz, the *Birmingham Post-Herald*, second vice president.

Board of directors: Ralph W. Callahan, *The Anniston Star*, chairman; George M. Cox, *The Mobile Press Register*; W. E. (Gene) Hardin, *The Greenville Advocate*; Joseph H. (Joe) Adams, *The Southern Star*, Ozark; H. Brandt Ayers, *The Anniston Star*; Ewell H. Reed, *The Arab Tribune*; Norman H. Bassett, *The Tuscaloosa News*; Barrett C. Shelton Jr., *The Decatur Daily*; and James Thomason, *The Industrial Press*, Ensley.

1967-1968

Porter Harvey, *The Advertiser-Gleam*, Guntersville, president; W.H. (Bill) Metz, the *Birmingham Post-Herald*, first vice president; Joel P. Smith, *The Eufaula Tribune*, second vice president; and Ed Dannelly, *The Andalusia Star-News*, chairman of the board.

Board of directors: George M. Cox, *The Mobile Press Register*; Joseph H. (Joe) Adams, *The Southern Star*, Ozark; H. Brandt Ayers, *The Anniston Star*; Robert E. Sutton Jr., *The Democrat-Reporter*, Linden; Norman H. Bassett, *The Tuscaloosa News*; Robert Bryan, *The Cullman Times*; and Barrett C. Shelton Jr., *The Decatur Daily*.

1968-1969

W.H. (Bill) Metz, the *Birmingham Post-Herald*, president; Joel P. Smith, *The Eufaula Tribune*, first vice president; Karl Elebash Jr., *The Graphic*, Tuscaloosa, second vice president; and Porter Harvey, *The Advertiser-Gleam*, chairman of the board.

Board of directors: George M. Cox, *The Mobile Press Register*; James H. (Jimmy) Faulkner Jr., *The Baldwin Times*, Bay Minette; Joseph H. (Joe) Adams, *The Southern Star*, Ozark; Phillip A. Sanguinetti, *The Anniston Star*; Robert E. Sutton Jr., *The Democrat-Reporter*, Linden; John W. Bloomer, *The Birmingham News*; Robert Bryan, *The Cullman Times*; and Leroy Simms, *The Huntsville Times*.

1969-1970

Joel P. Smith, *The Eufaula Tribune*, president; Karl Elebash Jr., *The Graphic*, Tuscaloosa, first vice president; Robert Bryan, *The Cullman Times*, second vice president; and W.H. (Bill) Metz, the *Birmingham Post-Herald*, chairman of the board.

Board of directors: J. Fred Nall, *The South Alabamian*, Jackson; James H. (Jimmy) Faulkner Jr., *The Baldwin Times*, Bay Minette; Orsen B. Spivey, *The Geneva County Reaper*, Geneva; Phillip A. Sanguinetti, *The Anniston Star*; Norman H. Bassett, *The Tuscaloosa News*; John W. Bloomer, *The Birmingham News*; Claude E. Sparks, *The Franklin County* Times, Russellville; and Leroy Simms, *The Huntsville Times*.

1970-1971

Karl Elebash Jr., *The Graphic*, Tuscaloosa, president; Robert Bryan, *The Cullman Times*, first vice president; W.E. (Gene) Hardin, *The Greenville Advocate*, second vice president; and Joel P. Smith, *The Eufaula Tribune*, chairman of the board.

Board of directors: J. Fred Nall Sr., *The South Alabamian*, Jackson; E.R. (Bob) Morrissette Jr., *The Atmore Advance*; Orsen B. Spivey, *The Geneva County Reaper*, Geneva; Roswell Falkenberry, *The Selma Times-Journal*; Norman H. Bassett, *The Tuscaloosa News*; John W. Bloomer, *The Birmingham News*; Claude E. Sparks, *The Franklin County Times*, Russellville; and Barrett C. Shelton Jr., *The Decatur Daily*.

1971-1972

Robert Bryan, *The Cullman Times*, president; W.E. (Gene) Hardin, *The Greenville Advocate,* first vice president; Ewell H. Reed, *The Arab Tribune*, second vice president; and Karl Elebash Jr., *The Graphic*, Tuscaloosa, chairman of the board.

Board of directors: J. Fred Nall Sr., *The South Alabamian*, Jackson; Orsen B. Spivey, Spivey Newspapers, Geneva; James W. (Jim) Oakley Jr., *The Centreville Press*; Claude E. Sparks, *The Franklin County Times*, Russellville; Karl Elebash Jr., *The Graphic*, Tuscaloosa; E.R. (Bob) Morrissette Jr., *The Atmore Advance*; Roswell Falkenberry, *The Selma Times-Journal*; Barrett C. Shelton Jr., *The Decatur Daily*; and John W. Bloomer, *The Birmingham News*.

1972-1973

W.E. (Gene) Hardin, *The Greenville Advocate*, president; Ewell H. Reed, *The Arab Tribune*, first vice president; Barrett C. Shelton Jr., *The Decatur*

Daily, second vice president; and Robert Bryan, *The Cullman Times*, chairman of the board.

Board of directors: E.R. (Bob) Morrissette Jr., *The Atmore Advance;* Jack Venable, *The Tallassee Tribune*; John W. Bloomer, *The Birmingham News*; David Marion, *The Athens News Courier*; J. Fred Nall Sr., *The South Alabamian*, Jackson; Orsen B. Spivey, *The Geneva County Reaper*, Geneva; James W. (Jim) Oakley Jr., *The Centreville Press*; and Claude E. Sparks, *The Franklin County Times*, Russellville.

1973-1974

Ewell H. Reed, *The Arab Tribune*, president; Barrett C. Shelton Jr., *The Decatur Daily*, first vice president; Orsen B. Spivey, *The Geneva County Reaper*, Geneva, second vice president; and W.E. (Gene) Hardin, *The Greenville Advocate*, chairman of the board.

Board of directors: Claude E. Sparks, *The Franklin County Times*, Russellville; Frank Helderman Jr., *The Gadsden Times*; John W. Bloomer, *The Birmingham News*; James W. (Jim) Oakley Jr., *The Centreville Press*; Phillip A. Sanguinetti, *The Jacksonville News*; Goodloe Sutton, *The Democrat-Reporter*, Linden; Roger W. Pride Jr., *The Butler County News*, Georgiana; Jack Venable, *The Tallassee Tribune*; E.R. (Bob) Morrissette Jr., *The Atmore Advance*; David Chancey, *The Headland Observer*; and John Cameron, *The Onlooker*, Foley.

1974-1975

Barrett C. Shelton Jr., *The Decatur Daily*, president; Orsen B. Spivey, *The Geneva County Reaper*, Geneva, first vice president; Claude E. Sparks, *The Franklin County Times*, Russellville, and *The Red Bay News*, second vice president; and Ewell H. Reed, *The Arab Tribune*, chairman of the board.

Board of directors: Don Thrasher, *The Northwest Alabamian*, Haleyville; Pat McCauley, *The Huntsville Times*; Alvin Bland, *The Luverne Journal and News*; John A. Burgess, *The Opp News*; Fallon Trotter, *The Mobile Press Register*; John W. Bloomer, *The Birmingham* News; Jack Venable, *The Tallassee Tribune*; Frank Helderman Jr., *The Gadsden Times*; James W. (Jim) Oakley Jr., *The Centreville Press*; Phillip A. Sanguinetti, *The Jacksonville News*; Goodloe Sutton, *The Democrat-Reporter*, Linden; and David Chancey, *The Headland Observer*.

1975-1976

Orsen B. Spivey, *The Geneva County Reaper*, Geneva, president; Claude E. Sparks, *The Franklin*

County Times, Russellville, first vice president; Phillip A. Sanguinetti, *The Anniston Star*, second vice president; and Barrett C. Shelton Jr., *The Decatur Daily*, chairman of the board.

Board of directors: David Poynor, *The Greene County Democrat*, Eutaw; John B. Stevenson, *The Randolph Press*, Wedowee; Marcia M. Sears, *The Shelby County Reporter*, Columbiana; Shelton Prince Jr., *The Daily Mountain Eagle*, Jasper; Frank Helderman Jr., *The Gadsden Times*; Jack Venable, *The Tallassee Tribune*; Fallon Trotter, *The Mobile Press Register*; David Chancey, *The Headland Observer*; John A. Burgess, *The Opp News*; Pat McCauley, *The Huntsville Times*; Marcia M. Sears, *The Shelby County Reporter*, Columbiana; Alvin Bland, *The Luverne Journal and News*; and Don Thrasher, *The Northwest Alabamian*, Haleyville.

1976-1977

Claude E. Sparks, *The Franklin County Times*, Russellville, president; Phillip A. Sanguinetti, *The Anniston Star*, vice president; E.R. (Bob) Morrissette Jr., *The Atmore Advance*, second vice president; and Orsen B. Spivey, *The Geneva County Reaper*, Geneva, chairman of the board.

Board of directors: Shelton Prince Jr., *The Daily Mountain Eagle*, Jasper; Marcia M. Sears, *The Shelby County Reporter*, Columbiana; John B. Stevenson, *The Roanoke Leader*; Jack Venable, *The Tallassee Tribune*; Luke Slaton, *The Moulton Advertiser*; Bill Nelson, *The Athens News Courier*; Frank Helderman Jr., *The Gadsden Times*; James Morgan, *The Luverne Journal and News*; Marcia M. Sears, *The Shelby County Reporter*, Columbiana; David Poynor, *The Greene County Democrat*, Eutaw; Steve Stewart, *The Monroe Journal*, Monroeville; Joseph H. (Joe) Adams, *The Southern Star*, Ozark; and William J. (Bill) Hearin, *The Mobile Press Register*.

1977-1978

Phillip A. Sanguinetti, *The Anniston Star*, president; E.R. (Bob) Morrissette Jr., *The Atmore Advance*, first vice president; James W. (Jim) Oakley Jr., *The Centreville Press*, second vice president; and Claude E. Sparks, *The Franklin County Times*, Russellville, chairman of the board.

Board of directors: Luke Slaton, *The Moulton Advertiser*; Bill Nelson, *The Athens News Courier*; James Morgan, *The Luverne Journal and News*; Steve Stewart, *The Monroe Journal*, Monroeville; William J. (Bill) Hearin, *The Mobile Press Register*; Don Woodward, *The Advertiser-Gleam*,

Guntersville; Shelton Prince Jr., *The Daily Mountain Eagle*, Jasper; John W. Bloomer, *The Birmingham News*; John B. Stevenson, *The Roanoke Leader*; Jim McKay, *The Demopolis Times*; and Millard Grimes, *The Opelika-Auburn Daily News*.

1978-1979

E.R. (Bob) Morrissette Jr., *The Atmore Advance*, president; James W. (Jim) Oakley Jr., *The Centreville Press*, first vice president; Shelton Prince Jr., *The Daily Mountain Eagle*, Jasper, second vice president; and Phillip A. Sanguinetti, *The Anniston Star*, chairman of the board

Board of directors: Don Woodward, *The Advertiser-Gleam*, Guntersville; Ed Lowry, *The Greensboro Watchman*; John W. Bloomer, *The Birmingham News*; John B. Stevenson, *The Roanoke Leader*; Jim McKay, *The Demopolis Times*; Millard Grimes, Grimes Newspapers; Luke Slaton, *The Moulton Advertiser*; Pat McCauley, *The Huntsville Times*; W.E. (Gene) Hardin, *The Greenville Advocate*; Mike Breedlove, *The South Alabamian*, Jackson; David Marion, *The Troy Messenger*; and Vernon Payne, *The Baldwin Times*, Bay Minette.

1979-1980

James W. (Jim) Oakley Jr., *The Centreville Press*, president; Shelton Prince Jr., *The Daily Mountain Eagle*, Jasper, first vice president; Marcia M. Sears, *The Shelby County Reporter*, Columbiana, second vice president; and E.R. (Bob) Morrissette Jr., *The Atmore Advance*, chairman of the board.

Board of directors: Edwin Reed, *The Arab Tribune*; Ed Lowry, *The Greensboro Watchman*; Luke Slaton, *The Moulton Advertiser*; Pat McCauley, *The Huntsville Times*; W.E. (Gene) Hardin, *The Greenville Advocate*; Mike Breedlove, *The South Alabamian*, Jackson; Dave Marion, *The Troy Messenger;* Vernon Payne, *The Baldwin Times*, Bay Minette; Angus McEachran, the *Birmingham Post-Herald*; Jay Thornton, *The Daily Home*, Talladega; Bruce Morrison, *The Selma Times-Journal*; and Jack Venable, *The Tallassee Tribune*.

1980-1981

Shelton Price Jr., *The Selma Times-Journal*, president; Marcia M. Sears, *The Shelby County Reporter*, Columbiana, first vice president; Don Woodward, *The Advertiser-Gleam*, Guntersville, second vice president; and James W. (Jim) Oakley Jr., *The Centreville Press*, chairman of the board.

Board of directors: Luke Slaton, *The Moulton Advertiser*; Pat McCauley, *The Huntsville Times*;

Edwin Reed, *The Arab Tribune*; Angus McEachran, the *Birmingham Post-Herald*; Bruce Morrison, *The Selma Times-Journal*; Jack Venable, *The Tallassee Tribune*; Charles Land, *The Tuscaloosa News*; Jay Thornton, *The Daily Home*, Talladega; James G. (Jim) Martin, *The Montgomery Advertiser* and *Alabama Journal*; Mike Breedlove, *The South Alabamian*, Jackson; David Marion, *The Troy Messenger*; and William J. (Bill) Hearin, *The Mobile Press Register*.

1981-1982

Marcia M. Sears, *The Shelby County Reporter*, Columbiana, president; Don Woodward, *The Advertiser-Gleam*, Guntersville, first vice president; Millard Grimes, *The Enterprise Ledger*, second vice president; and Shelton Prince Jr., *The Selma Times-Journal*, chairman of the board.

APA Board of directors: Luke Slaton, *The Moulton Advertiser*; Sam Harvey, *The Advertiser-Gleam*, Guntersville; Angus McEachran, the *Birmingham Post-Herald*; Robert E. Sutton Jr., *The White Bluff Chronicle*, Demopolis; Pat McCauley, *The Huntsville Times*; Charles Land, *The Tuscaloosa News*; Jay Thornton, *The Daily Home*, Talladega; James G. (Jim) Martin, *The Montgomery Advertiser* and *Alabama Journal*; Mike Breedlove, *The South Alabamian*, Jackson; William J. (Bill) Hearin, *The Mobile Press Register*; Jack Venable, *The Tallassee Tribune*; and Karol R.L. Fleming, *The Geneva County Reaper*, Geneva.

1982-1983

Don Woodward, *The Advertiser-Gleam*, Guntersville, president; William J. (Bill) Hearin, *The Mobile Press Register*, first vice president; Luke Slaton, *The Moulton Advertiser*, second vice president; and Marcia M. Sears, *The Shelby County Reporter*, Columbiana, chairman of the board.

Board of directors: Luke Slaton, *The Moulton Advertiser*; Tom Wright, *The Decatur Daily*; Sam Harvey, *The Advertiser-Gleam*, Guntersville; Charles Land, *The Tuscaloosa News*; Angus McEachran, the *Birmingham Post-Herald*; Jay Thornton, *The Daily Home*, Talladega; Robert E. Sutton Jr., *The White Bluff Chronicle*, Demopolis; James G. (Jim) Martin, *The Montgomery Advertiser* and *Alabama Journal*; Jack Venable, *The Tallassee Tribune*; John A. Burgess, *The Opp News*; Karol R.L. Fleming, *The Geneva County Reaper*, Geneva; and Charles Beasley, *The Onlooker*, Foley.

1983-1984

William J. (Bill) Hearin, *The Mobile Press Register*, president; Luke Slaton, *The Moulton Advertiser*, first vice president; Mike Breedlove, *The South Alabamian*, Jackson, second vice president; and Don Woodward, *The Advertiser-Gleam*, Guntersville, chairman of the board.

1984-1985

Luke Slaton, *The Moulton Advertiser*, president, Mike Breedlove, *The South Alabamian*, Jackson, first vice president; and Jay Thornton, *The Daily Home*, Talladega, second vice president. (William J. Hearin, publisher of *The Mobile Press Register* and immediate past president of APA, would have served as chairman of the board under APA by-laws, but Hearin withdrew his newspaper's membership from the press association in 1984 after the APA board of directors filed a neutral brief in a case involving the legal qualifications of newspapers to publish legal notices).

Board of directors: Jim Crawford, *The Colbert County Reporter*; Ginger Grantham, *The Hanceville Herald*; Sam Harvey, *The Advertiser-Gleam*, Guntersville; Ed Fowler, *The Tuscaloosa News*; James E. Jacobson, *The Birmingham News*; John O'Mara, *The Anniston Star*; Bo Bolton, *The Demopolis Times*; H. Doyle Harvill, *The Montgomery Advertiser* and *Alabama Journal*; Jack Venable, *The Tallassee Tribune*; Jim Cox, *The Clarke County Democrat*, Grove Hill; Ferrin Cox, *The Elba Clipper*; and Terry Everett, Gulf Coast Media, Baldwin County.

Alabama Newspaper Advertising Service: Ben Shurett, *The Troy Messenger*, president; and James W. (Jim) Oakley Jr., *The Centreville Press*, vice president.

ANAS Board of directors: Guy Hankins, *The TimesDaily*, Florence; Larry Beasley, *The Hartselle Enquirer*; Ben Kennamer, *The Sand Mountain Reporter*, Albertville; David Poynor, *The Times-Record*, Fayette; Eleanor Abercrombie Foster, *The Alabama Messenger*, Birmingham; Mike Kelley, *The Independent Advertiser*, Clanton; Bill Joyner, *The Selma Times-Journal*; W.E. (Gene) Hardin, *The Greenville Advocate*; Lon Williams, *The Alexander City Outlook*; Mike Pippin, *The Brewton Standard*; Mike Mullins, *The Headland Observer*; and Bill Beckner, *The Mobile County News*, Bayou La Batre.

Journalism Foundation: James E. Jacobson, *The Birmingham News*, president; and Paul R. Davis, *The Auburn Bulletin*, *The Lee County* Eagle, Auburn, and *The Tuskegee News*, second vice president.

Journalism Foundation Board of directors: Mike Freeman, *The Selma Times-Journal*; Doug Pearson,

The Daily Mountain Eagle, Jasper; Mike Mullins, *The Headland Observer*, James W. (Jim) Oakley Jr., *The Centreville Press*; Linda H. Breedlove, *The South Alabamian*, Jackson; Ginger Grantham, *The Hanceville Herald*; Les Walters, *The Hamilton Progress*; Edwin Reed, *The Arab Tribune*; Jay Thornton, *The Daily Home*, Talladega; Shelton Prince Jr., *The Selma Times-Journal*; John Cameron, *The Independent*, Robertsdale; and Ralph Sears, *The Shelby County Reporter*, Columbiana.

1985-1986

Mike Breedlove, *The South Alabamian*, Jackson, president; Jay Thornton, *The Daily Home*, Talladega, first vice president; Steve Stewart, *The Monroe Journal*, Monroeville, second vice president; and Luke Slaton, *The Moulton Advertiser*, chairman of the board.

Board of directors: Don Brown, *The TimesDaily*, Florence; Ginger Grantham, *The Hanceville Herald*; Dave Marion, *The Sand Mountain News*, Rainsville; Ed Fowler, *The Tuscaloosa News*; James E. Jacobson, *The Birmingham News*; John O'Mara, *The Anniston Star*; Bo Bolton, *The Demopolis Times*; H. Doyle Harvill, *The Montgomery Advertiser* and *Alabama Journal*; Lon Williams, *The Alexander City Outlook*; Jim Cox, *The Clarke County Democrat*, Grove Hill; Ben Shurett, *The Troy Messenger*; and Terry Everett, Gulf Coast Media, Baldwin County.

Alabama Newspaper Advertising Service: James W. (Jim) Oakley Jr., *The Centreville Press*, president; and Bill Joyner, *The Selma Times-Journal*, vice president.

ANAS Board of directors: John Fitzwater, *The TimesDaily*, Florence; Larry Beasley, *The Hartselle Enquirer*; Ben Kennamer, *The Sand Mountain Reporter*, Albertville; David Poynor, *The Times-Record*, Fayette; Mickey Townsend, *The Birmingham News*; Mike Kelley, *The Independent Advertiser*, Clanton; W.E. (Gene) Hardin, *The Greenville Advocate*; Michael Hand, *The LaFayette Sun*; Mike Pippin, *The Brewton Standard*; Jim Specht, *The Geneva County Reaper*, Geneva; and Bill Beckner, Mobile County Publications.

Journalism Foundation: Paul R. Davis, *The Lee County Eagle*, Auburn, *The Auburn Bulletin* and *The Tuskegee News*, president; and Mike Freeman, *The Selma Times-Journal*, vice president.

Journalism Foundation Board of directors: Linda H. Breedlove, *The South Alabamian*, Jackson; Don Brown, *The TimesDaily*, Florence; Kelly Bryan, *The St. Clair News-Aegis*; Ginger Grantham, *The Hanceville Herald*; Mike Mullins, *The Headland Observer*; James W. (Jim) Oakley Jr., *The Centreville*

Press; Doug Pearson, *The Daily Mountain Eagle*, Jasper; Shelton Prince Jr., *The Selma Times-Journal*; Edwin Reed, *The Arab Tribune*; Ralph Sears, *The Shelby County Reporter*, Columbiana; and Les Walters, *The Hamilton Progress*.

1986-1987

Jay Thornton, *The Daily Home*, Talladega, president; Steve Stewart, *The Monroe Journal*, Monroeville, first vice president; Jack Venable, *The Tallassee Tribune*, second vice president; and Mike Breedlove, *The South Alabamian*, Jackson, chairman of the board.

Board of directors: Don Brown, *The TimesDaily*, Florence; Bill Nelson, *The Athens News Courier*; Dave Marion, *The Sand Mountain News*, Rainsville; Doug Pearson, *The Daily Mountain Eagle*, Jasper; James E. Jacobson, *The Birmingham News*; John W. Stevenson, *The Randolph Leader*, Roanoke; Bo Bolton, *The Demopolis Times*; H. Doyle Harvill, *The Montgomery Advertiser* and *Alabama Journal*; Lon Williams, *The Alexander City Outlook*; Jim Cox, *The Clarke County Democrat*, Grove Hill; and Terry Everett, Gulf Coast Media in Baldwin County.

Alabama Newspaper Advertising Service: Mike Kelley, *The Chilton County News*, Clanton, president; and Bill Beckner, *The Mobile County News*, Bay La Batre, vice president.

ANAS Board of directors: Larry Beasley, *The Hartselle Enquirer*; Ben Kennamer, *The Sand Mountain Reporter*, Albertville; Joe Junkin, *The Tuscaloosa News*; Mickey Townsend, *The Birmingham News*; Larry Camp, *The Daily Home*, Talladega; Tommy Campbell, *The Choctaw Advocate*, Butler; Linda H. Breedlove, *The South Alabamian*, Jackson; Michael Hand, *The LaFayette Sun*; Jim Seymour, *The Prattville Progress*; Jim Specht, *The Geneva County Reaper*, Geneva; and Cleretta Thomas Blackmon, *The Mobile Beacon*.

Journalism Foundation: Paul R. Davis, *The Auburn Bulletin*, *The Lee County Eagle*, Auburn, and *The Tuskegee News*, president; and Edwin Reed, *The Arab Tribune*, vice president.

Journalism Foundation Board of directors: Steve Mitchell, *The Baldwin Times*, Bay Minette; Don Brown, *The TimesDaily*, Florence; Kelly Bryan, *The St. Clair News-Aegis*; Ginger Grantham, *The Hanceville Herald*; Eddie Dodd, *The Abbeville Herald*; Charles Land, *The Tuscaloosa News*; Luke Slaton, *The Moulton Advertiser*; Shelton Prince Jr., *The Selma Times-Journal*; Ralph Sears, *The Shelby*

County Reporter, Columbian; and Les Walters, *The Hamilton Progress*.

1987-1988

Steve Stewart, *The Monroe Journal*, Monroeville, president; Jack Venable, *The Tallassee Tribune*, first vice president; James E. Jacobson, *The Birmingham News*, second vice president; and Jay Thornton, *The Daily Home*, Talladega, chairman of the board.

Board of directors: Don Brown, *The TimesDaily*, Florence; Bill Nelson, *The Athens News Courier*; Dave Marion, *The Sand Mountain News*, Rainsville; Doug Pearson, *The Daily Mountain Eagle*, Jasper; James H. Denley, the *Birmingham Post-Herald*; John W. Stevenson, *The Randolph Leader*, Roanoke; Tommy Campbell, *The Choctaw Advocate*, Butler; Richard H. (Dick) Amberg Jr., *The Montgomery Advertiser* and *Alabama Journal;* Paul R. Davis, *The Auburn Bulletin* and *The Lee County Eagle*, Auburn, and *The Tuskegee News;* Jim Cox, *The Clarke County Democrat*, Grove Hill; Rebecca Parish Beasley, *The Clayton Record*; and Terry Everett, Gulf Coast Media.

Alabama Newspaper Advertising Service: Mike Kelley, *The Chilton County News*, Clanton, president; and Ben Kennamer, *The Sand Mountain Reporter*, Albertville, second vice president.

ANAS Board of directors: Ken Lightsey, *The Franklin County* Times, Russellville; Larry Beasley, *The Hartselle Enquirer*; Gary Gengozian, *The Times-Journal*, Fort Payne; Joe Junkin, *The Tuscaloosa* News; Wayne Rasco, *The Shelby County Reporter*, Columbiana; Mike Handley, *The Sumter County Journal*, York; Linda H. Breedlove, *The South Alabamian*, Jackson; Nell Walls, *The Valley Times-News*, Lanett; Jim Seymour, *The Prattville Progress;* Jim Specht, *The Geneva County* Reaper, Geneva; and Cleretta Thomas Blackmon, *The Mobile Beacon*.

Journalism Foundation: Charles Land, *The Tuscaloosa News*, president; and Pat McCauley, *The Huntsville Times*, vice president.

Journalism Foundation Board of directors: Don Brown, *The TimesDaily*, Florence; Ginger Grantham, *The Hanceville Herald;* James Harkness, *The Daily Sentinel;* Luke Slaton, *The Moulton Advertiser*; Ralph Sears, *The Shelby County Reporter*, Columbiana; Bill Brown, *The Montgomery Advertiser*; Rhonda Freeman-Baraka, *The Tuskegee News;* Steve Mitchell, *The Baldwin Times*, Bay Minette; Eddie Dodd, *The Abbeville Herald;* Paul R. Davis, *The Auburn Bulletin* and *The Lee County Eagle*, Auburn, and *The Tuskegee News;* and Jim Morgan, *The Alexander City Outlook.*

1988-1989

Jack Venable, *The Tallassee Tribune*, president; James E. Jacobson, *The Birmingham News*, first vice president; Paul R. Davis, *The* Auburn Bulletin and *The Lee County Eagle*, Auburn, and *The Tuskegee News*, second vice president; and Steve Stewart, *The Monroe Journal*, Monroeville, chairman of the board.

Board of directors: Larry Beasley, *The Hartselle Enquirer*; Doug Pearson, *The Daily Mountain Eagle*, Jasper; James H. Denley, the *Birmingham Post-Herald*; Tommy Campbell, *The Choctaw Advocate*, Butler; John W. Stevenson, *The Randolph Leader*, Roanoke; Richard H. (Dick) Amberg Jr., *The Montgomery Advertiser* and *Alabama Journal*; Ellen Williams, *The Wetumpka Herald*; Linda H. Breedlove, *The South Alabamian*, Jackson; Rebecca Parish Beasley, *The Clayton Record*; Bill Beckner, Mobile County Publications; and Pat Courington Jr., *The Sand Mountain Reporter*, Albertville. (Courington named to complete the term vacated by Dave Marion, formerly of *The Sand Mountain News*, Rainsville.)

Alabama Newspaper Advertising Service: Ben Kennamer, *The Sand Mountain Reporter*, Albertville, president; and Ken Lightsey, *The Franklin County Times*, Russellville, vice president.

ANAS Board of directors: Lee Woodward, *The Huntsville News;* John Childs, *The Oxford Sun;* Mike Handley, *The Sumter County Journal*, York; Nell Walls, *The Valley Times-News*, Lanett; Cleretta Thomas Blackmon, *The Mobile Beacon;* Jim Specht, *The Geneva County Reaper*, Geneva; Steve Oden, *The Moulton Advertiser*; Gary Gengozian, *The Times-Journal*, Fort Payne; Jim Seymour, *The Prattville Progress;* and Jim Cox, *The Clarke County Democrat*, Grove Hill.

Journalism Foundation: Pat McCauley, *The Huntsville Times*, president; and Luke Slaton, *The Moulton Advertiser*, vice president.

Journalism Foundation Board of directors: Jay Thornton, *The Daily Home*, Talladega; Bill Brown, *The Montgomery Advertiser* and *Alabama Journal*; Steve Mitchell, *The Baldwin Times*, Bay Minette; Jim Morgan, *The Alexander City Outlook*; Tom Wright, *The Decatur Daily*; David Poynor, *The Times-Record*, Fayette; and Bill Cornwell, *The Daily Sentinel*, Scottsboro.

1989-1990

James E. Jacobson, *The Birmingham News*, president; Paul R. Davis, *The Auburn Bulletin, The Lee County Eagle*, Auburn, and *The Tuskegee News*, first vice president; Terry Everett, *The Union Springs Herald*, second vice president; and Jack Venable, *The Tallassee Tribune*, chairman of the board.

Board of directors: Steve Ainsley, *The Times-Daily*, Florence; Larry Beasley, *The Hartselle Enquirer*; Pat Courington Jr., *The Sand Mountain Reporter*, Albertville; Doug Pearson, *The Daily Mountain* Eagle, Jasper; John W. Stevenson, *The Randolph Leader*, Roanoke; Richard H. (Dick) Amberg Jr., *The Montgomery Advertiser* and *Alabama Journal*; Linda H. Breedlove, *The South Alabamian*, Jackson; Jim Leavell, *The News-Herald*, Chickasaw; James H. Denley, the *Birmingham Post-Herald*; Tommy Campbell, *The Choctaw Advocate*, Butler; Ellen Williams, *The Wetumpka Herald*; and Rebecca Parish Beasley, *The Clayton Record*.

Alabama Newspaper Advertising Service: Jim Seymour, *The Prattville Progress*, president; and Gary Gengozian, *The Fort Payne Times-Journal*, vice president.

ANAS Board of directors: Steve Oden, *The Moulton Advertiser*; Bill Cornwell, *The Daily Sentinel*, Scottsboro; Hal Hodgens, *The Western Star*, Bessemer; Mike Handley, *The Sumter County Journal*, York; Nell Walls, *The Valley Times-News*, Lanett; Ed Lowry, *The Greensboro Watchman;* Lee Woodward, *The Huntsville News*; Mike Mullins, *The Headland Observer*; John Childs, *The Oxford Sun*; Jim Cox, *The Clarke County Democrat*, Grove Hill; Cleretta Thomas Blackmon, *The Mobile Beacon*; and Alvin Bland, *The Luverne Journal and News*.

Journalism Foundation: Bill Brown, *The Montgomery Advertiser* and *Alabama Journal*, president; and Tom Wright, *The Decatur Daily*, vice president.

Journalism Foundation Board of directors: Shelton Prince Jr., *The Selma Times-Journal*; Joel P. Smith, *The Eufaula Tribune*; Kerry Bryan, *The Leeds News*; Bill Cornwell, *The Daily Sentinel*, Scottsboro; Rhonda Freeman-Baraka, *The Tuskegee News*; Eddie Dodd, *The Abbeville Record*; Steve Stewart, *The Monroe Journal*, Monroeville; and W.E. (Gene) Hardin, *The Greenville Advocate*.

1990-1991

Paul R. Davis, *The Auburn Bulletin*, *The Lee County Eagle*, Auburn, and *The Tuskegee News*, president; Terry Everett, *The Union* Springs Herald, first vice president; Charles Land, *The Tuscaloosa News*, second vice president; and James E. Jacobson, *The Birmingham News*, chairman of the board.

Board of directors: Steve Ainsley, *The TimesDaily*, Florence; Larry Beasley, *The Hartselle Enquirer*; James H. Denley, the *Birmingham Post-Herald*; Tommy Campbell, *The Choctaw Advocate*; Ed Lowry, *The Greensboro Watchman*; Mike Kelley, *The Clanton Advertiser*; Richard H. (Dick) Amberg Jr., *The Montgomery Advertiser* and *Alabama Journal*; Linda H. Breedlove, *The South Alabamian*, Jackson; Ellen Williams, *The Wetumpka Herald*; Rebecca Parish Beasley, *The Clayton Record*; and Cleretta Thomas Blackmon, *The Mobile Beacon*.

Alabama Newspaper Advertising Service: Gary Gengozian, *The Times-Journal*, Fort Payne, president; and Nell Walls, *The Valley Times*-News, Lanett, vice president.

ANAS Board of directors: Steve Oden, *The Moulton Advertiser*; Bill Cornwell, *The Daily Sentinel*; Hal Hodgens, *The Western Star*, Bessemer; Lee Woodward, *The Huntsville News*; Horace Moore, Mid-South Newspapers; John Childs, *The Oxford Sun*; Alvin Bland, *The Luverne Journal and News*; Jim Cox, *The Clarke County Democrat*, Grove Hill; Mike Handley, *The Sumter County Journal*, York; Randy Ponder, *The Mobile County News*, Bayou La Batre; Mike Mullins, *The Headland Observer;* and Kenneth Boone, *The Alexander City Outlook*.

Journalism Foundation: Tom Wright, *The Decatur Daily*, president; and Steve Stewart, *The Monroe Journal*, Monroeville, vice president.

Journalism Foundation Board of directors: Jerry Turner, *The Demopolis Times*; Bill Cornwell, *The Daily Sentinel*, Scottsboro; Joel P. Smith, *The Eufaula Tribune*; Stan Voit, *The Auburn Bulletin* and *The Lee County Eagle*, Auburn; Horace Moore, *The Northwest Alabamian*, Haleyville; Eddie Dodd, *The Abbeville Herald*; Lee Woodward, *The Huntsville News*; Don Brown, *The Tuscaloosa News*; Jay Thornton, *The Daily Home*, Talladega; W.E. (Gene) Hardin, *The Greenville Advocate*; Kim Price, Bay Area Newspapers, Mobile; and Mark Singletary, *The Andalusia Star-News*.

1991-1992

Terry Everett, *The Union Springs Herald*, president; Charles Land, *The Tuscaloosa News*, first vice president; Sam Harvey, *The Advertiser-Gleam*, Guntersville, second vice president; and Paul R. Davis, *The Auburn Bulletin*, *The Lee County Eagle*, Auburn, and *The Tuskegee News*, chairman of the board.

Board of directors: Steve Ainsley, *The TimesDaily*, Florence; Pat Courington Jr., *The Sand*

Mountain Reporter, Albertville; Victor H. Hanson III, *The Birmingham News*; Mike Pippin, *The Selma Times-Journal*; Ellen Williams, *The Wetumpka Herald;* Joseph H. (Joe) Adams, *The Southern Star*, Ozark; Larry Beasley, *The Hartselle Enquirer*; Ed Lowry, *The Greensboro Watchman*; Mike Kelley, *The Clanton Advertiser*; Richard H. (Dick) Amberg Jr., *The Montgomery Advertiser* and *Alabama Journal*; Linda H. Breedlove, *The South Alabamian*, Jackson; and Cleretta Thomas Blackmon, *The Mobile Beacon*.

Alabama Newspaper Advertising Service: Gary Gengozian, *The Times-Journal*, Fort Payne, president; and Nell Cowart, *The Valley Times-News*, Lanett, vice president.

ANAS board of directors: Steve Oden, *The Moulton Advertiser*; Roger Quinn, *The Gadsden Times*; Hal Hodgens, *The Western Star*, Bessemer; David McElroy, *The Demopolis Times*; Kenneth Boone, *The Alexander City Outlook*; Ferrin Cox, *The Elba Clipper*; Marvin Pike, Gulf Coast Newspapers, Baldwin County; Lee Woodward, *The Huntsville News;* Horace Moore, *The Times-Record*, Fayette; John Childs, *The Oxford Sun*; Alvin Bland, *The Luverne Journal and News*; and Jim Cox, *The Clarke County Democrat*, Grove Hill.

Journalism Foundation: Steve Stewart, *The Monroe Journal*, Monroeville, president; and Joel P. Smith, *The Eufaula Tribune*, vice president.

Journalism Foundation Board of directors: James H. Denley, the *Birmingham Post-Herald*; Bill Cornwell, *The Daily Sentinel*, Scottsboro; Kenneth Boone, *The Alexander City Outlook*; Stan Voit, *The Auburn Bulletin* and *The Lee County Eagle*, Auburn; Horace Moore, *The Northwest Alabamian*, Haleyville; John Cameron, *The Selma Times-Journal*; Lee Woodward, *The Huntsville Times*; Don Brown, *The Tuscaloosa News*; Jay Thornton, *The Daily Home*, Talladega; W.E. (Gene) Hardin, *The Greenville Advocate*; Kim Price, *The Shelby County Reporter*, Columbiana; and Mark Singletary, *The Andalusia Star-News*.

1992-1993

Charles Land, *The Tuscaloosa News*, president; Sam Harvey, *The Advertiser-Gleam*, Guntersville, first vice president; Linda H. Breedlove, *The South Alabamian*, Jackson, second vice president; and Terry Everett, *The Union Springs Herald*, chairman of the board.

Board of directors: Tom Wright, *The Decatur Daily*; Ed Lowry, *The Greensboro Watchman*; Mike Kelley, *The Clanton Advertiser*; Bill Hardin, *The*

Greenville Advocate; Patrice Stewart, *The Monroe Journal*, Monroeville; Cleretta Thomas Blackmon, *The Mobile Beacon*; Steve Ainsley, *The TimesDaily*, Florence; Pat Courington Jr., *The Sand* Mountain Reporter, Albertville; Victor H. Hanson III, *The Birmingham* News; Mike Pippin, *The Selma Times-Journal*; Kenneth Boone, *The Alexander City Outlook*; and Joseph H. (Joe) Adams, *The Southern Star*, Ozark.

Alabama Newspaper Advertising Service: Jim Cox, *The Clarke County Democrat*, Grove Hill, president.

ANAS Board of directors: Richard Haston, *The Madison County Record*; Horace Moore, *The Northwest Alabamian*, Haleyville; Cathy O'Berry, *The Western Star*, Bessemer; Lane Weatherbee, *The Piedmont Independent*; Hollis Curl, *The Wilcox Progressive Era*, Camden; Alvin Bland, *The Luverne Journal and News*; Mark Singletary, *The Andalusia Star-News*; Marvin Pike, Gulf Coast Newspapers, Baldwin County; Steve Oden, *The Moulton Advertiser*; Roger Quinn, *The Gadsden Times*; Kenneth Boone, *The Alexander City Outlook*; and Ferrin Cox, *The Elba Clipper*.

Journalism Foundation: Joel P. Smith, *The Eufaula Tribune*, president; James H. Denley, the *Birmingham Post-Herald*, vice president; and Steve Stewart, *The Monroe Journal*, Monroeville, chairman of the board.

Journalism Foundation board of directors: Lee Woodward, *The Huntsville News*; Don Brown, *The Tuscaloosa News*; Michelle Cox Gerlach, *The Atmore Advance*; Mike Smelley, *The Tuskegee News*; Kim Price, *The Shelby County Reporter*, Columbiana; Lamar Smitherman, *The Prattville Progress*; William C. (Bill) Green Jr., *The Huntsville Times*; Bill Cornwell, *The Daily Sentinel*, Scottsboro; Kenneth Boone, *The Alexander City Outlook*; Stan Voit, *The Auburn Bulletin* and *The Lee County Eagle*; Horace Moore, *The Northwest Alabamian*, Haleyville; and John Cameron, *The Selma Times-Journal*.

1993-1994

Sam Harvey, *The Advertiser-Gleam*, Guntersville, president; Linda H. Breedlove, *The South Alabamian*, Jackson, first vice president; Pat McCauley, *The Huntsville Times*, second vice president; and Charles Land, *The Tuscaloosa News*, chairman of the board.

APA/ANAS Board of directors: Steve Oden, *The Moulton Advertiser*; Frank Helderman, *The Gadsden Times*; Victor Hanson III, *The Birmingham News*; Mike Pippin, *The Selma Times-Jour-*

nal; Kenneth Boone, *The Alexander City Outlook*; Joseph H. (Joe) Adams, *The Southern Star*, Ozark; Tom Wright, *The Decatur Daily*; Ed Lowry, *The Greensboro Watchman*; Mike Kelley, *The Clanton Advertiser*; Bill Hardin, *The Greenville Advocate*; Patrice Stewart, *The Monroe Journal*, Monroeville; and Cleretta Thomas Blackmon, *The Mobile Beacon*.

Journalism Foundation: James H. Denley, the *Birmingham Post-Herald*, president; Stan Voit, *The Auburn Bulletin* and *The Lee County* Eagle, Auburn, vice president; and Joel P. Smith, *The Eufaula Tribune*, chairman of the board.

Journalism Foundation Board of directors: Ed Fowler, *The Daily Home*, Talladega; David Moore, *The Arab Tribune*; Rebecca Parish Beasley, *The Clayton Record*; William C. (Bill) Green, *The Huntsville* Times; Kenneth Boone, *The Alexander City Outlook*; John Cameron, *The Mobile Press Register*; Lee Woodward, *The Huntsville News*; Don Brown, *The Tuscaloosa News*; Michelle Cox Gerlach, *The Atmore Advance*; Mike Smelley, *The Tuskegee News*; Kim Price, *The Shelby County Reporter*, Columbiana; and Lamar Smitherman, *The Prattville Progress*.

1994-1995

Linda Hayes Breedlove, *The South Alabamian*, Jackson, president; Doug Pearson, *The Daily Mountain Eagle*, Jasper, first vice president; Mike Kelley, *The Clanton Advertiser*, second vice president; and Sam Harvey, *The Advertiser-Gleam*, Guntersville, chairman of the board.

APA/ANAS Board of directors: Horace Moore, *The Times-Record*, Fayette; David Proctor, *The Clay Times-Journal*, Lineville; Howard Bronson, *The Mobile Press Register*; Tom Wright, *The Decatur Daily*; Bill Hardin, *The Greenville Advocate*; Patrice Stewart, *The Monroe* Journal, Monroeville; Frank Helderman Jr., *The TimesDaily*, Florence; Janie Halter, *The Fort Payne Times-Journal*; Victor H. Hanson III, *The Birmingham News*; Mike Pippin, *The Selma Times-Journal*; Kenneth Boone, *The Alexander City Outlook*; and Joseph H. (Joe) Adams, *The Southern Star*, Ozark.

Journalism Foundation: Stan Voit, *The Auburn Bulletin* and *The Lee County Eagle*, Auburn, president; Lee Woodward, *The Huntsville* News, vice president; and James H. Denley, the *Birmingham Post-Herald*, chairman of the board.

Journalism Foundation Board of directors: Deangelo McDaniel, *The Moulton Advertiser*; Joe Distelheim, *The Anniston Star*; Rick Loring, *The*

Daily Sentinel, Scottsboro; Michelle Cox Gerlach, *The Atmore* Advance; Mike Smelley, *The Tuskegee News*; Lamar Smitherman, *The Prattville Progress;* Bill Green, *The Huntsville Times*; Kenneth Boone, *The Alexander City Outlook*; Ed Fowler, *The Daily Home*, Talladega, David Moore, *The Arab Tribune*; John Cameron, *The Mobile Press Register;* and Rebecca Parish Beasley, *The Clayton Record*.

1995-1996

Doug Pearson, *The Daily Mountain Eagle*, Jasper, president; Mike Kelley, *The Clanton Advertiser*, first vice president; John W. Stevenson, *The Randolph Leader*, Roanoke, second vice president; and Linda H. Breedlove, *The South Alabamian*, Jackson, chairman of the board.

APA/ANAS Board of directors: Kim Price, *The Shelby County* Reporter, Columbiana; Mike Hudgins, *The Sand Mountain Reporter*, Albertville; Ann Smith, *The Eufaula Tribune*; Frank Helderman Jr., *The TimesDaily*, Florence; Hollis Curl, *The Wilcox Progressive Era*, Camden; Kenneth Boone, *The Alexander City Outlook*; Tom Wright, *The Decatur Daily*; Horace Moore, *The Times-Record*, Hamilton; David Proctor, *The Clay Times-Journal*; Patrice Stewart, *The Monroe Journal*, Monroeville; Howard Bronson, *The Mobile Press Register*; and Richard H. (Dick) Amberg Jr., *The Montgomery Advertiser*.

Journalism Foundation: Lee Woodward, *The Huntsville News*, president; David Moore, *The Arab Tribune*, vice president; and Stan Voit, *The Auburn Bulletin* and *The Lee County Eagle*, Auburn, chairman of the board.

Journalism Foundation Board of directors: Kathy Silverberg, *The TimesDaily*, Florence; Richard Walker, *The Opelika-Auburn News*; Marilyn Handley, *The Monroe Journal*, Monroeville; Stan Tiner, *The Mobile Press Register*; David Poynor, *The Cullman Times*; Ed Fowler, *The Daily Home*, Talladega; Deangelo McDaniel, *The Moulton* Advertiser; Joe Distelheim, *The Huntsville Times*; Michelle Cox Gerlach, *The Atmore Advance*; Mike Smelley, *The Tuskegee News*; Rick Loring, *The Daily Sentinel*, Scottsboro; and Lamar Smitherman, *The Prattville Progress*.

1996-1997

Mike Kelley, *The Clanton Advertiser*, president; John W. Stevenson, *The Randolph Leader*, Roanoke, first vice president; James H. Denley, the *Birmingham Post-Herald*, second vice president; and Doug Pearson, *The Daily Mountain Eagle*, Jasper, chairman of the board.

APA/ANAS Board of directors: Bob Ludwig, *The Huntsville Times*; Jim Cox, *The Clarke County Democrat*, Grove Hill; Horace Moore, *The Northwest Alabamian*; David Proctor, *The Clay Times-Journal*; Richard H. (Dick) Amberg Jr., *The Montgomery Advertiser*; W. Howard Bronson, *The Mobile Press Register*; Frank Helderman Jr., *The TimesDaily*, Florence; Michael J. Hudgins, *The Sand Mountain Reporter*, Albertville; Kim Price, *The Shelby County Reporter*, Columbiana; Hollis Curl, *The Wilcox Progressive Era*, Camden; and Ann Smith, *The Eufaula Tribune*.

Journalism Foundation: David Moore, *The Arab Tribune*, president; Lamar Smitherman, *The Prattville Progress*, vice president; and Lee Woodward, *The Huntsville News*, chairman of the board.

Journalism Foundation Board of directors: Tommy McGraw, *The Sumter County Record-Journal*, Livingston; Jill Tigner, *The Phenix Citizen*, Phenix City; J. Randolph Murray, *The Anniston Star*; Cy Wood, *The Valley Times-News*, Lanett; Deangelo McDaniel, *The Moulton Advertiser*; Joe Distelheim, *The Huntsville Times*; Kathy Silverberg, *The TimesDaily*, Florence; Marilyn Handley, *The Monroe Journal*; Stan Tiner, *The Mobile Press Register*; David Poynor, *The Cullman Times*; and Ed Fowler, *The Daily Home*, Talladega.

"I started into the newspaper business at the age of 15 — serving as a printer's devil on my hometown paper in southern Kansas. I've had my finger nails eaten off with the lye water used in those days to wash off the forms. I worked my way through the state university as a printer and makeup man on *The Daily Kansan*.

"I believe I can still hold my own in the back shop of any country newspaper. I've worked as owner, managing editor and ad manager on newspapers located in mining towns, old lumber towns, panic-stricken agricultural communities, drought-stricken and boll weevil-infected communities.

"I've worked on bankrupt papers, second papers, hand-set papers and papers that have had the finest of equipment and unlimited financial backing."

—*Doyle L. Buckles, APA field manager*
Sept. 1, 1939-Dec. 18, 1947
(Published in Buckles' first "confidential bulletin,"
later renamed The Ala-Pressa, *on Sept. 11, 1939.)*

FIELD MANAGERS AND EXECUTIVE DIRECTORS

W. Roy Brown

1934-1935
Field manager

The Alabama Press Association did not have a field manager until 1934 — 62 years after its founding. APA activities for more than 60 years had been planned and carried out by elected officers, appointed committees and volunteer workers.

APA had its first field manager, W. Roy Brown, in 1934. Brown's employment was made possible by the federal government when the Graphic Arts Code for Alabama was put into effect. The government, through the National Recovery Act, employed an administrator for the Graphic Arts Code, and it was through this that APA was able to use the same individual as its field representative.

The APA office was temporarily in Ozark, hometown of APA president Jesse Adams of *The Southern Star*, but later was moved to Montgomery. The arrangement with the NRA and the Press Association came to an end with the close of the federal program in 1935, and the Press Association was again without a field manager.

Not much information exists on APA's first field manager, who apparently only served in the post from 1934 to 1935. A photograph was published in the Aug. 17, 1934, issue of *The Southern Star* in Ozark that was captioned "Alabama Editors Hold Annual Meeting in Chicago." According to *The Southern Star*, APA president Jesse Adams and field manager W. Roy Brown "led the visitors from Alabama to the World's Fair in Chicago" for the 63rd annual APA convention.

Doyle L. Buckles

Sept. 1, 1939, until his death on Dec. 18, 1947
Field manager

On Sept. 1, 1939, APA and the University of Alabama entered a cooperative program which employed Doyle L. Buckles, weekly newspaper editor from Medford, Wis., as field manager and placed APA headquarters on the University campus. Under the arrangement, Buckles was to devote half his time as field manager and the other half as director of the University News Bureau.

Doyle L. Buckles

The University of Alabama administration successfully utilized teachers to direct publicity from 1928-1930, according to retired UA News Bureau director Edward (Ed) O. Brown III of Tuscaloosa in his 1958 master's thesis, "History of the University of Alabama News Bureau, 1928-1956." The hiring of Buckles initiated a cooperative staff venture between the Alabama Press Association and the University of Alabama that lasted until 1973.

Buckles came to Alabama with years of experience in newspapering in his native Kansas, in Nebraska, Iowa and Wisconsin. He was qualified to guide the newspapers of Alabama into more profitable channels, which he did, and he revitalized APA. Buckles had edited or managed papers at Fairbury, Neb., Alliance, Neb., Mitchell, Neb., and Medford, Wis.

Over the years Buckles had won 30 national and state awards for excellence in newspaper production, including a first-place award in the National Editorial Association's competition for achievement in community service. The award came while Buckles was editing a weekly Nebraska newspaper, *The Mitchell Index.*

The Tuscaloosa News reported in its Sept. 14, 1939, edition that Buckles would serve half of his time as field manager of the Press Association and the other half would be devoted to News Bureau duties. In September 1939 APA opened its offices jointly with News Bureau offices in the Union Building with Buckles in charge. He was directly responsible to the dean of the Extension Division.

Buckles also held an appointment as instructor in journalism. *The Tuscaloosa News* reported in 1939, "While Mr. Buckles will offer no journalism course this term, he may be called on to teach one. Randolph (Randy) Fort, assistant professor of journalism, director of the News Bureau for the past two years, will retain a connection with that office for the time being."

Buckles died Dec. 18, 1947, in a Birmingham hospital. At a Dec. 21 meeting at the McLester Hotel, Buckles' assistant, Norman H. Bassett of Tuscaloosa, was appointed acting field manager and secretary-treasurer.

Buckles had been extremely popular with APA members, and he was credited with a revitalization of the Press Association in the 1940s. *AlaPressa* reported that "it was generally agreed that he had worked himself to death during the eight years he was secretary-treasurer, field manager of the association."

At the 1948 winter convention, Bassett, who later served as executive editor of *The Tuscaloosa News*, asked to continue serving in the position until a permanent field manager could be selected.

Bassett, who attended public schools in Dover, N.J., received his bachelor's degree in journalism at the University of Alabama in 1940. Following graduation he was telegraph and sports editor of *The Rome* (Ga.) *News Tribune* for 11 months during 1941. He returned to Tuscaloosa in 1942 to work at *The Tuscaloosa News* as telegraph editor and managing editor.

J. Russell (Russ) Heitman

July 1, 1948-September 1950
Secretary-field manager

J. Russell (Russ) Heitman of Lake Forest, Ill., became secretary-field manager, effective July 1, 1948. Heitman had recently earned his master's degree at Northwestern University.

AlaPressa described the new field manager: "Russ has 20 years of bedrock background in the newspaper and publishing business which eminently qualifies him for the job and the work we believe

Russ Heitman

can be done for our members. As a former owner and manager of a printing company, Russ knows the headaches and the angles of the production end of the business. He is a printer and has been successful in operating and publishing newspapers. He will be able to talk your language."

Heitman's work at the University of Alabama was, for the most part, with APA. Following the precedent established with Buckles in 1939, Heitman also was to be director of the News Bureau. But a request of long standing, that a full-time assistant be employed whose primary duties would be with the News Bureau, was fulfilled when Norman Bassett was named associate director of the News Bureau in 1948.

In September 1950, Heitman resigned as secretary-field manager to become head of the journalism department at Texas Technological College in Lubbock. Announcement was made at the 1950 summer convention in Biloxi of the appointment of Ernest Bronwin (Jack) Beisner, 29-year-old editor of *The Custer County Chief* at Broken Bow, Neb., as the new secretary-field manager. Beisner moved to Alabama in June and apparently worked with Heitman until September.

Ernest Bronwin (Jack) Beisner

September 1950-Oct. 31, 1956
Secretary-field manager

Ernest Bronwin (Jack) Beisner served as field manager, director of the University of Alabama News Bureau, member of the UA journalism faculty, secretary-treasurer for APA, and manager of the Alabama Newspaper Advertising Service from September 1950 to Oct. 31, 1956.

Jack Beisner

Before coming to Alabama, Beisner was editor of *The Custer County Chief* in Broken Bow, Neb. Beisner, a native of Willisville, Ill., was born April 15, 1921. He had been involved in journalism as a teenager when he worked as a junior high school stringer for *The St. Louis Post-Dispatch*. He received a double major in political science and journalism from the University of Illinois. Beisner graduated from college in 1943 and went directly into active service with the U.S. Coast Artillery Anti-Aircraft, serving in the South Pacific. After his return from Okinawa in 1946 Beisner edited *The Harvard* (Ill.) *Herald* briefly before going to Wyoming, Ill., where he edited *The Princeville Telegraph* and *The Wyoming Herald*.

Beisner taught journalism and instituted an agricultural journalism and community newspaper program at the University of Nebraska in Lincoln

before joining *The Custer County Chief* in Broken Bow.

Norman H. Bassett resigned in September 1950, shortly after Beisner arrived at APA. Bassett had received a favorable offer from *The Tuscaloosa News* as its news editor at an increased salary.

Beisner resigned as secretary-field manager effective Oct. 31, 1956, to accept an appointment as press officer for overseas duty with the U.S. Information Agency. After two months in Washington, D.C., Beisner, his wife Mary-Louise and their four children were stationed in Calcutta, India.

Jones W. Giles, assistant manager, was appointed acting field manager in 1956 following Beisner's resignation.

The Beisners returned to the United States in 1959, and from 1959-1966 Beisner edited twin weeklies, *The Times* and *The Gazette* — one Republican, the other Democrat — in Owego, N.Y.

In June 1966, Beisner joined the Los Angeles office of California Newspaper Publishers Association. Beisner later was asked to set up the office of Western Newspaper Foundation, an outgrowth of California Newspaper Publishers Association. Western Newspaper Foundation's stated mission was to conduct research and education in print journalism. He also taught graduate journalism courses at Pepperdine University.

In 1978, Beisner and his wife Mary-Lou fulfilled their dream of owning their own community newspaper. They purchased *The Times Of Northeast Benton County*, in Pea Ridge, Ark., near Bentonville. Beisner died Jan. 22, 1986, at age 64. His wife Mary-Lou continued to operate the paper until 1988 when she sold it to Mike Freeman, a former Alabama newspaper man who had been managing editor of *The Alabama Journal* and *The Selma Times-Journal*.

Jones W. Giles

1957-April 30, 1965
Secretary-field manager

Acting field manager Jones W. Giles was named secretary-field manager in 1957, and an assistant manager was hired to work primarily with the journalism department and the Extension Division in the journalism field. This was done in order to meet the University of Alabama's requirements that the secretary-field manager have the academic requirements to teach journalism courses.

Jones Giles

John Edward Weems, a former Texas newspaper man and journalism teacher, was appointed assistant APA manager and assistant professor in the University of Alabama journalism department in 1957. Weems' duties included editing *The Alabama Publisher*, which he assumed with the September 1957 issue.

❧❧❧

Giles resigned effective April 30, 1965, and was succeeded by assistant manager John Burton who served as acting manager

Giles later become assistant director of the University of Alabama Press. Giles, had edited and published several weekly newspapers in Alabama before joining APA. He bought his first newspaper, *The Red Bay News* in Franklin County, while still a student. He also edited and published *The Franklin County Times* in Russellville in partnership with his father, former APA president Milton C. Giles, from 1945 to 1953.

Giles, 49, died in July 1970 at Druid City Hospital in Tuscaloosa. APA president Karl Elebash Jr., publisher of *The Graphic* in Tuscaloosa, issued the following statement: "The newspaper fraternity of our state is deeply grieved by the death of Jones Giles. As an editor and publisher and later as executive secretary and manager of the Alabama Press Association, he served the cause of journalism well and with honor. He loved his work and his associates respected him because of it."

James W. (Jim) Hall Jr.

May 2, 1966-April 1, 1974
Secretary-manager
Executive director

The first APA manager to hold the title of secretary-manager, and the first to hold the title of executive director was James W. (Jim) Hall Jr., who began work on May 2, 1966. Hall had been a pub-

lic relations manager for South Central Bell in New Orleans.

The APA board of directors voted to change the title from secretary-field manager to secretary-manager in 1966.

Jim Hall

Hall, 34, earned a degree in journalism at the University of Alabama. He succeeded Jones W. Giles. Assistant manager John Burton had worked as acting manager after Giles' resignation in 1965.

While a student at UA, Hall had been involved in a number of honorary organizations and journalism organizations and had been editor of *The Crimson White*.

Hall completed work on a master's degree in journalism in 1968. He had been hired with the understanding that he would earn the degree and teach journalism.

In 1970, the APA board of directors changed the title again from secretary-manager to executive director. Giles was the last APA manager to use the title of field manager, the original title given to APA managers.

During Hall's tenure, Press Association leaders started the APA Journalism Foundation, and he oversaw the start of a 10-year drive to raise $100,000. Part of the incentive to raise the money came when the University of Alabama journalism department lost its accreditation. Part of the earnings on the small endowment would be used to provide grants to support, among other things, a new class in community journalism and a new lecture series at the University. Foundation grants also were awarded to Troy State University and Auburn University, two other state universities offering print journalism degrees.

Hall also worked to strengthen the value of Press Association publications, and he worked with the officers to strengthen the conventions and other programs.

In 1973, the APA office moved from the University of Alabama campus where it had been located since 1939. The APA board of directors made the decision after criticism in *The Montgomery Advertiser*.

The Advertiser said it was a conflict of interest for state money to indirectly support a private organization such as APA.

Hall resigned from his post, effective April 1, 1974, and APA president Barrett C. Shelton Jr. of *The Decatur Daily* appointed Juanita Smith, ANAS supervisor, as interim manager.

Shelton also appointed Norman Bassett, executive editor of *The Tuscaloosa News*, as a consultant to the board of directors. Bassett had worked as acting manager after the death of Doyle Buckles in 1947.

Hall later joined the staff of Troy State University as special assistant to the president from 1974 to 1979. In addition, he became dean of the School of Journalism there from 1976 to 1979. He was co-owner of *The Pike County Leader* in Troy from 1978 to 1979, and he was owner and publisher of *The Greene County Democrat* in Eutaw from 1981 to 1983.

Since 1983, Hall and his wife Martha have owned Jim Hall Media Services in Troy. Hall Media Services is a newspaper brokerage, appraisal and consulting service. To date they have brokered almost 100 newspapers.

Stephen E. (Steve) Bradley

July 1, 1974-July 21, 1978
Executive director

Stephen E. (Steve) Bradley became executive director of APA, effective July 1, 1974. Bradley, 30, was chosen from a field of applicants by screening committee members comprised of Barrett C. Shelton Jr. of *The Decatur Daily* and vice presidents Orsen B. Spivey of *The Geneva County Reaper* and Claude E. Sparks of *The Franklin County Times*.

Steve Bradley

In a 1995 interview, Bradley recalled the first days in the first off-campus APA office in Tuscaloosa. The APA office was near Mack's Bait Shop, adjacent to the main railroad track running through the city. Bradley said he remembered framed photos of past APA presidents crashing to the floor as the trains roared by.

Bradley grew up in Florence and worked for *The Florence Times-Tri Cities Daily* in the circulation and editorial departments. After earning a master's degree in journalism with a concentration in public relations at the University of Alabama in 1971, he joined Shell Oil Co. in the company's public relations department. Bradley had earned a bachelor's degree at UA in 1968 in liberal arts, with a history major and an English minor.

During his four years as executive director, Bradley focused on the association's legislative lobbying efforts and its financial-administrative structure. He concentrated on making money on conventions and other meetings, and he worked to build revenues from the ad placement service and the clipping service. In addition, the board raised dues by about 20 percent and raised clipping service fees to become more in line with other state press associations.

As a lobbyist, he led the effort to increase the state-set limit on legal advertising rates by 40 percent, the first price increase in 12 years and, among other things, he worked to defend the state's open meetings law. APA also successfully fought back several bills related to advertising taxes, particularly local bills.

Bradley also oversaw completion of the APA Journalism Foundation's $100,000 fund drive in 1978, his last year as executive director.

Bradley resigned on July 21, 1978, the first day of the APA summer convention, to go to work for Alabama Power Co. as assistant vice president-public information. He later moved up at Alabama Power to supervise the company's governmental affairs and public relations programs.

Bradley was vice president for public affairs in 1990, when he left Alabama Power to become president of Waste Management Inc. of Alabama for three years. Later, he became an executive at AmSouth Bank in charge of public relations and governmental affairs.

In 1995, Bradley started the first combination public relations and governmental affairs firm in the state, Bradley-Townsend Public Affairs, which has offices in Birmingham, Mobile and Montgomery.

William F. (Bill) O'Connor Jr.

July 24, 1978-December 1982
Executive director

William F. (Bill) O'Connor Jr. was named executive director effective July 24, 1978, the close of the APA summer convention. O'Connor, a

Tuscaloosa native, had been director of communications for the state Department of Mental Health in Montgomery for two years. Before that, he had been director of field services for the University of Alabama School of Communication from 1974 to 1975.

Bill O'Connor

He received a bachelor's degree in journalism and a master's degree in public relations from the University of Alabama.

Before joining the Department of Mental Health, O'Connor was director of field services for the University of Alabama School of Communication from 1974 to 1975.

While APA executive director, O'Connor continued APA's strong legislative lobbying stance in Montgomery. He worked to protect the state's open meetings law and to defeat a proposed tax on advertising. While he was executive director, the APA Journalism Foundation started the Professional Development Institute, a program to support workshops for newspaper staff members.

He also worked to strengthen the association's advertising placement service and hired its first full-time sales manager, Craig Woodward, in 1979. Woodward, who earned his degree in advertising from the University of Alabama, had worked at the APA office while he was in college. Woodward is the son of Don Woodward, general manager of *The Advertiser-Gleam* in Guntersville, an APA past president, and grandson of the late Porter Harvey, publisher of *The Advertiser-Gleam*, also an APA past president.

O'Connor resigned in late 1982 to work for the University of Alabama System as a lobbyist, and he taught public relations classes on the UA campus. He also worked as campaign consultant and political consultant and worked part-time for UA. In late 1995, O'Connor returned to full-time lobbying work in charge of the UA System's government affairs efforts.

William B. (Bill) Keller

Jan. 3, 1983-November 1990
Executive director

William B. (Bill) Keller was named APA executive director to succeed Bill O'Connor. Keller,

who had worked as director of information services at the University of Montevallo, started working for APA on Jan. 3, 1983, to start the first part of a two-part term with the Press Association.

Bill Keller

He had joined the University of Montevallo staff in 1977 after working a year as a reporter for *The Tuscaloosa News*. Keller had joined *The News* staff after completing his master's degree in journalism at the University of Alabama. His first newspaper work had been at his hometown newspaper, *The Sand Mountain Reporter*, in Albertville.

Keller had been an aircraft maintenance officer in the U.S. Air Force, after earning a bachelor's degree with a history major from UA. In 1983, he was awarded a doctorate in higher education administration from UA.

While Keller was executive director the first time, APA's business affiliate, Alabama Newspaper Advertising Service, began offering a new statewide classified advertising service, ALA-SCAN, in 1985. The new service provided enough income to allow ANAS to sell the APA Clipping Service in January 1987.

In 1984, Keller hired the second full-time advertising sales manager, Michael Ryland, to succeed Craig Woodward. Among other efforts, Ryland, a former weekly newspaper editor and publisher, led the work to plan ALA-SCAN.

In April 1987, Keller oversaw moving the APA office from Tuscaloosa to Birmingham to be nearer advertising clients. The office was moved to the Commerce Center in downtown Birmingham.

In 1987, APA started the APA Legal Hotline, a free media law advice service for member newspapers.

Lobbying included persuading the Legislature to pass a bill to remove the state cap on legal notice rates. APA also lobbied to defeat bills to tax advertising, bills to eliminate the publication of voters lists, and bills to weaken the open meetings law.

During Keller's tenure, APA also added news value to the association's publications, *AlaPressa* and *The Alabama Publisher*.

In 1984, Keller oversaw a drive to raise another $100,000 for the APA Journalism Foundation, a five-year drive.

In 1987, a second advertising sales staffer, Felicia Mason, joined the APA staff. Mason, a native of Pine Hill, had been advertising director of *The Crimson White*. At the APA office, not only did she work to develop new advertising clients, but she also led a series of ad sales training workshops around the state in the late 1980s.

Keller resigned in the fall of 1990 to work for Consolidated Publishing Co. as associate publisher of *The Daily Home* in Talladega and assistant to the publisher of *The Anniston Star*. He later became editor and publisher of *The Daily Home*, succeeding Jay Thornton, a past APA president.

Mike Ryland was named acting director on Oct. 11 by the APA Executive Committee, after the board launched a nationwide search. He assumed the post on Nov. 9.

Michael T. (Mike) Ryland

Jan. 1, 1991 until his death on March 5, 1992
Executive director

Michael T. (Mike) Ryland, advertising manager of APA and ANAS since 1984, became executive director on Jan. 1, 1991. He succeeded Bill Keller.

A search committee led by APA president Paul Davis publisher of *The Auburn Bulletin*, selected Ryland after a nationwide search.

As advertising manager, Ryland had coordinated the effort to start APA's successful statewide classified advertising program, ALA-SCAN, and he had also worked to lead more education and training programs for newspaper advertising sales staffers.

Ryland, a native of Brewton, had joined the APA/ANAS staff, succeeding Craig Woodward. From 1979 to 1983, he had worked at *The Independent* in Robertsdale as a reporter, editor and publisher. He was publisher there when it won

Mike Ryland

first place in General Excellence in APA's 1984 Better Newspaper Contest.

Later in 1984, he and his wife, Julie Spafford Ryland, had moved to Montevallo, where she worked in public relations at the University of Montevallo. While there, Ryland was a part-time newswriting instructor at the University of Alabama and a correspondent for *The Birmingham News* before joining APA.

He graduated from the University of Alabama in 1978 with a degree in journalism and was managing editor of *The Atmore Advance* before joining *The Independent*.

After Ryland became executive director, he promoted Felicia Mason, former advertising sales and marketing representative, to advertising manager to succeed him. Mason had joined the staff in 1987.

Following the findings from a long-range planning retreat in September 1990, Ryland began working to develop more workshops for newspaper staff members.

Under Mason's leadership, APA and ANAS began offering a new annual advertising conference that by 1995 was attracting almost 200 delegates. She also worked to diversify the display advertising clientele from about 10 in the early 1980s to almost 50 by 1996.

Mike Ryland died in the gallery of the Alabama House of Representatives on March 5, 1992. He was 34. Ryland and his wife Julie were expecting their first child.

Ryland collapsed and was taken to a local hospital where efforts to revive him failed. The House adjourned for an hour in his memory, and the Senate paused for silent prayer. He had been working on efforts to defeat a proposed tax on services including advertising. The services tax had been seriously considered as part of an overall tax reform effort.

The APA board of directors led by APA president Charles Land, publisher of *The Tuscaloosa News*, established the Michael Ryland Family Trust and made a $12,500 donation to start it. Donations came from newspapers and friends as well as from other press association executive directors and state press associations around the nation.

APA past president Terry Everett of *The Union Springs Herald* said, "He was probably the most intellectually honest person I've ever met." Ryland worked for Everett part of the time he was publisher of *The Independent*.

APA president Charles Land said, "Mike was highly intelligent, able and hard-working. He had a genuine understanding of and appreciation for newspapers. Most of his adult life was devoted to working with newspapers, either directly or indirectly. A lot of us have worked with him for a good many years and we're really going to miss him."

APA's business affiliate, the Alabama Newspaper Advertising Service, began offering a new internship named in honor of Ryland in 1995.

William B. (Bill) Keller

March 30, 1992 to present
Executive director

Bill Keller returned to the APA office March 30, 1992, to work as executive director again. The APA board of directors asked him to return shortly after the death of Mike Ryland.

Keller had continued to live in Birmingham when he was publisher of *The Daily Home*. His wife, Jeanetta, had been promoted to vice president for administration at Southern Progress Corp.

He had resigned in 1990 to join the management staff of Consolidated Publishing Co. of Anniston.

Keller said he would work to build on some of the initiatives Ryland had started to develop for the association.

In 1992, ANAS started DIS-COVER, a new statewide display advertising program similar to ALA-SCAN. Advertising manager Felicia Mason led the effort the start the new program. In 1994, she and advertising-marketing representative Brad English developed a political advertising sales effort that placed the most dollars per newspaper of any state press advertising service in the nation that year.

In 1994, the APA board of directors voted to move the office from downtown Birmingham to a new office on U.S. Highway 31 in Homewood. The APA Journalism Foundation bought the building and rented the second floor to APA and ANAS. It rented the first floor to a real estate company.

Keller's lobbying efforts in the 1990s focused on preservation of the requirement to publish voters lists and maintaining or strengthening the state open meeting laws and public records laws.

Keller also oversaw APA's celebration of its 125th anniversary in 1996.

Staffing had dropped to three full time and one part time in 1987, when APA sold the clipping service. By 1996, the staff had grown to five full time and one part time. In addition to Keller, Mason and English, who joined the staff in 1991, other staff members, their responsibilities and the year they joined the APA staff were Leigh Leigh Tortorici, ad sales and marketing specialist, advertising conference, 1991; Laura Barraza Hankins, classified advertising, convention, workshop and contest management, and bookkeeping, 1993; and Kristy Halley, advertising/administrative assistant, 1996.

Hankins graduated from the University of Alabama with a degree in public relations, and Tortorici graduated from the University of Alabama with a degree in advertising. Halley was a journalism major at Samford University in 1996.

CHAPTER 10

Chronology of Events

1871-1996

"The grand, beautiful and inspiring hymn of peace and material glory sung by our press is sweet to the ears of our people, but sweeter far is its song of one common flag and one common country.... No people can be prosperous unless wisely governed, and no people are so wisely governed as those who govern themselves; and of all of the agencies and institutions of free government, none is so powerful for good as an enlightened press."

Gen. James Berney Stanley
The Greenville Advocate

— *Gen. James Berney Stanley, 1844-1934*
Editor and Publisher, The Greenville Advocate
APA president, 1882-1886 — four consecutive terms
(From a speech, "The Press of Alabama," given by Stanley at the second meeting of the National Editorial Association, Odeon Building, Cincinnati, Ohio, February 1886)

CONVENTIONS, EXCURSIONS, RESOLUTIONS, LEGISLATION, PEOPLE AND EVENTS THAT SHAPED 125 YEARS OF THE ALABAMA PRESS ASSOCIATION...

March 17, 1871

Eight publishers and editors meet at the office of Maj. William Wallace Screws, editor of *The Montgomery Advertiser*, to make the first definite plans for organizing the press of Alabama. They set a convention for June 8, 1871, but receive no response from other Alabama editors. Screws suggests that the convention be postponed until October 1871 when the "State Fair and other important gatherings will render a visit to Montgomery much more pleasant and profitable to the delegates in attendance than it can be in the heated month of June."

No records have been found that the October 1871 meeting was ever held.

1872
Col. Seaborn Jones Saffold, president
The Selma Daily Times
First press convention
June 18, 1872
Montgomery

Officers are elected, a constitution is drawn up, and bylaws are adopted. Gen. Jones Mitchell Withers of *The Mobile Tribune* is elected president, but "for reasons stated, which deemed to be satisfactory by the convention, asks to be excused from serving as president."

Col. Seaborn Jones Saffold, *The Selma Daily Times*, is elected first president of the Alabama Press Association (then called the "Editors and Publishers Association of the State of Alabama".)

Dues are set at $2 per person, but only one vote is allowed per newspaper.

Committee is appointed to study the possibility of establishing a paper mill in Alabama — which led to the eventual construction in 1950 of Coosa River newsprint plant owned by Kimberly Clark.

1873
Col. Seaborn Jones Saffold, president
The Selma Daily Times
Second annual press convention
May 15-17, 1873
Birmingham

Delegates take up the question of standardization of advertising rates in an effort "to form a sort of cooperative system for the mutual protection of members against advertising agencies which beat down prices and boast of their ability to advertise in scores of Southern newspapers at prices that leave all the profits in their own pockets."

Alabama editors invite New York editors to visit in May 1873 for "a grand tour of the State of Alabama."

1874
Col. Seaborn Jones Saffold, president
The Selma Daily Times
Third annual press convention
May 19, 1874
Birmingham

New York editors spend one week in Alabama, visiting Blount Springs, Birmingham, Tuscaloosa, Selma and Montgomery. Eight Alabama editors accompany the New Yorkers to Washington, D.C., for a short visit.

1875
Col. Richard Holmes Powell, president
The Union Springs Herald
Fourth annual press convention
May 11-13, 1875
Huntsville

Delegates set annual dues at $2 per year. Some 35 Alabama editors and publishers travel to New York. "We were met at the border and carried to every place of interest in that great state," said Gen. James Berney Stanley, *The Greenville Advocate*.

1876
James Freeman Grant, president
The Jacksonville Republican
Fifth annual press convention
May 30-June 3, 1876
Montgomery

Editors travel to Blount Springs for a banquet and entertainment. Resolutions of tribute to Seaborn Jones Saffold of *The Selma Daily Times*, the Press Association's first president, are passed. (Saffold died June 12, 1875.)

1877
Willis Brewer, president
The Hayneville Examiner
Sixth annual press convention
May 2-3, 1877
Mobile

Convention delegates attend the funeral of Col. John Forsyth, editor of *The Mobile Register*. Forsyth died on the opening day of the sixth annual convention. "The general business (of the 1877 convention) would not be of general interest to the public and we therefore make no mention of it," *The Montgomery Advertiser* reports in its May 6, 1877, issue.

1878
Maj. William Wallace Screws, president
The Montgomery Advertiser
Seventh annual press convention
May 30, 1878
Montgomery

Not much business is transacted at seventh annual convention in 1878 because of the "absorbing interest felt in the (Democratic and Conservative Party) State Convention." Many Press Association delegates are also members of the Democratic State Convention.

1879
Maj. William Wallace Screws, president
The Montgomery Advertiser
Eighth annual press convention
May 28-29, 1879
Gadsden

Editors travel to Rome, Ga., on the Coosa River on the steamer "Magnolia."
' Resolutions are adopted setting forth "the great value of the Coosa River to the Commerce of the World," urging the press of Alabama "to make no delay in setting forth the necessity of its speedy opening from Greensport to Wetumpka," and calling upon senators and congressmen to "use their utmost endeavors in securing appropriations necessary for this great work."

1880
Maj. William Wallace Screws, president
The Montgomery Advertiser
Ninth annual press convention
April 23-26, 1880
Tuscaloosa

Delegates to 1880 convention in Tuscaloosa discuss problems of newsprint supply and price.

Committee charged with studying feasibility of a paper mill in Alabama recommends that a mill be constructed in Birmingham or Montgomery.

New rate schedule for advertising from outside the county in which newspapers are published is adopted.

1881
Maj. William Wallace Screws, president
The Montgomery Advertiser
10th annual press convention
May 17-18, 1881
Blount Springs

Resolution is adopted at the 1881 press convention urging Alabama newspapers to publish information that would encourage "foreign immigration" into the state. By "foreign," the editor meant from other sections of the country more than from abroad.

Editors and publishers take excursion to Nashville, Tenn., following the convention in Blount Springs.

1882
Gen. James Berney Stanley, president
The Greenville Advocate
11th annual press convention
April 20-21, 1882
Montgomery

Railroad expansion in Alabama is favored by delegates to the 1882 press convention. Resolution is adopted seeking support of the Alabama congressional delegation for a bill allowing the St. Louis, Montgomery and Florida Railroad Company to purchase federal lands along its route.

Delegates travel on a river steamer from Montgomery to Prattville. Gen. James Berney Stanley, editor and publisher of *The Greenville Advocate*, is elected president while on the steamer. Stanley begins his first of four terms as APA president.

1883
Gen. James Berney Stanley, president
The Greenville Advocate
12th annual press convention
May 22-23, 1883
Selma

For their 12th annual press convention in 1883, the editors and publishers visit Uniontown and Demopolis. From Selma, they take an excursion to Florida, visiting the Navy yard at Pensacola. The Alabama press delegation returns through Georgia by way of Brunswick, Savannah, Macon and Atlanta.

1884
Gen. James Berney Stanley, president
The Greenville Advocate
13th annual press convention
May 8-10, 1884
Eufaula

Delegates to the 1884 press convention endorse the World Exposition to be held in New Orleans and state that it is "manifestly important that the resources and industries of Alabama be properly represented" there.

Mrs. I.M.P. Henry, associate editor of *The Greenville Advocate*, is elected honorary member of the Press Association.

The Eufaula Weekly Times and News, in its May 13, 1884, account of the 13th annual convention, reports, "After the operetta last night, which was attended by a large and delighted throng of mingled visitors and citizens, the audience repaired almost in a body to Hart's Hall, where merry music invited the dancers to the floor."

1885
Gen. James Berney Stanley, president
The Greenville Advocate
14th annual press convention
April 7-8, 1885
Talladega

Editors and publishers take excursion to Renfro, a large lumber camp, on the Talladega and Coosa Valley Railroad, and Anniston.

Delegates travel to New Orleans Exposition aboard a special train.

1886
William M. Meeks, president
The Gadsden Times and News
15th annual press convention
May 27-28, 1886
Marion

Delegates visit Lincoln Institute, the State University for Colored People.

Resolution is adopted tendering the thanks of Gen. James Berney Stanley, *The Greenville Advocate*, retiring Press Association president, for his four consecutive terms in office.

1887
William M. Meeks, president
The Gadsden Times and News
16th annual press convention
May 25-26, 1887
Birmingham

Legal incorporation of the Press Association is accomplished in 1887 by act of the Legislature. A committee is appointed at the 1887 press convention to prepare a constitution and bylaws to go into force along with the new charter in 1888.

Editors take excursion to Mammoth Cave at conclusion of 16th annual convention.

1888
Harry G. McCall, president
The Shelby Sentinel, Columbiana
17th annual press convention
April 19-21, 1888
Selma

More professionalism and less politics is theme of the 17th annual convention. Resolution is adopted not to "recognize any resolution favoring or condemning any party, policy, platform or public official."

1889
Harry G. McCall, president
The Shelby Sentinel, Columbiana
18th annual press convention
June 27-29, 1889
Huntsville

Sixty delegates attend 18th annual convention in 1889.

Maj. William Wallace Screws, *The Montgomery Advertiser*, Professor James Archibald Bradford Lovett, *The Teacher at Work*, Huntsville (first education journal established in Alabama) and Rufus N. Rhodes, *The Birmingham News*, are selected as delegates to the National Editorial Association. (This is the first recorded instance of the Press Association's sponsorship of delegates to a national organization.)

1890
John C. Williams, president
Our Mountain Home, Talladega
19th annual press convention
June 11-12, 1890
Montgomery and Troy

Dissension occurs at the 19th annual convention in 1890. Press Association president Harry G. McCall of *The Shelby Sentinel* refers to attacks made on candidates in the last election by the press of the state.

McCall advocates that a censorship board consisting of one lawyer, one journalist and one other be appointed by the Legislature to stop such attacks. Delegates reject McCall's proposal for press censorship by a vote of 47-2.

Editors take excursion to Brunswick and Savannah, Ga.

1891
John C. Williams, president
Our Mountain Home, Talladega
20th annual press convention
June 24-26, 1891
Anniston

Name of the Press Association is changed from the Editors and Publishers Association to the Alabama Press Association. Changing the name is indicative of the altered nature of the APA at the end of its first 20 years of existence.

The Press Association becomes less of a convivial and only occasionally productive organization of editors and publishers to more of an organization designed to improve the quality of the press in Alabama and protect its interests. *The Birmingham Age-Herald* comments in an editorial on June 24, 1891, "The editors threaten to get down to business."

Editors and publishers take side trip to Gadsden.

1892
John C. Williams, president
Our Mountain Home, Talladega
21st annual press convention
Oct. 20-21, 1892
Birmingham

The year 1892 is a turning point for the APA, as evident by the program of the 21st annual convention.

For the first time there are workshop sessions on various aspects of the newspaper business. "Heretofore there has been too much frolic and feast, too much junket and jest to permit...business, and the annual convocations of the cofraternity have therefore fallen somewhat into discredit," *The Birmingham News* editorializes in its Oct. 21, 1892, edition.

1893
Edward Louis Collen Ward, president
The Bridgeport News
22nd annual press convention
June 14-15, 1893
Bridgeport

Workshops are again held at the 22nd annual convention in 1893.

Convention is followed by an excursion to Chattanooga by N and C train and a return trip down the not-yet dammed Tennessee River by steamer of the Tennessee River Transportation Co.

1894
Robert M. Rawls, president
The Athens Courier
23rd annual press convention
Sept. 12-13, 1894
Montgomery

APA takes the lead in urging the Alabama Legislature to pass a bill "for the establishment and maintenance of a public school system in Alabama."

Formation of Legislative Committee is high point of the 1894 convention. The committee is formed to promote and protect the interests of the press in Alabama by being present in Montgomery during legislative sessions when necessary, and keeping in contact with state legislators.

Problem of lynching in the South is discussed. Editors condemn the arrival in the South of a "committee of foreigners" to investigate lynching, stating that "we look upon the source from which their information has been drawn as utterly irresponsible." Yet, "if they come seeking to investigate with fairness and justice, and not with already prejudiced minds to denounce, then we bid them come and our famous hospitality will be extended to them and our aid given in their undertaking."

Outgoing APA president Edward Louis Collen Ward of *The Bridgeport News* in Jackson County in his address at the 23rd annual convention urges that the Press Association "better guard our portals and see that we have a larger membership at business meetings or a much smaller one on excursion occasions."

1895
Robert M. Rawls, president
The Athens Courier
24th annual press convention
Oct. 8-9, 1895
Birmingham

APA visits Havana, Cuba, in January 1895 as its "midwinter tour." It is the first APA-sponsored trip to Cuba, a short time before the Spanish-American War. "The Alabama Press Association party left Cuba with higher ideas of American freedom than they ever had entertained before," *The Montgomery Advertiser* reports.

"These annual gatherings...are no longer given up to fun and frolic, but are devoted strictly to promoting the interests of the Association as a whole and of the profession generally," *The Birmingham News* reports in its Oct. 8, 1895, edition.

APA secretary J. Asa Rountree recommends that an advertising association be formed to help the newspapers secure out-of-state advertising and protect them from frauds. Committee is formed at the 1895 convention to study formation of an advertising association. The committee does not recommend formation of such an agency, but suggests that a few newspapers "might want to go together and hire someone to take care of their national advertising." It is to be several years (1906) before the weekly newspapers form an advertising association.

Following the 1895 convention, delegates attend the Atlanta Exposition.

1896
Moncure Woodson Camper, president
The Florence Times
25th annual press convention
Oct. 14, 1896
Huntsville

APA delegates again support changing of the state libel law. Delegates to 1896 convention urge Legislature to make changes and amendments in the law which would make it more in accord with laws in other states which require some element of malice to create libel.

Delegates ask that a newspaper be able to make a correction and give full reparation in its columns if it had published a report without intention to injure, instead of being held responsible in damages for errors or mistakes innocently made by the newspaper.

1897
Moncure Woodson Camper, president
The Florence Times
26th annual press convention
June 8-9, 1897
Florence

J.C. Lawrence, *The Marion Standard*, gives program at 1897 convention on "how the press could aid the development of the state."

Editors and publishers visit the Tennessee Exposition in Nashville. One day is known as "Alabama Press Day."

1898
Moncure Woodson Camper, president
The Florence Times
27th annual press convention
May 10-13, 1898
Tuscaloosa

Interest in improving the transportation of the state is reflected in resolutions rejoicing in completion of the Mobile and Ohio railroad line to Tuscaloosa and endorsing construction of a Warrior River canal.

Delegates leave on Southern Railway for Washington, D.C., to look at the workings of national legislation and "let the powers that be, know Alabama is still on the map." Delegates also travel to New York and to Newport News for christening of the "Alabama."

1899
Rufus Napoleon Rhodes, president
The Birmingham News
28th annual press convention
June 14, 1899
Birmingham

By 1899 the Legislative Committee apparently has met with success in changing the state libel law. William E.W. Yerby, *The Greensboro Watchman*, refers to "the new libel law as a great improvement over the old one in that a man who thinks himself libeled can recover for actual damages."

Percy Clark, *The Selma Telegraph*, "spoke ardently for an intelligent ballot." ("Intelligent ballot" was an euphemism for restricting Negro suffrage, particularly in the use of a literacy test).

Delegates travel to Niagara Falls and Toronto, Canada. Train furnished by Louisville and Nashville and Erie railroads.

1900
Rufus Napoleon Rhodes, president
The Birmingham News
29th annual press convention
July 17-18, 1900
Birmingham

Delegates take excursion to Denver, Colo., before returning to Alabama on July 25. The party visits Silver Plume, Manitou, Colorado Springs, the summit of Pike's Peak and Cripple Creek. A Denver newspaper reports that the railroad agent in charge of the train "was unaware of the large proportion of wives, sisters and children in the party, and, expecting men only, filled up his commissariat accordingly with liquids. He was obliged to buy many gallons of ice cream when the joke on him was discovered."

On the return trip, the editors receive many courtesies from citizens of St. Louis and resolve to do all in their power to contribute to the success of the World's Fair in St. Louis in 1903.

1901
William Edward Wadsworth Yerby, president
The Greensboro Watchman
30th annual press convention
June 20-21, 1901
Montgomery

The convention drawing up the new Alabama state constitution meets in Montgomery simultaneously with the 1901 APA convention. There is added to the proposed constitution a line stating that "No law shall ever be passed to curtail or restrain the liberty of the press."

Delegates take 15-day outing to San Francisco, where they are entertained by a ride on the bay through the Golden Gate, musical receptions, a trolley ride over the city, inspection of the ships in the bay, and a trip through Chinatown. *The San Francisco Call* features the APA visit in a page 1 story on June 28, 1901, headlined "Press Club Thronged With The Editors From That Far and Famous Sunny South."

1902
William Edward Wadsworth Yerby, president
The Greensboro Watchman
31st annual press convention
May 22-23, 1902
Mobile

Five issues of *The Alabama Press Reporter* are published in 1902. The publication contains reports on advertisers who did not pay their bills, and warnings against "deadbeat advertisers." This is the first reference to an official publication of the Alabama Press Association. (Copies of *The Alabama Press Reporter* have not been located).

Some discussion of abuses of passes given by the railroads to APA members takes place at the 1902 convention. Resolution is adopted to expel "any newspaper man who imposed on railroads." Delegates discuss the problem of the practice of trading railroad transportation for advertising.

Alabama editors visit Boston, Providence and New York, but records of that excursion have not been located.

1903
William Edward Wadsworth Yerby, president
The Greensboro Watchman
32nd annual press convention
May 21-22, 1903
Anniston

"Of the 175 members, 73 were present" at the 1903 convention, according to APA minutes. Minutes also reflect that "130 newspapers were represented in the total membership, 24 having been added since the last meeting."

Alabama editors and publishers travel by special train of four Pullman sleepers and a baggage car on July 14, 1903, for a tour of Canada. The Alabamians are given a drive over the city of Toronto, a boat trip on the bay and an elaborate lunch in the pavilion on Island Park.

1904
Charles Herd Greer, president
The Marion Standard
33rd annual press convention
June 29-30, 1904
Bessemer

Dissension occurs at the 1904 convention.

An Executive Committee meeting in November 1903 had charged APA secretary J.Asa Rountree of *The Dixie Home Manufacturer* with abuses of free railway passes secured for the association on its excursion to Canada in July 1903. Executive Committee charges that Rountree had been obtaining railway passes for individuals who were not APA members. Rountree also is accused of charging a higher sum than necessary for the excursion and pocketing commissions for securing accommodations.

Resolution is adopted condemning Rountree "for using the adopted Press Association through the trust and confidence reposed in him as its secretary for his personal graft." Resolution further states that Rountree's conduct made him "unworthy of membership in the Association." Rountree resigns as APA secretary. (It appears that Rountree was not actually expelled from the APA as his name appears on the lists of members attending the conventions in later years.)

A special train, consisting of four Pullman sleepers "with 120 members and their ladies" takes the delegates to St. Louis on July 1, 1904. Most of the editors remain in St. Louis for a week, during which time they visit the World's Fair and other attractions.

1905
Robert E. Lee Neil, president
The Selma Times
34th annual press convention
July 20-21, 1905
Coden

Delegates discuss formation of advertising agency for weeklies. The weekly editors call in Vic-

tor H. Hanson of *The Montgomery Advertiser* to help them formulate plans, as Hanson is considered "a past master of getting business and advertising rates" and "the evangelist of advertising in the South," *The Montgomery Advertiser* reports.

Friendly spirit pervades the 34th annual convention. An entire afternoon session turns into a huge tribute to William Wallace Screws of *The Montgomery Advertiser*, founding father of the APA, on his 40th anniversary with the newspaper.

1906
Robert E. Lee Neil, president
The Selma Times
35th annual press convention
July 25-26, 1906
Gadsden

Formation of advertising agency for weeklies is launched at the 1906 convention.

Delegates take excursion to Jacksonville, Fla., and Atlantic Beach, Fla., following the 35th annual convention.

1907
Howard S. Doster, president
The Prattville Progress
36th annual press convention
July 18-19, 1907
Montgomery

The 1907 convention is described by Gen. James Berney Stanley of *The Greenville Advocate* as "one of the stormiest sessions the association ever held. That was when Gov. B.B. Comer had just dealt the association a hard blow by prohibiting railroad passes." The anti-pass legislation passed during Comer's administration affects the APA after 1907 for, despite public statements to the contrary, in the next few years the pace of the Press Association slowed and membership declined.

Resolution urges stronger legal notice publication laws and stronger enforcement provisions. Resolutions lead to changes in state's civil libel statues.

The year 1907 ends a 15-year period in the history of the APA which is marked by a new seriousness of purpose, expanding membership and constructive actions, and marred by several violent controversies. It is doubtful that the controversies did much harm to the Alabama Press Association, however.

Following the 1907 convention, delegates leave for a week's outing on the Alabama River.

1908
J.C. Lawrence, president
The Union Springs Breeze
37th annual press convention
July 22-23, 1908
Bessemer

Reorganization of the APA occurs at the 1908 convention. The state is divided into five geographical groups with a vice president from each area. The five vice presidents are to hold area meetings at least once a year. During one session of the annual conventions, the newspapers are to divide into two classes: Class A, weeklies and monthlies, and Class B, dailies, to transact business affecting the two types of newspapers.

Following the convention, delegates travel to Brunswick, Ga., spending part of their time on Brunswick Island.

1909
C.G. Fennell, president
The Guntersville Democrat
38th annual press convention
June 16-17, 1909
Dothan

In his opening address at the 1909 convention in Dothan, outgoing APA president J.C. Lawrence of *The Union Springs Breeze* comments that it will not be possible for the state's weeklies to settle upon good advertising rates until nearly all the newspapers in the state are members of the Press Association. Lawrence praises the development of schools of journalism throughout the country and says he hopes there soon will be one in Alabama.

Maj. William Wallace Screws, editor of *The Montgomery Advertiser*, submits in pamphlet form a history of Alabama newspapers on which he had been working for several years.

Convention delegates travel to Panama City and St. Andrews Bay, Fla.

1910
McLane Tilton Jr., president
The Pell City Progress
39th annual press convention
June 16-17, 1910
Mobile

Delegates leave Mobile for Fort Morgan aboard the "Winona," revenue cutter of the Treasury Department. But after traveling about 10 miles, the party finds the New York steamer "Algonquin" grounded. The party returns to Mobile without having reached Fort Morgan.

1911
Luman Handley Nunnelee, president
The Centreville Press
40th annual press convention
June 11-12, 1911
Montgomery

The 40th annual convention was scheduled June 11-12, 1911, in Montgomery and was to be followed by a tour of Tuskegee. *The Prattville Progress* reports in its June 15, 1911, edition that the convention is postponed because of lack of interest by members. *The Progress* comments that the Alabama press "is not exercising a great influence in Alabama" and influence of the press is "at its lowest ebb."

Records do not reflect if the 1911 convention was ever held.

1912
Luman Handley Nunnelee, president
The Centreville Press
41st annual press convention
June 22, 1912
Birmingham

Concerns of Alabama newspapers are reflected in the program of the 1912 convention: "Should We Continue the $1 Rate for Weeklies at the Present Cost of Labor and Materials" by A.B. Tucker, *The Thomasville Echo*; "How to Increase an Interest in Our Association" by William E.W. Yerby, *The Greensboro Watchman*; "The Religious Press" by J.B. Cumming, *The Alabama Christian Advocate*; and "The Relation of the Daily to the Weekly Press" by Maj. William Wallace Screws and Franklin Potts Glass, *The Montgomery Advertiser*.

APA vice president A.B. Tucker of *The Thomasville Echo* announces that he was advised by an agent of Southern Railway and also by state officials that it is "perfectly legal" for newspapers to exchange advertising space for railroad transportation.

Delegates leave by special train for the Democratic National Convention in Baltimore.

The Birmingham News comments that the 1912 convention shows "the revival of the Press Association" to be complete. More than one-fourth of the 200 Alabama newspapers are represented at the convention.

1913
Luman Handley Nunnelee, president
The Centreville Press
42nd annual press convention
May 29-30, 1913
Birmingham

More independence of the press from politics and politicians, increased rates for advertising, and abolishing of free advertisements are chief topics of discussion at the 1913 convention.

Only 25 delegates attend the 42nd annual convention. It is decided that because of the poor attendance, another meeting will be held in Birmingham at State Fair time in the fall. (No records have been found indicating that the second meeting was ever held.)

1914
Christopher James Hildreth, president
The New Decatur Advertiser
43rd annual press convention
May 27-28, 1914
Birmingham

Small turnout again occurs at the 1914 convention. The question of equal suffrage is discussed at length with Julia Gillespie, *The Cullman Tribune*, and Mrs. Lee Moody, *The Bessemer Weekly*, leading the fight for women's suffrage.

Mrs. Gillespie appeals to the Alabama press to "sweep away some of the cobwebs and prejudice against suffrage." When an equal suffrage resolution is introduced, many delegates out of "chivalry" refuse to take a stand — however, the vote is 11-8 favoring suffrage.

Delegates to 1914 convention commend the work of the Alabama Good Roads Association in "educational efforts to improve the people's highway system."

1915
Col. Harry Mell Ayers, president
The Anniston Star
44th annual press convention
July 20-21, 1915
Montgomery

Effects of war in Europe are felt at the 1915 convention. Delegates express desire for presidential action to remove the embargo on cotton.

The Montgomery Advertiser editorializes for the Alabama press to become more strongly organized. "The hour has struck not only for the press of Alabama to be self-respecting, but for the manifestation of its influence and power in a way which will command respect from others," *The Advertiser* comments. "The Press Association, when united with a singleness of purpose and that singleness of purpose the welfare of the press of Alabama, can and will count heavily in all the affairs of the state."

1916
Col. Harry Mell Ayers, president
The Anniston Star
45th annual press convention
July 27-28, 1916
Birmingham

APA president Harry M. Ayers, *The Anniston Star*, urges editors to "emphasize more strongly the business end of our vocation...and bring those in other walks to realize that journalism is governed by the rules of income and outgo that make for the success or failure of any other business." Ayers also urges compulsory school attendance and local taxation amendments.

The Alabama Journal in Montgomery reports "a large attendance" at the 1916 convention. "Practically every section of the State was represented when the first business session was opened."

Delegates endorse locating a Federal Farm Loan Bank in Birmingham and a nitrate plant project in Muscle Shoals.

Gen. James Berney Stanley, *The Greenville Advocate*, gives a speech titled "Reminiscences of the Alabama Press." Newspapers are "pre-eminently the educators and enlighteners of the people," Stanley tells 1916 convention delegates. "Needless to say that the newspapers of today, no less than their predecessors of yesterday, will do their full share and more in utilizing any and all good to the greatest advantage of all the people."

1917
Edward Doty
The Tuscaloosa News, president
46th annual press convention
May 17-18, 1917
Gadsden

Patriotism is the tone of the 1917 convention. A major problem during World War I is high price of newsprint. Delegates endorse the idea of cooperative buying of newsprint.

Following the Gadsden convention, delegates board special L&N train furnished by Alabama Power Co. Delegates travel to Anniston to visit home of Lt. Gov. Thomas E. Kilby. Barbecue is served at the Kilby home, and delegates receive "Extra" edition of *The Anniston Star* announcing that Anniston is selected "site for a great training camp." It is to be known as Fort McClellan.

1918
A.W. McCullock, president
The Gadsden Journal
47th annual press convention
July 18-20, 1918
Birmingham

Delegates again express concern over price of newsprint, which has increased 100 percent in two years. Federal government also has ordered 10 percent reduction in use of white paper.

The Birmingham News urges editors and publishers to be more businesslike, eliminating unnecessary departments and improving the necessary ones and "not to apologize for raising rates."

1919
Oscar M. Dugger Sr., president
The Andalusia Star
48th annual press convention
June 26-27, 1919
Andalusia

Andalusia Chamber of Commerce pays all personal expenses of the 60 delegates to the 1919 convention. Delegates refuse to endorse a state income tax. Resolutions are adopted endorsing the League of Nations, the division of unused land among returning veterans and erection of a memorial to Alabama soldiers killed in World War I.

Banquet is dominated by discussion of women's suffrage. "Decorations for the banquet, and even the ice cream, were in suffrage colors," APA minutes reflect.

1920
Frank N. Julian, president
The Sheffield Standard
49th annual convention
May 27-28, 1920
Montgomery

Shortage of paper and high cost of newsprint is main topic of discussion at 1920 convention. Some speakers at convention recommend reducing circulation and raising advertising rates. Also discussed is "installation of a cost system to inform publishers whether or not a profit is being made."

It is during the 1920 convention that the first recorded discussion of having a permanent manager and headquarters for the APA takes place.

Delegates travel to Sheffield and Muscle Shoals to see construction of dam.

1921
William Theodore Hall, president
The Dothan Eagle
50th annual press convention
May 5-6, 1921
Albany and Decatur

Reform of state libel laws is chief topic of discussion at 1921 convention. Lt. Gov. Nathan L. Miller tells delegates: "Truth should be a bar to legal punishment. It should be a complete defense."

(Under the existing libel law, a newspaper can be prosecuted in any county where it circulates. If a suit fails in one county, it can be tried in a number of counties. Truth under Alabama law is only a mitigating circumstance, not a full defense.) In one instance, a prosecution had followed publication of a grand jury report.

APA committee is appointed to draft proposed changes in state's libel laws.

1922
Capt. William Thomas Sheehan, president
The Montgomery Advertiser
51st annual press convention
May 10-11, 1922
Montgomery and Auburn

Small convention turnout, fewer than 50 delegates, causes E.W. Barrett of *The Birmingham Age-Herald* to call again for the legalization of swapping of railroad advertising for passes.

During roundtable discussion of newspaper problems, the question of libel laws again is discussed. In one instance, a man who was shot at while operating a moonshine still sued a newspaper because it referred to him as a "shiner."

Delegates travel from Montgomery to Auburn where a barbecue is given by town and college officials.

1923
Forney G. Stephens, president
The Southern Democrat, Oneonta
52nd annual press convention
May 24-26, 1923
Mobile and Baldwin counties

APA holds joint convention with Mississippi Press Association. Frances Golson, editor of *The Wetumpka Herald*, is appointed to write the complete account of the convention, which is to be printed in newspapers throughout the state.

Delegates appoint advertising rate committee.

1924
W.R. Jordan, president
The Huntsville Morning Star
(Jordan died while in office and was succeeded by J.S. Benson, *The Progressive Age*, Scottsboro)
53rd annual press convention
June 13-14, 1924
Florence

The Birmingham Age-Herald hails opening of 53rd annual convention with editorial in praise of small dailies and weeklies in the state. *The Age-Herald* comments that "the country editor is thinking more for himself than ever before. He is broadening in his motives and purposes, is drawing firmer and sounder distinctions between the real and the spurious, and is more than ever speaking in terms of principle."

Advertising rate committee that was appointed in 1923 is given credit for a great deal of success in standardizing rates among the smaller newspapers in the state.

A decision is made to draft a code of ethics for the Press Association.

The question of employing a full-time APA secretary, first discussed at the 1920 convention, again is discussed.

Delegates vote to hold the 1925 convention on the Gulf Coast and tentative decision is made to establish "a summer camp at some point on the coast for a permanent meeting place."

1925
J.C. McLendon, president
The Luverne Journal
54th annual press convention
June 18-23, 1925
Foley

"Banquets, balls, trips to the Gulf of Mexico and Mobile, fish fries, barbecues, swimming, boating and fishing all come in for a share of the time in Baldwin County," says *The Onlooker* of Foley in reporting the week's activities of the APA during its 54th annual press convention in Foley in 1925.

The Onlooker reports in its June 25 edition that "Frank Barchard of *The Onlooker* offered to give the APA a site on Perdido Bay upon which to locate a summer home. The matter of building a permanent vacation place in Baldwin County has been under consideration by the state editors for some time and it is expected that some definite steps will be taken."

Delegates adopted resolution commending Gen. James Berney Stanley of *The Greenville Ad-*vocate, who had served for 60 years as only editor of the Greenville newspaper. The resolution notes that Stanley, who served four consecutive terms as APA president, "has long been a mentor of Alabama newspaper editors and dean of the Alabama Press Association."

• • •

The period from 1908 to 1925 is one of ups and downs for the APA. Attendance at annual conventions varies widely depending upon the meeting place and business conditions.

The ending of trading of railroad advertising for passes makes it difficult for some weekly editors to afford to attend meetings far away from their hometowns. This, coupled with the disruptions in economic life and especially the problems of newspapers during World War I such as newsprint shortages, does not help the APA.

Some progress, however, is made toward reform of Alabama's libel laws and standardization of advertising rates for the smaller papers.

Often the once-a-year conventions which combined business and pleasure are so loaded down it is nearly impossible to fulfill the planned program in only two days. Beginning in 1926, this situation is remedied by having a summer outing and two winter business meetings, one for the northern half of the state and one for the southern half.

1926
Webb Stanley, president
The Greenville Advocate
55th annual press convention
June 2-4, 1926
Auburn

Little business is transacted at 55th annual press convention in Auburn in 1926. Delegates endorse resolution to build a "Press City" in Florida to be used as a convention center and a "home for retired editors."

New meeting schedule goes into effect in 1926, remaining operational until 1933. Southern midwinter meeting is held in Montgomery on Jan. 16, 1926. Editors discuss improvement of education in Alabama and how to make the Black Belt lands more productive. A sales tax is suggested as the best way to finance education.

Northern midwinter meeting is held Jan. 30, 1926, in Birmingham. Victor H. Hanson of *The Birmingham News* suggests that publishers of weekly papers adopt uniform advertising and subscription rates.

1927
Robert B. Vail, president
The Baldwin Times, Bay Minette
56th annual press convention
May 7-15, 1927
New York City

APA travels to New York City for its 56th annual convention. Outgoing president Webb Stanley of *The Greenville Advocate* and Horace Hall of *The Dothan Eagle* work out plans for editors and publishers to make a round trip to New York by railroad and ocean at a cost of $25.75 per person, including meals.

Delegates stay at the Waldorf-Astoria Hotel and spend three days touring the city. "A visit to one of New York's night clubs and a dozen other things were participated in that are not mentioned, but suffice it to say that every hour was filled to the brim with experiences that combined to make the trip one that stood out in the lives of those who went," Stanley reports.

Somewhere at sea between Savannah, Ga., and New York, Robert B. Vail of *The Baldwin Times* in Bay Minette becomes the first APA president to be inducted into office on ocean liner.

Northern midwinter meeting is Jan. 8, 1927, in Birmingham. Southern midwinter meeting is Jan. 26, 1927, in Montgomery. Establishment of Linotype training at Alabama School of Trades is heartily endorsed by APA members, who ask the Legislature to enlarge the department.

1928
E. Cody Hall Sr., president
The Alexander City Outlook
57th annual press convention
April 18-26, 1928
Cuba

Dothan is point of assembly for 57th annual press convention in 1928. Delegates make first visit to Cuba since the 24th annual convention in 1895. "Very few suffered from seasickness, but everyone in the party was thrilled when the island of Cuba was sighted," it was reported in minutes.

Some of the editors and publishers, looking forward to seeing a bull fight, are disappointed upon learning that the sport was discontinued in 1898. However, Havana night clubs, a Spanish ball game, the jai-alai, and cock fighting make up for the editors' disappointment. Delegates vote to place marble plaque in the Reporters' Building in Havana.

Election of officers and a business meeting is held on the ship on the return trip from Cuba. E.

Cody Hall Sr. of *The Alexander City Outlook* becomes second APA president to be inducted on the high seas.

Southern midwinter meeting is Jan. 14, 1928, in Montgomery. Northern midwinter meeting is Jan. 28, 1928, in Birmingham.

Victor H. Hanson, publisher of *The Birmingham News*, provides loving cups to be awarded to the top weekly newspaper in Alabama. The loving cups are a precursor to APA's Better Newspaper Contest. Cups are first awarded in 1929.

Grover C. Hall Sr., editor of *The Montgomery Advertiser*, receives Pulitzer Prize, the first ever awarded in Alabama, for best editorial writing.

1929
W. Emmett Brooks, president
The Brewton Standard
58th annual press convention
May 10-23, 1929
New York City, Montreal

Train and steamer trip to New York from Savannah is duplication of the 1927 trip. Somewhere on the high seas between New York and Savannah, W. Emmett Brooks, editor and publisher of *The Brewton Standard,* becomes third APA president to be inducted on ocean liner. The 1929 excursion is extended to include a trip by train from New York to Montreal.

Northern midwinter meeting is Jan. 12, 1929, in Birmingham. Southern midwinter meeting is Jan. 26, 1929, in Montgomery. Competition and prices and job printing as an adjunct to a newspaper are main topics of discussion.

First APA Press Institute is held at Alabama Polytechnic Institute, Auburn, in August 1929. Program is of a practical nature and deals with the ever-important subject, "how to increase revenues." Gen. James Berney Stanley of *The Greenville Advocate* gives speech titled "Some Reminiscences of the Alabama Press Association."

The Mountain Eagle, Jasper, and *The Southern Star,* Ozark, receive the first Victor H. Hanson loving cups in 1929 as best weekly newspapers in Alabama.

1930
Marcy B. Darnall, president
The Florence Herald
59th annual press convention
June 14-21, 1930
Washington, D.C.

Delegates travel to Washington, D.C. for 59th annual convention, June 14-21, 1930.

Midwinter meeting for southern division is Jan. 11, 1930, in Montgomery. Midwinter meeting for northern division is Jan. 25, 1930, in Birmingham.

Second APA Press Institute is held at Alabama Polytechnic Institute, Auburn, Aug. 14-16, 1930, with theme of "Making a Better Newspaper." Hiring of a field manager again is discussed in 1930.

Professor John H. Casey, community newspaper specialist from the University of Oklahoma, attends the institute. "I learned that there was some sentiment for undertaking the employment of a field manager for the organization in cooperation with one of the state's educational institutions, probably Alabama Polytechnic Institute at Auburn," Casey later writes. "I also was gratified to find that President (Bradford) Knapp was kindly disposed to the idea in general. My impression was, however, that the publishers of the state would have to initiate the movement."

(Records indicate that before the 1930 Press Institute, the hiring of a field manager and permanent headquarters for the association had been publicly discussed during at least two earlier press conventions — in 1920 and 1924.)

At the 1930 Press Institute, the practice of selecting the "All-Alabama Weekly Newspaper Eleven" is inaugurated.

The Chilton County News, Clanton, and *The Florence Herald* are awarded the Victor H. Hanson loving cups in 1930 as the best weekly newspapers in the state.

1931
Jack M. Pratt, president
The Pickens County Herald
60th annual press convention
Aug. 13-14, 1931
Auburn

Convention is held at Alabama Polytechnic Institute in 1931 in conjunction with the third annual APA Press Institute.

The Press Institute is discontinued after 1931, but is revived in 1941 at the University of Alabama. Theme of 1931 institute is same as that of 1929 — going deeper into the matter of reducing expenses, and at the same time actually doing what the 1930 slogan suggested, "Making a Better Newspaper."

"All-Alabama Weekly Newspaper Eleven" announced at the institute.

The Greenville Advocate is awarded the Victor H. Hanson loving cup in 1931 as "the best all-round weekly newspaper." Award is presented at barbe-

cue-banquet in Auburn at close of 60th annual convention. Gen. James Berney Stanley of *The Advocate* calls it "the greatest honor *The Greenville Advocate* has ever received."

Midwinter meeting for northern division is in Birmingham Jan. 10, 1931. Midwinter meeting for southern division is in Montgomery Jan. 14, 1931.

1932
Forney G. Stephens, president
The Southern Democrat, Oneonta
61st annual press convention
July 21-22, 1932
Montgomery

"Back to the times which were old, and maybe good," is theme of 61st annual convention in Montgomery, and Jefferson Davis Hotel is site of the 1932 convention. "The hotel has agreed to give 'hard-time' rates and has asked the privilege of making no charge for rooms for your ladies," *The Ala-Pressa* reports.

"There is really no reason why the two days and one night in Montgomery should cost over $5.00 unless you are especially prosperous and inclined to be extravagant," Chamber of Commerce secretary Jesse B. Hearin writes in 1932 issue of *The Ala-Pressa*.

The Covington News in Andalusia is awarded the Victor H. Hanson loving cup at 1932 convention. (The loving cups are no longer awarded after 1932.)

Midwinter meeting for northern division is in Birmingham Jan. 16, 1932. Midwinter meeting for southern division is Jan. 30, 1932, in Montgomery.

1933
Jesse B. Adams, president
The Southern Star, Ozark
62nd annual press convention
July 21-23, 1933
Tuscaloosa

Not wishing to have an expensive excursion for the 62nd annual convention in 1933, APA chooses to meet at the University of Alabama. Diversions supplied by tour of Gulf States Paper Mill and boating on the Warrior River.

Resolution is adopted at the 1933 convention pledging the APA "to work with renewed zeal for the advancement of our schools and our citizens, through our newspapers, realizing that education must be sold to the public."

Only one midwinter meeting is held, the southern division, Jan. 28, 1933, in Montgomery. Business problems of newspapers growing out of the Depression are major concern of Alabama editors at 1933 midwinter meeting.

1934
Jesse B. Adams, president
The Southern Star, Ozark
63rd annual press convention
Aug. 17-20, 1934
Chicago

Following their old custom of traveling, delegates to the 63rd annual convention travel to Chicago and stay at the Hotel Sherman in Chicago. Delegates make the trip to Chicago's World Fair with the "Alabama Press Special" which is run from Birmingham to Chicago over the Illinois Railway System. Delegates participate in "Alabama Day" at the World's Fair.

The dream of a field director for APA is realized in 1934. It is made possible by the federal government when the Graphic Arts Code for Alabama is put into effect. The government, through the National Recovery Act, employs an administrator for the Graphic Arts Code, and it is through this that the APA is able to use the same individual as its field representative.

Field manager is W. Roy Brown. Office is temporarily located in Ozark, hometown of APA president Jesse B. Adams of *The Southern Star*. Office later is moved to Montgomery sometime in 1934 or 1935. The arrangement with the NRA and Alabama Press Association comes to an end with the close of the federal program in 1935, and the Press Association again is without a field manager.

1935
W. Bruce Shelton, president
The Tuscaloosa News
(Shelton resigned after two months and was succeeded by Webb Stanley,
The Greenville Advocate)
64th annual press convention
Jan. 25-26, 1935
Montgomery

Bruce Shelton of *The Tuscaloosa News* resigns after two months as APA president and is succeeded by Webb Stanley of *The Greenville Advocate*. (APA records do not explain the reason for Shelton's resignation.)

Organization of National Recovery Administration codes for Alabama dominates the 1935 convention. Discussion centers on the organization of

an Alabama regional code authority as it would affect weekly and small newspapers.

Delegates adopt resolution expressing sorrow at death of Gen. James Berney Stanley, *The Greenville Advocate's* founder, owner and editor for 70 years. Stanley was one of the 30 founders of the Alabama Press Association when the first convention was held in Montgomery in 1972.

APA urges passage of shield law. At concluding session, delegates adopt resolution by unanimous vote to support a bill by Rep. W.P. Calhoun of Houston County that was pending before the Legislature. The bill "would relieve newspaper reporters and employees from the necessity of divulging the sources of information and communications given them in confidence for the purpose of publication."

Resolution leads to legislation passing the state's respected shield laws, laws that protect reporters from divulging the sources of confidential information.

Midsummer meeting is held in Alexander City July 19-21, 1935. Delegates are guests of Col. Benjamin Russell, owner of Camp Dixon and president of the Alexander City Chamber of Commerce.

1936
Robert Gaston Bozeman Sr., president
The Evergreen Courant
65th annual press convention
June 14-22, 1936
Cuba

Squalls and high seas are encountered by the some 400 Alabama newspaper representatives, their families and friends as they travel to Havana for the 65th annual convention. Robert Gaston Bozeman Sr., *The Evergreen Courant*, becomes the fourth APA president to be inducted on the high seas. It marks APA's third trip to Cuba — the first was in 1885; the second visit was in 1928.

Midwinter meeting is held in Montgomery Jan. 10-11, 1936. It is at this midwinter meeting that APA becomes involved in formation of the State Chamber of Commerce.

Industrial committee is appointed to promote formation of State Chamber of Commerce, with Clifford L. (Cliff) Walton of *The LaFayette Sun* as chairman. Resolution is drafted pledging APA's full cooperation in promoting Alabama and its interests through industry. A resolution and widespread travel around the state by Walton lead to establishment of the chamber in 1937.

Public Relations Committee for APA is named to compile a weekly newsletter.

1937
Robert Gaston Bozeman Sr., president
The Evergreen Courant
66th annual press convention
Jan. 15-16, 1937
Montgomery

"More Industries for Alabama" is theme of 66th annual convention in 1937.

State Chamber of Commerce is officially organized in spring 1937. Clifford L. (Cliff) Walton, *The LaFayette Sun*, does considerable travel over the state as a representative of the APA, interviewing leaders and creating interest in sentiment for a Chamber of Commerce.

As its part in encouraging more industry in Alabama, APA endorses: Presentation of resources of Alabama to the outside world; encouragement of the location of new industries of all kinds; adoption of legislation favorable to the location of new industries; and elimination of any unfair or discriminatory taxes which might handicap Alabama in its bid for new industry.

W. Emmett Brooks, editor and publisher of *The Brewton Standard*, speaks on "Circulation Audit for Alabama Weeklies" and stresses that audited circulation would bring about stabilization and uniformity in advertising rates. He points out that dailies throughout the country are audited and that advertising agencies selected newspapers by using lists from audit agencies.

1938
Clifford L. (Cliff) Walton, president
The LaFayette Sun
67th annual press convention
Jan. 13-14, 1938
Birmingham

Establishment of a circulation audit bureau for Alabama weekly newspapers is discussed again at the 1938 convention. Delegates also discuss a proposal to standardize advertising rates based on circulation. Tentative agreement is reached "on efforts toward standardizing advertising rates in the state." Plan is adopted for a voluntary assessment of $1 per member to defray costs of administering a plan of circulation audits.

Hiring of a full-time executive secretary is discussed in 1938. APA had been without a field manager since W. Roy Brown briefly served in the post in 1934-1935.

Accomplishments of the 1938 convention foreshadow full-scale revival of the Alabama Press Association as an important force that begins with the appointment of a full-time executive secretary in 1939.

1939
Milton C. Giles, president
The Sheffield Standard, The Franklin County Times, Russellville, and *The Red Bay News*
68th annual press convention
Jan. 6-7, 1939
Montgomery

A proposal to appoint a full-time APA manager dominates business of the 1939 annual convention in Montgomery, Jan. 6-7. Committee is appointed to seek a manager and permanent headquarters.

On Sept. 1, 1939, Doyle L. Buckles, a former weekly newspaper publisher in Wisconsin, is named field manager. Under a cooperative program with the University of Alabama, Buckles is to devote half his time as field manager and the other half as director of the University of Alabama News Bureau.

University of Alabama agrees to pay half Buckles' salary and to provide office space. Some APA members have reservations about the plan and prepare a statement explaining that "...in the interest of maintaining the complete and absolute freedom of the press of Alabama, we are against Mr. Buckles' dual employment. There is too much possibility for political finagling."

On Sept. 11, 1939, Buckles starts mimeographing a confidential bulletin with two slogans in the nameplate: "Always for Alabama, All Ways," and "It's Our Business to Help Your Business."

Buckles writes APA president Milton C. Giles, *The Sheffield Standard,* in November 1939, "It looks like it might be a long process to build up the proper spirit of cooperation among the publishers."

According to one report at the time the field manager was selected, the APA had only 19 members in 1939 — 12 paid newspaper members and seven associate members.

1940
Hunter H. Golson, president
The Wetumpka Herald
69th annual press convention
Jan. 19-20, 1940
Birmingham

In January 1940, the confidential bulletin started by Doyle L. Buckles becomes *"The Ala-*

Pressa," with a subtitle of "Official House Organ of the Alabama Press Association."

In March 1940 the subtitle is changed to "Confidential Bulletin," and later to "*Ala-Pressa*, Confidential Bulletin of the Alabama Press Association." Some years later, the hyphen in "*Ala-Pressa*" is dropped, and the bulletin becomes "*AlaPressa.*"

Despite the worst blizzard in 20 years, 124 delegates attend the 1940 annual convention, reported to be "so full of practical business-building and newspaper-improvement ideas" that delegates urge that a similar program be held in Montgomery at the 1941 convention.

While impossible for all publishers to make the entire trip, more than 100, headed by field manager Doyle L. Buckles, make a 1,500-mile "blitz tour" of Alabama during the week of July 21, 1940, to "Sell, Alabama to Itself" and to enhance the prestige of the APA.

First summer convention, 1940
Gulf Shores

First summer convention is held in 1940. The press delegation spends two days of "rest and relaxation on the Gulf Shores of Baldwin County, boat riding and deep sea fishing." It is the beginning of what is to become the annual summer convention of the APA.

At the end of 1940, APA has membership of more than 100 who had paid dues that year totaling $934.10. Doyle L. Buckles writes in Dec. 16, 1940, issue of *AlaPressa* that 1940 has been a year of enlistment, with APA membership at its highest in history.

In compliance with requests of many Alabama publishers, Professor Randolph (Randy) Fort, head of the Department of Journalism at the University of Alabama, announces on Nov. 11, 1940, that 13 contests for Alabama newspapers will be sponsored by the journalism department. The first winners will be announced in 1941 at the 70th annual convention.

It will be called the "Better Newspaper Contest."

1941
James H. (Jimmy) Faulkner Sr., president
The Baldwin Times, Bay Minette
70th annual press convention
Jan. 24-25, 1941
Montgomery

"There is an entirely new spirit among weekly newspapermen of Alabama," *The Alabama Journal* comments in its coverage of the 1941 convention.

"The Alabama Press is on a new road to influence, self-respect and independence; and it is one of the most gratifying things that could happen in Alabama."

The University of Alabama Department of Journalism begins sponsoring 13 contests for Alabama newspapers, and the first winners are announced at the 1941 convention. (Known as the "Better Newspaper Contest," it is discontinued in 1947 and is not resumed until 1953.) *The Anniston Times* is named best weekly in Alabama. Second place goes to *The Lee County Bulletin* in Auburn.

The annual Press Institute, last held at Alabama Polytechnic Institute, Auburn, in 1931, is revived by APA in 1941. In opening the institute, chairman Col. Harry M. Ayers of *The Anniston Star* says resumption of the Press Institute is "a milestone in the history of journalism in the state and is the beginning of closer contact between the publishers of Alabama." (The Press Institute is not held again until 1948.)

Summer convention, Decatur and Huntsville
July 18-20, 1941

Only one short business session is held at the 1941 summer convention, and the remainder of the time is devoted to "boat rides on the Tennessee River, barbecues and dancing at Monte Sano Park, fishing, golfing, loafing, meeting old friends and attending banquets."

1942
Charles G. Dobbins, president
The Anniston Times
71st annual press convention
Jan. 16-17, 1942
Birmingham

The 1942 convention is devoted to business and problems of wartime newspaper production.

Better Newspaper Contest winners are announced by professor Phil Beedon, head of the University of Alabama Department of Journalism. *The Lee County Bulletin*, Auburn, is named outstanding weekly, followed by *The Baldwin County Times*, Bay Minette. Besides winning first place in the best all-around division, *The Lee County Bulletin* wins seven first-place awards, two seconds, and three honorable mentions in the 12 contests it entered.

Field manager Doyle L. Buckles is presented a plaque by APA past president Milton C. Giles of *The Franklin County Times* engraved "God's Gift to Alabama Newspapers and the State Itself."

Summer convention, Montgomery
July 24-25, 1942

Sen. Lister Hill and Gov.-elect Chauncey Sparks headline a "war council" banquet during the 1942 summer convention.

1943
Ben A. Green, president
The Tuscaloosa News
The Tallassee Tribune
72nd annual press convention
Jan. 29-30, 1943
Montgomery

Convention is called a "war conference." Delegates hear Gov. Chauncey Sparks pledge his sincere cooperation with the press in solving war problems and building up the state. Sparks praises Alabama press, saying he has "never met a finer group."

Sparks is chosen by APA as its "first honorary non-paying member" and is presented a "make-up rule to carry in his pocket and signify membership," *The Birmingham Age-Herald* reports.

Summer convention, Birmingham
Aug. 13-14, 1943

Roundtable discussions of timely war problems dominate the summer "warvention." The manpower problem, which had seriously hit all newspapers, is a topic for the roundtables. Increased costs of newsprint and overhead focus attention on the importance of increasing circulation and advertising rates.

1944
Parker W. Campbell, president
The Progressive Age, Scottsboro
73rd annual press convention
Jan. 28-29, 1944
Birmingham

"The Alabama Press Association takes great pride in the splendid records made by its members during another long war year, filled with increasing handicaps due to manpower and newsprint shortages and other abnormal conditions over which they had no control," APA field manager Doyle L. Buckles writes in his 1944 convention report.

Summer convention, Birmingham
Aug. 18-19, 1944

Summer program features a "citation banquet" at which tributes and citations were extended to the Alabama publishers by state and federal war leaders.

1945
George A. Carleton, president
The Clarke County Democrat, Grove Hill
74th annual press convention
May 11, 1945
Birmingham

Because of Office of Defense Transportation restrictions, no formal convention is held in 1945. Instead, a meeting of the Executive Committee is held which served as the annual convention.

Summer convention is not held in 1945

1946
Bonnie D. Hand, president
The LaFayette Sun
75th annual press convention
Jan. 18-19, 1946
Birmingham

Nationally known newspaper men are principal speakers at the 75th annual (victory) convention. APA president George A. Carleton of *The Clarke County Democrat* in Grove Hill opens the 1946 convention with a prayer and silent standing tribute to publishers who had made the "supreme sacrifice" on the battle and home fronts.

Special tribute is made to the late Lt. Marcy B. Darnall Jr., USN, of *The Florence Herald* who was reported missing in action.

Summer convention, Panama City, Fla.
July 18-20, 1946

"Informal three-day summer recreational convention" is attended by 100 members and guests.

1947
Neil O. Davis, president
The Lee County Bulletin, Auburn
76th annual press convention
Feb. 14-15, 1947
Montgomery

APA field manager Doyle L. Buckles dies Dec. 18, 1947, in a Birmingham hospital. At a Dec. 21, 1947, meeting, Norman H. Bassett is appointed acting field manager and secretary-treasurer.

Better Newspaper Contest is discontinued after 1947 and is not resumed until 1953.

Summer convention, Biloxi, Miss.
July 18-20, 1947

Delegates adopt resolution seeking greater recreational facilities within the state of Alabama in order that future summer conventions of the "Press Association and other state organization could be held on home shores."

1948
E.H. (Ed) Pierce, president
The Mountain Eagle, Jasper
77th annual press convention
Feb. 13-14, 1948
Birmingham

Citing the "high cost of living," *AlaPressa* reports that registration to the 1948 winter convention will be $7.50, which would include one banquet ticket. "Even at this inflated figure, it looks like we'll have to dig down in the endowment fund for a couple hundred bucks to pay for the convention expenses," *AlaPressa* reports.

Committee is named to find permanent successor to field manager Doyle L. Buckles, who also served as director of the University of Alabama News Bureau. Norman Bassett agrees to continue serving as acting field manager until a permanent field manager is named.

J. Russell Heitman of Lake Forest, Ill., is named field manager, effective July 1, 1948. Heitman, with 20 years' experience in the newspaper business, had recently earned his master's degree at Northwestern University.

The Press Institute, last held in 1941, is revived and held May 21-22, 1948, at the University of Alabama in cooperation with the Department of Journalism and Extension Division. The 1947 institute is called the Doyle L. Buckles Memorial Press Institute in honor of APA's popular field manager who died in 1947.

Institute is not held again until spring 1950.

Summer convention, Panama City, Fla.
July 23-24, 1948

1949
J.C. Henderson, president
The Alexander City Outlook
78th annual press convention
Jan. 21-22, 1949
Birmingham

Group insurance plan for weeklies is adopted at the 1949 winter convention. APA enters into agreement with Employers Life Insurance Co., Birmingham, by which members may participate in group insurance program.

New publication, *The Alabama Publisher,* is established in 1949 by field manager J. Russell Heitman.

Summer convention, Point Clear
Sept. 9-10, 1949

Summer convention at the Grand Hotel in Baldwin County is "all play and no work," *AlaPressa* reports.

1950
Edmund R. (Ed) Blair, president
The Pell City News, The Southern Aegis, Ashville
79th annual press convention
Feb. 9-11, 1950
Montgomery

The Lee County Bulletin in Auburn wins national award for best editorial in a weekly newspaper by the National Editorial Association. Judges say, "*The Lee County Bulletin* deserved to win for the clear and well written editorial campaign which it carried on to repeal the poll tax and to break down the restrictions used to keep Negroes from voting."

Theme of the Doyle L. Buckles Memorial Press Institute at the University of Alabama, May 19-20, 1950, is "Building Alabama."

J. Russell Heitman resigns as field manager to become head of the Department of Journalism at Texas Technological College in Lubbock, effective September 1950.

Summer convention, Biloxi, Miss.
Aug. 4-5, 1950

Announcement is made at the 1950 summer convention that Jack Beisner has been appointed to succeed Russell Heitman as APA secretary-field manager. Beisner came to Alabama from *The Custer County Chief* at Broken Bow, Neb.

1951
Clarence B. Hanson Jr. president
The Birmingham News
80th annual press convention
Jan. 26-27, 1951
Birmingham

Delegates to 1951 convention vote to review APA constitution. Delegates also approve recommendation from Executive Committee to set up a three-person committee to take whatever steps necessary to incorporate a profit-making business affiliate to handle intrastate advertising for APA members. Alabama Newspaper Advertising Service, a one-order, one-bill ad placement service, is established.

Following a board of directors meeting, APA officers are authorized to incorporate the Press Association as a non-profit trade association under the laws of the state. Application for incorporation is filed by field manager Jack Beisner in Tuscaloosa County probate judge's office on Feb. 26, 1951, one month after the action is authorized by APA delegates at their 80th annual convention in Birmingham.

New contract is approved between APA and the University of Alabama to allow the field manager "more free time for APA work and eliminate his teaching duties."

The Alabama Publisher is changed from a quarterly to a monthly publication in 1951.

Agreement is reached between APA board of directors and L.O. Brackeen, director of publicity at Alabama Polytechnic Institute, Auburn, for compilation and preparation of a history of APA from 1871 to 1951.

Incoming APA president Clarence B. Hanson Jr. of *The Birmingham News* names committee to establish a business affiliate for APA. Members of the committee, as incorporators for the affiliate, Alabama Newspaper Advertising Service Inc. (ANAS), are E.H. (Ed) Pierce, *The Mountain Eagle*, Jasper, president; Bonnie D. Hand, *The LaFayette Sun*, vice president; and Edmund R. (Ed) Blair, *The Pell City News*, secretary-treasurer.

ANAS officers enter agreement with Jack Beisner to be manager of ANAS, and to be assistant secretary-treasurer.

ANAS is incorporated on Feb. 12, 1951, and goes into operation in spring 1951. Beginning April 1, 1951, ANAS begins servicing newspaper advertising orders.

Summer convention, Mobile
Jan. 21-23, 1951

1952
Cecil H. Hornady, president
The Talladega News
81st annual press convention
Jan. 17-19, 1952
Montgomery

Delegates approve dues increase.

Mimeographed copy of history of Alabama Press Association, 1871-1951, is distributed by L.O. Brackeen, director of publicity at Alabama Polytechnic Institute, Auburn.

Alabama Clipping Bureau, which becomes a profitable sideline to ANAS, is established.

APA officers in 1952 take as their goal making membership the highest in the Press Association's history.

Freedom of Information Committee is established in 1952, led by James E. (Jimmy) Mills, editor of the *Birmingham Post-Herald*.

Summer convention, Panama City, Fla.
July 10-12, 1952

Of the 22 living APA presidents, 11 are present and receive Past President lapel pins at the 1952

summer convention, presented by master of ceremonies Jep V. Greer of *The Sylacauga News*.

Board of directors meets and approves establishment of an Executive Committee to act in the name of the board.

1953
William E. (Bill) Brooks Jr. president
The Brewton Standard
82nd annual press convention
Jan. 22-24, 1953
Birmingham

Delegates to 1953 winter convention approve reestablishment of Better Newspaper Contest. First winners are announced at 1954 summer convention in Biloxi.

Legislative activities occupy the time of officers, secretary-field manager and Legislative Committee in 1953. "Statement of legislative policy" is adopted at the 1953 winter convention stating that APA "will never advocate or seek passage of any legislation which (a) will give special privilege to the newspaper industry or its members, or (b) will produce revenue for newspapers without rendering a distinct and beneficial public service."

Although clipping service has not developed into a good revenue producer in 1953, ANAS has a good year. Volume of advertising handled more than doubles from 1952, and in late 1953 a full-time assistant manager is hired to spend majority of the time selling advertising.

Summer convention, Mobile
July 16-18, 1953

1954
Steele E. McGrew, president
The Limestone Democrat
The Alabama Courier, Athens
83rd annual press convention
Jan. 21-23, 1954
Montgomery

APA minutes reflect that "for the first time, the members made special plans for their wives. In appreciation of the many wonderful ladies who attend the conventions and help in so many ways to make the Association what it is today, the APA awarded prizes for their attendance."

ANAS has most successful year to date in 1954 with 64 percent gross increase in receipts over 1953.

Summer convention, Biloxi, Miss.
July 22-24, 1954

The Better Newspaper Contest, discontinued in 1947, is reinstituted in 1954. *The Monroe Jour-*

nal in Monroeville and *The Mountain Eagle* in Jasper win first place awards.

1955
George H. Watson, president
The Shades Valley Sun, Homewood
84th annual press convention
Jan. 20-22, 1955
Huntsville

In 1955 APA surpasses all previous membership figures. Increase includes a substantial jump in number of weekly newspapers — from 78 in 1954, to 112 in 1955.

Legislative Committee chairman Harold S. May of *The Florence Herald* reports that "the committee had been faced with more anti-newspaper legislation than had ever been considered by the Alabama Legislature previously, with unique success — all measures the APA Legislative Committee desired to have amended were so amended, and anti-newspaper measures the APA wished to defeat were defeated, and almost all legislation the APA committee favored was passed."
Summer convention, Fairhope
July 21-23, 1955

1956
Ben G. George, president
The Demopolis Times
85th annual press convention
Jan. 19-21, 1956
Birmingham

More than 200 delegates attend 1956 winter convention. Past APA presidents are presented gavels.

A legislative success in 1956 is the successful fight against bills which would have enforced a 3 percent tax on advertising revenue and a measure designed to prohibit advertising of alcoholic beverages in newspapers.

Jack Beisner resigns as APA secretary-field manager effective Oct. 31, 1956, to accept appointment as press officer for overseas duty with U.S. Information Agency. Jones W. Giles, assistant manager, is appointed acting manager.
Summer convention, Mobile
July 19-21, 1956

1957
George M. Cox, president
The Mobile Press Register
86th annual press convention
Jan. 10-12, 1957
Montgomery

On the legislative front, 1957 is "a trying year for the APA," president George M. Cox of *The*

Mobile Press Register reports at 86th annual convention. "We were shot at from all directions, but the Legislative Committee again came through."

Special committee is set up by Alabama Milk Control Board to study possible revision of the board's controls on milk advertising after APA charges that advertising of milk distributors is being censored. APA asks for reversal of Milk Control Board policy.

Tuscaloosa News publisher and editor Buford Boone, an active APA member, is honored in 1957 for his editorials written during integration at the University of Alabama. He becomes the second Pulitzer Prize recipient ever in Alabama. Boone follows Grover C. Hall Sr. of *The Montgomery Advertiser* as the second Alabamian to win the highest award in American journalism. Cited is Boone's Feb. 5, 1956, editorial, "What A Price for Peace," concerning the efforts of Autherine Lucy to gain admission to the University of Alabama.

Jones W. Giles is named secretary-manager of APA in 1957, and an assistant manager is hired to work primarily with the Department of Journalism and Extension Division at the University of Alabama in the journalism field. This is done to meet the University's requirement that the secretary-field manager have the academic qualifications to teach journalism courses.

John Edward Weems, former Texas newspaper man and journalism teacher, is appointed assistant APA manager and assistant professor in University of Alabama Department of Journalism. Weems' duties include editing *The Alabama Publisher*, which he assumes with September 1957 issue.
Summer convention, Edgewater Park, Miss.
Aug. 8-10, 1957

1958
C.G. Thomason, president
The Industrial Press, Ensley
87th annual press convention
Feb. 6-8, 1958
Tuscaloosa

Field manager Jones W. Giles reports a marked increase in functions of the APA to delegates at the 1958 winter convention. Membership reaches new high, with president George M. Cox of *The Mobile Press Register* reporting that paid membership for 1957 is 163.

JoAnn Flirt, a reporter with *The Montgomery Advertiser*, is named APA assistant manager in September 1958. Field manager Jones Giles says

that one of Flirt's main duties is editing *The Alabama Publisher.*
Summer convention, Lookout Mountain, Tenn.
June 26-28, 1958

1959
William M. (Bill) Stewart, president
The Monroe Journal, **Monroeville**
88th annual press convention
Jan. 22-24, 1959
Birmingham

Resolution is introduced by Col. Harry M. Ayers of *The Anniston Star* that blasts a Washington, D.C. newspaper for refusing to print a pro-segregation letter as paid advertising is adopted by 1959 winter convention delegates. Resolution condemns *The Washington Post* and *Times-Herald* for refusing to carry "the Putman Letter" as paid advertising. ("The Putnam letter" was a letter to President Dwight Eisenhower by Carleton Putnam, a retired Washington executive, criticizing the U.S. Supreme Court decisions requiring racial integration of public schools.)

Resolution calling for an "AlabamaNewspaper Hall of Fame is introduced in 1959 by L.O. Brackeen, director of publicity at Alabama Polytechnic Institute, Auburn, and Webb Stanley, *The Greenville Advocate.* Resolution is adopted suggesting that a committee work with the Department of Archives and History in Montgomery to establish a permanent "Hall of Fame," or some other suitable method of honoringAlabama newspapers.
Summer convention, Dauphin Island
June 11-13, 1959

Delegates approve plans for the Alabama Newspaper Hall of Honor. Four outstanding editors will be honored at the 1960 annual convention and two each future year.

Committee meeting at Dauphin Island recommends four individuals to be honored for induction in 1960: Hunter Howell Golson, *The Wetumpka Herald*; Frazier Titus Raiford, *The Selma Times-Journal*, William Wallace Screws, *The Montgomery Advertiser*; and James Berney Stanley, *The Greenville Advocate.*

Legislation adversely affecting newspapers is discussed.

L.O. Brackeen of Alabama Polytechnic Institute, who had written original "History of the Alabama Press Association, 1871-1951," announces revision of the history, from 1871 to 1959, to be distributed at 1960 convention.

1960
James E. (Jimmy) Mills, president
Birmingham Post-Herald
89th annual press convention
Feb. 9-11, 1960
Montgomery

Alabama Gov. John Patterson and Tennessee Gov. Buford Ellington address 1960 convention delegates.

L.O. Brackeen, director of publicity at Auburn University, officiates during ceremonies installing first members of Alabama Newspaper Hall of Honor — James Berney Stanley, *The Greenville Advocate*; William Wallace Screws, *The Montgomery Advertiser*; Frazier Titus Raiford, *The Selma Times-Journal*; and Howell Hunter Golson, *The Wetumpka Herald.*
Summer convention, Dauphin Island
June 14-18, 1960

1961
Harold S. May, president
The Florence Herald
90th annual press convention
Feb. 9-11, 1961
Huntsville

Delegates to 1961 convention receive day-long tour of Redstone Arsenal and George Marshall Space Flight Center.

Legislative Committee is successful in 1961 legislative session of helping kill a bill which would have prohibited advertising of alcoholic beverages in daily or weekly newspapers.
Summer convention, Dauphin Island
July 13-15, 1961

1962
J. Glenn Stanley, president
The Greenville Advocate
91st annual press convention
Feb. 8-10, 1962
Birmingham

Delegates to 1962 convention adopt plan to secure a salesman, with headquarters in Birmingham, to sell advertisers of Alabama and adjoining states on Alabama newspapers. APA incoming president Glenn Stanley, *The Greenville Advocate*, comments: "It is going to cost money. But that money is an investment."

APA enters court case in 1962 in which James E. (Jimmy) Mills, editor of the *Birmingham Post-Herald*, is charged with violating Alabama's election law by electioneering on election day. APA submits amicus curiae (friend of the court) brief maintaining that Mills should be acquitted. Mills is charged with violation of Alabama's Corrupt Practices Act and that he "did electioneer or solicit for and in support of a proposition that was being voted on."

"In our judgment we have violated no law," Mills says. "The editorial complained of was fair comment on a question of vital public interest. Had we failed to make it we would have been guilty of defaulting on our responsibility as a newspaper to the people of Birmingham and the area surrounding it."

Summer convention, Florence
July 12-14, 1962

1963
Herve Charest Jr., president
The Tallassee Tribune
92nd annual press convention
Feb. 21-23, 1963
Montgomery

Gov. George C. Wallace addresses 1963 convention delegates. Editors and publishers comment they are surprised how "temperate" Wallace was in his speech. "I was most pleased with his speech," says Jimmy Mills, editor of the *Birmingham Post-Herald*. "It was much more temperate than I had expected. Perhaps we have been over-exaggerating the governor's attitude on the race issue."

Charles I. Reynolds, manager of Alabama Newspaper Advertising Service, is introduced at 1963 convention. Every newspaper in state, with exception of three small dailies, pledge support to the sales program designed to bring new advertising to ANAS newspapers. Reynolds resigns after several months. Sales committee of ANAS comments that the salary paid Reynolds and the expense incurred during his two and a half months were "the best investment" that ANAS and APA had ever made.

E. Hal Davidson joins APA staff as ANAS salesman in September 1963.

Delegation of Alabama daily and weekly newspaper publishers attends luncheon at the White House with President John F. Kennedy. The luncheon is one in a series of luncheons which the president held with leaders of the press from various states. Racial outbreaks in Birmingham dominate "at least 99 percent" of the discussion with President Kennedy, says APA president Herve Charest Jr. of *The Tallassee Tribune*.

Summer convention, Dauphin Island
July 18-20, 1963

1964
E.M. (Sparky) Howell, president
The Onlooker, Foley
93rd annual press convention
Feb. 6-8, 1964
Tuscaloosa

Delegates to 1964 convention adopt a resolution endorsing fund-raising campaign to bring Battleship "USS Alabama back" to permanent home in Port of Mobile.

APA field manager Jones W. Giles misses Tuscaloosa convention because of severe case of pneumonia and is granted leave of absence by APA board of directors.

An achievement of the Legislative Committee led by Bonnie D. Hand of *The LaFayette Sun* is securing passage of an increase in legal advertising rates.

Permanent site for Alabama Newspaper Hall of Honor is established at Auburn University Ralph B. Draughon Library in fall 1964 as memorial to the late L.O. Brackeen, long-time APA historian and Auburn University news bureau director.

Summer convention, Decatur
July 23-25, 1964

1965
Ralph W. Callahan, president
The Anniston Star
94th annual press convention
Feb. 11-13, 1965
Birmingham

APA field manager Jones W. Giles reports at 1965 convention that membership fell from 152 to 148 in 1964 because of mergers and discontinuance of some publications. Membership includes 20 daily newspapers and 90 weeklies.

Guest speakers at Birmingham convention include Gov. George C. Wallace and nationally syndicated newspaper columnist Ann Landers.

A voluntary program of employee insurance which will be made available to APA members by American Fidelity Assurance Co. is outlined to convention delegates.

Resolution on journalism education is adopted by delegates. Resolution pledges APA's support in promoting recruitment of young Alabamians for careers in journalism.

APA president Ralph W. Callahan, *The Anniston Star*, appoints committee to study and recommend improvements both in APA and ANAS.

APA field manager Jones W. Giles resigns effective April 30, 1965.

APA takes stand in fall of 1965 opposing proposed speaker ban forbidding Communists from speaking at Alabama colleges and universities. "The Alabama Press Association is firmly and positively opposed to the communist ideology," says APA president Ralph W. Callahan. "But we cannot condone any attempt to curb free speech and free expression in Alabama."

Summer convention, Decatur
July 22-24, 1965

1966
Edward A. (Ed) Dannelly Jr., president
The Andalusia Star-News
95th annual press convention
Feb. 10-12, 1966
Birmingham

Services to APA members suffer during latter part of 1965 and early 1966 as the Press Association is without a secretary-field manager.

ANAS president W.H. (Bill) Metz of the *Birmingham Post-Herald* announces during business meeting of 1966 convention the hiring of a salesman during the Alabama election campaign year, and that ANAS is in good financial shape.

Reviewing APA's accomplishments, Ralph W. Callahan of *The Anniston Star*, outgoing APA president, says major problems facing the APA is hiring a secretary-manager to replace Jones Giles who resigned in 1965.

Callahan makes recommendations for APA goals in 1966: Work with Dr. Frank Rose, University of Alabama president, to secure new journalism building; work out joint summer meeting with Alabama Associated Press Association; effect immediate improvement in the APA quarters at the University of Alabama; meet with APA auditor to work out more detailed and comprehensive financial reports; and continue to search for qualified APA manager.

James W. (Jim) Hall Jr., a graduate of the University of Alabama who was in public relations work in New Orleans, is named APA secretary-manager and begins work on May 1, 1966. With appointment of new manager in 1966, APA begins process of revitalization that is not fully realized until the next year.

U.S. Supreme Court rules in 1966 to strike the Alabama law forbidding the state's newspapers from publishing election day editorials.

Summer convention, Kowaliga Beach
(near Alexander City)
July 14-16, 1966

1967
Porter Harvey, president
The Advertiser-Gleam, Guntersville
96th annual press convention
Jan. 26-28, 1967
Mobile

Convention delegates hear panel discussion on offset printing. Porter Harvey, *The Advertiser-Gleam*, Guntersville, moderates panel for weekly publishers and Barrett C. Shelton Jr., *The Decatur Daily*, moderates discussion for daily newspapers.

James E. (Jimmy) Mills, who had recently retired as editor of the *Birmingham Post-Herald*, is chiefly responsible for resolution adopted at the 1967 convention which states the APA's determination that both the fair trial and fair press be protected — establishing the APA's position.

Past APA presidents are honored in 1967 with unveiling of "Past Presidents Gallery" in central office of University of Alabama campus. Collection is incomplete, with pictures available of only 27 of the 72 past presidents.

Summer convention, Florence
July 13-15, 1967

1968
W.H. (Bill)Metz, president
Birmingham Post-Herald
97th annual press convention
Feb. 8-11, 1968
Montgomery

A Code of Ethics is among the final items given approval at the 1968 winter convention. Code calls for upgrading profession of journalism and newspaper content. Code deals with advertising as well as editorial and news content.

James E. (Jimmy) Mills, retired editor of the *Birmingham Post-Herald*, objects to the code on the grounds that "every editor and publisher in the business has his own code of ethics," and "I don't think we need a code to say we are honest men of integrity. I don't think we need to apologize for what the newspapers have stood for all these years." Outgoing APA president Porter Harvey, *The Advertiser-Gleam*, Guntersville, says the code "should not be interpreted as an apology, but merely as a written statement of beliefs."

Delegates to 1968 convention vote to take steps to form APA Journalism Foundation to improve quality and quantity of young men and women entering the newspaper field. Setting up a corporation to establish the Journalism Foundation is approved by convention delegates. Committee headed by H. Brandt Ayers, *The Anniston Star*, initiates proceedings for establishing the Journalism Foundation in 1966. Journalism Foundation is chartered in July 1968.

Summer convention, Nassau, the Bahama Islands
July 11-14, 1968

1969
Joel P. Smith, president
The Eufaula Tribune
98th annual press convention
Feb. 13-15, 1969
Huntsville

APA Journalism Foundation president H. Brandt Ayers, *The Anniston Star*, announces at 1969 Huntsville convention the establishment of Journalism Foundation and start of fund solicitation campaign.

APA, along with Southern Newspaper Publishers Association, enters as a friend of the court in a suit by *The Anniston Star* against Anniston city officials. Suit brought by *The Star* seeks access to city records. Suit is settled in favor of *The Star*. City is ordered to open up its records to the newspaper and to pay court costs.

New service offered to APA members is book service. Through the service, members may purchase best sellers at 15 percent discount.

APA wages legislative battle over attempts to pass local laws doing away with necessity of publishing voter lists. APA Legislative Committee also objects to method used by a House committee in approving a series of bills which would allow cities to adopt proposed building and zoning codes without publishing them in full in a newspaper. The committee reported out the bills in a secret session.

"In effect, what the House committee has done is approve a set of bills which would make it much harder for the people to find out what their own city hall is doing, and have done it in a manner that attempts to prevent the people from knowing what they did," says Legislative Committee chairman Barrett C. Shelton Jr., *The Decatur Daily*.

Offset printing seminar is held in May 1969 with cooperation of suppliers of equipment.

More than 60 APA members and guests attend sessions in plant of *The Cullman Times*.

Summer convention, Point Clear
July 17-19, 1969

1970
Karl Elebash Jr. president
The Graphic, Tuscaloosa
99th annual press convention
Feb. 12-14, 1970
Tuscaloosa

New feature at 1970 convention is "$1.00 Half Hour" at which Herve Charest Jr., *The Tallassee Tribune*, and Ed Dannelly, *The Andalusia Star-News*, pass out dollar bills for every idea that could be used by other editors and publishers.

University of Alabama president Dr. David Mathews, luncheon speaker, says two objectives of his administration are to "seek accreditation of the journalism program as an immediate goal" and to "try to save Woods Hall for another 100 years."

"Unrelieved concern" for the lack of accreditation and the poor housing of the University's journalism department in Woods Hall is expressed by APA delegates attending the Tuscaloosa convention.

Third Pulitzer Prize ever awarded in Alabama is presented in 1970 to Harold E. Martin, editor and publisher of *The Montgomery Advertiser* and *Alabama Journal*, in recognition of Martin's reporting which exposed and brought to a halt a commercial scheme using Alabama prisoners for drug experimentation.

Summer convention, Gulf Shores
July 23-25, 1970

1971
Robert Bryan, president
The Cullman Times
100th annual press convention
Feb. 11-13, 1971
Birmingham

APA Centennial Anniversary Convention is held Feb. 11-13, 1971, in Birmingham with past president Herve Charest Jr., retired publisher of *The Tallassee Tribune*, giving the keynote address. APA past presidents and oldest newspapers are recognized at the winter convention.

At the 1971 Alabama Newspaper Hall of Honor ceremony, a special program is published as a commemorative salute by Auburn University to those inducted and to the 100 years of the APA. The program includes photos and biographical

information on the 28 persons who had been inducted to the Newspaper Hall of Honor. Included in the Oct. 2, 1971, program is a message from APA president Robert Bryan, *The Cullman Times*, and the original resolution establishing the Hall of Honor.
Summer convention, Biloxi, Miss.
July 29-31, 1971

1972
W.E. (Gene) Hardin, president
The Greenville Advocate
101st annual press convention
Feb. 10-12, 1972
Mobile

APA agrees to terminate relationship with University of Alabama in 1972. Harold E. Martin, editor and publisher of *The Montgomery Advertiser*, reports in fall 1972 that taxpayer money is used to subsidize activities of the APA by paying half the salary of the APA manager and providing free office space.

APA begins rental agreement for office space occupied in Manly Hall on University campus and assumes full responsibility for APA manager's salary.
Summer convention, Disney World, Orlando, Fla.
July 20-22, 1972

1973
Ewell H. Reed, president
The Arab Tribune
102nd annual press convention
Feb. 8-10, 1973
Montgomery

APA officially ends ties with University of Alabama on Jan. 1, 1973. Outgoing APA president W.E. (Gene) Hardin, *The Greenville Advocate*, announces to APA membership that after Jan. 1, APA will be dependent only upon the membership for financial support.

Lease is signed by APA and University officials in which association agrees to pay $200 a month rent for space in Manly Hall on University campus. APA also assumes responsibility for all of the executive director's salary. Previously, the University had paid half the salary of the manager in return for services performed for the University.

In May 1973, APA moves from campus, to location on Queen City Avenue in Tuscaloosa. Board of directors discusses relocating the APA headquarters to either Birmingham or Montgomery. Office

remains in Tuscaloosa largely because of the difficulties involved in moving the clipping service.

Delegates to 1973 convention in Montgomery vote to double membership dues to finance independence of the Press Association.
Summer convention, Decatur
July 26-28, 1973

1974
Barrett C. Shelton Jr., president
The Decatur Daily
103rd annual press convention
Feb. 7-9, 1974
Huntsville

APA executive director James W. (Jim) Hall resigns, effective March 29, 1974. Stephen Bradley, who had been working in the public relations department of Shell Oil, becomes executive director on July 1, 1974.

Hall joins administrative staff of Troy State University later in 1974.

Gov. George C. Wallace delivers the keynote address at the 103rd annual convention in Huntsville in 1974. Delegates take side trips to the Space Center and to Jack Daniel's distillery in Lynchburg, Tenn., and Grand Ole Opry in Nashville.
Summer convention, Gulf Shores
July 18-20, 1974

1975
Orsen B. Spivey, president
The Geneva County Reaper, Geneva
104th annual press convention
Feb. 27-28, 1975
Birmingham

APA moves to new quarters on Tuscaloosa, Professional Plaza East, 921 Third Avenue East, Tuscaloosa, on May 5, 1975. Old address was 1925 Queen City Boulevard. Board of directors approved the move at the 1975 winter convention in Birmingham. "The present facilities are undesirable for several reasons and are not suited to the associations' needs," *AlaPressa* reports.
Summer convention, Point Aquarius Lodge and Country Club (near Pell City)
July 17-19, 1975

1976
Claude E. Sparks, president
The Franklin County Times, Russellville
105th annual press convention
Feb. 5-7, 1976
Mobile

Newspapers must be published 51 weeks with a Second Class mailing permit before they can print lucrative county voting lists, Circuit Judge Edgar Russell rules in Selma in April 1976. Russell said *The Wilcox American* in Camden cannot print voting lists in Wilcox County, and *The Selma News-Record* cannot do likewise in Dallas County, because the two papers are not old enough to meet state requirements for circulating voting lists. The cases were heard because two older newspapers, *The Wilcox Progressive Era* in Camden, and *The Selma Times-Journal* in Dallas County, protested awarding of the voting lists to the younger papers after they underbid the older papers for printing the lists.

Concerning the ruling, APA executive director Steve Bradley says that without the 51-week requirement, someone could start a newspaper just to publish the voting lists, and "the best interest of the public would not be served." Bradley tells *The Montgomery Advertiser* that "APA strongly opposes any attempt to place publications required by law in any newspaper not qualified to accept those notices" and that the APA would "fight any attempt to place those notices in an unqualified publication."

Mark L. Tucker, *The Chilton County News*, and Bonnie D. Hand, *The LaFayette Sun*, are inducted into the Alabama Newspaper Hall of Honor on the Auburn University campus Oct. 16, 1976, in a special ceremony that includes dedication of a permanent Newspaper Hall of Honor room at Ralph B. Draughon Library on the Auburn campus. A $5,000 grant from the APA Journalism Foundation and matching Auburn University funds make it possible to convert a little-used library classroom into a Newspaper Hall of Honor and reading room.

Billy Jack Jones, well-known Auburn historian and collector of Alabama newspapers, is appointed historian for the APA and curator for the new Newspaper Hall of Honor and reading room.

1976 summer convention, Gulf Shores
July 15-17, 1976

A resolution condemning action of the Alabama Public Service Commission is adopted unanimously in the closing session of the 1976 summer convention. The main thrust of the resolution protested the PSC's commitment "to a course designed to ultimately prevent Alabama Power Company from its constitutionally guaranteed right to advertise." The resolution also condemns those actions designed "to deny organizations under the Public Service Commission's jurisdiction their constitutionally guaranteed right to advertise information to customers and to the general public in the most cost-effective manner possible."

1977
Phillip A. Sanguinetti, president
The Anniston Star
106th annual press convention
March 11-13, 1977
Huntsville

106th annual convention, originally scheduled Jan. 20-22, 1977, is rescheduled to March 11-13, 1977, because of weather and road conditions.

1977 summer convention, Gulf Shores
Aug. 4-6, 1977

1978
E.R. (Bob) Morrissette Jr., president
The Atmore Advance
107th annual press convention
Feb. 24-26, 1978
Birmingham

APA executive director Steve Bradley resigns, effective July 21, 1978, to become assistant vice president-public information, with Alabama Power Co. William F. (Bill) O'Connor Jr., director of communications for state Department of Mental Health in Montgomery, is named APA executive director on July 24, 1978.

The Montgomery Advertiser and *Alabama Journal* again become active members of APA in 1977 after publisher Harold E. Martin resigns from the two papers. He is succeeded by his brother, James G. (Jim) Martin. The two papers withdrew membership from APA sometime prior to 1972. *The Advertiser* had reported in 1972 that the University was not only paying half the salary for the APA manager, but also was providing free office space.

Summer convention, Gulf Shores
July 14-16, 1978

1979
James W. (Jim) Oakley Jr., president
The Centreville Press
108th annual press convention
Feb. 16-18, 1979
Mobile

Delegates to 108th annual convention in 1979 hear speeches by Gov. Fob James, U.S. Sen. Howell Heflin and newspaper executive Rhea Eskew.

The first full-time advertising manager, Craig Woodward, is hired in 1979.

Summer convention, Gulf Shores
July 26-28, 1979

1980
Shelton Prince Jr., president
The Daily Mountain Eagle, Jasper
The Selma Times-Journal
109th annual press convention
Feb. 22-24, 1980
Huntsville

Speakers at the 109th annual convention in 1980 include Jody Powell, press secretary to President Jimmy Carter, and U.S. Sen. Donald Stewart.

Summer convention, Destin, Fla.
July 18-20, 1980

The 1980 summer convention is moved to Sandestin in Destin, Fla., because of damage to Gulf State Lodge in Gulf Shores, caused by Hurricane Frederic.

1981
Marcia M. Sears, president
The Shelby County Reporter, Columbiana
110th annual press convention
Feb. 27-March 1, 1981
Montgomery

Marcia M. Sears, editor of *The Shelby County Reporter* in Columbiana, becomes first woman president of APA.

Summer convention, Gulf Shores
July 24-26, 1981

1982
Don Woodward, president
The Advertiser-Gleam, Guntersville
111th annual press convention
Feb. 19-21, 1982
Birmingham

A dispute over publication of the voter's list in Baldwin County results in legal action in October 1982 between Gulf Coast Media Inc. and The Mobile Press-Register Inc. A declaratory judgment is sought by Gulf Coast Media in Baldwin County Circuit Court to determine whether *The Baldwin Press Register* meets all requirements necessary to carry legal advertising. Publication of the voters list is ultimately awarded to Gulf Coast Media, publishers of *The Baldwin Times* in Bay Minette, *The Independent* in Robertsdale, *The Onlooker* in Foley and *The Eastern Shore Courier* in Fairhope.

The four papers are permitted to publish the voters list under the stipulation that the list be published at no cost to the county unless the declaratory judgment ruling favored Gulf Coast Media.

Gulf Coast Media, in its written complaint, states "that the defendant, The Mobile Press Register Inc., is a corporation organized under the laws of the State of Alabama with its principal place of business in Mobile, Mobile County, Alabama." A date for hearing the case was not set.

Bill O'Connor, APA executive director, is named assistant to the chancellor for university relations, according to Dr. Thomas Bartlett, chancellor of the University of Alabama System. O'Connor assumes his new post Dec. 15, 1982. O'Connor had served as executive director of APA since August 1978.

William B. (Bill) Keller is named executive director of APA to succeed O'Connor. Keller, who had served as director of information services for the University of Montevallo, assumes the APA post Jan. 3, 1983.

Summer convention, Gulf Shores
July 23-25, 1982

1983
William J. (Bill) Hearin, president
The Mobile Press Register
112th annual press convention
Feb. 25-27, 1983
Mobile

The Coalition for the Preservation of Alabama Newspapers receives a $10,000 grant in 1983 to develop a statewide plan to preserve Alabama's newspaper files. Concern over potential loss of Alabama's unique newspapers led scholars, librarians, newspaper executives and archivists as well as leaders of colleges and universities to form a cooperative venture to preserve the newspapers. Work on the project begins July 15, 1983, with a survey to determine newspaper files held in Alabama.

APA and *The Abbeville Herald* file a complaint in 1983 against the Henry County circuit judge who cited an Abbeville woman with contempt of court for writing a Letter to the Editor critical of the judge. APA files the complaint with the Alabama Judiciary Inquiry Commission. Although Judge Billy Joe Sheffield withdraws his contempt order, he implies in his recision order that he could use the power of his office to stifle criticism.

Alabama Newspaper Hall of Honor inducts its first black newspaper executive, Frank P. Thomas Jr. of *The Mobile Beacon*, on Oct. 22, 1983. Other inductee is W. Emmett Brooks, editor and publisher of *The Brewton Standard*, who was APA president in 1929-1930.

Summer convention, Gulf Shores
July 15-17, 1983

1984
Luke Slaton, president
The Moulton Advertiser
113th annual press convention
Feb. 24-26, 1984
Huntsville

Delegates tour Alabama Space and Rocket Center, hear an update on politics by Lt. Gov. Bill Baxley, and attend a mock libel trial conducted by Cumberland School of Law.

Baldwin County Circuit Judge Henry J. Wilters Jr. rules in March 1984 in favor of The Mobile Press Register Inc., over Gulf Coast Media in a case involving publication of Baldwin County legal advertising. Gulf Coast Media, publishers of the four weekly newspapers in Baldwin County, had asked for a declaratory judgment concerning publication of legal advertising from Baldwin County in *The Baldwin People*, distributed each week in Baldwin County in *The Mobile Press Register*. Gulf Coast Media maintains that *The Baldwin People* does not qualify to carry legal ads from Baldwin County because it does not meet all requirements of state law.

The dispute began in 1982, when *The Press Register* bid for publication of the Baldwin County voter's list to run in *The Baldwin People*, formerly *The Baldwin Press Register*. APA board of directors votes in April 1984 to ask the Alabama Supreme Court to help clear the confusion over which newspapers are eligible to publish legal advertising in particular counties. In a called meeting, the board unanimously approves a motion to ask legal counsel David Olive to prepare a friend-of-the-court brief to submit in the dispute between Gulf Coast Media in Baldwin County and *The Mobile Press Register* in Mobile County.

The Mobile Press Register with APA immediate past president and chairman of the board William J. (Bill) Hearin as publisher, drops its membership in APA.

The former publisher of a prize-winning weekly newspaper is named ANAS manager in June 1984. Mike Ryland, former publisher of *The Independent* in Robertsdale, joins APA staff June 11, 1984. During Ryland's first week he worked with former manager Craig Woodward, who joined the firm of Gillis, Townsend and Riley in Birmingham as an account executive.

A program to produce new revenue for Alabama newspapers and provide a unique service to newspaper readers is tentatively approved by board members of the Alabama Newspaper Advertising

Service in 1984. At a Nov. 30, 1984, meeting, ANAS board members direct ANAS to survey member newspapers to determine how many papers are interested in participating in a statewide classified advertising network. The board agrees to discuss the program again at its meeting during the APA winter convention in February 1985.

Summer convention, Gulf Shores
July 20-22, 1984

1985
Mike Breedlove, president
The South Alabamian, **Jackson**
114th annual press convention
Feb. 22-24, 1985
Montgomery

Delegates hold session at 1985 convention on meeting direct-mail competition.

Daily and weekly newspapers in Alabama begin a new statewide classified advertising service the week of June 16, 1985. A total of 94 newspapers join the Alabama Statewide Classified Advertising Network (ALA-SCAN). The network enables an advertiser to purchase a classified ad in all 94 newspapers with one buy, by contacting any participating newspaper or the ANAS office. ANAS is the business affiliate of APA. Alabama joins many other state press associations already offering the service.

Alabama Supreme Court unanimously rules that a weekly supplement to *The Mobile Press Register* cannot publish legal notice advertisements from Baldwin County because it is not a separate newspaper. The court's opinion in May 1985 overturns a ruling by a Baldwin County circuit judge who said the supplement, *The Baldwin People*, qualified to publish legal advertisements under Alabama law. Gulf Coast Media Inc., owner of the four newspapers in Baldwin County, had appealed the lower court ruling.

Summer convention, Gulf Shores
July 12-14, 1985

1986
Jay Thornton, president
The Daily Home, **Talladega**
115th annual press convention
Feb. 28-March 2, 1986
Birmingham

Delegates hear candidates for governor and lieutenant governor. Sessions are also held on developments at the federal level affecting newspapers — developments such as forecasts of even higher postal rates and the new hazardous substance labeling requirements.

Board of directors adopts a resolution in 1986 endorsing a monument to late Supreme Court Justice Hugo Black. Resolution notes that Black is the state's only native to become a member of the U.S. Supreme Court and that he was a staunch defender of freedom of the press.

The Daily Home in Talladega becomes the first Alabama daily to increase the newsrack single copy price to 50 cents. Publisher Jay Thornton says the increase in August 1986 is intended to combat the cost of stolen papers and to fight inflation.

Wiregrass Today, the first new Alabama daily in a number of years, publishes its first copy on Sunday, Nov. 2, 1986. Although seven dailies in Alabama converted from weekly or twice-weekly publication since 1970, *Wiregrass Today* is the first new Alabama newspaper to start as a daily in recent memory.

Decisions are made at a Dec. 5, 1986, APA board of directors meeting to sell the APA clipping service and to move Press Association headquarters to Birmingham. The 1986 decision ends discussions that began as early as 1973, when the APA office moved from the University of Alabama campus but remained in Tuscaloosa.

Summer convention, Gulf Shores
July 18-20, 1986

1987
Steve Stewart, president
The Monroe Journal, Monroeville
116th annual press convention
Feb. 20-22, 1987
Mobile

"Publishers can look forward to at least two programs that can more than pay for their trip to the convention," according to the October 1986 issue of *AlaPressa* promoting the 1987 convention. Jim Boone, president of Boone Newspapers Inc., headquartered in Tuscaloosa, leads a panel on cost-saving and revenue-generating techniques.

Two historic decisions are made by the Press Association in 1987: APA and its for-profit affiliate, the Alabama Newspaper Advertising Service, approve sale of the clipping service, and a move of the APA headquarters from Tuscaloosa to Birmingham. APA moves to new quarters in the Commerce Center on First Avenue North in Birmingham the weekend of May 29, 1987.

APA Clipping Bureau is sold to Magnolia Clipping Service of Jackson, Miss., on Jan. 1, 1987.

Magnolia, which opened an office in Tuscaloosa on Jan. 2, hired most of the APA Clipping Bureau's full-time and part-time employees.

APA Legal Hotline is established in 1987. Beginning in winter of 1987, Alabama newspaper executives are able to phone a law office in Montgomery for free legal advice. APA attorney Dennis Bailey and two other attorneys from the Montgomery firm of Rushton, Stakely, Johnston and Garrett are available during normal business hours to answer questions on routine media law matters.

Less than three weeks after the new Dothan daily celebrates its first anniversary, *Wiregrass Today* ceases publication. Publisher Wayne Chancey announces that stockholders of the new daily made the decision to publish the last edition on Nov. 19, 1987.

Summer convention, Perdido Beach
July 17-19, 1987

APA is one of the first organizations to meet at the Perdido Beach Hilton, the newest resort hotel, in 1987.

1988
Jack Venable, president
The Tallassee Tribune
117th annual press convention
Feb. 26-28, 1988
Huntsville

The 117th annual convention at the new Huntsville Marriott, next to the Alabama Space and Rocket Center, features two presidential candidates and marks the APA's first trade show in memory. The Rev. Pat Robertson, Republican presidential candidate, attends the Saturday night reception at the Space and Rocket Center and speaks briefly. Rep. Richard Gephart, D-Mo., speaks following the Sunday morning membership meeting

APA makes $10,000 donation in 1988 to Alabama Department of Archives and History to catalog and microfilm Alabama's newspapers. APA is part of the Coalition for the Preservation of Alabama Newspapers, which began coordinating the project in 1983.

A number of weeklies and small dailies increase their single copy price from 25 cents to 50 cents in 1988. "The days of 25-cent cups of coffee and 25-cent candy bars have passed, and so have the days of 25-cent newspapers," *The West Alabama Gazette* of Millport reports in a story announcing the price increase.

AlaPressa reports in its August 1988 issue that a committee of APA officers and presidents of Alabama Newspaper Advertising Service and APA Journalism Foundation, APA's affiliate organizations, are exploring options to buy or build office space for APA.

APA and ANAS, with a staff of four full-time employees and one part-time employee, were renting a 1,200 square foot office in downtown Birmingham. APA president Jack Venable of *The Tallassee Tribune*, who appointed the committee during the 1988 summer convention, says the committee is seeking expert opinion on the advantages and disadvantages of ownership. The APA staff began working with the committee to collect information on financing, ownership, space needs and other factors from other state press associations, as well as other in-state trade associations.

Alabama newspapers participating in ALA-SCAN, APA's statewide classified classified service, begin receiving the statewide classifieds already typeset in 1988. APA staff announces plans to begin electronic transmission of the ads to participating newspapers, computer to computer. ANAS sets a record in 1988 with 52 ads placed in one week.

Summer convention, Perdido Beach
July 15-17, 1988

1989
James E. (Jim) Jacobson, president
The Birmingham News
118th annual press convention
Feb. 17-18, 1989
Grand Hotel, Mobile Bay

APA's 1989 winter convention features second consecutive trade show and the first convention at the historic Grand Hotel since early 1970s.

Citing newsprint and production cost increases, Alabama newspapers, both weeklies and dailies, continue to raise single copy price to 50 cents in 1989.

Eleven daily and weekly Alabama newspaper executives travel to Washington, D.C., in 1989 in the APA's first group visit to the state's congressional delegation. The publishers discussed HR 2140, a bill to lift restrictions on the regional Bell phone companies. Publishers explain to congressional delegation that they support the Bell companies' efforts to convince Congress to take the lead in setting policy on the emerging issue. Publishers also urge congressmen to encourage the Bell companies to go ahead and set up new computer phone-access gateway systems to help create a demand and market for the computer-available information.

Summer convention, Perdido Beach
July 21-23, 1989

1990
Paul R. Davis, president
The Auburn Bulletin, The Lee County Eagle,
Auburn, and *The Tuskegee News*
119th annual press convention
Feb. 23-25, 1990
Auburn

Southern history writer Dr. Wayne Flynt of the Auburn University history department is Saturday luncheon speaker at the 1990 convention in Auburn. Flynt discusses Alabama history and his view of the future of the state, as well as the role of Alabama newspapers in the state's history and the role newspaper could play in guiding the state's future development.

On Oct. 19, 1990, a group of Alabama editors and reporters flies from Miami to Havana, Cuba, to start a week-long APA Study Tour. It marks the fourth visit to Cuba in APA history. While not on the travel agenda, the 10 newspaper editors see Fidel Castro in 1990 during a dedication ceremony for a new school for the blind. Trip includes a visit to the journalism school at the University of Havana and a visit to the offices of Cuba's largest newspaper, *Granma*.

Bill Keller, APA executive director since January 1983, joins staff of Consolidated Publishing Co. in Anniston on Nov. 12, 1990, as associate publisher of *The Daily Home* in Talladega and assistant to the publisher of *The Anniston Star*. APA president Paul Davis, *The Auburn Bulletin*, says APA Executive Committee will meet with presidents of ANAS and APA Journalism Foundation to begin search for Keller's successor

Michael T. (Mike) Ryland is named acting director during an Oct. 11, 1990, meeting of APA Executive Committee. Ryland was manager of Alabama Newspaper Advertising Service. Ryland becomes acting APA director effective Nov. 9, 1990.

Summer convention, Perdido Beach
July 13-15, 1990

1991
Terry Everett, president
The Union Springs Herald
120th annual press convention
Feb. 23-26, 1991
Riverchase Galleria, Wynfrey Hotel, Hoover

Effective Jan. 1, 1991, Mike Ryland is named APA executive director, and Felicia Mason is promoted to manager of ANAS. Mason has served as ANAS sales/marketing representative since 1987. Search committee selects Ryland after interviewing finalists for the job in December 1990. Brad English is named new sales and marketing advertising representative of ANAS to fill the vacancy created when Mason is named ANAS manager.

The Birmingham News becomes second Alabama newspaper in three years to win a Pulitzer Prize. News editorial writers Ron Casey, Harold Jackson and Joey Kennedy are awarded the 1991 Pulitzer Prize for a series of editorials on tax reform in Alabama. *The Alabama Journal* in Montgomery won a Pulitzer for public service in 1988 for its series on infant mortality.

Two other Alabama newspapers had previously been awarded Pulitzers in Alabama newspaper history — *The Montgomery Advertiser* had received two, and *The Tuscaloosa News* had received one.

Summer convention, Perdido Beach
July 12-14, 1991

1992
Charles Land, president
The Tuscaloosa News
121st annual press convention
Feb. 21-23, 1992
Tuscaloosa

APA winter convention returns to Tuscaloosa for first time since 1970.

APA executive director Mike Ryland dies March 5, 1992, at age 34. Ryland collapsed while sitting in the House gallery at the State House in Montgomery during a debate about taxes. The House adjourned for an hour in his memory, and the Senate paused for silent prayer. APA board of directors establishes Michael Ryland Family Trust and makes $12,000 donation to get it started. Ryland's wife, Julie, was expecting their first child in August 1992.

Bill Keller returns as APA executive director on March 30, 1992. Keller, APA executive director from 1983 to November 1990, had joined Consolidated Publishing Co. in Anniston as associate publisher of *The Daily Home* in Talladega and assistant to the publisher of *The Anniston Star*.

The new chief executive officer, president and publisher of *The Mobile Press Register*, William Howard Bronson Jr., brings the Mobile dailies back into the APA in 1992. Former APA president William J. (Bill) Hearin, had dropped *The Press Register*'s membership in 1984 after the APA board of directors decided to file a neutral brief in a case involving the qualification of newspapers to publish legal notices. The brief asked the Alabama Supreme Court to clarify the law. Hearin was APA president in 1983-1984,

Having two corporations, a non-profit association and a for-profit affiliate, seemed inefficient, APA president and *Tuscaloosa News* publisher Charles Land said during a board meeting in 1992. ANAS president Jim Cox, publisher of *The Clarke County Democrat* in Grove Hill, agreed.

Land asks APA accountant Mike Echols and APA legal counsel Dennis Bailey to study the tax-related issues, and asks executive director Bill Keller to talk with other state press association managers.

APA members approve a change in ANAS bylaws during the 1992 summer convention. Effective February 1993 after the APA winter convention, membership of the new board of directors of Alabama Newspaper Advertising Service will be the same as the APA board. It was a governance structure already used by most state press associations and their business affiliates. APA and ANAS leaders say the change will mean clearer management of the association's income from ANAS services to help the association meet member needs. In recent years, with two different boards, the APA board had to go to the ANAS board to request money to support association programs.

ANAS was established by APA in 1951 after the Press Association had started making more income from its one bill, one check ad placement service. ANAS earned income for APA by paying a proportionate share of rent, salaries and other expenses. While expenses charged to ANAS reduced its taxable income, ANAS paid substantial state and federal income taxes. The third affiliated corporation, the APA Journalism Foundation, maintained a strict separation from the other corporations.

APA sponsors trip to Russia Aug. 23-31, 1992. *Gadsden Times* publisher Frank Helderman Jr. says the Russian people, despite their hardships, are open and friendly. "Frankly, I felt more welcome in Moscow and St. Petersburg than in many cities in my own country," Helderman says.

In December 1992, *Birmingham Post-Herald* editor Jimmy Denley is named to head a committee to study office space options for the APA office. Denley, who was also vice president of the APA Journalism Foundation, says the committee's first meeting will be in Tuscaloosa on Jan. 16, 1993, just before the UA-APA Day Program. The committee would study other rental options as well as possible building ownership. It would also study how the office space could be used for member services. In 1992 the APA was located on the 11th floor of a downtown office building.

Summer convention, Perdido Beach
July 10-12, 1992

The late Mike Ryland, former APA executive director who died unexpectedly on March 5, 1992, is honored at the summer convention. Ryland's wife, Julie, and his mother, Helen Ryland, are presented framed memorial resolutions from APA.

1993
Sam Harvey, president
The Advertiser-Gleam, Guntersville
122nd annual press convention
Feb. 19-21, 1993
Huntsville

AlaPressa reports in October 1993 issue that the APA office might move to its own building in 1994, "if the right building at the right price goes on the market." The APA and ANAS Executive Committees, meeting with the building-facilities committee, agree in principal that APA should buy its own building. The vote is unanimous. Committee members say the building should contain about 3,000 square feet of space and should contain a multi-purpose room large enough for board and committee meetings, advertising presentations and small workshops.

Alabama Journal executive editor Bill Brown goes in early on Friday, April 16, 1993, to see the last issue of *The Alabama Journal* printed with the headline, "Thanks for the Memories." The final issue reproduces a photograph of newsroom staff members taken when they learned they had won the Pulitzer Prize in 1988. *The Alabama Journal*, Montgomery's 104-year-old Pulitzer Prize-winning afternoon daily, merged with its sister morning publication, *The Montgomery Advertiser*, on April 19, 1993.

Publisher Richard H. (Dick) Amberg Jr. says the merger reflects national trends to strong morning newspapers. The combined newspaper is called *Montgomery Advertiser*, or more completely, the "*Montgomery Advertiser* Incorporating *The Alabama Journal*.*"

Alabama newspapers begin offering anonymous phone-in response columns in 1993. The "Sound-Off" type columns were started first at *The Mobile Press Register* and *The Arab Tribune*.

More ads show up on the front page of newspapers in 1993, a trend that design experts said was expected to increase. Mario Garcia, director of design and graphics at the Poynter Institute in St. Petersburg, Fla., says the 1990s will bring an increase in front page ads. Tradition held that page one ads take away from news content, but proponents say readers are just as interested in ads as they are in news.

Advertiser-Gleam publisher Porter Harvey of Guntersville, who celebrated his 90th birthday in May 1993, makes national news in the summer of 1993 when he bungee jumps from a 176-foot tower with an elastic cord attached to his back. Harvey had challenged other family members to join him in Chattanooga, Tenn., on Aug. 28, 1993, and 30 members of the family came, representing four generations and six states. Of the group, 16 bungee jumped, including his son, Sam Harvey, *Advertiser-Gleam* editor, and grandson, Craig Woodward, a past APA advertising manager.

Summer convention, Perdido Beach
July 16-18, 1993

1994
Linda H. Breedlove, president
The South Alabamian, Jackson
123rd annual press convention
Feb. 25-27, 1994
Mobile

Publishers and editors hear the latest trends in newspaper ties to electronic information delivery during the 1994 winter convention in Mobile. Speakers discuss how newspapers will be affected by changes in the information selling business, especially selling information by telephone.

Linda H. Breedlove, associate publisher of *The South Alabamian* in Jackson, becomes second woman to be elected APA president. The first woman president was Marcia M. Sears, former publisher of *The Shelby County Reporter* in Columbiana, in 1981.

AlaPressa reports in its January 1994 issue that if inspections, legal reviews and other details go as planned, the APA Journalism Foundation will soon own a 22-year-old building in Homewood. The APA/ANAS staff would rent the second floor of the 5,100 square foot building on U.S. 31 from the Journalism Foundation, and a real estate company would rent the first floor.

On Saturday, April 25, 1994, movers loaded boxes and furniture in the old downtown Birmingham office of APA and moved them to the APA's new suburban location on U.S. 31 in Homewood on Independence Drive.

The move is the culmination of more than six years of on-again, off-again studies about the pros and cons of owning a building. Work on the moving project was coordinated with the APA building committee and approved by the Journalism Foundation board. Committee chairman Jimmy Denley of the *Birmingham Post-Herald* helped select the building. APA and ANAS pay rent to the Journalism Foundation, as does the first-floor tenant.

Former APA executive director Steve Bradley said in 1994 that Jim Boone, then publisher of *The Tuscaloosa News*, had suggested the same financial structure almost 20 years earlier — that the Journalism Foundation should own a building and rent space to APA and ANAS.

The Randolph Leader office in Roanoke becomes official headquarters for national news coverage of a Wedowee High School principal and the controversy tied to his comments about interracial dating by students.

The APA 125th anniversary committee meets in September 1994 to begin plans for Press Association's anniversary celebration in 1996. Organizational meeting is held at APA headquarters in Birmingham Sept. 16, 1994. Committee agrees that compilation of APA history be given highest priority. Journalism professor Ed Williams of Auburn University agrees to write updated history.

Summer convention, Perdido Beach
July 22-24, 1994

1995
Doug Pearson, president
The Daily Mountain Eagle, **Jasper**
124th annual press convention
Feb. 24-26, 1995
Riverchase Galleria, Wynfrey Hotel, Hoover

Gov.-elect Fob James leads discussion on upcoming four years of state government during 1995 winter convention.

Winter convention delegates get chance to look over photographs and publications from APA's past. 125th anniversary committee has display of APA artifacts and historic documents.

Most weekly and daily newspapers begin cost-cutting measures to offset sharp increases in newsprint prices during 1996. By June 1995, newspapers are paying about 80 percent more for newsprint than in January 1994. One newsprint mill announced in June 1995 that it would raise the price of newsprint to $743.85 a metric ton, which nearly doubled the prevailing price in early 1994.

The Clanton Advertiser and *The Greenville Advocate* become the first newspapers in Alabama to sell non-weekend newspapers for more than 50 cents. Both raise single copy prices to 75 cents on June 1, 1995.

Two long-time APA leaders and past presidents die in 1995 — Bill Stewart, 74, president of *The Monroe Journal*, and Porter Harvey, 90, publisher of *The Advertiser-Gleam* in Guntersville.

Two Alabama dailies, *The Montgomery Advertiser* and *The Mobile Press Register*, are named finalists in Pulitzer Prize competition in 1995.

Summer convention, Perdido Beach
July 14-16, 1995

1996
Mike Kelley, president
The Clanton Advertiser
125th annual press convention, Montgomery
Feb. 23-25, 1996

History and the future of the newspaper industry are the focus of APA's 125th Anniversary Convention in 1996. Convention delegates gather in the same city where the Press Association was founded in 1872 as the Editors and Publishers Association of Alabama.

The convention begins on Friday, Feb. 23, 1996, with a reception at the Montgomery Museum of Art sponsored by *The Montgomery Advertiser*.

Saturday morning, two workshops reflect on the history of the APA. Historians and political scientists discuss the role that newspapers played in the state's history. In the second program, delegates review some leading newspaper law cases that started in Alabama and affected the entire country.

All day Saturday, the Alabama Department of Archives and History displays several historic newspapers in Alabama in the foyer outside the meeting area.

At Saturday's luncheon, delegates hear several of the state's senior members discuss how the business has changed over the years. The oldest participant is James E. (Jimmy) Mills, 95, retired editor of the *Birmingham Post-Herald*, and J.C. Henderson, 91, retired editor and publisher of *The*

Alexander City Outlook. Auburn University journalism professor Ed Williams, who was writing a new history of APA for the 125th anniversary in 1996, interviewed the senior members. The book was to be published later in 1996.

Special keepsake edition of *The Alabama Publisher* is published after the winter 1996 conventions. The special edition features photographs and stories about the 1996 conventions.

On Saturday afternoon, winter convention delegates tour *The Montgomery Advertiser's* new plant behind the convention hotel, the new Embassy Suites in downtown Montgomery.

On Saturday night, delegates attend a reception and banquet in the hotel. Kathryn Tucker Windham of Selma, a former newspaper reporter and editor, is guest speaker.

During the 1996 winter convention, APA recognizes the oldest member newspapers, the oldest active editors and publishers, multi-generation newspaper families, and others. Past presidents are also recognized.

Delegates attending the winter convention receive commemorative paper weights and other keepsakes.

Summer convention, Perdido Beach
July 12-14, 1996

CHAPTER 11

Alabama Newspaper Hall of Honor

"This period has seen transportation develop from the horse and buggy and the steamboat and sailing ship to ocean liners, jet planes and railroads and automobiles that offer the utmost in luxury and comfort. It has seen communication developed from the first crude telegraph systems to wireless telephone and telegraph. It has seen this newspaper evolve from a sheet in which two pages were set by hand and laboriously printed on a Washington hand press, into a plant in which the presses are driven by electricity and some of them are automatic. It has seen the general equipment of the country newspaper plant develop to the extent that should an old-time printer step into the plant, he wouldn't know which way to turn nor what to do."

George A. Carleton
The Clarke County Democrat,
Grove Hill

— *George A. Carleton (1889-1972)*
Editor and Publisher
The Clarke County Democrat, *Grove Hill*
APA president, 1945-1946
Alabama Newspaper Hall of Honor inductee, 1979
(From editorial written on 100th anniversary
of the founding of the newspaper, April 7, 1955)

A RESOLUTION CALLING FOR AN "ALABAMA Newspaper Hall of Fame" was introduced in 1959 by L.O. Brackeen, director of publicity at Alabama Polytechnic Institute, Auburn, and Webb Stanley,

business manager of *The Greenville Advocate.* "Alabama has had some outstanding newspaper publishers and editors whose lives and memories should be preserved," stated the resolution which was unanimously adopted by the Alabama Press Association.

Delegates attending the 1959 summer convention at Dauphin Island on June 11-13, 1959, approved plans for the Alabama Newspaper Hall of Honor. Under Hall of Honor plans, four outstanding editors would be honored at the annual convention in 1960, and two in each future year.

In addition the Alabama Press Association, through its officers and Hall of Honor Committee, encouraged Alabama editors and publishers to write and prepare in pamphlet form histories of their newspapers. Copies of the histories were to be placed in the Hall of Honor as they became available.

Members of the committee submitting the Hall of Honor plans for approval were L.O. Brackeen, chairman, Alabama Polytechnic Institute, Auburn; Webb Stanley, *The Greenville Advocate*; Cecil H. Hornady, *The Talladega News;* Bonnie D. Hand, *The LaFayette Sun*; and George A. Carleton, *The Clarke County Democrat*, Grove Hill.

Before the 1959 summer meeting, APA president Bill Stewart of *The Monroe Journal*, Monroeville, named a six-member committee to nominate those to be voted upon for the Hall of Honor. They included L.O. Brackeen of Alabama Polytechnic Institute, chairman; Cecil H. Hornady, *The Talladega News;* Bonnie D. Hand, *The LaFayette Sun;* Glenn Jones, *The Troy Messenger,* Walter F. Miller, *The Colbert County Reporter,*

Tuscumbia; and George A. Carleton, *The Clarke County Democrat*.

The committee met at Dauphin Island and recommended four individuals to be honored at the 1960 winter convention: Hunter Howell Golson, publisher of *The Wetumpka Herald* until his death in 1946, Frazier Titus Raiford, editor and publisher of *The Selma Times-Journal* who died in 1937, Maj. William Wallace Screws, editor of *The Montgomery Advertiser* until his death in 1913, and Gen. James Berney Stanley, editor of *The Greenville Advocate* for 70 years, who died in 1934. Upon recommendation of the committee, the four deceased editors and publishers were approved for induction to the first Alabama Newspaper Hall of Honor.

Brackeen, APA historian, also announced a project to acquire and preserve histories of Alabama newspapers and called on editors to submit their histories to him.

Brackeen officiated during ceremonies at the 1960 winter convention installing the first members of the Alabama Newspaper Hall of Honor. When the Hall of Honor Committee made its recommendation to APA, the idea was to locate the Hall of Honor in the Alabama Department of Archives and History in Montgomery.

At that time in 1959, space was not available in Archives, and the Hall of Honor remained homeless for at least four years. Its materials were kept at APA headquarters in Tuscaloosa and in the Department of University Relations on the Auburn University campus.

Auburn University officials offered space to house the Hall of Honor in the Ralph Brown Draughon Library. APA members accepted the offer, and on Oct. 10, 1964, the dedicatory ceremony took place. Auburn University has served as host each fall since 1964 for the APA Hall of Honor ceremony in the Draughon Library.

1960

Gen. James Berney Stanley (1844-1934)
Editor and publisher
The Greenville Advocate
APA president, 1882-1886 (four terms)

Maj. William Wallace Screws (1839-1913)
Owner, editor, president
The Montgomery Advertiser
APA president, 1878-1882 (four terms)

Frazier Titus Raiford (1872-1937)
Editor and publisher
The Selma Times-Journal

Hunter Howell Golson (1884-1946)
Editor and publisher
The Wetumpka Herald
and other weekly newspapers
APA president, 1940-1941

1961

Benjamin McGowan Bloodworth (1896-1953)
Editor
The Decatur Daily

Isaac Grant (1828-1907)
Editor and publisher
The Clarke County Democrat, Grove Hill

Charles Herd Greer (1860-1939)
Editor
The Sylacauga News
APA president, 1904-1905

1962

Harry Martin Doster (1892-1952)
Editor and publisher
The Prattville Progress

Johnson Jones Hooper (1815-1862)
Editor
The East Alabamian, LaFayette
The Chambers County Tribune, LaFayette
and other Alabama newspapers

1963

William Lee Gammell (1890-1954)
Editor and publisher
The Clayton Record

Franklin Potts Glass (1858-1934)
Editor
The Montgomery Advertiser
The Bibb Blade, Six Mile
The Selma Times

Grover Cleveland Hall Sr. (1888-1941)
Editor
The Montgomery Advertiser

1964
Jesse B. Adams (1902-1952)
Editor and publisher
The Southern Star, Ozark
APA president, 1933-1935 (two terms)

Olin Hampton Stevenson (1871-1937)
Editor and publisher
The Roanoke Leader

1965
Marcy B. Darnall Sr. (1872-1960)
Editor and publisher
The Florence Herald
APA president, 1930-1931

Milton C. Giles (1893-1957)
Editor and publisher
The Franklin County Times, Russellville
The Red Bay News
APA president, 1939-1940

1966
Oscar M. Dugger Sr. (1872-1947)
Editor and publisher
The Andalusia Star
APA president, 1919-1920

Julian O. Hall (1900-1939)
Editor
The Dothan Eagle

1967
Victor Henry Hanson (1876-1945)
Publisher
The Birmingham News

William Edward Wadsworth Yerby (1864-1940)
Editor and publisher
The Greensboro Watchman
APA president, 1901-1904 (three terms)

1968
Edward Seymour Cornish (1861-1936)
Editor and publisher
The Demopolis Times

Mary H. Raiford (1876-1959)
Editor and publisher
The Selma Times-Journal

1969
Col. Harry M. Ayers (1885-1964)
Editor and publisher
The Anniston Star
APA president, 1915-1917 (two terms)

Charles Glenn Jones (1908-1961)
Editor and publisher
The Troy Messenger
The Troy Herald
The Pike County Sentinel, Burndidge

1970
Edmond Cody Hall Sr. (1880-1941)
Editor and publisher
The Alexander City Outlook
APA president, 1928-1929

Robert Henry (Harry) Walker Sr. (1875-1952)
Editor and publisher
The Limestone Democrat, Athens

1971
Reese Thomas Amis (1888-1964)
Editor
The Huntsville Times

William Randolph Shelton (1860-1924)
Editor and publisher
The Decatur Daily

1972
Earl Lee Tucker (1904-1964)
Editor and publisher
The Thomasville Times

George Robert Cather (1836-1913)
Editor and publisher
The Ashville Aegis

1973
Rufus N. Rhodes (1856-1910)
Editor and publisher
The Birmingham News
APA president, 1899-1901 (two terms)

John H. Singleton (1883-1963)
Editor and publisher
The Enterprise Ledger

1974
Thomas Eastin (1785-1865)
Editor and publisher
The Halcyon, St. Stephens

J. Glenn Stanley (1894-1967)
Editor and publisher
The Greenville Advocate
APA president, 1962-1963

1975
John Crenshaw Burruss (1821-1910)
Editor and publisher
The Universalist Herald, Notasulga
and Montgomery

Robert B. Vail (1892-1964)
Editor and publisher
The Baldwin Times, Bay Minette
The Atmore Record
APA president, 1927-1928

1976
Mark L. Tucker (1871-1942)
Editor and publisher
The Chilton County News, Clanton

Bonnie D. Hand (1913-1967)
Editor and publisher
The LaFayette Sun
APA president, 1946-1947

1977
James W. (Jim) Oakley Sr. (1911-1972)
Editor and publisher
The Centreville Press

Pearle Ennis Gammell (1892-1960)
Editor and publisher
The Clayton Record

1978
Forney Gilmore Stephens (1872-1939)
Editor and publisher
The Southern Democrat, Oneonta
APA president, 1923-1924 and 1932-1933 (two terms)

Grover Cleveland Hall Jr. (1915-1971)
Editor
The Montgomery Advertiser
The Alabama Journal

1979
George Alexander Carleton (1889-1972)
Editor and publisher
The Clarke County Democrat, Grove Hill
APA president, 1945-1946

Ralph Bradford Chandler (1891-1970)
Founder and publisher 1921-1926
The Birmingham Post
Founder and publisher 1929-1932
The Mobile Press
President and publisher 1932-1970
The Mobile Press Register

1980
Robert Gaston Bozeman (1896-1974)
Editor and publisher
The Evergreen Courant
APA president, 1936-1938 (two terms)

McClellan (Ted) Van der Veer (1895-1961)
Editor
The Birmingham News

1981
Louis A. Eckl (1909-1970)
Executive editor
The Florence Times
& Tri-Cities Daily

Robert M. Tucker Sr. (1905-1965)
Editor and publisher
The Chilton County News, Clanton

1982
F. Webb Stanley (1888-1970)
Business manager and co-publisher
The Greenville Advocate
APA president, 1926-1927
and 1935-1936 (two terms)

G. Whatley Carlisle Sr. (1868-1944)
Editor and publisher
The People's Ledger, Enterprise

1983
Frank P. Thomas Jr. (1913-1974)
Editor and publisher
The Alabama Citizen, Tuscaloosa
The Mobile Beacon

W. Emmett Brooks (1896-1977)
Editor and publisher
The Brewton Standard
APA president, 1929-1930

1984
Duard M. Le Grand Jr. (1915-1978)
Editor
Birmingham Post-Herald
1915-1978

S. Vincent Townsend (1901-1978)
Vice president and assistant to the publisher
The Birmingham News

1985
Harold S. May (1899-1972)
Editor and co-publisher
The Florence Herald
APA president, 1961-1962

John S. Graham (1848-1928)
Editor and publisher
The South Alabamian, Jackson

1986
W. Bruce Shelton (1892-1963)
Editor and publisher
The Tuscaloosa News
APA president, 1935-1936 (Resigned after two months and succeeded by Webb Stanley, *The Greenville Advocate*)

James E. Chappell (1885-1960)
Editor, president, general manager
The Birmingham News

1987
William Dorsey Jelks (1855-1931)
Editor and publisher
The Eufaula Times and News

Arthur F. Slaton Jr. (1919-1982)
Editor and publisher
The Moulton Advertiser

1988
James Buford Boone (1909-1983)
Publisher and president
The Tuscaloosa News

John W. Frierson (1897-1959)
President
The Birmingham Post Co.

1989
Clarence B. Hanson Jr. (1908-1983)
Publisher
The Birmingham News
APA president, 1951-1952

Barrett C. Shelton Sr. (1902-1984)
Publisher
The Decatur Daily

1990
Wilbur H. (Bill) Metz (1916-1985)
Vice president
Birmingham Post-Herald
APA president, 1968-1969

Edgar Hughleigh (Ed) Pierce (1904-1982)
Publisher
The Jasper Advertiser
The Mountain Eagle
APA president, 1948-1949

1991
Karol Ruth Latimer Fleming (1931-1983)
Editor and publisher
The Geneva County Reaper, Geneva
The Samson Ledger
The Hartford News-Herald

Steel E. McGrew (1909-1985)
Publisher
The Alabama Courier, Athens
The Limestone Democrat, Athens
APA president, 1954-1955

1992
Edward A. (Ed) Dannelly Jr. (1913-1984)
Editor and co-owner
The Andalusia Star-News
APA president, 1966-1967

John W. Bloomer (1912-1985)
Editor
The Birmingham News

1993
Graham M. McTeer (1930-1975)
Managing editor
The Auburn Bulletin

Perkins John Prewitt (1892-1953)
News editor
The Mobile Register
City editor
The Birmingham News

1994
George Anthony Cornish (1901-1989)
Reporter
The Demopolis Times
The Birmingham Age-Herald
Reporter, editor and executive editor
The New York Herald-Tribune

Charles Gordon Dobbins (1908-1988)
Reporter and editor
The Birmingham Age-Herald
The Anniston Times
The Montgomery Advertiser
The Montgomery Examiner
APA president, 1942-1943

1995
Robert E. Sutton Sr. (1889-1986)
Editor and publisher
The Democrat Reporter, Linden

William Thomas Sheehan (1874-1928)
Editor
The Montgomery Advertiser
APA president, 1922-1923

1996
Carroll Kilpatrick (1913-1984)
White House correspondent
The Washington Post
Associate editor
The Montgomery Advertiser
Reporter
The Birmingham News
The Birmingham Age-Herald

Jonathan Cincinnatus McLendon (1959-1946)
Editor and publisher
The Luverne Journal
APA president, 1925-1926

CHAPTER 12

Interviews with Alabama's Senior Newspaper Men and Women

Interviews conducted by Ed Williams, Auburn University Department of Journalism, at the Saturday luncheon of the APA 125th Anniversary Convention in Montgomery Feb. 24, 1996. Interviews taped by Auburn University Archivist Dr. Dwayne D. Cox, Ralph B. Draughn Library, and transcribed by Auburn University Archives.

Ralph W. Callahan, age 89
(Actively involved in Consolidated Publishing Co., Anniston, in 1996)
Born April 18, 1906
Consolidated Publishing Co.

At age 89, you are the most senior active newspaper executive in the state of Alabama. You have been involved in the newspaper business ever since you were a paper boy on the staff of The Anniston Star when you were 12 years old. To what do you attribute your health and longevity?

"The reason I'm here, really, is four four partial reasons. I have to thank my God, my wife, my golf, and turnip greens."

Ralph W. Callahan, age 89
The Anniston Star

Your first full-time job was on the staff of The Nashville Tennessean.

In 1925, one of history's most famous court cases was heard, the Scopes trial in Dayton, Tenn. John Scopes was charged with teaching the theory of evolution in a Tennessee public school, and the chief defense

attorney was Clarence Darrow. One of the prosecutors was William Jennings Bryan. You were working in the newsroom one Sunday afternoon when the telephone rang. Do you remember what the caller said that day in 1925?

"I surely do. I understand Kathryn Tucker Windham is going to talk about ghost stories tonight, so I'll tell you a ghost story. I was really too young to be at *The Tennessean*. I'd just gotten out of high school, but they were short on help and they gave me a job and it took them about nine months to fire me.

"I had been there a couple of weeks and of course, I didn't know anything about Nashville, and had no money really. So Sunday afternoon I'd go down to the office and went in that day and Paul Conway, who had at one time worked at *The Star*, was in the slot that afternoon and talking to a guy named Pennypacker who was our telegraph operator.

"Back in those days every newspaper had to have a person to man the telephone switchboard. To connect to a telephone the operator would pick up a ring on an incoming call and stick the cord in the right phone hole. Naturally you didn't have but one telephone. You had to have a switchboard, and they would pick up a cord and stick it in the right phone. I was there, and Paul was wondering what on earth he was going to have for Monday morning's paper. This was Sunday and the trial wasn't going on. In a few minutes the phone rang. Paul says, 'What, oh, he ain't dead.'

"Paul told me, 'Some person just called and asked what time William Jennings Bryan died.' Paul says, 'I told him that Bryan wasn't dead.'

"Anyways, we kept talking. 'What are you going to have on Monday morning?' I asked Paul.

"In a few moments the phone rang again. Paul says, 'What? I told you Bryan ain't dead.' He hung up.

"Paul says, 'We might have to run a story like Mark Twain's *I Ain't Dead Story.*'

"But we kept talking, and in a few minutes the phone rang for the third time. Before he picked it up Paul says, 'Ralph, run downstairs to the switchboard and trace this call and I'd like to get some comment on why they made this call.'

"While he was talking, I ran downstairs to the switchboard and said, 'Mary, let me in on this call that Paul Conway's got up there so I can trace it.'

"She said, 'What call?' I said, 'Paul's talking to somebody up there.'

"'Oh no he isn't. I have not rung a telephone in the newsroom for over an hour,' Mary told me.

"Well, I ran back upstairs to see Paul and told him, 'They say you are not connected.'

"Well, Paul said, 'Let's go back to the Mark Twain story.' He told me to call Joe Hatcher. The reason I had a job up there was that Joe Hatcher was one of the reporters who was down at Dayton covering the Scopes trial. So I called Joe Hatcher to get him to see Mr. Bryan and deny this thing. I called Joe and told him what was going on and wanted him to go see Mr. Bryan and get him to deny that he was dead. Bryan was staying in an old house that had a boarding house table for Sunday dinner.

"Joe says, 'Bryan's gone upstairs to take a nap. He says, 'I'll tell you what I'll do. Jim, his (Bryan's) chauffeur is here. I'll send Jim upstairs. Jim goes upstairs at Joe's request and about two minutes later he comes running down the stairs, 'Mr. Joe, Mr. Joe, Mr. Bryan — he dead.'

"The newsroom got awfully quiet. The mystery was never solved.

"I swear."

You worked very closely with the late editor and publisher of The Anniston Star, Col. Harry Mell Ayers. Do you remember a visit the two of you made in 1932 to see Franklin Roosevelt?

"Well, I sure do. Col. Ayers was my boss, my mentor, my friend. One morning he says, 'Ralph, I want to go talk to Mr. Roosevelt. He's fixing to run for president.'

"He was over there at his Warm Springs (Ga.) place. So I said, 'All right sir, I'll drive you over.' We drove over and at the door Lucy met us. They don't print it now, but Lucy was his girlfriend. Anyway, Lucy Mercer, she carried us through the house to a back porch which was screened. Mr. Roosevelt was sitting there in a wheelchair with a robe on, having some late coffee. And after some preliminary things, the colonel told him, 'Mr. Roosevelt, I like what you say and what you are doing and I want to be the first newspaper in the South to endorse you for president.' Well, Mr. Roosevelt thought that was pretty nice, I guess.

"Anyway, things went on for a little while and we thanked him for being available to talk to us and left. And *The Star* was the first newspaper in the South to endorse Roosevelt for president. That was in '32. On March 4, 1933, I was in the Willard Hotel sticking my head out the window to watch President Roosevelt ride down Pennsylvania Avenue."

You were APA president in 1965. How were officers elected prior to your presidency?

"I'm proud of the fact that during that administration we changed the way that you nominated officers for the press association. Before, it just had been an open meeting and anybody who wanted to nominate somebody would say, 'Yeah, I nominate Joe'.

"Well, I called Jack Venable's predecessor down at *The Tallassee Tribune*, Herve Charest, and I said, 'Herve, I would like for you to be head of a nominating committee provided one thing. If you will agree to nominate Bill Metz up at the *Birmingham Post-Herald* to head the list of officers.'

"Herve said, 'Sure, I'll do that.'

"So that's when the nominating committee started to being appointed to bring in a list of folks capable of running the press association. There was a time when the ex-presidents met and sat around a table and made nominations. Since 1965, we have had an organized nominating committee operating under Roberts Rules of Order, and I think it has worked very well."

When did the Alabama Press Association lose its weekly image and become a press association representing all the newspapers of Alabama?

"I think it was when the daily newspapers came into the fold and began to contribute money for operations that the press association began to grow. By the same token, there was an understanding, if not expressed, condition by which the presidency of the press association would alternate from weekly to daily every other year."

The year that you were president, you insisted that there be more formality at the convention banquet that year, and that the men wear tuxedos. What did the late Porter Harvey, publisher of The Advertiser-Gleam in Guntersville, tell you?

"He says, 'I've never worn a tuxedo, and I ain't gonna.'

"I said, 'Well, we'd like to change the image a good bit of this institution' and I said, 'Here's the name of a rental place in Birmingham.'

"Porter showed up in a black tie and did a great job. Porter was not only a good newspaper man, he was a good friend and I regret that he's gone. He could join this crowd real good."

Neil O. Davis, age 81
(Retired)
Born Aug. 15, 1914
Co-founder of *The Lee County Bulletin*, Auburn, in 1937
Editor and Publisher, *The Lee County Bulletin*, *The Auburn Bulletin*, 1937-1975

You graduated from Alabama Polytechnic Institute in 1935 and, with journalism professor Joseph Roop, founded The Lee County Bulletin in 1937. You said you attended your first Alabama Press Association Convention in 1938. Would you compare your first convention with the APA conventions of the 1990s?

Neil O. Davis, age 81
The Lee County Bulletin, Auburn

"Well, I'm not happy to say that at the press convention in 1938, most of the program was given on how they were going to sell more advertising and how to get more job printing. I was dismayed at how little attention was given to the things I was most interested in. So many of the community newspapers were at the time sort of run as adjunct printing more than the vice versa. There wasn't much said about news and editorial content. That didn't really happen until Doyle Buckles came on board (in 1939) as the field manager of APA."

You were on the APA committee that resulted in the hiring of Doyle Buckles as field manager in 1939, and placing APA headquarters on the University of Alabama campus. What do you recall about Buckles?

"Doyle Buckles had the mind of a typical Mid-westerner and I wondered at first, when he got here, how he was going to get along with this bunch of native Alabama editors and publishers. But after a few weeks, actually a few months, I was convinced he was just what the doctor ordered. Buckles brought some fresh perspectives; he was a combination, really, of a hard-headed newsman, and a good one, and a good businessman. Most of the publishers wanted somebody to tell them how to make a lot of money, how to sell more advertising and increase circulation, and he did a good bit of that. But Buckles kept trying to center the interest of the editors and publishers on a quality product.

"Buckles very subtly...he didn't say, 'This is something you need to do,' he just worked with the incoming officers to try to get programs dealing with newswriting coverage, the editorial product. Too few of the community papers had editorial pages. To tell you the truth, newspapers were, up until the late 1940s and 1950s, owned and operated by men who operated their papers as an adjunct to the print shop. They made their money on job printing and gave little attention to the newspaper.

"Several of the editors got into the profession through the back door of being printers. Most were interested in finding out how to sell ads and how to sell subscriptions. There was not much attention given to the news and editorial side of the papers, and I give Buckles credit for the fact that he, really, he didn't say, 'You've got your sights set in the wrong place,' or 'You need to do this or that,' he just gradually suggested, 'This is what you need to do for the next meeting.' And he organized district meetings around the state.

"Buckles brought a fresh perspective, a fresh point of view."

What was the reaction of the APA membership in 1930 to placing the press association's headquarters on the University of Alabama campus?

"It was widely popular and accepted, mainly because the press association didn't have any money, and the University of Alabama was going to pick up most of the cost. The APA at the time was charging dues of $12 a year, and I think it was very smart on the University's part to establish a relationship with the press of the state. I was for it. I thought it was a good deal for the Alabama Press Association, and certainly couldn't hurt the University of Alabama."

Racial outbreaks were occurring in Birmingham in 1963, and they dominated discussion when President John F. Kennedy invited all Alabama daily newspapers, six weekly publishers and APA officers to attend a luncheon at the White House. It was one of a series of luncheons that President Kennedy called with press associations of several Southern states. You attended that luncheon in 1963, but you weren't originally invited, were you?

"No, I wasn't. Mine was the only weekly newspaper in the state that had endorsed John F. Kennedy. We endorsed him before he was nominated. But we were not invited to the White House luncheon, although we were the only weekly newspaper in the state that had endorsed Kennedy. So, I wasn't very happy about that. I called a friend of mine in Washington who was the White House correspondent for *The Washington Post*. His name was Carroll Kilpatrick. For 20 some odd years he covered the White House for *The Post*, and our friendship dated back to college days.

"His senior year and my senior year was 1934-1935, his at the University of Alabama and mine at Auburn, and we formed a very warm and lasting friendship in those days. So I called him and told him what happened. I said, 'Carroll, can you do anything about it?' He said, 'I think so.' The result was in a few hours I had a telegram signed by John F. Kennedy inviting me to come. Brandy Ayers was there. His father (Col. Harry M. Ayers) was there. Brandy, I believe, was correspondent for *The Raleigh* (N.C.) *News and Observer* at the time.

"But anyway, Carroll had told people at the White House about my affinity for President Kennedy and had elaborated much too much, I'm sure, about what a great guy I was, what a great press supporter and so on. And what I enjoyed the most was the expression on the faces of my fellow Alabama newspaper editors and publishers, most of whom had a hand in putting together the guest list. For some reason they didn't think I ought to be included.

"There were three newspapers, that I recall, that had endorsed the Kennedy presidency, Mr. (Harry M.) Ayers at *The Anniston Star*, Mr. (Barrett) Shelton at *The Decatur Daily*, and Buford Boone at *The Tuscaloosa News*. *The Lee County Bulletin* was the fourth newspaper that supported Kennedy. I, for the life of me, don't know why they had it in for me so much that I should be the only one not invited of that group.

"After the meeting (with President Kennedy), as I was walking out of the White House, one of the aides tapped me on the shoulder and said, 'Would you come with me?'

"The brunt of what he said was that the attorney general, Robert Kennedy, would like to see me. His office was at the Justice Department building. I told him that I would like to go, but I was afraid that I would miss my flight back to Atlanta. He asked me what the schedule was and I told him. He said, 'Well, that won't be any problem. We'll have the attorney general's automobile out here and I'll drive you to the Justice Department building and by my calculation you ought to have about 30 minutes and then we'll take you to the Washington National Airport.'

"So I went. But anyway, I went into the attorney general's office and he was behind this huge desk. You will recall he was about 5-feet-5 1/2 to 6 inches tall and he looked like he was lost behind that thing.

"Well, what he wanted to talk about was developing a strategy for dealing with the situation at Birmingham. He wanted me to give him some names of persons that he could contact and plead with them to join with the administration in trying to bring some sense out of a terrible situation. So, I suggested such as the president of the Tennessee Coal and Iron Company, the president of the First National Bank of Birmingham, and Mr. Martin, president of Alabama Power Company.

"But anyway, I was more impressed by him (Robert Kennedy) than I was the president. He was all heart and into this thing so deeply, and he got so excited in talking about it. He came around from the back of his desk and he got up on it and crossed his legs like a child would do, sitting on that big desk and talking about the prospects.

"But other than that, I think the biggest thrill I got out of it was when I walked in, everybody else was there because they went together and I came later, and they all looked around at me and began wondering, 'How did you get here?'"

You represent a community journalism background. Do you think the problems and pressures of being a weekly community newspaper publisher and editor are different from those of editors and publishers of large metropolitan dailies?

"Well, the short answer is yes. I was an undergraduate at Alabama Polytechnic Institute in 1931-35, and I founded *The Lee County Bulletin* in 1937. I found out that in a small community it was best to write about the Chamber of Commerce projects, Rotary Club meetings, that sort of thing. But when you got into writing about such things as trying to point out that we were all captives of some myths about our own history, if I suggested that we need to do something about hookworm or pellagra, that was throwing off on the South. You don't do that. You are supposed to write, 'We have a great community.' You don't write about such things.

"Then, when I moved cautiously from that to suggesting that we need to do something about the poll tax, abolishing it.... Well, poor people that didn't vote would show up to become registered to vote for a few years found out that they owed $10, $12, $15. That's a lot of money. They didn't have it, so they couldn't pay it. They couldn't vote."

J.C. Henderson, age 91
(Retired)
Born March 6, 1904
Editor and Publisher, *The Alexander City Outlook*, 1944-1971

You're the 91-year-old retired publisher of The Alexander City Outlook. You had a successful career in community journalism, at one time owning, The

Opelika Eagle, The Dadeville Record, The Goodwater Enterprise Chronicle, The Camp Hill News, The Chambers County News at Lanett, The Chattahoochee Valley Times, The West Point News and The Outlook. But your career actually started at age 14, as a printer's devil working after school for your hometown newspaper, The Gainesville (Ga.) Eagle.

J. C. Henderson, age 91
The Alexander City Outlook

"Well, I started out with the newspaper career at age 14, and I worked after school setting type by hand. Each letter. You'd pick up a letter and it was 10 point Cheltenham type that you would have. Then you'd get your stick for a line and then you'd put a little lead strip to hold the letters together.

"Of course, you had to do all of that and then you'd get the type set up and you'd run it off in the old Washington hand-press and then you'd clean that type afterwards with Red Devil lye solution and you'd get your hands all ate up by Red Devil lye.

"But anyway, we started off like that. Of course, at that time the advertising in the newspaper was very limited. Most of it was patent medicines such as Carter's Little Liver Pills, Cardui women's medicines. So anyway that's the way...you didn't have much advertising except what you had out of patent medicine ads. But anyway later on, why, we got the first Linotype, I think was in the 19 (some-things) — gosh, I've forgotten how many years back it's been. But anyway, we finally got a Linotype machine, but that hand-set type was one of the big things that we did. Of course, I made a little extra money, why, working in the afternoon. But that started it off."

During the years that you owned The Alexander City Outlook, you wrote a popular column called "The Ole Crier," which you continue to write today. But didn't you write your first column when you were in high school?

"Yes. The editor — we had an editor that had these glasses that you put on your nose and he wore this, actually a dress shirt with the collar turned down. He told me to write a story on calculus. Well, of course, I was smart and I went into the dictionary to look and see what he was talking about. Anyway, I wrote the story just like it was written in Webster's Dictionary. I handed it over to him and he says, 'Ain't worth a damn.'

"He says, 'If I had wanted something like that I would have told you, but I wanted something to tell me you didn't know a damn thing about the

thing.' Anyway, that was the start of me writing the column (*The Outlook* News Crier). In getting the name 'Crier' I was reading a magazine in New York and I read where this fellow called himself the crier, and I adopted that name from the magazine in New York City."

I've been told that you and your late wife, Nellie Mae, used to have a lot of fun at the press conventions of yesteryear, that there were always bands, dances on Saturday nights, and that folks used to refer to you and some other couples as the 'wild gang.'

"Well we weren't so wild, but Bonnie Hand and Pearl (*The LaFayette Sun*), Ed Pierce and Y *(The Mountain Eagle*, Jasper), and Steele and Ellen McGrew (*The Limestone Democrat* and *Alabama Courier*, Athens)...all of them are dead now, bless their hearts...but anyway, we actually — every press convention we always had a band. Over the years that I was with the press association or attended it regularly, why, we always had an orchestra and all of us would dance, and we'd go to the Downtown Club. It wasn't so bad because we all had due bills at the Bankhead Hotel. My wife, I think, was in the same grade that Ralph (Callahan) was at Anniston High School, and I met her at her junior prom, I think it was at Oxford Lake.

The late Ed Dannelly, editor of The Andalusia Star-News, is probably one of the most popular and colorful characters in the history of the Alabama Press Association. Do you remember an incident involving Mr. Dannelly and a Rolls Royce?

Yes. We had a summer press convention at Kowaliga Beach in 1966. Of course, we had a new director, Jim Hall, and we had to borrow cabins from all over the lake and everybody was coming in and finally Mr. Dannelly came in with this Rolls Royce and everybody thought it was the governor coming in. But anyway, he borrowed it from one of his friends and they had a lot of fun after that."

James E. (Jimmy) Mills, age 95
(Retired)
Born July 28, 1900
Editor, *The Birmingham Post*
and *Birmingham Post-Herald*,
1930-1967

You are the senior newspaper man in the state of Alabama. You were editor of the old Birmingham Post and later the Birmingham Post-Herald from 1930 until your retirement in 1967.

You are probably best known for a landmark Supreme Court decision in *Mills vs. Alabama*. Until 1966, Alabama law forbid the state's newspapers from publishing election-day editorials. Birmingham was in the middle of a bitter change of government election in 1962, and an editorial ran in the Birmingham Post-Herald on election day

James E. (Jimmy) Mills, age 95
Birmingham Post-Herald

urging citizens to vote for an alternative form of government. The mayor-council proposition carried, but James E. Mills was arrested and charged with violating the Alabama Corrupt Practices Act.

At the time you wrote that editorial, were you making a deliberate challenge to the state law of the time?

"No, I wasn't making a deliberate challenge at all. I was just trying to throw out the present city government so we could replace it with some decent government."

Were you ever actually jailed on charges of electioneering?

"No, but I thought I might have an opportunity to have a lot of fun if I did go to jail. My predecessor as editor of the old *Birmingham Post*, Ed Leach who ended up as editor of *The Pittsburgh Press*, did turn jail time into a big party. The Alabama attorney general came up from Montgomery and demanded that he stop the press and end publication of a story. Ed told him he could just go to hell.

"So they arrested him, and Ed went to jail for a week and he had more fun and the people of Alabama had more fun for a week than they had ever seen before or since. He really had a big time. They brought him drinks, cigarettes and delicacies seldom seen in city jails. They even brought a band down to play for him. He had a great time.

"When the sheriff's deputy came up with the warrant for my arrest, he said, 'Well, you just sign your own warrant.' I thought about going to jail like Ed Leach did and then decided it wouldn't be worth it. I just won't have any fun. And we let the deputy go about his way."

Prior to your trial date, a judge ruled the anti-electioneering law to be unconstitutional, but the Alabama Supreme Court reinstated the charge.

Mills. vs. Alabama reached the U.S. Supreme Court on appeal, and the judgment was reversed on May 23, 1966, with an Alabama native, Justice Hugo Black, writing the opinion for the high court. Will you recall

where you were at the time you heard the news, and your reaction at the time?

"You know, at my age, my chief complaint is that I don't have a memory, but I'll never forget where I was or what I did. Elise (my wife) and I had been up to a meeting of the American Society of Newspaper Editors in Montreal that year. The meeting was over and we decided to take a little vacation up there. We wanted to go up to Quebec on the French side of the St. Lawrence River there. As we got over there, of course, we found most of the people speaking French only. We had a time driving, but we had a lot of fun.

"From our Quebec hotel window we could look down on the river and watch the big ocean vessels coming in.

"We were out one morning walking around town to see what we could see of interest and returned a little after noon and the telephone's red light was blinking and blinking, and there were several notes under our door.

"I had calls from New York and calls from Washington, and calls from Birmingham. I said, 'Mimi, (Elise Mills' nickname) all hell has broken loose someplace.'

"I had many calls and had to decide where to call first. One was from Jack Howard, calling from the New York office of Scripps Howard. I hurriedly got on the phone and and called him.

"Jack said, 'All is forgiven. You can come home.'

"I said, 'What did you say?'

"'All is forgiven. you can come home.'

"I said, 'Jack, I don't understand.'

"Jack said, 'Oh hell. The Supreme Court just handed down a decision in your behalf. You can come home.'

"Then, of course, I had all the other calls to answer, among them the Associated Press and United Press. I had to sit down then and figure out something to say that would make some sense. That's what I did. I prepared a statement I was willing to be quoted on in papers all cross the country. It was not easy. That finished our day — a big day never to be forgotten."

Bertie Gammell Parish, age 80
(Active as editor/publisher of *The Clayton Record* in 1996)
Born June 4, 1915
Editor and publisher, *The Clayton Record*, 1960-1996

You have many stories to tell because you grew up in the newspaper business. Your grandfather was a pressman at The Montgomery Advertiser. You followed both your parents as editor and publisher of The Clayton Record, and at age 80, you continue to be actively involved in the newspaper. After your mother died in 1960, do you recall what you said at the time?

"Oh, yes I do remember. I looked around because George Wallace and Billy Watson was his big mate there, came rushing to me. 'What are you going to do with it, what are you going to do with it?'

"I said, 'I'm going to print a paper. What can I do with it? It's like leaving a baby on your front doorstep. What are you going to do? You've got to raise that baby. So I stayed with it.'"

Will you share the story of what happened in 1972 when The Clayton Record received some national attention? It involved Gov. George Wallace, a Barbour County native who was a presidential candidate at the time.

"It was during 'Meet the Press' and old George was so keen. In those days he was just bubbling with energy. They asked him, 'Governor Wallace, what is your favorite newspaper?'

"Well, I thought surely he would say *The Chicago Tribune*, some big paper like that. He turned around without batting an eye and said, '*The Clayton Record*, Clayton, Alabama.'

"Well, that was just a howl."

Both of your parents, William Lee Gammell and Pearle Ennis Gammell, were inducted into the Alabama Newspaper Hall of Honor. Only one other husband and wife team in the history of the Hall of Honor hold such an honor, Frazier and Mary Raiford of The Selma Times-Journal. In the Hall of Honor proceedings, it mentions that your father was particularly fond of collecting and printing rattlesnake stories.

It is said that quite a collection of snake yarns and pictures were accumulated because of his interest. Do

you remember what your mother told him one day about printing all those snake stories?

"I've heard it over and over, yes. Mother, you know, she always liked to have the parties and the teas, and the receptions and all those, because she had me at the piano all the time. And she wanted all those things and Daddy, when he came up there, he liked fishing and hunting and his rattlesnakes.

"He said, 'Anybody that could kill a rattlesnake deserves to have their name in the paper.' He said, 'Any woman that plays bridge and plays cards, if you can put her name in the paper then we can certainly put that man's name in my paper, that killed a snake.'"

During the Great Depression, when people had no money, bartering for newspaper subscriptions was quite common. Joe Adams, editor and publisher of The Southern Star at Ozark, told me that he remembered as a boy growing up even in the late 1930s, seeing sacks of sweet potatoes, sticks of sugarcane and cans of sorghum syrup that people exchanged for subscriptions.

Jim Oakley Jr., former owner of The Centreville Press, says his father, the late J.W. Oakley, had a deal in the 1930s where he would exchange two gallons of syrup for a year's subscription to the paper. He ended up with about 3,000 gallons of sorghum syrup.

Do you remember bartering occurring at The Clayton Record?

"Oh, I remember...Mother — some lady had a cow and she would get milk from her to pay for the subscription, or butter, or something like that. Then Daddy would come home...and would say, 'Well so and so brought a dozen eggs in here to today to help pay for a subscription.'

"Mother would say, 'Oh, how nice that is.'

"So we did. We bartered and it was common. Everybody did it during the Depression.

"Some of you can't remember those days."

After your mother died in 1960 and you became editor and publisher of The Clayton Record, you said you had your doubts about whether you could write editorials. What did Stuart X. Stevenson, state editor of The Montgomery Advertiser, tell you?

"He said, 'Bertie Parish, listen, anybody that can talk as much as you can, can write.'"

Lancie M. Thomas, age 79
(Active as publisher of *The Mobile Beacon* in 1996)
Born Feb. 5, 1917
Editor and publisher, *The Mobile Beacon*, 1996

You and your husband, the late Frank P. Thomas, set an example for all newspaper people with your spirit

Bertie Gammell Parish, age 80, and husband Tom at Alabama Newspaper Hall of Honor. Both of Mrs. Parish's parents were inducted into the Hall at Auburn University's Ralph B. Draughon Library.

of community service, your perseverance and your courage. You worked with your husband since The Beacon's beginning in 1954, and before then with The Alabama Citizen in Tuscaloosa, which the two of you founded in 1943. It's hard enough to publish a newspaper anywhere, but The Mobile Beacon overcame a number of challenges.

Lancie M. Thomas, age 79
The Mobile Beacon

In 1956, while your husband was spending most of his time in Mobile with the new paper there, you were running the Tuscaloosa paper. You had a part in historic events at the University of Alabama. Autherine Lucy, a black woman from Birmingham, registered at the previously all-white university and attended it for three days. Miss Lucy ate lunch at the Thomas house daily, and you even accompanied her to class.

Each day, Miss Lucy stayed at The Citizen office with some friends. Whites threatened to burn the building and attack Miss Lucy and the staff. When a mob marched on The Citizen's office, they found it protected by several hundred blacks, who turned them back.

"Well, when the University of Alabama was integrated by Autherine Lucy, I was there on the campus when she registered. She had lunch at my home every day that she attended class, and I was the one that got her out of town safe back to Birmingham. My office was filled with pistols and guns, and they didn't know that I couldn't shoot one. I didn't dream about how dangerous it was for me. But I didn't think about it. I was only thinking about Autherine. I said, 'Because I'm safe. God is going to take care of me and I'm not worried. I'm going to be okay.'"

Why did you and your husband, who was inducted into the Alabama Newspaper Hall of Honor in 1983, decide to start a black newspaper?

"We wanted to report the news of blacks that the white papers did not cover — school news, wedding announcements and the first baby born in the black community. Back then (when the paper was founded), the only time you saw black people's names in the paper was for rape or murder."

Didn't you borrow $150 from a bank to start The Alabama Citizen in 1943?

"Yes. At times the going was tough. Friends said we couldn't make it. We have had some prob-

lems, but we've always been able to make it. We always worked together. And any time we didn't have a salary on the weekend to pay ourselves, I'd always tell my husband, 'Don't worry about it. I've got food at home, and I know how to make a meal. So we're going to live.'"

The Tuscaloosa newspaper (The Alabama Citizen) became a financial success, with a circulation of about 6,000, which enabled you and your husband to branch out, publishing a second Alabama Citizen in Selma for a time and, in 1954, to establish The Mobile Beacon. Your husband's health caused the two of you to combine the Tuscaloosa and Mobile newspapers, moving everything to Mobile a few years later.

Did you ever miss a week of publication?

"We had a fire — our building burned down in 1961. We still came out that week. We had the hurricane (Frederic in 1979). Most of the roof was off. We came out. Another time the pressman walked out. And we still put out the paper."

The Beacon is characterized by its glowing lighthouse nameplate with the motto, "The Light that Never Fails."

"That means that a newspaper never fails to give news to the public and hear the voices of other people. Nobody's too small or too large that you can't listen. Now, that's what we really built our paper on — little people. We've never catered to the upper-class folks. We give them all service, but there are a lot of newspapers and a lot of people in business who feel that if you are a doctor or a lawyer or a teacher or a professional person, you are IT. That's not our policy. Everybody is a human being."

You attended Tuskegee Institute (now Tuskegee University) and Alabama State College (now Alabama State University) in Montgomery, where you received a degree in home economics — not journalism.

"I've done everything and haven't been taught. I just learned myself."

You gave up your career as a teacher to work on the newspaper. Have you had any regrets?

"I would not have changed a thing. I have thoroughly enjoyed (being in the newspaper business). The service we have done in the community is far more than anything I could have done in the classroom."

CHAPTER 13

Alabama Newspapers

LISTED ALPHABETICALLY BY CITY

DAILIES

ALEXANDER CITY
The Alexander City Outlook
Ph: (205) 234-4281   Fax: (205) 234-6550
Box 999   Zip: 35010
Ship to: 139 Church Street
Contacts:
Bruce Wallace-P
Billy McGhee-AD
K.A. Turner-E

ANDALUSIA
The Andalusia Star-News
Ph: (334) 222-2402   Fax: (334) 222-6597
Drawer 430   Zip: 36420
Ship to: 207 Dunson St.
Contacts:
William T. "Bill" Beckner-P
Greg McCord-ME
Ruck Ashworth-AM
Charity S. Welcher-CAM

ANNISTON
The Anniston Star
Ph: (205) 236-1551   Fax: (205) 231-0027
Box 189   Zip: 36202
Ship to: 216 West 10th St.
Contacts:
H. Brandt Ayers-P & E
Phillip A. Sanguinetti-President
Chris Waddle-EE
Ken Warren-AM & CAM

ATHENS
The News-Courier
Ph: (205) 232-2720   Fax: (205) 233-7753
Box 670   Zip: 35611
Ship to: 410 West Green
Contacts:
Robert Bryan-P
Mike Jeffreys-GM
Sonny Turner-E
Linda Williams-AM
Connie Tucker-CAM

L E G E N D

AD	Advertising Director	**EPE**	Editorial Page Editor	**MD**	Marketing Director
AM	Advertising Manager	**EE**	Executive Editor	**MM**	Marketing Manager
CAM	Classified Manager	**GM**	General Manager	**NE**	News Editor
E	Editor	**ME**	Managing Editor	**P**	Publisher
RAM	Retail Ad Manager				

BIRMINGHAM
The Birmingham News
Ph: (205) 325-2222   Fax: (205) 325-2283
Box 2553   Zip: 35202
Ship to: 2200 4th Ave. North (35203)
Contacts:
Victor H. Hanson II-P
Victor H. Hanson III-GM
James E. Jacobson Sr.-E
Thomas Scarritt-EE
Carol Nunnelley-ME
Ron Casey-EPE
Elwin Ward-AD
Thomas J. Lager-MD
Carl Bates-CAM
Bobbi Brandenburg-MM

BIRMINGHAM
Birmingham Post-Herald
Ph: (205) 325-2344   Fax: (205) 325-2410
Box 2553   Zip: 35202
Ship to: 2200 4th Avenue North (35203)
Contacts:
James H. Denley-E (& President)
Karl Seitz-EPE
Elwin Ward-AD
Thomas J. Lager-MD

CULLMAN
The Cullman Times
Ph: (205) 734-2131   Fax: (205) 737-1020
300 4th Ave. S.E.   Zip: 35055
Ship to: Same
Contacts:
Robert Bryan-P
Sandra Massey-E
David Poynor-ME & EPE
Robbie Camp-AM
Kathy McLeroy-CAM

DECATUR
The Decatur Daily
Ph: (205) 353-4612   Fax: (205) 340-2366
Box 2213   Zip: 35609
Ship: 201 1st Ave. SE 35601
Contacts:
Barrett C. Shelton Jr.-P & E
Doug Mendenhall-ME
Tom Wright-EPE
Clint Shelton-Production Manager
Don Kincaid-AM
Darlene Ziegler-CAM

DOTHAN
The Dothan Eagle
Ph: (334) 792-3141   Fax: (334) 712-7979
Box 1968   Zip: 36302
Ship to: 227 North Oates St.(36303)
Contacts:
Stanley Warren-P
Terry Connor-ME
Bill Perkins-EPE

ENTERPRISE
The Enterprise Ledger
Ph: (334) 347-9533   Fax: (334) 347-0825
Box 1140   Zip: 36331
Ship: 106 North Edwards (36330)
Contacts:
Rick Martin-E & AD
Kenneth Tuck-NE

FLORENCE
Times Daily
Ph: (205) 766-3434   Fax: (205) 740-4717 (N)
                                       740-4700 (A)
Box 797   Zip: 35631
Ship to: 219 West Tennessee St. (35630)
Contacts:
Frank Helderman Jr.-P
Kathy Silverberg-E
Gary Thatcher-ME
David Palmer-EPE
Tim Thompson-AD
Carole Daniel-CAM

FORT PAYNE
Fort Payne Times-Journal
Ph: (205) 845-2550   Fax: (205) 845-7459
Box 349   Zip: 35967
Ship to: 811 Greenhill Blvd NW
Contacts:
Ben Shurett-P & E
Patrick Graham-ME & EPE
Sharon Kyle-AM
Nita Stevens-CAM

GADSDEN
The Gadsden Times
Ph: (205) 549-2000   Fax:(205) 549-2013(A)
                                          549-2105(N)
P.O. Box 188   Zip: 35999
Ship to: 401 Locust St. (35901)
Contacts:
Roger N. Hawkins-P   Fax: (205) 549-2109
Ron Reaves-ME
Arthur Shaw-EPE
Roger Quinn-AD

HUNTSVILLE
The Huntsville Times
Ph: (205) 532-4000   Fax:(205) 532-4420 (N)
                                          532-4461 (A)
Box 1487, West Station   Zip: 35807
Ship: 2317 S. Memorial Parkway (35801)
Contacts:
Bob Ludwig-P
Joe Distelheim-E
John Ehinger-EPE
Bill Joyner-AM
Steve Wilson-RAM
Jim Hollenbeck-CAM

JASPER
The Daily Mountain Eagle
Ph: (205) 221-2840   Fax: (205) 221-2421
Box 1469   Zip: 35501
Ship to: 1301 E. 19th
Contacts:
R. Douglas Pearson Jr.-P, E & EPE
Steve Cox-ME
Jerry Geddings-AM
Sandra Lawson-CAM

LANETT
Valley Times-News
Ph: (334) 644-1101   Fax: (334) 644-5587
Box 850   Zip: 36863
Ship to: 220 N. 12th St
Contacts:
Cy Wood-P & E
Bridge Turner-AM

MOBILE
Mobile Press Register
Ph: (334) 433-1551   Fax:(334) 434-8435 (A)
                                          (334) 434-8662 (N)
Box 2488   Zip: 36630
Ship to: 304 Government St. (36602)
Contacts:
W. Howard Bronson Jr.-P
Stan Tiner-E
Mike Marshall-ME
Bailey Thomson-EPE
Larry Wooley-AM
Eric Yance-CAM

MONTGOMERY
Montgomery Advertiser
Ph: (334) 262-1611   Fax: (334) 261-1502
Box 1000   Zip: 36101-1000
Ship to: 200 Washington Ave. (36104)
Contacts:
Richard H. Amberg Jr.-P
William B. Brown-E
Jim Tharpe-ME
Kenneth M. Hare-EPE
Leo Pieri-AM
Kathy Cowart-CAM

OPELIKA/AUBURN
The Opelika-Auburn News
Ph: (334) 749-6271   Fax: (334) 749-1228
Drawer 2208 Opelika   Zip: 36801
Ship to: 3505 Pepperell Parkway
Contacts:
Steve McPhaul-P
Philip Lucas-E
Roxanne Connor-NE
Kim Chandler-EPE
Jack Nolan-AD
Robert Delany-CAM

SCOTTSBORO
The Daily Sentinel
Ph: (205) 259-1020   Fax: (205) 259-2709
Box 220   Zip: 35768
Ship to: 701 Ft. Payne Hwy
Contacts:
Anita Bynum-P & E
Carmen Wann-ME
Sharon Womack-CAM

SELMA
The Selma Times-Journal
Ph: (334) 875-2110   Fax: (334) 875-5896
Box 611   Zip: 36701
Ship to: 1018 Water Ave. (36702)
Contacts:
E. Wilson Koeppel-P
Chuck Chandler-ME
Marcia Jowers-CAM

TALLADEGA/SYLACAUGA
The Daily Home
Ph: (205) 362-1000   Fax: (205) 249-4315
Box 977 Talladega   Zip: 35161
Ship to: #4 Sylacauga Hwy, Talladega (35160)
Contacts:
Ralph Callahan-President
Ed Fowler-P & E
Carol Pappas-ME
Zell Copeland-Asst. GM
Pam Adamson-AD
Alta Bolding-CAM
Rickey Garrett-CM

TROY
The (Troy) Messenger
Ph: (334) 566-4270   Fax: (334) 566-4281
Box 727   Zip: 36081
Ship to: 918 S. Brundidge St.
Contacts:
Rick Reynolds-P
Chris Day-E
Huck Treadwell-ME
Deedie Carter-AD
Janet Gates-CAM

TUSCALOOSA
The Tuscaloosa News
Ph: (205) 345-0505   Fax: (205) 349-0845
Box 20587   Zip: 35402
Ship to: 2001 6th St.   (35401)
Contacts:
Ron Sawyer-P
Bruce Giles-EE
Ken Stickney-EPE
Grady E. Smith Jr.-AD
Henry Burt-RAM
Newell Allen-CAM

WEEKLIES

ABBEVILLE
The Abbeville Herald
Ph: (334) 585-2331   Fax: (334) 585-6835
Box 609   Zip: 36310
Ship to: 135 Kirkland St.
Contacts:
J. Edward Dodd,III-P, AD & E

ALBERTVILLE
The Sand Mountain Reporter
Ph: (205) 878-1311   Fax: (205) 878-2104
Box 190   Zip: 35950
Ship to: 3760 U.S. Hwy 431
Contacts:
Michael J. Hudgins-P
Avis Holderfield-E
Debra Hedgepath-AM
Linda Allen-CAM

ARAB
The Arab Tribune
Ph: (205) 586-3188   Fax: (205) 586-3190
Box 605   Zip: 35016
Ship to: 619 S. Brindlee Mtn. Pkwy
Contacts:
Edwin H. Reed-P
David F. Moore-E
Dannie Elmore-GM
Phil Baker-RAM
Liz Stewart-CAM

ASHFORD
The Ashford Power
Ph: (334) 899-5126   Fax: (334) 899-8566
Box 481   Zip: 36312
Ship to: 515 Broadway Street
Contacts:
Guy Beasley-P
Jane McCardle-ME & AM
Vivian (Sissy) Stewart-CAM

ATMORE
The Atmore Advance
Ph: (334) 368-2123   Fax: (334) 368-2124
Drawer 28   Zip: 36504
Ship to: 301 S. Main St.
Contacts:
Michele Cox Gerlach-P, E & AD

AUBURN
The Lee County Eagle
Ph: (334) 821-7150   Fax: (334) 887-0037
Box 3240   Zip: 36831-3240
Ship to: 122 Tichenor Ave.
Contacts:
Alan Davis-Associate P
Don Norman-AD & CAM

BAY MINETTE
The Baldwin Times
Ph: (334) 937-2511   Fax: (334) 937-1637
Box 519   Zip: 36507
Ship to: Courthouse Square
Contacts:
Mike Mueck-P
Diane Martin-BM
Tara Salter-CAM

BESSEMER
The Western Star
Ph: (205) 424-7827   Fax: (205) 424-8118
Box 1900   Zip: 35021
Ship to: 1709 3rd Ave. North
Contacts:
Bob Tribble-P
Mike Oakley-E & GM
Cathy Calure-AM
Rhonda Brown-Production Manager

BIRMINGHAM
The Alabama Messenger
Ph: (205) 252-3672   Fax: (205) 252-3679
205 North 20th St., Suite 706
Frank Nelson Bldg.   Zip: 35203
Ship to: Same
Contacts:
Eleanor O. Foster-P
Karen W. Abercrombie-E & GM
Traci A. Smeraglia-AM & CAM

BIRMINGHAM
Birmingham Business Journal
Ph: (205) 322-0000   Fax: (205) 322-0040
2101 Magnolia Ave. So. #400
Ship to: same
   Contacts:
Tina Verciglio-Savas-P
Bill Stoeffhaas-Assoc. P
Mark Griggs-AD

BREWTON
The Brewton Standard
Ph: (334) 867-4876   Fax: (334) 867-4877
Box 887   Zip: 36427
Ship to: 407 St. Nicholas (36426)
Contacts:
George Turner-P & E
Marilyn Raines-AM
Lonna Jackson-CAM

BUTLER
The Choctaw Advocate
Ph:(205)459-2858/2836   Fax:(205)459-3000
   459-3383 wkends/after hours
Box 475   Zip: 36904
Ship to: 210 N. Mulberry St.
Contacts:
Tommy Campbell-P, E & ME
Lee Mosley-AM & CAM

CAMDEN
The Wilcox Progressive Era
Ph: (334) 682-4422   Fax: (334) 682-5163
Box 100   Zip: 36726
Ship to: 16 Water Street
Contacts:
M. Hollis Curl-P & E
Glenda Curl-GM

CARROLLTON
Pickens County Herald
Ph: (205) 367-2217   Fax: (205) 367-2217
Box 390   Zip: 35447
Ship to: Hwy. 17, Junkin Bldg.
Contacts:
Doug Sanders Jr.-P & AM
Belinda Tilley-CAM

CENTRE
Cherokee County Herald
Ph: (205) 927-5037   Fax: (205) 927-4853
107 West 1st Ave.   Zip: 35960
Ship to: Same
Contacts:
B.H. Mooney III-P
Paul W. Dale-GM, E
Vickie Robinson-AD
Lisa Battles-CAM

CENTREVILLE
Centreville Press
Ph: (205) 926-9769   Fax: (205) 926-9760
Box 127   Zip: 35042
Ship to: 119 Court Square West
Contacts:
Bob Tribble-P
Judy Farnetti-E, ME, & AM
Susan Nash-CAM

CHATOM
Washington County News
Ph: (334) 847-2599   Fax: (334) 847-3847
Box 510   Zip: 36518
Ship to: 305 Jordan St.
Contacts:
James A. Specht-P
Frank Harwell-E
Sherrie Farabee-ME
Shirley Helms-AM & CAM

CLANTON
The Clanton Advertiser
Ph: (205) 755-5747   Fax: (205) 755-5857
Drawer 1379   Zip: 35045
Ship to: 1109 7th St N.
Contacts:
Michael R. Kelley-P
Trey Hughes-E
Dan Cook-AD
Sharron Smith-CAM

CLAYTON
The Clayton Record
Ph: (334) 775-3254   Fax: (334) 775-8554
Box 69   Zip: 36016
Ship to: 109 E. College Ave.
Contacts:
Bertie G. Parish-P & E
Rebecca P. Beasley-ME
Sharon Martin-EPE
Annette Williams-AM
Fay Chance-CAM

COLUMBIANA
Shelby County Reporter
Ph: (205) 669-3131   Fax: (205) 669-4217
Box 947   Zip: 35051
Ship to: 115 Main St.
Contacts:
Mr. Kim N. Price-P & E
Leada Franklin-ME & EPE
Patti Bryan-AM
Stacy Cox-CAM

CULLMAN
The Cullman Tribune
Ph: (205) 739-1351   Fax: (205) 739-4422
219 Second Ave. S.E.   Zip: 35055
Ship to: Same
Contacts:
Delton Blalock-Co-P & E
Barbara Blalock-Co-P & BM

DADEVILLE
The Dadeville Record
Ph: (205) 825-4231   Fax: (205) 234-6550
Box 999 Alexander City   Zip: 35010
Ship to: 139 Church St., Alexander City (35010)
Contacts:
Bruce Wallace-P
Billy McGhee-AD
Janet Goodyear-Mayo-ME

DAPHNE
The Bulletin
Ph: (334) 626-9300   Fax: (334) 626-0144
Box 1560   Zip: 36526
Ship to: 25369 U.S. Hwy 98
Contacts:
Denny Thomas-P
Diane Martin-BM
Tara Salter-CAM

DEMOPOLIS
The Demopolis Times
Ph: (334) 289-4017   Fax: (334) 289-4019
Box 860   Zip: 36732
Ship to: 315 East Jefferson
Contacts:
Danny Smith-P & E
Inda Pugh-AD & CAM

DORA/SUMITON
The Community News
Ph: (205) 648-3231   Fax: (205) 648-3246
#6 Midway Plaza   Zip: 35062
Ship to: Hwy 78

ECLECTIC
The Eclectic Observer
Ph: (334) 541-3902   Fax: (334) 541-3903
Box 634   Zip: 36024
Ship to: 30 Main Street
Contacts:
Harold L. Whatley Jr.-P, AM & CAM
Gina M. Whatley-E, ME& EPE

ELBA
The Elba Clipper
Ph: (334) 897-2823   Fax: (334) 897-3434
Box A   Zip: 36323
Ship to: 419 W. Buford
Contacts:
Ferrin Cox-P & AD
Marvin McIlwain-E

EUFAULA
The Eufaula Tribune
Ph: (334) 687-3506   Fax: (334) 687-3229
Box 628   Zip: 36072-0628
Ship to: 514 E. Barbour (36027)
Contacts:
Joel P. Smith-P, E & EPE
Tom Davis-ME
Jack Smith-GM & Assoc. Editor
Carol Spence-AD

EUTAW
The Greene County Democrat
Ph: (205) 372-3373   Fax: (205) 372-2243
Box 598   Zip: 35462
Ship to: 214 Boligee St.
Contacts:
John Zippert-Co-P, E
Carol Zippert-Co-P
Ms. Laddi Jones-GM
Ed Jordan-AM
Ms. Ella Richardson-Reporter
Barbara Amerson-CM

EUTAW
Greene County Independent
Ph: (205) 372-2232   Fax: same
106 Main St.   Zip: 35462
Ship to: Same
Contacts:
Betty C. Banks-P
Leewanna Parker-E
Sharon Stuckey-GM

EVERGREEN
The Conecuh Countian
Ph: (334) 578-1155   Fax: (334) 578-1156
HCR 35, Box 6-G   Zip: 36401
Ship to: Old Greenville Hwy
Contacts:
Geary C. Risher-P
Sonja McNeil-E
Jim Allen-EPE
Christie Griffin-AM

EVERGREEN
The Evergreen Courant
Ph: (334) 578-1492   Fax: (334) 578-1496
Box 440   Zip: 36401
Ship to: 204 Rural St
Contacts:
Mrs. Maurice G. Bozeman-P
Robert Bozeman III-E & AM
Cheryl A. Johnston-GM & CAM

FAIRHOPE
Fairhope Courier
Ph: (334) 928-2321   Fax: (334) 928-9963
Box 549   Zip: 36533
Ship to: 325 Fairhope Ave
Contacts:
Denny Thomas-P
Diane Martin-BM
Tara Salter-CAM

FAYETTE
The Times-Record
Ph: (205) 932-6271   Fax: (205) 932-6998
Drawer 151   Zip: 35555
Ship to: 106 1st St. SE
Contacts:
Horace Moore-P
Michael James-E
Mrs. Jerrie Elliott-GM
Mrs. Barbara Cross-AM

FLOMATON
The Tri-City Ledger
Ph: (334) 296-3491 Fax: Same
Drawer F   Zip: 36441
Ship to: Hwy 31 South
Contacts:
Joe Thomas-P & E

FLORALA
The Florala News
Ph: (334) 858-3342   Fax: (334) 858-3786
421 South Fifth St.   Zip: 36442
Ship to: same
Contacts:
Gary Woodham-P & E
Merle Woodham-ME
Lisa Windham-AM & CAM
Lucile McRae-OM

FOLEY
The Onlooker
Ph: (334) 943-2151　　　Fax: (334) 943-3441
Box 1687　　　　　　　　Zip: 36536
Ship to: 217 N. McKenzie
Contacts:
Will Petrovics-P
Tara Salter-CAM

FORT DEPOSIT
The Lowndes Signal
Ph: (334) 227-4411
Box 384　　　　　　　　Zip: 36032
Ship to: 118 Ellis St.
Contacts:
Cecil B. Cross Jr.-P
F.B. Cross-E & AM

FORT PAYNE
The DeKalb Advertiser
Ph: (205) 845-6156　　　Fax: (205) 845-1105
Box 559　　　　　　　　Zip: 35967
Ship to: 200 Gault Ave., North
Contacts:
Jerry E. Whittle-P

GADSDEN
The Messenger
Ph: (205) 547-1049　　　Fax: (205) 547-1011
Box 858　　　　　　　　Zip: 35902
Ship to: 408 Cherry Street
Contacts:
Dr. Barbara Bryant-P

GARDENDALE
The North Jefferson News
Ph: (205) 631-8716　　　Fax: (205) 631-9902
Box 849　　　　　　　　Zip: 35071
Ship to: 125 Bell St.
Contacts:
Robert Bryan-P
Tim Lasseter-E
Becky Johnson-GM
Mona Richards-AD

GENEVA
The Geneva County Reaper
Ph: (334) 684-2287　　　Fax: (334) 684-3099
Box 160　　　　　　　　Zip: 36340
Ship to: 803 Town Ave.
Contacts:
Maurice Pujol-P
Brenda Pujol-Associate P

GEORGIANA
The Butler County News
Ph: (334) 376-2325　　　Fax: (334) 376-9302
Box 620　　　　　　　　Zip: 36033
Ship to: 22 Maranda St.
Contacts:
Roger Pride-P & E
Teresa Lowe-ME

GREENSBORO
The Greensboro Watchman
Ph: (334) 624-8323
Drawer 550　　　　　　Zip: 36744
Ship to: 1005 Market St.
Contacts:
Edward E. Lowry Jr.-P,GM, AM, & CAM
Willie Jean Lowry Arrington-ME

GREENVILLE
The Greenville Advocate
Ph: (334) 382-3111　　　Fax: (334) 382-7104
Box 507　　　　　　　　Zip: 36037
Ship to: 103 Hickory St.
Contacts:
Todd Carpenter-P, E & AM
Gregg Fuller-ME
Susan Rhodes-CAM

GROVE HILL
The Clarke County Democrat
Ph: (334) 275-3375　　　Fax: (334) 275-3060
Box 39　　　　　　　　Zip: 36451
Ship to: 261 North Jackson Street
Contacts:
James A. Cox-P, E, & AD
Mike Williamson-GM

GULF SHORES
The Islander
Ph: (334) 968-6414   Fax: (334) 968-5233
Box 1128   Zip: 36547
Ship to: 128 Cove Ave (36542)
Contacts:
Will Petrovics-P
Tara Salter-CAM
Diane Martin-BM

GUNTERSVILLE
The Advertiser-Gleam
Ph: (205) 582-3232   Fax: (205) 582-3231
Box 190   Zip: 35976
Ship to: 2218 Taylor St.
Contacts:
Sam Harvey-E
Don Woodward-GM & AD
Taunya Buchanan-CAM & CM

HALEYVILLE
The Northwest Alabamian
Ph: (205) 486-9461   Fax: (205) 486-4849
Box 430   Zip: 35565
Ship to: Highway 195, East
Contacts:
Horace Moore-P & GM
Melica Allen-E
Buford Thompson-AD
Linda Howell-CAM

HAMILTON
Journal Record
Ph: (205) 921-3104   Fax: (205) 921-3105
Drawer 1477   Zip: 35570
Ship to: 401 State Hwy 17
Contacts:
Horace Moore-P
Les Walters-GM & E
Dawn Milam/Vicky Massey-AM
Renae Watson-CAM
Ed Howell-NE
Kyle Bond-SE

HANCEVILLE
The Hanceville Herald
Ph: (205) 352-4775
Box 880   Zip: 35077
Ship to: 111 Commercial St.
Contacts:
Johnny Grantham-P
Jennifer Grantham-E
Violet Earing-AD

HARTFORD
Hartford News-Herald
Ph: (334)) 684-2287
Box 160 Geneva   Zip: 36340
Ship to: 803 Town Ave. Geneva
Contacts:
Maurice Pujol-P
Brenda Pujol-Associate P

HARTSELLE
Hartselle Enquirer
Ph: (205) 773-6566   Fax: (205) 773-1953
Box 929   Zip: 35640
Ship to: 407 W. Chestnut St.
Contacts:
Larry Beasley-P & RAM
Clif Knight-E

HEADLAND
The Headland Observer
Ph: (334) 693-3326   Fax: (334) 693-5224
Rt. 2, Box 707   Zip: 36345
Ship to: Hwy. 431 North
Contacts:
Guy Beasley-P & GM
Betty S. Gamble-AD
Betty Rowland-CAM
Terry Grimes-E & EPE

HEFLIN
The Cleburne News
Ph: (205) 463-2872   Fax: same
Box 67   Zip: 36264-0067
Ship to: 938 Ross Street
Contacts:
Randy Grider-E
Graham Boozer-AM

JACKSON
The South Alabamian
Ph: (334) 246-4494   Fax: (334) 246-7486
Box 68   Zip: 36545
Ship to: 1064 Coffeeville Road
Contacts:
Michael M. Breedlove-P & E
Linda H. Breedlove-Co-P
Cammie Breedlove-AM
Martha Wynn-CAM

JACKSONVILLE
The Jacksonville News
Ph: (205) 435-5021   Fax: (205) 435-1028
203 Pelham Rd. S.   Zip: 36265
Ship to: Same
Contacts:
P.A. Sanguinetti-P & E
Julia M. Brock-ME
Darlene Bates-AM
Lisa Smith-CAM

LAFAYETTE
The LaFayette Sun
Ph: (334) 864-8885   Fax: (334) 864-8310
Box 378   Zip: 36862
Ship to: 116 Lafayette St S.
Contacts:
Michael Hand-P & E
Lisa Edge-AM

LEEDS
The Leeds News
Ph: (205) 699-2214   Fax: (205) 699-3157
720 Parkway Dr.   Zip: 35094
Ship to: Same
Contacts:
Robert Bryan-P
Rebecca Comer Gunter-E
Leah Hollister-AM
Glenda Smith-OM & CAM

LINDEN
The Democrat-Reporter
Ph: (334) 295-5224   Fax: (334) 295-5563
Box 480040   Zip: 36748
Ship to: 108 East Coats Ave.
Contacts:
Goodloe Sutton Sr.-P, E & EPE
Betty Hurst-AM
Pat Windham-CAM

LINEVILLE/ASHLAND
The Clay Times-Journal
Ph: (205) 396-5760   Fax: same
Box 97   Zip: 36266
Ship to: 102 3rd Ave., No.
Contacts:
David Proctor-P & E
Linda McDonald-AD

LIVINGSTON
Sumter County Record-Journal
Ph: (205) 652-6100   F ax: (205) 652-4466
P.O. Drawer B   Zip: 35470
Ship to: 200 S. Washington St.
Contacts:
Tommy McGraw-P, E & AD
Herman B. Ward Jr.-GM

LUVERNE
The Luverne Journal
Ph: (334) 335-3541   Fax: (334) 335-3541
Box 152   Zip: 36049
Ship to: 506 Forest Ave.
Contacts:
James Morgan-P, GM & SE
Alvin Bland-E & EPE

MADISON
The Madison County Record
Ph: (205) 772-6677   Fax: (205) 772-6655
Box 859   Zip: 35758
Ship to: 202 Main
Contacts:
MCR, Inc.-P
Jeff Dickinson-ME
Bill Bates-AM

MARION
Marion Times-Standard
Ph: (334) 683-6318   Fax: (334) 683-4616
Box 418   Zip: 36756
Ship to: 414 Washington St.
Contacts:
Bob Tribble-P
Lorrie Blankenship-GM & AD
Charley Ann Reichley-E & EPE

MILLBROOK
The Community Press
Ph: (334) 285-6000
Box 568   Zip: 36054
Ship to: 83 Deatsville Hwy
Contacts:
Lamar Smitherman-P
Steve Sawyer-E & EPE
Gail Cobb-AM

MILLPORT
West Alabama Gazette
Ph: (205) 662-4296   Fax: (205) 662-4740
Box 249   Zip: 35576
Ship to: 100 Vernon Street
Contacts:
L. Peyton Bobo-P & EPE
Barbara J. Bobo-E & AD

MOBILE
Mobile Beacon
Ph: (334) 479-0629   Fax: (334) 479-0610
Box 1407   Zip: 36633
Ship to: 2311 Costarides (36617)
Contacts:
Mrs. Lancie M. Thomas-P
Mrs. Cleretta T. Blackmon-E & AD
E.M. Cockrell-NE

MONROEVILLE
The Monroe Journal
Ph: (334) 575-3282   Fax: (334) 575-3284
Box 826   Zip: 36461
Ship to: 126 Hines St.
Contacts:
Bo Bolton-P
Marilyn Handley-E

MONTGOMERY
The Montgomery Independent
Ph: (334) 213-7323   Fax: (334) 271-2143
Box 241207   Zip: 36124-1207
Ship to: 6005-B Monticello Dr. (36117)
Contacts:
Don Hatley-P
W. Thomas Johnson-Editor at Large
Wendi Lewis-ME
Nancy Lowe-AM

MOULTON
The Moulton Advertiser
Ph: (205) 974-1114   Fax: (205) 974-3097
Box 517   Zip: 35650
Ship to: 659 Main Street
Contacts:
Luke Slaton-P &E
Deangelo McDaniel-ME
Amy Thrasher-RAM
Pam Wallace-CAM

MOUNDVILLE
Moundville Times
Ph: (205) 371-2488   Fax: (205) 371-9010
Box 683   Zip: 35474
Ship to: 2nd Avenue
Contacts:
Larry Taylor-P
Austin Dare-ME & E

ONEONTA
The Blount Countian
Ph: (205) 625-3231   Fax: (205) 625-3239
Box 310   Zip: 35121
Ship to: 217 3rd Street South
Contacts:
Molly Howard Ryan-P & E
Lisa Ryan-ME
James Still-GM
Manuel Acevado-CAM

OPP
The Opp News
Ph: (334) 493-3595   Fax: (334) 493-4901
Box 409   Zip: 36467
Ship to: 200 Covington W. Ave.
Contacts:
Randy Pebworth-P
Tracey D. Nelson-E
Jennifer Cosby-AM

OZARK
The Southern Star
Ph: (334) 774-2715   Fax: (334) 774-9619
Box 1729   Zip: 36361-1729
Ship to: 428 E. Andrews Ave. (36360)
Contacts:
Joseph H. Adams-P & E
Dorothy Adams-AD

PELL CITY
St. Clair News-Aegis
Ph: (205) 884-2310   Fax: (205) 884-2312
Box 748   Zip: 35125
Ship to: 1820 Second Ave. N.
Contacts:
Robert Bryan-P
Gary Hanner-E
Dolores Porter-CAM

PHENIX CITY
The Phenix Citizen
Ph: (334) 298-0679   Fax: (334) 298-0690
Box 1267   Zip: 36868-1267
Ship to: 1606 Broad Street (36867)
Contacts:
Jill Tigner & Mike Venable-P
Mike Venable-E
Jill Tigner-AM

PIEDMONT
The Piedmont Journal-Independent
Ph: (205) 447-2837   Fax: same
115 N. Center Ave.   Zip: 36272-2013
Ship to: Same
Contacts:
Lane Weatherbee-P & E
Carol Weatherbee-AD

PRATTVILLE
The Prattville Progress
Ph: (334) 365-6739
Box 680840   Zip: 36068
Ship to: 152 W. Third St. (36067)
Contacts:
Lamar Smitherman-P
Brightman Brock-E
Gail Cobb-AM

RAINSVILLE
Weekly Post
Ph: (205) 638-4027   Fax: (205) 638-2329
Box 849   Zip: 35986
Ship to: 225 E. Main Street
Contacts:
Jerry Turner-P

RED BAY
The Red Bay News
Ph: (205) 356-2148   Fax: (205) 356-2787
Box 1339   Zip: 35582
Ship to: 120 4th Ave. SE
Contacts:
LaVale Mills-P & AM
Tony Launius-E
Glenda Tucker-Assistant P & CAM

ROANOKE
The Randolph Leader
Ph: (334) 863-2819   Fax: (334) 863-4006
Box 1267   Zip: 36274
Ship to: 524 Main Street
Contacts:
John W. Stevenson-P, E & EPE
Peggy Seabolt-AD & CAM

ROBERTSDALE
The Independent
Ph: (334) 947-7318   Fax: (334) 947-7652
Box 509   Zip: 36567
Ship: 21764 Media Drive
Contacts:
Diane Mueck-P
Tammy Leytham-EE & EPE
Diane Martin-BM
Tara Salter-CAM

ROCKFORD
Coosa County News
Ph: (205) 377-2525   Fax: (205) 3772422
Box 99   Zip: 35136
Ship to: Main Street
Contacts:
Lewis Scarbrough-P
Beckie Mosley-NE
Karen Pearce-AD

ROGERSVILLE
East Lauderdale News
Ph: (205) 247-5565/1902
Box 179   Zip: 35652
Ship to: Lee Street
Contacts:
James B. Cox-P & E
Phyllis D. Cox-P & AD

RUSSELLVILLE
Franklin County Times
Ph: (205) 332-1881   Fax: (205) 332-1883
Box 1088   Zip: 35653
Ship to: 142 Hwy. 43 Bypass
Contacts:
Stanley Allison-P & E
Tracie Smith-ME
Wayne Franklin-AM
Kim Black-CAM

SAMSON
The Samson Ledger
Ph: (334) 684-2287   Fax: (334) 684-3099
Box 160 Geneva   Zip: 36340
Ship to: 803 Town Ave. Geneva
Contacts:
Maurice Pujol-P
Brenda Pujol-Associate P

SHEFFIELD
Standard and Times
Ph: (205) 383-8476   Fax: (205) 383-8476
Box 1419, Tuscumbia   Zip: 35674
Ship to: 106 W. 5th St, Tuscumbia 35674
Contacts:
Jim Crawford Jr.- P & E
Estelle Crawford Whitehead-ME
Mary Hill-AD & CM

STEVENSON
North Jackson Progress
Ph: (205) 437-2395   Fax: (205) 437-2592
Drawer 625   Zip: 35772
Ship to: Highway 72 East
Contacts:
Larry O. Glass-P, AD & E
Machelle McCrary-CAM
Faye Glass-NE
Lee Glass-SE

SULLIGENT
Lamar Leader
Ph: (205) 698-8148   Fax: (205)698-8146
Box 988   Zip: 35586
Ship to: 55071 Hwy 17
Contacts:
Don Dollar-P, E, & AM
Rebecca Cox-GM & CAM

TALLASSEE
The Tallassee Tribune
Ph: (334) 283-6568   Fax: (334) 283-6569
Box 736   Zip: 36078
Ship to: 301 Gilmer
Contacts:
Jack Venable-P & E
Barbara Morrow-AD
Jane Parker-CM

THOMASVILLE
The Thomasville Times
Ph: (334) 636-2214   Fax: (334) 636-9822
Box 367   Zip: 36784
Ship to: 6 Highway 43 N.
Contacts:
Mike Breedlove & Jim Cox-Publishers
Dana Dunn-E
Tonya Joyce-AM

TUSCUMBIA
Colbert County Reporter
Ph: (205) 383-8471   Fax: (205) 383-8476
Box 1419   Zip: 35674
Ship to: 106 W. 5th St.
Contacts:
Jim Crawford Jr.-P & E
Estelle Crawford Whitehead-ME
Mary Hill-AD & CM

TUSKEGEE
The Tuskegee News
Ph: (334) 727-3020   Fax: (334) 727-3036
Drawer 60   Zip: 36083
Ship to: 112 Eastside Street
Contacts:
Paul R. Davis-P
Mike Smelley-Associate P, ME & AM
Guy Rhodes-E
Lizzie Dixon-CAM

UNION SPRINGS
Union Springs Herald
Ph: (334) 738-2360   Fax: (334) 738-2342
Box 600   Zip: 36089
Ship to: 104 E. Conecuh Ave.
Contacts:
Terry Everett-President
Thomas May-P, E & GM
Neal May-AM & CAM

VERNON
The Lamar Democrat
Ph: (205) 695-7029   Fax: (205) 695-9501
Box 587   Zip: 35592
Ship to: 125 1st Ave NE
Contacts:
Rex Rainwater-P
Howard Reeves-E & GM
Tammy Bardon-AM & CAM

WETUMPKA
The Wetumpka Herald
Ph: (334) 567-7811   Fax: (334) 567-3284
Box 29   Zip: 36092
Ship to: 300 Green St.
Contacts:
Ellen T. Williams-P, ME& EPE
Gerald M. Williams Sr.-E & AM
Mike Baker-Sales/Marketing
Barbara Yates-CAM
Gladys Hatcher-CM

Updated Nov. 4, 1996

Bibliography

Interviews, books, newsletters, documents, correspondence and publications

Alabama Official and Statistical Register, 1979, State of Alabama Department of Archives and History, Skinner Printing Co., Industrial Terminal, Montgomery. Chapter 10, Newspapers and Periodicals.

Alabama Press Association records at Birmingham headquarters: annual Rate and Data Guides, correspondence, minutes, issues of *AlaPressa* and *The Alabama Publisher*, Legislative Green Sheets, 1939-1996.

Alabama Press Association Rate & Data Guide, 100th Anniversary Edition (1971), official directory of newspapers published annually by Alabama Newspaper Advertising Service, business affiliate of the Alabama Press Association. (Rate and Data Guide includes revised history of APA, 1960-1971, by former APA executive director Jim Hall and his wife Martha Hall.)

Boyd, Minnie Clare. "Alabama In The Fifties: A Social Study," AMS Press Inc., New York, 1966.

Brackeen, L.O. "History of the Alabama Press Association (1871-1951)," (prepared and reproduced as a special project of Alabama Polytechnic Institute in cooperation with the Alabama Press Association, Dec. 22, 1951).

Brackeen, L.O. "History of the Alabama Press Association (1871-1959)," reproduced by Photographic and Duplicating Service of Auburn University, January 1960.

Brigham, Clarence S. "History and Bibliography of American Newspapers," Volume 1, American Antiquarian Society, Worcester, Mass., 1947.

Brown III, Edward (Ed) Owen. "History of the University of Alabama News Bureau, 1928-1956," A thesis submitted in partial fulfillment of the requirements of master of arts in the Department of Journalism in the Graduate School of the University of Alabama, 1958.

Burnham, Robert W. "A Brief History of the Alabama Press Association," (Written in 1949 by Burnham of Jacksonville, a senior in journalism at the University of Alabama, under the guidance of APA field manager J. Russell Heitman. History reprinted in July, August, September 1949 issue of *The Alabama Publisher*).

Clark, Thomas D. "The Southern Country Editor," University of South Carolina Press. 1991.

Clark, Thomas D. and Kirwan, Albert D. "The South Since Appomattox: A Century of Regional Change," Oxford University Press, New York, 1967.

Cunningham, Penelope Prewitt. "The Fourth Estate," (The writings of Perkins J. Prewitt, compiled by his daughter). Ralph B. Draughon Library, Auburn University, 1996.

Dobbins, Charles G. "Alabama Governors and Editors, 1930-1955," The Alabama Review, a quarterly journal of Alabama history published by the University of Alabama Press, Volume XXIX, Number 2, April 1976.

Ellison, Rhoda Coleman. "Early Alabama Publications," University of Alabama Press, 1947.

Ellison, Rhoda Coleman. "A Check List of Alabama Imprints, 1807-1870," University of Alabama Press, 1946.

Ellison, Rhoda Coleman. "History and Bibliography of Alabama Newspapers in the Nineteenth Century," University of Alabama press, 1954.

Gates, Grace Hooten. "An Epithet for *The Montgomery Advertiser* or How 'Grandma' Got Her Name," "The Alabama Review," A Quarterly Journal of Alabama History, published in cooperation with the Alabama Historical Association by the University of Alabama Press, Volume XLVII, Number 1, January 1994.

Gray, Daniel Savage, The Alabama Historical Quarterly, Fall 1975 (Vol. XXXVII), pages 183-191. published by Alabama State Department of Archives and History. "Frontier Journalism: Newspapers in Antebellum Alabama."

Grimes, Millard. "The Last Linotype: The Story of Georgia and Its Newspapers Since World War II," Mercer University Press and Georgia Press Association, 1985.

Hanson, Clarence B. Jr. "The Story of *The Birmingham News*, A Good Newspaper," (From the text of a talk given by Clarence B. Hanson Jr.'s uncle, Victor H. Hanson, on Nov. 5, 1913, to the Birmingham Rotary Club.)

Helmbold, F. Wilbur. "Early Alabama Newspapermen, 1810-1820," (Paper presented at the annual meeting of the Alabama Historical Association in Gadsden on April 18, 1858. (Reprinted in The Alabama Review, XII, January 1959.)

Hereford, Lady. "Banner day for free speech: (James E.) Mills case overturns law restricting election day editorials, upholds constitutional freedom of speech," Auburn University, research paper prepared for Newspaper Management course, Department of Journalism, 1995.

Hollingsworth, Annie May. "Johnson Jones Hooper: Statesman and Humorist," The Alabama Historical Quarterly, Vol. 1, No. 3, fall 1930.

Hollis III, Daniel Webster. "An Alabama Newspaper Tradition: Grover C. Hall and the Hall Family," University of Alabama Press, 1983.

Hollis III, Daniel Webster. "Grover Cleveland Hall: The Anatomization of a Southern Journalist's Philosophy," The Alabama Historical Quarterly, Volume XLII, spring and summer 1980.

Karolevitz, Robert F. "From Quill to Computer: The Story of America's Community Newspapers," National Newspaper Association, 1985.

McMurtrie, Douglas C. "A Brief History of the First Printing in the State of Alabama," by Douglas C. McMurtrie, director of typography, Ludlow Typographic Co., Chicago, Ill., (Reproduced by Alabama Polytechnic Institute, Auburn, by special permission of W.D. Fleming, president and treasurer, Birmingham Printing Co., for distribution at summer convention of Alabama Press Association in Panama City, July 10-12, 1952).

Oswald, John Clyde. "Printing In The Americas," Gregg Publishing Co., 1937.

Plott, William J. "A Checklist of Alabama Newspapers Published Since 1900," master's degree thesis, the University of Alabama, 1982.

Screws, William Wallace. "Alabama Journalism, Memorial Record of Alabama," Volume 2, pages 158-235, published in 1893 by Brant and Fuller, Madison, Wis.

Smith, Richard R. "Alabama: A Guide to the Deep South," written by WPA in state of Alabama, New York, 1941, (Newspapers and Radio" Chapter).

Suggs, Henry Lewis. "The Black Press in the South, 1865-1979," Greenwood Press, Westport, Conn., 1983. (Chapter 1, Alabama Newspapers, pages 23-64, by Dr. Allen Woodrow Jones, professor emeritus, archivist, Auburn University Department of History.)